Beacham's Guide to
International Endangered Species

Volume 1

Mammals Listed
1970 to July 1997

Edited by
Walton Beacham
Kirk H. Beetz

BEACHAM PUBLISHING CORP.
OSPREY, FLORIDA

Beacham's Guide to
International Endangered Species

Editors
Walton Beacham
Kirk H. Beetz

Photo Editor
Deborah Beacham

Book and Cover Design
Amanda Mott

Species Accounts
All of the gibbon entries and introduction were written by Lori K. Sheran and Allan Mootnick of the International Center for Gibbon Studies. Most of the other articles were compiled by the editors; some material was contributed by the Threatened and Endangered Species Information Institute, Golden Colorado.

Spine and Cover Photo Credits
Howler Monkey, Art Wolfe
Wild Bactrian Camel, Rich Block
Black Rhinoceros,
    Rick Weyerhaeuser
Douc Langur, Noel Rowe
Mhorr's Gazelle, Art Wolfe

Title Page Photo Credits
Vol. 1, Ring-tailed Lemur
    Noel Rowe
Vol. 2, Long-tailed Marsupial Mouse
    Babs & Bert Wells, NPIAW

Library of Congress Cataloging-in-Publication Data

Beacham's guide to international endangered species, volumes 1-2: mammals / edited by Walton Beacham, Kirk H. Beetz.
    Includes bibliographical references and indexes.
    Contents: v. 1-2. Mammals listed 1970 to July 1997

    Describes all international endangered or threatened species listed by the U.S. Fish and Wildlife Service through July 1997, and some other species listed by IUCN or included in CITES Appendices.

    ISBN 0-933833-34-2 (alk. Paper)

1. Endangered species. 2. Wildlife conservation. I. Beacham, Walton, 1943- . Beetz, Kirk H., 1952- .
QL82.B435   1997   97-35751
333.95'42--dc21   CIP

Printed in Singapore
First Printing, January 1998

Contents
Volume 1

MOUSE AND DWARF LEMURS

LEMURS

Introduction

Beacham's Guide to International Endangered Species represents our continuing commitment to provide data and photos of all species listed as threatened or endangered by the U.S. Fish and Wildlife Service. Our master list of protected species was derived from the U.S. Fish and Wildlife Service's "Foreign Listed Species Index by Status" as of July 1997. This can be retrieved online through FWS's web site address: http://www.fws.gov. Additionally, we have included some species that are not listed by FWS but are considered at risk by IUCN (The World Conservation Union) or listed by CITES. We have also included one previously-endangered kangaroo to address how species can be recovered.

Unique to these volumes are full entries for many subspecies that are treated generically in most reference sources. There are separate entries for species or subspecies of 7 chimpanzees, 7 gibbons, 10 langurs, 29 lemurs, 10 sifakas, 7 tamarins, and 5 rhinoceros, among many others. The 8 subspecies of tigers occur in different habitats thousands of miles apart, and their circumstances are vastly different, so that data about the subspecies is essential for understanding its degree of vulnerability.

In our goal to provide data about all USFWS listed species, we have included some that are believed to be extinct by most authorities, but which are still protected under the Endangered Species Act. Foreign species benefit from inclusion on the federal list because of restrictions placed on importation and sale of endangered wildlife and derived products within U.S. borders. Some of these animals live in remote areas of the world, and in areas that are ravaged by strife or war, making them inaccessible for scientific study by westerners. Consequently, their current status may be unknown, and species thought to be extinct may, in fact, survive.

Our sources of information include the IUCN *Red Data Books*, scientific journals, accounts and updates from the "Endangered Species Bulletin" (published by USFWS), conservation organizations, and individual scientists from around the world (see References for the complete list). We are particularly indebted to Noel Rowe, Lori Sheeran, and dozens of other field scientists who have provided us with their recent data. Where there is conflicting opinion about the taxonomy, status, and behavior of some species, we have stated the various positions of the authorities without attempting to resolve them. We have followed traditional taxonomic treatment, but this is more for the purpose of organizing material than taking a scientific position for classifying animals.

From these sources, we compiled 351 accounts, grouped by families, with an introduction. Each entry is alphabetized by its scientific name, using the genus, species, and, where applicable, subspecies name within its chapter. Volume 1 includes 183 accounts of primates, elephants, rhinoceros, tapirs, bears, camels, horses, zebras, and deer. Volume 2 includes 168 accounts of wild cattle, pronghorns, antelopes, duikers, oryx, sheep, goat antelopes, gazelles, chamois, wild pigs, cats, dogs, foxes, wolves, hyenas, marsupials, rabbits, hares, martens, civets, linsangs, otters, solenodons, hutias, beavers, porcupines, chinchillas, rats, mice, sloths, armadillos, pangolins, bats, and marine mammals. There is a glossary of scientific terms, a country index grouping animals by regions, and a comprehensive (Master) index of scientific and common names, as well as taxons and introductory sections.

For ease in locating and comparing information, each of the accounts is formatted to include the animal's description, behavior, habitat, distribution, threats, and conservation and recovery. The purpose of the distribution section is to locate a species by stating not only where it occurs but to give a sense of its population size. A population estimate can serve as an important measure of a species' need for protection, but for some species, population figures have not been recently, or ever, compiled, and one must rely on the size of its range to understand its relative scarcity. The section "Threats" explains the causes for a species' decline, most often of which is destruction or loss of habitat. The section "Conservation and Recovery" describes what, if anything, is being done to assist the animal's recovery. Captive breeding programs, especially for primates, have been particularly successful with reintroduction of species into the wild as an ongoing goal.

Of all the labors involved in compiling this guide, locating the photos was perhaps the most daunting and rewarding task. Never before have so many images of international endangered species been published in the same volume, and some are published here for the first time. It is only through the generosity and dedication of wildlife photographers to helping the cause of species at risk that we have been able to provide so many images. We wish to express sincere appreciation to all the photographers. Five individuals in particular contributed significant numbers of images, and we are featuring them in the Photographers Gallery, beginning on page xiii.

These two volumes covering mammals will be followed by a third volume covering all the other foreign species listed by USFWS. For data on species listed on USFWS's domestic species list, see Beacham Publishing's *WWF Guide to Endangered Species of North America* (in four volumes). For species that have become extinct in modern times, see Beacham Publishing's *WWF Guide to Extinct Species of Modern Times*.

Walton Beacham

International Conservation Treaties and Laws

Along with habitat loss, international trade is the major threat to many species that are threatened with extinction. CITES, the Convention on International Trade in Endangered Species of Wild Fauna and Flora, is an international agreement signed by more than 120 countries whose aim is to regulate international trade though a system of permits and controls. CITES recognizes that controlled trade in species, rather than prohibiting all trade, often works to the advantage of protecting them, and so it divides species into two categories, according to their degree of endangerment. These categories are called "Appendices" to the general agreement; every two years the signatory countries meet to evaluate the status of species, and to decide in which category (Appendix) species should be placed.

Appendix I provides the highest degree of controlled trade. Species that are near extinction, such as mountain gorillas, or those which are highly desirable for commercial products, such as sea turtles, or as pets, such as parrots, cannot be exported in whole or in part except under exceptional circumstances, and then only with high government approval. Exceptional circumstances are normally restricted to scientific study or breeding opportunities; under no circumstances can Appendix I species be exported or imported for commercial use.

Appendix II recognizes species that will be placed at risk if trade in them is not controlled. Alligators, for example, which were once common, then hunted to near extinction for commercial trade in their hides, were protected from trade by CITES until they had repopulated their numbers and could be removed from the protected list. Species listed in Appendix II may, with permits, be exported from their country of origin, and some commercial trade is allowed with proper permitting.

CITES also recognizes the sustenance rights of indigenous peoples to hunt species for survival. Eskimoes, for example, are permitted to take a limited number of walruses every season to provide their village with meat and oil.

The U.S. has three legal instruments for protecting international species: (1) CITES. (2) The Endangered Species Act, which requires all U.S. government agencies to apply the same conservation standards for species listed in foreign countries as those in the U.S. (3) The Lacey Act, which makes it unlawful to import, export, transport, sell, receive, acquire, or purchase any wild animal, alive or dead, including parts, products, eggs, or offspring; or any wild plants, including roots, seeds or other parts, of species listed as threatened or endangered by the U.S. Fish and Wildlife Service.

The Endangered Species Act regulates Federal activities abroad and requires that no agency of the U.S. government initiate or fund activities that might degrade the habitat of threatened or endangered species. Agencies most often affected by the regulations are the Department of Defense and the Army Corps of Engineers. Because of the impact of troops, artillery, and heavy equipment on habitats, and because of the location of many military bases in coastal regions, DOD has played an increasingly larger role in species protection abroad. Similarly, the Army Corps of Engineers is often involved with foreign governments to carry out infrastructure projects sponsored in part by the U.S. Because the construction of dams and roads can dramatically affect the environment of species, the Corps is compelled to conduct extensive environmental impact studies in areas where endangered species are believed to occur.

The protection of endangered species in foreign countries through U.S. law is difficult to enforce, and presents considerable legal, ethical, and moral dilemmas for U.S. authorities and lawmakers. Nations sometimes, or often, disagree about which species should be included in an Appendix, and a signatory nation to CITES may declare itself an exception to a specific listing. Norway, for example, never agreed to CITES' ban on whaling, and allowed its citizens to continue taking whales while most of the signatory nations forbid it. Persuading foreign nations to comply to international standards of conservation is a cooperative or coercive process; obviously, the U.S. is not going to commit troops to stop the killing of gorillas in Rwanda. However, as a part of treaty negotiations, wildlife conservation can sometimes become a beneficiary. A recent example is that China agreed to the conservation of its tigers as part of a compromise to maintain its Most Favored Nation status.

The most effective insurance for the survival of species is support by the local population. The concept of "sustainable harvesting" has won acceptance by a number of Third World governments. When a species is vital to the economy of the local people or to the country as a whole, then its survival is clearly recognized as an economic priority.

Photographers Gallery

Rich displays contraband seized by authorities

RICH BLOCK

Rich Block directs educational activities at the Indianapolis Zoo, including the application of "distance learning" technology and the interpretation of zoo exhibits. He also directs the zoo's research activities, and is co-host of a weekly television program "At the Zoo" (WRTV6).

From 1987-1992 Rich served as director of public programs for World Wildlife Fund, leaving that position to become executive director of the Dian Fossey Gorilla Fund. He returned to WWF in 1993 as senior fellow. His duties included developing membership and programs, marketing and licensing, public affairs and TRAFFIC. He was WWF's liaison with Microsoft in developing the CD-ROM *Dangerous Creatures*, and he assisted in producing HBO's *Going, Going, Almost Gone.*

Rich's wide experience includes curator of public relations at the Kansas City Zoo, curator of education at Zoo Atlanta, and faculty member in the University of Michigan School of Natural Resources and Environment. He lectures widely in the U.S. and abroad about wildlife conservation and the need for individual action. He has served as technical advisor to writers and publishers of books, films, and CD-ROMs on endangered wildlife, rain forests, and giant pandas. In 1991 and 1992 he served as education consultant to the President's Council on Environmental Quality for the "Environmental Challenge Awards."

Rich holds a B.S. in environmental studies, and an M.S. in natural resources from the University of Michigan, where he continues to serve as a member of the School of Natural Resources & Environment's Board of Governors.

DAVID HARING

David Haring has been associated with the Duke University Primate Center since 1986, first as a research technician, monitoring behavior and reproductive status of the tarsier colony and writing articles for a variety of newsletters and publications, including the AAZPA Newsletter. From 1991 to 1993 he served as Primate Technician responsible for the husbandry and maintenance of the Primate Center's aye-aye colony. He was also the international studbook keeper for captive *Propithecus*, co-editor of the DUPC newsletter, and author of husbandry manuals on DUPC's prosimians. He currently serves as colony manager.

David documented the development of two *Propithecus verreauxi* infants from birth to six months of age. Data from this study were utilized to implement management techniques which have significantly decreased infant mortality in the colony. Currently,

Wendy Shelp

fifty percent of the colony is captive born, with all births, except one, occurring since 1986.

David has traveled extensively throughout Madagascar photographing flora, fauna, villages, and indigenous people. His photographs of prosimians have appeared in numerous periodicals, including *Life, National Geographic, Natural History, Animal Kingdom, National Geographic World, Wildlife Conservation, Red Data Book on Lemurs, Walker's Mammals of the World, Scientific American,* and *Science.*

David contributes technical papers to journals such as *Primate Conservation, International Zoo Yearbook, Zoo Biology,* and *International Zoo Yearbook.*

Luiz Claudio Marigo

Luiz Claudio Marigo was born in Rio de Janeiro and studied Philosophy and Eastern Culture at the Rio de Janeiro Pontifcal Catholic University, as well as cinematography at the Visual Arts College. He has devoted the last 18 years to nature photography, illustrating and writing art-icles for numerous Brazilian and international magazines, including *Foto* (Sweden), *Periplo* (Spain), *BBC Wildlife* (U.K.), *Grands Reportages* (France), *Hōrzu* (Germany), *Wildlife Conservation* (U.S.A.), *Birds International* (Australia), and *Prio* (Japan). He has also authored or contributed to dozens of books, including *Amazon Wildlife* (Singapore), *Floresta Atlântica, Rainforests, Tropical Rainforests, The International Book of Forests* (U.K.), and *Wonders of the Jungle* (U.S.).

Luiz has traveled throughout Brazil photographing ecosystems, flora, and fauna, and has photographed wildlife in Antartica, Patagonia, the Andes, India, Africa, Europe, and the United States. In 1987 he was awarded first prize, and in other years various commended photographs, in the *Wildlife Photographer of the Year* competition organized by the BBC, the London Natural History Museum, and the Fauna and Flora Preservation Society. He has had many one-man shows in Brazil and other countries, and has taken part in group shows in London, Copenhagen, and Bonn, as well as at the Rio de Janeiro Fine Arts Museum and the São Paulo Art Museum.

C. Allan Morgan

C. Allan Morgan has been photographing animals professionally since 1972, when he left his job as an electronics design engineer. He photographs wildlife from insects to whales. From 1975 to 1979 he was the photographer for the Arizona-Sonora Desert Museum in Tucson, Arizona. In 1976 he began leading whale watching trips to Baja California, Mexico. Since that beginning, Allan has served either as a trip leader, naturalist or photographer in Alaska, Antarctica,

Argentina, Australia, Chile, Costa Rica, Greenland, Iceland, Japan, Panama, Russia, and Venezuela.

Allan especially enjoys photographing birds and marine mammals, although he says there is something fascinating about each and every life form. Allan lives in Tucson, Arizona where he operates his photography studio and maintains a large photo library of species.

NOEL ROWE

A. S. Barber

Noel Rowe is director of Primate Conservation, Inc. whose goal is to fund field research and conservation projects on the least known and most endangered primates. Since 1994 the organization has funded 57 projects in 17 countries through grants which are awarded twice per year.

Noel was born in Cincinnati and moved to Long Island in the 1970s to study marine science at Southampton College. After graduating, he worked at the New York Ocean Science Laboratory in Montauk for three years. He later attended C. W. Post College where he studied with Arthur Leipzig and earned an M.F.A. in photography.

After a 1981 research project with Earthwatch that took Noel to Madagascar where he photographed and studied lemurs, he enrolled in a graduate course in primate conservation with Dr. Patricia Wright at the State University of New York at Stony Brook. Noel was inspired to create a book that would contain photographs and descriptions of the 234 living species of primates. This mammoth undertaking resulted in the 1996 publication by Pogonias Press, founded by Noel, of *The Pictorial Guide to the Living Primates*. Many of the images from this book are reprinted with sincere appreciation to Noel.

Beacham's Guide to
International Endangered Species

Gorillas and Orangutans
Family: Pongidae

Mountain Gorilla   Rick Weyerhaeuser

Sumatran Orangutan   Noel Rowe

General Characteristics of the *Pongidae*

The *Pongidae* are the apes: gibbons, orangutans, gorillas, chimpanzees, and pygmy chimpanzees (the bonobos). These are the closest living relatives to human beings, other, closer relatives having become extinct. Genetic studies and blood tests indicate that of the apes, the chimpanzees are the closest relatives of humans, with their blood types so close to those of humans that some medical researchers suggest that chimpanzee blood could be a source of blood transfusions for humans. Some taxonomists are now placing gorillas and chimpanzees in the family *Hominidae,* the family of humans. Next closest to humans are the gorillas, then, much more distantly related, are the orangutans, and then much more distantly related than they, the gibbons, sometimes called the "lesser apes."

All of the apes walk on all fours; gorillas have calloused knuckles on their hands for walking on the ground. Gorillas are primarily terrestrial animals, rarely climbing trees and then not very high. Gorillas and chimpanzees can walk bipedally for short distances, and chimpanzees and bonobos can sit in a crouch while using their hands for gathering food or making tools. Orangutans walk bipedally with difficulty, characteristically holding their arms and hands upward and outward for balance. They move much more swiftly along the ground when on all fours, but they are speedier still when traveling up in tree branches. They prefer to remain in trees and will climb very high up in them. Except for the gibbons, apes find brachiation (swinging from tree branch to tree branch by the arms) difficult or impossible because they are too heavy.

The apes have in common great upper-body strength, long torsos, and feet with opposable big toes. They have lost the tails of their ancient primate ancestors, and like humans have bones fused to form a coccyx. Their lumbar vertebrae are fewer in number and thicker than in other primates, an adaptation for bearing the weight of a large upper body that is usually carried upright, even though it costs the spine much of its flexibility. The hands and wrists of apes are supple and highly maneuverable, allowing for great dexterity. They tend to have long hair that covers almost all of their bodies, short faces with prominent eyes, and small ears. Early in their evolution, the eyes of primates moved forward beneath their foreheads, allowing them to see straight ahead with both eyes at once, providing them with true stereoscopic vision — an advantage when moving quickly through an ever-shifting environment such as tree branches because stereoscopic vision provides a three-dimensional view that shows objects moving with depth as well as length and breadth. The movement of the eyes forward made room for the cranium to expand, and the brain within expanded, providing room for, among other traits, a more highly developed brain center for eyesight than had been possible before. The sense of smell of *Pongidae* species is more sensitive than that of humans, but in general less sensitive than that of other primates; this is the result of the eyes becoming more prominent than in other primates (except for humans) because the nasal passages have become smaller, even compressed, and the anatomy for the eyes took up more room on the face and skull. Their hearing may not be much better than that of humans. As with humans, their ears have dropped down on their heads and have become smaller than in the ancestral stock of primates. These are sometimes called "modern" traits, but this does not mean "superior." When biologists refer to modern characteristics in animals, they mean traits that have recently evolved as opposed to "primitive" traits, which were ones common among earlier ancestors of animals. In the case of the apes, they retain many primitive traits found in the fossils of the earliest known primates; for instance they retain clavicles, which serve to bear the weight of a body that swings through trees by the arms (even though the chimpanzees and gorillas cannot do so); they also retain five digits and their hands and feet and other skeletal structures that harken back to the bodies of small squirrellike primates that lived 55 million years ago. In fact, among primates, the colobus monkeys are overall more "modern."

Remarkable in their development are the brains of the apes. The enlarged skulls of the apes are home to large, complex brains with large cognitive and learning centers. The cognitive parts of their brains probably evolved because the ancestors of *Pongidae* lived in a widely varying, frequently changing environment that provided a wide variety of foods to the animals that could take advantage of them. The apes survived by becoming nonspecialists — rather than by depending on one principal resource for nourishment, they took advantage of whatever was available, from animal meat to tiny insects to fibrous plants. Their learning centers may have evolved in part to cope with a changing environment and to satisfy a need to keep track of food supplies. The apes to a large extent teach their young how to behave and to survive. Childhood and adolescence last for many years for apes, during which they learn what is good to eat and what is not, how to socialize with others of their species, and how to recognize and respond to danger. Much of this behavior is not instinctive but is shown to the young animals by adults. Their memory is also very good. For example, orangutans memorize their range, learning where the best sources of food are, especially fruit trees because such trees are uncommon compared to the number of other trees in their habitat. The discovery of a new fruit tree becomes a memory. In orangutans, memory and cognition coordinate so that an orangutan not only remembers where food sources are but even plans ahead so that it travels to fruiting trees in their proper season and has trees to travel to when the one currently being used for food runs out of fruit.

A long-held scientific view about intelligence has been that high intelligence — thinking intelligence — results from a complex social life. After all, humans have the most complicated social behavior of anyone and also have a correspondingly high capacity for thinking in order to cope with social complexities. Orangutans have long confused observers because testing them suggests that they are very intelligent animals, yet they seem to lead solitary lives without much interaction. However, field studies show that orangutans have complex social lives, but they are social lives unlike that of humans. They live in vast ranges in which they keep track of one another through loud cries, and they create and maintain an intricate hierarchy of dominance among males and females partly through their cries. Unlike humans who live in close proximity, their intimate social lives are conducted over many square miles. Each ape species is an animal with its own unique combination of physical and behavioral traits; their priorities are set by instincts that have evolved separately from humans for millions of years.

The evolution of the apes is mysterious. They, like other primates, evolved in moist tropical areas, the climate of which is conducive to rapid decay of corpses and thus very poor for forming fossils. In fact, there is a gap in the fossil history of primates of about 10 million years, from 14 to 4 million years ago, during which the apes evolved considerably. Scientists have engaged in a lively (often bitterly rancorous) debate about ape evolution for most of the second half of the twentieth century, and few agree about the exact details of their evolutionary tree. There is a broad consensus that of the ape family, the gibbons branched away first, then the orangutans. It is probable that the gorillas were next to part company from the line that would lead to humans, but some authorities argue that the chimpanzees actually parted before the gorillas. Exactly when the human line parted from the apes is not known, although paleontologists are striving mightily to find out. At present, evidence suggests that the human line parted company from the apes over 4 million years ago.

The Perplexing Case of *Homo sapiens*

The subject of much argument and little revelation is the relationship of humans to the apes. Since the 1950s, the dominant view has been that human beings, the species *Homo sapiens*, belong to a family separate from that of apes, *Hominidae*. Presently, many authorities argue that apes are in fact hominids and part of the evolutionary ancestors of the hominid line; thus, they place the apes in the family *Hominidae* and dispense with the family *Pongidae* altogether. Both sides of the argument have evidence that seems to support their views. For those who argue for a separate family there is fossil evidence indicating there have been many species of human and that these species broke away from their nearest ape ancestors several million years ago. For the other side, there is biochemical evidence that suggests that chimpanzees were part of the line that led to humans until perhaps as recently as 4 million years ago; their genes are very similar to those of modern humans, with some claiming (the evidence for this is incomplete) that only three percent of chimpanzee genes are different from those of *Homo sapiens*. The apes also bear anatomical and skeletal similarities to humans. For example, they have appendixes, a trait not found in other primates but shared by humans. Further, they have the fused bones and heavy lumbar vertebrae in their spines that, while not exactly like humans, seem much closer to human spines than to those of any other primates. In addition, they have similar hands, wrists, and forearms to those of humans. On the other hand, their skulls bear significant differences from those of humans such as a sagittal crest, their hips diverge markedly from those of humans, and their knees are structured much differently. Further, in spite of a romantic tendency to equate ape behavior with familiar human patterns of behavior, the behavior of the apes varies enormously from that of humans. For the present book, we have chosen to follow the taxonomy used by the United States Fish and Wildlife Service for its designation of endangered species and by the IUCN in its discussions of apes, placing the apes in the family *Pongidae*.

Mountain Gorilla

Gorilla gorilla beringei

Rick Weyerhaeuser

Status	Endangered
Listed	June 2, 1970
Family	Pongidae (Gorillas)
Description	Largest of the primates; heads have a prominent crest, low forehead and heavy ridges over the small eyes; hair is brownish-black.
Habitat	Lowland rain forest; mountain rain forest; and bamboo forest.
Food	Vines, ferns, bamboo shoots.
Reproduction	Single young every 3 to 4 years.
Threats	Poaching; agricultural development.
Range	Rwanda, Republic of Congo, and Uganda.

Description

The mountain gorilla, *Gorilla gorilla beringei*, is considered to be the largest and the most powerful of all the living primates. However, it is also considered to be one of the most gentle animals. An adult male may weigh 300 to 400 pounds or more and stand 5 feet 6 inches tall when fully erect, with an arm-spread greatly exceeding its height. The females are much smaller, weighing 150 to 250 pounds. Unlike many other primates, such as monkeys, gorillas have no tail but rather the few remaining caudal vertebrae are fused together in a small bone, the coccyx. They also have a pungent odor, like humans, emanating from a large cluster of specialized sweat glands under the armpits.

Their heads are massive and have a prominent crest with a low forehead and heavy ridges over the eyes. Their eyes and ears are small while the nostrils are large. Their hands are very large and the thumbs are larger than the fingers. Their hair is brownish-black to blue-black and the males over the age of ten have a predominate silvery-grey saddle.

Gorillas often stand erect but prolonged movement on two feet is rare. The normal walking position is on all fours with the knuckles on the ground.

One of the identifying features of this species is its nose. The nose of the mountain gorilla does not have a continuous ridge all around the nostrils, while the nose of the western lowland gorilla has a continuous ridge all around the nostrils that forms the shape of a heart.

Behavior

The mountain gorilla consumes as much as 50 pounds a day of vegetation, preferring the choicest parts of vines, ferns, bamboo shoots, and other plants. They usually get enough moisture from this food without drinking any water.

These gorillas roam the forest floor during the daylight hours in search of preferred food, especially termites, for consumption.

It is believed that the females do not reach sexual maturity until the age of 6 or 7, while males reach sexual maturity at about 9 or 10, when the hair starts to turn silver. There is no evidence of a breeding season, but mature females normally produce a single young every 3.5 to 4 years. If the young dies in infancy the time interval is reduced. Mortality is high, probably between forty and fifty percent of the progeny die during the infant and juvenile periods.

The mountain gorilla lives in groups of any number between 2 and 30 but generally average between 6 and 17. Each group is dominated by a silverback male.

Habitat

The mountain gorilla is found in three types of environment: lowland rain forest below 5,000 feet; mountain rain forest from 5,000 to 11,500 feet; and bamboo forest from 8,000 to 10,000 feet. An estimated three-quarters of the population inhabit the lowland rain forest and the remainder live in the mountain forests. The bamboo habitat is relatively unimportant to the subspecies, as it contains little suitable dry season forage and has a limited distribution.

The most favored habitat consists of secondary forest. The rotational felling of primary forest, and its subsequent regeneration, under the slash and burn system of shifting agriculture used in the past by primitive agriculturalists, created conditions that were very favorable.

The primary habitat may consist of dwarf elfin forest, which is permanently shrouded in mist in a perpetually cold and wet atmosphere. Dense forest is less favored than a more open type in which plenty of light can penetrate the canopy. This results in a luxuriant growth of herbaceous vegetation which provides the gorillas with their main source of food.

The heavy, mature males sleep on the ground but the others of a family group bend branches of a tree into a crude platform. A gorilla rarely takes more than a few minutes to make a nest which is not normally occupied more than once.

Distribution

The mountain gorilla is found in the remote forests bordering the Rift Valley between Republic of Congo and Tanzania. It inhabits a very small area of the Virunga Volcanoes on the borders of Rwanda, Uganda, and Republic of Congo.

The last survey was conducted in 1989 in the Virunga conservation area, where 324 individuals were counted. Another 320 gorillas were counted in Uganda at Bwindi Impenetrable Forest National Park, but it is not known if this species is *G. g. beringei*. A new survey is scheduled for late 1997 in Bwindi.

Threats

The number of gorillas that are routinely killed for food is thought to be substantial, although this appears to have little effect on the total population numbers. There is also an increasing demand for gorillas in the pharmaceutical industry and for medical research.

Losses through predation by leopards or other carnivores are believed to be insignificant. Of course, the main predator is man. Gorillas are also subject to a wide variety of diseases and other ailments such as viruses, bacterial infections, and various internal parasites which may be responsible for the majority of the deaths.

Threats to gorilla populations include predation, commercial exploitation, and habitat destruction. Local people are known to kill gorillas. In fact, Dian Fossey the former leading field researcher on gorillas, once found a group of five gorillas stoned to death in Virunga. Gorillas are killed for food, as a pest, and for their body parts. Gorilla parts are used for religious ceremonies, medicinal purposes, and for sport trophies.

Conservation and Recovery

Through Dian Fossey's tireless efforts to study the mountain gorilla and the world attention she brought to their cause, her base camp in the Virunga mountains evolved into a research facility and the focus of conservation efforts. Staffed through many periods of political turmoil, the researchers were forced to abandon their post in 1990 when full civil war erupted in Rwanda, and as of mid-1997 had not returned. With their departure, field conservation efforts have ceased.

Recovery of the mountain gorilla started in 1925 with the establishment of the Albert National Park, which was designed primarily for the long-term protection of the gorillas inhabiting the six dormant cones that constitute the Virunga Volcanoes. However, in 1958, 47,500 acres of forest land were relinquished to agriculture.

In 1932, the Kayonza Forest, otherwise known as the Impenetrable Forest, was designated as a forest reserve and then as a wildlife sanctuary in 1961. Foresting has been done in this area but through selective procedures there has been little more than a temporary disturbance. Gorillas are seldom molested in the reserve, although occasionally a few may be unintentionally killed in traps that were set for wild pigs. Their status in the Kayonza Forest appears to be satisfactory and steady at the present.

The conservation of gorillas and their habitat is of global concern. Those in captive populations may avoid extinction. The future of the gorilla in captivity requires national and international cooperation. The colonies of endangered species in zoos and other facilities can ensure the survival of the species. The development of successful breeding colonies requires that offspring are produced, and that the species retains its natural behavior and is able to reproduce and care for its young.

Recent advances in artificial reproduction are being used in attempts to increase captive populations of endangered primates. In vitro fertilization and embryo transfer techniques are being used to increase these populations.

Research programs in zoological parks have probably contributed the most to gorilla conservation in the areas of exhibit design, animal management and propagation, health care, field research, and educational programs.

The U.S. National Institute of Health funds seven primate centers in the United States. These centers house such vital data as primate behavior and development, husbandry, reproductive biology, nutrition, disease, and pathology.

Western Lowland Gorilla

Gorilla gorilla gorilla

Noel Rowe

Status	Endangered
Listed	June 2, 1970
Family	Pongidae (Gorillas)
Description	Brown-gray hair, black skin, humanlike gaze, big molars and jaw muscles, long arms, and broad hands.
Habitat	The tropical forests of west central Africa, near sea level.
Food	Mostly leaves and some ripe fruit.
Reproduction	Females bear young about every four years; about 50% of young do not survive to adulthood.
Threats	Loss of habitat to urbanization and agriculture, and to human predation.
Range	Gabon; scattered in the Central African Republic, Cameroon, Congo, Rio Muni and southern Nigeria.

Description

It seems almost impossible for field researchers not to be captivated by the gorilla's eyes. Many reports consistently note how looking into a gorilla's eyes seems the same as looking into a human's eyes. The eyes are deep set, bounded above by thick brow ridges and beneath by a broad nose and upward-curving bare patches that are themselves bounded by hair. The tendency of the gorilla to meet the eyes of humans with its own gaze may be part of what makes it not only appealing, but vulnerable. A hunter may respond to the gorilla's steady gaze with a bullet.

The western lowland gorilla may be distinguished from its relatives by its hair color, which is brownish gray for both male and female, and by hair length, which tends to be much longer than on its relatives, the mountain gorilla and the eastern lowland gorilla. Its face is shorter and its teeth smaller than the other gorillas. Like other gorillas, its chest tends to be bare, with its limbs and back covered with long, shaggy hair and its abdomen covered by shorter hair. It walks on four limbs — on the bottoms of its feet and the knuckles of its hands. Its arms are long, with broad hands, but its arms are somewhat shorter than those of a mountain gorilla. Although youngsters may be found high in trees — even swinging from tree to tree — bulky grownups tend to remain on the ground, sometimes nesting in the lower limbs of trees.

Newborns weigh about 5 pounds. Males grow to be about 400 pounds, and females grow to about 200 pounds in the wild. Full-grown males tend to be about 5 feet 6 inches in height, although they may be taller or shorter by a few inches. Full-grown females tend to be about 5 feet in height.

In the wild, the gorillas live to be about 35 years old. In captivity, they may reach 50 years of age. However, they do not necessarily fare better in captivity; they need much exercise and may become obese when confined to small areas and fed by humans, rather than feeding by moving about. Thus the animal one sees at a zoo may not well represent the species as a whole.

Behavior

Western lowland gorillas normally are not wide-ranging travelers. In conditions in which human presence is small, the gorilla can find plenty of food at hand in its heavily vegetated native forests, and it need not travel far to forage for food. A group of western lowland gorillas may need no more than 12 square miles for its range.

They live in family units, usually consisting of an adult male, a few females, and their young, usually about 10 individual animals altogether, although the group may comprise 2 to 35 individual animals. However, the western lowland gorilla rarely lives in groups larger than 10 and is commonly found in groups of 5 animals.

As with the other gorillas, the western lowland gorilla group's adult male is a "silverback," a male with a silver saddle across his back. When a female reaches sexual maturity, she leaves her original group to join another, becoming the mate of an adult male. It is the male that holds the group together, by attracting females and by protecting its group from intruders. The adult male is very strong and amazingly quick, able to cover several feet in the wink of an eye. Few predators ever challenge it, and it seems to deal with intruders either by challenging them or by moving the group out of harm's way. Its tendency to challenge human interlopers may contribute to its decline in numbers; when it charges (usually stopping itself short of physical contact — the impressiveness of the challenge is usually enough to persuade unwanted animals to move away), it presents a big target for a hunter intent on shooting it.

Other members of the group will stay close enough to the adult male so that he can come to their aid with a bounding charge. At rest, the females with the youngest infants will stay closest to the male, with lesser-burdened female members a few feet farther away, and maturing males at the outer edge of the group. Upon reaching maturity, the males will leave the group to live singly, eventually picking up females. The females may move from one adult male to another, attracted to the males who fight other males best. Since interloping males may kill the infants in a group, a male's ability to defend its females and their young is important. An interloping male runs a significant risk if he already has females of his own. Losing a confrontation with a male protecting its group may cause the females of the interloping male to seek out new silverbacks. In spite of these pressures on family groups, they tend to be more stable than the mountain gorilla and the eastern lowland gorilla. The generally smaller size of their family groups may be the reason for this.

Western lowland gorillas spend much of their days foraging for food, occasionally stopping to rest. They eat leaves and ripe fruit — more fruit than their near relatives. They are unable to metabolize unripe fruit. Because fruit is less available than leaves, and because fruit is a notable part of the western lowland gorilla's diet, it may be that the eating of fruit is what keeps the western lowland gorilla's family groups relatively small — each individual needs more range for food, and therefore a given area can support fewer western lowland gorillas than other gorilla subspecies.

Habitat

The western lowland gorilla prefers to live in dense primary and secondary forests and lowland swamps and montane forest up to 10,007 feet. It is an adaptable animal that can adjust to a wide variety of forest types.

Distribution

The western lowland gorilla's past territory was western central Africa, and it is now found in the forests of Angola, Cameroon, the Central African Republic, Congo, Gabon, Nigeria, and Rio Muni. It probably no longer exists in Republic of Congo (formerly Zaire). At one time, it would have had a wide range extending through the vast forests which once covered the territories of these modern nations. Today, its original habitat may be best seen in Gabon, a nation which is still mostly forested, and in the small reserves of Rio Muni, which is trying to preserve its wildlife even as its urban areas expand. Naturalists are still trying to learn about the populations of the western lowland gorilla; the animal's preference for densely forested areas have made it hard to count its numbers. Recent research suggests that the original numbers of gorillas that existed before the encroachment of human civilization may have been surprisingly high, maybe in the hundreds of thousands. This high number for the past population derives out of the number of western lowland gorillas found in Gabon's old-growth forests, where perhaps more than 30,000 of the gorillas live.

At present, the safest region for the western lowland gorilla is in southwestern Gabon, which not only has substantial forests, but has a human population whose customs forbid the eating of the flesh of primates. In northern Gabon, people generally regard gorilla meat as a delicacy, but the animal seems to be holding its own by living in remote, dense forests, and by being shy of humans. Gabon is still primarily forested, allowing gorillas a large range in which to live and propagate, and Gabon is thinly populated, keeping pressures from the expansion of human habitat to a minimum.

The western lowland gorilla does not fare nearly as well in other nations. Few — they are rarely seen — live in Angola, just north of the Zaire River. Nigeria was probably never an important home for the western lowland gorilla, and 100 to 250 individuals occur there, now. Their range in Nigeria is limited to the Afi River Reserve and the Boshi-Okwongo Forest Reserve. Possibly 500 (probably fewer) gorillas live in the Central African Republic. They have disappeared from traditional ranges such as the Mongoumba region, but are still to be found in the southwest of the country, near Ngama. In Cameroon, gorillas live across the south of the country and possibly in the northwest — although they may have disappeared from there since the late 1970s, when they were seen in the Takamanda Reserve. Pressures from human populations are squeezing the gorilla ranges, but it is possible that 2,000 or so still live in the country. They seem to be holding their own in the Campo Reserve in southwest Cameroon. In Rio Muni (once Equatorial Guinea), the western mountain gorilla has been reported in small, disparate areas, and seems to be doing best in Monte del Frio National Park. Poor enforcement of laws against harming the gorillas and poaching limits the number of western mountain gorillas in Rio Muni to between 1,000 to 2,000. The pressures on the Rio Muni populations of gorillas are so great that the western mountain gorilla may disappear from the country around the turn of the century. Up-to-date population estimates for Congo are hard to find, but in the 1980s between 2,000 and 3,000 western mountain gorillas were thought to be living there, in the southwest and northwest corners of the country, and at the headwaters of the Ogooué River.

These ranges are shrinking rapidly, except in Gabon and the reserves in Nigeria. Poaching and loss of habitat are reducing the populations rapidly, in spite of conservation efforts. There are at present still enough range left and enough western lowland gorillas left that the species may not only be preserved, but that its genetic diversity may also survive intact; this very much depends on conservation efforts.

Threats

The threats to the survival of the western lowland gorilla almost entirely originate with humans. The gorillas need well-forested territory in which to feed, propagate, and interact. Urbanization presses gorillas out of their ranges. When these ranges disappear, so does the gorilla. Agriculturalization is a problem for the western lowland gorilla everywhere but Gabon, where other enterprises prevail, and where a low human population density puts less pressure on the nation to produce food to feed its people than in neighboring lands. Not only does agriculture destroy gorilla habitats, but the gorillas also become pests for the farmers. The gorillas will eat leaves on farms, and thus farmers will destroy the animals.

The greatest threat to the western lowland gorilla comes from humans hunting it. Although the numbers of western lowland gorillas in Gabon seem promising, this subspecies is being killed off at such a rapid rate that it could still disappear in a few years. In northern Gabon, the gorilla is a delicacy and can even be found on restaurant menus. In a protein-poor part of the world, the western lowland gorilla may be hunted for food almost anywhere, even in southwestern Gabon, where the local peoples forbid the eating of primates. An even more destructive pressure on the western lowland gorilla is trophy hunting. Local people hunt gorillas for their body parts. Skulls attract foreign buyers. Hands are made into ashtrays (indeed, a gorilla may be killed for nothing other than taking its hands for ashtrays). Other parts may be used for display or for folk medicines. This money-driven hunting is the most immediate threat to the western lowland gorilla.

Conservation and Recovery

Most national governments in the natural territory of the western lowland gorilla have laws protecting it. Enforcement of these laws varies, and they are often not enforced at all. Even when the will is there, the resources for enforcement often are not. The dense, hard to travel regions that have long shielded the western lowland gorilla from casual human incursion also protect poachers from the law. They can track down gorillas, kill them and quickly butcher them, and disappear into the forest before their crime can be spotted. Selling gorilla body parts is often not illegal, but even where it is illegal, villagers openly peddle skulls, hands, teeth, and other parts of the gorilla.

The money for such harvesting of gorillas comes from outside their native regions, often from tourists, sometimes from collectors, and often from dealers in foreign lands that will sell gorilla parts in their shops. Another threat also comes from foreign zoos. The buying and selling of gorillas is now illegal in many places, but zoos continue to buy them. About two thirds of the gorillas in zoos were captured in the wild. These represent about one third of those originally captured, because two thirds die in transit. Other deaths would follow from the breakup of family groups. The capture of a silverback could result in the deaths of all of its young and perhaps its mates. The loss of a female means the loss of its young. The loss of any gorillas results in a reduction of the breeding population. In a species in which 50% of its young normally do not survive to mate, the precipitous loss of potential breeders can have a disproportionate effect on the species' future population.

In Gabon, it is illegal to hunt the western lowland gorilla. Its Ministry of Eaux et Forêts is actively trying to protect the animals on reserves and is trying to block the access of poachers to them. The national government has been wrestling since the early 1980s with ways to accommodate both its human population and its vast wilderness — the wildlife of which is perhaps the nation's greatest natural resource. It has funded research into western gorilla habitats in order to find natural boundaries that it can exploit for keeping the animals and humans apart.

Angola has been beset by civil war and political strife for decades; the government's good intentions toward the western lowland gorilla in the early 1970s, when it hoped to create a sanctuary for the animals, has not reached fruition. Cameroon's laws strictly forbid the hunting of the western lowland gorilla. Conservationists are working there to establish sanctuaries for the gorillas. The Central African Republic, also by law, protects the western lowland gorilla. The animal's density of population in the southwest of the nation is high enough that there is reason to hope that by protecting the animals they can establish a viable breeding population. Congo is trying to preserve its natural world as a tourist attraction and has cooperated with the international community on a number of environmental preservation projects. The ideal habitat for the western lowland gorilla has shrunk greatly in Congo, but suitably dense forestation still exists in the Conkouati area (from the coast to the Koubala Mountains), which is to be a national park. Nigeria's laws protect its western mountain gorillas, although conservationists complain that the laws are not enforced. Conservationists hope to negotiate with local villagers to end the hunting of the western lowland gorilla. The major problem in this effort is the potential conflict between the national government and the locals; an attempt to link up the known gorilla territories into a gorilla reserve could engulf whole villages, and villagers might rebel against being forced to observe the rules of the reserve in what they consider to be their homeland and territory.

Still, there is the potential that the gorillas, already situated in accessible areas, could be exploited as tourist attractions, which would bring badly needed money to the locals, as well as their government, and conservationists are hoping to use the potential economic benefit to persuade the government to act on behalf of its gorilla population and to persuade the local hunters that it is in their best interest to help the gorillas prosper. The western lowland gorilla population in Nigeria is small, but the government already has a system of reserves that could serve to protect its western lowland gorillas, possibly making itself into a major force in the preservation of the species. Rio Muni outlaws the capturing and selling of the western lowland gorilla, but the IUCN reports that the law is unenforced.

A number of actions could save Rio Muni's western lowland gorillas, two of which would be particularly significant: protecting them in the Campo area would expand the range of protection in Cameroon's Campo Reserve since the two areas are contiguous; the southeast area of Rio Muni is isolated from humans and has the right habitat for the gorillas, making it a prime spot for a national park. Unfortunately, urbanization is putting pressure on the wild habitat of the Campo area, and the preservation of the western lowland gorilla in the southeast and elsewhere requires immediate enforcement.

Eastern Lowland Gorilla

Gorilla gorilla graueri

Noel Rowe

Status	Endangered
Listed	CITES Appendix 1, IUCN.
Family	Pongidae (Gorillas)
Description	Black hair and skin; males weigh about 400 pounds and stand 5 feet 9 inches tall; females weigh 200 pounds.
Habitat	Tropical forest.
Food	Leaves
Reproduction	Single infant after gestation of about 260 days; female bears one young about every 4 years.
Threats	Loss of habitat killing by farmers as pests, and hunting.
Range	Republic of Congo (formerly Zaire)

Description

It is perhaps the large canines of the eastern lowland gorilla, *Gorilla gorilla graueri*, which it may display when threatened, that have encouraged its reputation among humans as a fierce, savage beast. While, like most wild animals, it can be dangerous, the eastern lowland gorilla normally does not disturb human beings and in general avoids them. Its humanlike eyes are captivating for field researchers, and the animal's steady, grave gaze suggests to some people that it possesses a humanlike intelligence. This suggestion of humanity within the gorilla has helped motivate efforts to preserve it from extinction.

The eastern lowland gorilla tends to be bigger than the western lowland gorilla, and it tends to have a broader chest, similar to that of the mountain gorilla. Its face is longer than that of the other gorillas, but its teeth are much like those of the mountain gorilla and larger than those of the western lowland gorilla. The fully grown male of the eastern lowland gorilla is "silverback," with a patch of silvery hair on its back, not as large as on other gorillas. Males tend to be double the weight of females, with disparity in sizes between males and females sometimes much larger than among other gorillas. This last feature may not be a truly distinguishing one for the eastern lowland gorillas — the animals were so close to extinction when scientific studies were conducted that the male-female size disparity may have been normal for all three subspecies of gorillas when they lived at their maximum populations in forests undisturbed by humans. Eastern lowland gorilla males reach about 400 pounds at maturity, although ones weighing as much as 600 pounds have been reported by researchers. Females tend to weigh about 200 pounds at maturity. The males tend to be about 5 feet 9 inches tall at maturity, although researchers report seeing much larger ones, including one that may have been 6 feet 4 inches tall. Females tend to be about 5 feet tall.

Behavior

Eastern lowland gorillas prefer to live in primary, secondary, and bamboo forests and marshes at 3,280 to 7,875 feet. Requiring habitat that is rich in plant life, they eat primarily leaves and a little fruit, which is uncommon in their forests. The sagittal crest on their heads, for attaching powerful jaw muscles, are large, particularly on males, and their huge jaw muscles and large molars probably are a hereditary consequence of a diet almost entirely of leaves. They eat during the day, steadily on the move while they eat. Their food intake is large, and they must eat almost every waking moment, which means the heavily vegetated forests of their native habitat are important for their survival. They never denude a particular eating spot, so the forest that sustains them is able to constantly renew itself — and their food supply.

The eastern lowland gorilla social life focuses on the silverbacks. Each social group has but one silverback, which mates with the females and defends the group from interlopers. Other adult males may try to invade the group, killing the young and persuading females to join their groups; a silverback defends against this with impressive displays of its size and strength, frighteningly quick charges at the interlopers, and by fighting, although it should be emphasized that fighting is rare. Young males slowly move out of a group. When infants, they live with their mothers close to the silverback at times of rest; as they grow older, they and their mothers move outward, supplanted by other mothers with infants. Eventually, young males find themselves at the outer edge of the group, when at rest, and upon reaching maturity the young male leaves the group to live first as a solitary male, and eventually with his own group of females, if he can attract any.

Females choose their silverbacks and have been known to switch groups. Important qualities that a female considers in choosing a silverback include the size of the male and the impressiveness of his ability to intimidate or fight other males. A suitably powerful male means protection for the female and her young, not only from other eastern lowland gorilla males, but from potential predators, most of which leave the big silverbacks alone.

Eastern lowland gorilla groups can be much larger than those of the mountain gorilla and the western lowland gorilla. Groups with as many 35 members have been found.

Habitat

The eastern lowland gorilla occurs in the tropical forests of eastern central Africa. The habitat is very leafy, with an abundance of vines and underbrush as well as trees.

Distribution

The eastern lowland gorilla's past population distribution is a matter of debate, with figures stemming more from conjecture and inference than scientific evidence. They may have once numbered 100,000 distributed throughout Republic of Congo, Uganda, and Rwanda. Today, the only gorillas to be found in Uganda and Rwanda are a tiny number of mountain gorillas, although it is possible that the few gorillas living in Uganda's Bwindi Forest Reserve are actually eastern lowland gorillas who have been misclassified as *berengei* rather than *graueri*. In modern Republic of Congo, the eastern lowland gorilla has lost nearly all of its habitat and lives in populations of 100 to 300 in the Maiko National Park, the Virunga National Park, and the Kahuzi-Biega National Park. It is in the Kahuzi-Biega National Park that the gorillas may be making a small population comeback.

Threats

The greatest problem for the survival of eastern lowland gorillas has been the expansion of human territory. Forests that would harbor the gorillas have been chopped down for lumber, for pastureland, and for cropland. The traditional ranges of the eastern lowland gorilla are nearly gone; if the forests are totally destroyed, gorillas will survive only in captivity.

Another significant pressure on the gorilla population is human trophy hunting. Locals kill the gorillas for their skulls, which they sell to tourists and city dwellers. With only a few thousand individuals remaining, the eastern lowland gorilla's genetic diversity is also in jeopardy, and a good breeding population is

continually weakened.

Conservation and Recovery

Republic of Congo has laws prohibiting the hunting of the gorilla. Naturalists and others have worked since the mid-1980s to insure that these laws are enforced and to create sanctuaries for the eastern lowland gorilla. In 1984 the Eastern Zaire Gorilla Conservation Project was created, which has worked to find ways to save the gorillas from extinction. The individual populations of the eastern lowland gorilla are scattered and small, and this dispersion places pressure on breeding diversity. Although there seem to be signs that the gorilla population is growing a little, the numbers are small enough, and the gorillas are vulnerable enough to hunters, that with the loss of any more habitat the eastern lowland gorilla could disappear from the wild in any given year.

From its first discovery, the gorilla has interested world audiences. The eastern lowland gorilla's long fangs and tendency to display its strength when threatened once encouraged people to believe it was a vicious killer capable of rending human beings limb-from-limb. In Edgar Rice Burroughs's *Tarzan of the Apes* (1914), an immensely popular work that has been read by millions of people for generations, Tarzan battles a ferocious and aggressive gorilla. Hunters would proudly stand beside their slain gorillas for photographs, which would perhaps prove their courage when facing a menacing and violent creature. Since the 1960s, much of the world's perception of gorillas has slowly changed. In America, television specials on PBS have shown an animal that is usually a peaceful herbivore, uninterested in confrontations with humans. Magazines discovered that real-life accounts of gorillas sold copies, thus bringing the endangered status of gorillas to the attention of their readers. Naturalist Dian Fossey came to prominence through PBS specials and magazine coverage of her studies of the nearly extinct mountain gorilla, and her murder brought a sense of urgency to her work. Motion pictures have helped present the plight of gorillas to worldwide audiences, with the popular success of *Gorillas in the Mist* (1988) being the most notable example. Worldwide publicity, generated in part by the film, has reduced the demand for gorilla body parts, and the capture and shipping abroad of living gorillas for zoos and theme parks. In the case of the eastern lowland gorilla, loss of habitat has been most responsible for its decline in numbers, but the trade in body parts and specimens could lead to its extinction in the wild.

Sumatran [=Abel's] Orangutan

Pongo abelii

Noel Rowe

Status	Endangered
Listed	June 2, 1970
Family	Pongidae (Primates)
Description	Large primate with long, shaggy hair, colored orange, brown-orange, or black. Face is pale when young, darkening as the orangutan ages.
Habitat	Tropical forests.
Food	375 varieties of foods, including fruit, vegetation, insects and small animals.
Reproduction	Gestation is one of the longest among primates, 260 to 270 days, usually resulting in a single birth.
Threats	Loss of habitat to logging and agriculture; hunting; collecting for zoos.
Range	Indonesia: Sumatra

Description

The orangutan formerly included two subspecies, but *Pongo abelii* has been elevated to a full species. *Pongo abelii* lives on Sumatra, and *Pongo pygmaeus* lives on Borneo (please see separate entry). The Sumatran species has fairer hair color than the Bornean species, with black-haired orangutans seemingly rarer than on Borneo; the black hair is often reddish. In addition, the Sumatran species has longer hair than its Bornean relative. It has a longer face and a thinner, lighter build than the Bornean species. Like that of the Bornean orangutan, the face of the Sumatran darkens to black as it ages, although it seems to remain somewhat paler than the darkest faces among the Bornean species. Most orangutans have orange hair, which has led to their common nickname, "the red ape." Their hair color varies from one orangutan to another, and the hair can be brownish and is sometimes black.

Behavior

The Sumatran orangutan is a solitary animal requiring large tracts of land with sparse populations. The center of the Sumatran orangutan's society is the dominant male, a large, mature male over ten years old. It probably takes over the territory of its father. Once it has secured its territory of several square miles, it makes great, booming calls, using its throat sack to give the calls resonance. Explorers have reported that the call can be startling and even frightening; still, all the territorial male is doing is letting other males know that it lays claim to a certain area and letting them know where it is — helping them avoid direct confrontations. Within the dominant male's territory are several female territories; these belong to mature females over seven years old. These are the females that the dominant male mates with, probably because mature females have the best chance of successfully bearing and raising their young. Adolescent and younger females are usually left alone by the dominant male. The mature females prefer to mate with the dominant male and will try to fight off the advances of other males; this is probably because the dominant male offers the best protection for their young. The dominant male will protect both mother and child from other orangutans and predators. The fully mature male is both very strong and very protective. Sexual unions involving dominant males are entirely consensual; the dominant males do not commit rape. The dominant males prefer to mate infrequently and only with fully mature females. This behavior puzzled observers for decades; young males mated far more often than the old males, which would make it seem that the young males were likelier to sire young than the supposedly dominant males. Some naturalists thought that the old territorial males did little other than bellow at each other, without producing young of their own. More recent work shows these ideas to be mistaken. For one thing, the rapes hardly ever result in pregnancy; for another, the young males tend to mate with immature females that are unlikely to become pregnant. In the unions between mature orangutans, the female is an active, willing participant; this enhances the chances that she will become pregnant.

The mothers are the primary care givers for their young. For the first year of its life, the youngster holds tight to its mother, never leaving her physical touch. As it matures, the youngster leaves its mother to find and eat on its own or to find playmates near its own age. Adolescence arrives at about seven years of age for males and somewhat earlier for females. Adolescent males are rambunctious and eager for sexual activity. Females prefer to mate with older males and tend to resist the advance of the adolescent males; this can result in rape, with the female struggling against the violent sexual union with the young male. Females usually do not become mothers until they are over ten years old; in their teens, males begin to settle down.

Habitat

Orangutans of Sumatra once lived in large tropical forests. They are now restricted to remote mountainous regions and a few swampy areas.

Distribution

The Sumatran orangutan has long lived

in the highland forests of Sumatra. Logging and especially agriculture have in the last thirty years destroyed most of its habitat, and its range is now restricted to a few wildlife reserves and patches of highland forests.

Threats

Slash-and-burn agriculture is responsible for most of the destruction of the Sumatran orangutan's forest. This old practice has been forcing the forests into retreat for centuries, but like much of the rest of the world, Sumatra has had a boom in its human population, accelerating the process of deforestation to the point that most of the forest has been eliminated in only the last few decades. The Indonesian government has met with a great deal of frustration in its efforts to save what is left of its natural heritage. It made it illegal to sell timber from the forests, so local people chopped down the trees and burned the timber, stubbornly continuing to clear the land for farming. Elsewhere, the slash-and-burn mode of agriculture continues, with people setting fire to the forestlands. In any case, the farming is primitive, with no thought to preserving the land; after a few years, a cleared plot of forestland has been depleted of its nutrients and eroded so badly that it cannot support most plant life; observers say these areas in what was once the forestlands of orangutans look like desolate, blasted heaths.

Logging is also a significant factor in the decline of the Sumatran orangutan. The animal is sometimes treated as a pest by loggers; where the orangutans live naturalists press for restrictions on logging, and some logging companies therefore kill the orangutans, eliminating one of the important reasons for halting their work.

Between agriculture and logging, the Sumatran orangutan has lost nearly all of its range. This has resulted in the isolation of individual orangutans from other ones because their forests have been broken up into small patches, and it has resulted in a decline in the fertility of the orangutans. Apparently, the orangutans have a mechanism for regulating the size of their population according to how much range is available to it; as the range has shrunk, so have the number of births as a percentage of the remaining population.

The Sumatran orangutan is also severely threatened by hunting. Mothers are killed and their babies are sold to exporters who sell them as pets in America, Canada, Europe, and other industrialized regions, and orangutans of all ages are sold to medical researchers. Orangutans are also purchased for use in zoos, circuses, motion pictures, and television. Penalties for poaching orangutans are high in Indonesia, but just one orangutan can earn a poacher the equivalent of a year's wages for most of his neighbors, and the animals earn importers several tens of thousands of dollars in Canada, Europe, the United States, and elsewhere. In the United States, the penalties for importing orangutans are high, increasing the price of illicitly imported orangutans greatly.

Conservation and Recovery

Indonesia has established wildlife reserves on Sumatra, but maintaining these reserves has proven to be a daunting task. Some reserved areas are open to tourists and have proven to be a significant attraction for foreigners and their international currency, which helps pay for the maintenance of Sumatra's reserves. If the Sumatran orangutan is to survive, the destruction of its forests must stop altogether. This is a matter of urgency; not all areas are well patrolled, and thus even the reserves are disappearing to logging and agriculture. Soon, there will not be enough forest remaining to support a viable breeding population of orangutans.

The orangutan breeds well in captivity, and zoos and wildlife parks have had good success in maintaining their orangutan populations. The problem for the Sumatran species is that it has been crossbred with Bornean orangutans; therefore, it is not a distinct species as it is in the wild. If the wild population disappears, as seems likely, then the Sumatran species will probably cease to exist.

Borneo [=Common] Orangutan

Pongo pygmaeus

Noel Rowe

Status	Endangered
Listed	June 2, 1970
Family	Pongidae (Primates)
Description	Long, shaggy orange to black hair; face is pale when young, darkening to black with age.
Habitat	Tropical forests.
Food	375 varieties of fruits, vegetation, insects and small animals.
Reproduction	Gestation is one of the longest among primates, 260 to 270 days, usually resulting in a single birth.
Threats	Loss of habitat and human predation.
Range	Indonesia (Borneo)

Description

The orangutan formerly included two subspecies, but they have both been elevated to a full species. *Pongo pygmaeus,* the Bornean species, is heavier, stouter, and more thickly muscled than its Sumatran counterpart, *Pongo abelii* (see separate entry), and its hair tends to be shorter and darker. Its face is darker, especially in adults, whose face becomes coal black.

Behavior

There are significant differences in behavior between the two species of orangutan, but many of these differences may be the result of stress forced on orangutan populations by the rapid destruction of their native ranges by humans. A significant physical difference that is related to behavior is the throat sack on adult males; it is much larger in the Bornean species. This throat sack increases in volume as a male ages. It is used when the male makes territorial cries — loud booming calls that carry far through a forest. Typically, a large mature male (one over 10 years old) stakes out for himself a large territory; other adult males are not allowed to settle within the territory. Rather than fight over territorial boundaries, the big males call out threateningly to each other; this allows them to avoid actually meeting each other because the cries let them know where the other local territorial males are. One naturalist reported observing a boundary along a ridge between the territories of two very large males: One day one male would come to the boundaries and make big, deep cries, its big throat sack adding resonance to the calls. The next day, the other big male would come to the boundary and make its big cries. The two were careful to alternate their coming to the boundary, thus avoiding actually confronting each other. On the other hand, Bornean orangutan territorial males do sometimes meet and dispute a border between their territories. Their confrontation involves a great deal of thrashing about; tearing off big tree limbs and waving them around seems to be a significant part of the confrontation ritual. What usually happens is one or the other male retreats, ending the dispute. On those occasions when neither male retreats, the confrontation takes a frightening turn; the males grapple with one another, biting and tearing at fingers and faces. Most old males bear facial scars from such conflicts; stiff or missing fingers are also common, their having been broken or bitten off. Old Bornean males can be very dangerous to humans; they need to have a space to call their own and they resent human intrusions, even in zoos. They will attack human faces and fingers, and because they are very strong, they can do great damage to a human being.

Differences in territorial behavior between Bornean and Sumatran orangutans illustrate the problems in trying to learn how a wild animal would behave without humans around when human activity has disrupted the entire population. Members of both species of orangutans are solitary animals, preferring to live alone, yet the Bornean orangutan accepts a great many intrusions into his or her territory. By the time naturalists began studying the orangutan in detail, logging was annihilating the Bornean orangutan's forests; this meant that hundreds, perhaps thousands, of orangutans were forced out of their longtime homes and inland into the territories of other orangutans. The result was that orangutans of both genders and all ages flowed through well-established territories on their search for new territory that they could claim as their own. Thus even large territorial males would journey into territories protected by established males. Often, the established male tolerates the intruding males, allowing them to feed and sleep in peace. Sometimes, the intruding males will be confronted; if the intruding male is big enough, strong enough, and determined enough, he can frighten the established male into keeping his distance, otherwise the intruding male tries to hide. In either case, the intruding male does not remain in the established male's territory but moves on. Females and youngsters are also usually tolerated, and they, too, move on after a day or two of feeding. The dispossessed females run the risk of rape by young, territoriless males, even when they struggle against the male. Are any of these behaviors normal? It seems unlikely because the extensive migration of orangutans through other orangutans' territories is caused by human destruction of the forest, but no one can be sure that the behavior is not normal.

Habitat

The Bornean orangutan was formerly found in lowland and highland tropical forests, but now is mostly restricted to remote, often mountainous areas where some of the old primary forest survives.

Distribution

The Bornean orangutan has long lived in

the dense forest of Borneo. Logging and agriculture have in the last thirty years destroyed most of its habitat, and its range is now restricted to a few wildlife reserves and highland forests.

Threats

The Bornean species of orangutan has one significant advantage over its Sumatran relative: Most of the local people revere the orangutan and disapprove of harming it. The Bornean orangutan population has been seriously disturbed by logging, which has worked its way into the center of Borneo from the coastal forests. The land has been clear cut and eroded, more or less ruining it for both agriculture and forest. The loss of range has resulted not only in the loss of thousands of animals to starvation but in a dramatically reduced reproductive rate among the surviving orangutans. Apparently, the orangutan population regulates its population density by reducing mating when too many individual orangutans live in a small area.

The Bornean orangutan is under constant threat of capture by poachers. Babies are sold as pets in America and Europe (the poachers kill the mothers), and orangutans of all ages are sold to medical researchers. Orangutans are also purchased for use in zoos, circuses, motion pictures, and television. The animal's high intelligence makes it easy to teach tricks that amuse audiences. Penalties for poaching orangutans are high in both Malaysia and Indonesia, but just one orangutan can earn a poacher the equivalent of a year's wages for most of his neighbors, and the animals earn importers several tens of thousands of dollars in Canada, Europe, and the United States.

Conservation and Recovery

Both Malaysia and Indonesia have established wildlife reserves on Borneo; the effectiveness of these reserves remains to be seen because the relentless logging of the island's forests often intrudes into the reserves. Some naturalists have established research centers that serve as halfway houses for captured orangutans; these centers try to reintroduce the orangutans to the wild. This effort began when local peoples would find orphaned orangutan young and smuggle them out of harm's way to naturalists who were studying the orangutans. With the aid of the local people, the researchers were able to reintroduce the young orangutans back into the wild with some success; these animals sometimes survived and even began breeding. However, orangutans raised in captivity are not always successful when introduced into the wild, and they tend to remain dependent on the research centers for food and security. In spite of the efforts of the local people and the researchers, the orangutans remain threatened by poaching and by logging. Researchers have had the disquieting experience of returning to a research camp after a short absence and discovering that the camp that had been in the middle of remote, dense jungle now was in the middle of a vast open area, devoid of trees because of logging.

Chimpanzees
Family: Pongidae

Pan troglodytes schweinfurthi   Craig Stanford

Human Characteristics of Chimpanzees

According to Jane Goodall, the world's authority on chimpanzees, chimps are the closest living relative to humans and much resemble humans in their biochemical, physiological, anatomical, and behavioral composition. Our life cycles are similar: female chimps in the wild can begin reproducing at 11 to 13 years; males can copulate at this same age but require another 2 to 3 years to carry out courtship. Males are not fully mature until age 20; middle age is reached by 35, and life expectancy is 50 to 55 years. Chimps also express similar feelings as humans of joy, grief, curiosity, and fear. Females complete their menstrual cycle every 38 days (on average), with 2 to 4 days of menstruation and 10 days of sexual receptiveness. Typically, a female will give birth to one young every 5 to 6 years; twins almost never occur. The young chimp remains socially dependent on its mother until another young is born, at which time the first child begins sleeping alone and learning independence. Females rarely leave their mothers for more than a couple of hours until they are 10 years old. Once she reaches puberty, she will begin mingling with other groups, where she may eventually establish residence for mating. Male offspring generally remain near their family group for their whole lives. The diet of chimpanzees is similar to humans. They eat fruits, seeds, vegetation, eggs, and meat. Their meat resources include pigs, baboons, other species of monkeys, squirrels, and rats. Chimps, next to humans, are the most adept with using tools. They extract termites from mounds with sticks; they use leaves as wash cloths and as ladles; they use stones as weapons; and they fashion tools for specific tasks, having different tools for different tasks.

Habitat

The chimpanzee is dependent on areas with large supplies of fruit, the essential part of its diet. It lives in rain forests, deciduous forests, or savannah with woodlands. Although preferring to live in primary forests, it seems to adapt to secondary forests when necessary — an advantage over many of the other primates that live in the same region that will die out if their primary forest habitat is replaced by secondary forest.

Threats

Deforestation, caused by logging and agriculture, has destroyed much of the suitable habitat of the chimpanzee. It is also killed for meat or as an agricultural pest, although there is little evidence that it raids farmlands. The chimpanzee is also hunted for capture, to be sold either as a pet or as a laboratory animal. Typically, hunters find a small family unit that is foraging away from the larger group that they belong to, and the hunters kill every member of the family group except an infant, which they take alive. Infants are valued over adults because they are small and tractable; adults are dangerously aggressive and strong. The taking of an infant usually involves the killing of six or seven other chimpanzees; perhaps as few as one in seven captured infants survive being shipped overseas to laboratories, zoos, or pet owners. Thus the capturing of chimpanzees for commercial sale involves the deaths of many other chimpanzees and has had a profoundly negative influence on their population in the wild.

Pygmy Chimpanzee

Pan paniscus

Bertrand Deputte

Status	Endangered
Listed	March 12, 1990 (First listed as threatened on October 19, 1976)
Family	Pongidae (Primates)
Description	Large lower limbs and narrow chest, with black overall body hair.
Habitat	Unbroken forest in equatorial Africa, also secondary forests.
Food	Fruit, leaves, nuts, seeds, some meat.
Reproduction	Slow reproductive rate, raising no more than 2 young to maturity. Gestation of 230 to 240 days.
Threats	Commercial logging, forest felling for agricultural purposes, human encroachment, and commercial trade.
Range	Republic of Congo (formerly Zaire)

Description

There are two species of the genus *Pan: Pan troglodytes* (common chimpanzee) and *Pan paniscus* (pygmy chimpanzee). The pygmy chimpanzee has longer limbs, a narrower chest, and smaller teeth than the common chimpanzee. Chimpanzees are covered with black hair and walk more erect than other apes.

The head-and-body length for adult females is 27.6 to 29.9 inches; for males, it is 28.7 to 32.7 inches. Females weigh about 68 pounds; the males weigh about 86 pounds. Its skin is black as is its hair, which is short. Its young have white tail tufts, but unlike common chimpanzees — which lose their white tail tufts before adulthood — the pygmy chimpanzees retain their tufts in adulthood. The hair on their heads grows sideways, creating tufts around their ears.

The chimpanzee was once considered one species (*Pan styrus* or *Simia styrus*) which was described by Linnaeus in 1758. In 1965 Maurice Wilson described the pygmy chimpanzee as a separate species, *Pan paniscus*.

Behavior

The pygmy chimpanzee is relatively somber and seldom bites unless provoked. Its call is quieter than that of the common chimpanzee. It avoids human beings, and when humans encroach upon territory occupied by pygmy chimpanzees, the animals leave it.

Chimpanzees are known to be loosely social and will develop defended territories; male hierarchy persists. Status is established through a display of hooting and throwing rocks or tearing off and shaking branches. A single community will have between 50 to 200 members; this community will split into groups of 6 to 15 members, including both genders, that will forage for food. Adult males sometimes forage alone.

Pygmy chimpanzees have a slow reproductive rate and females usually raise no more than 2 young to maturity. The females are not able to become pregnant before 13 years of age (sometimes later), and after giving birth will not become pregnant again for at least 3 years, perhaps as many as 7 years. The reproductive life of a female is about 26 years. When in heat females will mate successively with several males. Young are born 240 days after conception. Parental care is displayed primarily by females and orphaned babies will even be adopted. Young remain with the mother for about six years and may aid in the care of younger siblings.

Chimpanzees are known to be most active during the day and are seen in trees and on the forest floor during this time. They seem comfortable on the ground, and they not only travel on it but sometimes they will even wade through shallow water. They forage and feed both on the ground and in trees, with feeding taking up about 30 percent of their waking hours. The primary food source of the pygmy chimpanzee is provided by fruit, but it supplements its diet with leaves, nuts, seeds, and some meat, including reptiles, squirrels, duikers, and bats. They are also known to prey on the voracious glossy black driver ant (*Dorylus nigricans*). This vicious insect will attack intruders with a painful bite.

Habitat

The pygmy chimpanzee is dependent on areas of unbroken forest in equatorial Africa. It seems to prefer dry lowland forests, both primary and secondary, but it also inhabits savannahs and swamps. The pygmy chimpanzee is highly associated with the presence of fruit trees. In areas of wet forests, it is migratory, moving to dry forests in wet seasons and to the wet forest in dry seasons.

Distribution

The pygmy chimpanzee occurs only in Republic of Congo (formerly Zaire), in a region called the Zaire Basin, which is between the Zaire River to the north and the Kasai and Sankuru Rivers to the south, and between Lake Tumba and Lac Ndombe to the west and the Lomani River to the east. It is not found uniformly throughout this area but instead lives in patches scattered through the forest; this patchiness may be caused by hunting by humans, which can eliminate large chunks of the pygmy chimpanzee's population. Only a few of these patches have viable breeding populations, and these are threatened by hunters. Past distribution is unknown, although it is likely that it spread only a little farther than its present range. The key change in distribution is the pygmy chimpanzee's dramatic decline in population within its native territory.

Estimates of the surviving population of pygmy chimpanzees vary, but fewer than

10,000 seems likely.

Threats

Forest felling for agricultural purposes and commercial logging have destroyed much of the suitable habitat of the pygmy chimpanzee. Use of arboricides is an additional threat to this species. This habitat destruction and human encroachment are the primary factors contributing to the declining numbers.

The pygmy chimpanzee has been the victim of exportation for use in scientific research, entertainment, exhibitions, and zoos. Prior to the 1920s there was no scientific research pertaining to nonhuman primates. Anatomical research was an integral part of evolutionary research of the post-Darwin era and scientists struggled to place man in a zoological perspective with the rest of the biological world. Primatology of this time was a study of cadavers and fossils. Yet in the 1930s, Robert M. Yerkes, a psychologist from the United States, founded the first major American primate breeding laboratory, utilized the pygmy chimpanzee and common chimpanzee in his live-animal experiments, and reached a new era of laboratory primate research.

Conservation and Recovery

The Republic of Congo (formerly Zaire) has created the Salongo National Park to protect a small number of the pygmy chimpanzees. Another possible location for a park would be in the Lomako Forest, where local peoples do not hunt the pygmy chimpanzee because hunting primates is considered taboo.

Member nations of the Convention on International Trade in Endangered Species of Wild Fauna and Flora (CITES) have agreed that this species' situation complies with Appendix I of the Convention and export and import are prohibited by these nations unless such activity is not detrimental to the species. The pygmy chimpanzee is listed in Class A of the African Convention, which means it may only be hunted, captured, or exported with the express permission of the highest governmental authority responsible for wildlife in the Republic of Congo. Further, even in some non-African countries, importation of wild-caught chimpanzees is forbidden.

In zoos in the United States and some other countries there are fewer than a hundred pygmy chimpanzees, with untold numbers in research laboratories. Most of those held in zoos were captive-born, and breeding captive pygmy chimpanzees may help stave off its extinction. The international studbook for the pygmy chimpanzee is maintained at the Antwerp zoo (Koningen Astridplein 26, B-2000, Antwerp, Belgium).

Chimpanzee

Pan troglodytes

Rich Block

Status	Endangered
Listed	October 19, 1976; March 12, 1990
Family	Pongidae (Primates)
Description	Pink, brown, or black face that usually darkens with age; black hair, sometimes turning to gray on the backs of fully mature adults.
Habitat	Unbroken forest with fruit trees.
Food	Fruit, leaves, nuts, seeds, and some meat.
Reproduction	After gestation of 240 days, a single young is born.
Threats	Forest felling for agricultural use, commercial logging, commercial trade.
Range	Guinea, Ghana, Nigeria, Cameroon, Gabon, Congo, Central African Republic, Republic of Congo, Uganda, Tanzania.

Description

The genus *pan* includes two species of chimpanzee, *Pan troglodytes,* the common chimpanzee (please see the separate entries on the central chimpanzee, the eastern chimpanzee, and the western chimpanzee for individuating information on these subspecies) and the pygmy chimpanzee, *Pan paniscus* (see separate entry).

The chimpanzee is sexually dimorphic, with males significantly larger than females. Adult females may be from 28 to 33 inches in head-and-body length and may weigh 65 to 176 pounds. Adult males may be from 30 to 36 inches in head-and-body length and may

weigh 90 to 200 pounds. The higher weights are recorded from captive animals. Their faces are pink, brown, or black, and usually darken with age. Their hair is black, sometimes turning to gray on the backs of fully mature adults. Frequently, they lose hair on their heads as they age, creating bald spots, especially on the forehead. A chimpanzee may live up to 45 years.

Behavior

The chimpanzee displays a complex social order and forages in large groups. Socializing often consists of mutual grooming, in which chimpanzees will pick parasites and debris out of each other's hair; this seems to reenforce rank in a group's hierarchy. A male hierarchy persists and status is established through a display of hooting and throwing rocks or tearing off and shaking branches. In some areas the chimpanzee will form territories and will defend them. Gangs of males will patrol the territorial borders and will attack lone males that cross those borders, biting and beating them. Such encounters do serious injury to the offending male and usually result in its death within a few days. The chmpanzee is aggressive and strong, and it will even chase leopards down trees.

Chimpanzees display a slow reproductive rate and females usually raise no more than 2 young to maturity. The reproductive life of a female is about 26 years. When in heat, females will mate successively with several males. Young are born 230 to 240 days after conception. Parental care comes primarily from females, who will even adopt orphaned infants. Young remain with the mother for about six years and may aid in the care of younger siblings.

The primary food source of the chimpanzee is ripe fruit. The animal supplements its diet with leaves, nuts, seeds, and meat. It preys on the voracious glossy black driver ant (*Dorylus nigricans*). This vicious insect will attack intruders with a painful bite, but chimpanzees avoid the bite by using a simple tool. They strip sticks clean of bark and branches and thrust them into ant nests; when ants crawl onto the sticks, the chimpanzees raise the stick to their mouths and sweep it lengthwise through their lips, stripping the ants into their mouths before the ants have a chance to bite. The tool-making by chimpanzees is one of their most interesting practices, since it makes them one of a very few animals who make tools besides humans. Chimpanzees also use stones to crack open hard-shelled nuts; they place the nuts on large rocks and pound them with the stones. Some of the rocks archaeologists have discovered have rounded indentations in them created by centuries, perhaps millennia, of pounding by chimpanzees. Chimpanzees will also use large branches and debris in their competitions for rank within their groups. Males will wave and throw branches in an effort to intimidate other males. Jane Goodall noted that a chimpanzee near her camp learned that empty cans made loud noises when thrown or rolled on the ground, and that it used this knowledge to its advantage to intimidate other chimpanzees. Thus chimpanzees are not only tool users, but learners, as well. Laboratory research shows that they are problem solvers who use their intellect to figure out ways to overcome obstacles. Some researchers contend that chimpanzees can learn rudimentary aspects of languages (this still occasions much dispute among authorities), although there is no evidence of language use among chimpanzees in the wild.

Habitat

The chimpanzee occurs in flatlands and mountains, from sea level to 6,600 feet above sea level.

Distribution

Historically, the chimpanzee was known to have been distributed throughout 25 countries in equatorial Africa, from Senegal in the west to Tanzania in the east. The chimpanzee is distributed throughout areas in western and central Africa, including Guinea, Ghana, Nigeria, Cameroon, Gabon, Congo, Central African Republic, Republic of Congo, Uganda, and Tanzania.

Threats

Deforestation caused by logging and agriculture has destroyed much of the suitable habitat of the chimpanzee. Hunting, and capture for pets, zoo animals, and medical research have historically caused the depletion of chimp populations.

Conservation and Recovery

At the time of the United States Fish and Wildlife Service's determination of threatened status for the chimpanzee (October 19, 1976), a special regulation was provided to the effect that prohibitions generally covering all threatened species against possession and take would not be applicable to species in captivity in the United States on the effective date of rule, or to the progeny of this species legally imported into the United States after the effective date. This rule was applied to facilitate useful research activities of U.S. institutions, zoos and entertainment operations, without any effect on wild populations. When the chimpanzee's status was changed to endangered by the United States Fish and Wildlife Service (March 12, 1990), the exemption for animals bred in captivity was retained.

The chimpanzee is listed in CITES, Appendix I, which restricts international trade. It is also listed as vulnerable in the *IUCN Red List of Threatened Animals,* which means that the IUCN does not consider it in immediate danger of extinction, but that the IUCN considers it vulnerable to extinction in the near future. In some non-African countries importation of wild-caught chimpanzees is forbidden. Additionally, in many African nations wild chimpanzee populations are protected by laws.

In the U.S. and some other countries there are captive groups large enough to be maintained independently. An enhanced care and breeding potential of these groups could reduce the demand for additional wild individuals. Deprivation studies displayed that chimpanzees such as those held in laboratories may recover and be able to find companions, mate and therefore reproduce when reintroduced to a social group. This research may be highly valuable as reintroduction efforts are researched and management of wild populations becomes more focused.

Eastern Chimpanzee

Pan troglodytes schweinfurthi

Craig Stanford

Status	Endangered
Listed	March 12, 1990
Family	Pongidae (Gorillas and chimps)
Description	Black hair with long, thick whiskers on the chin and cheeks.
Habitat	Unbroken forest with fruit trees.
Food	Fruit, leaves, nuts, seeds, honey, insects, and small mammals.
Reproduction	Females usually raising no more than 2 young to maturity.
Threats	Forest felling; commercial trade.
Range	Burundi, Rwanda, Sudan, Tanzania, Uganda, and Republic of Congo (formerly Zaire).

Description

The common chimpanzee, *Pan troglodytes*, has three subspecies: the eastern chimpanzee (*Pan troglodytes schweinfurthi*), the central chimpanzee (*Pan troglodytes troglodytes*), and the western chimpanzee (*Pan troglodytes verus*); see separate entries. Of these, the eastern chimpanzee is the best known, with the Tanzanian population having been deeply studied by Jane Goodall and others. The eastern chimpanzee is sexually dimorphic, with males significantly larger than females. According to Goodall, the adult males she observed fell into two groups, "heavy and light," with the heavy males averaging 100 pounds and the light males averaging 82 pounds. Full-grown females (about 19 years old) weigh between 71 and 82 pounds.

The eastern chimpanzee's skin is less intensely black than that of the central chimpanzee, and it grows long, thick whiskers on its chin and cheeks. As with the other subspecies of the common chimpanzee, its skin darkens with age. Both genders will lose hair on their heads as they mature, but they do not become as bald as do central chimpanzees. As with its cousins, the hair of the eastern chimpanzee is black, sometimes turning to gray on the backs of fully mature adults.

Other common names include East African chimpanzee, long-haired chimpanzee, and common chimpanzee.

Behavior

There are behavioral differences among the subspecies of the common chimpanzee, mostly in their eating habits. Like the other subspecies, the eastern chimpanzee is a toolmaker. It creates sticks of about 26 inches in length (much longer than the sticks for the other subspecies) for use on ants and termites. The eastern chimpanzee will simply tear open and plunder the nest of slow moving ants (*Dorylus gerstaeckeri*), shoving its arm deep into the nest to grab ant larvae. Although their bites are less painful, the ants *Dorylus nigricans* are much faster moving and can quickly swarm up a chimpanzee's arm, inflicting many more bites, thus the eastern chimpanzee uses its long, denuded stick to probe this ant's nests and draw out ants to eat. The ants swarm over the stick, and when they near the chimpanzee's hand, the stick is withdrawn and swept through the chimpanzee's free hand (the other subspecies would pull the stick through their lips). The fistful of ants are shoved in the mouth and quickly chewed. The western chimpanzee uses a smaller stick and thus is able to probe the ant nest and withdraw its stick several times more often per minute than does the eastern chimpanzee, but the eastern chimpanzee seems to come out ahead; although only thrusting in and withdrawing its long stick from an ant nest only three times in a minute, it reaps about 900 ants per minute, as opposed to the 200 or so ants reaped by the western and central chimpanzees. Although they do not seem to be as ingenious in their modifications of sticks as tools as are the other chimpanzee subspecies, the eastern chimpanzee does seem to vary its sticks in size for use on termite mounds; there also seems to be less planning ahead when creating sticks as tools than with the other subspecies. The termite mounds are especially important sources of protein for the eastern chimpanzee because of their stability. The mounds remain in one place for many years and can therefore be counted on as feeding places.

Another primitive tool used by the chimpanzees is a stone — used to crack open the shells of nuts. Typically, the eastern chimpanzee will set the nut on a large rock and pound it with a stone. The rocks that are used as platforms often have rounded holes in them caused by their repeated use in cracking open nuts and suggesting that the chimpanzees have been using these rocks for hundreds of years. The chimpanzee eats a wide variety of vegetation, of which fruits are the most important part. Chimpanzees seem to be able to adjust to the absence of any food type from their diet except fruit. Where fruit-bearing trees are cut down, chimpanzees tend to disappear.

Meat is an important part of the eastern chimpanzee's diet. The central chimpanzee hunts small animals, most notably small monkeys, and it is known to cannibalize its young.

Habitat

The eastern chimpanzee lives in rain forests, deciduous forests, or savannah with woodlands.

Distribution

The eastern chimpanzee once lived in a huge continuous tropical forest in eastern Africa. Logging, agricultural development, and expanding human communities have broken up this forest, leaving the eastern chimpanzee living in scattered populations of as few as single isolated individual animals and possibly as many as 10,000 animals occurring in Burundi, Rwanda, Sudan, Tanzania, Uganda, and Republic of Congo.

Threats

Deforestation, caused by logging and agriculture, has destroyed much of the suitable habitat of the eastern chimpanzee. The eastern chimpanzee is also hunted for capture, to be sold either as a pet or as a laboratory animal.

Conservation and Recovery

The chimpanzee is listed in CITES, Appendix I: Trade Prohibited, which restricts international trade. It is also listed as vulnerable in the *IUCN Red List of Threatened Animals*, which means that the IUCN does not consider it in immediate danger of extinction, but that the IUCN considers it vulnerable to extinction in the near future. In some non-African countries importation of wild-caught chimpanzees is forbidden. Additionally, in many African nations wild chimpanzee populations are protected by laws.

In Burundi, 200 to 300 eastern chimpanzees survive, and they may not form a sufficiently large enough breeding population to sustain themselves. Most of them live in Kibira National Park. Although they are not extensively protected by law (but their exportation is forbidden), their main threat to survival comes not from hunters but from deforestation caused by agriculture. Perhaps 100 eastern chimpanzees live in the Nyungwe Forest Reserve in Rwanda, with fewer than 10 to be found in the rest of the country. Mining, road building, logging, and reforestation with nonnative trees and other plants threaten the chimpanzee's habitat in Rwanda. However, hunting of chimpanzees is rare, and they are protected under Rwandan law. Preservation of the forest in Nyungwe Forest Reserve offers hope that sufficient habitat will be preserved

to maintain the small chimpanzee population. Eastern chimpanzees may survive in southwestern Sudan. Estimates of their numbers vary from 100 to 400, although they may, in fact, already be extinct. The possible lack of breeding-age females may doom this small population; loss of habitat to human encroachment and their capture for pets are also threats. Efforts by the government to starve its rebellious southern population into submission may also threaten the chimpanzees, which could become sources of protein and whose habitat may be consumed by hungry people who may eat the fruits the chimpanzees depend on. Sudan provides sweeping protection of its chimpanzees under its laws, and they may survive in the Mbarizunga Reserves, the Bangangai Reserve, and Bire Kpatuos Reserves. In Tanzania, the eastern chimpanzee lives along the shores of Lake Tanganyika. Approximately 150 live in Gombe National Park, and are among the most famous animals in the world, having been extensively studied and frequently filmed for television nature shows. Perhaps 2,000 chimpanzees in all live in Tanzania, where they are threatened by loss of habitat to agriculture. The rich natural resources of Uganda have undergone extended periods of exploitation, and corrupt tyranny and civil war have made protection of its wildlife difficult. Eastern chimpanzees now exist only in the western part of Uganda, where they may number more than a thousand. Small populations scattered in places such as the Kigezi Game Reserve and Kabalega National Park are unlikely to survive because too much of their required forest habitat has been lost. On the other hand, Uganda is doing a good job of protecting the chimpanzees in its Kibale Forest Reserve. The significant problem there is the question as to whether enough chimpanzees of breeding age survive to maintain the animal's genetic diversity, probably a key to its adaptability to changes in its environment. Much of Republic of Congo's (formerly Zaire's) primary forest has been cut down, but chimpanzees appear to live in the region south of Sudan to Lake Tanganyika and in the northwest. Only a small number live scattered in Ituri Forest. It seems that no one knows how many chimpanzees actually live in Republic of Congo, at present, but some naturalists hope that more than 10,000 may survive in areas that are still forested. (This may seem like a large number, but hunting could wipe it out in five years.) In addition to relentless deforestation, hunting is a threat to the chimpanzee in Republic of Congo. It is hunted for its meat, to be sold in towns and cities, and for its live young, to be sold to foreign laboratories. Republic of Congo has undertaken a program of conservation of wildlands in order to promote tourism, and it protects chimpanzees under law — although the laws are difficult to enforce. It has had its greatest success in Virunga National Park, where primary forest has been preserved. The chimpanzees also live in the Garamba and Kahuzi-Beiga national parks, where they are supposed to be protected, but poaching in those parks may overwhelm the foresters protecting them. The overall outlook for the survival of the eastern chimpanzee in the wild is poor, with it being only five years or so away from extinction, even though it is a very famous animal. Efforts to conserve the subspecies in a few countries show promise and may delay extinction or, as naturalists hope, save the subspecies from the short-term threats of hunting and deforestation.

Although in the United States and some other countries there are captive groups of chimpanzees large enough to be maintained independently, the eastern chimpanzee may be impossible to maintain as a distinct subspecies because of too much cross-breeding with captive members of the other two subspecies. Thus captive breeding programs may be unable to save the eastern chimpanzee from extinction.

Central Chimpanzee

Pan troglodytes troglodytes

Noel Rowe

Status	Endangered
Listed	March 12, 1990
Family	Pongidae (Primates)
Description	Largest of the three subspecies of the common chimpanzee.
Habitat	Unbroken forest in equatorial Africa with presence of fruit trees.
Food	Fruit, leaves, nuts, seeds, honey, insects, and small mammals.
Reproduction	Slow reproductive rate with females usually raising no more than 2 young to maturity.
Threats	Forest felling; commercial trade as pets and as laboratory animals.
Range	Angola, Cameroon, Central African Republic, Congo, Equatorial Guinea (Rio Muni), Gabon, and Nigeria.

Description

The common chimpanzee, *Pan troglodytes*, has three subspecies: the central chimpanzee (*Pan troglodytes troglodytes*), the eastern chimpanzee (*Pan troglodytes schweinfurthi*), and the western chimpanzee (*Pan troglodytes verus*). Of these, the central chimpanzee is the largest, with adult males sometimes weighing more than 190 pounds. The central chimpanzee is sexually dimorphic, with males significantly larger than females. Males stand 47 inches and weigh 130 pounds and females stand 45 inches high and weigh 105 pounds, on average. Because females are nearly as tall as males but weigh much less, they appear notably slimmer than the males.

In addition to being larger than the other subspecies of the common chimpanzee, the central chimpanzee may be distinguished by the very black color of its skin, which is much blacker than the other subspecies. Already very black when the central chimpanzee is young, the skin darkens even more with age. Both genders tend to become bald on their heads as they mature. Male baldness takes the shape of a triangle that extends back over the head from the forehead, with the base of the triangle over the brow and the point aiming into the crown. Females tend to go completely bald on their heads, hence the sometimes-used name "bald chimpanzee." As with its cousins, the hair of the central chimpanzee is black, sometimes turning to gray on the backs of fully mature adults.

Other common names include Central African chimpanzee, bald chimpanzee, and common chimpanzee.

Behavior

There are behavioral differences among the subspecies of the common chimpanzee, mostly in their eating habits. Like the other subspecies, the central chimpanzee is fond of honey and will raid beehives, often by thrusting their arms into the honeycomb if the bees are the stinging honeybees, eating the bees as well as the honey. They are diligent in their pursuit of honey and will use sticks as tools for getting at even the last drops. For a raided beehive of sweat bees (a stingless variety, genus *Triogna*), they will use sticks to prod into hard-to-reach places after they have plundered most of the honeycomb. When attacking the hives of stinging bees (mostly *Apis mellifera*), they may thrust their arms into the honeycomb, grab as much as they can, and then run away from the swarm of angry bees that arise to repel the intruder. The central chimpanzee then eats its booty while other member of its group then raid the hive. They also eat the honey and larvae of the carpenter bee (genus *Xylocopa*). This insect has a nasty sting, so it is approached with care. It is a solitary insect that burrows into wood; it stores honey in its tunnel, where a larva may develop. The chimpanzee will thrust a stick, stripped of its leaves, into the tunnel; if the adult carpenter bee is inside, it will stick its stinger out of the hole, for defense. The chimpanzee stabs the adult bee with its stick and eats it; the chimpanzee then

bites away the wood until the nest is revealed and it eats both the honey and the larva.

The central chimpanzee is an ingenious toolmaker that seems to plan ahead for the tools it needs for different targets. It creates sticks of varying lengths, thicknesses, and flexibility for its different insect prey, bees, ants, and termites. Like the western chimpanzee, the central chimpanzee will dig open the nests of ants that live in the ground, first by scraping away dirt and debris over the entrance to the nest and then by thrusting its arm as far as it will go into the swarming nest, reaching for the larvae that are kept in the deepest part of the nest. This is a painful process because the guarding ants will attack the arm with strong bites, but the reward of a handful of succulent larvae seems to be enough for the chimpanzee to be willing to accept the bites. Some species of ants swarm over a grasping arm too quickly, biting too much to make the dig-and-plunder method of raiding a nest worthwhile. For these ants, the central chimpanzee uses sticks of about eight inches in length (shorter than those used by the eastern chimpanzee), which it will clean of twigs and leaves before using. The chimpanzee shoves it into a nest, waits for ants to swarm up it, and before the ants reach its hand, it pulls the stick out and then sweeps it through its mouth, sucking off the ants and chewing them before they can bite. It will repeat this process ten to twelve times per minute, eating perhaps as many as 200 ants each minute, making this activity a significant source of protein.

Another primitive tool used by the chimpanzees is a stone — used to crack open the shells of nuts. Typically, the central chimpanzee will set the nut on a large rock and pound it with a stone. The rocks that are used as platforms often have rounded holes in them caused by their repeated use in cracking open nuts and suggesting that the chimpanzees have been using these rocks for hundreds of years. The chimpanzee eats a wide variety of vegetation, of which fruits are the most important part. Chimpanzees seem to be able to adjust to the absence of any food type from their diet except fruit. Where fruit-bearing trees are cut down, chimpanzees tend to disappear.

The central chimpanzee hunts small animals, most notably small monkeys that are torn apart and their meat devoured. Sometimes the chimpanzees will wait for another predator such as a baboon or a leopard to make a kill, then they will gang up in a group of several members and drive the predator off, then taking its kill for themselves. The central chimpanzee, a large and very strong animal, will even drive leopards out of their trees where they have taken their prey. Large males tend to get the choice pieces in such group endeavors, but females in estrus are often deferred to and given meat by the males.

Habitat

The central chimpanzee lives in rain forests, deciduous forests, or savannah with woodlands from sea level to 6,600 feet.

Distribution

The central chimpanzee once lived in a huge continuous tropical forest from coastal western Africa to central Africa. Logging, agricultural development, and expanding human communities have broken up this forest, sometimes eliminating it altogether in a country, leaving the central chimpanzee

living in scattered populations of as few as single isolated individual animals and possibly as many as 50,000 animals in Angola, Cameroon, Central African Republic, Congo, Equatorial Guinea (Rio Mundi), Gabon, and Nigeria.

Threats

Deforestation caused by logging and agriculture has destroyed much of the suitable habitat of the central chimpanzee. The central chimpanzee is also hunted for capture, to be sold either as a pet or as a laboratory animal. Typically, hunters find a small family unit that is foraging away from the larger group that they belong to, and the hunters kill every member of the family group except an infant, which they take alive. Infants are valued over adults because they are small and tractable; adults are dangerously aggressive and strong. An adult male central chimpanzee can easily kill a man. The taking of an infant usually involves the killing of six or seven other chimpanzees; perhaps as few as one in seven captured infants survive being shipped overseas to laboratories, zoos, or pet owners. Thus the capturing of chimpanzees for commercial sale involves the deaths of many other chimpanzees and has had a profoundly negative influence on their population in the wild.

Conservation and Recovery

The chimpanzee is listed in CITES, Appendix I: Trade Prohibited, which restricts international trade in the species. It is also listed as vulnerable in the *IUCN Red List of Threatened Animals*, which means that the

IUCN does not consider it in immediate danger of extinction, but that the IUCN considers it vulnerable to extinction in the near future. In some non-African countries importation of wild-caught chimpanzees is forbidden. Additionally, in many African nations wild chimpanzee populations are protected by laws.

Angola may have a few hundred central chimpanzees north of the Zaire River, although civil war has made scientific investigation difficult and therefore the numbers are not really known. Angola protects its central chimpanzees by law, but hunting for meat may pose a threat to the chimpanzee population. Central chimpanzees exist in small groups scattered through western and southeastern Cameroon, and people hunting them for meat is their greatest threat to survival, although they may be freely traded in Cameroon. Fewer than a thousand central chimpanzees are to be found in the Central African Republic, thinly scattered in the country's southwest. These animals seem to be little disturbed by human beings, and they are protected under the Central African Republic's laws. Congo (Brazzaville) protects its central chimpanzees under law and by creating forest reserves for wildlife. Harming chimpanzees is considered a serious offense, and even wounding a chimpanzee must be reported to legal authorities. Even so, Congo allows exportation of chimpanzees by permit. As many as 3,000 central chimpanzees may survive, mostly in northern Congo. Social unrest and even civil war has threatened endangered species in several African nations, but in Equatorial Guinea long periods of unrest in the human population has resulted in the interruption of logging operations and movements of people away from rural and forested areas, giving central chimpanzees periods of relative peace. Hunting the chimpanzees for trade is a significant problem in Equatorial Guinea, and deforestation by logging, agricultural development, and human communities threaten the central chimpanzee's habitat. In Gabon, the central chimpanzee is hunted for its meat, and it is under severe pressure in nearly populated areas — where forest animals are the most important source of protein for local people. Deforestation also has reduced the central chimpanzees' numbers in Gabon, although the chimpanzees have shown a remarkable ability to recover their numbers in logged areas if secondary forests are allowed to replace the lost primary forest, often returning their population to near normal after six or seven years. Gabon still has a large primary forest and chimpanzees are found throughout it, perhaps numbering about 50,000 animals. Although the chimpanzee is fully protected from harm under Gabon's laws, poaching is a very big problem, and along with loss of forest habitat to agriculture, forms a significant threat to the animal's survival in that country. Nigeria has lost nearly all of its central chimpanzees, and its western chimpanzee population appears to be extinct. The few surviving central chimpanzees are found in mountain forests, near Cameroon. They are hard to find, but may be increasing in numbers because of central chimpanzees crossing the border from Cameroon, where they are being pressured out of their forest. The chimpanzees are hunted for their meat in Nigeria, but inaccessibility in some mountain areas may be protecting them. Overall, the outlook for the central chimpanzee is better than that for the western chimpanzee. The central chimpanzee still exists in healthy numbers in Gabon and Congo, and conservation efforts, especially the creation and enforcement of wildlife refuges, may preserve sound breeding populations in those countries.

In the United States and some other countries there are captive groups of chimpanzees large enough to be maintained independently, and there is some hope of maintaining the central chimpanzee subspecies as an independent breed. Although it is often cross-bred with captive members of the other two subspecies, the central chimpanzee still exists as a distinctive animal in zoological collections and enough exist in these collections to create a captive breeding population that retains the central chimpanzee's unique genetic heritage.

Western Chimpanzee

Pan troglodytes verus

Michael Durham, Metro Washington Park Zoo

Status	Endangered
Listed	March 12, 1990
Family	Pongidae (Gorillas and chimps)
Description	Smallest of the three subspecies of the common chimpanzee.
Habitat	Unbroken forest in equatorial Africa with presence of fruit trees.
Food	Fruit, leaves, nuts, seeds, and meat.
Reproduction	Slow reproductive rate with females usually raising no more than 2 young to maturity.
Threats	Loss of habitat; commercial trade as pets and as laboratory animals, extensive hunting.
Range	Benin, Gambia, Ghana, Guinea, Guinea Bissau, Ivory Coast, Liberia, Mali, Senegal, Sierra Leone.

Description

The common chimpanzee, *Pan troglodytes*, has three subspecies: the western chimpanzee (*Pan troglodytes verus*), the central chimpanzee (*Pan troglodytes troglodytes*), and the eastern chimpanzee (*Pan troglodytes schweinfurthi*). Of these, the western chimpanzee is the smallest. The western chimpanzee is sexually dimorphic, with males significantly larger than females. Adult females average about 28 inches in head-and-body length and average 65 pounds, whereas adult males average about 30 inches in head-and-body length and average about 90 pounds. (Please note that the western chimpanzee is little studied in the wild and its size and weight are not well recorded.) Captive western chimpanzees tend to weigh more than wild ones. In addition to being smaller than the other subspecies of the common chimpanzee, the western chimpanzee may be distinguished by the different coloration of its face. Its face tends to be paler, even pink, but the skin around its eyes is a very dark brown or black, creating an effect that looks to humans like a mask. Even as its skin darkens with age, the skin around the eyes remains significantly darker. The hair on their head also varies from the other subspecies. When young, its hair has a central division, but unlike the other subspecies it does not tend to go bald with age, and even when there is some balding, it is not extensive. It develops a long, grey beard as it ages. As with its cousins, the hair of the western chimpanzee is black, sometimes turning to gray on the backs of fully mature adults. Other common names include West African chimpanzee, masked chimpanzee, or common chimpanzee.

Behavior

There are behavioral differences among the subspecies of the common chimpanzee, mostly in their eating habits. The western chimpanzee is fond of honey and will raid beehives by chewing into them if their residents are the stingless sweat bees (*Trigona*) or by thrusting their arms into the honeycomb if the bees are the stinging honeybees (*Apis mellifera*), eating the bees as well as the honey. They seem to accept the bee stings as a matter of course. Like the other common chimpanzees, the western one eats a variety of insects, mostly ants and bees, as well as insect larvae. They eat many kinds of ants, including the fierce driver ant, which will swarm over its prey and debilitate it with numerous stinging bites. The chimpanzees scoop these ants up and eat them in mouthfuls. The tailor ant is another favorite; the chimpanzees will grab the ant nest — consisting of woven-together leaves filled with workers, soldiers, and larvae — and eat it in gulps, apparently savoring the flavor.

The western chimpanzee will dig open the nests of ants that live in the ground, first by scraping away dirt and debris over the entrance to the nest and then by thrusting its arm as far as it will go into the swarming nest,

reaching for the larvae that are kept in the deepest part of the nest. This is a painful process because the guarding ants will attack the arm with strong bites, but the reward of a handful of succulent larvae seems to be enough for the chimpanzee to be willing to accept the bites. Some species of ants swarm over a grasping arm too quickly, biting too much to make the dig-and-plunder method of raiding a nest worthwhile. For these ants, the western chimpanzee uses sticks of about eight inches in length, which it will clean of twigs and leaves before using. The chimpanzee shoves it into a nest, waits for ants to swarm up it, and before the ants reach its hand, it pulls the stick out and then sweeps it through its mouth, sucking off the ants and chewing them before they can bite. It will repeat this process ten to twelve times per minute, eating perhaps as many as 200 ants each minute, making this activity a significant source of protein. The western chimpanzees have been observed making specific shapes of sticks for specific problems presented by individual ant nests and beehives, and they will modify their tools to suit changing conditions in a nest they are raiding.

Another primitive tool used by the chimpanzees is a stone — used to crack open the shells of nuts. Typically, the western chimpanzee will set the nut on an exposed tree root (the other subspecies tend to use large rocks) and pound it with a stone. The chimpanzee eats a wide variety of vegetation, of which fruits are the most important part. Chimpanzees seem to be able to adjust to the absence of any food type from their diet except fruit. Where fruit-bearing trees are cut down, chimpanzees tend to disappear.

The western chimpanzee hunts as a social unit. Prey are usually small animals, most notably small monkeys. The western chimpanzees will spread out and sweep through a small area, driving monkeys before them in what seem to be preplanned group hunts. The prey are trapped and torn apart by the western chimpanzees. Large males tend to get the choice pieces, but females in estrus are often deferred to and given meat by the males.

Habitat

The western chimpanzee lives in rain forests, deciduous forests, or savannah with woodlands containing large supplies of fruit, which form the essential part of its diet.

Distribution

The western chimpanzee once lived in a huge continuous tropical forest from far-western to central Africa. Logging, agricultural development, and expanding human communities have broken up this forest, sometimes eliminating it altogether in a country, leaving the western chimpanzee living in scattered populations of as few as 20 and possibly as many as 8,000 in Benin, Gambia, Ghana, Guinea, Guinea Bissau, Ivory Coast, Liberia, Mali, Senegal, and Sierra Leone.

Threats

Deforestation caused by logging and agriculture has destroyed much of the suitable habitat of the western chimpanzee. It is also killed for meat (especially in Liberia). The western chimpanzee is also hunted for capture, to be sold either as a pet or as a laboratory animal. Typically, hunters find a small family unit that is foraging away from the larger group that they belong to, and the hunters kill every member of the family group except an infant, which they take alive. Infants are valued over adults because they are small and tractable; adults are dangerously aggressive and strong. The taking of an infant usually involves the killing of six or seven other chimpanzees; perhaps as few as one in seven captured infants survive being shipped overseas to laboratories, zoos, or pet owners. Thus the capturing of chimpanzees for commercial sale involves the deaths of many other chimpanzees and has had a profoundly negative influence on their population in the wild, and at present may represent the most significant cause of decline to near extinction of the western chimpanzee.

Conservation and Recovery

The chimpanzee is listed in CITES, Appendix I: Trade Prohibited, which restricts international trade in the species. It is also listed as vulnerable in the *IUCN Red List of Threatened Animals*, which means that the IUCN does not consider it in immediate danger of extinction, but that the IUCN considers it vulnerable to extinction in the near future. In some non-African countries importation of wild-caught chimpanzees is forbidden. Additionally, in many African nations wild chimpanzee populations are protected by laws.

Gambia's native population of western chimpanzees was eradicated around 1900. Presently, naturalists are trying to reintroduce the chimpanzee into the wild on Baboon Island in the River Gambia National Park. Although these animals have been raised mostly in captivity, having been poached in other countries for export to zoos, they seem to be adapting well to their wild environment.

A small number (perhaps 200) of western chimpanzees may survive in Ghana's Bia National Park. Although Ghana has laws protecting its chimpanzees, hunting for meat, as well as loss of habitat to logging, are threats to their short-term survival. Guinea offers little protection for the western chimpanzee, although the animal's population was once large there, numbering perhaps 8,000 in the late 1980s. In the early 1960s, hunting the chimpanzee for export created a booming industry that reduced the western chimpanzee's numbers by the tens of thousands in Guinea, and such hunting continues, making the outlook for the animal's survival in that country very bleak. In the Ivory Coast, western chimpanzees survive in a small population in the Tai National Park, as well as in Comoe, Marahoue, and Mount Peko national parks and the Mount Nimba Strict Nature Reserve. Studies of the population in Tai National Park are the sources of much of what is known about the western chimpanzee's behavior. The western chimpanzee may still exist in very small numbers scattered around Liberia. People in Liberia eat chimpanzees, and government efforts to protect the tiny population of remaining chimpanzees seem to have been derailed by the nation's interminable civil war. It is possible that the western chimpanzee has been hunted into extinction in Liberia, by now. About 500 western chimpanzees live in southern Mali, scattered in low-density populations. The local people in Mali seem to be well aware of the locations of chimpanzees but do not seem to pose a threat to them, wanting them neither for meat nor for sale. The western chimpanzee is protected from hunting, killing, and sale by law in Mali. Senegal may have about a hundred surviving western chimpanzees (although only about 30 have been observed), mostly living in Niokolo-Koba National Park

near Mt. Assirik. Loss of habitat to economic development may eliminate the chimpanzee population in Senegal. Sierra Leone took action to protect its western chimpanzee population in the early 1970s, eventually banning hunting them in 1978. By then, the animal's numbers had declined to fewer than two thousand. Although poaching for exportation is still a big problem for the western chimpanzee in Sierra Leone, a hundred or so seem to be protected in that nation's Gola Forest Reserves.

Although in the United States and some other countries there are captive groups of chimpanzees large enough to be maintained independently, there is little hope of maintaining the western subspecies as an independent breed. Rather, it is cross-bred with captive members of the other two subspecies, especially the central chimpanzee.

Gibbons
Family: Hylobates

Female Pileated Gibbon (*Hylobates pileatus*)　　　　John W. Haug

General Characteristics of the *Hylobates*

Gibbons (*Hylobates*) are small, arboreal apes inhabiting the tropical and subtropical forests of southeast Asia. They weigh 12 to 34 pounds and possess long arms and legs relative to their body size. Wild gibbons are almost exclusively arboreal, and their use of brachiation (arm-swinging), climbing, leaping, and bipedal walking has enabled them to master the complex forest canopy. One consequence of their dexterity and relatively small body size is the exploitation of food sources found at terminal branches, a niche which larger and less agile monkeys and apes cannot readily utilize. Adults of both sexes have long, sharp canines that are used in defense and in preparing and accessing food.

Although gibbons have a long evolutionary history and indigenous people have coexisted with, and written about, gibbons for hundreds of years, the West did not become aware of this ape group until du Halde (1735) and de Buffon (1766) published the first gibbon descriptions. Subsequently, some species were described in the 1800s (e.g. black gibbons), while others such as *H. hoolock* were not described until much later.

Carpenter (1940, 1964) published the first account of gibbon behavior in which he described the monogamous, territorial, and frugivorous nature of these animals. For almost thirty years after Carpenter's pioneering gibbon study, *H. lar* remained the only well-known species in the genus. Ellefson (1968, 1974) conducted the first long term field study on *H. lar* in Malaysia, followed by the longer studies on *H. lar* and *H. syndactylus* of Aldrich-Blake, Chivers, and Raemaekers. To date, all gibbon species have been studied to some extent in the wild, and the genus *Hylobates* has become one of the best known in the order Primates.

Brachiation

Gibbons are strongly arboreal and of all the apes the most persistent brachiators (arm swingers), which accounts for their anatomy and behavior. Two physical features are particularly emphasized for their relationship to brachiation ability: the gibbons' small body size and their elongated forearms. Brachiation characterizes all gibbons and is the preferred mode of locomotion. *H. lar* and *H. syndactylus* use brachiation to traverse 60-75% of their daily travel routes. Brachiation enables gibbons to cover quickly the home range along complex, preferred arboreal pathways.

Territoriality and Vocalizations

Territorial behavior among gibbons serves several functions, but predominant among them is the protection of nutritional and reproductive resources. The monitoring of territory boundaries is an activity of high energetic costs. For example, *H. klossii* mated males spend 13% of their daily activity budget in territory defense and monitoring. The protection of the territory may result in dangerous physical altercations. There is a high frequency of damage to adult male gibbons' canines (*H. lar*), possibly indicative of intergroup aggression.

A second frequently cited function of territoriality is its connection with monogamy. Monogamy results from the exclusion of unmated individuals by territorial males so that each territory contains only one adult of each sex. From this perspective, the territory size is set by the area required for the adult female to successfully rear her offspring, while the male conforms to the distribution of females across space and the intolerance of a female toward other females encroaching on her territory.

Average territory size differs from species to species, and ecology and habitat saturation impact this size in an as yet untested fashion. The existence of neighbors limits the outward expansion of a family's territory, while nutritional requirements at certain times of the year or during different stages of the life cycle may stimulate a family's drive to expand its territory size. The maximum gibbon density in mature habitats for those species studied in the wild is 17.4 to 21.7 individuals per square mile.

Although the various functions of territoriality are not always immediately distinguishable, the most obvious defense of the gibbon family's territory is clearly the morning vocalization (given singly or in a series) and accompanying display, which includes rapid brachiation, jumping, and branch shaking. Gibbon vocalizations are characterized by repetitiveness, stereotypy, and dueting with complex interactions between the sexes.

Both sexes in a family participate in protecting a geographic area by displaying and vocalizing at other families; mated males approach, chase, and displace solitary males, and females similarly confront solitary females.

A "song bout" consists of the first to last loud note produced with no period of silence of more than ten minutes between the notes. The gibbon song bout is often divided into distinct forms, which can be further subdivided into their component parts. The major forms are the mated male solo song, the mated female solo song, the duet between the mated male and mated female, and the solo song of the unmated male. A song bout may contain a combination of solo songs and/or duets, depending on the species. Technically, the species *H. hoolock* and *H. moloch* do not duet. The mated pair of these two species may sing simultaneously but not in synchrony.

Younger family members become increasingly agitated and may join in singing parts of the male's or the female's duet. In this fashion youngsters of both sexes learn the appropriate sex roles and the sequences of an entire duet. The faithfulness of each species to its prescribed musical score, together with pronounced sexual divocalism make the voices of gibbons seem a powerful guide to the isolation of species by appropriate pairing and restriction to territories.

During the duet, family members may engage in such territorial behaviors as branch shaking, rapid brachiation, and rigid posturing. These activities are typically directed toward the territory of neighboring families, but they are not necessarily precipitated by a physical encounter with a neighboring family or an unfamiliar gibbon. The reaction of neighbors to a family's territorial song may depend on the degree to which the singing family has trespassed on territory boundaries.

The duets function to indicate the family's existence and willingness to protect resources within the territory, whether food or reproductive access, from other gibbons. Additionally, because in most species the morning song bout involves a complex interaction between the family's adult male and adult female, it is hypothesized that dueting reinforces the pair bond.

After the morning or early afternoon duets are finished gibbons are vocally silent, probably to avoid predators. As a consequence, it is often difficult to locate a gibbon family after the duets have been completed. Finding them after dawn may entail listening for branches breaking and falling — a possible indicator of a gibbon's presence in the canopy.

Gibbons' anti-predator defense is to remain silent most of the day so that predators are less likely to find them. If a predator does find them, they flee silently.

Family Structure and Monogamy

Gibbons live in nuclear families which average four individuals: one adult male, one adult female, and their sexually immature offspring. The typical family consists of the two breeding adults, a juvenile or subadult offspring, and an infant that is still dependent on the parents.

Female lar gibbons' menstrual cycle varies from 15-27 days, and gestation in captivity has been recorded from 197-210 days (*H. lar*) to 235 days (*H. syndactylus*). For roughly four months after birth, young rely exclusively on the mother's milk, and the mother carries the infant constantly. Between 4 and 6 months, the infant becomes interested in solid food and begins spending time off the mother's body. Captive individuals are weaned at 1 to 1.5 years. Wild gibbons give birth every three or four years; captive gibbons may breed as often as every one or two years.

Sexual maturity in the wild is attained at 6 to 9 years, but may occur earlier in captivity (4 to 5 years). Captive gibbons have been observed to mate year round, even the day before and day after giving birth. Newly introduced captive gibbons tend to mate more frequently.

There may be a breeding or birth season for wild gibbons, but the relevant data has not been collected for all species. Mating seasonality is suggested by the occurrence of sexual swellings in female gibbons. Seasonality is also implied by family structure of wild gibbons. Each wild pair may produce up to 4 offspring, but captive animals may produce 10 or more offspring, in part because of their longer life span and shorter interbirth interval. Maximum lifespan in the wild is approximately 25 years (the estimated maximum age for *H. lar* and *H. syndactylus*). The oldest documented captive gibbon is an Abbotts Mueller's gibbon (*H. muelleri abbotti*) that was born in 1949 and is housed at the Wellington Zoo.

When the young gibbon reaches sexual maturity, it is "peripheralized" from the family's main activities by the parents. Peripheralization may entail active repulsion of the young animal from the family by the same-sexed parent or exclusion from family activities. These peripheralizing animals may be observed near the core of the family, but they infrequently interact with the family proper. Studies indicate that peripheralization can be a passive, gradual occurrence, taking years to complete or it can be a more dramatic, physical interaction.

The eventual goal of peripheralization appears to be the dispersal of the sexually mature offspring. Females from neighboring families are attracted to the lone male by his solo song, which advertises his willingness to establish a new breeding unit. The young male travels across the territories of several nearby families in his search for a mate. Young females may also range across neighboring territories during this time.

Females do not always leave the natal family upon reaching sexual maturity. They may be tolerated and possibly even incorporated into the natal family if territory resources permit, while males apparently attempt to establish their own territory.

Parental assistance in obtaining a territory has been observed in gibbons. This entails the demarcation of a small territory immediately adjacent to the parents', with the new territory boundaries gradually expanding so that the newly established pair usurps small portions of neighboring territories. Whether such attempts occur without parental assistance is not known.

By remaining near his parents, a young individual may inherit his natal territory, which is probably superior to any territory the younger animal could obtain on his own. This occurrence will be more likely if the end of the parents' (or the father's) lives occurs close to the timing of the dispersal event. It may be possible for the offspring to recognize the potential for this venue by assessing the capabilities of the parents (i.e. by observing how much time is spent patrolling territory boundaries) or by the frequency of inter-male conflicts. This could cue the individual as to potential profit in remaining close to the natal group. One young male kloss' gibbon inherited his father's territory and mated with his mother.

The dispersing individual may also benefit in predator avoidance and food procurement by remaining close to familiar areas. Presumably individuals will be most familiar with those areas immediately adjacent to the natal territory, resulting in a preference for these areas in establishment of the individual's own territory.

Because gibbons are philopatric, most populations are probably inbred. This may be the case even if a male or female ranges over several territories before selecting a mate. The chromosomal evidence indicates that gibbons have probably been inbred at least since the evolution of the existing species. Habitat fragmentation in recent years has increased the tendency for inbreeding by isolating populations in small patches of forest.

When a newly bonded male and female have established themselves as a pair, the boundaries of their territory begin to become permanent. This process may take several years to complete, and reduces the gibbons' reproductive lifespan. The female calls add a distinct territorial threat to the otherwise tolerated calls of lone males. This threat is frequently met by direct physical attack from established neighboring families. Only if the new pair is able to repel such attacks can it form its own territory and establish a new breeding unit. Once established, visual and vocal displays are usually sufficient to maintain territory boundaries.

Because male reproductive fitness is often better served through polygyny, many primatologists describe gibbon monogamy as "female enforced." This view is supported by the way in which mated animals respond to "strangers" of both sexes. A mated female will repulse strangers of both sexes, while a mated male tends to respond more aggressively to unmated males, which suggests that he may tolerate additional adult females if his current mate also would. Some primatologists suggest that female distribution across territories and interfemale aggression are the overriding factors which sustain monogamy in gibbons.

Diet and Feeding Behavior

Gibbons are typically found in monsoon, evergreen rainforests, but they occasionally inhabit more seasonal, mixed evergreen and deciduous or semi-deciduous environments; but they never inhabit completely deciduous forests. Within these preferred forest formations, gibbons live where tree diversity is high and where *Dipterocarpaceae* trees are common. The preference for diverse forests ensures a consistent supply of sugar-rich fruit available throughout the year. Dietary shifts are possible during lean times because at least one tree species will be fruiting at any given time. Mature *Dipterocarpaceae* trees are at least 130 feet tall, with horizontal branching patterns. These trees also provide the locomotion supports favored by gibbons for various activities such as dueting, sleeping, and playing.

Wild gibbons are strictly arboreal and do not come to the ground to eat or drink. Instead, they obtain necessary liquids from the fruits ingested and from licking rain water from bark, their own fur, and from leaves. They occasionally drink water from tree hollows, or use a low-hanging branch to sip from a stream.

Gibbons generally feed when hanging from a terminal branch by one hand, and picking food with the other hand and bringing it back to their mouth. Usually, one or both feet are used to steady or bend the branch containing the food. When a gibbon eats small berries, new leaves, buds or flowers, it either picks the bits of food individually with its hand and carries it to its mouth or, if the small items are in clusters, it pulls the branch to its mouth and eats directly from the branch. Large new leaves are eaten by folding the two sides of the leaf together, grasping the leaf halves near the stem end, and tearing the meaty leaf halves along the leaf rib from base to tip. Gibbons usually sit on their ischial callosities while feeding.

Usually gibbons seek food at a height of more than ten meters above the ground, utilizing two techniques for gathering it: foraging or stationary feeding bouts. Gibbons, who spend about 40% of their time feeding, use foraging to collect fruits, leaves, or invertebrates, and stationary feeding to collect fruits.

Gibbons feed throughout the day but have a concentrated feeding bout in the morning. Their activity level declines throughout the day until they move to their sleeping trees. (This pattern is called a unimodal activity curve.)

All gibbon species exhibit a preference for fruit, particularly figs, which is the food gibbons seek out for the day's first feeding bout. Generally, figs and other fruits must be available throughout the year for gibbons to inhabit a particular area. As a result, gibbons usually inhabit forests with high floral diversity which ensures that there is always a supply of fruit. Because gibbons lack the ability to digest toxins that may be found in some fruits, this could be a key factor restricting gibbons to the more diverse and less seasonal forests, where toxic effects can be reduced by frequently changing foods. Gibbons' biomass varies from 92.4 to 300 pounds per square mile of home range. Biomass is usually higher in drier, more seasonal forests.

Gibbons compete with squirrels, birds, and other primates in their exploitation of fig fruits and leaves, but gibbons eat near ripe or fully ripe figs, while other nonhuman primates eat unripe ones. Gibbons ingest their largest daily dose of figs at dawn, possibly to avoid competing with monkeys who tend to eat later in the day. Gibbons lack plant detoxification abilities, so it is not possible for them to exploit mature leaves while many sympatric monkeys can; however, few systematic studies of gibbon digestive abilities have been conducted.

A nuclear family social structure appears to maximize utilization of small, patchily distributed food resources. A small, dispersed family of gibbons can better exploit these resources than can a large, compact monkey troop. A gibbon family carefully monitors the fruiting status of all trees in an area large enough to meet the family's dietary requirements, but small enough to be searched frequently and protected by the family. The family gains an intimate knowledge of each tree within the territory.

The ultimate factor determining a monogamous social structure for gibbons may have been reliance on a highly selective diet of relatively high-quality, well dispersed fruits which in turn were selected for a small, territorial group structure.

Threats to Gibbons

Extant gibbons are restricted to primary or good-quality forests. They are threatened throughout their range by deforestation, poaching, and the illegal pet trade. Human population pressures and expansion means that impoverished local people exploit the forest for firewood and food. The body parts of gibbons and other animals such as tigers form the basis for some traditional medicines, particularly in China, and these increasingly rare animals' parts command exorbitant prices. Gibbons are popular pets throughout the world, and poachers and animal dealers often kill the parents to obtain infants for the illegal pet trade. As adults, gibbons become intractable and dangerous, so owners abandon them or turn them over to zoos. Unfortunately, these individuals cannot be rehabilitated to the wild and are often unsuitable mates and/or parents in captivity (see below).

For example, Indonesian primates are threatened by loss of habitat as a result of forest clearance. Indonesian forests are being converted to agricultural fields to help sustain its exploding human population. Most gibbon species have lost huge amounts of their original habitats: siamangs have lost 66%; agile gibbons 66%; lar gibbons 55%; Mueller's gibbons 38%; Kloss' gibbons 31%; and silvery gibbons 96%. Little of gibbons' remaining habitat falls within protected areas such as park boundaries.

Dwindling numbers of gibbons in the wild also generate concern because research on endangered species indicates that monogamous, territorial mammals are more susceptible to extinction than are species with alternative mating systems. This inclination is partially attributable to the mating system and partially due to length of the interbirth interval and the developmental stage of neonates.

The number of breeding individuals (or effective population size) can become quite small when there is a deficit of one sex because monogamy requires one male for every female. Polygyny, conversely, enables one male to inseminate several females, so theoretically every female of the appropriate age will become pregnant. Some females of breeding age in a monogamous mating species may not mate, particularly when there is not a one-to-one sex ratio. Individuals who had lost their mates but were capable of sexual reproduction may not mate even though they occupy and defend a prime territory. There may be several potential breeders in gibbon populations who are not contributing to the effective population size.

Disruptions of habitat stress females and may reduce their reproductive outputs. Environmental destruction can prolong the process of procuring a breeding-suitable territory when males and females are attempting to establish themselves as a pair. Gibbons living in optimal environments may produce as few as four offspring per pair; habitat disruption reduces this number further and lengthens the interbirth interval.

Gibbons have been described as "behaviorally rigid", and they appear unable to adjust rapidly to ecological alterations. Gibbons exhibit site tenacity even when humans are destroying the forest around them, a tendency which has been attributed to their locomotion pattern, their passive mode of predator avoidance, and their territorial nature. Wild gibbons are almost never observed on the ground, so large gaps in the canopy effectively isolate populations. Generally, where a patch of rainforest has been destroyed its resident gibbons have been destroyed as well.

Conservation

Gibbons are becoming increasingly rare in the wild, so it is desirable to breed them in captivity with the goal of eventually returning them to their countries of origin. Unfortunately, gibbons do not adjust well to captivity, and breeding programs for most species, with the exception of *H. lar, H. syndactylus* and *H. concolor leucogenys,* have been unsuccessful. Many captive gibbons have developed profound behavioral disturbances as a consequence of mistreatment or inappropriate handling at early life stages. Such animals are often fearful of, or aggressive toward, potential mates and/or offspring. They also are apparently stressed by close proximity to other gibbon groups and by the more terrestrial environment that they are forced to occupy in captive settings. Thus, based on current captive conditions it is unlikely that depleted wild populations can be "restocked" with the offspring produced in captivity. Gibbon survival into the next millennium is unlikely if deforestation trends in Asia continue at current rates.

Captive breeding is a part of the recovery effort of all gibbons, but attention is being focused on the rarest gibbons first. Siamangs and lar gibbons are common enough in captivity that their breeding is no longer considered a priority. Moloch and pileated gibbons are among the rarest, but to complicate the picture, some species are fairly common while some subspecies are not. For example, *H. lar* as a species is common in captivity, but *H. lar yunnanensis* and *H. lar carpenteri* are extremely rare. The goal of captive breeding is to concentrate on the rarest species and attempt to match breeding partner. The use of computer analysis helps to prevent inbreeding or subspecific hybridization.

Lori K. Sheeran, Ph.D.

Agile Gibbon
Hylobates agilis

H. a. agilis   Tad Motoyama

Status	Endangered
Listed	June 2, 1970
Family	Hylobatidae (Gibbons)
Description	Black to brown to buff, with white brows in adult females and white brows and cheek patches in immature and adult males.
Habitat	Warm, moist, evergreen forests with a continuous canopy.
Food	Figs and other fleshy fruits; leaves, buds, flowers, small animals and animal matter.
Reproduction	Reproduction occurs approximately every 3-4 years in the wild.
Threats	Habitat loss, hunting and poaching.
Range	Peninsular Malaysia, Sumatra, southwestern Borneo

Description

The Agile gibbon's, *Hylobates agilis'*, relatively small pelage ranges from black to brown to buff. Adult and immature males and immature females have white brows and cheek patches, and the male or female can be of any color phase. Adult females lose the cheek patches but retain a pale brow. The agile gibbon has been referred to as the dark-handed gibbon or active gibbon. The three subspecies are known as the lowland agile gibbon (*H. a. unko*), mountain agile gibbon (*H.a. agilis*), and Bornean agile gibbon (*H. a. albibarbis.*)

The Bornean agile gibbon is found in southwestern Borneo. Adults are brown with dark-brown to brown-black underparts, hands, feet, and cap, a white brow, and their lower back is golden-buff. One adult female specimen had a head-and-body length of 18.13 inches, a foot length of 5.8 inches, and weighed 13.2 pounds. The dimensions of an adult male specimen were 18.13 inches for head-and body length with a 5.26 inch foot length. Two adult females had total lengths of

31.9 inches and 30.96 inches, foot lengths of 5.77 inches and 5.53 inches, and one female's weight was 12.12 pounds. An adult male was 32.4 inches long, had a foot length of 5.60 inches, and weighed 13.3 pounds.

H. agilis agilis (Mountain agile gibbon) is distributed in the Barisan mountains of western Sumatra to the south of Lake Toba. It is also found in the mountainous regions of western Malaysia. Adults of this subspecies are black, brown, or buff, and may have darker under parts. Approximately 82% of one wild population was found in brown and buff color phases. An adult male specimen had a head-and-body length of 18.33 inches and weighed 13.78 pounds. Two adult males ranged from 31.6 to 31.9 inches total length, 5.69 to 5.96 inches in foot length, and 13.03 to 16.03 pounds.

H. agilis unko (Lowland agile gibbon) is found in the lowlands of eastern Sumatra and western Malaysia. Approximately 72% of the wild *H. a. unko* populations are black and have paler cheek patches in appearance to *H. a. agilis*. There are few other consistent variations between *H. a. unko* and *H. a. agilis*. An adult female *H. a. unko* specimen had a head-and-body length of 18.5 inches and weighed 12.78 pounds. The corresponding figures for an adult male specimen were 19.3 inches and 16.29 pounds.

Behavior

Hylobates establish and defend territory through a series of vocalizations and displays, and a ritualistic song is conducted nearly every morning. Agile gibbons engage in a complex duet between both sexes. *H. agilis* sing on average 1.90 song bouts per singing day, with an average song duration of 16.45 minutes. Unmated adult males sing solos. The adult female's great call is similar to that of female *H. lar* and female *H. moloch*.

Gibbons' anti-predator defense is to remain silent most of the day so that predators are less likely to find them. If a predator does find them, they flee silently.

Female lar gibbons' menstrual cycle ranges from 15-27 days, and gestation in captivity has been recorded from 197-225 days. Wild gibbons give birth every three or four years; captive gibbons as often as every one to two years. Gibbons live in nuclear families which average four individuals: one adult male, one adult female, and their sexually immature offspring. The typical family consists of two breeding adults, a juvenile or subadult offspring, and an infant that is still dependent on the parents. Newborn infants are able to cling to their mother's ventrum. Sexual maturity in captive gibbons varies but can occur as early as four to five years of age. Gibbons are thought to become sexually mature in the wild between the ages of six to eight years.

Captive gibbons have been observed to mate year round, even the day before and day after giving birth. Newly introduced captive gibbons tend to mate more frequently. There may be a breeding or birth season for wild gibbons, but the relevant data has not been collected for all species. Mating seasonality is suggested by the occurrence of sexual swellings in female gibbons. Seasonality is also implied by family structure of wild gibbons.

One study observed the following dietary proportions for wild *H. agilis*: 17% figs, 41% other fruit, 39% leaves, 3% flowers, and 1% invertebrates. Captive agile gibbons have a preference for spinach over other leafy materials.

Habitat

H. agilis inhabits warm, moist, evergreen forests with a continuous canopy in southwestern Borneo, in the Barisan mountains of western Sumatra, and in the lowlands of eastern Sumatra and western Malaysia. Wild gibbons, including *H. agilis* are strictly arboreal, and populations are restricted to good quality forests.

Distribution

Agile gibbons are found in isolated populations in Sumatra, southwestern Borneo, and the Malaysian Pennisular.

Threats

The main threat facing primates in Indonesia, as elsewhere in the tropics, is loss of habitat as a result of forest clearance. Indonesian forests are being converted to agricultural fields to help sustain its exploding human population. Forests are also being lost to industrial development, especially to logging, which is the second most important source of revenue in Indonesia after oil.

Illegal animal markets are common throughout gibbons' range, where endangered species, including gibbons, may be purchased as pets. In parts of the world Indonesian primates were still being purchased by zoos and for biomedical research, but in the United States the exportation guidelines established by CITES limit trade in primates.

Reduced numbers have also resulted in reduced reproductive viability. Because gibbons are monogamous, requiring one male for every female, female gibbons may not mate if the sex ratio is unequal. Individuals who have lost their mates but are capable of reproduction may not find another mate but remain defenders of the territory. The combination of lost habitat, poaching, and reduced reproduction have pushed gibbon species to the brink of extinction.

Conservation and Recovery

Although gibbons are legally protected on state lands in Indonesia, poaching remains a problem. Malaysia has banned all export of gibbons, but international laws are only sporadically enforced. Conservationists estimate that for each infant gibbon that survives to be sold on the black market, 10 other gibbons have died.

Crested [=Black] Gibbon

Hylobates concolor

Noel Rowe

Status	Endangered
Listed	June 2, 1970; June 14, 1976
Family	Hylobatidae (Gibbons)
Description	Medium to large sized gibbon with short dense black fur; males may have pale cheek patches; females are buff to tawny with a black occipital stripe.
Habitat	Warm to cold, lowland tropical, and montane subtropical forests.
Food	Figs and other fleshy fruits; leaves, buds, flowers, small animals.
Reproduction	Reproduction occurs approximately every 3-4 years in the wild after a gestation period of 197-222 days.
Threats	Habitat loss, poaching, hunting.
Range	Vietnam, Republic of Lao, Cambodia, China.

Description

Crested gibbons, *Hylobates concolor,* are characterized by dense hair compared to other genus members. Adult males have black fur. Adult females are buff to gold to gray-tan but can have an orange cast during the dry season. Females have a black occipital streak of various sizes and may have a faint white face ring. The crown hair of males and females stands erect, with the male's hair being longer in the crown's center. All subspecies and species have a long, slender nose.

Females have a long, slender clitoris and males have a long baculum. Adult males of *H. concolor* and *H. leucogenys* possess a throat sac. Young begin life with buff fur but turn black beginning at the age of 6 months and will complete the color change at approximately 2 years of age. Females develop the light-colored coat by puberty's end at 7 to 8 years. Males remain dark throughout life after the gold infant coat is lost.

The eight subspecies are marked as follows.

The adult males of two species have white or pale cheek patches (the "cheeked gibbons": *H. gabriellae, H. l. leucogenys, H. l. siki*). The adult males of the remaining subspecies are solid or nearly solid black (the "black gibbons": *H. c. lu, H. c. concolor, H. c. furvogaster, H. c. jingdongensis,* and *H. c. hainanus*).

H. c. hainanus is found on Hainan Island, P.R.C. Males have short, black fur, and the crown hair is not obvious. Females have obvious black crown patches, but all other body hair is a brown-yellow and there are no dark regions on the chest, abdomen, or limbs. Ma, Wang, and Poirier note a body weight range of 12.78 to 22.05 pounds for adults of both sexes.

H. c. concolor is found in Vietnam, Republic of Lao, and Yunnan Province, P.R.C. The males are black with long fur. Females have gray or yellow body hair and black-brown or black crown patches. Females have dark fur on the back and ventrum. An adult male specimen had a head-and-body length of 22.23 inches. A female specimen had a head-and- body length of 19.70 inches. Ma, Wang, and Poirier found body weight ranges from 16.9 to 22 pounds for adults of both sexes.

H. c. lu is found in the extreme western region of Laos. Males are solid black except for a silver stripe on the side of the head. Museum specimens are variable in the intensity of this streak, and Delacour's description of it may include individuals undergoing coat color changes. Females have buff fur heavily grizzled with black hairs. There are no figures for body length and weight, but Geissmann has published other body dimensions.

H. c. jingdongensis is found only in the Wuliang Mountains, central Yunnan Province, P.R.C. Adult males have long crown hair (1.95 to 2.54 inches). Females have golden-yellow hair with a slight orange tint. Their appendages are black-brown, with gray-white areas on the face and throat. The occipital patch is brown-black. Adults of both sexes have body weights ranging from 15.21 to 19.18 pounds.

H. c. furvogaster is found in western Yunnan Province, P.R.C. Males have short, black body hair. Females have black fur in the chest, ventrum, and armpit regions, and the crown patch is black and covers most of the head. The ears are bordered by long, black hairs. Adults of both sexes have body weights ranging from 11.03 to 17.64 pounds.

H. l. leucogenys is found in N. Republic of Lao, N. Vietnam, and S. Yunnan Province, P.R.C. The males' cheek patches connect at the chin and extend up to the top of the ear. Females are buff to creamy orange often diffused with tan, gray, or black hairs, with a medium-length black, occipital streak. Females can have brown-black genitals and black hairs on the tips of fingers and toes. A trace of the occipital streak can extend between the scapulae. One adult male was 31.2 inches long from head-to-foot and weighed 18.04 pounds. An adult female specimen had a head-and-body length of 22.4 inches and a 6-inch foot length. Females are sometimes larger than males.

H. l. siki is found in central Vietnam and central Republic of Lao. Males have small white cheek patches that extend as far up as the eye's corner, and thin white hair partially encircles the upper lip and totally encircles the lower lip, terminating in a black chin. Adult females are more similar in appearance to adult female *H. l. leucogenys* than to *H. gabriellae* females.

H. gabriellae are found in South Vietnam and Cambodia east of the Mekong. Males have small, light buff cheek patches that extend to the bottom of the orbital ridge. *H. gabriellae* females are generally smaller than *H. l. leucogenys* females and have a black fringe at the ears. Generally, females are buff to strawberry-buff and can have a slight grizzling of darker hairs on the chest, on edges and tips of fingers and toes, and on the outer forearm. Usually, there is no white fringe around the face. Females are typically smaller than males. Adult females may have slight red-brown genital hairs. A five-year-old male at the Los Angeles Zoo had a head-to-foot length of 24.9 inches and weighed 7.94 pounds. An adult female at the Los Angeles Zoo had a head-to-foot length of 30.8 inches and weighed 12.68 pounds.

Delacour reported that crested gibbons live in groups larger than 2 to 6 animals. Haimoff, *et al.* describe a polygynous mating system and state that a more folivorous diet is causally linked to polygyny. However, there is debate over the accuracy of Haimoff's interpretation. Lan, *et al.* and Sheeran characterized a monogamous family grouping consisting of one mated adult pair and up to four offspring. However, Bleisch and Chen and Liu, *et al.* note that wild crested gibbons are often found in fragmented forests where dispersal options are limited. This may result in unusually large groupings, in some instances with multiple adults of both sexes.

Other taxonomic treatments have included *Hylobates leucogenys* and *Hylobates gabriellae*.

Behavior

Hylobates establish and defend territory through a series of vocalizations and displays, and a ritualistic song is conducted nearly every morning. Crested gibbons engage in a complex duet between both sexes. *H. c. jingdongensis* sing on average 1.14 song bouts per singing day, with an average song duration of 12.02 minutes. The crested gibbon song is high-pitched and tonally pure. Unmated adult males sing solos. There may be slight variation in song for the various species and subspecies.

Female lar gibbons' menstrual cycles range from 15-27 days, and gestation in captivity has been recorded from 197 to 225 days. Wild gibbons give birth every 3 or 4 years; captive gibbons as often as every 1 to 2 years. Gibbons live in nuclear families which average 4 individuals: one adult male, one adult female, and their sexually immature offspring. The typical family consists of 2 breeding adults, a juvenile or subadult offspring, and an infant that is still dependent on the parents. Newborn infants are able to cling to their mother's ventrum. Sexual maturity in captive gibbons varies but can occur as early as 4 to 5 years of age. Gibbons are thought to become sexually mature in the wild between the ages of 6 to 8 years.

Wild crested gibbons have been observed eating figs and other fruits, leaves, buds, flowers, and insects. Crested gibbons appear to be more folivorous than other gibbons because fruits are relatively uncommon in the subtropical environments where some populations are found.

Habitat

H. concolor is found in lowland tropical, and montane subtropical forests. Crested gibbons can tolerate temperatures ranging from 37 to -2 degrees Celsius, and their dense fur may be an adaptation to low temperatures encountered by those populations living at high elevations.

The hoolock gibbon, lar gibbon, and some species of the crested gibbon group (*H. concolor*) inhabit more seasonal environments. However, no gibbon species has been found in completely deciduous forests. There is debate about whether these populations were pushed into suboptimal habitats by human population pressures, or whether they have a long evolutionary history of occupying these regions. *H. concolor*, for example, appears to be well-adapted to the seasonal, montane environments it occupies.

Distribution

Crested gibbons are distributed in Republic of Lao, Vietnam, and Yunnan and Hainan Provinces, P.R.C. In historical times its range extended northward to the Yangtze River. Fossil gibbons date within the Pleistocene epoch (2 million to 10,000 years ago) and have been recovered in Jiangsu, Guangxi, Sichuan, and Yunnan Provinces, P.R.C.

Threats

The greatest threat to the survival of wild crested gibbons is habitat destruction attributed to the modernization of Asia. Populations become fragmented and isolated in pockets of remaining forest where they are susceptible to poaching and inbreeding. Crested gibbons are hunted throughout their range as a meat source. In some cases, its body parts are used to manufacture traditional medicines. A thriving illegal pet trade also exists for this increasingly rare gibbon. There may be as a few as 300 to 1,000 individuals remaining in the wild in the P.R.C. *H. c. hainanus*, the subspecies endemic to Hainan Island, P.R.C., has dwindled to 15 individuals, and its extinction is imminent.

Hoolock Gibbon

Hylobates hoolock

Perth Zoo, Western Australia

Status	Endangered
Listed	June 2, 1970; June 14, 1976
Family	Hylobatidae (Gibbons)
Description	Large gibbon; males have black pelage with a pale brown streak; females have copper-tan pelage.
Habitat	Drier forests
Food	Figs and other fleshy fruits; leaves, buds, flowers, small animals and animal matter.
Reproduction	Reproduction occurs every three to four years in the wild after a gestation period of 197-225 days.
Threats	Habitat loss, poaching, hunting.
Range	Eastern India (Assam), Bangladesh, Burma, South Yunnan, P.R.C.

Description

Male hoolock gibbons, *Hylobates hoolock*, have black fur with a pale brow streak that curls up at the ends. The female pelage is copper-tan with dark-brown hair on the sides of the face, chest, and genitals. The female's face ring is wide above the eyes, turns upwards at the ends, and becomes thin as it encircles the muzzle. Shorter hairs on the sides of the neck give this gibbon's face a triangular appearance. The muzzle is larger compared to other gibbon species with a thin tuft of fur at the chin. Ischial callosities are heavily furred. The chest region is narrow. Infants are a pale gray white with a yellow tinge (McCann, 1933). Infants darken as they age, and both sexes pass through a black stage. Females turn pale at puberty, while males remain black throughout life.

There are 2 subspecies of the hoolock gibbon. *H. h. hoolock* (Western hoolock gibbon) is found in eastern India (Assam) and in Bangladesh. The males have a long, black pre-pubital tuft and the brows are a single pale streak. Females' crown hair is parted in the middle. Hands and feet are the same color as the limbs, with a black fringe on the edge of the hand, fingers, and toes. An adult male had a head-and-body length of 18.8 inches. An adult female had a foot length of 5.91 inches.

H. h. leuconedys (Eastern hoolock gibbon) is found in Burma and in South Yunnan Province, P.R.C. Males' hair is black with a brown cast, but the legs are blacker than the body. Males have a white or brown pre-pubital tuft, pale separated brows that flick up at the ends, and the chin has many white-beige hairs. Females are copper-tan and their hands and feet are slightly paler than their limbs. The hands and feet have few dark hairs. The crown hair grows outwards and slightly upwards but is not parted down the middle (Mootnick et al., 1987). One adult female (ICGS #HHL303) had a foot length of 5.7 inches. Ma, Wang, and Poirier (1988) note that adults of both sexes weigh 11.7 to 18.7 pounds and are from 17.4 to 22.5 inches long.

Hylobates establish and defend a territory through a series of vocalizations and displays, and a ritualistic song is conducted nearly every morning. Female hoolock gibbons produce a belch-like growl as part of their song. The pattern of their call is a short "who-hah" with a rapidly accelerating series of alternating low and high notes. Hoolock gibbons engage in a complex duet between both sexes. Families sing on the average of 1.12 song bouts per singing day, with an average song duration of 14.4 minutes. Unmated adult males sing solos.

Common names include the hoolock (or white-browed) gibbon for the species, western hoolock for *Hylobates hoolock hoolock,* and eastern hoolock for *Hylobates hoolock leuconedys.*

Behavior

One observed population of hoolock gibbons spent 67% of their feeding time eating fruits, 32% eating flowers and leaves, and 1% feeding on insects.

Gibbons feed throughout the day but have a concentrated feeding bout in the morning. Their activity level declines throughout the day until they move to their sleeping trees. (This pattern is called a unimodal activity curve.)

Habitat

H. hoolock normally inhabits warm, moist, forests, but is sometimes found in forests with low annual rain and temperature ranges of 8 to 37 degrees Celsius. One consequence of the displacement of hoolock gibbons into drier habitat may be smaller family size.

Distribution

The hoolock gibbon was once widely distributed throughout Eastern India, through Bangladesh to China and south to the Irrawaddy River in Burma. Today hoolock gibbons are found in the Assam region of India, Bangladesh, Burma, and Yunnan Province, China. Once common throughout northern and eastern forests of Bangladesh, they are now restricted to the semi-evergreen forest of Sylhet Division (Khan, 1984).

H. hoolock is divided into a western and eastern race. The western race is distributed between the Brahmaputra and Chindwin rivers. The eastern race is found between the Chindwin and Salween rivers.

Hoolock gibbons have not been well-studied in the wild, but they appear to have a smaller average family size (3.00 individuals) than do most other gibbons. This may be related to their occupation of drier and floristically less diverse forests compared with most other gibbon species.

Hoolock gibbons are endangered throughout their range. Burma has not been surveyed, so the numbers remaining there are unknown. In China, they number 100 to 150 individuals and they are very scarce in Assam. *H. hoolock* is found in countries where the human population is rapidly expanding and governments are in the process of development and modernization.

There are no known hoolock gibbons in captivity outside of the countries of origin. The only known hoolock gibbons to have bred in captivity were *H. h. hoolock* at the Stanley Park Zoo, Vancouver. The oldest known eastern hoolock gibbon was housed at the International Center for Gibbon Studies. She was born in 1950 and died at the age of 42. The oldest known western hoolock gibbon was housed at the International Center for Gibbon Studies. She was born in 1956 and died at the age of 26.

Threats

Deforestation, 'jhuming' or shifting cultivation, and killing primates for food are the main factors responsible for the decline in the population of hoolock gibbons. *H. hoolock* are kept as pets and are used in the manufacture of traditional medicines.

Conservation and Recovery

There is no specific recovery program for Assam or Bangladesh. Assam is an area of civil unrest. India does not permit the exportation of gibbons.

Kloss' [=Mentawai] Gibbon

Hylobates klossii

Noel Rowe

Status	Endangered
Listed	June 2, 1970; June 14, 1976
Family	Hylobatidae (Gibbons)
Description	Medium sized gibbon with short, black fur.
Habitat	Warm, moist, evergreen forests with a continuous canopy.
Food	Figs and other fleshy fruits; leaves, buds, flowers, and small animals.
Reproduction	Reproduction occurs every 3 to 4 years in the wild.
Threats	Loss of habitat, poaching, hunting.
Range	Indonesia (Mentawai Islands)

Description

H. klossii (Kloss' gibbon) has no subspecies, but there are some variations in its hair length and body size on different islands. Both sexes have blackish fur and remain this color at all life stages. There is no sexual dimorphism or dichromatism. They have short hair, a broad chest, and long legs, thumbs, and large toes. Kloss' gibbons have a short muzzle, and hair on top of the adult's head is flat. Infants are the same color as the parents, but head hair stands erect. In the past, *H. klossii* was sometimes called the dwarf siamang (*H. syndactylus*) until its closer evolutionary relationship to the subgenus

Hylobates was noted. One specimen had a head and body length of 17.8 inches and weighed 14.53 pounds.

Behavior

Hylobates establish and defend territory through a series of vocalizations and displays, and a ritualistic song is conducted nearly every morning. Kloss' gibbons engage in a complex duet between both sexes. *H. klossii* sing on average 0.88 song bouts per singing day, with an average song duration of 35 minutes. Unmated adult males sing solos. The pattern of *H. klossii*'s song is quiver hoots and moans in males; the female's song has a slow rise-and-fall bubble lasting approximately 45 seconds. The female's song is similar to the songs of female *H. pileatus* and *H. muelleri*. Whitten describes the Kloss' gibbon song.

Whitten observed feral Kloss' gibbons for 2 years, noting that 72% of their total feeding time is devoted to fruit, 2% to leaves, 0% to flowers, and 25% to arthropods. Twenty-three percent of total feeding time was concentrated on figs.

Kloss's gibbons, like all gibbons, feed throughout the day but have a concentrated feeding bout in the morning. Their activity level declines throughout the day until they move to their sleeping trees. (This pattern is called a unimodal activity curve.) Males sing before dawn; the females chorus about 2 hours later.

Habitat

Kloss' gibbon inhabits warm, moist, evergreen or semi-evergreen forests. Populations are restricted to good-quality forests with a continuous canopy.

Kloss' gibbon is particular to its lodging site and will relocate because of increasing odor, shifting winds, disturbances by humans and perhaps by predators, pressure from neighboring groups, and fluctuations in food viability.

Distribution

Kloss' gibbons are restricted to the Mentawai Islands.

Threats

Human activities are exacting a toll on this species. Humans hunt these gibbons, keep them as pets, and use their body parts in the practice of the aboriginal Mentawai religion. Humans also modify the forest through selective logging, deforestation, and trail cutting, and these practices impact on *H. klossii's* habitat.

The main threat facing primates in Indonesia, as elsewhere in the tropics, is loss of habitat as a result of forest clearance. Indonesian forests are being converted to agricultural fields to help sustain its exploding human population. Forests are also being lost to industrial development, especially to logging, which is the second most important source of revenue in Indonesia after oil.

Illegal animal markets are common throughout gibbons' geographical range, where endangered species, including gibbons, may be purchased as pets.

Conservation and Recovery

The plight of Indonesian wildlife was a focus of a workshop held in Cisarua Bogor, Indonesia on May 3-5, 1994. The Indonesian Forest Protection and Nature Conservation (PHPA) staff, Indonesian Primate Society members, and Indonesian Zoological Parks Association (PKBSI), IUCN/SSC Captive Breeding Specialist Group, and participants from around the world worked on developing management strategies for wild and captive Java primates. The recommendations that emerged from the conference included surveying the most important gibbon sites, and training and educating forest rangers and local NGOs, with the goal of collecting data by monitoring primate populations and ecology. The goal is to strengthen law enforcement in protected areas, and to increase awareness and increase participation of local people in the conservation of gibbons and langurs.

Lar Gibbon

Hylobates lar

Rich Block

Status	Endangered
Listed	June 2, 1970; June 14, 1976
Family	Hylobatidae (Gibbons)
Description	Medium-sized gibbon, creamy buff to brown to black, with white hands, feet, and face ring.
Habitat	Warm, moist, evergreen forests.
Food	Figs and other fleshy fruits; leaves, buds, flowers, and small animals.
Reproduction	Reproduction every 3 to 4 years after gestation of 197 to 210 days.
Threats	Loss of habitat, hunting, poaching.
Range	Indonesia (Sumatra), Myanmar, Malaysia, Thailand, China

Description

Lar gibbon (*Hylobates lar*) males weigh 9.02 to 16.03 pounds and females weigh 8.60 to 13.43 pounds. The lar gibbon has five subspecies. Both sexes have white hands and feet, and a complete face ring of varying degrees. Males and females can be dark or light in color, ranging from creamy buff to brown to black. Depending on the subspecies, the hair on their heads lies flat or points upward, and hair texture ranges from straight to frizzy.

H. lar vestitus (Sumatran lar gibbon) is found in Sumatra, north of Lake Toba. They vary in color from red-buff to red-brown.

These species have darker shades on their forearms, calves, crown, and throat. They have a white medium-sized face ring. The genital region is darker. This species also has white on the hands which can extend past the wrist. A Smithsonian male specimen's head and body was 18.72 inches long, and another male weighed 12.13 pounds. A female weighed 11.03 pounds and head and body length was 18.13 inches.

H. l. lar (Malayan lar gibbon) is found in Malaysia south of the Perak river. Members of this subspecies are generally dark chocolate brown, with the exception of a quarter of the population, who are creamy-buff. There is a thin white face ring above the eyes, connecting into a larger face ring at the sides of the muzzle. A male specimen at Smithsonian is 17.94 inches long. Hair on the withers is 1.40 to 2.15 inches long.

H. lar carpenteri (Carpenter's lar gibbon) is found in northwest Thailand and southern China. They have long hair, which is either dark brown with a slight grayish appearance, or whitish buff. They have a thin white face ring with the pubic region similar in color to the rest of the body hair. Hair length is 3.08 to 4.02 inches.

H. lar entelloides (Mainland lar gibbon) is found in Thailand and northern Malaysia, near the Thepha River on the Malay peninsula, and Sungei Myanmar. This gibbon is either black, brown or buff, and some specimens can have the widest face ring of the lar gibbons depending on their geographical region. This subspecies covers such a wide range that in the future it probably will be broken into additional subspecies. A male measured 17.08 inches and weighed 12.96 pounds; and a female head and body measured 18.72 inches; a female at ICGS weighed 16 pounds. Both color phases are darker than *H. l. lar*. Their hands and feet are whitish and can be mottled with body hair color.

H. lar yunnanensis (Yunnan lar gibbon) is found in Menglian, Ximeng, and Cangyuan Counties in southern and southwestern Yunnan Province. The dark phase is either black or brown with a blackish-brown pre-pubital region. The pale phase is creamy in color and is darker and more brownish on the throat, neck, and inner aspects of the arms, legs, chest and abdomen. It has a reddish-brown pre-pubital region. Hair length is 4.29 to 5.85 inches. Four individuals (male and female) weighed 8.6 to 11.03 pounds and had a head and body length of 14.4 to 19.7 inches.

Behavior

Hylobates establish and defend territory through a series of vocalizations and displays, and a ritualistic song is conducted nearly every morning. Lar gibbons engage in a complex duet between both sexes. *H. lar* sing on average 1.12 song bouts per singing day, with an average song duration of 12.48 minutes. Unmated adult males sing solos.

Female lar gibbons' menstrual cycle varies from 15 to 27 days, and gestation in captivity has been recorded from 197 to 210 days.

Wild populations of lar gibbons were observed spending 61% of total feeding time eating fruits and flowers, 30% leaves, and 9% animal matter.

Habitat

The lar gibbons are distributed in tropical and subtropical forests of Peninsular Malaysia, Sumatra, Thailand, Myanmar, and Yunnan Province, P.R.C. Some populations tolerate forests with low annual rainfall and relatively low temperatures, but lar gibbons probably thrive most optimally in tropical, lowland rain forests.

Distribution

H. l. lar is found in S. Peninsular Malaysia. *H. l. carpenteri* inhabits northwest Thailand and is near extinction. *H. l. entelloides* is distributed through east Myanmar and central Thailand. *H. l. vestitus* is found in north Sumatra. *H. l. yunnanensis* is distributed in W. Yunnan Province, China in small populations that may number as few as 30 to 40 individuals.

Threats

Lar gibbons are threatened throughout their range by habitat destruction, poaching, and the illegal pet trade. In China, their body parts are used in the manufacture of traditional medicines. Although data are sparse related to the current status of the lar gibbon and its five respective subspecies, it is believed that excessive logging of habitat has reduced the lar gibbon's range and abundance. As it is forced into smaller areas, competition for space and food increases dramatically.

Conservation and Recovery

The Thai government has inaugurated a program to restore gibbon habitat with a goal of reintroducing captive gibbons into the wild.

Moloch Gibbon

Hylobates moloch

John W. Haug

Status	Endangered
Listed	June 2, 1970
Family	Hylobatidae (Gibbons)
Description	Medium-sized gibbon with long, dense fur at the neck, sides of the head, and on the shoulders, and white-gray hair on the brow and surrounding the chin.
Habitat	Fragmented rain forests of western and central Java at elevations below 1,000 meters.
Food	Figs and other fleshy fruits; leaves, buds, flowers, small animals and animal matter.
Reproduction	Reproduction occurs approximately every 3-4 years in the wild after a gestation period of 197-210 days.
Threats	Habitat loss and pet trade.
Range	Indonesia (Java)

Description

The Moloch gibbon, *Hylobates moloch*, has long, dense fur at the neck, sides of the head, and on the shoulders. They may have a distinct charcoal to gray cap, a dark-gray chest plate, and dark- gray hair in the genital region. They have white- gray hair on the brow and surrounding the chin. Both sexes are virtually identical in body color, which is silver gray. Infants are lighter in color and change to silver gray in a short period of time (Groves, 1972). *H. moloch* is sometimes confused with *H. muelleri* because of similarities in coloration. An adult male was 32.76 inches long (head to toe) and weighed 18.54 pounds. An adult female was 32.96 inches long (head to toe) and weighed 18.04 pounds, with a foot length of 53.66 inches.

Behavior

Hylobates establish and defend territory

through a series of vocalizations and displays, and a ritualistic song is conducted nearly every morning. Moloch gibbons do not engage in a duet between the sexes, but adults of each sex do sing solos. *H. moloch* sing on average 0.64 song bouts per singing day, with an average song duration of 12.30 minutes. Their vocalization is not as loud and is of higher pitch than what is heard in most other gibbon species. The female's "great call" is similar to that of *H. agilis* and *H. lar* females.

Wild moloch gibbons have been observed eating figs and other fruits, leaves, buds, flowers, and small animals and animal products. Sixty-2 percent of their feeding budget is devoted to fruit and flowers, 38% to leaves, and 0.2% to animal matter.

Habitat

H. moloch is only found in the warm, moist, lowland, fragmented rain forests of western and central Java at elevations below 3,280 feet. They are restricted to good quality forests with a continuous canopy.

Distribution

The past and present range of *H. moloch* is central and western Java. The drier climate in eastern Java has prevented molochs from inhabiting this region.

Threats

Moloch gibbons depend on dense forest habitat for survival, and they are severely threatened by the forests' conversion to agricultural fields and human predation. Java has lost as much as 96% of its rain forests, and only 37% of the moloch gibbon's habitat falls within protected areas.

Conservation and Recovery

The plight of Indonesian wildlife was a focus of a workshop held in Cisarua Bogor, Indonesia on May 3-5, 1994. The Indonesian Forest Protection and Nature Conservation (PHPA) staff, Indonesian Primate Society members, and Indonesian Zoological Parks Association (PKBSI), IUCN/SSC Captive Breeding Specialist Group, and participants from around the world worked on developing management strategies for wild and captive Javan primates. The recommendations that emerged from the conference included surveying the most important gibbon sites, and training and educating forest rangers and local NGOs, with the goal of collecting data by monitoring primate populations and their ecology. The goal is to strengthen law enforcement in protected areas, and to increase awareness and increase participation of local people in the conservation of Javan primates.

Mueller's Gibbon

Hylobates muelleri

Art Wolfe

Status	Endangered
Listed	June 2, 1970; June 14, 1976
Family	Hylobatidae (Gibbons)
Description	Small- to medium-size gibbon ranging from gray to brown and sometimes black underparts, with white brows.
Habitat	Warm, moist, evergreen forests with a continuous canopy.
Food	Fruits, flowers, leaves, animal matter.
Reproduction	Reproduction occurs every 2-4 years in the wild; gestation period lasts 195-210 days.
Threats	Habitat loss, hunting, poaching.
Range	Indonesia (Borneo)

Description

The three subspecies of Mueller's gibbon, *Hylobates muelleri*, vary in appearance.

H. m. muelleri (Eastern Mueller's gibbon) of southeastern Borneo is pale gray with a black cap, ventrum, hands, feet, and inner aspects of the limbs. They have a faint white face ring. An adult female specimen weighed 13.03 pounds and had a foot length of 5.46 inches.

H. m. funereus (Northern Mueller's gibbon) of northern Borneo is dark gray or gray-brown with black underparts and cap. Toes and fingers are black and lower limbs are pale or buff-gray. An adult female specimen weighed 9.92 pounds and had a foot length of 5.15 inches.

H. m. abbotti, (Abbott's Mueller's gibbon) found in western Borneo, is mouse-gray all over the body with short hair. Those populations bordering *H. m. funereus* populations sometimes have black hair on the throat and/or a slightly darker cap and chest, reflecting subspecific hybridization in overlap zones.

There is sometimes confusion in the identification of captive Mueller's gibbons. *H. m. muelleri* and *H. m. abbotti* are sometimes mistaken for *H. moloch* because of similarities in coat color. *H. m. funereus* is occasionally misidentified as *H. agilis albibarbis* for the same reason.

Behavior

Hylobates establish and defend territory through a series of vocalizations and displays, and a ritualistic song is conducted nearly every morning, in which the female Mueller's gibbon plays the major role. The pattern of *H. muelleri's* call is a series of single hoots in males; the female's call is a short rising note lasting less than 18 seconds. *H. muelleri* sing on an average of 1.18 song bouts per singing day, with an average song duration of 14.90 minutes. Both mated and unmated adult males sing solos. Mitani describes the song of Mueller's gibbon.

Habitat

Mueller's gibbon is found in the Southeast Asian rain forests of Borneo. The temperature displays little seasonal variation and ranges from 68 to 82 degrees Fahrenheit. *H. muelleri* is strictly arboreal and is restricted to good quality forests with a continuous canopy.

Distribution

H. muelleri is distributed in north, southeastern, and west Borneo.

Threats

The main threat facing primates in Indonesia, as elsewhere in the tropics, is loss of habitat as a result of forest clearance. Indonesian forests are being converted to agricultural fields to help sustain its exploding human population. Forests are also being lost to industrial development, especially to logging, which, after oil is the second most important source of revenue in Indonesia.

Conservation and Recovery

The plight of Indonesian wildlife was a focus of a workshop held in Cisarua Bogor, Indonesia on May 3-5, 1994. The Indonesian Forest Protection and Nature Conservation (PHPA) staff, Indonesian Primate Society members, Indonesian Zoological Parks Association (PKBSI), IUCN/SSC Captive Breeding Specialist Group, and participants from around the world worked on developing management strategies for wild and captive Javan primates. The recommendations that emerged from the conference included surveying the most important gibbon sites, and training and educating forest rangers and local NGOs, with the goal of collecting data by monitoring primate populations and ecology. One intention is to strengthen law enforcement in protected areas, and to increase awareness and participation of local people in the conservation of gibbons and other primates.

Pileated [=Capped] Gibbon

Hylobates pileatus

Noel Rowe

Status	Endangered
Listed	June 2, 1970; June 14, 1976
Family	Hylobatidae (Gibbons)
Description	Males have short black hair and a white brow band that encircles the face, fingers and toes; females are silver-buff with a black inverted triangle on the ventrum and cap.
Habitat	Warm, moist evergreen or semi-evergreen forests with a continuous canopy.
Food	Figs and other fleshy fruits; leaves, buds, flowers, and small animals.
Reproduction	Reproduction occurs approximately every 3 to 4 years.
Threats	Habitat loss, poaching, hunting.
Range	Southeast Thailand, Cambodia

Description

Pileated gibbon, *Hylobates pileatus*, adult males have short, black hair with a thick, white brow band that becomes thin as it encircles the face. Fingers and toes are white, with a slight fringe running halfway up the sides of the hands and feet. There is a white prepubital patch. The crown cap is encircled by a grizzled white streak on the sides of the head that becomes faint on the back of the head. Some adult males have a faint gray grizzling on the lumbar region.

Adult females are silver-buff with a black inverted triangle on the ventrum that branches off to the underarm area and stops short of the genital area. The female's cap is large and black, with long, silver-buff hair curved over the temples. They have a black, heavily-furred throat. The black coloration extends upwards to the bottom of the ears and narrows in front of the ear to connect with the cap. They have a thin, white brow which sometimes extends laterally around the orbital ridge, and there can be a trace of a white facial ring. Both sexes have a lateral tuft along the crown's sides. Infants are slightly paler silver-buff than are the adult females.

One adult male was 33.54 inches long from head-to-foot, weighed 17.33 pounds, and had a foot length of 6.47 inches. A second adult male was 33.93 inches long from head-to-foot, weighed 23.04 pounds, and had a foot length of 6.32 inches. An adult female was 30.03 inches long from head-to-foot, weighed 14.02 pounds, and had a foot length of 5.23 inches. A larger adult female was 35.5 inches long from head-to-foot, weighed 19.05 pounds, and had a foot length of 6.24 inches. Adult males' arms can be longer than adult females'.

Behavior

Wild pileated gibbons eat figs during 26% of their total feeding time, and divide up the remainder of their feeding budget on other fruit (45%), insects (15%), young leaves (11%), and young shoots (2%).

Habitat

H. pileatus inhabits warm, moist, evergreen or semi-evergreen forests. Populations are restricted to good-quality forests with a continuous canopy.

Distribution

H. pileatus is distributed in southeast Thailand and in Cambodia and inhabits tropical, semi-evergreen forests.

H. pileatus and *H. lar* overlap geographically in southeast Thailand. Brockelman and Gittins have documented hybrids in this overlap zone.

It is estimated that fewer than 25,000 individuals survive in Thailand; their status in Cambodia is unknown.

Threats

Pileated gibbons are threatened by the destruction of their habitat, poaching, the illegal sale of immature individuals, and the use of their body parts in traditional medicines.

In 1977, there were some 22,000 square miles of good forest, or about 18% of its probable former habitat, remaining in southeast Thailand.

Conservation and Recovery

In 1994, the Royal Forest Department of Thailand teamed with the World Conservation Union to host a population/habitat workshop for Thailand's pileated and lar gibbons. At the conclusion of the workshop, the field biologists, conservationists, and government officials agreed to work toward the protection of reserves, increased monitoring of gibbon populations, and the halt of pet trade.

Siamang Gibbon

Hylobates syndactylus

H. s. continentis   Alan Mootnick

Status	Endangered
Listed	June 2, 1970; June 14, 1976
Family	Hylobatidae (Siamangs)
Description	Large-sized gibbon with long dense fur at the neck, sides of the head, and on the shoulders; and white-gray hair on the brow and surrounding the chin.
Habitat	Warm, moist, evergreen forests.
Food	Leaves, figs and other fleshy fruits; buds, flowers, small animals and animal matter.
Reproduction	Reproduction occurs every three to four years in the wild after a gestation period of 189 to 239 days.
Threats	Habitat loss, hunting, and poaching.
Range	Indonesia (Sumatra), Malaysia

Description

Both sexes of *Hylobates syndactylus* have long, black hair which often includes faint white or cream chin hairs. The crown hair lies flat and swirls laterally above the brow. Siamangs are the largest gibbon. They have a stocky build, a broad chest, and exhibit sexual dimorphism in size. Both subspecies have webbed second and third toes. Males have a short penis and a large prepubital tuft; females have a short clitoris. Both sexes have a large inflatable throat sac. Infants are the same color as the parents.

There are few visual features which can reliably be used to distinguish the 2 subspecies. There is, however, some evidence that *H. s. syndactylus* (Sumatran siamang) can be distinguished from *H. s. continentis* (Malayan siamang) by its larger cranium, tooth row, and overall body size. One adult female *H. s. syndactylus* had a head-to-foot length of 36.66 inches, a foot length of 6.59 inches, and weighed 24.5 pounds. An adult male of the same subspecies weighed 32.57 pounds. An adult female *H. s. continentis* weighed 22.05 pounds, while an adult male of the same subspecies weighed 27.06 pounds.

Chromosomal features distinguishing the two siamang subspecies have been found in C-banding, G-banding, or silver staining. Siamang DNA is being analyzed further for subspecific differences as of 1994.

Behavior

Hylobates establish and defend territory through a series of vocalizations and displays, and a ritualistic song is conducted nearly every morning. Siamangs engage in a complex duet between both sexes. They sing on average 0.31 song bouts per singing day, with song durations ranging from 3 to 35 minutes. Unmated adult males sing solos. Both sexes have a large, inflatable throat sac that enables them to produce dog-like barks, accounting for their inclusion among the loudest land mammals. Their songs are audible for distances of more than 1.24 miles. Siamangs produce resonating "booms" punctuated by a series of loud "barks" from the female and "screams" from the male. Their duet begins at mid-morning, and is probably the most complex song of all the *hylobatids.*

Male siamangs provide indirect paternal care to their offspring through territorial defense and protection from predators. They also participate directly in caring for the young by carrying them, playing with them, and sharing food with them.

Wild siamangs' diet consists of 44% fruits and flowers, 48% leaves, and 8% animal matter.

Wild siamangs are more folivorous than are the other gibbons, and this apparently has an impact on their ranging and activity pat-terns, particularly where they are sympatric with other gibbon species or with orangutans (*Pongo pygmaeus*). MacKinnon notes: ". . .the greater size of the siamang enables it to dominate [other] gibbons in food tree disputes, but the bioenergetic consequences of their greater size restrict them to a shorter day range whilst having to consume more food." Raemaekers found that siamangs feed longer, travel less, and rest more than do sympatric lar gibbons (*H. lar*).

Habitat

Siamangs inhabit warm, moist evergreen forests with a continuous canopy.

Distribution

There is fossil evidence of siamangs in Java, but today they are restricted to the montane and southern, lowland swamp-forests of Sumatra (*H. s. syndactylus*) and central and western peninsular Malaysia (*H. s. continentis*).

Threats

The main threat facing primates in Indonesia, as elsewhere in the tropics, is loss of habitat as a result of forest clearance. Indonesian forests are being converted to agricultural fields to help sustain its exploding human population. Most gibbon species have lost huge amounts of their original habits: siamangs have lost 66% of theirs. As this species is forced into smaller areas, competition for space and food increases dramatically.

Siamangs are also hunted; however, relative to the other gibbons, siamangs are more numerous and have a stronger likelihood of surviving into the next century.

Conservation and Recovery

The plight of Indonesian wildlife was a focus of a workshop held in Cisarua Bogor, Indonesia on May 3-5, 1994. The Indonesian Forest Protection and Nature Conservation (PHPA) staff, Indonesian Primate Society members, and Indonesian Zoological Parks Association (PKBSI), IUCN/SSC Captive Breeding Specialist Group, and participants from around the world worked on developing management strategies for wild and captive Java primates. The recommendations that emerged from the conference included surveying the most important gibbon sites, and training and educating forest rangers and local NGOs, with the goal of collecting data by monitoring primate populations and ecology. The goal is to strengthen law enforcement in protected areas, and to increase awareness and increase participation of local people in the conservation of gibbons and langurs.

Siamang are easily bred in captivity, but sometimes mates are incompatible. Some individuals are also emotionally too disturbed to be suitable mates or parents. This is particularly true of individuals that were reared in isolation from other gibbons.

Old World Monkeys:
Leaf, Langur, and Colobus Monkeys
Family: Cercopithecidae
Subfamilies: Cercopithecinae and *Colobinae*

Francois' Langur (*Trachypithecus francoisi*)   Noel Rowe

General Characteristics of the *Cercopithecidae*

The members of the family *Cercopithecidae* are the Old World monkeys. These are the most recently radiated of the primates, having expanded from Africa into Asia to the Far East after a great ice age about 14,000 years ago. The Old World monkeys include the newest primates — animals that have become unique species only since that ice age. Although most Old World monkeys are tropical creatures, the family as a whole has adapted to a wide variety of climates, including tropical rain forests, open grasslands, frigid mountainsides, and in Japan, to arctic-like cold, icy lands.

The secret to the success of the family of Old World monkeys is the adaptability of their basic physical form and their behavior. They have soft, long dense fur that in some species is colored for camouflage, that in others serves to distinguish adult from youngster, male from female, and one subspecies from another, and that in others has adapted from the tropical coat of their origins to one that will retain heat and resist the cold such as with Japanese macaque (*Macaca fuscata*). They have hands capable of manipulating small objects, such as food; most species use their hands to hold food for examination, in order to determine whether the food is fit to eat. They have long, usually powerful arms that enable them to climb great heights and to carry or drag heavy objects such as branches to be waved about to scare off predators. The strength of the arms coupled with the dexterity of the hands give most Old World monkeys the very valuable ability to find food in one place and then carry it to another, safer place where it may be eaten. The proportion of the legs to the rest of the body varies among species. In general, the longer the leg in proportion to the body, the more likely the monkey is to travel by leaping; in general, the shorter the leg is in proportion to the body, the more likely the monkey is to travel among trees by climbing, and along the ground or along branches by walking on all fours.

Perhaps the most remarkable aspect of the behavior of Old World monkeys is one they have in common with other higher primates: the capacity for learning. It takes at least two and half years for an Old World monkey to reach sexual maturity, and usually it takes much longer. During those years before sexual maturity, the animal observes the behavior of adults and learns about food resources, how to socialize with members of its own species, and how to behave sexually. It is this latter aspect that makes many species of *Cercopithecidae* difficult to breed in captivity: an animal raised in captivity may have no idea of how to go about wooing a member of the opposite gender, and inept sexual advances are likely to be rejected. Another aspect of the learning capacity of Old World monkeys is their ability to adjust to a changing environment; for example, it is possible for many species to discover a new food resource and for individual members of a given species to show others what the new food resource is, with those that learn of the new resource being able to add it to their eating patterns. It is this last aspect of learning that may explain the rapid radiation of the *Cercopithecidae* after the ice age 14,000 years ago, as well as its swift speciation into numerous kinds of monkeys: They can adjust their survival skills when their environment changes. Even so, one should keep in mind that this humanlike aspect of *Cercopithecidae* behavior does not mean that they are like humans; they are still primarily instinct-driven creatures.

Species of Old World monkeys tend to live in groups, usually of about seven to thirteen members, although some species will congregate into huge troops of more than one hundred members, usually at night. Nearly all Old World monkeys are daytime (diurnal) animals who forage and mate in daylight. Fruit is the major ingredient of the diet of nearly all Old World monkeys; most have a varied diet that in addition to fruit includes flowers, buds, insects, and other small animals. The *Colobinae* are notable for their adaptations for eating leaves.

The Subfamily *Cercopithecinae*

The members of the subfamily *Cercopithecinae* are probably the most familiar of all monkeys to Americans, and perhaps humanity in general. In America, the familiarity stems in part from the use of rhesus monkeys (or rhesus macaques) in scientific research. This small creature from northern India and Tibet has been a staple of biological research for several decades. There was even a time that when a scientist said the word *monkey,* he meant specifically the rhesus monkey and no other. The popularity of the rhesus monkey for scientific research has greatly reduced its numbers in the wild, and for macaques in general, capture for laboratory research is a significant factor in their declining populations.

One of the reasons species of *Cercopithecinae* are used in biological research is that their metabolisms are similar to that of humans and are in general typical for primates. For instance, their digestive systems have the same basic elements as that of humans (excluding the appendix) and take up only about a third of their torso. This alone makes them attractive for medical studies of such matters as digestive diseases which may afflict humans.

Cercopithecinae is composed of baboons (five species), guenons (seventeen species), macaques (fifteen species), mangabeys (four species; please note that there is some disagreement among authorities about how many species of each of these kinds of animal actually exist, and the number of species in each group is being revised as new information about them is acquired by scientists; in addition, as species become extinct, the number of surviving species will be reduced), as well as the Allen's swamp monkey, the patas monkey, and the talapoin monkey. The members of *Cercopithecinae* are sometimes referred to as "the typical monkeys." They have in common dense coats of fur, often with manes on the neck and shoulders. They are quadrupedal, with primarily terrestrial species such as the baboons having longer limbs than primarily arboreal species. Using their tails as counterweights, arboreal species are able to move among tree branches on their hind limbs alone, allowing them to move their hands freely, especially when gathering food. However, only the patas monkey has adapted to an erect posture that allows it to square its shoulders above its center of gravity and to stand upright, which it does when scanning its locality. The terrestrial species, baboons especially, are too heavy in their upper bodies to sit or stand upright; when feeding, they often stand on three limbs, allowing one hand to move freely to bring food to the mouth. The jaws of *cercopithecine* species are very strong, bringing great pressure on the molars; their jaws tend to be long, with the molars having an extensive surface area. This helps them to grind their food. Distinguishing features of a *cercopithecine* species are cheek pouches, which tend to hold as much volume as the individual animal's stomach. The monkeys will stuff these pouches full, particularly when in a threatening area, and then retreat to a relatively safe place to eat the food; *Colobines* do not share this characteristic. The name *cercopithecine* means "tailed ape," and the tail was once thought to be something that distinguished the monkeys from the apes such as chimpanzees, but this is not the case. As they have spread through the Old World, *cercopithecines* have adapted to their new environments, and in cold climates the monkey's tails can be very short because blood circulation in the tails of *cercopithecines* is poor and the tails can freeze in cold weather. Thus, those species in cold climates have evolved by losing most of their tails.

The behavior of *cercopithecines* varies widely among their species. For instance, most respond to danger by fleeing, but baboons may respond by trying to take a bite out of the threat. When a predator is sighted, *cercopithecines* will usually cry out, warning one another of the danger. They then may make threatening gestures at the predator or run away; baboons use the cry not only to alert them to flee, but sometimes to rally them as a group. They can swarm over a foe and their bites can be deadly. In addition to living in groups, *cercopithecines* tend to be territorial, with territories defined by groups that live in them rather than by individual animals. They usually respond to intruders of their own species nonviolently — with cries, jumping up and down, and perhaps wagging nearby branches; even so, they all seem capable of violence against their own kind and may fight with intruders.

The subfamily *Cercopithecinae* probably evolved from macaques or a macaquelike species that lived in Africa. The macaques spread out of Africa and through much of Asia. As the great ice age ended about 14,000 years ago, the forests of Africa began to spread over what had been cold, dry territory. As the forest spread, so did the *cercopithecines*, adapting to their new ranges and becoming the distinct species of the present. The details of their speciation have yet to be revealed, partly because the fossils of their ancestors are rare and partly because scientific interest in their natural history is relatively recent; originally, most scientific interest was in their suitability for medical research.

The Subfamily *Colobinae*

The subfamily *Colobinae* includes thirty-seven (disputed) species of colobus and leaf monkeys; these last include the langurs. There are two genera of Colobine monkeys. *Colobus* have black and white hair, a three-chambered stomach, and no genital swelling during estrus; *Procolobus* have red fur, a four-chambered stomach, and exhibit genital swelling. Taxonomy is disputed for *Procolobus pennantii*; some authorities argue that there are 9 subspecies that include *P. p. kirki* and *P. p. tholloni*, while others treat *kirki* and *tholloni* as full species.

The colobine monkeys inhabit Central Africa; the others have spread through southern Asia. Evolutionary theorists are especially excited by colobine monkeys because they are the most recently evolved of primates and because the colobus monkeys and Asia's proboscis monkey (*Nasalis larvatus*) still seem to be in the process of evolving to adapt to their environments. The proboscis monkey lives in an arboreal range, yet retains terrestrial physical adaptations; the colobus monkeys are very recently radiated and are still adjusting to the variety of the new environments. Anatomically, the *Colobinae* are distinguished from other monkeys by their large digestive tracts that include sacculated stomachs that harbor symbiotic bacteria that break down leaves into amino acids the monkeys can digest. The upper digestive tract is large in order to hold leaves long enough for them to be fermented by the bacteria, and it is distinct from the lower tract which uses acids for digestion. Colobine monkeys have small thumbs, reduced to stubs in the colobus species of Africa. This is probably an adaptation to brachiation, the process of swinging from tree branch to tree branch by the arms. The hands have become hooklike for grabbing tree limbs as the monkeys swing along.

The Colobine species were once most abundant in Africa, but they spread into Europe and Asia, and now they are most abundant in southern Asia; their European and Middle Eastern species are extinct, leaving a geographical gap from East Africa to India between the African and Asian species. All the African species are threatened to some degree by the activities of humans. Their forest habitats have been greatly reduced by logging, agriculture, and industry, and they are hunted for food and for their colorful, soft coats. In Asia, the degrees of persecution vary, but most species are losing their habitats to humans.

Colobine monkeys tend to eat foods that other Old World primates would reject, especially leaves. Leaves comprise more than half the diet for about half the colobine monkey species, and are important in the diets of others. Immature leaves tend to be preferred over mature leaves; where soil and climate conditions are good for tree growth, the colobine monkeys will eat many mature leaves, but where conditions are poor for the trees, the colobine species tend to be selective, eschewing mature leaves and eating young ones only from selected tree species that provide the most nourishment in their leaves. Fruits are another important food for colobine monkeys, as are — especially for African species — nuts and seeds. Many species also eat insects, lizards, birds, and small mammals, although these comprise a small proportion of their diet.

Colobine monkeys live in groups that vary greatly in size from one species to another, with some tropical forest species having groups with scores of members. Group members usually share in the raising of young, with females taking about four years to mature and males taking about five years to mature. During their years before maturity, colobines learn about group behavior, what cries mean what, how to respond to predators, and how to respond to intrusions of outsiders into group territories. They tend to be very curious, constantly studying their surroundings and inquiring into anything new that appears in their range. An interesting aspect of colobine behavior is that colobine youngsters are actually taught by mature group members, often including their fathers. Instead of just watching an adult to learn how to behave, youngsters have adults who take time to show them what to do in certain situations, such as when in danger.

Colobine groups are territorial, but they are not as aggressive in defending their territories as are *cercopithecines*. Indeed, some species seem very relaxed; for instance, langur groups sometimes congregate peacefully together, forming huge troops of up to 120 members. When rival groups meet and one or the other wants to protect its territory (this would be important in regions where food is scarce), the confrontation usually consists of loud cries and rapid movement through trees, including big leaps. The presence of predators may also trigger noisy displays of leaping, as well as cries that alert other group members. Most colobines do not seem to initially regard humans as predators; when encountering humans for the first time, some species were slaughtered by the thousands because they would expose themselves while satisfying their curiosity about the new creatures in their habitat. All of these colobine species learned to regard humans as predators and avoid humans when they live in areas frequented by humans. Those that live in areas where humans are rare may still display curiosity and not fear when they see humans.

Pagai Island [=Pig-tailed] Mangabey

Nasalis [=Simias] concolor

R. Tenaza

Status	Endangered
Listed	June 2, 1970
Family	Cercopithecidae (Old World monkey)
Description	Most are very dark, almost black, with lighter speckles along the back of the neck, shoulders, and upper back; the face is black and fringed by white hairs.
Habitat	Tropical forest with a high canopy.
Food	Mostly leaves, probably supplemented by fruits and flowers.
Reproduction	Single births are probable.
Threats	Hunting by humans.
Range	Indonesia (Mentawai Islands)

Description

Female adult Pagai Island mangabeys, *Nasalis concolor*, may be slightly smaller than male adults. Adult females are 1.5 to 1.75 feet in head-and-body length, with tails of 4 to 6 inches; adult males are 1.6 to 1.75 feet in head-and-body length, with tails of 5.25 to 7.7 inches. Adults weigh about 15.5 pounds.

Most Pagai Island mangabeys are very dark brown, with light speckles scattered across their necks, shoulders, and backs. Apparently dark-haired parents can have light-brown or creamy haired young, so the light-colored Pagai Island mangabeys do not represent a different species or subspecies but simply represent a color variation within the Pagai Island mangabey community. It is possible that the distinct color variation could represent the potential for a new subspecies — one that might have evolved into a unique pattern on an isolated island had the habitat not been disrupted by humans.

This subspecies was treated as *Simias* until 1975. Other common names include pig-tailed langur monkey and simakobu.

Behavior

The Pagai Island mangabey's behavior varies considerably between areas where humans frequently hunt them and areas where human intrusion is uncommon. In the well hunted areas, the basic living unit is that of a family, with one adult male, one adult female, and their progeny. The adult pair are monogamous. They seldom make vocalizations, although when two family units approach each other, the adult males will each bark once, with the two families then retreating from each other. These Pagai Island mangabeys take great care to move through their forest quietly; they seldom leap — a noisy action — but will take wide detours in order to pass silently from one tree to another. When they are disturbed by humans, they climb into the high canopy and then remain motionless for as long as two hours.

Where humans are uncommon, Pagai Island mangabeys form groups consisting of one adult male and three or so adult females. They are noisy, announcing their movements to other mangabeys. The males show off by making high leaps. When food is plentiful, there may be as many as 570 of these Pagai Island mangabeys per square mile; otherwise, the number may be as few as 20 per square mile.

Habitat

The Pagai Island mangabeys live in primary rain forests with high canopies.

Distribution

The Pagai Island monkey is found on the Mentawai Islands of Indonesia, southwest of Sumatra.

Threats

Humans seem to be the only significant enemies of the Pagai Island mangabeys, which have already been exterminated on some of their native islands. The Pagai Island mangabeys are hunted for food.

Conservation and Recovery

Indonesia has taken steps to preserve its wildlife on its largest islands, but islands like the Mentawais are hard to patrol and keep secure from human interlopers. The Pagai Island mangabey needs large undisturbed forests either on one or more of the larger Mentawai Islands, or it needs one or more of the smaller Mentawai Islands to be secured from hunting and preserved from logging.

Proboscis Monkey

Nasalis larvatus

C. Leimbach

Status	Endangered
Listed	June 14, 1976
Family	Cercopithecidae (Old World monkeys)
Description	Reddish brown or orange-white monkey, with gray or cream-color underparts and reddish facial skin.
Habitat	Mangrove swamps, peat swamps, and riverine forests.
Food	Fruit, flowers, leaves, seeds and aquatic vegetation.
Reproduction	Single young is born after a gestation period of 166 days.
Threats	Destruction of mangrove habitat.
Range	Indonesia (Borneo: Brunei), Malaysia

Description

The proboscis, or nose, of the Proboscis monkey, *Nasalis larvatus*, grows to 4 inches in the adult male, falls over the mouth and is sometimes so obtrusive that the animal must move it out of the way in order to eat. The tongue-shaped nose is reddish brown, but swells and turns red when the monkey is agitated. The female's nose is only slightly enlarged.

The shoulders, cheeks, throat, and nape are pale orange. The legs, belly, rump patch, and tail are whitish gray. The face is pink in adults and dark blue in infants. The penis is red and the scrotum is black. The coat is reddish brown or orange-white, with gray or cream-color underparts. Males measure from 28.7 to 29.9 inches and weigh up to 47 pounds; females measure from 24.0 to 25.2 inches and weigh 22 pounds.

This monkey has partially webbed hind feet and is a good swimmer, even underwater. As with most monkeys, it is an excellent climber and tree swinger.

Behavior

The proboscis monkey forms groups of 4

to 20 individuals comprised of one adult male and a number of females and juveniles. Territories are restricted to less than a square mile. The group feed together but individuals sleep separately.

Mating occurs year round; a single young is born after a gestation period of 166 days.

The proboscis monkey is a day feeder who eats fruit, flowers, leaves, seeds and aquatic vegetation.

Habitat

The Borneo habitat includes coastal nipa palm, mangrove, lowland, riverine, and peat swamp forest below 804 feet.

Distribution

The population is rapidly declining. In 1986, estimates placed the population at 250,000 individuals; by 1994 that number had declined to just a few thousand.

Once endemic throughout Borneo, populations now occur only in the districts of Sabah and Sarawak (Malaysia), in Brunei, and the central-southern region of Kalimantan (Indonesia), and perhaps on several small islands along the coast. Reserves where the species occurs include Samunsam Wildlife Sanctuary, Tanjung Puting National Park, and Kutai National Park.

Threats

The dense mangrove swamps where this species occurs once protected it from human predation, but mangrove wood has become valuable in the production of cellulose, tan-nins, charcoal, and construction material, and the swamps are being quickly destroyed. Pollution and increased river traffic also contribute stress.

Conservation and Recovery

Stopping human predation is mandatory if this species is to survive. Hunting still occurs, even in the wildlife preserves.

Tonkin Snub-nosed Monkey

Pygathrix [=Rhinopithecus] avunculus

Juvenile *P. avunculus*   Tilo Nadler

Status	Endangered
Listed	October 19, 1976 (Threatened)
	September 27, 1990
	(Endangered)
Family	Cercopithecidae (Old World monkey)
Description	Brown-black with yellowish white to orange underparts; elbows have a patch of the same color; the crown and ears are white to yellowish; the facial skin is blue, and the lips are pink.
Habitat	Bamboo jungle.
Food	Leaves; probably eats other vegetation and some meat.
Threats	Habitat loss.
Range	Vietnam

Description

The adult Tonkin snub-nosed monkey, *Pygathrix [=Rhinopithecus] avunculus* measures 21.3 to 25.6 inches from nose to tail, with its tail adding another 23 to 33 inches. The weight range is 18.7 (females) to 30.9 (males) pounds.

They are brown-black with yellowish white to orange underparts, and the elbows have a patch of the same color. The crown and ears are white to yellowish; the facial skin is blue, and the lips are pink. The brown tail has a contrasting whitish yellow or orange grey tip. Infants are born whitish grey and gradually darken. Males have a black penis and white scrotum.

Behavior

This animal lives in Vietnam near the border with China. Neither the Vietnamese nor the Chinese government wants strangers moving about in the area where the two nations fight skirmishes, so naturalists have had little access to the habitat of the animals.

The Tonkin snub-nosed monkey lives in

troops; these may have once had as many as 600 members, although that would now be impossible (there are not enough surviving). The troops would be divided into small groups, each with one adult male and perhaps five adult females, along with their young. Child care seems to be the province of the females, while the males protect against predators.

Studies of some monkeys suggests that about half of their diet consists of fruit, a third of young leaves, and the remainder seeds.

Habitat

The Tonkin snub-nosed monkey seems to favor primary forest on limestone hills at elevations from 656 to 3,937 feet.

Distribution

The Tonkin snub-nosed monkey is found in two small forests, one of which overlaps the Tuyen Quang and Bac Tai provinces, in northern Vietnam. It is very remotely possible that its range extends into China. The last field study conducted in 1995 indicated only roughly 150 individuals remain.

Threats

Slash-and-burn agriculture has destroyed much of the Tonkin snub-nosed monkey's territory. The loss of habitat is likely the most significant factor in the animal's decline toward extinction. Its body parts are used in regional folk medicine, and its coat is lovely and prized for clothing, so commercial hunting may be contributing to the animal's dwindling numbers.

Conservation and Recovery

Internationally, the Tonkin snub-nosed monkey is regarded as one of the most endangered of primates. It is listed in CITES, Appendix I: Trade Prohibited, which means that by treaty it may not be traded in whole or in part internationally. The government of Vietnam has a great many problems to deal with, so it has not protected its wildlife as much as outsiders would like. However, the government has taken some modest steps to attempt the short-term survival of this monkey. The government of Tuyen Quang province has established the Na Hang Nature Reserve to protect the Tonkin snub-nosed monkey.

Yunnan Snub-nosed Monkey

Pygathrix [=Rhinopithecus] bieti

Noel Rowe

Status	Endangered
Listed	September 27, 1990
Family	Cercopithecidae (Old World monkey).
Description	Black fur on its upper and outer body, with white to white-orange fur on its undersides; pink facial skin, a black brow, and a forward-drooping crest.
Habitat	Mountain needle and evergreen forests.
Food	Primarily leaves and pine needles, but occasionally lichens, pine cone seeds, flowers, worms, insects, and birds and their eggs.
Threats	Human predation and loss of habitat.
Range	China (Yunnan Province), Tibet.

Description

The Yunnan snub-nosed monkey, *Pygathrix [=Rhinopithecus] bieti*, measures 29 to 32.7 inches not counting the tail, with the tail adding another 20.4 to 29.4 inches. Males are considerably larger than females, with adult males weighing about 33 pounds and females weighing about 20 pounds.

The monkey's fur is black or dark gray on most of its body, including the paws and arms beyond the elbow. It has yellow tinted hairs scattered across it shoulder. The hair on the shoulders can grow up fourteen inches long and is much prized for human clothing. These monkeys have pink facial skin, a black brow, and a forward-drooping crest. The black tail has a tuft at the end, similar to a cow's tail.

Taxonomy for this species is disputed. It was elevated from a subspecies of *P. roxellana* in 1988.

Behavior

Not much is known of this animal's behavior. It lives in groups that may have once included as many as 600 members, but now numbers from 23 to 200. Males guard their group and warn of danger. Young may be cared for by their mothers for as long as two years, when they may become sexually mature. The Yunnan snub-nosed monkey may be migratory, moving to the east side of the Yun-ling Mountains in cold seasons and the west side in warm seasons. Their diet is mostly leaves and pine needles. They may not care for fruit. Their diet sometimes includes lichens (in winter when other food is scarce), pine cone seeds, flowers, and some small animals: worms, insects, birds and bird eggs.

Mating season is August to September with the birth season from March to May. Gestation lasts 170 days.

Habitat

The Yunnan snub-nosed monkey lives in broadleaf, deciduous, evergreen, conifer, montane and temperate forests at altitudes up to 14,765 feet. The environment is cold and frosty for about two thirds of the year, but the monkey seems to prefer the colder climate and only descends below 4,600 feet to take advantage of leaf growth in the spring.

Distribution

The Yunnan snub-nosed monkey lives in mountains in Yunnan, China, and eastern Tibet.

Threats

The Yunnan snub-nosed monkey is hunted for use in Southeast Asian folk medicine; it is also hunted for its luxuriant fur; and it is hunted for food. Its habitat has been extensively cleared for agriculture in the second half of the twentieth century, leaving it with a constricted range that is probably too small to support it in large numbers. Recent published estimates of its total numbers vary from 200 to 600, although 200 is the likeliest number. Although China has taken steps to protect its monkeys, the Yunnan snub-nosed monkey has the misfortune of living outside of protected areas. Without protection, it is almost certainly doomed and is one of the most endangered of all primates. It could quite literally be exterminated in a day.

Conservation and Recovery

The state of decline of China's monkeys has alarmed primatologists and has attracted the attention of major conservation organizations such as the IUCN. It is included in CITES, Appendix I: Trade Prohibited, which means that by international treaty it is forbidden to trade in the Yunnan snub-nosed monkey in whole or in part. China has enacted laws prohibiting the hunting of the monkey, but poaching is a significant problem. The monkey's parts and coat are highly valued for folk medicine, clothing, and display. The Yunnan-snub nosed monkey fares poorly in captivity and needs a range that is protected from habitat destruction and human predation.

Guizhou Snub-nosed Monkey

Pygathrix [=Rhinopithecus] brelichi

Noel Rowe

Status	Endangered
Listed	September 27, 1990
Family	Cercopithecidae (Old World monkey)
Description	Gray-brown with almost black paws, forearms, and tail; thighs are gray; chest and abdomen are yellowish gray.
Habitat	Subtropical evergreen forests.
Food	Leaves, fruits, seeds, bark, insects, bird's eggs, and small birds.
Threats	Commercial hunting and loss of habitat.
Range	China: Guizhou Province

Description

The head-and-body length of the adult Guizhou snub-nosed monkey, *Pygathrix [=Rhinopithecus] brelichi*, is 26 to 30 inches; its tail adds another 22 to 30.4 inches. It probably weighs in the neighborhood of 30 pounds. The Guizhou snub-nosed monkey's coat is valued as a fashion item because it is colorful, long, and soft. Its basic fur color is gray-brown. This becomes a very dark gray on its paws, forearms, and tail, and pales to gray on its thighs. The tip of its tail and the space between its shoulders are yellowish-white, and its underbody is yellowish gray.

The upper arms, the inside of the shoulders, and the brow are yellowish orange. The crown of the head is brown, and the top of the ears is white. The facial skin is blue, and the lower lip is pink. Males have a white patch of fur on the back between their shoulders; the scrotum and nipples are white.

Other common names include, gray snub-nosed monkey, Brelich's snub-nosed monkey, white-shoulder-haired snub-nosed monkey, white-shoulder-haired snub-nosed golden monkey, or Guizhou snub-nosed langur.

Behavior

The Guizhou snub-nosed monkey lives in troops as small as 30 and as large as 430; these large troops are divided into subgroups that usually consist of one adult male, five adult females, and their offspring. Some males are solitary, living outside of the subgroups. The males of a troop defend it against predators such as raptors.

The diet of the Guizhou snub-nosed monkey consists primarily of leaves, but it includes fruits, seeds, bark, insects, bird's eggs, and small birds.

Habitat

The Guizhou snub-nosed monkey inhabits subtropical evergreen or deciduous broadleaf or coniferous forests at 3,281 to 7,546 feet.

Distribution

The Guizhou snub-nosed monkey occurs in one reserve in the province of Guizhou.

Threats

The Guizhou snub-nosed monkey is threatened by hunting and by habitat loss. Its body parts are used in Chinese folk medicine and its fur coat is valued for clothing, so the monkey is hunted commercially by poachers. Its forest habitat has been extensively cleared for agriculture, leaving it little room in which to live. Fewer than 1,000 are believed to remain.

Conservation and Recovery

The Guizhou snub-nosed monkey is protected from harm under Chinese law, and its limited amount of remaining forest is protected from clearing. Violations of the laws carry penalties of imprisonment and fines. Although the Guizhou snub-nosed monkey is still very endangered, in recent years China's efforts to preserve it seem to have helped, and its population is slowly increasing. Chinese attempts to breed this species in captivity have been unsuccessful. Preservation of its wild habitat is its only hope for long-term survival.

Douc [=Red-shanked Douc] Langur

Pygathrix nemaeus

Noel Rowe

Status	Endangered
Listed	June 2, 1970
Family	Cercopithecidae (Old World monkey)
Description	Pale golden brown face with long white hair fluffing out from its cheeks and throat; its crown, back, and chest are mixed with white, gray, and black hairs; paws, hindlegs, and hindquarters are dark gray, almost black.
Habitat	Tropical rain forest.
Food	Primarily leaves, but includes other vegetation such as fruit and buds.
Reproduction	Gestation lasts up to 165 days and results in a single birth.
Threats	Loss of habitat, commercial hunting, and hunting for food.
Range	Cambodia, Laos, and Vietnam.

Description

The adult male douc langur, *Pygathrix nemaeus*, measures 21.7 to 24.8 inches in length, not counting the tail, which adds another 23.6 to 28.9 inches. Females measure 23.1 inches with tail length of 23.5 inches. Males weigh 24 pounds with females weighing 18.1 pounds. The species has a remarkably fine coat that is thick and fluffy. It head, back, and chest are an overall gray, created by the mixing of white, gray, and black hairs. Its face is a pale golden brown, with white around its mouth and eyes. Long white hair fluffs out from its cheeks and throat, and between the throat and the chest is often a band of orange, long hair. The tail, forearms, and genital region are white, as is the triangular patch at the tail's base. The penis is red; the scrotum is white. Infants are gray with a black face and two pale stripes beneath the eyes.

Other common names include douc monkey, and red-shanked douc monkey.

A new form, *P. nigripes* (black-shanked douc langur), has been documented that may be elevated from a subspecies of *P. nemaeus*. It has a pale face, gray legs and forearms, and a white belly and genital region. A study of its behavior began in 1966, and it is listed as endangered under *P. nemaeus*.

Behavior

Much about the douc langur's behavior has yet to be learned, yet what little has been recorded makes the animal a captivating one to study. Adults males, either singly or as a pair, will form groups comprising several adult females and offspring. Females are in estrus for only a short time, perhaps 48 hours; males will indicated their interest in mating by staring at the prospective female, then staring at a patch of ground suitable for the sex act. The female, if receptive, then lies prone on the ground and stares over her shoulder at the male during sexual intercourse. Pregnancy lasts no more than 165 days and usually results in the birth of one infant. The youngster is cared for primarily by its mother, but it will be passed around to the other members of its group. Although the females will do most of the handling, the males also sometimes hold the youngster. One observer of a youngster born in a zoo records that when a three-month-old infant's mother died, the father took over the principal care of the youngster; the youngster spent 70% of its time with its father, and 30% with the females of the group. The douc langur is closely related to the *colobus* monkeys of Africa, and it seems that as is the case with several *colobus* species, the male takes an extraordinary interest in the rearing of the young. In any case, for the douc langur, child rearing is a group activity.

Douc langur is a fussy eater. It wants leaves that are mature but not old, and it wants fruit that is not yet ripe. Before eating something, the douc langur will examine it closely and will discard it if it is an old leaf or ripe or overripe fruit. Foraging seems to be a group activity, but the douc langur needs to be observed much more in the wild than it has for the dynamics of foraging and group movement become clear. It is probable that the douc langur established group territories.

Habitat

The douc langur lives in dense primary and secondary tropical rain forest at elevations of 984 to 6,562 feet.

Distribution

The douc langur lives in central and southern Vietnam and central Laos; it probably also lives in Cambodia.

Threats

The loss of habitat to warfare, logging, and slash-and-burn agriculture is the greatest threat to the douc langur's survival. The douc langur is hunted for food by local peoples, and it is hunted for its spectacular coat by commercial hunters.

Conservation and Recovery

Perhaps the single most important factor favoring the douc langur's survival is its own determination to live. The douc langur tries to adapt to whatever replaces its forest; for example, it will try to live in urban areas if there is no forest available. Its cooperative care of its young is also favorable; the loss of a mother, a father, or even most of a group does not necessarily doom a youngster: It still may be cared for by other douc langurs. Vietnam has established a nature reserve in an area where douc langurs live and is trying to prevent the further clearing of the forest within the reserve. Poaching of wildlife on the reserve is a big problem, and Vietnam may not at present have the resources to police its reserve and prevent the poaching. The douc langur is held in several zoos and has been bred with a fair amount of success in the United States, although the gene pool is presently probably too small for captive breeding to ensure the douc langur's long-term survival.

Sichuan Snub-nosed Monkey

Pygathrix [=Rhinopithecus] roxellana

Ron Garrison, San Diego Zoo

Status	Endangered
Listed	September 27, 1990
Family	Cercopithecidae (Old World monkey)
Description	Its back and tail are dark brown, almost black, with long golden hair spread across the shoulders. The rest of its body and the tip of its tail are orange.
Habitat	Mountain forests between 4,600 and 10,500 feet.
Food	Primarily leaves and pine needles, but it will eat fruit, flowers, bark, worms, insects, small birds, and bird eggs.
Threats	Habitat loss and commercial hunting.
Range	China

Description

Male adult Sichuan snub-nosed monkeys, *Pygathrix [=Rhinopithecus] roxellana,* are larger than female adults. Body length without the tail varies from 26.8 to 29.9 inches; the tail adds 25.4 to 28.4 inches. Males weigh 33 to 86 pounds, whereas females weigh 14 to 22 pounds. The back and tail are dark brown, almost black, with long whitish orange hairs spread across the shoulders. The face, except for a white muzzle, chest, and legs are a dark orange which darkens in males as they age. The tip of the tale is a pale orange. The skin of the face is pale blue.

Taxonomy is disputed. The subgenus name *Rhinopithecus* was formerly the genus name. Other common names include the golden snub-nosed monkey, Roxellane's snub-nosed monkey, orange snub-nosed monkey, Sichuan snub-nosed langur, or moupin langur.

Behavior

The Sichuan snub-nosed monkey migrates up mountains in warm weather and down the mountains in cold weather. It seems to bear cold very well, even in snow. It gathers together in large groups with as many as 600 members. Females always outnumber males in such troops. The troops are divided into smaller, male-dominated groups, usually consisting of one adult male, five adult females, and their offspring. The dynamics of this social unit and the process of mating are little understood, at present. The males are the protectors against predators.

The Sichuan snub-nosed monkey is dependent on the leaves and needles of the trees in its native habitat. Depending on the seasonal availability of other foods, it will eat fruit, flowers, worms, insects, small birds, and their eggs. Mating season is October to December with births occuring from April to June.

Habitat

The Sichuan snub-nosed monkey lives in mountain forests, from 4,600 to 10,500 feet in elevation. The forests are evergreen, coniferous, and bamboo. They are adapted to the longest winter and the coldest temperatures that any primate can withstand besides humans. They prefer altitudes of 6,562 to 9,187 feet with winter temperatures ranging from 32 to 48 degrees Fahrenheit.

Distribution

The Sichuan snub-nosed monkey is found in the Chinese provinces of Hubei, Shaanxi, Gansu, and Szechwan (Sichuan).

Threats

The Sichuan snub-nosed monkey has long been hunted for its meat. Its body parts are used in Southeast Asian folk medicines and it is heavily poached for the medicinal market. Its dense, soft coat is valued for clothing; thus, it is hunted for its pelt as well. Its ancient forest has been larger cleared for agriculture, restricting it to patches of mountain forest. Loss of the forest would almost certainly doom the species.

Conservation and Recovery

China has protected the Sichuan snub-nosed monkey's remaining forest habitat and has made it illegal to disturb that habitat or to harm the monkeys in it. Violations are punishable with fines and prison terms. China's efforts seem to have had some success. The population of the Sichuan snub-nosed monkey seems to be increasing, topping 10,000 monkeys. This number is large enough that scientists can hope to find healthy populations that they can study; little is known about the Sichuan snub-nosed monkey's life, and what can be learned about it could not only help conservationists save the monkey from extinction, but to save its close *Rhinopithecine* relatives, as well.

Entellus [=Sacred] Langur

Presbytis [=Semnopithecus] entellus

George Holton

Status	Endangered
Listed	June 14, 1976
Family	Cercopithecidae (Old World monkeys)
Description	Silvery gray fur with a black face.
Habitat	Hot dry desert areas, cold alpine scrub, as well as dense wet tropical evergreen forest.
Food	Primarily leaves, fruits, and flowers, and occasionally insects.
Reproduction	Gestation lasts about 200 days, usually resulting in a single birth.
Threats	Loss of habitat and hunting by humans.
Range	Bangladesh, India, Pakistan, Sri Lanka, and Burma.

Description

The Entellus langur, *Presbytis entellus,* is the best studied of the *Presbytis* species. Adults are 16 to 30.7 inches in length from tip of nose to base of tail, with the tail adding another 27.3 to 38.5 inches. Males are somewhat heavier on average than females, weighing 23.4 to 43.6 pounds, whereas females weigh 14.8 to 34.4 pounds. There are at least 15 subspecies (naturalists disagree over exactly how many). Some taxonomists consider the genus *Semnopithecus* to be a subgenus of *Presbytis;* others include all species of the genus *Trachypithecus* in *Semnopithecus.*

There is some variation in coat among the subspecies. For instance, a subspecies on Sri Lanka has erect hairs on its crown, whereas the other subspecies do not. Coloration tends to be uniform, a silvery gray with a black face. The adults of *Presbytis* species tend to resemble one another, so naturalists often look at their young to distinguish them: Their young tend to have markedly different colorings. In the case of the entellus langur, it is black or very dark brown at birth. This coloration will give way to the silvery gray of the adults as the youngster matures.

Other common names include Hanuman langur, named after the Hindu monkey-god Hanuman, and gray langur.

Behavior

The entellus langur lives in mixed-gender groups of up to 70 members and all-male groups that may have over 100 members. In areas where food is plentiful, the mixed-gender groups have only one adult male; this male has exclusive breeding rights to the adult females in his group. Females typically stay with the group they were born into, and territories are inherited by daughters from their mothers. Adult males are forced out of their original groups and wander widely through the territories of other groups. These free males often bind together, forming all-male groups looking for food and the opportunity to take over a group. When these males try to usurp a dominant male, a fight ensues in which even the adult females participate. The females help to drive off challengers to the adult male's dominance because new adult males often kill all the infants in their new groups, hastening their mother's reproductive cycle. The females fight to protect the investment they have made in their offspring, even after a new dominant male has taken over the group. Females have been badly mauled by placing themselves between infanticidal males and their infants.

Where food is scarce, the entellus langurs have groups with several adult males, as well as many females. Infanticide is unknown in such groups.

Females initiate mating, and one will pull the hair of a male that she is interested in but who ignores hers; she will even hit and bite him. Gestation is long, lasting 200 days, resulting in a single birth, although twins rarely occur. Infant care is shared among the females of the birth group, although the infant spends most of its time with its mother; the male may also participate to a small degree in caring for the youngster. Females eventually become sexually mature members of their birth group; males are driven away just before they reach sexual maturity.

The entellus langur prefers to eat tree products, although it is at home on the ground as much as it is in trees and often travels and forages on the ground. In India, it has formed an unusual relationship with chital (*Axis axis*), a large deer. Where a group of entellus langurs settle in a tree, the deer come and wait below; they apparently listen for the entellus langurs or try to catch their scent, and then seek the entellus langurs out. The entellus langurs eat the tender parts of leaves and throw the rest away; most of what is discarded is edible for the chital, so it waits for the discarded food to be dropped on the ground. The entellus langurs seem unafraid of the chitals; they even push away chitals, sometimes grabbing them by the horns. The chital and entellus langurs share the chore of guarding against predators such as leopards and tigers; the chital has a keen sense of smell, and the entellus langur has keen eyesight, and therefore by eating together they increase their chances of discovering an approaching predator.

Habitat

The entellus langur inhabits tropical, subtropical, dry thorn scrub, pine, semievergreen, and alpine forest and urban areas and live from sea level to 14,000 feet in altitude, representing the widest range for any primate other than humans. It seems tolerant of arid climates (less than 4 inches of rain per year) to wet climates (about 80 inches of rain per years). It also tolerates a wide range of temperature, from nearly freezing to 120 degrees

Fahrenheit. Where its wild range has been lost to human encroachment, the entellus langur has adapted to living among humans and may even be found in urban areas. In spite of its remarkable adaptability, the entellus langur plainly prefers dense forests over other habitats and only thrives within such forests.

Distribution

This highly adaptable animal has found homes for itself in deserts to rain forests in Pakistan, India, Bangladesh, Sri Lanka, and Burma.

Threats

The entellus langur is losing its range to expanding human settlements and agriculture. It is thought of as a pest throughout its range because of its willingness to enter human occupied areas and eat what it finds, and it is therefore hunted as an agricultural and domestic nuisance. Humans also hunt the entellus langur for food, and it is hunted for sale in Southeast Asian folk medicine.

Conservation and Recovery

India has laws protecting the entellus langur from harm, and it and its neighbors have wildlife reserves in which the langur dwells. Poachers are a problem in these protected areas, but the reserves may be sufficiently protected to enable the entellus langur to survive, at least for the near future. In India, the entellus langur is a sacred animal and wanders freely through human habita-

tions.

The entellus langur species is listed in CITES, Appendix I: Trade Prohibited, which means that by treaty, it may not be traded in whole or in part internationally. Even so, its parts may be finding their way out of its native countries and into others with a demand for the parts as ingredients in folk medicine.

Mentawai Island Langur

Presbytis potenziani

Ron Tilson

Status	Threatened (IUCN Endangered)
Listed	October 19, 1976
Family	Ceropithecidae (Old World monkeys)
Description	Back and tail are black, the underside is orange or brown, the brow, cheeks, chin, throat, and upper chest are grayish white.
Habitat	Rain forests and mangrove forests.
Food	Leaves
Threats	Predation by humans and loss of habitat.
Range	Indonesia (Mentawai Islands)

Description

The Mentawai Island langur, *Presbytis potenziani*, measures 17 to 19.7 inches long, not counting the tail, which is another 22.8 inches in length. It weighs 14.1 to 14.3 pounds. It is a colorful animal, with its black back and tail setting off the bright orange to brown of the lower chest and abdomen, and the grayish white of the brow, cheeks, chin, throat, and upper chest. The tail's tip is sometimes white. The Mentawai Island langur has a small crest of erect hairs along its crown. The genital region is yellowish white and males have a white scrotum. Neonates are whitish gray with a dark stripe down the back.

Other common names include Mentawai leaf monkey, Mentawai Islands sureli, long-tailed langur, and red-bellied sureli.

Behavior

The behavior of the Mentawai Island langur has been poorly observed. It lives in groups of about seven members. These monogamous groups appear to have one adult male and one adult female. This species is the only monogamous colobine monkey. The species appears to mate for life, with their family groups forming the foundation of their social behavior. Mating can occur any time of the year. The period for gestation is not accurately known, but it may be about 165 days;

it results in a single birth. Females probably take four years to reach maturity, with males probably taking five years. Males leave their birth groups just before they become sexually mature. Females probably leave their birth group, too, in order to form a monogamous union, but this is not certain.

Groups have territories that overlap with other groups. Each group has a core area within its territory where overlapping is not tolerated. A territorial call is described as a loud and repetitive *bagok*. The diet consists of leaves, fruits and seeds. These monkeys are one of the few primates that can tolerate the leaves of the dipterocarp tree family.

Habitat

The Mentawai Island langur lives in primary and secondary evergreen rain forests and mangrove forests.

Distribution

This species occurs in Indonesia's Mentawai Islands.

Threats

The Mentawai island langur is hunted by humans for food, and it is this hunting, more than any other factor, that accounts for its decline. Its habitat is being logged, which is constricting its range and breaking up its population into patches too small to successfully maintain itself through normal breeding. It has already disappeared from one of its native islands.

Conservation and Recovery

In recent years, Indonesia has acted to protect some of its wildlife, but the long-tailed langur lives in an area with few protections. The hunting of it for food needs to be regulated, and it needs reserves where logging and agriculture are prohibited.

François' Langur

Trachypithecus [=Presbytis] francoisi

Noel Rowe

Status	Endangered
Listed	October 19, 1976
Family	Cercopithecidae (Old World monkey)
Description	Overall shiny black coat with a white streak from the corners of the mouth to the ears. It has sharply erect hairs on its crown, forming a crest, and two whorls of fur on the nape of its neck.
Habitat	High elevation rain forests.
Food	Leaves, fruits and flowers.
Reproduction	Gestation probably lasts about 165 days, resulting in a single birth.
Threats	Habitat loss.
Range	China, Laos, and Vietnam.

Description

Taxonomy is disputed for François' langur. It was formerly in the genus *Presbytis*. Some taxonomists include this species in *Semnopithecus*. Four subspecies (*T. f. hatinhensis, T. f. laotum, T. f. leucocephalus,* and *T. f. poliocephalus*) may be recognized as full species after further study.

An adult male François langur measures between 19.1 and 25.0 inches in length, not including the tail, which adds another 32.3 to 34.9 inches. It weighs approximately 13 pounds. Females measure 21.7 to 23.2 inches with a tail length of 32.7 to 34.9 inches. Its coat is a shiny black, with white from the corners of the mouth to the ears; on its head is a crest of erect hairs, and on the nape of its neck are two whorls.

Other common names include François' leaf monkey, white-sideburned black leaf monkey, or François' black leaf monkey.

Behavior

Very little is known of the habits of the François' langur. It seems to live in groups similar to those of the entellus langur (*Presbytis entellus*; please see separate entry). These groups can be large, with as many as 70 members; in general the groups are smaller, with one adult male, several females, and their young. Young adult males probably band together to form all-male groups where they remain until they manage to take over a mixed-gender group (although this behavior has not yet been observed).

The groups are territorial, and it is likely that territories overlap somewhat, with only a core area within the larger territory protected against outside groups. This core area would contain special trees for sleeping and eating. The females would pass the territory on to their daughters; males move from group to group but females tend to remain with their birth group. The entire group would participate in caring for youngsters, but the birth mother would usually care for her young about 70% of the time.

Langurs have specially adapted digestive systems for processing leaves, and the François langur undoubtedly eats many different kinds of leaves. Other likely parts of its diet would be fruits, probably unripe, flowers, buds, and stems.

Habitat

The François' langur occurs on high cliffs overlooking rivers and on high, rocky mountainsides amid very wet rain forests.

Distribution

The François' langur has been seen in southeastern China, Laos, and northern Vietnam.

Threats

Loss of habitat is probably the principal threat to the François' langur's survival. Its forest is being cut for timber and burned to make way for agriculture. It has some value in regional folk medicine and is probably hunted for that reason, and it may be a food source for local people.

Conservation and Recovery

The François langur has the misfortune in living in one of the most fought over territories among humans. Wars have been fought there for hundreds of years, and even now China and Vietnam skirmish and sometimes all-out fight over the territory. This warfare makes it very difficult for scientists to observe the François langur and through observations learn how to protect the monkey. Strangers are unwelcome in the area; naturalists could fall victim to soldiers or poachers.

Vietnam has taken steps to protect its wildlife, although its resources for such protection are small. China has made the hunting of its langurs illegal, and violations are punishable by fines and imprisonment. At present, the populations of François' langur seem to live outside of reserves and parks where they could have extra protection.

Golden Langur

Trachypithecus geei

Bruce Bunting

Status	Endangered
Listed	June 14, 1976
Family	Cercopithecidae (Old World monkey).
Description	Orange-white red to orange underparts; a cap of short erect hairs protrude slightly beyond the cheek hairs; face is mostly bare, with dark brown skin.
Habitat	Dense tropical forests.
Food	Leaves, fruits, flowers, buds, stems, and salty dirt.
Reproduction	Births are usually single.
Threats	Loss of habitat.
Range	Bhutan and India.

Description

Taxonomy is disputed for the golden langur. It was formerly in the genus *Presbytis.* Some taxonomists include this species in *Semnopithecus;* others include it as a subspecies of *T. pileatus.*

Adult males are larger than adult females. Males are 24 to 29 inches long, not counting the tail, which adds another 31 to 37 inches. They weigh 22 to 26.5 pounds. Females are 19 to 24 inches long, not count-

ing the tail, which adds another 28 inches. They weigh about 21 pounds. The golden langur has an elegant coat of long fluffy fur that is mostly golden orange-white, with the undersides being red to orange. The cheeks are sometimes reddish-orange. It has a cap of short erect hairs that protrude slightly beyond the cheek hairs. Its face is mostly bare, with dark brown skin. Neonates are orange brown or gray.

Another common name is golden leaf monkey.

Behavior

The golden langur has been observed in mixed gender groups, and all male groups have been reported. The mixed gender groups usually have only one, occasionally two, adult males; this male has exclusive breeding rights to the adult females in his group. The mating season occurs from January to February; birth season follows in July and August. Females typically stay with the group they were born into, and territories are inherited by daughters from their mothers. Just before reaching sexual maturity, males are forced out of their original groups and wander widely through the territories of other groups. These free males often bind together, forming all-male groups looking for food and the opportunity to take over a group. When these males try to usurp a dominant male, a fight ensues in which even the adult females participate. The females help to drive off challengers to the adult male's dominance because new adult males often kill all the infants in their new groups, hastening their mother's reproductive cycle. The females fight to protect the investment they have made in their offspring, even after a new dominant male has taken over the group. Females have been badly mauled by placing themselves between infanticidal males and their infants.

The golden langur prefers to live in trees, although it is comfortable on the ground. Its diet consists mostly of tree leaves, although it also consumes fruits, flowers, buds, and stems. It probably also eats insects, although this is not certain. This species has been reported to raid cardamom plantations.

Habitat

The golden langur occurs in moist evergreen, dipterocarp, riverine, savanna, and deciduous forest up to 7,874 feet.

Distribution

The golden langur lives in forests in the state of Assam in India and in Bhutan.

Threats

The golden langur's native forests have been logged for timber and cleared for agriculture. This has shrunk its range and broken its population up into patches of forest, making it difficult for males to migrate to new groups and through their breeding, keep the gene pool diverse. It now exists in small numbers (exact counts are hard to come by, but the population probably numbers in the hundreds). In general, local people do not hunt the golden langur, although its body parts may be used in folk medicines in nearby Southeast Asian nations.

Conservation and Recovery

The golden langur is protected under Indian law and is found in wildlife reserves in India and Bhutan. If Bhutan and India are successful in protecting their reserves from the pressures of expanding human populations, the golden langur has good prospects for long-term survival. Efforts to breed the golden langur have met with small success.

Capped Langur
Trachypithecus pileatus

Craig Stanford

Status	Endangered
Listed	June 14, 1976
Family	Cercopithecidae (Old World monkey)
Description	Gray base color with brown to orange chest and abdomen and an upright shock of hair on their heads.
Habitat	Deciduous, evergreen, and bamboo forests and swamps.
Food	Mostly leaves but also fruit and flowers, as well.
Reproduction	Single offspring after gestation of 168 days.
Threats	Loss of habitat.
Range	Bangladesh, Burma, and India.

Description

Adult male capped langurs, *Trachypithecus pileatus*, tend to be larger than females. A male can be 21.0 to 28.0 inches long, not counting the tail, which can add another 32.7 to 37.6 inches; the male can weigh between 25.5 and 31 pounds. Adult female capped langurs can be 19.3 to 26 inches long, not counting the tail, which can add another 33.8 to 40.4 inches; the female weighs about 22 pounds. The scrotum is absent in this species. There is some variation among the capped langur's five subspecies, but adults tend to look similar to the other *Trachypithecus* species: They have gray bodies with brown to orange underbodies. Variations include white or orange cheeks, black or dark gray paws, orange paws, a darker lower back than upper back, and a black tail base. Naturalists find it easier to tell species apart by the coloration of their young, which varies greatly from species to species. The capped langur's young are creamy white up to 5 months, with a pink face; at 5 to 14 months they acquire adult coloration. The capped langur gets its name from the shock of upright hair that sprouts from its head beyond its cheek hairs.

Other common names include capped

leaf monkey and bonneted leaf monkey. The genus *Semnopithecus* includes only 1 species. Some taxonomists consider it to be a subgenus of *Presbytis*. Others include all species of the genus *Trachypithecus* in *Semnopithecus*.

Behavior

The capped langurs live in groups of 2 to 13 members with one adult male. They are territorial, with territories of about 160 acres in size. Group territories may overlap, but each group has a core area of trees for sleeping in as well as feeding that comprise 20% to 50% of their total territory and which they will defend against interlopers. They spend most of their lives in trees, rarely descending to the ground. They move about by leaping.

Mating behavior for capped langurs is poorly recorded, but it seems to follow a fairly typical langur pattern: A male stares at a female; if she is willing, she assumes a prone position and they mate. Gestation could take up to 168 days, resulting in the birth of a single infant. The group as a whole assumes responsibility for raising the youngster, although most of its time will be spent with its mother.

As with other langurs, the capped langur has a specially adapted digestive tract that allows its primary diet, leaves, to sit and be slowly broken down by symbiotic bacteria. Its diet consists mostly of leaves. The capped langur is known to eat fruits and flowers, as well. It spends almost 30% of its feeding time on two species of trees. During the rainy season when fruit is abundant, 50% of their feeding is on fruit, especially figs. They drink water form tree cavities.

Habitat

The capped langur lives at high elevations, up to 3,281 feet, in Burma and low ones in Bangladesh and India. It is found in dense forests of evergreen trees, deciduous trees, and bamboo. Typically, the environment is wet, although this may not be crucial to making the habitat suitable for the capped langur. On the other hand, an abundance of mature leaves seems to be essential to the animal's survival.

Distribution

The range of the capped langur extends from Assam in India, through Bangladesh, and into central Burma.

Threats

The capped langur's forests are being clear cut for timber and burned for slash-and-burn agriculture. The result is that the capped langurs live in patches of what was once continuous forest. Their territories are broken up, and their breeding populations are fragmented. The loss of trees has also created a shortage of food for the capped langur, and some have taken to seeking nourishment in human occupied areas, making them seem to be agricultural pests. They are thus hunted as pests; they are also hunted by humans for food. It is possible that they are also hunted for sale as ingredients for Southeast Asian folk medicine.

Conservation and Recovery

The capped langur is a somewhat ne-
glected species; it is unspectacular and often
shares territories with more attractive monkey species. Little is known of how it is faring
in Burma, whose government dislikes intrusions of outsiders. In Bangladesh, it is a
source of protein for humans. India has a
good park and wildlife reserve system, but it
is perhaps to fragmented for the capped
langur too form a regenerating breeding
population.

Purple-faced Langur

Trachypithecus vetulus

Noel Rowe

Status	Threatened
Listed	October 19, 1976
Family	Cercopithecidae (Old World monkey)
Description	The coat is brown, darkening at the extremities; the throat is white or yellow.
Habitat	Lowland and highland forests up to 6,700 feet in elevation.
Food	Mostly leaves, supplemented with flowers and fruits.
Reproduction	Pregnancy lasts about 200 days and usually results in a single birth, although twins do rarely occur.
Threats	Loss of habitat.
Range	Sri Lanka.

Description

The taxonomy for the purple-faced langur is disputed. The species was reclassified in 1980 as *Tracypithecus vetulus;* formerly it was classified as *Presbytis senex.* Adult male purple-faced langurs measure between 19.5 to 23.9 inches from tip of nose to base of tail; the tail adds between 24.3 to 33.6 inches. Females measure from 119.1 to 21.3 inches with tail length of 26.2 to 32.3 inches. Males weigh 12.5 to 20.8 pounds; females weigh 11.3 to 16.5 pounds. Their basic coat is brown, darkening as it approaches the hands and feet; some-times the coat is nearly black. Their throat is white or yellow. The crown can be pale brown or yellow, and the tail's tip can be pale brown or yellow, too. Sometimes they have scattered spots of white on their backs and thighs.

Other common names include purple-face leaf monkey and wanderoo.

Behavior

The purple-faced langur has well-defined territories that are 2 to 25 acres in size; where food is abundant, territories are smaller, and where it is scarce, territories are larger. Males seem to be the principal custodians of territorial boundaries, and are reportedly so exactly that they even chastise their own group members for violating a boundary. When different groups meet at territorial boundaries, the females join the males in vigorous crying and threatening gestures in defense of their territories.

Groups have one adult male, occasionally two males, a few adult females, and their young; a group will have 6 to 20 members. The adult male has the exclusive breeding rights to the group's adult females. Gestation lasts about 200 days and usually results in a single birth; twins occur rarely. Mating occurs from October to January with young born from May to August. Youngsters are cared for primarily by their mothers, but other group females will share in the holding, feeding, and protecting of the young. Youngsters are weaned between 7 and 8 months of age. Females remain with their group, inheriting the group's territory from their mothers. Males will be forced out of the group before they reach sexual maturity. Such males often band together in groups and wander through territories looking for a dominant male to usurp. Confrontations between dominant males and their challengers can be violent. When a dominant male is driven out of his group, the new dominant male may kill the group's infants, in order to speed up the adult females' sexual receptivity and to breed young of his own. Females resist the infanticide and can be hurt themselves by getting between the new dominant male and their infants.

The purple-faced langur is diurnal and arboreal, avoiding the ground. It prefers to live in forests with high canopies. It mostly eats tree leaves, but will eat fruits and flowers. They have been observed raiding potato and cauliflower crops.

Habitat

The purple-faced langur lives in primary, secondary, semi-deciduous dry, riverine, coastal, scrub, and montane cloud forest up to 7,200 feet. Most of its mature forest habitat is gone, and it is trying to adapt to man-made parks and other areas with new trees.

Distribution

The purple-faced langur probably once ranged over all of Sri Lanka, from its mountainous evergreen forests to its oceanside mangrove forests. It now lives primarily in the island's highlands.

Threats

The population of the purple-faced langur may already be too small to maintain the genetic diversity necessary for the species' long-term survival. Its habitat has been largely cut down for timber and to make way for agriculture.

Conservation and Recovery

The purple-faced langur lives in national parks where it seems to be adapting to human activity. Preservation of the parks is essential to the animal's survival.

Western Black-and-white Colobus

Colobus polykomos

Noel Rowe

Status	Vulnerable
Listed	*IUCN Red List*
Family	Cercopithecidae
Description	Black with a white beard and a long white mane.
Habitat	Rain forests to dry forests.
Food	Mostly immature leaves; fruits, mature leaves, leaf and buds.
Reproduction	1 young; gestation of 170 days.
Threats	Predation by humans, bird's of prey, chimpanzees, and leopards.
Range	Gambia, Guinea, Guinea Bissau, Ivory Coast, Liberia, Senegal, and Sierra Leone

Description

The adult western black-and-white colobus, *Colobus polykomos,* is between 23 and 26.8 inches long, with its tail adding another 28 to 39 inches to its length. It typically weighs between 18.3 and 21.8 pounds. Its coat features beautiful long hair, black everywhere except for the face and mane, which are bright white. The cheek hairs fluff out wide, and the mane is prominent, giving this monkey an impressive appearance. It is for this coat that thousands of western black-and-white colobuses have been killed by humans.

Behavior

Western black-and-white colobuses live in groups consisting of 5 to 21 members. A typical group has but one fully adult male that dominates social behavior. Males born into the group are usually forced out by the dominant male before they are themselves fully mature. They then try to join another group, and if successful, they may eventually challenge for group leadership. Females seem to remain with their birth group for life, so the migration of males is vital for genetic mixing. The females socialize in part by grooming one another. They also share in the care of their infants; the infants have an extensive white coat that seems to be attractive to adult western black-and-white colobuses; when the coat changes at about 3 months of age, the youngster loses much of its appeal for group members other than its mother.

The western black-and-white colobus is strongly territorial. Territories are 30 to 40 acres in size and seldom overlap. Males will defend these territories against other groups by putting on aggressive shows of loud cries and big leaps. If the show does not deter invaders, the males may become physically violent, striking the outsiders with their hands.

Primarily arboreal, the western black-and-white colobuses move through upper trees while searching for food. They do not swing from branch to branch, but instead walk along branches and leap from tree to tree. When they leap, they stretch their arms and legs forward, so that they look as though they are gliding; they will fall as much as 15 feet to reach the branches of a new tree.

They call to each other as part of their communication. One very loud cry seems to be a declaration of location and a warning to outsiders that a particular territory is occupied. Another cry signals that an individual western black-and-white colobus has lost its group. It elicits cries from its group, helping it find them. Other cries signal various levels of alarm, with one particular cry sending the colobuses fleeing into dense tree cover. When a group flees, the dominant male covers their retreat, offering threatening behavior to possibly deter the feared interloper.

When mating, a male and female will retreat from their group. The sexually mature females will mate with all the sexually mature males. After a pregnancy of 170 days, the female will retreat from the group to give birth. She is accompanied by a male. After the passage of no more than one day, they return to the group with the newborn. The infant is carried against the female's tummy, held in place by one of her hands; after several days, the infant's grip has strengthened enough that it can cling with little risk of falling. After 5 weeks, a youngster moves about vigorously, while playing games. All members of the group seem to tolerate having the youngster jump on them or pull their hair, and the youngster's safety seems to be a communal concern. It will be weaned after 15 months; males mature in 4 years and females mature in 2 years.

Habitat

The western black-and-white colobus lives in moist forests. It needs an abundance of tree leaves and prefers forests with interconnected canopies.

Distribution

The western black-and-white colobus has been found in Gambia, Guinea, Guinea Bissau, the Ivory Coast, Liberia, Senegal, and Sierra Leone. Estimates of its current numbers are hard to find, but naturalists generally agree that the western black-and-white colobus' population is in sharp decline. It may have once numbered in the millions; it now numbers in the thousands or perhaps hundreds.

Threats

In the nineteenth century, the western black-and-white colobus was slaughtered to provide fashionable clothing for world markets. The numbers killed for this purpose are astounding, with almost 200,000 being killed in a year. Fashions changed after World War I, and the coats of other animals replaced that of the western black-and-white colobus in the world of fashion. Nowadays, the western black-and-white colobus is still hunted for its coat to provide tourists with rugs and wall hangings. Presently, the greatest threat to the monkey's survival is the loss of its habitat. It once had an immense forested territory that included most of West Africa and central Africa. Those ancient forests have given way to logging, farms, and human settlements. Less than twenty percent of their forested range still survives, in patches here and there, and those patches are disappearing daily.

Conservation and Recovery

In order to avoid extinction, the trade in the skins of the western black-and-white colobus needs to be curtailed. The monkey also needs legally protected reserves. It does not fear humans and allows them to approach closely, making it an easy target for hunters; thus it needs places where people are not allowed to shoot even though it is an easy, perhaps tempting, mark.

The *IUCN Red List of Threatened Animals* lists the western black-and-white colobus as vulnerable.

Black Colobus

Colobus satanas

Noel Rowe

Status	Endangered
Listed	October 19, 1976
Family	Cercopithecidae (Old World monkey)
Description	Long, soft and black hair except for its face, which has black skin.
Habitat	Forests and meadows.
Food	Seeds and various parts of plants.
Reproduction	Pregnancy lasts for 195 days, producing one young.
Threats	Deforestation and hunting.
Range	Cameroon, Equatorial Guinea, Gabon, and Congo.

Description

The adult black colobus monkey, *Colobus satanas*, is between 25 and 26.4 inches long, not counting its tail, with a long furry tail of 31.5 inches in length, and it weighs 24 pounds. Its hair is shiny black, with crown hairs erect but droopy, with those above its forehead pointing forward. Infants have a brown coat, not white as in other colobuses.

Other common names are satanic black colobus, and satan monkey.

Behavior

Although the black colobus may be found in open areas, a trait that distinguishes it from most other members of its genera (it can eat plants that are found in meadows and that other colobus monkeys would find unpalatable), it lives most of its life high in trees. It rarely swings from branch to branch by its arms, but instead walks on the branches or leaps from one branch to another.

The female of the species indicates her interest in mating by smacking her tongue. During coitus, she lies prone. Her pregnancy probably lasts approximately 195 days. A few days before giving birth, the pregnant female and one of the males from her group leave the group. She will give birth to a single infant; the male probably stands guard for her, but he may also help in holding the infant after it is born. In about a day, the male, female, and born. In about a day, the male, female, and infant will return to the group, where the other females will take particular interest in the infant. Its mother will carry the youngster on her abdomen, at first holding it in place with one of her hands, but later letting it hang on with the firm grip it develops in a few weeks. After its hair turns from brown to black, the youngster is still watched after and cared for by the group, including the males. Its play consists primarily of survival techniques that it will practice endlessly (hiding, looking for predators, running away). Youngsters receive a great deal of indulgence from mature group members, even while the youngsters pull their hair, jump on their backs, and involve them in repetitive games. Gradually, a youngster turns from playing with adults to playing with other youngsters, and at about 15 months of age it is fully weaned. Males reach sexual maturity in 4 years, but females reach sexual maturity in only 2 years.

Males will leave their group, perhaps voluntarily, before they reach sexual maturity. They will lead solitary lives or will join a few other young males to form a small, all-male group. Eventually, they join a larger male-and-female group. It is possible that the group's dominant male will reject a young male's efforts to join his group; a confrontation between the two involves jumping, waving arms, and crying out. A young male that does not get the message risks death at the hands of the dominant male. Females seem to remain with their parental group, rarely moving into another. Thus, male migrations among groups are essential to maintaining the genetic diversity of the species.

Although each group has a dominant male, the groups do not feature the rigid hierarchy found in other such groupings, for instance as with gorillas. For example, sexu-

ally mature new males, not just the dominant male, may be able to mate with females. Sometimes a young male pushes the dominant male out of its station in the group; when this happens, infants are at risk because the new dominant male may kill them. The dynamics of this process are not clear, but if the infants were fathered by the previous dominant male, the new dominant male may be disposing of the infants in order to have the females focus on his progeny. Dominant males lead their groups in the direction of food, although any group member may discover the food, and in times of danger it remains to confront the threat while the rest of the group flees. This makes them good targets for hunters.

There were once as many as 80 members in a black colobus group, but in the second half of the twentieth century groups have been no larger than 15 members. Their territories are ill-defined and vary in size from 170 acres in coastal rain forests to 445 acres in inland mountain forests. Black colobuses are fairly respectful of one another's territories, and they seem to know where their territorial borders are, thus minimizing overlapping territories (for many other colobus monkeys, territories frequently overlap). When groups meet at their territorial borders, they cry out, jump up and down, and shake branches. Such confrontations may become physical (perhaps when food is in short supply or territories have been squeezed by the loss of habitat), but usually end with the groups moving along to feed. The group confrontations may serve to preserve territorial boundaries.

The territories are important in maintaining sufficient growth of food plants to sustain a group. Groups of black colobus move fairly leisurely from one feeding area to another, ranging perhaps 700 yards in one day. They move about and feed both night and day, with only about 22 percent of their time devoted to eating (this may vary with the density of a forest and amount of its food supply), and about 50 percent of their time relaxing. They may remain in place for three days before moving on.

Habitat

The black colobus lives in rain forests, gallery forests, and dry forests, and may sometimes be found in open ground near forest cover. Unlike most colobuses, its diet does not focus on leaves. Instead, it emphasizes seeds, stems, and other plant parts, although young (but never old) leaves still are part of its diet. This diet enables it to adapt to a range that would be inhospitable to those colobuses with limited diets, and it may be one reason why the black colobus still survives after centuries of human predation when others of its genera have not — it has more places it can live and hide in.

Distribution

The past distribution of the black colobus monkey is vague, but it may have ranged in a continuous forest from the coast of West Africa well into Republic of Congo (formerly Zaire). It is now restricted to a broken up forest in Cameroon, mainland Equatorial Guinea, Gabon, and the Congo (although it may now be absent from the Congo). Only Gabon has a large swatch of forest that is essentially unchanged from what it was a century ago, primarily because Gabon's population is not expanding enough to put pressure on the forest's central area.

Threats

Unfortunately, notoriety is not always good for wild animals. In the nineteenth century, people wanted coats made from colobus skins, especially those of the black colobus, and the animal was slaughtered relentlessly for decades, nearly eradicating it by the 1920s. Even today, the skins are valued for rugs and wall hangings, and the black colobus monkey continues to be hunted for the fur trade. People also eat the monkey, and in regions where monkey meat is popular, the black colobus monkey has been annihilated. Even so, it faces an even worse threat, the destruction of its habitat by logging and for agricultural development. The human populations of its ancient range have boomed, so the expanding population has cut down the forests and pressed the black colobus monkey into an ever constricting range that cannot support the species in large numbers.

Conservation and Recovery

One of the problems conservationists have in formulating a plan to save the black colobus from extinction are the sketchy figures on its population's size. Some probably still live in Cameroon's Douala-Edea Reserve, where it was doing well in 1972, but which has suffered a dramatic loss of suitable habitat since then. It is possible, but unlikely that some still live in Cameroon's Campo Reserve. Some may survive in the mountains of Equatorial Guinea — they may even be abundant; they need to be counted. Equatorial Guinea's forests have also been shrinking rapidly, thereby shrinking the monkey's habitat. In Gabon, the black colobus's range has diminished considerably since 1970. Even so, its best breeding population is probably in the Lopé Reserve, where several groups may still live. The Forêt des Abeilles in central Gabon may still have some groups of the monkey, as well. Because Gabon has much of its primeval forest still intact, and because its southern peoples have a taboo against eating the meat of primates, the black colobus has its best chance for survival in the still remote inner reaches of its central forest. Reports of the monkey in the Congo are disparate, and the monkey may (but not certainly) be extinct there.

The black colobus is poorly protected by law in the nations where it lives. If it is to survive for even another decade, the deforestation of its habitat must be curtailed. Naturalists disagree over whether the colobus can survive in secondary forests, and until the matter is settled, primary forests need to be preserved as its habitat. There is some hope for this because it shares a range with a number of other endangered species such as the western lowland gorilla. Thus the preservation of the black colobus's range is also the preservation of the ranges of many other valuable animals — in economic terms, this mean that its range is a gold mine of tourist revenue, international research funding, and potential pharmaceuticals just waiting to be properly conserved and developed. For the countries involved, the preservation of the monkey's habitat could result in decades of steady foreign currency income.

Local education programs that teach people about the long-range value of their wildlife would benefit the black colobus monkey. Moving it to CITES, Appendix I: Trade Prohibited would also discourage the trade in the monkey's skins. At present, the black colobus is listed in Class B of the African Convention, which means permission from a relevant governmental authority should be obtained for hunting the animal. This restriction, in the case of the black colobus, seems to have been ineffective.

Bouvier's Red Colobus

Procolobus badius bouvieri

Western Red Colobus *(Procolobos badius)*   Noel Rowe

Status	Endangered
Listed	*IUCN Red List of Threatened Animals.*
Family	Cercopithecidae (Old World monkey)
Description	White cheek and chin hair; white or orange forehead; the rest of its head, and its neck, paws, back, tail tip are nearly black red.
Habitat	Dense and gallery forests.
Food	Tree leaves; possibly fruit, buds, flowers, and insects.
Reproduction	Little is known of its reproductive processes. If it is like some of its close relatives, then pregnancy lasts over 6 months and results in the birth of one infant.
Threats	Loss of habitat to logging; hunting.
Range	Congo

Description

The body length, not counting the tail, of adult Bouvier's red colobuses, *Procolobus badius bouvier*, is between 17.5 and 26.5 inches. Their tails add another 22.5 to 31.5 inches. They weigh between 11 and 25 pounds. They feature an intricately patterned coat that is beautiful to the human eye and may serve the more practical purpose of making it hard to fix one's gaze on an individual animal as it moves among the branches of its home forests. Its dark face is outlined by white cheek and chin hair, as well as white or orange hair over its forehead. Its head, neck, back, paws, tail tip have nearly black red hair, and the area of its tail's base is dark brown to red with black dots above, and pale orange underneath. Its sides have reddened orange hair with gray or black dots, and its chest and abdomen may have white or pale orange hair. Although its thighs have yellow tinted brown-to-black hair, the rest of its legs, as well as its arms, have reddened pale orange hair. The hair is long and soft.

Behavior

Very little is known of the Bouvier's red colobus' behavior, because it is very rare and hard to find and therefore little studied. They live in groups of up to 80 members, and groups have territories as large as 320 acres. Its other habits are likely to resemble those of Preuss's Red Colobus (*Procolobus preussi*); see separate entry.

Habitat

Bouvier's red colobus lives in dense forests and gallery forests. It requires thick tree foliage and a large supply of leaves.

Distribution

The Bouvier's red colobus once had a large region of contiguous forestlands in which to live. It now probably only exists in the Lefini Reserve in the Congo, but some suggest that a few may live near the confluence of the Zaire River and the Oubangui River (this could result from misidentification).

Threats

In the nineteenth century, the Bouvier's red colobus was slaughtered by the thousands to provide fashionable coats, rugs, and wall hangings for world markets. This, combined with local peoples hunting them for food, nearly wiped them out. They now exist in small numbers in Congo. Their habitat has nearly disappeared, and what is left of it is being burned to make way for agriculture.

Poachers continue to hunt the Bouvier's red colobus for meat.

Conservation and Recovery

The Lefini Reserve in the Congo may be the last refuge of the Bouvier's red colobus. Nearly all of the reserve is grassland created by burning of forestland; grasslands are unsuitable habitat for the monkey. Although the Congo has laws intended to protect the wildlife in the Lefini Reserve, the laws are not well enforced. The forest continues to be felled, and hunters have killed much (probably most) of the wildlife in the reserve. The Congo has very difficult social and economic problems, some of which have been caused by the looting of its natural resources, and it may not have enough funds to pay for the kind of care and protection the Bouvier's red colobus needs.

The Bouvier's red colobus monkey is listed in Class B of the African Convention. It is also listed in CITES, Appendix II: Trade Restricted, and can only be traded with government approval. The *IUCN Red List of Threatened Animals* lists it as endangered. It is very near extinction.

Elliot's Red Colobus

Procolobus badius [=rufomitratus] ellioti

Tana River Red Colobus (*Procolobus rufomitratus*)   Lysa Leland

Status	Insufficiently Known.
Listed	*IUCN Red List*
Family	Cercopithecidae
Description	Gray to dark-gray, with the head covered with red hair and the shoulders, back, and outer arms covered with reddish-brown hair.
Habitat	Rain forests, gallery forests, mountain forests, and swamp forests.
Food	Leaves and perhaps other plant parts.
Reproduction	Gestation is over 6 months, resulting in the birth of one infant.
Threats	Loss of habitat to logging and fires; hunting for food by humans.
Range	Uganda and Republic of Congo (formerly Zaire).

Description

Elliot's red colobus probably resembles its close relative, the Tana River red colobus (*Procolobus rufomitratus*); please see separate entry. Thus, the adult Elliot's red colobus probably measures between 18 and 26 inches in length, not counting the tail, with its tail probably adding another 20 to 30 inches. It would weigh between 11 and 25 pounds.

Its hair is long, soft, and colorful. Its coloration is uncertain, but is similar to that of the Tana River red colobus. It may have a base color of dark hair, from gray to dark-gray, with the head covered with red hair and the shoulders, back, and outer arms covered with reddish-brown hair.

Behavior

Very little is known about the behavior of this rare animal. It lives in groups of unknown size, but seemingly small, perhaps averaging 15 members. A group has a mixture of males and females, young and old, with perhaps one male dominant. As with other red colobuses, the Elliot's red colobus is probably territorial by group.

Females have genital swelling when ovulating. They are likely to be the aggressors when choosing a mate. Once a male responds they may move a little away from their group and mate, with the female in a prone position. Pregnancy probably lasts over 6 months and results in a single birth. Care of the youngster is shared among the other females of the group. It is likely that behavior within a group resembles that of the Elliot's red colobus' close relative, the Tana River red colobus (please see separate entry).

Habitat

This monkey makes its home in rain forests, gallery forests, mountain forests, and swamp forests. It seems able to endure very cold and very hot climates. Leaves make up a significant portion of its diet, but it is not known what else they may eat.

Distribution

The Elliot's red colobus once ranged in Uganda and The Republic of Congo (formerly Zaire), but the denuding of its forest habitat has probably made it extinct in Uganda. At present, it lives east of the Zaire River in Republic of Congo, with its northern range bounded by the Aruwimi-Ituri River and its southern range bounded by the Elila River. It is not known how far east its range extends, but it probably extends near to the eastern edge of its forest.

Threats

The Elliot's red colobus lives in a very troubled part of the world, which may account for why little has been discovered about its numbers in the wild. Authorities seem to agree that the monkey is now rare, and with the destruction of its habitat and hunting by humans, its population is quickly shrinking. It stands at risk of extinction at almost anytime, depending on whether the logging of its lands continues and how urgently humans need it for food.

Conservation and Recovery

Some Elliot's red colobuses live in Republic of Congo's Kahuzi-Biega National Park and Maiki National Park. Since its numbers are unknown, whether or not either park has a breeding population is uncertain. If Zaire succeeds in protecting the parks from logging, fires, and human predation, the monkey has a chance for survival.

The Elliot's red colobus is listed in Class B of the African Convention of 1969, which means it may only be killed, captured, or traded by permission of an appropriate government agency. It is also listed in CITES, Appendix II: Trade Restricted, which means that international trade in the monkey or its parts is regulated and monitored by international conservation agencies such as the IUCN.

Oustalet's Red Colobus

Procolobus badius [=rufomitratus] [=pennantii] oustaleti

Tana River Red Colobus (*Procolobus rufomitratus*)   Lysa Leland

Status	Insufficiently Known.
Listed	*IUCN Red List*
Family	Cercopithecidae (Old World monkey)
Description	Gray to dark-gray, with the head covered with red hair and the shoulders, back, and outer arms covered with reddish-brown hair.
Habitat	Rain forests, gallery, mountain, and swamp forests.
Food	Leaves and perhaps other plant parts.
Reproduction	One infant after gestation of 180 to 200 days.
Threats	Loss of habitat to logging and agriculture; hunting for food and skins by humans.
Range	Central African Republic, Sudan, and Republic of Congo (Zaire).

Description

The Oustalet's red colobus, *Procolobus badius oustaleti*, has soft, long hair and probably looks like its better known close relative the Tana River red colobus, *Procolobus rufomitratus*. Thus, it may have a base color of dark hair, from gray to dark-gray, with the head covered with red hair and the shoulders, back, and outer arms covered with reddish-brown hair. This beautiful coat was once very fashionable, making Oustalet's red colobus the target of extensive hunting for its skin. Although the market for the skins is not what it once was before the 1920s (with thousands of the monkey killed for their coats annually), the skins are still traded, primarily to tourists for use as rugs or wall hangings. However, the monkey is now so rare that such trade is small.

The adult Oustalet's red colobus' head-and-body length is probably between 18 and 26 inches; its tail likely adds another 20 to 30 inches. It weighs between 11 and 25 pounds. Its face is black and framed by gray whiskers on the cheeks and chin. It is likely to be sexually dimorphic, with males larger than females, having proportionally bigger heads than females, and having larger fangs than females.

Behavior

The behavior of this scarce animal is largely unrecorded. It lives in groups of unknown size, but seemingly small, perhaps averaging 15 members, although much larger groups may have existed before their range was reduced by deforestation. A group has a mixture of males and females, young and old, with perhaps one male dominant. As with other red colobuses, the Oustaleti's red colobus is probably territorial by group. Confrontations between groups seem to consist mostly of threatening performances such as jumping and flashing fangs; this behavior may help groups establish their boundaries with one another.

Females have genital swelling when ovulating. Whether they mate with several males during ovulation or only one is not as yet known. Pregnancy probably lasts between 180 and 200 days, resulting in the birth of one infant. Care of the youngster is shared first among the other females of the group and later, as the youngster becomes more independent, by the group's males, as well. It is likely that behavior within a group resembles that of the Oustalet's red colobus' close relative, the Tana River red colobus (please see separate entry).

Habitat

This colobus requires a densely foliaged forest with room for several groups to cohabitate — at least a few hundred acres. Leaves seem to be the most important part of its diet, which may also include buds, fruits, and flowers. Not enough is known about this monkey to pin down the specifics of its habitat. Clearly, if humans are to help the Oustalet's red colobus survive, they need to discover what it requires in its habitat.

Distribution

The ancient range of the Oustalet's red colobus included most of Republic of Congo (formerly Zaire), much of the Central African Republic, and possibly southern Sudan, although this last region is known by only one skin taken from an animal killed there. It presently lives in northern Republic of Congo, north of the Arumimi-Ituri River.

Threats

The Oustalet's red colobus is scarce. Its range is being extensively clear cut by logging, leaving it little room for foraging. Humans still hunt it, and its skin is reportedly still for sale locally. With its numbers unknown, it is hard to judge how close to extinction it is, which is why the Red List of Threatened Animals notes its status as "unknown." Even so, we know that its relatives need extensive territory in which to survive, and the Oustalet's red colobus' forest is shrinking so fast that it may be gone in a year or two. Since the Oustalet's red colobus is not bred in captivity, the loss of its forest would mean its extinction.

Conservation and Recovery

The Oustalet's red colobus needs a reserve

in which they have dense forestlands and are safe from humans hunting them. Thus the Oustalet's red colobus is in urgent need of study before its forest disappears, because it is unlikely it can be saved without conservationists knowing its behavior and biology.

The Oustalet's red colobus is listed in Class B of the 1969 African Convention, and may be killed, captured, or traded only by permission of an appropriate government agency. It is also listed in CITES, Appendix II: Trade Restricted, and monitored by international conservation agencies such as the IUCN (The World Conservation Union).

Temminck's Red Colobus

Procolobus badius temminckii

Tana River Colobus *(Procolobos rufomitratus)*   Lysa Leland

Status	Rare
Listed	*IUCN Red List*
Family	Cercopithecidae (Old World monkey)
Description	Red-brown hair on head, back, and outer arms; gray or gray-brown elsewhere.
Habitat	Rain forests, mountain forests, and mangrove swamps.
Food	Immature leaves, leaf buds, flowers, and fruits.
Reproduction	Gestation lasts between 6 and 6.5 months and results in the birth of one infant. Breeding takes place year round.
Threats	Loss of habitat; hunting.
Range	Gambia, Guinea, Guinea-Bissau, and Senegal.

Description

The adult Temminck's red colobus, *Procolobus badius temminckii*, is between 18 and 27 inches long, not including the tail. Its tail adds another 16 to 36 inches to its length. It is sexually dimorphic, with males much larger than females. Males weigh between 20 and 27 pounds; females weigh between 15.5 and 20 pounds. The Temminck's red colobus is covered by long hair. Its head, back, and arms are covered with reddish-brown hair. The face is dark and fringed with gray hair. The rest of the body is covered by grayish brown hair.

Typical of colobus monkeys in general, Temminck's red colobus has tiny thumbs on each hand. The other four digits are long fingers that have a powerful grip.

Behavior

During mating, the male and female

retreat away from their group, and the female lies prone. It is unclear whether the female mates with several males, similar to leaf monkeys, or simply mates with one male of her choosing.

Temminck's red colobuses live in loose groups of about 25 members, including males and females, young to old. They are territorial, with each group having a territory of 22 to 50 acres. Females seem to be able to move from one group to another without much trouble (the dynamics of this need further study). On the other hand, males have a difficult time joining a group. Before they reach sexual maturity, males will either voluntarily leave their parental group or will be driven out by the group's dominant male. These young males will remain solitary for a time and then sometimes join with a few other males for traveling and feeding. Eventually, they try to enter a group of males and females. The males in the group often take exception to the attempt of an outside male to join their ranks and they often become violent, striking the newcomer to drive it away, and the newcomer is sometimes killed by the resident males.

Temminck's red colobuses seem to be able to accept significant variations in its diet, although leaves are always important. They require leaves for food, but they typically mix their diets with fruits, buds, and flowers as they are available. Although they tend to be arboreal, they spend much of their time on the ground foraging for food or traveling.

When not in cover, they are vulnerable to predation by hawks, but they sometimes venture into open areas, either for traveling or for food.

Habitat

The Temminck's red colobus lives primarily in forests, but also may be found in grasslands. It may be found in wet forests, even swamps, and in dry forests with seasonal rainfall, and seem at home in densely packed woods such as tropical forests and more spacious woods with little ground cover such as mountain forests.

Distribution

The Temminck's red colobus once ranged in a vast tropical forest that extended from the West African coast deep into central Africa — exactly how far east the population extended is not known. It now exists in scattered patches of forest in Gambia, Guinea, Guinea-Bissau, and Senegal, although the status of the population in Guinea is uncertain.

Threats

The primary threat to the Temminck's red colobus is loss of habitat to logging and agriculture. Logging accentuates the Temminck's red colobus' troubles because the leaves the animal most favors are found on the trees the timber industry most favors. Hunting is also a problem. As with other red colobus monkeys, the Temminck's red colobus' coat has been popular for making clothing, and hunting for its coat has driven the animal to extinction through most of its ancient range. People hunting it for food seems to be less of problem for this red colobus than for others of its genus.

Conservation and Recovery

There are good reasons to hope for the Temminck's red colobus' recovery and survival. Gambia's Abuko National Park has a good breeding population, and Gambia by law completely forbids the hunting, capturing, or exporting of the Temminck's red colobus. Enforcement of this 1977 law could very well save Gambia's population of the animal. Senegal's Basse Casamanse National Park and Saloum Delta National Park have what seem to be healthy populations of the Temminck's red colobus, with perhaps 600 of the monkey in the latter park. The Water and Forest Service of Senegal may issue permits for trapping or exporting the animal, but the Senegalese government has been careful to care for the monkey.

The Temminck's red colobus is listed in Class B of the African Convention of 1969 and in CITES, Appendix II: Trade Restricted. The *IUCN Red List of Threatened Animals* lists it as rare.

Miss Waldron's Bay Colobus

Procolobus badius waldroni

Western Red Colobus *(Procolobos Badius)*   Noel Rowe

Status	Endangered
Listed	*IUCN Red List*
Family	Cercopithecidae (Old World monkey).
Description	Reddish brown (bay) on its head, arms, abdomen, and legs and is otherwise gray to black, including the tail.
Habitat	Dense, high forests.
Food	Leaves.
Reproduction	Gestation lasts 180 to 195 days, resulting in the birth of one infant.
Threats	Loss of habitat; hunting by humans.
Range	Ghana and Ivory Coast.

Description

The adult Miss Waldron's Bay colobus, *Procolobus badius waldroni*, is between 18 and 27 inches long, head-to-tail, with its tail adding another 16 to 36 inches. It is sexually dimorphic, with males much larger than females. Males weigh between 20 and 27 pounds; females weigh between 15 and 20 pounds (these figures for weight are derived from those typical of Miss Waldron's Bay colobus' genus; there are few examples of the monkey to draw on). Miss Waldron's Bay colobus is covered by long hair, with its crown, outer arms and legs, and abdomen covered by reddish-brown hair and the rest of the body save for the face covered by gray to black hair. The face is dark and fringed with light gray hair.

Behavior

Little is known of the behavior of Miss

Waldron's Bay colobus. Like other colobus monkeys, the genital area of the female swells during ovulation. It is likely that the female chooses her mate or mates, and it is likely that she assumes a prone posture for coitus as do other colobus monkeys.

Miss Waldron's Bay colobus monkeys may live in groups that include males and females, young and old. Females are probably able to move from one group to another without much trouble, the way the females of their close cousins, the Temminck's red colobus, do. Whether males trying to join a new group face the same violence the Temminck's red colobus is not known. It is probable that before they reach sexual maturity, young males will leave their parental group. Such males will remain solitary for a time and then sometimes form small groups with a few other males. Eventually, they try to enter an established group of males and females.

The diet of Miss Waldron's Bay colobus includes some mixture of leaves and fruits, including seeds.

Miss Waldron's Bay colobus lives high in the forest canopy and sometimes leaps through the air from one tree to another, thrusting out its hands at a branch after falling as much as 15 feet.

Habitat

Miss Waldron's Bay colobus is dependent on a habitat of dense, high forest with a tall canopy. Its diet requires leaves, which unfortunately come from the very trees the timber industry values most.

Distribution

Evidence of Miss Waldron's Bay colobus range has been found only in Ghana and Ivory Coast. It may still survive in southeastern Ivory Coast and does still survive in western Ghana.

Threats

Miss Waldron's Bay colobus is under relentless pressure from humans. Its once large forest has been almost completely destroyed by logging, agriculture, and human settlements. Its long-haired coat is prized, and its meat has been a staple of the diet of the indigenous peoples of its region. Ceaseless hunting of the monkey for its meat has eliminated its population through nearly all of its remaining habitat.

Conservation and Recovery

Ghana has taken steps to preserve Miss Waldron's Bay colobus. It has established the Bia National Park, the Nini-Souhien National Park, and the Ankasa Resource Reserve, each of which once harbored Miss Waldron's Bay colobus. The monkey is likely gone from the Ankasa Resource Reserve, and no traces have been found in the Nini-Souhien National Park. Even so, the Nini-Souhien National Park preserves some of Miss Waldron's Bay colobus' traditional high forest habitat. Poaching and loss of genetic diversity are major threats to its welfare. By law, Ghana prohibits the hunting, trapping, and exporting of its Miss Waldron's Bay colobuses. With enforcement of the laws and with study of the animal's habits and biology so that it may be provided with the environment it needs, Miss Waldron's Bay colobus may survive its presently dire condition.

In 1996, Primate Conservation, Inc. funded two surveys of Miss Waldron's Bay colobus, which are being conducted in the forests on the eastern portion of Ivory Coast adjoining Ghana, and in the forests of western Ghana. Initial survey reports in September 1997 indicate no evidence of Miss Waldron's Bay colobus in the eastern part of Ivory Coast.

Miss Waldron's Bay colobus is listed in Class B of the African Convention of 1969, and in CITES, Appendix II: Trade Restricted. The *IUCN Red List of Threatened Animals* lists it as endangered.

Uhehe [=Pennant's] Red Colobus

Procolobus pennantii gordonorum

Tana River Red Colobus (*Procolobus rufomitratus*)   Lysa Leland

Status	Endangered
Listed	*IUCN Red List*
Family	Cercopithecidae (Old World Monkey)
Description	A long-haired monkey with gray-to-black hair on its head, back, and the outsides of its limbs, with pale orange to orangish red hair elsewhere.
Habitat	Forests at elevations between 1,800 and 2,000 feet above sea level.
Food	Leaves and fruit.
Reproduction	Sexual unions are instigated by females.
Threats	Loss of habitat to logging, agriculture, and wildfires; hunting for food.
Range	Tanzania

Description

The adult uhehe red colobus monkey, *Procolobus pennantii gordonorum*, is similar in dimensions to other red colobus monkeys: It is between 18.5 and 22.5 inches long, not including the tail. Its tail adds another 20.5 to 37.5 inches to its length. It typically weighs between 12 and 22 pounds. Male skulls have a sagittal crest that is not present in females. Its back, head, and outer limbs are covered by gray-to-black hair, with the rest of its body except for the pubic region covered by pale to deep orangish red hair. The pubic region is covered by white hair. The hair on the head tends to fluff out, while the hair on the body tends to lay back, toward the tail. Over most of the body — but not the chin — the hair is long, even luxuriant.

Like other red colobus monkeys, the uhehe has only vestigial thumbs. The other four digits are long fingers that have a powerful grip. This grip and the uhehe's long arms enable it to swing easily from branch to branch.

Other common names include Pennant's red colobus, Gordon's red colobus, and Iringa red colobus.

Behavior

Males and females reach sexual maturity between 4 and 5 years of age. Females are the sexually aggressive gender among the uhehe. When interested in mating with a particular male, she will smack her tongue. A receptive male will gaze at her eyes. The female lies prone during mating. Mating may take place at any time of the year. A newborn infant typically weighs almost 1 pound; it is cared for by all the mature females of its group. Typically, females in a group will suckle the infants of others as well as their own and will keep watch on the infants of others.

Red colobus monkeys are typically territorial, but the uhehe seems more relaxed about protecting its territory than others of its genus. Territories of different groups of uhehe's may overlap considerably. On those rare occasions when one group of uhehe's takes exception to the presence of another, the older males confront those of the rival group and drive them off; the confrontation seems to involve displays of threatening postures.

A group of uhehes comprises about 25 members, and the places where they survive are scattered and small. The groups are so isolated from one another that it is nearly impossible for them to interbreed. Typically, a newly sexually mature male leaves his group, becoming solitary. The dynamics of its entering a new group need further study, but it does eventually join a new group and become eligible for the attentions of the group's sexually mature females. The isolation of groups means that they are not exchanging males, and they are not maintaining a birthrate that would sustain them. Therefore, they are disappearing — even before the negative effects of inbreeding can take hold.

A group of uhehes includes a mixture of males and females. Their principal social interactions are breeding, caring for young, and confronting rival groups. Most of their days involve little social interaction, especially during feeding periods. They devote most of their waking hours to concentrating on feeding because their diet consists primarily of leaves of low nutritional value, requiring them to eat a great deal in order to survive. Feeding is a sedentary activity, with groups sitting for hours in one place while dining. There is little violence within a group, with members being careful not to bump into each other; indeed, they are respectful of a space around each monkey, avoiding entering it even while searching for a branch on which to sit and feed.

Uhehes are arboreal animals who can move swiftly among tree branches and do not break stride or hesitate before leaping from one tree to another. When disturbed, a group of the monkeys can disappear quickly — although noisily — into their forest habitat. Always while moving, they look very serious, as if intently concentrating.

Habitat

Uhehes live in mountain forests, at elevations between 1,800 and 2,000 feet. These forests tend to be wet but cool. The monkey's long hair may serve to protect them from the chill.

Distribution

The uhehe is native to the Uzungwa Mountains in Tanzania. It once ranged all through these mountains at high elevations, and it likely (but this is not known for a certainty) numbered in the many thousands in the middle of the twentieth century. It now exists in patches in the mountains, especially at the highest elevations.

Threats

The uhehes are so little known, and so rare, that they are missing from reference books on monkeys and endangered species. In the mid-1980s, perhaps 2500 uhehes existed. Their present number is unknown, but it has almost certainly declined. Their traditional range is split by the Tanzania-Zambia Railway, isolating in north and south pockets. The railway has brought with it people. They have (probably accidentally) set wildfires that have grievously reduced the size of the forest habitat the uhehe needs in order to survive. Further, logging has outright eliminated pockets of forest, and other small populations of uhehes have been wiped out by hunters. Its outlook for survival is very bleak.

Conservation and Recovery

The Selous Game Reserve still retains a small population of uhehes, and the age distribution within groups in the reserve may mean that there is a healthy breeding population of the monkeys. The Mwanihana Forest Reserve is also a possible haven for the uhehes, but it is giving way to agriculture, notably rubber plantations.

Tanzania has made efforts to protect the uhehe by requiring by law that people have certificates in order to even own a uhehe skin or any uhehe body parts, and a permit is required for exporting the uhehe. Enforcement of the laws protecting the uhehe may help it survive, but much more needs to be known of its numbers, distributions, and needs such as kinds and amounts of food, as well as minimum numbers of the animal required for a self-sustaining population. The territory required by a single group of uhehes is unclear, but seems similar to that of other red colobus monkeys, about 70 acres. This means that loss of habitat must shrink the population of uhehes since each group has a minimum range it must have in order to survive. Stopping the burning (apparently the most significant cause of lost forest lands in the uhehe's range), logging, and agriculturalization of its habitat is essential to the uhehe's survival. There is no captive breeding program for the uhehe.

The uhehe is listed in Class A of the African Convention and in CITES, Appendix II: Trade Restricted. This nearly extinct animal needs to be moved to CITES, Appendix I: Trade Prohibited. The *IUCN Red List of Threatened Animals* lists it as endangered.

Zanzibar Red Colobus

Procolobus kirkii

Lysa Leland

Status	Endangered
Listed	June 2, 1970
Family	Cercopithecidae (Old World monkey)
Description	Long-haired monkey with a shaggy white crest on its head and white shaggy hair on its shoulders and chest, with the rest of the coat black to dark orange-brown.
Habitat	Mangrove swamps, marshes, and other wet areas.
Food	Leaves, buds, and fruit.
Reproduction	Gestation lass 180 to 195 dayst, resulting in a single infant.
Threats	Loss of habitat to logging and agriculture; hunting for food and as a pest.
Range	Zanzibar Island, Tanzania.

Description

Taxonomy is disputed for the Zanzibar red colobus, *Procolobus pennantii kirkii*. There may be 9 subspecies of *Procolobus pennantii*, including *P. p. gordonorum*, *P. p. kirkii*, *P. p. tephrosceles*, and *P. p. tholloni*. However, some taxonomists recognize *P. p. kirkii* and *P. p. tholloni* as full species.

The adult Zanzibar red colobus is between 18.5 and 22.5 inches long, not including the tail. Its tail adds another 20.5 to 37.5 inches to its length. It typically weighs between 12 and 22 pounds. Its coat is spectacular, with a base color of dark hair, from black to brown-orange, and the top and cheeks of the head, the shoulders and upper chest, and the genital area covered with white hair. The hair is long and often appears fanned out, giving the Zanzibar red colobus monkey an ethereal appearance.

Of particular interest are its hands, which have only vestigial thumbs, typical of colobus monkeys in general. The other four digits are long fingers that have a powerful grip, enabling the monkey to swing easily from branch to branch.

Another common names is Kirk's red colobus monkey.

Behavior

Females are the sexually aggressive gender. A female's efforts to attract the attention of a male features tongue-smacking. A receptive male will respond with smacking noises of his own. Eye contact seems essential to the signaling of desire. If a male fails to respond, the female trying to get his attention may become violent, even hitting him. The female lies prone during mating, which may occur at any time of the year. A newborn infant typically weighs almost 1 pound and has a strong hand grip with which it clings to its mother while traveling. Soon after birth, the infant is passed to other females. Typically, females in a group will suckle the infants of others as well as their own and will keep watch on the infants of others.

Colobus monkeys are typically territorial, and the Zanzibar red colobus seems to follow this tendency of its genus, but this has been hard to observe. The reason for this is that a typical group of Zanzibar red colobus comprises about 35 members, and the places where they survive are scattered and small, rarely leaving enough habitat to support several groups and therefore providing little opportunity for them to interact. A typical home range for a group is about 70 acres. If they are typical of red colobus monkeys, they would show little tolerance for other Zanzibar red colobus monkeys. Typically, the older males would confront the interlopers and chase them off. Also if they are typical, such confrontations would be frequent.

The groups include a mixture of males and females with very little social interaction, especially during feeding periods. Their diet consists primarily of leaves of low nutritional value, and they spend most of their time concentrating on eating enough food to survive. Feeding is a sedentary activity, with groups sitting for hours in one place while dining. There is little violence within a group, with members being careful not to bump into each other; indeed, they are respectful of a space around each monkey, avoiding entering it even while searching for a branch on which to sit and feed.

Although their niche is in watery areas, the Zanzibar red colobus monkeys are primarily arboreal, and live up in the trees above the water. They move swiftly among tree branches and do not break stride or hesitate before leaping from one tree to another. When disturbed, a group of the monkeys can disappear quickly — although noisily — into their forest habitat.

Habitat

Zanzibar red colobus monkeys live in swamp-forests on Zanzibar Island in Tanzania, and on Pemba Island, 46 miles to the north, where some have been relocated. They prefer areas with ground water and require a densely leafed forest canopy in which to feed and move.

Distribution

The Zanzibar red colobus is native to Zanzibar Island, located in the Indian ocean, and where Zanzibar City, the capital of Tanzania, is located. It may now be found on a few nearby islands and on Pemba Island, where some of the monkeys have been relocated, 46 miles north of Zanzibar Island.

Threats

Loss of habitat is the principal threat to

the survival of the Zanzibar red colobus. Its forest range is being logged, felled for charcoal production, cleared for agriculture, and burned in order to drive out pigs and other animals for hunters. The Zanzibar red colobus is hunted for its meat and for sport, and it is sometimes killed because farmers think it raids their crops.

Conservation and Recovery

In the mid-1970s, perhaps 150 Zanzibar red colobus monkeys existed. Today, their population has recovered greatly, comprising more than 1,500 monkeys, but the numbers may presently be once again in decline. Tanzania has set aside a 20 square mile wildlife refuge, Jozani Forest, on Zanzibar Island in 1960, which has helped the monkeys, although poaching is still a problem. It needs more thorough protection and careful management by the Tanzanian government. The Zanzibar red colobus monkey is listed in Class A of the African Convention and in CITES, Appendix I. The *IUCN Red List of Threatened Animals* lists it as endangered.

These international sanctions may help to preserve the animal, but its most urgent concern is its loss of habitat, rather than being hunted. Although logging has been moderate by the region's standards, the loss of trees means less food and fewer places to hide and rest. It also means that a species that needs many acres of space for its population will necessarily decline in number as that space is lost.

Uganda Red Colobus

Procolobus pennantii tephrosceles

Noel Rowe

Status	Vulnerable
Listed	*IUCN Red List*
Family	Cercopithecidae (Old World monkey)
Description	Head, sides, and limbs are ruddy brown, the back and tail are dark, the undersides are light gray or brown; the cheeks and chin have light gray whiskers.
Habitat	Rain forests, gallery forests, and mountain forests.
Food	Leaves.
Reproduction	One infant after gestation longer than 180 days.
Threats	Loss of habitat.
Range	Tanzania and Uganda

Description

The significant difference in sizes of Uganda red colobuses, *Procolobus pennantii tephrosceles*, probably results from sexual dimorphism, although naturalists suspect that what is called the "Uganda red colobus" may actually be two or three separate species that simply have not been studied enough for observers to distinguish among them. Differences in coat patterns may be explained by the natural variation among members of a single species; they also may be accounted for

if the Uganda red colobus is not one species but two or three. In general, its head, sides, and limbs are ruddy brown, the back and tail are dark, the undersides are light gray or brown, and the cheeks and chin have light gray whiskers. The head-and-body length, not counting the tail, is between 18 and 30 inches; the tail adds 20 to 38 inches and is more likely to be on the long side than the short. Males are bigger than females and weigh up to 28 pounds, with females weighing up to 20 pounds.

Behavior

The Uganda red colobus lives in groups averaging 50 members in Uganda's Kibale Forest Reserve, averaging 25 elsewhere, probably because of restricted habitat. A group has a mixture of males and females, young and old. The females do most of the migrating from group to group; these changes in group affiliations seem to be done easily and suggest that group societies are loosely defined.

Uganda red colobuses spend 45 percent of their time feeding and 30 percent of their time resting. They are territorial, with territories being about 85 acres in size. Groups seem respectful of one another's territories.

It is probable that females initiate mating by smacking their tongues at a male. They have genital swelling when ovulating. A female lies prone during coitus. Gestation lasts over 180 days and results in a single birth. Care of the youngster is shared among the other females of the group.

Habitat

The Uganda red colobus eats a wide variety of tree leaves and must have an abundance of trees in its range in order to survive. It will live in rain, gallery, or mountain forests, and spends most of its life in trees.

Distribution

The Uganda red colobus probably ranged through a large range of contiguous forests that included rain, gallery, and mountain forest and that extended through Uganda, Tanzania, Burundi, and Rwanda. It is unlikely that it survives in Burundi or Rwanda, and it exists in patches in Tanzania. The population in Uganda is also patchy, with the most significant population restricted to central Kibale Forest Reserve, where about 1,000 individuals are thought to occur.

Threats

The Uganda red colobus is in dire straits primarily because of the loss of nearly all of its habitat. Logging of the monkey's remaining habitat continues, even on government reserves in Uganda, where timber poaching is a significant problem. Further, trees not well suited to the timber market are poisoned, cutting down the diversity of leaves on which the monkey feeds and preventing the formation of a high canopy in which it may seek shelter. Additionally, a significant portion of Uganda's Kibale Forest Reserve has been cleared for agriculture. Uganda has undergone much social and political turmoil since gaining its independence, and it has been hard for it to protect its natural resources. In spite of the present era's relative calm, Uganda could use outside funding and research to help protect what natural resources that have not yet been looted; some Uganda red colobuses likely survive in Kibale Forest Reserve and patches of surviving forest that have not been logged or have only been slightly logged.

Conservation and Recovery

Tanzania has a few hundred Uganda red monkeys. Much of its forest reserve acreage is unsuitable habitat for the Uganda red colobus. During colonialism, the nation's reserves were planted with tree species that are alien to the monkey's diet. Its reserves have been violated by illegal agriculture development and fires set to create charcoal. Hunting of the Uganda red colobus in Tanzania for food and skins is a problem, but is rare. At present, the few hundred Uganda red colobuses in Tanzania seem secure in well-protected reserves.

Although the Uganda red colobus has been observed in Burundi and Rwanda in the past, it is probable (but not certain) that it has been pressed into extinction in those countries. To avoid being pressed into extinction in its remaining havens, the national parks and wildlife reserves of Uganda and Tanzania need to be protected. Much of the hope for the monkey's survival depends on the cooperation of local peoples and thus education programs such as those undertaken in Cameroon and Kenya would be of great benefit. At present, Tanzania seems to be coping with the aftermath left by colonial administrations and there is good reason to hope its population of the Uganda red colobus will survive, provided that it has not been so reduced in size that it has lost its genetic diversity. Too much inbreeding would make the monkeys susceptible to epidemic disease. In Uganda, people are coping with the reconstruction of their nation after years of civil war and governments of appalling cruelty. Further, the nation is having to construct a new economy out of chaos; the poaching of timber and wildlife brings income to impoverished people. Thus, while the Kibale Forest Reserve is home to the largest Uganda red colobus population, that population is shrinking because people are destroying its forests in order to survive themselves. Good protection of the Kibale Forest Reserve would probably ensure the Uganda red colobuses' survival into the indefinite future.

Both Tanzania and Uganda have given the Uganda red colobus full legal protection, and by law the monkey may not be killed or captured in either country. Further, it is illegal to exploit any of the wildlife in the Kibale Forest Reserve. Uganda is trying to protect the reserve with the resources it has for law enforcement. Tanzania seems to be successfully protecting its small populations of the Uganda red colobus in the Gombe National Park and the Mahale Mountains National Park (it also has a few scattered populations outside of the parks). The Uganda red colobus is listed in Class B of the 1969 African Convention and in CITES, Appendix II: Trade Restricted. At present, foreign trading of the monkey does not seem to be a problem. As with other red colobuses, the Uganda red colobus does not do well in captivity, in part because its nutritional needs and its behavior are poorly understood.

Thollon's Red Colobus

Procolobus pennantii tholloni

Uganda Red Colobus (*P. p. tephrosceles*)   Noel Rowe

Status	Insufficiently Known.
Listed	*IUCN Red List*
Family	Cercopithecidae (Old World monkey).
Description	Gray to dark-gray, with the head covered with red hair and the shoulders, back, and outer arms covered with reddish-brown hair.
Habitat	Wet forests.
Food	Leaves and perhaps other plant parts.
Reproduction	One young after gestation of 180 to 195 days.
Threats	Loss of habitat to logging and agriculture; hunting for food and skins by humans.
Range	Republic of Congo

Description

Thollon's red colobus, *Procolobus pennantii tholloni,* has a black face framed by gray whiskers on the cheeks and chin. It may have a base color of dark hair, from gray to dark-gray, with the head covered with red hair and the shoulders, back, and outer arms covered with reddish-brown hair. Its hair is long and satiny.

The adult Thollon's red colobus' head-and-body length is between 18 and 26 inches; its tail adds another 20 to 30 inches; it weighs between 11 and 25 pounds. It is likely to be sexually dimorphic, with males larger than females.

Behavior

The behavior of this uncommon animal is largely unrecorded. It lives in groups of unknown size, although groups with as many as 80 members are possible. A group has a mixture of males and females, young and old, with perhaps one male dominant. As with other red colobuses, the Thollon's red colobus is probably territorial. Each group would have its own territory, although territories might overlap. The sizes of individual territories have not been recorded.

Mating behavior may resemble that of the Tana River red colobus monkey. Pregnancy probably lasts between 180 and 195 days, resulting in the birth of one infant. Care of the infant is shared among the other females of the group and possibly immature males, as well. As the youngster becomes more independent, the group's adult males may also participate in looking after it. It is likely that behavior within a group resembles that of the Thollon's red colobus' close relative, the Tana River red colobus monkey.

Habitat

This monkey requires a dense forest with a high canopy. Leaves are the most important part of its diet, which may also include buds, fruits, and flowers. Not enough is known about this monkey to pin down the specifics of its habitat.

Distribution

The ancient range of the Thollon's red colobus is not known, but it is possible that it never ranged widely. It presently resides in a forest located between the Kasai-Sankuru River and the Zaire River in Republic of Congo.

Threats

The Thollon's red colobus lives in a very troubled part of the world. The monkey is now rare, and with the destruction of its habitat and hunting by humans, its population is quickly shrinking. It stands at risk of extinction at almost anytime, depending on whether the logging of its lands continues and how urgently humans need it for food.

Conservation and Recovery

The Thollon's red colobus' population numbers are unknown, but its small, shrinking range suggests that it is scarce. Logging in its range needs to be regulated and hunting needs to be curtailed. The Solongo area's forest still has stands of intact habitat suited to the monkey, and the forest's easily defined zone makes it a good candidate for preservation as a park or wildlife reserve.

The Thollon's red colobus is listed in Class B of the 1969 African Convention. It is also listed in CITES, Appendix II: Trade Restricted.

Preuss's Red Colobus

Procolobus preussi

Noel Rowe

Status	Endangered
Listed	January 23, 1984
Family	Cercopithecidae (Old World monkey)
Description	Back and head are black; its sides, outer limbs, and cheeks are red-orange; its chest, abdomen, inner limbs, and underparts are white-orange; its tail is blackish red.
Habitat	Coastal rain forests with a very high canopy.
Food	Primarily leaves, but buds, fruits, and flowers as well.
Reproduction	Mating occurs year 'round; single infant after gestation of about 6 months.
Threats	Loss of habitat to logging.
Range	Cameroon

Description

Preuss' red colobus, *Procolobus preussi*, is sexually dimorphic, with males much larger than females. The males have proportionally larger heads than the females and have larger fangs; the jaw of males is more muscular than that of females, which suggests that biting may be a significant form of defense since males usually do the fighting for a group. Not counting the tale, the Preuss's red colobus ranges in length from 22 inches to 25 inches; its tail adds another 29 to 30 inches. Males weigh between 20 and 28 pounds; females weigh 14.5 to 22 pounds.

Similar to other red colobus monkeys, the Preuss's red colobus has long, soft, even luxuriant hair. The hair is black with light gray dots on its back and head, red orange on its sides, outer limbs, and cheeks, white-orange on its chest, abdomen, inner limbs, and other underparts, and almost black red on its tail. Its face is black and sometimes framed by gray whiskers.

Taxonomy is disputed for this species. It was elevated from a subspecies of *P. badius*. A population that was discovered in 1993 in the Niger Delta may be described as a new subspecies.

Behavior

Preuss's red colobus lives in groups with as many as 50 members. Each group has a dominant male who takes the role as the group's primary defender against interlopers and predators. There is not a strong hierarchy within the group, which features a loose social structure. When eating the monkeys face away from each other and concentrate on the branch before them, thus limiting social interaction. Much of the monkey's social behavior is focused on youngsters. Soon after birth, an infant is passed to females other than its mother; any of these females may suckle and care for the infant, although the mother seems to take charge of the infant when her group is on the move. She then clutches the infant to her abdomen.

Males leave their birth group before reaching maturity, and they join with other young males to form a loose, small group of their own. Eventually, the young male will try to join a full group of males and females. The dynamics of this have been little observed in the Preuss's red colobus monkey; most of its close relatives handle the matter by having the new male show obeisance to the group's dominant male, perhaps by lifting its hind quarters up toward the principal male. It is possible that females, too, migrate from one group to another, but this would be a casual matter, with females possibly wandering from one group to another fairly often.

Habitat

Preuss's red colobus occurs in tall primary forests near water, not in second growth forests.

Distribution

Preuss's red colobus once ranged from the coastal forests of Cameroon into southeast Nigeria. It probably is extinct in Nigeria. It now lives in a strip of forest approximately 74 miles long and 37 miles wide in Cameroon along the border with Nigeria.

Threats

Preuss's red colobus requires a habitat with a high forest canopy, which makes it vulnerable to the effects of logging. In areas where the high canopy has been lost, Preuss's red colobus has not adapted and has instead died out. It also is hunted for food, which is responsible for its disappearance from some areas, including the Barombi Mbo Forest.

Conservation and Recovery

With financial assistance from the British Overseas Development Agency and the World Wide Fund for nature, Cameroon has established the Korup Reserve to protect the region in which the Preuss' red colobus monkey lives and has undertaken an education program to teach people about the rarity and value of the monkey. It is illegal to hunt, capture, or trade the monkey in Cameroon. The steps Cameroon has taken to protect the Preuss's red colobus monkey are encouraging; the Korup Reserve may have a population of 8,000 — a size sufficient for a healthy breeding population. Even so, hope must be tempered with caution — continued habitat loss still means that the monkey is threatened with extinction.

Tana River Red Colobus

Procolobus rufomitratus

Lysa Leland

Status	Endangered
Listed	June 2, 1970
Family	Cercopithecidae (Old World monkey)
Description	Red head with red-brown back and outer arms and dark gray pelage.
Habitat	Wet forests of Kenya's Tana River floodplain.
Food	Primarily immature leaves but also unripe fruit, buds, flowers, and mature leaves.
Reproduction	Gestation lasts over 180 days, producing one infant.
Threats	Loss of habitat to agriculture and hunting the monkey for its coat.
Range	Kenya

Description

The adult Tana River red colobus, *Procolobus rufomitratus*, is between 18 and 26 inches long, not including the tail. Its tail adds another 20 to 30 inches to its length. It typically weighs between 11 and 25 pounds. Its coat is spectacular, with a base color of dark hair, from gray to dark-gray, with the head covered with red hair and the shoulders, back, and outer arms covered with reddish-brown hair. The hair is long and soft, which once led to extensive hunting of the monkey for its coat, which was exported and made into clothing.

Behavior

There is disagreement among naturalists about the mating habits of the Tana River red colobus monkey. This monkey has yet to be bred successfully in captivity (captured adults have survived no more than 2 years in captivity), and its wild mating has been little observed. It is probable that females are the sexually aggressive gender. When receptive, her genital area swells. During mating, the male and female retreat away from their group, and female lies prone. It is unclear whether the female mates with several males, similar to leaf monkeys, or simply mates with one male of her choosing. The Tana River red colobus's infant raising behavior strongly suggests that the female mates with only one male. After birth, the male takes much interest in the care of the infant. As the infant matures, it runs to its father nearly as often as to its mother, and it plays games with both parents; these games seem to consist of survival behavior such as spotting predators, fleeing out of sight, and rushing to either parent for protection. The father is notably patient, allowing even pulling of its hair by the youngster without indication of anger.

The Tana River red colobus is territorial. It lives in groups of 12 to 20 members, with each group having a territory of 20 to 25 acres. Confrontations between groups are rare. A group will have a mixture of males and females of varying maturity. Males will usually leave their parental group before reaching sexual maturity and will live solitary or with a few other young males. They are eventually absorbed into new groups, after presenting their hindquarters — indicating submission — to the group's dominant male.

Although their niche is in watery areas, the Tana River red colobus are primarily arboreal, preferring leafy forests with dense ground cover. Their presence has been recording in savannah, and they seem willing to venture into open areas that offer leafy plants to eat and bushes to hide in. Grassy areas provide them with little or no food. They move swiftly among tree branches and do not break stride or hesitate before leaping from one tree to another. The leaps feature two different postures. In one posture, the monkeys thrust their arms and legs forward and grab the first large branch they come across. In the other posture, they pull their arms and legs in close to their bodies and land amid thick foliage.

Habitat

Tana River red colobus monkeys live in forests in the Tana River flood plain in Kenya. They require areas with numerous trees and seem to prefer dense canopies in rain forests over more open forestlands.

Distribution

The Tana River red colobus monkey is native to the Tana River flood plain in Kenya and once was found throughout extensive forestlands. It now exists in scattered patches of forest in a range of about 100 miles along the river. Once numbering in the thousands, it now is down to perhaps 100 in population.

Threats

In the nineteenth century, the Tana River red colobus was slaughtered by the hundreds of thousands to provide fashionable coats for world markets. By the 1970s, fewer than 2,000 still survived. By the 1980s, only a few hundred survived.

Conservation and Recovery

Although Kenya has created the Tana River Reserve to protect wildlife in the river's flood plain, only about 4 square miles of it has the type of habitat the Tana River red colobus monkey needs. Agriculture has destroyed most of the area's forests. Further, the building of a dam upstream has changed the flood plain's habitat considerably because the plain no longer floods, which means that area's ecology is drastically changed: Without floods plant regeneration has been slowed considerably, and trees are not reproducing as rapidly as they had. This means that the small patches of remaining forest are not producing as much of the new growth that the monkey depends upon for its diet. Efforts to create a captive population have so far failed.

The Tana River red colobus is listed in Class A of the African Convention and in CITES, Appendix I: Trade Prohibited. The *IUCN Red List of Threatened Animals* lists it as vulnerable.

Foa Red Colobus

Procolobus rufomitratus foai

Tana River Red Colobus (*Procolobus rufomitratus*)   L. Leland

Status	Insufficiently known.
Listed	*IUCN Red List*
Family	Cercopithecidae (Old World monkey)
Description	Gray to dark-gray, with the head covered with red hair and the shoulders, back, and outer arms covered with reddish-brown hair.
Habitat	Rain, mountain, and swamp forests.
Food	Leaves and perhaps other plant parts.
Reproduction	Gestation is 180 to 195 months, resulting in the birth of one infant.
Threats	Loss of habitat to logging and fires, as well as hunting for food and skins by humans.
Range	Republic of Congo (formerly Zaire)

Description

The foa red colobus, *Procolobus rufomitratus foai*, probably resembles its better known close relative the Tana River red colobus monkey (*Procolobus rufomitratus*; see separate entry). Thus, the adult foa red colobus' head-and-body length is probably between 18 and 26 inches, and its tail probably adds another 20 to 30 inches. It would weigh between 11 and 25 pounds. It is likely to be sexually dimorphic, with males larger than females and having larger fangs than females.

Its hair is long and soft. Its coloration is uncertain, but is colorful, like those of its relatives. It may have a base color of dark hair, from gray to dark-gray, with the head covered with red hair and the shoulders, back, and outer arms covered with reddish-brown hair.

Behavior

The behavior of this scarce animal is largely unrecorded. It lives in groups of unknown size, but seemingly small, perhaps averaging 15 members, although groups with as many as 80 members may once have existed before their range was constricted by deforestation. A group has a mixture of males and females, young and old, with perhaps one male dominant. As with other red colobuses, the foa red colobus is probably territorial by group.

Females have genital swelling when ovulating. Whether they mate with several males during ovulation or only one is not as yet known. Pregnancy probably lasts 180 to 195 days and results in a single birth. Care of the youngster is shared among the other females of the group. It is likely that behavior within a group resembles that of the foa red colobus' close relative, the Tana River red colobus monkey.

Habitat

This monkey once made its home in rain forests, gallery forests, mountain forests, and swamp forests. Leaves make up a significant portion of its diet, but it is not known for certain what else they may eat, although buds, unripe fruits, and flowers may supplement their mainly leafy fare.

Distribution

The ancient range of the foa red colobus is unknown. It is thought that it adapted to a wide range of forest environments, from wet to dry, from warm to cool. It seems to require dense foliage and a high forest canopy. Currently, it lives west of Lake Tanganyika, but how far west it extends is unknown, although logging is shrinking its potential habitat and thus its potential range.

Threats

The foa red colobus is threatened by loss of habitat due to logging, and by hunting from the native population who values the meat for food.

Conservation and Recovery

Authorities seem to agree that the foa red colobus is now rare, and with the destruction of its habitat and hunting by humans, its population is quickly shrinking. It stands at risk of extinction at almost anytime, depending on whether the logging of its lands continues and how urgently humans need it for food. The foa red colobuses need a wildlife reserve in which they are safe from loss of their habitat and free from human predation. Educating the local people about the value of the monkey and the need to preserve it cannot reasonably begin before naturalists have learned more about its habitat needs and behavior, but such education may ultimately be vital to saving it from extinction. Thus the foa red colobus is in urgent need of study. As with other red colobus monkeys, the foa red colobus is not a good candidate for breeding in captivity even if its nutritional and behavioral needs were known; without such knowledge the monkey is unlikely to survive long in zoos.

The foa red colobus is listed in Class B of the African Convention and in CITES, Appendix II: Trade Restricted.

Olive [=Van Beneden's] Colobus

Procolobus verus

Noel Rowe

Status	Rare
Listed	*IUCN Red List*
Family	Cercopithecidae (Old World monkey)
Description	Small monkey with olive-gray hair on its upper areas and whitish gray to pale gray hair on its lower, under parts.
Habitat	Rain forests and other densely overgrown areas, especially ones with thick growths of tropical trees.
Food	Leaves and fruit.
Reproduction	Sexual unions are instigated by females, who exhibit perineal swelling when receptive.
Threats	Habitat loss to logging and agriculture.
Range	Ghana, Guinea, Ivory Coast, Liberia, Nigeria, Sierra Leone.

Description

The adult olive colobus, *Procolobus verus,* is between 17 and 21.5 inches long, not including the tail. Its tail adds another 22.5 to 25 inches to its length. It typically weighs between 9 and 10.4 pounds. Its upper body features olive-gray hair that becomes grayer as it extends over the limbs toward the extremities. The rest of its body may grayish white to pale gray. The hair forms a front-to-back crest on the animal's head.

Behavior

Olive colobuses are diurnal and arboreal. They prefer feeding sites in thick growth below 49 feet, using their coat very effectively as camouflage. They live in groups averaging 8 members, although ones as small as 5 and as large as 20 have been observed. Olive colobuses associate with groups of monkeys of another species, moving with them through the forest canopy. It especially associates with large groups of Diana monkeys (*Cercopithecus diana*), which sound alarm calls when they spot a predator. It has been observed that one olive colobus group associated with Diana monkeys 80% of the time over a 3-year period.

Mating behavior for this animal is largely unrecorded but it is thought that gestation lasts 150 to 180 days. One behavior that is striking is that female olive colobuses carry their infants in their mouths (the young of most of its colobus relatives cling with their hands to their mothers' hair when traveling). A group seems to consist of a mixture of males and females. Olive colobuses are arboreal animals who can move swiftly among tree branches and who rarely come to the ground. They seem to get their water from dew and from tree hollows that have some rain, and their diet seems to consist primarily of leaves. They also consume seeds, flowers, and some fruit.

Habitat

The olive colobus favors rain forests with very high tree canopies, and they live primarily in tropical areas. There is some evidence that the species will adapt to somewhat open lands such as failed farms if there is a great amount of dense brush.

Distribution

The olive colobus once inhabited a great range from Sierra Leone in west central east into Nigeria. The vast forests that were its home have by and large disappeared, and it now survives in pockets of forest scattered through its ancient range, including Ghana, Guinea, Ivory Coast, Liberia, Nigeria, and Sierra Leone.

Threats

Although the olive colobus' traditional range is large, massive deforestation, primarily for logging, has drastically reduced its habitat. Once found in Benin and Togo, it has probably disappeared from those countries. Ghana has enacted laws that protect the olive colobus from being trapped, hunted, or captured. The Ivory Coast has some olive colobuses in its Tai National Park of over 1300 square miles. It requires that hunters have licenses to hunt the olive colobus. Liberia still has a large part of the olive colobus' habitat intact, but people there hunt it extensively for food, driving it near to extinction. Although Liberia has made efforts to protect its endangered wildlife, a long civil war has made law enforcement nearly impossible. Sierra Leone is now almost deforested.

Conservation and Recovery

In its Gola Forest Reserves, the olive colobus may still be found; it is also protected by law in Sierra Leone, and Sierra Leone has an education program intended to teach people about the value of endangered wildlife, hoping to discourage hunting of the olive colobus and other endangered animals. For the olive monkey to survive, rain forest needs to be set aside and protected for it, so that it will have sufficient habitat to survive and breed. Laws against hunting it need to be enacted and enforced.

It does not breed well in captivity, and captive breeding does not seem to be a viable option for sustaining this monkey.

The olive colobus is listed in Class A of the African Convention of 1969 and in CITES, Appendix II: Trade Restricted.

Mouse and Dwarf Lemurs

Family: Cheirogaleidae

Fat-tailed Dwarf Lemur (*Cheirogaleus medius*)   Noel Rowe

General Characteristics of the *Cheirogaleidae*

The family *Cheirogaleidae* is composed of the mouse lemurs and dwarf lemurs, which are prosimians — primitive primates. All members of *Cheirogaleidae* are protected by Malagasy law and CITES, Appendix I: Trade Prohibited. *Cheirogaleidae* has four genera containing seven species: the fat-tailed dwarf lemur (*Cheirogaleus medius*), the greater dwarf lemur (*Cheirogaleus major*), the gray mouse lemur (*Microcebus murinus*), the brown mouse lemur (*Microcebus rufus*), the Coquerel's dwarf lemur (*Microcebus coquereli*), the hairy-eared dwarf lemur (*Allocebus trichotis*), the fork-marked lemur (*Phaner furcifer*), and the smallest living primate, the pygmy mouse lemur (*Microcebus myoxinus*), which weighs just over one ounce (30.6 grams). All of these species are at least to some degree threatened by habitat loss: Their native forests are being annihilated. The most endangered is the hairy-eared dwarf lemur, thought to be extinct until it was rediscovered in 1990 in a lowland forest in northern Madagascar. Its habitat is nearly gone, and it is very hard to find because its remaining numbers are very low. It is likely to be driven to extinction before 2000. The other two most threatened species are the Coquerel's dwarf lemur and the fork-marked lemur; of these, the fork-marked lemur may have the better chance for survival because it is found in four of the Malagasy Republic's national parks and in five of its special reserves, although law enforcement is having much difficulty preventing poaching and preventing illegal logging and farming on the protected lands.

At one time, the family *Cheirogaleidae* had representatives spread throughout Madagascar and were among the most successful lemurs before humans began destroying their native forests. All *Cheirogaleidae* species are arboreal and rarely touch the ground; they will travel on the ground to cross a gap between trees or dart to the ground to quickly snatch insects to eat. Because they are very tiny (about 2 ounces to about 1 pound) they have much trouble regulating their body temperature and rely heavily on a warm environment to retain sufficient body heat to stay alive. This has resulted in some of them having a period of dormancy during cool seasons, roughly half a year. While dormant they are in tree holes or other places where their small size makes them very hard to discover, which probably protects them from natural predators.

The dwarf and mouse lemurs are nocturnal creatures, and as a consequence they have a flat layer of tissue called a *tapetum* behind their retinas. The *tapetum* has riboflavin crystals that reflect light back into the retinas and that bend the light into more easily seen colors, especially yellow. This *tapetum* helps the dwarf and mouse lemurs see in the dark, and it also reflects light from fires and flashlights; naturalists look for the glowing eyes that reflect the light from their lamps when they are looking for dwarf or mouse lemurs to study. The dwarf and mouse lemurs eat both plants and animals, with plants usually making up the greater part of their diet, except for the genus *Microcebus*, whose diet comprises fruits and insects.

The members of *Cheirogaleidae* tend to be solitary feeders that wander off on their own at night. They tend to live on their own, except for the fork-marked lemurs, which seem to form monogamous pairs that keep track of each other at night by crying out to one another, and perhaps the Coquerel's dwarf lemur, in which male-female pairs may also remain close to each other while feeding. They tend to be territorial, with males having larger ranges than females, and with some overlapping of ranges, particularly among a male and a few females. When the dwarf and mouse lemurs breed, they will usually have two or three infants; how adults care for these infants varies among the species. The species of *Microcebus*, the gray mouse lemur, the brown mouse lemur, and the Coquerel's dwarf lemur, are primarily insectivorous.

Hairy-eared Dwarf Lemur

Allocebus trichotis

Bernhard Meier

Status	Endangered
Listed	June 2, 1970; June 14, 1976.
Family	Cheirogaleidae (Dwarf lemurs)
Description	Grayish-brown above and pale gray below, with a reddish-brown tail.
Habitat	Eastern rain forest inland from Mananara, Madagascar.
Reproduction	Birth season is January-February.
Food	Primarily omnivorous.
Threats	Habitat loss due to logging and agricultural development.
Range	Eastern Madagascar

Description

The hairy-eared dwarf lemur, *Allocebus trichotis,* is known to science through fewer than ten specimens. One of the interesting aspects of this animal is its periodic reappearance in its range long after scientists have decided it was extinct. In 1874, it was thought to have altogether disappeared and was known by only one specimen in a museum. Then another was captured in the wild. By 1964, the hairy-eared dwarf lemur was thought to be long extinct, but it reappeared in eastern Madagascar, near Mananara, in 1989, giving the world its sixth, seventh, and eighth examples of itself — all living. What little is known about the hairy-eared dwarf lemur comes primarily from these three animals. At present, the hairy-eared dwarf lemur still inhabits a small patch of forest and is certainly one of the world's most endangered species.

Adult males measure 4.9 to 5.3 inches in body length, with its tail adding 6.3 to 7.7 inches. They weigh from 2.6 to 3.5 ounces. Females measure 5.1 to 5.7 inches with a tail length of 5.9 to 6.5 inches, and weigh from 2.8 to 3.2 ounces. The hairy-eared dwarf lemur gets its name from the large tufts of fur sprouting out of its small ears, as well as from its small size. Its fur is gray-brown, except for its underbody and tail. The underbody is light gray, and the tail is gray with a red tinge.

Like other members of its family (*Cheirogaleidae* — commonly called "mouse lemurs"), the hairy-eared dwarf lemur has trouble regulating its body temperature, falling into torpor in cold weather and during dry seasons (usually May through September), essentially hibernating until the weather warms or water returns. While hibernating, it survives on the fat stored all over its body — not just in the tail as other dwarf lemurs do.

Another common name is tsidy ala.

Behavior

The hairy-eared dwarf lemur is nocturnal, feeding and moving at night and sleeping by day. In captivity it eats 70% insects, along with sweetened rich broth and fruit. Little is known of its diet in the wild, but it probably feeds on flower nectar, the juices of small plants, and insects. It frequently jumps from place to place while foraging. Owls, also nocturnal eaters, are its primary natural predator.

Although they forage for food singly, the hairy-eared dwarf lemurs are social animals whose females congregate in small groups to sleep in tree hollows by day and whose males sleep singly or in pairs. Their nests are carefully lined with dry leaves. Their social behavior includes territoriality, with males having somewhat larger ranges than females and with male and female territories overlapping. They mark their territories as they travel; they rub urine on their feet and the scent marks their territories as they walk. It is

likely that like other mouse lemurs, the hairy-eared dwarf lemur makes high-pitched cries (many beyond human hearing) to communicate with others of its kind while moving about at night. This would include a screeching to warn of the presence of predators.

Breeding is seasonal, with births occurring from January to February. It is possible, but not certain, that the hairy-eared dwarf lemur can breed twice a year. The young are weaned at seven weeks of age, and are independent and behave like adults at eight to ten weeks of age.

Habitat

The hairy-eared dwarf lemur inhabits lowland rain forest. The presence of flowering plants — probably trees — seems to be a requirement for this lemur's habitat.

Distribution

The hairy-eared dwarf lemur's range is the subject of disagreement — too little is known of its wild habitat. It may once have ranged through the rain forests of northeastern Madagascar, possibly ranging through northern Madagascar to the western mountains, and southward to the middle of the island. It now lives in a tiny region of primary rain forest near the town of Mananara, on the east coast of Madagascar; one was found about ten miles from Mananara, and another was found about 20 miles from Mananara.

Threats

Local people consider mouse lemurs in

general to be bad eating, so the hairy-eared dwarf lemur is not hunted for food. Given the animal's rarity, there is some danger of poaching for capture and sale overseas. The great threat to the animal is the loss of its habitat. The region in which it lives is being rapidly denuded of its native forests to be replaced by agricultural development and expanding human communities.

Conservation and Recovery

The rain forest habitat needs to be preserved as part of any effort to conserve this species. It is listed (as a member of the family *Cheirogaleidae*) in CITES, Appendix I: Trade Prohibited, which means that by treaty it is not to be traded in whole or in part internationally. It also is listed (as a lemur) in class A of the African Convention, which means that by treaty it may not be hunted, killed, captured, or traded without permission of the nation's highest authority responsible for wildlife. The Malagasy Republic also has laws protecting the lemur from human predation.

Greater Dwarf Lemur

Cheirogaleus major

Noel Rowe

Status	Endangered
Listed	June 2, 1970
Family	Cheirogaleidae (Dwarf lemurs)
Description	Grayish brown or reddish brown fur; weighs no more than 1 pound.
Habitat	Rain forests
Food	Ripe fruits, nectar, pollen, and insects; possibly small vertebrates.
Reproduction	2 to 3 young, born in December or January, after gestation of 70 days.
Threats	Loss of habitat; predation by owls and civets.
Range	Madagascar

Description

The greater dwarf lemur's, *Cheirogaleus major*, small size may be one reason why it is doing somewhat better than most other lemurs: it is able to hide in small holes, making it hard for humans to find, although human hunters will sometimes poke holes with sticks, hoping to disturb a lemur that will then be killed. It weighs 12.5 to 16 ounces, and it has a head-and-body length of 7.5 to 11 inches, with a tail length of 6.5 to 10 inches.

Its upper body is grayish to reddish brown, with sometimes redder hindquarters. Its underbody is lighter than its upper body. The fur tends to be soft, laid back over a loose-skinned body. Its tail tends to be large in diameter relative to the body, with fluffed-out fur. The eyes are large, round, and set forward on the forehead. The nose is fleshy with oval nostrils.

Behavior

The greater dwarf lemur is nocturnal, sleeping during the day in trees, either in tree holes or in nests it has made from leaves, twigs, and grasses. It usually sleeps among several other greater dwarf lemurs. At dusk, it parts company from the lemurs it has slept with, and during the night it forages alone. Its diet consists primarily of ripe fruit, but it often eats nectar and pollen, and less frequently insects. It is possible that it eats small vertebrates such as lizards. It moves slowly, on all fours most of the time.

The animal may be territorial, with individual greater dwarf lemurs having territories of 1.8 acres, with male and female territories overlapping. Territories are marked by feces and urine on branches; whether or not territories are actually defended is uncertain. When two or more greater dwarf lemurs have been observed together, the interaction has been peaceful, with mutual grooming.

During the dry winter months, the greater dwarf lemur has a period of dormancy, during which it survives off the fat that it has stored in its tail. The length of the period of dormancy is uncertain, either because of inaccurate observations or because individual greater dwarf lemurs vary their dormancy according to their needs and the length of the dry season. Usually, the period of dormancy is reported to last about 3 months, but periods as short as 3 days have been recorded.

The birth season is November to February; gestation lasts 70 days, resulting in the birth of 2 or 3 infants. Care of the infants seems to be a female responsibility. She moves them about by carrying them in her mouth. Their eyes open after 2 days of age; they are weaned after 45 days of age; and they become sexually mature after 7 to 10 months of age.

Habitat

The greater dwarf lemur lives in high-canopied rain forests, seldom descending below 10 feet. (There is some disagreement about this, with one authority asserting that the greater dwarf lemurs move among the reeds and bushes of the forest.) It usually nests high in the trees for sleeping, although it sometimes retreats into hollows among tree roots.

Distribution

Exactly how large the greater dwarf lemur's range was before the destruction of its rain forests is uncertain, although there are reports of its being found deep in central Madagascar and through most of the island's southern forests, almost to the west coast Its southern range is now a hot, dry desert and its central rain forests have been exterminated; both these environmental calamities have been caused by humans. The greater dwarf lemur now lives in patches of rain forest along Madagascar's east coast, from the far northern coast all the way to the edge of the desert in the south.

Threats

Among the most abundant of lemur species, the numbers of greater dwarf lemurs have precipitously declined in recent years because of the eradication of most of its rain forest habitat. About forty years ago, centuries of slash-and-burn agriculture, combined with logging and the felling of trees for charcoal, began to turn southern Madagascar into a large desert. Many southerners migrated northward and, along with logging companies, began to destroy the island's central forests, a process that is now nearly complete; these central areas are showing signs of desertification. These human activities forced the greater dwarf lemur into a narrow strip of rain forest along the east coast of Madagascar; this remnant of Madagascar's recently large forests is also being stripped bare, leaving patches of rain forest. Within these patches, the animal seems to thrive, but it is increasingly restricted to small parks and reserves. These are threatened by illegal logging and farming.

Conservation and Recovery

The government of the Malagasy Republic has long recognized the importance of its wildlife, but its people's poverty has forced it to make significant compromises — for instance surrendering prime wildlands to mining for the foreign currency selling minerals will bring. Lack of funds to hire and train personnel for its many parks and reserves has also been a problem for the government, although since 1980, international wildlife and scientific organizations have increasingly invested money in the preservation of Madagascar's remaining wild areas. Several areas that have been set aside for protection have at least a few greater dwarf lemurs in them. The most important of these are probably the Nosy Mangabe Special Reserve in the Bay of Atongil in northeastern Madagascar, which is home to small numbers of the greater dwarf lemur; the Périnet-Analamazaotra reserve, nineteen miles east of Moramanga in central eastern Madagascar, which is home to a dense population of greater dwarf lemurs (about 176 per square mile); and the developing Ranomafana national park in central eastern Madagascar, south of the Périnet-Analamazoatra reserve, is home to greater dwarf lemurs and several other lemur species, providing the opportunity to see how the greater dwarf lemur night have interacted with other, sometimes competing, species before the presence of humans altered their habitat.

Fat-tailed Dwarf Lemur

Cheirogaleus medius

Noel Rowe

Status	Endangered
Listed	June 2, 1970
Family	Cheirogaleidae (Dwarf lemurs)
Description	Overall coat is gray with red or brown highlights, with the underbody colored white, brown, or orange.
Habitat	Dry forests.
Food	Fruits, flowers, nectar, pollen, insects, and small vertebrates.
Reproduction	Gestation lasts 62 days, resulting in 1 to 4 (usually 2) young, born in December or January.
Threats	Loss of habitat. Owls and weasels are its principal natural predators.
Range	Madagascar

Description

The adult fat-tailed dwarf lemur's, *Cheirogaleus medius*, head-and-body length is 8.5 inches, with its tail adding another 8 inches. Its weight fluctuates greatly from season to season, apparently depending on how much fat it has stored. On average, adults weigh 9 ounces, but an individual animal's weight can vary from 6 to 16 ounces. The fat-tailed dwarf lemur's body temperature also varies from 70 to 90 degrees Fahrenheit.

The tiny creature's tail is often about one inch thick when it is storing fat and sometimes looks as big as the rest of the animal. The fat-tailed dwarf lemur's head is round, with prominent round eyes and a small, bulbous nose with nostril slits along its sides. The fur is gray, tinged with red or brown, and the underbody is usually white but sometimes brown or orange. The eyes, cheeks, and mouth are surrounded by lighter colored fur.

Behavior

Little has been recorded about the fat-tailed lemur's habits, although new opportunities for its study afforded by breeding it in captivity may soon change this. It is a nocturnal animal that forages alone, eating fruit, flowers, nectar, pollen, insects, and probably small vertebrates such as lizards. It seems utterly without territories, although it marks tree limbs with trails of feces — perhaps just to let others know of its presence. During the day it sleeps in trees, usually in hollows.

During its active season, the fat-tailed dwarf lemur stores fat in its tail and legs, making the tail especially appear huge compared to the rest of the body. The animal lives off this fat during its long dormancy period of up to 6 months, during the dry season. When dormant, the fat-tailed dwarf lemurs rest in tree hollows, having covered themselves with leaves; they pile up in heaps on top of one another during this period.

Males have been observed to fight over estrous females. Gestation averages 62 days, resulting in the birth of 1 to 4, usually 2, young. Infants are weaned after 61 days.

Habitat

Fat-tailed dwarf lemurs live in dry forests and have been observed foraging in savannah and brush lands. They seem to require the presence of trees for roughly half the year, when they are dormant.

Distribution

The fat-tailed dwarf lemur's range once extended from the far north of Madagascar, throughout western Madagascar, and across the south of the island. It now lives in patches of forest in the north, west, and southeast of the island.

Threats

The fat-tailed dwarf lemur's forests are being cut down for agriculture and for making charcoal and are being logged, as well. As a result, its population has been steadily decreasing every year.

Conservation and Recovery

The fat-tailed dwarf lemur is found in parks and preserves scattered from the far north, along the west coast, and to the southeast of Madagascar. The famous Berenty Private Reserve in southeastern Madagascar is home to a population of the lemurs, which can be seen at night in the spiny desert part of the reserve; these lemurs are said to be tame. Another private reserve, Analabe, near the coast in central western Madagascar also is home to fat-tailed dwarf lemurs. These private reserves are examples of how money can be made from the tourism Madagascar's wildlife attracts, without harming the animals, themselves. The Ankarana Special Reserve in far northern Madagascar has a population of the fat-tailed dwarf lemurs, an indication of how far their distribution may once have been. To the south of Ankarana, in northwestern Madagascar, southeast of the city of Mahajanga (also known as Majunga), a healthy population lives in the Ankarafantsika Strict Nature Reserve. They are also found in the Beza-Mahafaly Special Reserve, in southern Madagascar. Protection of these wildlife areas varies from good to almost nonexistent, and people are constantly putting pressure on them by illegally felling of trees, by setting them afire to clear land for agriculture, and by poaching the animals. The fight to save these protected lands has become desperate in some cases, but the Malagasy government and foreign investors have made a special effort to save Ankarafantsika.

Captive breeding programs are meeting with much success, which is unusual for a species of lemur. The Duke Primate Center, in particular, has managed to have a population boom among its fat-tailed dwarf lemurs. In all, over 90 percent of captive fat-tailed dwarf lemurs were born in captivity, a remarkable achievement.

Coquerel's Dwarf Lemur

Microcebus [=Mirza] coquereli

Noel Rowe

Status	Endangered
Listed	June 2, 1970
Family	Cheirogaleidae (Dwarf lemurs)
Description	Overall grayish brown with yellowish underbody, with a tail much longer than the rest of the body.
Habitat	Dry deciduous forests.
Food	Opportunistic feeder, including fruit, the secretions of insect larvae, tree sap, leaves, buds, insects, frogs, lizards, bird eggs, and small birds.
Reproduction	1 to 4 young after gestation of 84 to 89 days.
Threats	Loss of habitat; predation by owls.
Range	Madagascar

Description

Coquerel's dwarf lemur, *Microcebus [=Mirza] coquereli*, has soft, downy fur that is grayish brown on the back and sides and yellowish gray on the underbody, with pale fur on the face. An adult has a head-and-body length of 9.5 inches, with a 12-inch tail. Authorities disagree on the average weight, putting it between 10.5 and 14 ounces. Its squarish head features tall, wide, rounded ears, indicating that sound is important to its movements and possibly for locating prey — logical because it hunts at night. Its somewhat angled back eyes are small in comparison to its prominent, bare nose.

Behavior

The Coquerel's dwarf lemur is nocturnal. It spends its days sleeping in spherical nests about 12 inches in diameter, made of interlaced leaves and branches. Coquerel's dwarf lemurs will often build their nests in clusters of half a dozen. A given nest may have one occupant, a mother and her young, or two or three adults of both genders. The nest may be located in branches 6 to 33 feet above the ground. At night, the animals forage, apparently alone, and gather for socializing, which involves calls and mutual grooming. They are territorial, with each animal defending a territory of its own; female territories are larger than those of males. A territory consists of a core area and a surrounding peripheral area. The core area is the focus of an individual Coquerel's dwarf lemur's activities, with the peripheral area being infrequently visited. The peripheral area usually overlaps the peripheral areas of other Coquerel's dwarf lemurs, but the core area is usually defended from most members of the same gender. Both males and females will tolerate core area overlaps from members of the opposite sex, and females will tolerate overlaps from their offspring. A male's core area is about 3.7 acres, while a female's may exceed 7 acres; a male's peripheral area is about 9.9 acres, while a female's is about 11.1 acres.

It seems as though every authority that has written about Coquerel's dwarf lemur disagrees with every other one about its breeding habits. Breeding seems to be seasonal; mating may occur in October, with births following about three months later. On the other hand, mating may actually occur much earlier, with births occurring in late November. Mothers care for their young in their nests; males have not been observed helping them.

The Coquerel's dwarf lemur seems to be an opportunistic feeder, a trait that may be helping it stave off extinction. It alters its diet from season to season and from locale to locale, and it seems to be able to weather hard times if insects and their larvae are available. Their willingness to vary their diet may be the reason why they adapt very well to secondary forests when primary forests are unavailable. In food-rich forests, including secondary ones, they may achieve high population densities; in a forest with many cashew nut trees, the density may have been as high a 1,000 per square mile.

Habitat

The Coquerel's dwarf lemur prefers a tall deciduous forest near a large body of water. The floor of the forest would ideally have an abundance of reeds and brush.

Distribution

The Coquerel's dwarf lemur's past distribution is hard to determine, but may have extended north-to-south throughout the deciduous forests of Western Madagascar. It presently lives in patches of forest in the far northwest of Madagascar and in south-central western Madagascar.

Threats

The forests of the Coquerel's dwarf lemur are being eradicated by logging, clearing for cattle grazing and cultivation, and harvesting for charcoal. Fires, often deliberately set, are destroying much of the Coquerel's dwarf lemur's remaining forest range. These forests are not, in general, being replaced by new forest growth, and the animal requires a forest habitat.

Conservation and Recovery

The northern patches of forest inhabited by the Coquerel's dwarf lemur are not well protected and are disappearing; the prospects for the animal's survival in northern Madagascar are very slim. In the south-central patches of forest, the Coquerel's dwarf lemur appears in three protected areas; the Bemarah Strict Nature Reserve, farther south in the Analabe Private Reserve, and slightly farther south in the Andranomena Special Reserve. Until recently, these areas were not well protected, although Bemarah is receiving special attention from the Malagasy government and private conservation organizations. Each area is under pressure from people clearing their forests for agriculture.

Experiences at the Duke Primate Center indicate that the Coquerel's dwarf lemur can breed well in captivity, although the animal is rarely bred elsewhere in captivity. If the three reserves in which the animal is presently found are not adequately protected, then captive breeding may be its best hope for survival.

Gray Mouse Lemur

Microcebus murinus

Noel Rowe

Status	Endangered
Listed	June 2, 1970
Family	Cheirogaleidae (Dwarf lemurs)
Description	Soft, fluffy upper body fur is gray to grayish brown or reddish; underbody is grayish white.
Habitat	Rain forests, dry forests, swamps, and scrublands.
Food	Fruits, flowers, nectar, sap, gum, leaves, insects, and lizards; possibly small birds.
Reproduction	Gestation lasts 59 to 62 days, resulting in 2 to 3 young. Females can give birth twice a year.
Threats	Loss of habitat; predation by owls.
Range	Madagascar

Description

An adult gray mouse lemur, *Microcebus murinus*, is 4.5 to 5.25 inches in head-and-body length, with a tail of 5.25 inches. It generally weighs about 2 ounces, but stores fat on its body and can weigh as much as 3.5 ounces. It consumes its store of fat during dry seasons when food is scarce. It does not regulate its internal body temperature well, and as a consequence, its temperature can vary from 77 to 95 degrees Fahrenheit depending on ambient temperatures. When its body temperature becomes low, it becomes torpid and dependent on its reserves of fat.

It is usually gray, grayish brown, or reddish brown on its back and sides, and grayish white on its underbody and between its eyes. Its fur is soft and fluffy, and its tail is bushy. The ears are low on the side of the head, slightly behind the eyes. The ears are oval and are mobile, moving independently to pick up sounds; the gray mouse lemur can hear ultrasound. The eyes are dark and round, set close together; they shine when light, as from a flashlight, is pointed at them. The nose is narrow and dark, with prominent nostrils.

Other common names include lesser mouse lemur and least mouse lemur.

Behavior

Perhaps what one first notices about a gray mouse lemur is how it moves: It tends to sprint, punctuating the sprinting with leaps of up to 10 feet. Its tiny size allows it to live among the fine branches of trees, seeking food where heavier animals cannot go. Thus, in a high canopied forest, the gray mouse lemur may live over a hundred feet above the ground, sprinting along thin branches and leaping from one slender branch to another. The lower the fine branches are to be found, the lower the gray mouse lemur is to found, until, in the absence of trees, it lives on the ground. It seems to prefer dense forests, both rain forests and dry forests, but it seems to most require dense ground growth; even where there are no trees, it will try to make do with dense brush and grass, especially reeds. It also makes an effort to adapt to what humans do to the land in its range, and it is not only found in secondary forests, but in garbage dumps and gardens. However, it is healthiest when living among tall trees.

Although it sometimes forages alone, it is a highly social animal. It is a nocturnal animal, and during the day it sleeps in groups, sometimes in nests made of leaves and sometimes in tree hollows. The nests are usually high among tree branches and are hard to see from the ground because they are small and their leaves tend to blend them in with their surroundings; when trees are unavailable, nests are built on the ground. When asleep, the grey mouse lemurs curl up and lie atop one another. At night they forage and hunt, but they also gather together to groom and to make cries to each other. They are territorial, but the territories are shared and seem more governed by how much food is available in a given radius than by other factors; overlap-ping of territories, especially of males and females, is common. A grey mouse lemur marks its territory in part by urinating on its hands and then rubbing the urine on its feet, leaving a scent trail wherever it wanders. Males also use scent glands near the anus.

The gray mouse lemur is an eclectic eater, but its diet consists mostly of fruit and insects. It will eat flowers, nectar, sap, gum, and leaves, where available, and preys on lizards, especially chameleons, and possibly small birds. When eating, it sits upright. Its dexterous hands will often hold the food.

An individual female is able to give birth twice a year. Gestation lasts about two months, usually resulting in twins, although triplets are common. The mother eats the afterbirth and then grooms her young thoroughly. An infant lemur's eyes open after 4 days of life. After about two weeks it is able to move about, and it is weaned after 45 days. Play is very important for the young, who sprint, climb, and leap about, often climbing on their mother and even tweaking her ears. This play teaches them hunting skills. Gray mouse lemurs become sexually mature between 7 and 10 months of age.

Habitat

The gray mouse lemur seems to prefer tall forests with ample ground cover, but it is known to inhabit virtually treeless savannah and scrublands, where it builds its nests on the ground. It lives in greater densities in forested areas and seems to breed better in forests; individual animals are heavier and in better health in forested lands.

Distribution

The gray mouse lemur is still found in patches of wildlands throughout the inland areas of Madagascar, extending from the Ankarana Special Reserve in the north to the Beza-Mahafaly Special Reserve in the south.

Threats

The gray mouse lemur is one of the most widespread of all lemurs, but its once great forests are mostly gone, and even the scrublands to which it has adapted are giving way to desertification. Preservation of the gray mouse lemur requires preservation of central Madagascar's ecosystem, and the preservation of the ecosystem is important to humans, as well. When the land becomes so biologically poor that the gray mouse lemur cannot live on it, the land will have little left to offer people.

Conservation and Recovery

At present, little is being done specifically to conserve the gray mouse lemur. It lives in several protected wildlife areas, most notably the Ankarana Special Reserve at the northern end of the gray lemur's range, the Beza-Mahafaly Special Reserve south of the Onilahy river in southern Madagascar, and the Berenty Private Reserve in southeastern Madagascar. The special reserves are closed to most exploitation, and in general special permission is required in order to enter them. Berenty is a tourist attraction, and the gray mouse lemur is a favorite for those who wish to observe animals active at night: They are tiny animals with eyes that shine out of the dark when lamps catch them in their glow.

Although the gray mouse lemur breeds very well in captivity, few zoos have adopted it for breeding programs.

Pygmy Mouse Lemur

Microcebus myoxinus

Russell A. Mittermeier

Status	Endangered
Listed	June 2, 1970
Family	Cheirogaleidae (Mouse lemurs)
Description	Grayish brown to red; face is fine boned with a prominent nose; eyes are set close together, ears are oval and set low on the head.
Habitat	Rain forests, and possibly dry deciduous forests and scrublands.
Food	Fruits, flowers, nectar, insects.
Reproduction	1 to 3 young after gestation of about 60 days.
Threats	Loss of habitat.
Range	Madagascar

Description

Little has been recorded about the pygmy mouse lemur, *Microcebus myoxinus*, and the data in this article should be taken as approximations that need to be confirmed by further study. Taxonomy for the pygmy mouse lemur was disputed until 1992 when it was described fully. It is now accepted as a full species rather than a variant of the gray mouse lemur (*Microcebus murinus*; see separate entry).

An adult pygmy mouse lemur is 2 to 4 inches in head-and-body length, with a tail of 5.4 inches. It generally weighs about 1.5 ounces, but it probably stores fat on its body during the wet season and lives partly off the fat during the dry season, which means its weight fluctuates considerably depending on how plentiful food is. Like other mouse lemurs, it does not regulate its internal body temperature well, and when the temperature of its environment drops, particularly during dry periods, its body temperature becomes low, and it becomes torpid. This would not be true hibernation, but the pygmy mouse lemur would nonetheless be dependent on its store of fat for survival.

Its fur is soft and usually grayish brown or reddish brown. The pygmy lemur's face is fine boned with a prominent nose. The eyes are round and set close together, slightly separated by the bridge of the nose. The ears are oval and set low on the head. Pygmy mouse lemurs are the smallest of all primates.

Behavior

The pygmy mouse lemur is nocturnal, and forages alone at night. During the day it sleeps in small groups of two or three members in nests made of leaves or in tree hollows. Like the gray mouse lemurs, pygmy mouse lemurs curl up and lie atop one another while asleep. They are probably territorial, but their territories probably overlap one another. They probably mark their territories with urine, feces, and scent glands.

Like its close relatives the gray mouse lemur (*Microcebus murinus*) and the brown mouse lemur (*Microcebus rufus*; see separate entry), the pygmy mouse lemur is apparently a great leaper, capable of leaping as much as 10 feet from one tree branch to another. Its low weight allows it to venture high into tree tops where thin branches would not support the weight of most other lemurs, and it seems to inhabit a forest from its canopy to its middle level. It is possible that it descends to the ground and may even be able to survive in a terrestrial habitat, making its nests on the ground where trees are absent. Even so, its only confirmed environment is in a dense forest.

The pygmy mouse lemur is a good, fierce hunter that tracks the movements of its prey at night with keen hearing and eyes adapted to gathering light in the dark. Its principal prey are insects, but spiders, lizards, and small birds are also likely prey. During the wet season, it principally eats fruit, relying more on prey and other foods such as flowers when fruits are scarce.

Habitat

The pygmy mouse lemur lives in dense forest, but the full diversity of habitats it can live in is not yet known.

Distribution

The pygmy mouse lemur is found in a very limited area of west central Madagascar, but the full extent of its range, which could be similar to that of the gray mouse lemur, is not yet recorded.

Threats

The pygmy mouse lemur's woodlands are being cleared by logging and for cultivation and the grazing of livestock. Local peoples are somewhat in conflict with migrants from the south, who have brought with them the practice of slash-and-burn agriculture. Until more is known about the pygmy mouse lemur's adaptability, it must be assumed that the loss of its forest will mean its extinction. Human predation does not appear to be a problem for the small, elusive animal.

Conservation and Recovery

It is possible that a population of pygmy mouse lemurs lives in the Ankarana Special Reserve, where scientific study is emphasized and visitors must have government permits. The reserve and all the wildlands near it are shrinking because of logging, the felling of trees to make charcoal, and clearing for agriculture.

Brown Mouse Lemur

Microcebus rufus

Noel Rowe

Status	Endangered
Listed	June 2, 1970
Family	Cheirogaleidae (Dwarf and mouse lemurs)
Description	Coat is mostly brown to gray; the underbody is white.
Habitat	Rainforests
Food	Fruit, flowers, and insects.
Reproduction	Gestation lasts 60 days.
Threats	Loss of habitat.
Range	Madagascar

Description

The brown mouse lemur, *Microcebus rufus*, is shaped like a mouse, with a pointy snout. Its eyes are round and set forward on the face, with the mobile, oval ears set not far behind. Its fur is thick and woolly. It gets its name from the gray-brown to gray coloring of most of its fur, although its underbody is white. Its head-and-body length is 5 inches, with its tail adding another 4.5 inches. It weighs about 2 ounces, although its weight can fluctuate from 1.3 to 3 ounces, depending on how much fat it has stored in its tail. Dur-ing wet periods, the brown mouse lemur deposits fat in its tail, but during dry periods it is supplements its diet with the fat stored in the tail.

Other common names are rufous mouse lemur and brown lesser mouse lemur.

Behavior

The brown mouse lemur is a fierce little creature that sometimes attacks insect prey larger than itself; it also eats fruit. It has an acute sense of smell, which it uses to find fruits and prey in the dark. The agility of the brown mouse lemur is remarkable; it can dart through branches speedily. Its leaping ability is also remarkable, for it can leap as far as 10 feet from one branch to another.

The brown mouse lemur is a solitary forager. A nocturnal animal, it sleeps during the day high in trees in spherical leaf nests, in tree hollows, or in abandoned bird nests. Mothers sleep with their infants. During cool, dry periods, the brown mouse lemur will sometimes become torpid and live off its fat; this state probably occurs because the animal has trouble controlling its body temperature, which drops perilously when the weather is cool. Although the brown mouse lemur is one of the most populous of lemurs, little has been recorded of its behavior because it moves at night and is very hard to see.

Mating season in the wild is from September to October with births of 1 to 3 young occurring in November/December. In captivity, 2 birth seasons have occurred.

Habitat

The brown mouse lemur prefers rain forests and is usually found living on the forest fringes. It is possible that it can adapt to secondary forests.

Distribution

The brown mouse lemur is found throughout eastern Madagascar, from the far north to the far south.

Threats

Its forest habitat is being cut down at a great rate, and its eastern forest habitat now exists in patches rather than as continuous forest.

Conservation and Recovery

The brown mouse lemur lives on several wildlife reserves. The one that remains the most intact is Nosy Mangabe Special Reserve, which is on an island occupied only by scientists who are there to study the wildlife. Ranomafana National Park, where brown mouse lemurs are most easily seen, is open to tourism.

Fork-marked Lemur

Phaner furcifer

Jean-Jacques Petter, Paris Zoological Park

Status	Endangered
Listed	June 2, 1970
Family	Cheirogaleidae (Dwarf and mouse lemurs)
Description	Dense golden or brown fur with a deep-brown stripe on its back which splits on the nape into a stripe above each eye extending down to the nose. Hands, feet and tail are darker.
Habitat	Deciduous forests and wooded open areas associated with the presence of baobabs.
Food	Tree gum, fruit, nectar, and insects.
Reproduction	Mating is seasonal, occurring in June. Single births occur in November.
Threats	Destruction of habitat by burning and cutting.
Range	Northwestern Madagascar

Description

The fork-marked lemur, *Phaner furcifer*, is distinguished by dense golden or brown fur notable for the deep-brown stripe on its back which splits on the nape into a stripe above each eye extending down to the nose. The hands, feet, and tail are darker in color than the rest of the body. From head to tail this lemur measures 8.9 to 11.2 inches. Its weight is from 12.3 to 21.2 ounces. The tail is 11.8 to 14.6 inches long. This species is somewhat solitary and territorial, with male territories more likely to overlap than those of females. The fork-marked lemur is known for its loud, piercing vocalizations.

The fork-marked lemur is also known as tanta, tantaraolana, vakiandrina, and vakivoho.

Behavior

The fork-marked lemur feeds primarily on gums, scraping bark off with modified incisors and lapping resinous sap. It also feeds on fruit, nectar, and insect secretions.

The fork-marked lemur is nocturnal. This species spends the day in holes in trees or in dense foliage. When active, the male fork-marked lemur makes about 30 loud calls per hour. These calls probably help it keep track of other members of its species. Males use their throat gland to mark females. No territorial scent marking has been reported.

Young are born in holes in trees and are then cared for by their mothers. When moving about, the mothers carry their infants in their mouths.

Habitat

The fork-marked lemur is restricted to the deciduous forest and wooded open areas of Ankarana Special Reserve, Madagascar. Dominant canopy trees include the *Dalbergia* species and the *Cassia* species, various figs, and the babobab, *Adansonia madagascariensis*. The shrub layer includes numerous palms; epiphytes (air plants) are few but include many specimens of a vanilla orchid with its leafless, green stems which cling to tree trunks.

Distribution

This species is known only from scattered patches in Madagascar (mostly in the west) and occurs in Ankarana Special Reserve, 40 miles south of Diégo Suarez to the southwest of Anivorano. Population densities of 80 to 2254 per square mile have been recorded. The higher numbers have been reported on the basis of counting a small number of animals in gum-rich areas and do not reflect the animal's overall density in its ranges.

The fork-marked lemur has only recently begun to be studied closely by scientists. Its subspecies and their distribution are little understood. At least four subspecies have been identified by naturalists C. P. Groves and Ian Tattersall, and other subspecies may soon be identified.

Threats

The fork-marked lemur's habitat is being destroyed by wildfires and deforestation for agriculture.

Conservation and Recovery

The fork-marked lemur is protected from killing and capturing under the laws of the Malagasy Republic and may be found in several wildlife reserves. Poaching is a significant problem. It is listed in class A of the African Convention and in CITES, Appendix I: Trade Prohibited.

Lemurs
Family: Lemuridae

Ring-Tailed Lemur (*Lemur catta*)

Rich Block

General Characteristics of the *Lemuridae*

The lemurs of Madagascar represent a frustrating near miss for biologists: Until the last few thousand years, the island had a vastly diverse population of lemurs, all probably descended from early lemurlike primates that may have drifted on debris to Madagascar 50 to 60 million years ago. The many lemurs that evolved could have told biologists much about how creatures evolve to take advantage of opportunities offered by their environment, but with the arrival of humans, most of the large lemurs were killed or died from loss of habitat, and many of the remaining lemurs are so rare that they are hard to keep track of for scientific study and are fast dying out as humans eliminate their native forests. Fossils from the period when the lemurs would have been evolving are very rare, probably because the climate of Madagascar at the time was unsuited to the making of fossils. Consequently, biologists have only the living lemurs to study in order to learn about their evolution, but the once great diversity of types of lemur has been lost.

Of the surviving families of lemurs, *Lemuridae* is the most diverse and is usually divided into four genera: *Eulemur* (typical lemurs), *Hapalemur* (gentle lemurs), *Varecia* (ruffed lemurs), and *Lemur* (ring-tailed lemurs). Until 1988, all species that are now classified as *Eulemur* were regarded as *Lemur*. Authorities disagree about the classification of the sportive lemurs, *Lepilemurinae*; some (including the *IUCN Red Data Book*) regard the sportive lemurs as a distinct family, *Megaladapidae*.

Subfamily *Lemurinae*

The typical lemurs walk on all fours, with their rumps somewhat higher than their shoulders because their hind limbs are longer than their forelimbs. The hind limbs are probably an adaptation for leaping great distances because their longer length gives them greater leverage than short legs would. Hence, typical lemurs often leap to escape threats, and they often leap to get from one tree to another. With the exception of the ring-tail lemur (*Lemur catta*), typical lemurs are primarily arboreal and avoid the ground, descending to it only occasionally. On the other hand, like domesticated cats to which they are often compared, ring-tailed lemurs choose to go their own way regardless of what the other typical lemurs do, and spend much of their lives on the ground.

The typical lemurs have lower incisors and canines that thrust somewhat forward, forming a comb of teeth that are used for grooming as well as opening food. In general, typical lemurs eat fruits, flowers, buds, and leaves, supplemented by insects. They also tend to be territorial, with each individual species having evolved behavior that enables individual animals or groups of them to defend their territory from members of their own species that live outside their territory. Most typical lemurs form groups, and these groups are usually the focus for establishing and retaining territories.

Subfamily *Hapalemurinae*

Only two species of *Hapalemurinae* survive, the grey gentle lemur (*Hapalemur griseus*), which has four distinct subspecies, and the greater bamboo lemur (*Hapalemur simus*). These lemurs have a specialized diet of bamboo; their upper canines are designed to strip open bamboo shoots. Like typical lemurs, they have lower teeth that project forward and form a comb. Their fur is thick, and their ears are furry. The walk on all fours and sometimes leap; those that live near water can swim. They tend to live in small groups. They are threatened by the destruction of the bamboo and reeds on which they depend for food and shelter, and they are hunted for their meat.

Subfamily *Lepilemurinae* (or *Megaladapidae*)

For authorities who regard the sportive lemur to be part of the *Lemuridae* family, the subfamily *Lepilemurinae* has only one species (*Lepilemur mustelinus*) and numerous subspecies. If the sportive lemur is treated as a separate family *Megaladapidae,*then each member is treated as a full species. One of the largest lemurs, *Megaladopsis,* was probably a sportive lemur. An adult *Megaladopsis* weighed 110 pounds, was arboreal, and moved by climbing with its powerful limbs; it did not swing (brachiate) or leap.

Sportive lemurs are widely adaptable to a variety of forest types. They eat mostly leaves, but also eat fruits, flowers, and even bark. Like the typical lemurs, sportive lemurs have long hind legs that can propel them nearly twenty feet through the air. They are arboreal, traveling from tree to tree by leaping, and their ability to leap a great distance means that they can sometimes survive in sparse wooded forests where there are small open spaces between trees. They are active at night, sleeping in tree hollows during the day.

Crowned Lemur

Eulemur coronatus

Noel Rowe

Status	Endangered
Listed	June 2, 1970
Family	Lemuridae (Lemurs)
Description	Bright orange crown that crosses above its forehead in a V shape; males are overall brown; females overall gray.
Habitat	Both deciduous dry forests and evergreen rain forests.
Food	Fruits and, rarely, leaves.
Reproduction	Gestation lasts approximately 125 days, probably resulting in a single birth.
Threats	Loss of habitat and human predation.
Range	Madagascar

Description

The crowned lemur's, *Eulemur coronatus*, genders are distinguished by their coloration; both sexes are notably beautiful animals. The adult male crowned lemur has an overall orange-to-tan coat with highlights of dark gray through the back and reddish brown on the hands and feet. It underbody is white, as are its muzzle, circles around its eyes, and the insides of its ear. The cheeks are a pale orange that blends upward into a rich orange V across its forehead, dipping toward the face. Its cap is a deep, dark gray. The adult female crowned lemur is overall silver gray, with a white underbody, throat, and cheeks. Its face is a mix of white and gray. Like the male, it has a rich orange V that begins at one ear, dips toward the face, and then climbs to the other ear. There is also a splash of orange near the base of its tail. Some all-white females (save for the orange crown) have been reported. Both adult males and adult females are 12.5 to 14 inches from head to tail, with a tail length of 16.5 to 20 inches. They weigh about 4.5 pounds. The face features a long muzzle, like that of a chihuahua, tipped by black whiskers and a small black nose. The eyes are set well apart and are recessed back of the muzzle. The ears extend outward and extend vertically along nearly the entire sides of the head.

Another common name is Ankomba.

Behavior

Not much about the crowned lemur's habits have been recorded, although scientific studies are underway and are likely soon to yield much more information about the animal's natural history. There is a sense of urgency to the studies, which have been inspired in part by the impending extinction of the crowned lemur.

Crowned lemurs live in loose groups consisting of 3 to 11 males and females, with a mixture of adults and young. These groups have territories that vary in size according to the abundance or scarcity of food. Males scent-mark their territory with anal glands. They also mark territory by rubbing their foreheads on objects, a behavior that is prevalent a few days before females come into estrus. Crowned lemurs do not seem particularly defensive about their territories and can be pushed out of them by intruding members of other species of lemurs. On the other hand, group members are very protective of infants and will vigorously defend them. Although there seems to be no dominance hierarchy among crowned lemurs, a group is led by an adult female. Being leisurely diners, crowned lemurs can linger far behind their leader, with the group slowly coalescing during a rest period. The crowned lemurs are vocal animals, letting one another know where they are with loud chirps and yelps.

Crowned lemurs are cathemeral, active both night and day. They live according to a twenty-four hour cycle that features foraging for food punctuated by periods of rest. They eat almost exclusively fruit, taking what is seasonally available. When fruit is scarce in their habitat, they raid cultivated orchards or fall back to leaves or insects.

Crowned lemurs spend much of their time walking on the ground — much more time than most other species of lemurs. Being accustomed to traveling on the ground may account for their willingness to adapt to life in partially cleared forest; the canopy may be lost, and trees may be too far apart for jumping from one to another, which would exclude many other lemur species, but the crowned lemur is willing to walk from tree to tree.

Mating seems to be seasonal, with times of birth differing among crowned lemur groups according the season of greatest abundance of fruit in their particular region, mostly between September and November, but as late as May. A newborn clings to its mother's underbody when she is moving about, but moves to her back when it gets older. Sexual maturity is reached in about 20 months.

Habitat

The crowned lemur's preferred habitat is deciduous dry forest, typical of much of far northern Madagascar. It is attempting to adapt to the destruction of its forests by moving into montane rain forest.

Distribution

The crowned lemur lives in far northern Madagascar, from the northernmost tip to as far south as the Ankarana Special Reserve.

Threats

Clear-cut logging has destroyed most of the crowned lemur's habitat. In 1988 to 1989, a foreign logging company clear-cut nearly an entire forest, wiping out populations of crowned lemurs and other animals. Humans hunt the crowned lemurs for food. One of the ways crowned lemurs are trying to adapt to the loss of their native habitat is to inhabit farmlands, and farmers therefore kill them as pests that raid their crops.

Conservation and Recovery

The crowned lemur is found Montagne d'Ambre National Park, where intense poaching is threatening it. It exists in its greatest densities in the Ankarana Special Reserve near the west coast, but is threatened there by illegal logging. It is also found in the Analamera Special Reserve, near the east coast, where the rainy season helps to protect it by making roads to it impassable. The World Wildlife Fund is working to develop the Analamera Special Reserve into a wildlife park that tourists could visit; the special reserve needs more protection from poachers and from logging companies. Hit-and-run logging companies have illegally felled much of the reserve's forest.

Brown-collared Lemur

Eulemur fulvus collaris

Noel Rowe

Status	Endangered
Listed	June 2, 1970; June 14, 1976; June 24, 1976.
Family	Lemuridae (lemurs)
Description	Males have a brown neck, face, ears, and top of head, females are gray. Both sexes have pale orange cheeks which are bushy in the male.
Habitat	Rain forests.
Food	Fruits and leaves.
Reproduction	Generally a single infant after a 120-day gestation period.
Threats	Hunting, trapping, and loss of habitat due to agricultural development.
Range	Southeastern Madagascar

Description

The brown-collared lemur is one of six subspecies of the brown lemur (*Eulemur fulvus*). It weighs between 4.5 and 6 pounds. The males tend to have a black neck, face, ears, and top of head, while these parts are gray in the female. Both sexes have pale orange cheeks which are bushy in the male. The upperparts are dark brown or gray-brown with a darker stripe down the spine. The underparts are paler.

Behavior

The collared lemur is diurnal and generally feeds on fruit and leaves, flowers, bark, sap, dirt and insects, especially centipedes and millipedes.

Females become sexually mature at 10 months and males at 24 months of age. After a 120-day gestation period, females generally give birth to a single infant. The birthing season is August through November.

Brown lemurs, *E. fulvus*, form mixed

groups of 13 to 18 members. The group appears to be cohesive with no particular hierarchy.

Habitat

The brown-collared lemur is found in primary closed canopy forest and deciduous forest above 1,312 feet.

Distribution

The brown-collared lemur is distributed in southeastern Madagascar, from Taolanaro (Fort Dauphin) northward to the Mananara River. Its exact limits are not well established.

Threats

The brown-collared lemur is hunted for food, and it is trapped to sell as pets. Deforestation is a greater threat than hunting; the brown-collared lemur's region is rapidly being denuded by clear-cutting.

Conservation and Recovery

The brown-collared lemur is common in the Andohahela Special Reserve, located 25 miles north of Fort Dauphin, containing 155,857 acres with a wide altitudinal range, from 330 feet to the 6,417-foot Pic d'Andohahela. There is currently underway in this reserve a management and conservation development program proposed and funded by the Department of Water and Forests, the University of Madagascar, the World Wildlife

Fund, and USAID. The Malagasy government is protecting the brown-collared lemur by only allowing accredited scientists with officially sanctioned projects into the animal's habitat. The brown-collared lemur has been inserted in the Berenty Private Reserve, but there they are in danger of interbreeding with the red-fronted lemur (*Eulemur fulvus rufus*).

In June of 1994, there were 39 brown-collared lemurs captive in 6 institutions. Of these animals, 95% were captive born.

Sclater's [=Blue-eyed] Lemur

Eulemur macaco flavifrons

Noel Rowe

Status	Endangered
Listed	June 2, 1970; June 14, 1976; June 24, 1976.
Family	Lemuridae (Lemurs).
Description	Males are black and females are reddish-tan; both sexes have blue eyes and no ear tufts.
Habitat	Humid evergreen forests of north-west Madagascar.
Food	Primarily omnivorous.
Reproduction	Generally give birth to a single infant after a 125-day gestation period.
Threats	Hunting, trapping, and habitat destruction for agricultural development.
Range	Northwestern Madagascar

Description

Sclater's lemur, *Eulemur macaco flavifrons*, is a subspecies of the black lemur, *Eulemur macaco* (see separate entry). They measure 13.8 to 15.8 inches from snout to tail. The tail is 17.7 to 19.7 inches long. They generally weigh 4.5 to 5.5 pounds.

Males are black, sometimes with a brown tint to the fur, most notably on the abdomen and chest. The females have a reddish-tan coat. Both sexes have bright blue or blue-green eyes and no ear tufts.

Behavior

Sclater's lemurs travel in multimale and multifemale groups consisting of 6 to 10 members. They become sexually mature at approximately 20 to 24 months of age. After a 125-day gestation period, they generally give birth to a single infant, usually in the period from August through November. Immediately following birth, the infants are able to grip the mother's fur strongly; initially they ride ventrally, but after about 4 weeks they switch to the mother's back. At 2 months of age, although still carried by its mother when moving with the group, the infant explores its environment and begins tasting various foods. By 6 months of age, the infant no longer rides on its mother's back and is completely independent.

This subspecies' diet is dominated by fruits during the rainy season and by leaves during the dry season. Water is primarily obtained by drinking from tree holes. Sclater's lemurs are active throughout the day and night, but seem to forage for food primarily at night. This may be a response to the threat posed by humans during daylight, but it may simply be the animals' ordinary behavior.

Habitat

This subspecies is found in the humid evergreen forests of northwest Madagascar.

Distribution

Sclater's lemur is reported to occur in northwest Madagascar from the Andranomalaza River in the north to the Sandrakota River in the south. They do not occur in any protected areas.

Threats

Sclater's lemur is very rare and near extinction. It is hunted and trapped for trade. This subspecies is additionally threatened by habitat destruction for agricultural development. Only small patches of its forest habitat remain, and these are threatened with imminent destruction.

Conservation and Recovery

Sclater's lemur was believed to be extinct until it was rediscovered in 1983 in a tiny range in northwestern Madagascar.

In 1988, France's Strasbourg University and the Mulhouse Zoo proposed a conservation program for Sclater's lemur to the Malagasy Government. This plan included captive breeding efforts, field studies, creating a special reserve within its range, and training a Malagasy student to work on the project. Cologne Zoo, Saarbruken Zoo, and the Duke University Primate Center have joined this program.

In December 1993, there were 34 captive Sclater's lemurs in four institutions: Koln Zoo, Mulhouse Zoo, Ivoloina, and the Duke University Primate Center. In the four institutions that house these animals, 65% of the animals are captive born and 35% are wild born; there were 5 captive births from December 1992 to December 1993, and only 1 death occurred within the first 30 days of life.

All lemur species are listed in CITES, Appendix I: Trade Prohibited. Sclater's lemur is also listed in class A of the African Convention

Black Lemur

Eulemur macaco macaco

Black lemur female   David Haring

Status	Endangered
Listed	June 2, 1970; June 14, 1976
Family	Lemuridae (Lemurs)
Description	Males are jet black with black ear tufts; females are light brown with white ear tufts.
Habitat	Primary and secondary ever-green forests and plantations.
Food	Fruit, flowers, leaves, and bark.
Reproduction	Single infant after a 128-day gestation period.
Threats	Habitat destruction due to agricultural development, logging practices, and incidental death.
Range	Northwest Madagascar, Nosy Bé Island, and Nosy Komba Island.

Description

The black lemur, *Eulemur macaco macaco*, is 13.8 to 15.8 inches long, measured from snout to tail; the tail is 17.7 to 19.7 inches long. This species generally weighs about 4.41 pounds. Males are jet black with black ear tufts; females are light brown with long white ear tufts and have darker faces. Both males and females have brown eyes.

Behavior

Although two to three hundred black lemurs are held in captivity, very little is known about their behavior in the wild. They live in groups with 5 to 15 members, most of whom are male. Females seem to dominate the group social life. Groups join together during the night.

The black lemur is cathemeral. It is arboreal, moving with great agility among branches, and prefers to live in unbroken forest canopy. Even so, it adapts well to agricultural lands and seems to achieve population densities greater on plantations than in their natural habitat. They are unafraid of humans and because of this they have become tourist attractions on Nosy Komba. There the locals only kill the animal if it is a crop pest, otherwise harming them is considered taboo. In villages, the black lemur eats bananas offered them by the locals and by tourists, who are able to get close to the animals without fear because of the black lemur's calm, passive nature. When not being fed by humans, the black lemur eats fruits, flowers, leaves, and bark.

Habitat

The black lemur is found in primary and secondary humid forests of northwest Madagascar and on the islands of Nosy Bé and Nosy Komba.

Distribution

The black lemur lives in a small area (about 4.5 square miles) in the Lokobe Natural Reserve and on Nosy Bé Island.

Threats

The black lemur is threatened by habitat destruction caused by agricultural development, logging, and incidental fire from slash-and-burn agriculture. It is also hunted to stop its raiding of agricultural crops.

Conservation and Recovery

Poaching is reported to be a problem in the Lokobe Natural Resere on Nosy Bé, but it may be secure in the mountainous Tsaratanana Reserve on the mainland because of the region's remoteness from humans.

Captive breeding programs have resulted in a high degree of success for the black lemur. Populations bred in captivity are considered to be self-sustaining. The international studbook for captive breeding is kept at the St. Louis Zoological Park.

The hunting of black lemurs is restricted under the laws of the Malagasy Republic. The black lemur is also listed in class A of the African Convention.

Mongoose Lemur

Eulemur mongoz

David Haring

Status	Endangered
Listed	June 2, 1970
Family	Lemuridae (Lemurs)
Description	Brown backs, gray heads and shoulders, and reddish brown sides; white chests and throats; males tend to have orange bellies and reddish-brown to gray tails; females tend to have white bellies and black tails.
Habitat	Primarily dry deciduous forest; also rainforests and secondary forest.
Food	Nectar, flowers, fruits, leaves.
Reproduction	Gestation lasts 128 days, usually resulting in a single birth.
Threats	Loss of habitat and human predation.
Range	Madagascar

Description

Adult mongoose lemurs, *Eulemur Mongoz*, are about 13.8 inches in head-and-body length, with tails of equal length or a bit longer. They weigh 3.6 to 4 pounds. The genders are sexually dichromatic: Both tend to have overall dark brown to dark gray coats, with brown to red-brown backs, reddish brown sides, and dark gray heads and shoulders. Their chests and throats tend to be white. Males have light gray faces with a splash of white across their noses; their chins and cheeks are orange; their bellies are or-

ange, shading toward yellow; their tails are reddish brown and gray. Females have black faces, with a splash of white across their noses; chin and cheeks are white; their heads tend to be darker gray than the heads of males; their bellies are white; their tails are black. Some adult males have coloring more like that of females than that of the majority of males. The fur is long and soft.

Behavior

In the 1980s and 1990s, naturalists have

made special efforts to find and observe this extremely rare and very elusive animal, but much of their data is contradictory. One important confusion that seems to have been sorted out is that of the mongoose lemur's period of activity: Some observers have declared it to be nocturnal and others have declared it to be diurnal. Naturalist Ian Tattersall and others put together long term observations and noted that the mongoose lemur was nocturnal during the dry season and diurnal during the rainy season, which indicates that the mongoose lemur's period of activity changes with changes in the climate. Although reasons for this have not been established, a likely possibility is that predators, including humans, are much more active in the dry season than the wet season, so the mongoose lemur adjusts to moving at night during the period when predators, mostly diurnal animals, are most active, thus making it harder for predators to track their movements.

In their Madagascar range, mongoose lemurs form small family groups, with an adult male, an adult female, and one or two offspring. The adult male and adult female remain bonded for several years, probably for life. The family groups have territories of 3 acres. Family groups can be either rarely aggressive when they meet or highly agitated when they meet. On the islands of Moheli and Anjouan, mongoose lemurs gather in large groups that lack social structure, and males and females do not form long-term bonds. Mutual grooming seems to be the only social interaction among the lemurs. These differences between the mongoose lemurs of Madagascar and those of the Comoro Islands indicate that social behavior is learned in the species; it may also indicate that social behavior is affected by the environment, because the Madagascar mongoose lemurs live mostly in dry forests whereas those on the Comoro Islands live in rain forests; it may indicate that under severe pressure from humans, the social structure of the mongoose lemur breaks down — the mongoose lemurs on the Comoro Islands have lost almost all their habitat and are nearer to extermination than those on Madagascar; another possibility is that naturalists are observing two different subspecies that are distinguished by their behavioral differences.

Mating may be seasonal, resulting in births in October. The young are weaned at 5 months of age, and they may become sexually mature at 18 months of age.

Habitat

The mongoose lemur prefers to live in dry deciduous forests with a cycle of dry and wet seasons. When dry forests are unavailable, as on the islands of Moheli and Anjouan, they will live in rain forests. In areas that have been cleared of primary forest that has been replaced by secondary forest, they will live in relatively low population densities. They seem unable to adapt to areas that are devoid of trees; their diet consists almost entirely of tree products.

Distribution

The mongoose lemur lives in a small coastal range in northwestern Madagascar and on the Comoro Islands of Moheli and Anjouan. It was probably brought to the islands several hundred years ago by humans.

Threats

The mongoose lemur is very dependent on the food trees provide it, especially flowering trees during the dry season. When the trees disappear, the mongoose lemur dies. All of its range is being clear-cut by logging, the gathering of wood to make charcoal, and farmers creating new grasslands on which to graze their livestock, and slash-and-burn agriculture. Woodlands are also burned in the dry season in order to drive out lemurs that are then killed for food. The loss of habitat and hunting by humans have made the mongoose lemur extremely rare.

The forests on Anjouan are very nearly wiped out; only tiny patches on steep terrain exist. There and on Moheli, the mongoose lemurs are killed for entertainment, even though some local peoples have taboos against eating them. The thousands of migrants from Madagascar are killing and eating the few remaining mongoose lemurs on the two smaller islands.

Conservation and Recovery

The Ankarafantsika Strict Nature Reserve and the nearby Ampijeroa Forestry Station have some mongoose lemurs, although most live near but outside these protected areas. The small staff in Ankarafantsika has been fighting a desperate but losing battle to protect the reserve from poaching and destruction by loggers, charcoal makers, and slash-and-burn farmers. The World Bank and other international organizations are trying to relieve pressure from the reserve by investing in local economic development; the underlying idea is that if local people have sources of income not dependent on abusing the land and are able to adequately feed, clothe, and house themselves, that they will be less likely to exploit wildlands. The success of this effort remains to be seen; it has not worked elsewhere, for instance in Brazil, where people with jobs not related to environmental exploitation eat endangered primate species in restaurants, rather than hunting the animals themselves.

Red-bellied Lemur

Eulemur rubriventer

Russell A. Mittermeier

Status	Endangered
Listed	June 2, 1970
Family	Lemuridae (Lemurs)
Description	Long, rusty brown fur; males have red-brown underbodies and white eye patches; females have white underbodies and cheeks.
Habitat	Rainforests
Food	Fruit, flowers, and young leaves, according to seasonal availability, and possibly insects.
Reproduction	Gestation lasts 123 days, usually resulting in a single birth.
Threats	Loss of habitat and human predation.
Range	Madagascar

Description

Adult red-bellied lemurs, *Eulemur rubriventer*, have a head-and-body length of about 16.5 inches, with tails of 18 inches; their weight is 4.5 to 5 pounds. The genders are somewhat dichromatic. Both have rusty brown or chestnut brown fur on their upper bodies, black tails, and dark faces. Males have white eye patches and red-brown underbodies; females have white to creamy-white underbodies and cheeks. Their heads are oval-shaped — longer from side-to-side than top-to-bottom. The fur is long. Their muzzles are catlike, with prominent nose bridges; their eyes are well apart and slightly angled; their oval-shaped ears are small, high on the head, and held close to the head.

Behavior

Almost every account of the red-bellied lemur includes the phrase or its equivalent: "poorly known." The animal is very rare and very thinly distributed throughout its range. It prefers to live in dense rain forest at high elevations; the terrain is often steep and wet and very hard for humans to traverse, making observing them in their natural habitat very difficult. Further, their coloration is ideal for the forests they inhabit; they live high in a thick tropical forest canopy, and their colors blend in with the background of branches and trunks. It is possible to be under one and not to see it.

Red-bellied lemurs form monogamous male-female bonds that appear to last for life. A typical group would consist of the bonded adult pair and two or three of their young, making groups of 4 or 5 members. Unattached males may form groups of 3 to 5 members. Breeding may be seasonal, with births possibly occurring in September and October. Gestation lasts 123 days, usually resulting in a single birth, although twins are common. The father shares in the carrying of youngsters as the family group travels, and youngsters sleep with their father as often as they sleep with their mother.

Red-bellied lemurs are cathemeral, meaning that they live on 24-hour cycles rather than diurnal or nocturnal ones. They alternate moving, foraging, and resting throughout the day and night. They live in the highest region of the canopy of the rain forest and therefore need to beware of raptors; a group posts a sentinel — any adult or nearly adult member of the group — to watch for predators while the other group members feed, play, or rest. Red-bellied lemurs seem to always have a guard posted.

Authorities disagree markedly over whether the red-bellied lemurs are territorial, with a few asserting that they exhibit little or no territorial behavior, but most asserting that they are very territorial. One possible explanation for this difference in observations may be that animals in a forest that has been recently damaged by humans have had their territories and even groups disrupted by the loss of habitat and therefore show little territoriality, whereas those in undisturbed habitat are able to mark and defend a territory for months or even years. Both males and females mark their territorial borders with glands located near their anuses, and males have a scent gland on their heads that they also use to mark boundaries. Boundary disputes between groups tend to be very noisy, but there seems to be no record of outright physical attacks.

The diet of the red-bellied lemur varies according to season and what is available in its territory. In the central eastern rain forests, red-bellied lemurs will feed on the flowers of eucalyptus trees, foreign imports from Australia. They tend to feed in these trees at night because their open structure of branches makes them vulnerable to raptors during the day. When fruits are plentiful, the red-bellied lemurs will eat almost nothing else. As seasons change, they will shift the proportions of their diet to favor flowers and will even eat young leaves. They play a part in the health of their forest: They spread pollen from flower to flower. Sometimes, they will descend all the way to the ground and eat dirt. Perhaps they do this to supplement their mineral intake, or perhaps they do it because minerals in the soil counteract toxins in the leaves they eat.

Habitat

Red-bellied lemurs live high in the canopy of rain forests on high elevations, along mountainsides and even the tops of mountains.

Distribution

The range of the red-bellied lemur is along the eastern highlands of Madagascar, usually far from the coast (it nears the coast at the Bay of Antongil), extending from the region of the Tsaratanana Strict Nature Reserve in the north to the spiny desert in the south.

Threats

Madagascar's eastern rain forests are being wiped out by slash-and-burn agriculture, the taking of trees to make charcoal, and logging. Efforts by the Malagasy government and wildlife protection groups are being met with much resistance from the local population in the south. The red-bellied lemur is presently very rare and only thinly distributed through the once-extensive but now narrow band of patchy eastern rain forest. Human predation as well as loss of habitat are reducing the red-bellied lemur's numbers to unsustainable levels.

Conservation and Recovery

The red-bellied lemur may be found in the Tsaratanana Strict Nature Reserve, although the reserve is under pressure from illegal clearing for cultivation and grazing of livestock, illegal logging, and poaching. It lingers in the steepest, most remote parts of the reserve. The red-bellied lemur also may be found in the new Ranomafana National Park, which is being developed by the Malagasy government, the World Wildlife Fund, and other organizations as a tourist attraction. Much of the national park is now spiny

desert, an environmental catastrophe that has encompassed most of southern Madagascar and which is moving northward. Much of the land around the national park is now unusable and the park itself is endangered. The red-bellied lemurs live in difficult to access high stands of old forest within the eastern area of the park.

Golden Bamboo Lemur

Hapalemur aureus

Noel Rowe

Status	Endangered
Listed	June 2, 1970
Family	Lemuridae (Lemurs)
Description	Dark reddish brown fur overall, with golden orange underbelly, bottom of the tail, and bands on the face.
Habitat	Rainforest that contains tracts of bamboo.
Food	Shoots and leaf bases of giant bamboo, bamboo grass, and fungi.
Reproduction	Probably seasonal; probably resulting in the birth of a single young.
Threats	Loss of habitat and human predation.
Range	Madagascar

Description

The discovery of the golden bamboo lemur, *Hapalemur aureus*, was first recorded in 1985; in 1987, two expeditions set out to find it in hopes that it was the long missing greater bamboo lemur (*Hapalemur simus*; see separate entry) that had not been seen for about 15 years. These expeditions found both the greater bamboo lemur and a new, colorful one called "golden" because of its bright orange-gold coat on its underbelly and chest.

The sides and back of the golden bamboo lemur are covered with dark reddish brown fur, which darkens and extends over the crowns of their heads and extends in transverse stripes down the upper half of the tail. Alternating with the reddish brown stripes are faint bands of golden orange, and the under half of the tail is dark golden orange. The face is delicate and finely featured, like a cat's, with a black or dark brown muzzle, a golden orange chin, and puffy golden orange fur ascending over the cheeks, eyes, and to the top of the bridge of the nose. The ears are set well back on the head and are small, almost disappearing into the surrounding fur.

Widely divergent measurements for the golden bamboo lemur have been recorded, perhaps because of confusion with the greater bamboo lemur (*Hapalemur simus*) and grey gentle lemur (*Hapalemur griseus*; please see separate entries), both of which share the golden bamboo lemur's range. For an adult, head-and-body length is probably 13.4 to 15.6 inches; tail length is probably 14 to 16 inches; weight is probably 3.6 pounds.

All lemurs were listed as endangered on June 2, 1970, and even though the golden bamboo lemur not discovered until the 1980s, it is covered until the general listing.

Behavior

Golden bamboo lemurs live in family groups formed by 2 paired adults and their progeny; these groups have 2 to 6 members. They have a territory of as much as 200 acres for their group. This territory is marked by scent glands under their arms. They also make clamorous calls, especially at dusk, to let other groups know of their claim to their territory. Within the group, the calls are soft, intended to let each other know where they are amid the trunks and leaves of bamboo.

They mostly eat the shoots and leaf bases of giant bamboo (*Cephalostacyum viguieri*), but also eat bamboo grass, fungi, and possibly vines associated with the bamboo. Their primary food, the shoots of the giant bamboo, contains cyanide and is not eaten by other local animals; a single golden bamboo lemur eats enough cyanide in a single day to kill a human being. When feeding, the mother will peel bamboo for her infant to eat.

Golden bamboo lemurs are active primarily at dawn and dusk, and may be active part of the night. The adult female leads the group's movements, trailed by the male and nearly mature young. They can move stealthily through their bamboo habitat, sometimes

with slothlike slowness if trying to avoid danger. On the other hand, they will sometimes move about by leaping from trunk to trunk, feet first, in their dense bamboo forest.

Habitat

The golden bamboo lemur lives in tracts of bamboo along rivers in a rain forest.

Distribution

The golden bamboo lemur lives in patches of bamboo forest in Ranomafana National Park.

Threats

Much of the region around the golden bamboo lemur's small remaining range is turning arid, having been denuded of its trees and plants, with the soil having been used up by farming and eroded by floods. This desertification is a threat to the golden bamboo lemur in more than one way: Rivers have been drying up; if the golden bamboo lemur's river falls or dries, the animal is very likely doomed. The desertification makes local people eager to find new, usable land to exploit, and the forests of Ranomafana National Park are very attractive. The forests are illegally logged, the park's land is illegally burned to make way for agriculture (a plot of land may only support crops for three years), and lemurs are poached for food. One technique is to set bamboo afire, driving panicked lemurs into the water, where they are captured by hunters. Only 100 to 200 of the golden bamboo lemur exist; they could easily be exterminated in a season, and some naturalists expect it to be extinct before the year 2000.

Conservation and Recovery

The golden bamboo lemur may hold the distinction of having inspired a great national park. There had been talk for years of plans to create a national park near the village of Ranomafana, but the discovery of new species of lemur unique to the Ranomafana area seems to have spurred the Malagasy government into taking action, creating Ranomafana National Park, with the assistance of the World Wildlife Fund. The park is becoming a prime tourist attraction and is bringing badly needed money to its region. Even so, there much resentment over a large tract of old forest and other patches of forest now being off limits to exploitation, and illegal logging, illegal clearing of land for agriculture, and poaching threaten the park and especially the golden bamboo lemur, which has little habitat left.

Alaotran [=Grey] Gentle Lemur

Hapalemur griseus alaotrensis

David Haring

Status	Endangered
Listed	June 2, 1970; June 14, 1976.
Family	Lemuridae (Lemurs)
Description	Stoutly built lemur with long, bushy tail the same length as the body, with a dark gray-brown coat and forearm marking gland.
Habitat	Evergreen forests and grassland vegetation of Madagascar.
Food	Shoots and leaves of reeds and pith and buds of *Papyrus.*
Reproduction	Breeding is seasonal, with single births in January and February.
Threats	Deforestation resulting in erosion, mineral depletion, and watershed loss.
Range	Madagascar

Description

Taxonomy is disputed for *Hapalemur griseus alaotrensis,* Alaotran gentle lemur, which may be a separate species. This lemur is about 11 inches in length from the tip of the snout to the base of the tail. Its long, bushy tail is generally the same length as the body. They weigh approximately 2 pounds. The coat is dark gray-brown, similar to that of its relative, the eastern grey gentle lemur (*Hapalemur griseus griseus*; see separate entry) but even darker. Gentle lemurs have a forearm marking gland as well as one located axially; both are covered with epithelial spines.

The Alaotran gentle lemur is also commonly known as bandro and lesser bamboo lemur.

Behavior

Never coming down to the ground, the alaotran gentle lemurs move about by leaping and sometimes rest while clinging vertically. They are good swimmers. Diurnal feeders, their diet consists of bamboo shoots, stems, and leaves. This species eats ten species of plants, including the shoots and leaves of

Phragmites communis.

The alaotran gentle lemurs live in groups that vary in size according to the season. They gather in groups of 3 or 4 in July; these groups increase in size to about twelve members in October. At the height of the rainy season, usually February, the alaotran gentle lemurs gather in groups of 30 to 40 members. These large gatherings may be connected to the birthing season of January and February.

Immediately after its birth, an infant is carried on the mother's back. Mothers have been observed swimming while carrying their youngsters on their backs.

Habitat

The alaotran gentle lemur inhabits the reed beds (which are open and treeless) around Lake Alaotra in central Madagascar. This habitat is highly atypical for primates and is a significant distinguishing feature of this particular subspecies.

Distribution

The alaotran gentle lemur lives in the reed beds of Lake Alaotra in central Madagascar.

Threats

Habitat destruction is the primary threat to the alaotran gentle lemur. Its homes of reeds are cut for making fish traps, screens, mats, and even fences. In addition, every year the reed beds around Lake Alaotra are burned and humans club the fleeing alaotran gentle lemurs to death and then eat them or capture the fleeing lemurs to sell as food.

Conservation and Recovery

The Malagasy Republic protects the alaotran gentle lemur under law, but these laws seem to have no effect on local habitat destruction and hunting of the animal. This lemur is listed in CITES, Appendix I: Trade Prohibited, which outlaws international trade in the species or its parts.

Duke University Primate Center has imported five pairs of Alaotran gentle lemurs from Madagascar for research purposes. The Jersey Wildlife Preservation Trust also maintains this lemur in captivity and is establishing itself as the center for major research on this subspecies.

Eastern Grey Gentle Lemur

Hapalemur griseus griseus

David Haring

Status	Endangered.
Listed	June 2, 1970; June 14, 1976.
Family	Lemuridae (lemurs).
Description	Lemur with a long tail and overall dark gray-brown coat.
Habitat	Rain forests with bamboo.
Food	Omnivorous, feeding primarily on bamboo.
Reproduction	Gestation lasts 135 to140 days and usually result in single births.
Threats	Loss of habitat due to deforestation and erosion.
Range	Eastern Madagascar

Description

The eastern grey gentle lemur, *Hapalemur griseus griseus*, is about 11 inches in length from the tip of the snout to the base of the tail. The long, bushy tail measures from 12 to 16 inches. The coat is dark gray-brown with light gray underparts. The tips of the ears, which have no tufts, are light gray merging to medium gray that continues across the brow, down the face, and around the neck. The four feet and tail are also medium gray. Females weigh about 31.5 ounces and males 33.1 ounces. The *Hapalemur griseus* species has a forearm marking gland as well as one located axially; both are covered with epithelial spines.

Other common names are grey gentle lemur, lesser bamboo lemur, bokombolo, and kotrika.

Behavior

The gentle lemurs are adapted to vertical clinging and leaping. Groups consist of 3 to 6 members; each group has a male-female pair of adults with adolescents and infants. Multiple family groups of up to 40 individuals have been recorded. Both the male and the female eastern grey gentle lemur will care for and carry the infant, which is carried by mouth.

The eastern grey gentle lemurs usually

bear 1 or 2 young in a nest constructed in a tree cavity after gestation of 135 to 140 days. The mother may carry the young as she forages for food or she may leave them in the tree cavity nest. Sexual maturity is reached at 24 months, and females will bear their first young 2 to 3 months later.

The eastern grey gentle lemurs are predominantly diurnal, resting at midday. They spend about 48% of their days continuously browsing on bamboo shoots and leaf stems. They also eat young leaves of trees, berries, and grass stems. Although they seem to prefer forests with canopies, during a day they will range from the ground throughout the midlevels of the forest to its high canopy. They may travel as far as 1,400 feet in search of food.

Habitat

Madagascar is dominated by evergreen forest and grassland vegetation. It has a tropical climate with abundant rainfall and warm seasonal temperatures. The normal habitat of the eastern grey gentle lemur is the rain forest of eastern Madagascar, where bamboo or bamboo vines are present, from near Fort Dauphin northward to the Tsaratanana massif, but the secondary forest dominated by bamboo may support high numbers of this subspecies. In fact, the eastern grey gentle lemur thrives on the secondary bamboo thickets which grow once cultivation has ceased.

Distribution

The eastern grey gentle lemur occurs in southeast Madagascar from Fort Dauphin to the Tsaratanana massif. This lemur also occurs in the reserve at Périnet.

Threats

Deforestation is the eastern grey gentle lemur's greatest threat. Most of its ancient range, from almost all-the-way south to all-the-way north along the east coast of Madagascar has been denuded. In some areas, long abandoned agricultural land has been completely taken over by bamboo; in these small areas, the eastern grey gentle lemur has been reported to be recovering its population. Humans hunt the eastern grey gentle lemurs for food and capture them to be kept as pets.

The forests are being exploited for their natural fuel reserves and cleared for roads and towns. Poor felling practices in addition to poor management techniques are no alleviation to the plight of forest dwelling primates.

In addition, hill rice cultivation is accounting for the slow land clearing and deforestation of Madagascar.

Conservation and Recovery

Habitat loss is a serious problem for the eastern grey gentle lemur, but a few naturalists have hope that it may survive where other species would not: Where the primary forest is replaced by bamboo, the eastern grey gentle lemur seems to adapt to the new environment and may even thrive in it. Other naturalists disagree, asserting that the eastern grey gentle lemur does very poorly wherever its primary forests disappear, regardless of whether or not the forest is replaced by bamboo. This latter view seems, at present, to be the more scientifically supportable one.

The eastern grey gentle lemur lives in several wildlife reserves in the Malagasy Republic. Poaching is a significant problem for the eastern grey gentle lemurs in these reserves.

Duke University Primate Center maintains a research population of the eastern grey gentle lemur. As of September 1997 the population numbered 16 with 15 of these captive born. There have been several second generation births.

The eastern grey gentle lemur is listed in Appendix I of CITES: Trade Prohibited, and is protected in Madagascar.

Grey Gentle Lemur

Hapalemur griseus meriodinalis

David Haring

Status	Endangered
Listed	June 2, 1970; June 14, 1976.
Family	Lemuridae (Lemurs)
Description	Primate with long, bushy tail, dark gray-brown coat, with a forearm marking gland.
Habitat	Evergreen forests and grassland vegetation of Madagascar.
Food	Omnivorous, feeding primarily on bamboo.
Reproduction	Young are born in a nest in a tree cavity.
Threats	Loss of habitat due to deforestation and erosion.
Range	Madagascar

Description

Rediscovered in 1986, after about a hundred and thirty years, this bamboo lemur or gentle lemur, *Hapalemur griseus meriodinalis*, is about 11 inches in length from the tip of the snout to the base of the tail. The long, bushy tail is generally the same length as the body. The coat is dark gray-brown. *Hapalemur griseus* subspecies have a forearm marking gland as well as one located axially; both are covered with epithelial spines.

Gentle lemurs have yet to be studied in detail, but their front teeth appear specialized to exploit bamboo shoots and leaves. The upper canine is short and broad, and the premolar behind it is relatively large and not separated from the canine by a gap as it is in most primates.

Behavior

Much has to be learned about this subspecies' behavior. It seems to give birth in a nest in a tree cavity. The mother may carry her young as she forages for food, or may leave it in the tree cavity nest.

The grey gentle lemur is diurnal and feeds primarily on the bamboo, *Cephalostacyum perrieri*. Gentle lemurs detach a bamboo shoot with their incisors, clamp it between the upper and lower canines and premolars, and pull the shoot sideways with their hands, stripping off the fibrous outer layer. Then they push the tender interior portion into the side of the mouth and chew it.

Habitat

The *meriodinalis* subspecies of the grey gentle lemur inhabits a small forest area on the southeast coast of Madagascar. Because it has only recently been described, its habitat requirements are little known.

Distribution

The *meriodinalis* subspecies is known from a small area of forest on the southeast coast of Madagascar about six miles north of Fort Dauphin.

Threats

Deforestation is an immediate threat to this subspecies' survival. Wood is felled to provide local people with fuel. The forest is also being cleared for roads and expanding human settlements. Unrestricted capture of the animal for scientific purposes is also a threat.

Conservation and Recovery

The grey gentle lemur is protected by Malagasy law. It is listed in CITES, Appendix I: Trade Prohibited.

The few *meriodinalis* grey gentle lemurs that have been taken into captivity have not adapted very well.

Western Grey Gentle Lemur

Hapalemur griseus occidentalis

David Haring

Status	Endangered
Listed	June 2, 1970; June 14, 1976.
Family	Lemuridae (Lemurs)
Description	Lemur with long, bushy tail, dark gray-brown coat, and a forearm marking gland.
Habitat	Evergreen forest and grassland vegetation of Madagascar.
Food	Omnivorous diet, feeds primarily on bamboo.
Reproduction	Young are born in a nest in tree cavities.
Threats	Habitat alteration due to agricultural development and livestock ranching.
Range	Western Madagascar

Description

The western grey gentle lemur, *Hapalemur griseus occidentalis*, is about 11 inches in length from the tip of the snout to the base of the tail. Its long, bushy tail is generally the same length as the body. The coat is gray-brown, somewhat lighter than the coat of its relative the eastern grey gentle lemur (*Hapalemur griseus griseus*; please see separate entry). It is a little lighter than the eastern grey gentle lemur, weighing about 25 ounces. Like other grey gentle lemurs, it has a forearm marking gland as well as one located axially; both are

covered with epithelial spines.

Other common names are bekola, kofi, or ankomba valiha.

Behavior

The western grey gentle lemur is active during the day, and it has been observed traveling alone or in groups of up to 4 members. They forage on the ground and live in the trees of their forests. This lemur feeds primarily on the bamboo. The western grey gentle lemur usually bears its young in a nest in a tree cavity. The mother may carry her young as she forages for food or may leave it in the tree cavity nest.

Habitat

The western grey gentle lemur inhabits humid, swampy forest associated with bamboo thickets.

Distribution

The western grey gentle lemur is known from two isolated western locations in Madagascar, one in the Sambirano region between Moramandia and Beramanja, and the other between Maintirano and Belo-sur-Tsiribihina, north of Morondava, near Lake Bemamba.

Threats

Deforestation is the animal's principal threat to survival. The forests are being exploited for their natural fuel reserves and are also being cleared for roads and towns. Forest lands are also being burned to clear the way for grasses for the grazing of livestock. The western grey gentle lemur seems to be very sensitive to forest loss and its numbers are plummeting because of it.

Conservation and Recovery

The western grey gentle lemur is listed with the other lemurs in CITES, Appendix I: Trade Prohibited, meaning that international trade in the animal or its parts is forbidden by treaty. It protected by Malagasy law, but

enforcing the law in the western grey gentle lemur's range is proving to be very difficult. It is known to live in the Manongarivo Special Reserve; less certain, but possible is that it may live in the Bemarah Nature Reserve. Grey gentle lemurs have been reported in the Ankarana Special Reserve; these may be members of the western gentle lemur subspecies.

Greater [=Gentle] Bamboo Lemur

Hapalemur simus

David Haring

Status	Endangered
Listed	June 2, 1970; June 14, 1976; June 24, 1976.
Family	Lemuridae (Lemurs)
Description	Individuals have charcoal grey upperparts with paler, grey-brown underparts and white ear tufts; largest species in the genus *Hapalemur.*
Habitat	Humid rain forests in a small area of eastern Madagascar.
Food	Primarily feeds on bamboo, but has been seen eating a variety of fruits, as well as grass.
Reproduction	Seasonal breeders, usually giving birth to a single infant.
Threats	Hunting, habitat destruction by slash and burn agriculture, and the cutting of bamboo.
Range	Eastern Madagascar

Description

The greater bamboo lemur, *Hapalemur simus*, is the largest species in the genus *Hapalemur*. Its total body length including tail measures 35.5 inches. Adult males generally weigh 5 pounds.

Greater bamboo lemurs have reddish charcoal gray upperparts with paler, gray-brown underparts. The muzzle is usually dark and the ears are moderately tufted with white hairs. They have brachial glands near the elbow and males have glands on the side of the neck.

Other common names broad-nosed gentle lemur, varibolo, and tan-tang.

Behavior

The greater bamboo lemur is arboreal and cathemeral, although it is most active at night. Its diet consists mainly of bamboo, particularly the woody pith inside the main stem, a source of fiber but low in protein. It has also been seen eating flowers, fruits, and leaves.

The greater bamboo lemur forms groups of up to 30 members (4 to 12 is average) comprised of one to several males and several females. All *Hapalemurs* are seasonal breeders and usually give birth to a single infant.

The greater bamboo lemur has a loud call that sounds like a whistle, and a loud ascending call that begins with a motorlike purr.

Habitat

The greater bamboo lemur is found in the rain forests of southeastern Madagascar where there are considerable quantities of the giant bamboo, *Cephalostachium viguieri*.

Distribution

This species was distributed in the past throughout northern, northwestern, central, and eastern Madagascar. Currently, it is only found in the humid rain forest east of Fianarantsoa. Their population numbers less than 1,000.

Threats

The threat to the greater bamboo lemur's short-term survival is great. Once spread throughout much of Madagascar, it now exists in patches in southeastern Madagascar, near Ranomafana and Kianjavato. Its population decline has been precipitous, and with the loss of the last of its range it will likely become extinct before the year 2000.

The greater bamboo lemur is hunted and trapped for trade and food, but habitat destruction by slash-and-burn agriculture and the cutting of bamboo have been the major threats to the greater bamboo lemur. Nearly all of the bamboo in its habitat in southeastern Madagascar has been destroyed during the years 1986 to 1996. The ancient forest that was large even in the 1970s, is down to a few miles in width and will likely be utterly denuded in a few more years. Even so, poachers may be the ones to kill the very last greater bamboo lemurs; these lemurs are hunted for sport and for food, and they are captured for pets.

Conservation and Recovery

Currently, Ranomofana National Park is the only protected area in which the greater bamboo lemur is known to occur. These are estimated to be approximately 1,000 in number living in the park. (Some naturalists disagree, putting the total wild population at less than 400.) Increased protection for the park is needed and searches for new populations in other areas should be conducted. The captive breeding program at the Paris Zoo should be expanded and a captive breeding program should be established in Madagascar as well.

All lemur species are listed in CITES, Appendix I: Trade Prohibited. The greater bamboo lemur is listed in Class A in the African Convention. The Malagasy government protects the greater bamboo lemur under law, but the law has proven ineffective. Even so, the Malagasy Republic has taken conservation steps that may prove effective: It has divided the Ranomofana National Park into four protected zones, each surrounded by a buffer of land that humans are not supposed to settle in or cross. It seems as though each zone will be like a small fortress, the object being to keep people out and preserve the last bits of wildland from being burned and settled by humans.

In December 1993 there were only two greater bamboo lemurs in captivity at the Paris Zoo. This pair were both wild born and have bred twice while in captivity, but all of the offspring have died.

Duke University Primate Center has applied in 1997 for a CITES permit to bring a pair of greater bamboo lemurs to its center for study.

Ring-tailed Lemur

Lemur catta

Noel Rowe

Status	Endangered
Listed	June 2, 1970; June 14, 1976; June 24, 1976.
Family	Lemuridae (Lemurs)
Description	Brownish-gray with white underparts; white face with a black muzzle and black rings around the eyes and a black and white ringed tail.
Habitat	Brush and scrub forests, and closed canopy deciduous forests.
Food	Fruits, leaves, flowers, bark, sap, herbs.
Reproduction	Single infant after a 134 to 138 day gestation period.
Threats	Hunting, trapping, loss of habitat.
Range	Southwestern Madagascar.

Description

The adult ring-tailed lemur, *Lemur catta*, measures 15 to 18 inches from the tip of its nose to its tail; the tail adds another 22 to 24 inches. It generally weighs 5 to 7.5 pounds. Both males and females of this species have brownish-grey fur on the body, arms, and legs, whiter underparts, a white face with a black muzzle, black rings around the eyes, and a characteristic black and white ringed tail (hence its common name).

The taxonomy of the ring-tailed lemur is disputed. Formerly grouped with all the species now treated as *Eulemur, Lemur catta* has been regarded as one monotypic species since 1988.

Other common names are maki and hira.

Behavior

Females usually dominate ring-tailed lemur groups, which have 5 to 30 members (averaging 15 members), but dominant male hierarchies also exist. Conflicts are ritualized, and ring-tailed lemurs wave their scent smeared tails in the direction of their rivals.

Males have scent glands on their forelegs, with which they anoint their tails; they then raise their tails and flick them forward, sending a mass of smelling secretions at the opposition. These distinctive tails, carried erect when the lemur is walking, serve also as signals of where individual animals are, helping group members keep track of each other. They spend much of their lives on the ground, even though they feed mostly in trees. They spend about 70% of their time in trees, and when traveling in trees, they leap from branch to branch. Ground travel serves primarily for patrolling territorial boundaries. The ring-tailed lemur feeds on fruit, leaves, flowers, bark, and sap from a variety of plants, but particularly from the kily tree (*Tamarindus indica*). When not feeding or patrolling their territories, ring-tailed lemurs take long naps, often huddled together in large groups, or extensively groom one another. The ring-tailed lemur is diurnal.

Ring-tailed lemurs become sexually mature at approximately 24 months of age; mature females can give birth annually. After a 134-138 day gestation period, they generally give birth to a single infant (although twins are sometimes produced, both in the wild and in captivity) from August through Septmber. Immediately following birth, the infant clings to its mother's front; within three days, it moves around actively on its mother; and by about two weeks of age it regularly rides on her back. At two and a half months of age, although still carried by its mother when moving with the group, the infant explores its environment, plays with other offspring, and begins tasting various foods. By four months of age, the infant no longer rides on its mother's back, and is completely independent. When mature, females remain in their natal area, while males transfer between troops.

Habitat

The ring-tailed lemur lives primarily in dry areas, favoring scrub forests and deciduous forests. It is also found in the dry, rocky, and mountainous areas in the southern portion of the central plateau where patches of deciduous forests remain.

Distribution

The ring-tailed lemur is found in southwestern Madagascar, scattered in patches. The northern limit of its range appears to be the forests south of Morondava on Madagascar's west coast. It ranges farther into the interior highlands than any other lemur.

Threats

The ring-tailed lemur is hunted and trapped for trade and food and is often kept as a pet. This hunting has almost wiped out the species in the southern part of its range and is threatening it throughout the rest of its range.

The animal's native forests are disappearing quickly, being clear-cut for timber and for fuel, as well as to make way for agriculture and expanding human communities. The Malagasy government has instituted management plans in the wildlife reserves of Andohahela, Andiringitra, and Beza which may save some of the forest.

Conservation and Recovery

The ring-tailed lemur lives in six protected areas within its range and is the most studied of all lemurs — partly because it lives in easily accessible areas and partly because it is often fearless, with a catlike attitude that whatever it sets its feet upon must belong to it, making it easy for people to see it, especially when it is walking in groups with tails held characteristically high. In the Berenty Private Reserve, the ring-tailed lemurs have become accustomed to the presence of tourists, and they are reported to have developed a fondness so severe for the bananas that tourists bring them that they will swarm over a tourist who brings a banana into sight.

In December of 1993, there were 935 ring-tailed lemurs in 139 institutions. Of these animals, 98% were captive born. The ring-tailed lemur's commonness in captivity may create the illusion for some people that it is common, even thriving, in the wild. This is not so; it is presently very vulnerable to extinction in the wild. Its commonness in zoos may be accounted for in part to its being able to adjust to limited living space and institutional food, whereas most lemur species cannot make those adjustments and die quickly when captive.

The lemur is listed in CITES, Appendix I: Trade Prohibited, which means it is not to be traded internationally. It also is listed in class A of the African convention, which means it may not be hunted, trapped, killed, or traded without permission of the highest appropriate governmental authority, and even then only under very limited conditions. The Malagasy government is having trouble enforcing its laws against poaching the animal.

Gray-backed Sportive Lemur

Lepilemur dorsalis

Russell A. Mittermeier

Status	Endangered
Listed	June 2, 1970
Family	Megaladapidae (Sportive lemurs)
Description	Coat is brown to dark brown, with the underbody slightly lighter than the rest of the body; the face is dark gray or brown.
Habitat	Rain forest.
Food	Leaves, bark, and flowers.
Reproduction	Gestation lasts 140 days, resulting in 1 young, born in September or October.
Threats	Loss of habitat to logging; hunting by humans; predation by owls and feral cats.
Range	Madagascar

Description

The gray-backed sportive lemur, *Lepilemur dorsalis*, is one of the smaller sportive lemurs at a head-and-body length of approximately 10 inches and a weight of approximately 17.5 ounces. Its tail is slightly shorter than the length of the rest of its body. Its fur is a dull brown, sometimes very dark; its underbody is lighter than its overall coloration. The fur is dense and downy, even on the face. The head is rounded, with outward-pointing oval ears set forward and close to its eyes. The eyes are round; the vision is keen. It has a small, moist nose set above a receding mouth.

Behavior

Active at night, the gray-backed sportive lemur sleeps during most of the day, although it sometimes emerges from its sleeping place to cling to a tree trunk. The mainland gray-backed sportive lemurs sleep in small groups in tree hollows, but those on the island of Nosy Bé sleep out in the open, perhaps because natural predators are uncommon on the island. On the mainland, human hunters will probe tree hollows with sticks in hopes of disturbing gray-backed sportive lemurs, which will emerge from their sleeping places when prodded.

In the evening, the gray-backed sportive lemurs will leave their sleeping place to forage in their individual, small territories. Each gray-backed sportive lemur marks its territory by urinating and by using scent glands on its posterior. Their frequent cries to each other probably further define an individual territory. As is the case with other species of sportive lemurs, male and female territories probably overlap. Gray-backed sportive lemurs eat mostly leaves, which they digest with the aid of symbiotic bacteria in their gut. They also eat flowers and bark, and they may eat fruit. When active, they run on all fours along branches or on the ground; they leap from tree to tree.

The gray-backed sportive lemur's mating season extends from May into July. After a gestation of 135 to 140 days, a single infant is born. Its mother carries the infant in her mouth when moving it. The infant is quickly active and shows some independence in a few days; it is weaned after 4 months. It becomes sexually mature after 18 months.

Habitat

The gray-backed sportive lemur requires a rain forest habitat with an abundance of leaves.

Distribution

The gray-backed sportive lemur lives on the island of Nosy Bé (sometimes spelled "Nossi-Bé") and on the northwest coast of Madagascar.

Threats

The gray-backed sportive lemur is already very rare. Its remaining habitat is being logged and cleared for cultivation and livestock grazing. It is hunted by humans, who prize its reportedly tasty meat.

Conservation and Recovery

The gray-backed sportive lemur lives in the reserves of Manongarivo and Lokobe, the latter on the island of Nosy Bé. Both reserves are being destroyed by illicit logging. Malagasy law forbids this destruction and forbids the killing of the gray-backed sportive lemur, but it has had much difficulty in enforcing the laws protecting the animal and its range. The animal has not lived long in captivity, probably because its diet is poorly understood.

Milne-Edwards' Sportive Lemur

Lepilemur edwardsi

Russell A. Mittermeier

Status	Endangered
Listed	June 2, 1970
Family	Megaladapidae (Sportive lemurs)
Description	Overall coat is dark brown, with dark gray undersides, reddish tail, and dark grayish brown face.
Habitat	Dry deciduous forest.
Food	Leaves, fruit, seeds, and flowers.
Reproduction	Gestation may last 140 days, probably resulting in 1 young.
Threats	Loss of habitat.
Range	Madagascar

Description

The adult Milne-Edwards' sportive lemur, *Lepilemur edwardsi*, weighs between 28 and 35.25 ounces; it probably is about 14 inches in head-and-body length, with a tail that is probably 12 inches long. The Milne-Edwards' sportive lemur has been little studied, and these dimensions and other details about it may be revised as more is learned and recorded. It has dense, woolly fur, mostly colored dark brown, with grayish brown with cream spots on its underbody, and a reddish tail. The head is somewhat flattened and squarish, with a prominent, narrow muzzle. The eyes are set well apart, and the large, oval-shaped ears are set well back on the head.

Another common name is boenga.

Behavior

The behavior of the Milne-Edwards' sportive lemur has been little recorded, probably because it is very rare and difficult to locate in sufficient numbers for scientific study. It is nocturnal, spending its days asleep in tree hollows. At night it forages for food; whether or not it also socializes is unclear. It seems to be territorial, and if it is like other sportive lemur species, marks its territories with urine and scent glands, and it chatters in the dark to other nearby Milne-Edwards' sportive lemurs. Leaves make up the bulk of its diet, but it also eats fruits, meaty seeds, and flowers. Mating is probably seasonal, and it probably results in a single birth. The mother is likely to be the primary caregiver for her infant.

Habitat

Dry, deciduous primary forest is the animal's preferred habitat.

Distribution

The Milne-Edwards' sportive lemur is found in patchy populations in central western Madagascar.

Threats

The Milne-Edwards' sportive lemur's habitat is being destroyed for cultivation and livestock grazing.

Conservation and Recovery

The Milne-Edwards' sportive lemur lives in the wildlife reserves of Ankarafantsika, Bemaraha, and Namoroka. Each of these reserves is being destroyed by slash-and-burn agriculture, as well as fires set to eliminate trees in order to create more grasslands for the grazing of livestock; Namoroka is especially threatened. With the help of the World Bank, the Malagasy Republic's Department of Water and Forests has created a management plan for Ankarafantsika, including plans for reforestation to create wood for local needs and thus ease some of the pressure from the reserve's forest.

White-footed Sportive Lemur

Lepilemur leucopus

Leanne T. Nash

Status	Endangered
Listed	June 2, 1970
Family	Megaladapidae (Sportive lemurs)
Description	Overall coat is light to dark gray, with white to light gray undersides and a light brown tail.
Habitat	Gallery forest.
Food	Leaves and flowers.
Reproduction	One pregnancy per year; mating occurs in May to July; gestation lasts about 135 days, resulting in 1 young.
Threats	Loss of habitat.
Range	Madagascar

Description

The adult white-footed sportive lemur, *Lepilemur leucopus*, weighs approximately 19.5 ounces. Head-and-body length is about 12 inches, with a somewhat shorter tail. Its coat is a swirling blend of color, light to dark gray on its back and sides, stirring into white to light gray on its undersides. Swirls of white rise across its cheeks and over its eyes, and its ears are surrounded by white. The tail is light brown. The head is rounded, marked by a thick nose and large, round eyes. Its ears are broad and rounded.

Another common name is songiky.

Behavior

The diet of the white-footed sportive lemur consists primarily of leaves; when leaves are unavailable, it eats flowers. Field observations at Bega-Mahafaly Special Reserve indicate that this lemur ate kily (Tamarind) flowers when available, and leaves at all other times. The lemurs also ate younger stems and the tiny leaves of Euphorbia, which has a latex that is an eye irritant to humans.

The white-footed sportive lemur is nocturnal, foraging at night in its small territory. Although there are not good data on behavior, adults are likely to sleep alone or with members of the opposite sex during the day. Territories vary in size, perhaps according to the size of the individual animal. White-footed sportive lemurs appear to make no effort to scent mark their individual territories, and seem tolerant of intruders, although they will sometimes cry out to make sure their ownership of the territory is known to others.

White-footed sportive lemurs seem to be slower moving than other species of sportive lemur, with their movements perhaps dictated by the immediate abundance of food. They walk on all fours and leap from tree trunk to tree trunk while retaining an erect posture. They may sometimes hop on two legs.

Mating season extends from May to July, with pregnancies lasting about 135 days. The mother seems to be the principal care giver for her infant. The youngster becomes sexually mature at about 18 months of age. Females may remain in their mother's range.

Habitat

The white-footed sportive lemur lives in gallery forests with abundant brush on the ground.

Distribution

Except for wildlife reserves and terrain too steep for logging or agriculture, the white-footed sportive lemur's traditional range is almost devoid of the forests and food plants the animal needs in order to survive. It now lives in at least four (perhaps no more than four) patches scattered in reserves across southern Madagascar.

Threats

The white-footed sportive lemur is threatened by the loss of its habitat to logging, fires set by people to clear land for grass and grazing, and by the clearing of forest for agriculture. The habitat is also threatened by the desertification that has overcome much of southern Madagascar.

Conservation and Recovery

The white-footed sportive lemur is doing well in the Berenty Private Reserve in southeastern Madagascar and in the Beza-Mahafaly Special Reserve in southwestern Madagascar. Its range in Beza-Mahafaly is well marked by fences and is well guarded. It is found in the Andohahela Strict Nature Reserve, to the northeast of Berenty; with the cooperation of the University of Madagascar, international wildlife organizations are helping to fund the hiring and training of guards in order to put an end to illegal tree felling and other abuses in the reserve. As a "strict" nature reserve, Andohahela is supposed to be off limits to all but scientists given permission to do research by the government and the reserve's guards.

Small-toothed Sportive Lemur

Lepilemur microdon

Lelia Porter

Status	Endangered
Listed	June 2, 1970
Family	Megaladapidae (Sportive lemurs)
Description	Short, soft fur, reddish brown over the back, but with a dark stripe along the middle of the back, with creamy yellow sides, a dark brown tail, and gray undersides.
Habitat	Secondary forest with dense saplings and bamboo.
Food	Leaves, fruits, and flowers.
Reproduction	Probably breeds once a year, with a gestation of 140 days, resulting in a single birth.
Threats	Loss of habitat.
Range	Madagascar

Description

The small-toothed sportive lemur, *Lepilemur microdon*, has short but fluffy fur. Its coat has a dark red line down the back, amid red-brown over the rest of the back; the underbody is gray; the sides are a creamy yellow; the tail is dark brown. Its eyes are set far apart on the face and are very large, as well as round. Its muzzle spreads out in the shape of a triangle from under and between the eyes, with a small, rounded nose above the mouth. Its ears are spread wide from the side of its head.

Another common name is microdon.

Behavior

This animal has become very rare, and as a consequence it has been little studied. It seems to be a solitary, nocturnal creature that feeds primarily on leaves, but eats fruit and flowers, as well.

Small-toothed sportive lemurs have been observed to be active during winter months. They rest next to their tree cavity by day and return to the nesting hole before dark. Field observations indicate females share sleeping sites with their offspring.

Habitat

The small-toothed sportive lemur prefers secondary forest with dense saplings and bamboo.

Distribution

The small-toothed sportive lemur's range begins in the far southeast of Madagascar and extends about two thirds of the way north along the eastern edge of the island.

Threats

The animal's forests are being cleared by slash-and-burn agriculture. The resulting loss of habitat is diminishing the small-toothed sportive lemur numbers, making it rare. Humans hunt them for food.

Conservation and Recovery

Much has yet to be learned about the small-toothed sportive lemur's natural history. It lives in the Andohahela Strict Nature Reserve and Analamazaotra Special Reserve; the Andohahela reserve has recently been the subject of special scientific attention and money from international wildlife organizations, and it is possible that the financial contributions and the research will help naturalists uncover the secrets of one of Madagascar's most mysterious animals.

Weasel Sportive Lemur

Lepilemur mustelinus

Illustration, Stephen Nash

Status	Endangered
Listed	June 2, 1970
Family	Megaladapidae (Sportive lemurs)
Description	Coat is brown, with pale under-parts, cheek, and beard.
Habitat	Rain forest.
Food	Leaves.
Reproduction	Gestation probably lasts between 135 and 140 days, resulting in a single birth.
Threats	Loss of habitat.
Range	Madagascar

Description

Although the best-studied member of the sportive lemur genus (*Lepilemur*) is the gray-backed sportive lemur (*Lepilemur dorsalis*; see separate entry), the weasel sportive lemur, *Lepilemur mustelinus*, is often treated as the archetype for the whole genus. It is one of the largest sportive lemur species at 13 to 14 inches in length, with a 12 inch tail, and weighing 28 to 35 ounces. It has dense fur that is brown overall, with a pale brown underbody and pale cheeks and beard; its face is gray or brown with a lighter throat and cheeks. It has a black median stripe, and the tail becomes dark toward the tip.

Behavior

As with most sportive lemur species, little is recorded of the weasel sportive lemur's behavior, although scientific interest in it may be increasing. The animal is probably nocturnal and probably forages for leaves; it is probably entirely arboreal. During the day it may sleep in groups of 2 or 3, in tree holes 10 to 40 feet high during the dry season, and on nests made of leaves during the rainy season. When active, it moves about by leaping. It is not sociable, with most interactions such as grooming occurring only between a mother and her young. The weasel sportive lemur is territorial, with territories among the largest for sportive lemurs, about 3.7 acres. It is likely that male and female territories overlap.

Habitat

At present, the weasel sportive lemur is found only in rain forests, but it may once have ranged into dense brushlands.

Distribution

The weasel sportive lemur's range extends along the east coast of Madagascar, from south of the Maningory river northward to the area of the town of Sambava. Its distribution probably extended in recent times farther north, beyond the rain forest.

Threats

Most of the forest in the weasel sportive lemur's range has been destroyed to make way for agriculture and expanding human settlements. What remains are patches of forest, all of which are threatened with eradication.

Conservation and Recovery

The Malagasy government has been trying for over a decade to protect wildlands within the range of the weasel sportive lemur.

It is found in small numbers in the Marojezy Strict Nature Reserve and the Tsaratanana Strict Nature Reserve, both at the northern limit of its present-day range. Both of these reserves require that visitors have special permission from the government to enter, because the government is trying to keep their ecosystems pristine for scientific research. They are both under pressure from agricultural incursion and a burgeoning human population. Both these reserves need careful protection.

Red-tailed Sportive Lemur

Lepilemur ruficaudatus

Quentin Bloxam

Status	Endangered
Listed	June 2, 1970
Family	Megaladapidae (Sportive lemurs)
Description	Grayish brown back blending into reddish brown on the tail; white to pale gray underbody.
Habitat	Dry gallery forest and possibly dense brushlands.
Food	Leaves and fruits.
Reproduction	Gestation lasts between 120 and 150 days, resulting in a single birth.
Threats	Loss of habitat and human predation.
Range	Madagascar

Description

The red-tailed sportive lemur, *Lepilemur ruficaudatus*, weighs 21 to 32 ounces. Its head-and-body length is about 12 inches, with a tail of 10 inches. The fur is woolly, light or grayish brown overall, becoming reddish brown on the tail. The face and throat are pale gray to pale brown.

Behavior

Mating is seasonal for the red-tailed sportive lemur, occurring in May to July, resulting in single births in September to November. The mother is the primary care giver, at first carrying her infant in her mouth when she wants to move it; later it clings to her fur as they move. An infant is weaned at 4 months of age and leaves its mother before it is one year old. Sexual maturity probably comes later, when it is about 18 months old.

The red-tailed sportive lemur is nocturnal and solitary, sleeping in tree hollows during the day and foraging at night. It prefers to eat leaves, but includes fruits in its summer diet.

Habitat

The red-tailed sportive lemur prefers to live in dry gallery forests that have much seasonal variation in the foods available to it.

Distribution

The red-tailed sportive lemur lives in southwestern Madagascar from the area south of the Onilahy River, northward to the Tsiribihina River, which may mark the northern limit of its range.

Threats

Fires both natural and set by humans have devastated much of the red-tailed sportive lemur's habitat. The forest timber is harvested for use as fuel. Humans hunt the red-tailed sportive lemur for food.

Conservation and Recovery

The red-tailed sportive lemur is very difficult to maintain in captivity and only two or three captive births have occurred. It has been found in at least two wildlife reserves, the Analabe Private Reserve near the Tsiribihina River and the Andranomena Special Reserve south of Analabe. The Andranomena Special Reserve is especially threatened by fires; both need more fire fighters and rangers, posted signs that let people know that they are on protected land, and possibly even fencing.

Northern Sportive Lemur

Lepilemur septentrionalis

Illustration, Stephen Nash

Status	Endangered
Listed	June 2, 1970
Family	Megaladapidae (Sportive lemurs)
Description	Mostly dark gray fur, with a darker stripe down the head and back, with light gray hind limbs.
Habitat	Primarily dry deciduous forest, but sometimes in rain forest.
Food	Leaves
Reproduction	Gestation probably lasts 135 to 140 days, resulting in a single birth.
Threats	Loss of habitat and human predation.
Range	Madagascar

Description

The northern sportive lemur, *Lepilemur septentrionalis*, has long, muscular legs, plump, round torso, and a round head. Its eyes are in a large-boned eye socket that bulges out its flat forehead. The eyes are set well apart on the face and are round and predominantly red. The nose is narrow and prominent, ending well forward of the mouth below. The ears are set low on the sides of the head, thrusting outward, cup shaped. The hands and feet are heavily furred, with digits that are shorter than found on other species of sportive lemurs.

The fur is overall dark gray, with a darker stripe down the head and back. The hind limbs are light gray, but the tail is a mixture of dark and light gray with a darker brown tip. Its head-and-body length is approximately 11 inches, with a tail of approximately 10 inches. An adult weighs 24.5 to 28.25 ounces.

Behavior

Little is known about the behavior of the

northern sportive lemur, a rare animal that is difficult to observe. It is nocturnal, foraging alone for leaves. During the day, it sleeps in tree hollows or nests made of leaves, usually 18 to 25 feet above the ground. It thrives best in high canopy forests far from humans, attaining population densities of perhaps 1,400 per square mile; where humans have been active, such as the Analamera Special Reserve, the density drops to 150 per square mile. It requires a forest habitat and disappears altogether when the forest disappears.

Habitat

The northern sportive lemur seems to prefer living in dry deciduous forest, but it is also found in some patches of rain forest. This suggests that before humans wiped out most of its regional forests, the northern sportive lemur may have had a much wider distribution into the rain forests that existed to the south of its present range.

Distribution

The northern sportive lemur lives in the far north of Madagascar, approximately in a triangle formed among the Montagne d'Ambre National Park to the north, the Ankarana Special Reserve to the southwest, the Analamera Special Reserve to the southeast.

Threats

All of the northern sportive lemur's range is being deforested, and it presently lives in scattered patches of forest that are being destroyed by rampant illegal logging, slash-and-burn agriculture, and clearing for livestock grazing. The soil is being so badly depleted that desertification of large regions is a significant threat. The northern sportive lemur is hunted for food, although its population has shrunk so much that few remain in its range.

Conservation and Recovery

The northern sportive lemur occurs in Montagne d'Ambre National Park, in far northern Madagascar, in the Ankarana Special Reserve to the southwest of Montagne d'Ambre, and in the Analamera Special Reserve near the coast southeast of Montagne d'Ambre. The Malagasy government is developing the park for tourism, but it has not yet become a tourist attraction. The special reserves are intended to protect entire ecosystems and are intended for scientific research; visitors must obtain government permits in order to lawfully enter them. The Analamera Special Reserve has benefitted from being inaccessible during the rainy season, discouraging humans from exploiting it during that period. When accessible, it is illegally logged, and much of it is burned to make way for cultivation and livestock grazing. Overgrazing quickly destroys the soil. World Wildlife Fund has established campsites and trails within the reserve for visitors (who must have the proper permits). Visitors are also allowed into the Ankarana Special Reserve, which is administered by the WWF. It is reportedly under very heavy pressure from recent illegal logging.

Black and White Ruffed Lemur

Varecia variegata variegata

Rich Block

Status	Endangered
Listed	June 2, 1970; June 14, 1976; June 24, 1976.
Family	Lemuridae (Lemurs)
Description	Large, thick-coated lemur with varied patterns of black and white coloration.
Habitat	Rain forests of eastern Madagascar.
Food	Fruit, seeds, leaves, nectar.
Reproduction	Gestation period is 90 to 102 days. Young are born in a nest; twin births are the most common.
Threats	Hunting, trapping, and loss of habitat due to agricultural development.
Range	Eastern Madagascar

Description

There are two subspecies of ruffed lemurs, *Varecia variegata variegata* and *V. v. rubra*. The black and white ruffed lemur, *V. v. variegata*, measures 22 inches from snout to tail. The tail is 23 to 26 inches long. It generally weighs 7.5 to 8.5 pounds.

All black and white ruffed lemurs have long, silky fur, which is particularly dense around the ears, cheeks, and throat. The muzzle is long and the face is covered with light hair. The coat is black and white; in *V. v.*

rubra, the coat color is mostly red, with a black crown and a white nape.

Behavior

In the wild, black and white ruffed lemurs have been observed in small social groups as well as monogamous pairs. Loud calls by the male and female coordinate the pair's activities and announce their presence to others. The females are responsible for defending the territory. Black and white ruffed lemurs make loud calls to advertise their territory and to announce their movements. A range for a pair is about 486 acres; a pair will travel 0.62 miles in a day. The black and white ruffed lemur lives in the canopy of its rain forest habitat. Movement is primarily quadrupedal, with occasional leaping from one tree branch to another.

Most of the information about reproduction for black and white ruffed lemurs comes from studies of captive animals. Both males and females reach sexual maturity at approximately 18 to 20 months of age. The gestation period is 90 to 102 days. Up to five offspring may be produced in a litter, but twins are most common. Unlike other lemur species, when *Varecia* infants are born, they do not cling to their mother's fur. Instead, they are left in either arboreal or in terrestrial nests that are constructed by the female. At 2 to 3 weeks of age, the mothers frequently leave their infants "parked" in branches high up in trees. The infants begin to follow their mothers at three weeks of age. At seven weeks of age, they are as active and mobile as the adults. The infants reach adult size at about six months of age.

Black and white ruffed lemurs are thought to be primarily frugivorous. Their diet, which varies seasonally, consists of mostly fruit, supplemented with small amounts of nectar, seeds, and leaves. They have also been observed eating soil. They are most active in the early morning and late afternoons and often hang upside down by their feet to feed.

Habitat

The black and white ruffed lemur lives in primary rain forests up to 3,937 feet. Ruffed lemurs are one of the first species to disappear after logging because they eat large fruits from large trees, which are usually the first to be cut.

Distribution

The black and white ruffed lemur ranges from slightly north of the Mananara River upwards to a point near the Antainambalana River, covering about three fourths of Madagascar's east coast. In the 1930s, it was introduced to the island of Nosy Mangabey and continues to live there.

The number of black and white ruffed lemurs that remain in the wild is unknown. It appears to occur at low densities throughout its range, with the exception of the population on Nosy Mangabé, where as many 150 live in densities of 12 to 19 per square mile. (In 1983, one observer put the island's black and white ruffed lemur population at about 900, with a density of 109 per square mile, but this is at variance with every other counting of the population.) The black and white lemur is heavily poached on Nosy Mangabé and its numbers are therefore declining. On the mainland, poaching and habitat destruction are racing each other to exterminate the black and white ruffed lemur first. In December 1993, there were 390 black and white ruffed lemurs in 95 institutions. Of these individuals, 93% were captive born; 7% were wild born; there were 52 captive births from December 1992 to December 1993; and 19 deaths occurred within the first 30 days of life.

Threats

The black and white ruffed lemur is

heavily hunted and trapped for food, and this subspecies is endangered by deforestation for agricultural development.

Conservation and Recovery

The black and white ruffed lemur is already found in several protected reserves throughout Madagascar. Better protection of wildlife is needed in most of these areas.

Currently, there are three national programs that coordinate the captive breeding of the ruffed lemurs. As a result of successful captive breeding at Duke University Primate Center, reintroduction of five black and white ruffed lemurs is planned for October 1997. These animals will be taken to an area approximately 50 miles from the Ivoloina Zoo in Madagascar.

All lemur species are listed in Appendix I of CITES. The black and white ruffed lemur is classified as Class A of the African Convention.

Macaques, Baboons, Mangabeys, and Guenons

Family: Cercopithecidae
Subfamily: Cercopithecinae

Stump-tailed Macaque (white infant, black adult)   Noel Rowe

General Characteristics of the *Subfamily Cercopithecinae*

The members of the subfamily *Cercopithecinae* are probably the most familiar of all monkeys to Americans, and perhaps humanity in general. In America, the familiarity stems in part from the use of rhesus monkeys (or rhesus macaques) in scientific research. This small creature from northern India and Tibet has been a staple of biological research for several decades. There was even a time that when a scientist said the word *monkey*, he meant specifically the rhesus monkey and no other. The popularity of the rhesus monkey for scientific research has greatly reduced its numbers in the wild, and for macaques in general, capture for laboratory research is a significant factor in their declining populations.

One of the reasons species of *Cercopithecinae* are used in biological research is that their metabolisms are similar to that of humans and are in general typical for primates. For instance, their digestive systems have the same basic elements as that of humans (excluding the appendix) and take up only about a third of their torso. This alone makes them attractive for medical studies of such matters as digestive diseases which may afflict humans.

Cercopithecinae is composed of baboons (five species), guenons (seventeen species), macaques (fifteen species), and mangabeys (four species; please note that there is some disagreement among authorities about how many species of each of these kinds of animal actually exist, and the number of species in each group is being revised as new information about them is acquired by scientists; in addition, as species become extinct, the number of surviving species will be reduced), as well as the Allen's swamp monkey, the patas monkey, and the talapoin monkey. The members of *Cercopithecinae* are sometimes referred to as "the typical monkeys." They have in common dense coats of fur, often with manes on the neck and shoulders. They are quadrupedal, with primarily terrestrial species such as the baboons having longer limbs than primarily arboreal species. Using their tails as counterweights, arboreal species are able to move among tree branches on their hind limbs alone, allowing them to move their hands freely, especially when gathering food. However, only the patas monkey has adapted to an erect posture that allows it to square its shoulders above its center of gravity and to stand upright, which it does when scanning its locality. The terrestrial species, baboons especially, are too heavy in their upper bodies to sit or stand upright; when feeding, they often stand on three limbs, allowing one hand to move freely to bring food to the mouth. The jaws of *cercopithecine* species are very strong, bringing great pressure on the molars; their jaws tend to be long, with the molars having an extensive surface area. This helps them to grind their food. Distinguishing features of a *cercopithecine* species are cheek pouches, which tend to hold as much volume as the individual animal's stomach. The monkeys will stuff these pouches full, particularly when in a threatening area, and then retreat to a relatively safe place to eat the food; *Colobines* do not share this characteristic. The name *cercopithecine* means "tailed ape," and the tail was once thought to be something that distinguished the monkeys from the apes such as chimpanzees, but this is not the case. As they have spread through the Old World, *cercopithecines* have adapted to their new environments, and in cold climates the monkey's tails can be very short because blood circulation in the tails of *cercopithecines* is poor and the tails can freeze in cold weather. Thus, those species in cold climates have evolved by losing most of their tails.

The behavior of *cercopithecines* varies widely among their species. For instance, most respond to danger by fleeing, but baboons may respond by trying to take a bite out of the threat. When a predator is sighted, *cercopithecines* will usually cry out, warning one another of the danger. They then may make threatening gestures at the predator or run away; baboons use the cry not only to alert them to flee, but sometimes to rally them as a group. They can swarm over a foe and their bites can be deadly. In addition to living in groups, *cercopithecines* tend to be territorial, with territories defined by groups that live in them rather than by individual animals. They usually respond to intruders of their own species nonviolently, with cries, jumping up and down, and perhaps wagging nearby branches; even so, they all seem capable of violence against their own kind and may fight with intruders.

The subfamily *Cercopithecinae* probably evolved from macaques or a macaquelike species that lived in Africa. The macaques spread out of Africa and through much of Asia. As the great ice age ended about 14,000 years ago, the forests of Africa began to spread over what had been cold, dry territory. As the forest spread, so did the *cercopithecines*, adapting to their new ranges and becoming the distinct species of the present. The details of their speciation have yet to be revealed, partly because the fossils of their ancestors are rare and partly because scientific interest in their natural history is relatively recent; originally, most scientific interest was in their suitability for medical research.

Stump-tailed Macaque

Macaca arctoides

E. R. Luna

Status	Threatened
Listed	October 19, 1976
Family	Cercopithecidae (Old World monkey)
Description	Hair is dark to reddish brown, with face and rump naked and dark red.
Habitat	Dense forests at elevations up to 6,400 feet.
Food	Fruit, young leaves, buds, grains, insects, papayas, mangoes, rice, maize, and sugar cane.
Reproduction	Gestation lasts 166 to 185 days, resulting in a single birth.
Threats	Loss of habitat to logging and agriculture, hunting for food, killing by humans during military conflicts, and capture for sale to zoos or for medical research.
Range	China, India, Malaysia, possibly Vietnam.

Description

Adult male stump-tailed macaques, *Macaca arctoides*, measure 20.4 to 25.6 inches in length; females measure 19.1 to 23 inches, not counting their tail, which is small, only 0.6 to 2.7 inches long. Males tend to be larger than females, weighing 21.8 to 22.5 pounds, whereas females weigh 16.5 to 20 pounds. The stump-tailed macaque's coat varies from dark to reddish brown. The hair is long but not dense, and the tail is almost bare. The face and rump are bare, and they are pale in the young, becoming dark red in adults. The

adult's face is blotched with black or brown, as well as dark red. Adults tend to become bald on their foreheads and then scalps.

This species is also called the bear macaque.

Behavior

The stump-tailed macaque spends most of its waking time on the ground, but it sleeps in trees. It spends it day foraging, with a rest period at midday. The stump-tailed macaques live in groups with 5 to 40 members, with a mix of adult males, adult females, and their young. They communicate with a variety of facial and arm gestures, as well as 17 types of vocalization. The most common vocalization is a coo used when approaching other group members to avoid aggression and initiate grooming or other friendly interactions. The groups are usually led by a single dominant male. Some naturalists have reported that the groups migrate seasonally, perhaps according to the seasonal abundance of food.

Sexual intercourse is a difficult process, and it seems to take place even when the female is not in estrus. After the male has completed his part of the mating, he must wait with his female partner sitting in his lap because swelling in the vagina will not allow him to withdraw his penis. During this period, subdominant males will excitedly hit and pull the hair of the mating male. Pregnancies result in single births. Group behavior toward the young is poorly documented, perhaps because most observations on young have been in captivity, not in the wild with the large groups the animal normally forms. A youngster is weaned between 6 and 12 months of age. Females take 4 years to reach sexual maturity, but males take 6 to 8 years. Their life span in captivity tops 30 years.

The stump-tailed macaque eats a wide variety of foods and is opportunistic in its feeding habits. It eats fruit, young leaves, buds, grains, insects, and other small animals such as birds. They are said to be clever hunters. They sometimes eat crops such as papayas, mangoes, rice, maize, and sugar cane, making them pests to some farmers.

Habitat

Although the stump-tailed macaque can be occasionally found at low elevations, its prefers to live in mountains, up to 6,400 feet in elevation. The forests it prefers are dense, even though it spends little waking time in trees and feeds primarily on ground-level foods. Where its habitat has been replaced by agriculture, it sometimes tries to adjust to the new environment and will try to live among the crops.

Distribution

The stump-tailed macaque still survives in eastern India. It probably inhabits mountainous areas in southern China, and it has been observed in northern Malaysia. Its range once extended across northern Indochina into Vietnam, but its survival there is doubtful.

Threats

The stump-tailed macaque is rare throughout its range. In Indochina and Malaysia it has suffered terribly from human warfare, which has denuded some of its range and seriously disrupted the rest of it. In southern China, it is a crop pest. It is hunted for food through most of its range (apparently excepting Malaysia) and is hunted and trapped for capture for commercial sale everywhere. It is has been sold by the thousands to medical researchers and is in demand for zoos. In addition, its habitat is rapidly disappearing because of logging and agricultural expansion. Clear-cut logging has left much of the animal's natural range denuded of trees; agricultural has replace the animal's dense forests with crops. The sum result is that the stump-tailed macaque's population is sparse and exists in patches. The incursion of agriculture has made it hard for the stump-tailed macaque to migrate and thus mix its genes throughout its population; the patchiness of its remaining populations means that hunters are able to wipe it out piecemeal.

Conservation and Recovery

Both India and Malaysia have well-run wildlife reserves in the stump-tailed macaque's range. In India's case, poaching is a significant problem. As long as Western medicine maintains a demand for the stump-tailed macaque for laboratory research, the poaching is likely to remain a problem. In northern Malaysia, the drug trade interferes with studies of wildlife and the maintenance of wildlife reserves. Malaysia has very tough laws against the drug trade, and these laws are vigorously enforced; thus there is hope that Malaysia will be able to keep the growers and sellers of drug crops at bay and be able to protect some of its wildlife. This may come too late for the stump-tailed macaque, which may already be extinct in Malaysia. Through Indochina, constant warfare has made it very difficult for naturalists to keep track of wildlife, and although the stump-tailed macaque was once reported to live in Vietnam, it has probably disappeared from this part of its range.

Formosan Rock [=Taiwan] Macaque

Macaca cyclopis

Tsuey-shay Chen

Status	Threatened
Listed	October 19, 1976
Family	Cercopithecidae (Old World monkey)
Description	Covered with dark brown hair and sporting a beard.
Habitat	Rocky areas along the seashore and mountains with open ground and few trees.
Food	Berries, fruits, with roots, buds, immature leaves, insects, crustaceans, and shellfish.
Reproduction	Gestation lasts about 165 days, resulting in a single birth.
Threats	Hunting by humans for food and for scientific research.
Range	Taiwan

Description

Male Formosan rock macaques, *Macaca cyclopis,* tend to be a little larger than females. Males are 17.7 to 21.7 inches in length, not counting the tail, with the tail adding another 10.2 to 17.7 inches, and they weigh approximately 13.2 pounds. Females are 15.7 to 19.7 inches in length and they weigh approximately 10.9 pounds. Their faces are brown, with bare foreheads and beards; their coat is dark brown.

Behavior

The Formosan rock macaque is almost entirely terrestrial. This may not be what the Formosan rock macaque prefers; it is quite possible that it prefers forests, but humans have forced it into remote areas with few trees. For centuries, the Formosan rock macaque lived near and among humans; it has learned to avoid humans because it is now hunted for food and for medical research.

It lives in groups with multiple adult males and adult females, and there is a hierarchy among the males and the females. The females form the core of a group; they rarely migrate, and they instead form elaborate kinship relationships that determine where each one is in the female hierarchy. The dominant male usually has exclusive rights to mating with females. The mating season occurs from November to January followed by the birth season in April to June. Females 5 to 9 years old usually give birth every other year; older females give birth every year. Pregnancy lasts roughly 165 days, and it results in the birth of single infant. All members of a group share in the care of the infant, including the subdominant males, although the males' primary duty is to protect the young against predators. A youngster is weaned in 6 months to a year, the length of time varying with each youngster. Female Formosan rock macaques become sexually mature in 3.5 years; males become sexually mature in 4.5 years. The males are forced to leave their birth group before sexual maturity.

Habitat

The Formosan rock macaque lives among rocks on the seashore and in remote mountain areas with mixed coniferous-hardwood temperate forest as well as bamboo and grassland at elevations of 328 to 11,812 feet.

Distribution

The Formosan rock macaque once roamed most of Taiwan, but it is now restricted to remote mountain and seashore areas.

Threats

The Formosan rock macaque has several factors working against its survival. It lives on Taiwan; the government of Taiwan has been sanctioned by the United States for its disregard for international treaty obligations to protect endangered species. Taiwan is a hotbed for trade in animals and animal parts for southeast Asian folk medicine, and the government has made little effort to put a halt to the destructive trade in endangered animals for use in folk medicine. However, the folk medicine is not alone in exploiting the Formosan rock macaque. Western medicine uses the Formosan rock macaque for medical research. Further working against the Formosan rock macaque's survival is hunting by humans for food; as Taiwan's population has grown, so has the demand for animal protein. In addition to the Formosan rock macaque's being hunted for medical use and for food, expanding human agriculture has pushed the monkey into inhospitable areas of their native island. The Formosan rock macaque's habitat has largely been turned into farms.

The Formosan rock macaque's population has been fragmented, making the establishment and maintaining of a viable breeding population difficult, perhaps impossible. It is possible that there are already too few macaques alive to maintain the species' genetic diversity.

Conservation and Recovery

This species has little chance for survival in Taiwan. It has been transplanted to the Izu islands of Japan, where it may fare better.

Japanese Macaque

Macaca fuscata

Dennis Rausch

Status	Threatened
Listed	October 19, 1976
Family	Cercopithecidae (Old World monkey)
Description	Hair is shaggy, overall coloration varies from brown to gray, with the face and rump bare.
Habitat	Highland forests and along the coast in temperate to very cold climate; the northern Japanese macaques live in snow.
Food	Fruits, young leaves, buds, grain, nuts, bark, mushrooms, insects, snails, crayfish, and birds' eggs.
Reproduction	Single birth after gestation of approximately 173 days.
Threats	Loss of habitat.
Range	Japan

Description

Adult male Japanese macaques, *Macaca fuscata,* are somewhat larger than adult females. The adult male is 21.1 to 23.9 inches in length, not counting the tail, which is another 3.2 to 4.9 inches long; the adult males weigh 24.2 to 39.7 pounds. The adult females are 18.6 to 23.7 inches in length, not counting the tail, which is 2.8 to 4.1 inches long. The female weighs 8.3 to 39.7 pounds.

The Japanese macaque's fur is thick and fluffy, giving the animal the look of a stuffed toy; the length of the hair varies seasonally, with the Japanese macaque growing long, shaggy hair for winter. The fur color varies from brown to gray. The face and rump are bare and tend to be red in adults. It is possible that the facial color varies according to how much sunlight it has been exposed to. The face features a long beard.

This species is also known as the snow monkey and red-faced macaque.

Behavior

Although the Japanese macaque has been

associated with human beings for centuries, remarkably little is known about its behavior; this is changing at present because of a strong public interest in Japan and the United States in the animal's life and welfare created by television nature programs depicting the northern Japanese macaques — the "snow monkeys." Recent discoveries include the extraordinary capacity for creative thinking of the Japanese macaque and its capacity for learning new behavior and passing on that new behavior to subsequent generations. The most famous example of the creative problem solving of the Japanese macaque involves a physically handicapped female snow monkey who learned how to make some food more palatable (and perhaps tastier) by washing it in water; this innovation, never before seen in the Japanese macaque was slowly imitated by other snow monkeys. It has become learned behavior that is taught to youngsters, and it serves as an example of the kind of adaptive behavior that would be lost if the Japanese macaque disappears from its wild habitat. In recent times, the coastal Japanese macaques have also been observed adding a new food to their diet: seaweed.

The Japanese macaque forms close family units in which members care for one another. Members of the family unit that are sick, injured, or crippled, including those with birth defects, are to some degree cared for and watched after by other family members. Youngsters especially remain attached to their mothers and may help them find food as they grow into old age. The seeming humanlike behavior of problem solving, teaching and learning new behavior, and care for the infirm is controversial because it has led some people to speculate on whether the Japanese macaque has humanlike intelligence and possibly even a culture.

The Japanese macaque organizes itself into groups of 40 to 194 members; these groups remain associated with territories usually varying in size from 7.5 to 15.5 square miles, although the territories are occasionally smaller. Groups as large as 700 members have been recorded; in each case where a group reached 600 to 700 members, portions of the group broke away to form groups of less than 100 members. They live along remote seashores and in forested highlands; whether this is a product of inherited behavior or caused by humans pressing them out of more preferred regions is unclear. They are agile animals that move easily among the rocks of their seashore territories and move readily among tree branches in forested highlands. It is possible that they would prefer to be arboreal throughout their range, but that they have little choice but to be terrestrial in their seashore environment because humans dominate the inland where trees might be found. They are adaptable to different climates, with southern populations inhabiting temperate areas and northern populations living in snow. The snow monkeys seek out sources of warmth such as hot springs; they seem to like immersion in water and are good swimmers.

Females are the focus of a social group, and inheritance of territories is matrilinear. Males move about more than females and may change group affiliation when adults. The females may be sexually receptive several times a year. Gestation lasts about 173 days and results in a single birth. The mother is the primary care giver for an infant, but the entire group assumes some responsibility for raising the youngster and passing on survival behavior. A youngster is weaned between 6 and 12 months of age; females reach sexual maturity at 3.5 years of age, whereas males reach sexual maturity at 4.5 years of age. The female's primary ages of reproductivity are 6 to

18 years old.

The diet of the Japanese macaque is broad, and the animal seems open to trying new foods. Fruits, especially berries, are the preferred diet of the Japanese macaque. According to local availability, it also eats nuts, grains (including crops), young leaves, buds, bark, mushrooms, insects, spiders, snails, crayfish, and birds' eggs.

Habitat

The Japanese macaque is found in subtropical to subalpine, deciduous, broadleaf, and evergreen forest of Japan below elevations of 4,922 feet.

Distribution

The Japanese macaque occurs on all of Japan's islands except Hokkaido.

An introduced population of 150 individuals brought to Texas in 1972 has grown to more than 400.

Threats

The Japanese macaque population has been in decline for several decades and is presently diminishing rapidly. As Japan's human population continues to expand, the Japanese macaque's wilderness areas are being taken over by human communities and agriculture, pressing the animal into territories too small for it to maintain its numbers. An adaptable creature, the Japanese macaque sometimes lives in farm areas, feeding off the crops. The reaction of farmers to this is varied; some regard it as a pest, but other see it as good luck. The government tries to compensate its farmers for the losses they incur from the feeding of endangered species such as migrating birds; this has encouraged some farmers to provide a portion of their crops to the wild animals. Even so, the Japanese macaque may be killed as a farm pest. The animal is also losing its habitat to logging. Japan has few forested regions left, but these are being cut down for timber. Loss of forests means a significant loss of range in which to live and of foods which may sustain a Japanese macaque population.

Japan is striving to manage its wildlife areas well, in spite of sometimes overwhelming pressures from human communities. Poaching is a problem for the Japanese macaque because of Southeast Asian folk medicine, which is practiced in Japan, although to a lesser degree than in China, Taiwan, and Korea; the Japanese macaque's body parts are used in some folk medicines. The animal may also be kept as a pet; it is intelligent and looks like a toy, making it attractive to some people. Every animal taken as a pet is one less animal that can breed and perpetuate the species; in addition, they are highly social animals that require the company of many of their kind, so they do not fare well as lonely pets.

Their most significant natural predator is the lynx, although it is possible that birds of prey also eat them. At present, these natural predators seem to be insignificant in the Japanese macaque's decline.

Conservation and Recovery

Japan protects the Japanese macaque under law, and its scientific community is acutely aware of and concerned about the plight of the animal.

Lion-tailed Macaque

Macaca silenus

Rich Block

Status	Endangered
Listed	June 2, 1970
Family	Cercopithecidae (Old World monkey)
Description	Black coat with a big gray to silvery white, lionesque mane around its head. Its tail has a tassel at its tip.
Habitat	Tropical forest.
Food	Fruits, nuts, flowers, buds, leaves, sprouts, cardamon pulp, caterpillars, and insects.
Reproduction	Single birth after gestation of 162 to 186 days.
Threats	Loss of habitat and hunting by humans.
Range	India

Description

The lion-tailed macaque, *Macaca silenus*, is an impressive-looking animal with a thick, powerfully built body. Adult males tend to be larger than adult females, with males measuring 20.1 to 24 inches in length; tail length is 10.0 to 15.2 inches. Females measure 18.1 inches in length, with the tail measuring 10.0 to 12.6 inches. Males weigh 11 to 22 pounds, while females weigh 6.6 to 13.2 pounds. The lion-tailed macaque's fur is black except for a great, fluffy fringe of hair around the head, which is gray to silvery white. Its face is black with grayish eyelids. Neonates have brown hair and pale pink skin. This macaque gets its name not from its lionlike mane, but from the tassel of hair at the end of its tail. When one of these animals is in its quadrupedal stance and giving a person a hard, fierce stare, it looks impressively regal.

Behavior

The behavior of the lion-tailed macaque differs from that of other macaques in two significant respects: It assiduously avoids humans, and the dominant males of groups make loud cries when their groups are on the move. This loud cry serves to pull the members of a group together, and it probably serves to let other groups know where the group is.

Much has yet to be learned about the lion-tailed macaque's behavior. For instance, it has been reported to live in groups with only one adult male and yet has also been reported to live in groups with more than one adult male. A possible explanation for this is that in small groups a dominant male can drive away all other adult males, whereas in large groups this would take too much time and energy, forcing the dominant male to tolerate subordinate adult males; this is speculation, much more observation of lion-tailed macaque groups is required to clarify their social structure. Groups usually have 10 to 20 members, although 4 to 34 have been reported.

The lion-tailed macaque does not appear to be particularly territorial, although groups tend to remain in areas of 100 to 500 acres during a year. Groups seem fairly tolerant of each other and avoid confrontations by avoiding each other (hence the value of the dominant male crying out loud enough for others to hear him and to stay out of the way). Some research suggests that a group may have a core area within its range that other groups usually avoid.

Lion-tailed macaques spend about 99% of their lives in trees. During dry periods that occur a couple of times per year, they descend to drink from streams. Anything that alarms them will send them scampering back up high into the treetops. Most of the year, they do not need to descend to find water because rain is so abundant that plenty of fresh drinking water may be found cupped in leaves and in tree hollows.

The dominant male of a group seems to have exclusive mating rights to the females in the group. Groups coalesce around their females because males tend to be the ones who move from one group to another. There is some evidence to suggest that males will not mate with female relatives, which means that they have a powerful incentive to migrate to groups other than their birth group. When is estrus, females have pronounced genital swelling. Mating peak season is from January to February. Births occur year round. Gestation lasts 162 to 186 days and results in a single birth. Youngsters are weaned at 6 to 12 months of age. Sexual maturity occurs at between 2.5 and 4 years of age, with females apparently reaching sexual maturity a year before males do. Reaching sexual maturity does not mean instant mating; females usually do not bear young until their fifth year of age, often not until their eighth year. This means that the lion-tailed macaques have a slow rate of reproduction, making it hard for them to reestablish themselves in areas where their numbers have been severely reduced.

The lion-tailed macaque is omnivorous, although most of its diet is vegetarian. It prefers fruits and where fruits are plentiful they may comprise 90% of the animal's diet. It is a somewhat opportunistic feeder and can adjust some to what it environment offers. It eats nuts, seeds, flowers, buds, grasses, sprouts, leaves, cardamon pulp, caterpillars, insects, toads, and lizards. It is possible that it raids crops for grains, but this has not been recorded and would seem to be very rare, if it ever actually occurs.

Habitat

The lion-tailed macaque lives in a wet, mountainous evergreen, broadleaf forest. It prefers areas with very tall trees (95 feet high) and lives most of the time in the treetops. It is found at elevations up to 4,922 feet.

Distribution

The lion-tailed macaque occurs in the southern reaches of the Western Ghat mountain range along the west coast of southern India.

Threats

The lion-tailed macaque is very endangered. It has been thought since the early 1970s that fewer than 400 (probably less than 300) survive in the wild, with perhaps 300 more surviving in captivity, but there is one report from the 1980s that suggests that there may be 2,000 to 3,000 of them in the northern part of their range; this would mean that the total number of lion-tailed macaques would be no more than 3,500. Most naturalists disagree with this number, generally asserting that 100 to 300 altogether exist in the wild, putting the lion-tailed macaque very near extinction. The principal reason for the animal's decline has been the loss of its habitat to agriculture, industry, mining, and roads. It is also hunted by humans for food and for its fur, and it is captured for sale as a pet, for sale to zoos, or for sale for medical research. It does not seem to figure greatly in the rapacious southeast Asian folk medicine market that threatens many other monkeys.

Conservation and Recovery

Ascertaining how many lion-tailed macaques actually exist in the wild and where they exist are essential to creating a plan for preserving them. India has created wildlife sanctuaries for many of its endangered species, including one in the southern part of the lion-tailed macaque's range.

Breeding programs have met with some success and offer promise for preserving the lion-tailed macaque in captivity even if it disappears from the wild; this would require a large enough captive breeding population to maintain the species' genetic diversity and probably an international studbook so that zoos and artificial preserves can mix and match mates. This is complicated by the lion-tailed macaques high intelligence, which has created a complex social structure in which several different animals need to be present in order to encourage mating and then to raise the resulting young. Further, lion-tailed macaques plainly dislike humans and are very uncomfortable among humans, making their care in captivity difficult.

Naturalists in general regard the state of the lion-tailed macaque with alarm; it is feared by most that the animal will be extinct in the wild before the year 2000 and that the captive population will follow within a generation.

Toque Macaque

Macaca sinica

Anne Zeller

Status	Threatened
Listed	October 19, 1976
Family	Ceropithecidae (Old World monkey)
Description	Overall coat is gray or yellow-to-red brown, with a pale underbody. The hair on the head swirls out of the central crown.
Habitat	Rain forest, dry forest, and scrubland.
Food	Fruit, young leaves, grains, and insects.
Reproduction	Gestation lasts between 150 and 170 days, resulting in a single birth.
Threats	Loss of habitat.
Range	Sri Lanka

Description

Adult male toque macaques tend to be larger than females. Adult males are 17.4 to 21 inches long, not counting the tail, with the tail adding another 21.6 to 24.5 inches; adult females are 17.0 to 17.8 inches long, not counting the tail, with the tail adding another 18.3 to 22.4 inches. Adult males weigh 9.7 to 18.5 pounds; adult females weigh 7.5 to 9.5 pounds. Their fur is yellowish or reddish brown, gray, or olive-gray; their faces are light brown. Their heads feature a swirling crown of hair.

Behavior

Toque macaques live in groups of 8 to 43 members. These groups have an assortment of adult males, adult females, and their young. The males are dominant and get first chance at food the group discovers. Adult females generally push out young females in the competition for food. Although most foods are scattered when found, making it unlikely that the dominant members of the troop can exclude any others from eating, in periods of food shortages, the young females will starve to death, followed, if the shortage is severe enough, by adult females, then young males. During good food periods, adult females will often kill female youngsters; this seems to be a behavior designed to increase the adult female's chance of getting food during hard times because the young female could grow up to be a strong, dominant adult. The killings decrease during hard times, probably because the adult females are too busy looking for food. In spite of this, adult females outnumber adult males by two to one. The males must migrate from their birth group to another one, and they are frequently killed by dogs when alone. They are also subject to exclusion by other groups, which could result in their not being able to share in food resources, resulting in their starvation.

The toque macaque spends about 75% of its time in trees and seems nervous even in well-covered shrubland. During the night, it sleeps high in trees. During the day, they often live among the entellus langur (*Presbytis entellus*; please see separate entry). They play with the entellus langurs, share grooming with them, rest and eat with them; the relationship seems to provide the small toque macaque with additional security.

Fruits and seeds are the favored foods of the toque macaque, but it will eat young leaves, and probably buds. It also eats insects. With little natural habitat left, it is probably inevitable that the toque macaque invades farmlands for food. They will eat grain crops and the fruits of some orchards.

Habitat

The toque macaque lives in lowland, gallery, and semi-deciduous forest near permanent water at elevations up to 5,000 feet.

Distribution

Toque macaques occur in central and eastern Sri Lanka.

Threats

Most of the toque macaque's native forests have been logged and replaced with plantations, and agriculture has taken over its shrublands. The ideal territory for a toque macaque group is about 60 square miles in size, but their groups are squeezed into territories as small as one fifth of a square mile. Although the USFWS lists the toque macaque as "threatened," a step better than endangered, most naturalists who have studied the animal consider it to be in immediate danger of extinction because of the loss of its habitat.

Only 15% of female and 10% of male toque macaques reach full maturity. They die from hunger, from infanticide, and from predators such as dogs.

Conservation and Recovery

The toque macaque has the misfortune of living in a region that has long been the scene of civil unrest. Warfare and terrorism have made it hard to establish reserves to protect wildlife. For its long-term survival, the toque macaque needs a reserved range of several hundred square miles; one in which trees are preserved and in which water is plentiful either from rainfall or in streams.

Tibetan Macaque

Macaca thibetana

Noel Rowe

Status	Threatened
Listed	October 19, 1976
Family	Cercopithecidae (Old World monkey).
Description	Grayish brown fur, hairy ears, and a crown of radiating erect hairs.
Habitat	Montane forests at elevations between 2,500 and 6,400 feet.
Food	Primarily vegetarian, supplementing its diet with birds' eggs and small animals.
Reproduction	Gestation probably lasts 150 to 170 days, usually resulting in only a single birth.
Threats	Loss of habitat to logging, agricultural development, and military activities, as well as capture and sale for medical research.
Range	China and Tibet.

Description

The Tibetan macaque, *Macaca thibetana*, has been little studied, and most of the current information requires more scientific study. Adult Tibetan macaques measure 24 inches in length, not counting their short tails, which are 2 to 3 inches long. Males weigh 26.5 pounds and are probably larger on average than females. The Tibetan macaque has long, dense gray fur, and furry ears, probably adaptations to its cold environment; its short tail is also probably an adaptation to a cold climate. The Tibetan macaque has a crown of stiff hair that radiates out from the center, and a long beard.

Other common names include Tibetan stump-tailed macaque, or Père David's macaque.

Behavior

The Tibetan macaque is little observed in the wild, and when writing about it, naturalists tend to make inferences based on what is known of the bonnet macaque (*Macaca radiata*), which has similar behavior. It is known that the Tibetan macaque seems equally comfortable on the ground and in trees, and divides its time between them. It probably forms social groups of up to 70 members, with several adult males, several adult females, and their young. Mating habits are not recorded, but females are probably sexually receptive several times during a seasonal mating period. Gestation likely lasts between 150 and 170 days and probably results in a single birth. Youngsters are weaned between 6 and 12 months of age, with females reaching sexual maturity between 2.5 and 4 years of age, and males reaching sexual maturity between 4 and 7 years of age.

The Tibetan macaque is found in all types of forests within its mountainous range, and it seems to try to adapt to agricultural development when such development intrudes into its natural habitat. It probably eats fruits and young leaves, as well as other kinds of vegetation, and its is known to eat birds' eggs and small animals. It is reported that these macaques are fed by humans near temples.

Habitat

The Tibetan macaque inhabits a chilly range that has seasonal variations in temperature. Winters are generally cold and snowy; food can become scarce, but the animal seems to make do with roots and other foods it can dig up. Seasonal scarcity of naturally occurring foods can make nearby agricultural areas tempting targets for feeding. The Tibetan macaque does not seem particularly choosy about the kinds of forests it inhabits, and will not only live in old-growth forests but in the patchy woods that sometimes appear after an area has been logged.

Distribution

The Tibetan macaque lives in the mountains of eastern Tibet and western China.

Threats

The Tibetan macaque is rapidly losing its habitat to logging and agricultural development. It is possible that it numbers among the many macaques that are captured and sold for medical research.

Conservation and Recovery

The Tibetan macaque seems to be an intelligently adaptive animal, but is unable to live without some sort of woodland haven. Therefore, it needs a reserve where logging and agriculture are prohibited. If more were known about its biology and behavior, more specific measures could be identified for helping it to survive.

Drill

Mandrillus leucophaeus

Irwin Bernstein

Status	Endangered
Listed	October 19, 1976
Family	Cercopithecidae
Description	Baboon-like with a dark brown coat, black face surrounded by white hair; rump is blue or purple.
Habitat	Lowland rain forests, coastal and riverine forests.
Food	Fruits and invertebrates; lizards, seeds, roots, and fungi.
Reproduction	Females rarely breed.
Threats	Loss of habitat; extensive hunting.
Range	Cameroon, Equatorial Guinea (Bioko), and Nigeria.

Description

The taxonomy is disputed. Until 1989, the drill was included in the baboon genus *Papio*. Male drills, *Mandrillus leucophaeus*, have much larger fangs than the females. These fangs are probably used in display confrontations between rival males. The males weigh up to 37.5 pounds and are much more heavily built than female drills. Males may have a head-and-body length of 28 inches, with a tale length of 4.7 inches. Females measure 26 inches with a tail length of 3.2 inches and weigh 22 pounds.

The drill is dark brown, with a black face and a white fringe of hair. The muzzle is long and has lateral ridges. The naked rump is blue to purple, and there is red on the inner thighs. The drill resembles baboons in body shape, hair distribution, and facial structure, but it eschews environments that other baboons favor.

Behavior

The drill's diet is not well known, but it is known to eat fruits, seeds, roots, fungus, and small invertebrates. It eschews open areas, but it is possible that it may occasionally raid fruit crops in agricultural areas.

It lives in small groups of about 20 members (sometimes fewer); these groups may associate with one another to form troops of as many as 180 members. The small group usually has only one adult male and the group will retain its cohesiveness even when associating with several other groups with their own adult males. Each male periodically cries out, helping its group members to find and coalesce around him. Mature males are known to live alone, and they sometimes form their own groups of females or take over the group of another male. The process of takeover has not been well observed, but it likely involves elaborate facial displays intended to show off the males' fangs and to express hostility. Violent confrontations between rival males are possible.

The drill lives primarily on the ground, but will occasionally climb into trees to harvest fruit or to eat. Its day is spent primarily foraging, with its nights spent at rest and socializing.

Habitat

The drill lives mostly in coastal forests and riverine forests, as well as inland in lowland rain forests. It probably once extensively inhabited inland rain forests in Cameroon, Equatorial Guinea, Gabon, and Nigeria. Although considered by many naturalists to be a form of baboon (hence the *Papio* genus designation), unlike most baboons the drill avoids open areas. Although they prefer old primary forests, they have been known on rare occasions to make do with new secondary forests, particularly if the secondary were selectively logged instead of clear cut, thus leaving some old trees to form the basis of the forest.

Distribution

The drill lives between the Sanaga River to the south in Cameroon and the Cross River to the north in Nigeria, with the subspecies *Papio leucophaeus poenis* living on the island of Bioko (also called Ferndando Póo), which is part of Equatorial Guinea. This area is very small, but the drill may once have extended farther south to the Zaire River in Gabon. The population in Nigeria (subspecies *Papio leucophaeus mundamensis*) was severely threatened by habitat loss, having become restricted to small patches of forest. Before 1987 the drill was believed to be extinct in Nigeria and on Bioko, with the only confirmed population confined to Korup National Park in Cameroon. Surveys conducted in Nigeria between 1987 and 1990 confirmed that drills survived in four forest blocks. A survey of Bioko in 1989 found drills in two patches of habitat. These populations are believed to be a distinct subspecies.

Wild populations are estimated at between 2,000 and 10,000 individuals. The Bioko population is around 500 animals. About 60 drills are held in zoos worldwide, while 57 are in a captive breeding and rehabilitation facility in the Afi River Reserve in northern Cross River State in Nigeria.

Threats

The destruction of the drill's habitat has been thorough, leaving it almost nowhere to live. Loss of habitat to logging has almost certainly doomed the drills in Nigeria. Hunting now is driving the drill toward complete extinction, with the drill having already disappeared from almost all of its traditional range south of the Sanaga River and over half of its range in Cameroon north of the Sanaga. It is hunted for food and is considered to be good eating; its meat is valued for its sweet flavor. It is also hunted as a crop pest. The loud cries of the male group leaders make the drill easy to locate, and because the groups tend to coalesce around the male, dozens of them may be shot down all at once.

With so few drills remaining in the wild, fragmentation of habitat, which permanently isolates drill groups, impedes mating and reduces the strength of genetic material.

Conservation and Recovery

Nigeria has created wildlife reserves in its areas where drills have been found, but the effectiveness of these reserves has yet to be fully evaluated, and whether drills still live in them is doubtful. Cameroon has tried to regulate the hunting of its drills, but the popularity of the animal's meat and the ease with which it can be slaughtered have made enforcement of the regulations very difficult.

Several dozen drills are held in captive collections around the world. The individual drills are selective in choosing a mate, but the Hannover Zoo in Germany has had some success with breeding them and maintains an international studbook for helping other zoos crossbreed drills with those in other collections. Even so, the genetic diversity among the captive drills may be too low, making long-term survival of zoo-bred drills doubtful.

By far, the most successful effort to rescue wild drills in distress is at the Drill Rehabilitation and Breeding Center, which started in 1991 with 5 drills in Calabar, Nigeria. These animals, and most of the drills at the facility, were captured when hunters killed their mothers. Donated by citizens of Cross River State, these drills were raised to maturity and have begun propagating. The first captive-bred drill was born in 1994, and 16 more have been born since then.

"Drill Ranch," as it is called, credits its success to the involvement of the local people who have developed a sense of responsibility to protect drills. A village-based initiative to reduce poaching recruited 10 men, mostly former hunters, to form anti-poaching patrols, and to participate in community education.

Once the Afi Mountain Wildlife Sanctuary is secured from poaching, the center expects to release some of the captive population back into the wild. Because these drills are the progeny of younger mothers who have not lost their instincts for survival in the wild, and because they are being released into their original habitat, the center expects good results.

The center is also considering lending breeding animals to zoos that hold drills so that they can improve the genetic stock of their population.

Mandrill

Mandrillus sphinx

Irwin Bernstein

Status	Endangered
Listed	October 19, 1976
Family	Cercopithecidae
Description	Ground monkey with heavy body and short arms; male's face and hindquarters are brightly colored.
Habitat	Dense wet forests and brushlands.
Food	Omnivorous.
Reproduction	Estrus lasts 33 days. Gestation lasts between 172 and 176 days.
Threats	Loss of habitat due to logging and agricultural development.
Range	Cameroon, Congo, Equatorial Guinea, and Gabon.

Description

The mandrill, *Mandrillus sphinx*, is a ground monkey. It was included in the *Papio* genus until 1989. Its heavy body and comparatively short arms are much more adapted to forest floor dwelling than to life in trees. The male's face and hindquarters are renowned as the brightest colored of any mammal. The nose is red and the cheek swellings are prominent and colored a bright blue. A yellow band covers the underside of the chin. The hindquarters have blue patches with pink portions on each side. Females and juveniles have a duller blue snout and a buffy beard. From the tip of the snout to the end of the tail, the mandrill measures 22.0 (females) to 31.9 inches (males). The tail is 2.8 to 3.9 inches long. Females weigh 25.3 pounds; males weigh 59.3 pounds. The mandrill has a recorded longevity exceeding 40 years.

Mandrills were part of the baboon genus, *Papio*, which is why their scientific name is sometimes given as *Papio sphinx*, but some naturalists believe they should be in a separate genus, *Mandrillus*, which they would share with the drill (please see separate entry). They are larger than baboons, but their posture, hair distribution, skeletal proportions, and dentition are similar to baboons. They also make facial expressions that echo those commonly found among baboons. On the other hand, they tend to prefer environments eschewed by baboons and their social organization may also differ, although much more information is needed in order for the differences to be made clear.

Behavior

Mandrills are diurnal and are both arboreal and terrestrial. They travel on the ground or in the lower reaches (no higher than 16 feet) of trees. During fruiting season, they will travel some distance in search of their preferred food. They like to forage along streams and in mature secondary forests without dense undergrowth. They have an eclectic diet of fruits, seeds, roots, leaves, buds, fungi, insects, and small vertebrates. When food is hard to come by — usually in dry seasons — the mandrill sometimes raids farmlands.

Those that live in small groups of 15 to 50 members have one adult male. In multimale-multifemale groups the group size averages 95 members, with males having a distinct hierarchy. Not much is understood of their social life, but their associations with each other seem to be flexible with considerable movement among groups and shifting affiliations among groups that may create troops of as many as 200 members. They communicate with facial expressions and complex cries. For instance, the yawn that bares fangs is a way of warning another individual mandrill away, and the cries seem to tell mandrills of their associations.

The mating season occurs from July to October followed by births from December to April. Among mandrills, aunts (real or surrogate) may assist in feeding and transporting the young.

Mandrills are one of the few Old World monkeys to have cutaneous glands. The sternal gland is located in the triangular area in the middle of the mandrill's chest. Males

older than 7 years scent-mark, but the alpha male will scent-mark frequently.

Habitat

The mandrill is found in primary and secondary dense rain forests as well as coastal and gallery forests. It is able to adapt to regenerating forests and secondary growth; however, agricultural areas are intolerable to the mandrill.

Distribution

The mandrills have been exterminated in much of their traditional range, a large forest that once extended from central Gabon along the coast of equatorial West Africa. Most of them now live in the central forest of Gabon, much of which has yet to be disrupted by human developments. In small numbers, they still live in patches of forest in Cameroon, southwestern Congo, and Equatorial Guinea (Rio Muni). There are rumors of sightings of the mandrill in Nigeria and Togo.

Threats

In both Cameroon and Guinea the mandrill is hunted for food. This species provides the favorite meat of 20 percent of the Fang people in Equatorial Guinea. Additionally, their bright coloration makes them a highly popular zoo attraction. Illegal exportation to zoos and "investigation centers" are a serious threat to the mandrill.

The forests in which the mandrill is found are being logged for timber, cleared for plantations and shifting agriculture, and cut for logging access roads. In Cameroon, the coastal forests are being destroyed at a rapid rate due to their accessibility for logging and fertile soil. In Equatorial Guinea, the range of the mandrill had been significantly reduced by felling by 1967 and has been further reduced.

While captive breeding programs in zoos have seen some success for this species, a new problem confronts survival, one of sex distortion. It has been observed, more often than not, by zoo professionals that in captivity there seems to be disproportionate female births. Distorted sex ratios can make efforts to rebuild an already small population futile.

Conservation and Recovery

Captive breeding programs for the mandrill seem hopeful and have seen some success. The mandrill is also protected within Wong-Wonue National Park in Gabon. Some live in the Campo Reserve in Cameroon, where they have some hope of protection from hunters.

Gelada Baboon

Theropithecus gelada

Irwin Bernstein

Status	Threatened
Listed	October 19, 1976
Family	Cercopithecidae (Old World monkey)
Description	Gray to dark brown; males have white sideburns and a blackish brown "cape;" both sexes have pink skin on the front of the neck running down to the chest.
Habitat	Alpine meadows, rocky gorges and other treeless areas.
Food	Grass, grass seeds and grass bulbs.
Reproduction	Gestation lasts for about six months and lactation extends through about eighteen months.
Threats	Alteration of habitat due to agricultural development and human settlement.
Range	Ethiopia

Description

Theropithecus seems to be a divergent from the genus *Papio* (true baboons). Most believe the speciation occurred sometime during the Pliocene epoch, when these species invaded grassland habitats. Of the known three species of *Theropithecus*, only *Theropithecus gelada* persists.

The gelada baboon is gray to dark brown in color. Its hair is sexually dimorphic: Males have white sideburns and a blackish brown "cape" or mane, consisting of a series of long hairs. Females lack the sideburns and mane. Both sexes have pink skin on the front of the

neck running down to the chest. This skin is in an hourglass-shape and is surrounded by white fur in males, but is surrounded by raised vesicles in females.

The gelada baboon has a caved-in snout. It is rather large and heavily built. From the tip of the snout to the base of the tail, males measure from 27.2 to 29.1 inches; females measure from 19.7 to 25.6 inches. The tail is 15.7 to 19.7 inches long in males, and in females the tail measures from 12.8 to 15.7 inches. Males average 44.1 pounds; females 25.8 pounds.

Females remain estrous for 32 to 36 days. Pregnancy can be distinguished by a swelling of the chest vesicles and simultaneous brilliant pink coloration of these vesicles. Gestation lasts for about 150 to 180 days and lactation extends through about eighteen months. The chest patch becomes scarlet during weeks 4 to 8 of pregnancy. The nipples are located close together on the chest, which allows for young to take in both nipples when feeding.

Behavior

Communication of primates is most generally displayed with physical color patterns and facial expressions. Male gelada baboons will reveal their white teeth and gums of the upper jaw with a simple inversion of the upper lip (a "lip flip"); simultaneously, the scalp is retracted to reveal the eyelids. These displays are used to express rage, fear, or jealousy. Males will round up straying females with a barking vocalization along with the lipflip.

The social system of the gelada baboon is one in which individuals will organize themselves into "quasi-military" units, consisting of up to 300 members. Within smaller groups the females have a hierarchy. Those higher on the hierarchical ladder will protect (or deprive) inferiors from males. Success and failure in fights between males for the attention of females may result in change of the order of command within the troop.

Primates display a primarily omnivorous diet, displayed in the uniform development of the cusps and lack of specialization of dentition. However, the gelada baboon is strictly herbivorous (or more precisely granivorous); as a result the cheek teeth possess defined ridges used to mince vegetation. The main foods of this species are grass, grass seeds, and grass bulbs. Blades of grass are picked, bunched into the palm, and transferred to the mouth. Seeds are stripped from the stems with the teeth or by individually plucking each seed with the index finger and the thumb. This species is diurnally and terrestrially active.

Habitat

The gelada baboon is limited to the central mountains at elevations between 4,593 to 14,436 feet in Ethiopia. At night this species takes shelter on cliffs along gorges. During the day the gelada baboon may be observed feeding on grass in montane grasslands. It seems to prefer open lands and is found in alpine meadows, rocky gorges, and other treeless areas and is the most terrestrial non-human primate, spending almost all of its life on the ground. It is a poor tree-climber.

Distribution

The genus *Theropithecus* is thought to have diverged from the genus *Papio* in the Pliocene epoch. Fossil evidence from this era indicates *Theropithecus* ranged from as far north as Ternifine on the Mediterranean coast of Africa to Swartkrans and Makapan in South Africa.

Now, the gelada baboon is restricted to northern Ethiopia and inhabits the Ethiopian plateau exclusively. It occurs in the Simien National Park in Ethiopia.

Threats

The gelada baboon is primarily affected by agricultural development and human encroachment and settlement in its range. Agricultural practices have forced this baboon into less suitable habitat. Grass density is lower and as a direct result population size decreases. Habitat destruction is severe on the Amhara Plateau and has resulted in heavy topsoil erosion. With intense agricultural development the gelada baboon's habitat is being altered by eucalyptus plantations.

The gelada baboon is additionally threatened by take of individuals for exportation. Traditionally, every 8 years Galla tribesmen shoot large numbers of males for their manes. These manes are used to make headdresses and capes which are worn during ceremonies.

The gelada baboon suffers from a severely restricted distribution. Local populations are reduced due to habitat restriction by agriculture and settlement. In the late 1970s the world population of the gelada baboon was estimated to be about 600,000. In 1973, 440,000 individuals were estimated from the highlands. Of five observed populations 2 were considered to have been heavily cultivated (W. Geech and Debra Libanos), 1 had undergone some degree of habitat disturbance (Bole) and 2 others were relatively undisturbed (Sankaber and E. Geech) when comparing population size and densities. Habitat disturbance has a direct correlation to population success.

Conservation and Recovery

Killing or capturing the gelada baboon for any reason is illegal in Ethiopia. However, exportation of the animal was still active in the late 1960s and early 1970s. Between 1968 and 1972, 1,231 gelada baboons were imported into the United States from Kenya and Tanzania (where the species does not occur); report falsification is suspected.

The gelada baboon is held in zoos and has been bred in captivity with much success.

Tana River Mangabey

Cercocebus galeritus

Peter Waser

Status	Endangered
Listed	June 2, 1970
Family	Cercopithecidae (Old World monkey)
Description	Long, soft hair, gray at the roots and mainly gray-green and brown to almost black at the tips, yellowish-gray limbs, with yellow colored rings on its long tail.
Habitat	Tropical rain forest of the Tana River.
Food	Primarily fruit, but also leaves, mushrooms, grubs and insects.
Reproduction	Births occur between November and January.
Threats	Conversion of habitat for agricultural and cattle ranching.
Range	Kenya

Description

The Tana River mangabey, *Cercocebus galeritus*, is covered with long, soft hair which is gray at the roots and mainly gray-green and brown to almost black at the tips. It is yellow on its lower back and the medial-lateral portion of its limbs is yellowish-gray. Its tail has yellow rings.

Males measure from 19.7 to 24.6 inches in head-and-body length, with a tail length from 3.0 to 29.9 inches. Females measure from 17.3 to 20.7 inches with tail length of 1.6 to 23.6 inches. Males weigh about 22.5 pounds; females 11.9 pounds.

The Tana River mangabey is also known as the agile mangabey, or golden-bellied mangabey.

Behavior

This mangabey lives in troops of 17 to 36, and the troops may have 1 to 6 adult males each. Troops sometimes combine to create groups of as many as 60 members. Home ranges seem to overlap among groups. The mangabey varies its movements between the ground and the trees, but it seems to require tree cover. It communicates through a series of high-pitched screeches.

The diet of the Tana River mangabey is primarily frugivorous, but also includes leaves, mushrooms, grubs, and insects, and many other foods, such as lizards. These mangabeys use 61 species of plants for food, but the palm tree, *Phoenix reclinata*, provides 62% of the diet.

The estrous cycle lasts for 30 days and gestation varies. Females will reach sexual maturity by their fourth year, while males will not become sexually mature until they are six or seven. For a female, the period between births is one-and-a-half and two years. Birth season occurs from November to February.

Habitat

The Tana River mangabey is endemic to the primary and secondary forests and *Acacia* woodlands along the Tana River. This area is seasonally flooded.

Distribution

This species is distributed along the Tana River in Kenya and probably is fewer than 1,000 in number. There once was a great forest along the Tana River, and in those days the Tana River mangabey may have numbered in the tens of thousands. They now live in patches of forest and travel across open areas from one patch to another.

Threats

For many years tribesmen have converted the gallery forests for agricultural and cattle ranching purposes, using the slash-and-burn method. In response to forest felling, the Tana River mangabey has left its riverine habitat and has ventured about 4 miles inland to an inaccessible area. Furthermore, the river has been dammed, thus changing the pattern of seasonal floods that once renewed the forests and their food sources along the river.

Conservation and Recovery

The Tana River mangabey is protected by the Kenyan Game Department. No capture permits may be issued for this species for any reason. The largest number of the Tana River mangabeys live in Kenya's Tana River Game Reserve.

This species is listed as endangered in the *Red Data Book* maintained by the IUCN. It is listed under CITES, Appendix I: Trade prohibited, which means that by treaty the Tana River mangabey may not be traded internationally. The animal is listed in the 1969 African Convention in class A, which means that it may only be hunted by the permission of the highest government authority, and even then, the hunting must be either for scientific study or a pressing national interest.

White-collared Mangabey

Cercocebus torquatus

Noel Rowe

Status	Endangered
Listed	October 19, 1976
Family	Ceropithecidae
Description	Long tail and pronounced snout; gray above and white underneath
Habitat	Mangrove, coastal galleries and inland swamp forests.
Food	Fruit, leaves, animal prey.
Reproduction	Single young after gestation of 168 days.
Threats	Loss of habitat due to logging.
Range	Liberia, Ghana, Sierra Leone, Ivory Coast, Nigeria, Cameroon, Gabon, and Angola.

Description

Taxonomy is disputed for *Cercocebus torquatus*, which includes *C. t. atys* as a subspecies (see separate entry). Some taxonomists believe *C. atys* is a full species. Mangabeys have long legs and pronounced snouts. The white-collared mangabey measures 22 to 24.6 inches from snout to the end of the tail; the tail is 23.7 to 29.5 inches long; its weight averages 23.7 pounds. The white-collared mangabey has a reddish-brown cap, a white collar, and white eyelids. The back is dark brown to black and the dark tail has a white tip. The underparts are white.

This mangabey is also known as the collared mangabey, red-capped mangabey, and smoky mangabey.

Behavior

The white-collared mangabey has a complex social behavior that involves groups of 14 to 23 members mixing with other groups, sharing dominant males, and creating subgroups within large groups. The white-collared mangabey forms associations with the troops of other primates, including mona monkeys, white-throated guenons, western red colobuses, and black-and-white colobuses.

This mangabey is diurnal, arboreal, and terrestrial. They have been known to travel on the ground in single file and feed on the forest floor and in emergent trees along the way.

Sexual maturity occurs at 32 months but first breeding does not occur until 54 months.

A single young is born after gestation of 168 days; the interval between births is about 13 months.

Habitat

The white-collared mangabey inhabits mangrove, coastal galleries, and inland swamp forests, with proximity to water. It prefers to live in old forests with high canopies.

Distribution

The white-collared mangabey is represented by two populations separated by 500 miles. This could reduce genetic vigor, as the possibility of these populations overlapping and reproducing is nil. The white-collared mangabey occurs from Sierra Leone to Angola, including Liberia, Ghana, Ivory Coast, Nigeria, Cameroon and Gabon. It occurs in Tai National Park, Bia Forest Reserve, Omo Forest Reserve, and Korup Reserve.

Threats

The white-collared mangabey has been ravaged by hunting and trapping for food, but logging is the principal reason for its decline throughout Equatorial Africa. In the western part of its range, large scale felling is occurring, especially in the Ivory Coast. In Sierra Leone, less than 4 percent of the white-collared mangabey's habitat remains.

Conservation and Recovery

Cameroon requires that hunters have permits to hunt or trap the white-collared mangabey, and it maintains a population of the animal in its Korup National Park. Cameroon is receiving financial help from international conservation organizations to maintain and protect the park. Congo (Brazzaville) is having trouble protecting its white-collared mangabeys because of a shortage of funds needed to employ rangers. Equatorial Guinea does not protect its mangabeys. The white-collared mangabey may only be exported by a government issued permit in Gabon, but hunting is unrestricted. The white-collared mangabey is virtually extinct in Gabon, with only a small number living in the Sette Cama Forest Reserve. Nigeria requires that hunters or exporters of white-collared mangabeys have government permits, but the law is little enforced. Nigeria lacks the funds to employ an adequate number of game wardens to protect the mangabey and also has an exploding population that is short on animal protein, making the mangabey's status in Nigeria precarious. About a forty square mile area within Nigeria's Okomu Forest Reserve is protected by law from hunting and logging, and there is hope that the white-collared mangabey may survive there.

A small number of white-collared mangabeys have been bred in captivity, including a few second-generation births, but lack of genetic diversity in captive collections is a significant problem.

Sooty Mangabey

Cercocebus torquatus atys

Noel Rowe

Status	Endangered
Listed	October 19, 1976
Family	Ceropithecidae (Old World monkey)
Description	Long and silky mostly gray hair.
Habitat	Primary rain forest
Food	Fruit, nuts, seeds, and leaves.
Reproduction	Births occur between November and January; usually one young is born at a time.
Threats	Loss of habitat and hunting by humans for food and for the fur coat.
Range	Sierra Leone, Liberia, Ivory Coast, Nigeria, and Ghana.

Description

The adult sooty mangabey, *Cercocebus torquatus atys*, has a head-and-body length of 18 to 26.5 inches; the tail adds 16 to 31 inches. Adults weigh 10 to 27.5 pounds. The sooty mangabey may be distinguished from the white-collared mangabey (please see separate entry) by its sooty-gray face. Its overall coat is gray with a gray-white underbody. The fur is long and silky and puffs out around the face, with the upper half of the head dark gray and the lower half pale gray. Even the muzzle is pale gray. Its eyes are set close together; the nose is long and flat, stretching about three quarters of the way down a prominent, rounded muzzle. Large incisors help it to consume foods such as palm nuts that are too hard for other local animals to eat.

Some taxonomists recognize this mangeby as a full species, *Cercocebus atys*.

Behavior

Sooty mangabeys live primarily in groups

of 13 to 36 members, although membership in groups is fluid, and groups sometimes unite into larger troops with as many as 60 members. Home ranges seems to overlap among groups. In turn, these sooty mangabey troops will form associations with other primates such as guenons, with whom the sooty mangabeys will share lookout duties for warning of danger; they make loud, high-pitched cries. These associations with other primate species succeed in part because the sooty mangabey does not have to compete directly with them for food: The large incisors of the sooty mangabey enable it to eat foods other primates cannot eat. The sooty mangabey forages by day and rests by night.

Habitat

The sooty mangabey inhabits primary rain forests with high canopies.

Distribution

Distribution is presently a mystery to naturalists who have yet to search out how far the sooty mangabey ranges. This problem is complicated by disagreements over the sooty mangabey's taxonomy, leading some observers to note sightings of it as a member of another species. It has a smaller range than *C. torquatus*, and is believed to extend from Sierra Leone, Liberia, Ivory Coast, and Nigeria to Ghana.

Threats

Primary forests in the sooty mangabey's range have been largely cut down by loggers.

The sooty mangabey is also hunted by humans as a source of meat and for the commercial value of its soft fur.

Conservation and Recovery

The sooty mangabey may possibly still survive in the Okomu Forest Reserve in Nigeria; hunting is forbidden within a 26-square-mile central area of the reserve. The white-collared mangabey, *Cercocebus torquatus*, is protected by law in Nigeria.

Diana Monkey

Cercopithecus diana

Noel Rowe

Status	Endangered
Listed	October 19, 1976
Family	Cercopithecidae (Old World monkey)
Description	Slender monkey with well-developed cheek pouches and soft, dense fur. It is gray with a chestnut back, a white stripe on its thigh, with a black face, hands, feet, and tail.
Habitat	Rain forests of West Africa.
Food	Mostly fruit, but will eat leaves and insects.
Reproduction	Single offspring any time of year after gestation of 7 months.
Threats	Loss of habitat, hunting.
Range	Ghana, Guinea, Ivory Coast, Liberia, and Sierra Leone.

Description

The Diana monkey, *Cercopithecus diana*, measures 17.3 to 24.2 inches from head to tail. The tail adds another 27.6 to 33.5 inches. Males weigh about 11 pounds, with females weighing slightly more, 11.9 pounds. The two subspecies of the Diana monkey, which some taxonomists believe includes *C. roloway* and some consider to be a valid species, share similar coats that make them difficult for humans to distinguish one from another, but their rumps typically vary in color.

Diana monkeys are gray agouti, with a brownish red back, a black tail, and white underparts. They have a distinctive white stripe on the thigh and a red or cream-colored rump. The face is black, with a white beard.

Behavior

The Diana monkey, typical of the subfamil *Cercopithicinae*, has large cheek pouches. When a Diana monkey finds a large food source it shoves the food into its cheeks and then flees; the monkeys are very competitive for food, and once a supply is found, they may swarm over it. If the monkey that found the food could not fill its cheek pouches, it is possible that its companions would take most of the food away. The cheek pouches hold about a stomach-sized volume, and thus when filled may assure a Diana monkey of a full meal. It typically pushes the food out of its cheeks with the back of its hand, then holds the food in its hand and examines it, apparently to determine whether it is digestible. Sometimes it cleans debris from the food. The Diana monkey has an extended jaw that provides a large surface area for its molars, helping it to chew tough foods such as leaves. It also eats flowers and insects.

Group size ranges from 5 to 50 members and consists of one male with multifemale groups in which the females bond and the male is peripheral to the group. Diana monkeys are diurnal and arboreal. They associate with Campbell's guenon and lesser spot-nosed guenons. Olive colobuses will follow the Diana monkey's group movements and will intersperse within the group. Western red colobuses will move to be closer to a Diana monkey group upon hearing the calls of chimpanzees.

The Diana monkey prefers to live in the highest forest canopy, but when subspecies share an area, or other primates also want to live in the high canopy, groups of Diana monkeys adjust by shifting to lower areas of the canopy.

Habitat

The Diana monkey prefers to live in primary rain forest, but it is adaptable and can live in secondary forests, as well as riverine forests and even semi-deciduous forests, just as long as there is some canopy available to it. It needs large quantities of fruits and thus requires many fruit trees in its range. In

general, it needs a warm climate.

Distribution

The Diana monkey has historically been distributed through large, high canopy forests in West Africa. These forests have been almost entirely logged in Sierra Leone and are falling to logging and agriculture in Ghana, Guinea, the Ivory Coast, and Liberia. There have been reports of sighting of the Diana monkey in Cameroon and Republic of Congo (formerly Zaire). Its present numbers are unknown, but are likely to be small. The Diana monkey breeds well in captivity, and there may be a hundred or so in U.S. zoos.

Threats

The Diana monkey is a severely endangered species; its population plummeted as logging and road building made access to its territories easier for humans. Their calls as they travel and their vivid coats make them easy prey for someone with a gun, and they are often hunted for food, especially in Liberia. Commercial hunters from Liberia even hunt the monkey in Sierra Leone, shipping the meat back home. Even though hunting is a very important reason for the decline of the Diana monkey, an even more significant reason is deforestation. Throughout its range, logging has drastically reduced the forest canopy. Replanting logged forest with eucalyptus trees in some areas makes it impossible for the Diana monkey to live in the new secondary forest because the eucalyptus is unpalatable and crowds out other tree species.

Conservation and Recovery

The life cycle of the Diana monkey needs to be studied more closely in order for effective conservation measures to be established. Plainly, its forest habitat needs to be preserved and human predation curbed or ended in order for it to have a chance for survival. It is almost extinct in Sierra Leone, where very little suitable habitat remains. Hunting has driven it to near extinction (possibly already to extinction) in Ghana and possibly in Guinea and the Ivory Coast. Data on the monkey in Liberia is hard to come by, but if commercial hunters must go out of the country to find the animal, its status in Liberia is unlikely to be good.

The Diana monkey is listed in class A of the African convention and in CITES: Appendix II: Trade Restricted. None of these restrictions has slowed the traffic in the monkey's meat or skins. Moving the Diana monkey to CITES, Appendix I: Trade Prohibited might discourage the trade in the monkey outside of Africa, but stopping cross-border trade in Africa would require the nations involved to enact and enforce their own laws. Outsiders are unlikely to be allowed to interfere.

Red-bellied Monkey
[=White-throated Guenon]
Cercopithecus erythrogaster

Noel Rowe

Status	Endangered
Listed	October 19, 1976
Family	Cercopithecidae (Old World monkey)
Description	Long arms and tail, rounded head, dark brown coat with a reddish or grayish chest and abdomen, a prominent white neck collar, and a black face.
Habitat	Dense lowland rain forest.
Food	Mostly fruit, but will eat leaves and insects.
Reproduction	1 young after gestation of over 140 days.
Threats	Loss of habitat mostly to logging, but also to oil and mineral exploration, road building, and agriculture. Humans vigorously hunt it for food.
Range	Nigeria and Benin.

Description

The white-throated guenon, *Cercopithecus erythrogaster,* is a member of the colorful and varied family of guenons. Its overall coat is a dark brown, with a belly that varies from red in Benin to gray in Nigeria. It is called the "white-throated guenon" because of a prominent white ruff that engulfs its neck. Amid the white ruff is a rounded, black face. Its tail may have red markings. Little scientific observation of this animal has been published, so many of its specifics are unknown. Males weigh about 6.3 pounds, with females weighing 5.3 pounds. Head and body length is 18.0 inches.

Taxonomy is disputed among taxonomists. Some include *C. sclateri* in this species as a subspecies.

Behavior

Very little is known about the habits of the white-throated guenon. It is diurnal and arboreal. It will go where it can to find food in its now very limited environment, even if it means going into the open in daylight, where raptors as well as humans may be able to easily hunt it. The monkey ventures onto the ground only when it needs to in search of food.

It lives in small groups of less than 30 members with one adult male. Small groups usually observed may be the result of the animals' near extermination by hunters and the small forest patches in which it now lives; perhaps before humans intruded significantly into its habitat, the monkey usually lived in larger groups.

The white-throated guenon's social behavior may resemble that of other guenons, but this has not been confirmed by thorough research. The single adult male organization suggests that as with other guenon species, the adult male is responsible for the group's security, keeping watch for predators. It may also, like other guenons, share territory and security chores with other arboreal primates such as other guenon species or colobus monkeys — the adult male of the white-throated guenon group would possibly watch for threats from below such as leopards, snakes, and humans, while the adult male of the other primate group might watch for predators from above such as eagles. It is likely that females in a given group are related by birth and that they share in the chores of rearing their offspring and that the adult male participates in the game play that teaches youngsters how to react to danger. Pre-adult males likely try to help care for the young by carrying them and protecting them from outside threats, which could include other males trying to take over the group from the current resident adult male. They are likely to be highly intelligent like other guenons and to be dependent upon the teaching of others to learn how to cope with their environment.

Habitat

The white-throated guenon prefers to live in very densely vegetated areas. It spends most of its time in trees, seldom descending below seven feet above the ground; it lives mostly in high forest canopy, 50 feet high. One hope for its survival is offered by its willingness to adapt to changing forest conditions. Although it prefers primary rain forest, it will live in secondary forests, and will extend its range into brushlands and farmlands if at least some dense forest is nearby, to which it can retreat for shelter.

Distribution

The white-throated guenon is found in patches of what once was a continuous forest in southwestern Nigeria, between the Niger River and the city Ijebu-Ode. It is unlikely that the monkey exists west of Ijebu-Ode, even though one specimen has been found in southeastern Benin. However, little is known about the white-throated guenon that naturalists may be mistaken about the exact boundaries of its range. In any case, it probably has always had a wide distribution in southwestern Nigeria. Presently, it at best numbers a couple thousand, with a population so fragmented by logging and other human intrusions such as road and agriculture, that it may no longer have a single breeding population large enough to perpetuate the species. On the other hand, it is possible that in Okomu Forest there may be sufficient numbers to maintain genetic diversity to successfully breed over the short term.

Threats

The greatest threat to the white-throated guenon is the loss of its habitat to logging. By now, only small patches of forest survive where once it extended from the coast into central Nigeria. This loss of habitat alone may already have doomed the white-throated guenon to extinction. Hunting for food is also a significant problem because the guenon lives in a region where humans find animal protein hard to come by.

Conservation and Recovery

The white-throated guenon lives in reserves in Nigeria, but these reserves are illegally logged. For its survival, the white-throated guenon needs the active intervention of human beings: the reserves need to be protected from further logging and mineral development, as well as from farming, and local people need to find other sources for protein. It is possible that enough of the Okomu Forest is left (perhaps 70 square miles in a reserve) to enable the white-throated guenon to survive there.

There are not enough white-throated guenons in captivity to have a good captive-breeding program. Nigerian zoos have had several white-throated guenons in their collections, and the animals seem able to live long lives (about twenty years) in captivity, but only one pair has mated and produced offspring.

The white-throated guenon is protected under class B of the African Convention, which means it may hunted legally only by permit from an authoritative government agency (for example, a national forest service or a ministry of the interior). Even so it is hunted illegally, without permits. The monkey has been listed in CITES, Appendix II: Trade Restricted, which means international trade in the monkey or its parts must be by government permit and must be monitored by international conservation organizations. This listing may be withdrawn because some naturalists believe the white-throated guenon to already be extinct (and thus would be beyond the protection CITES offers).

Red-eared Nose-spotted Monkey [=Red-eared Guenon]

Cercopithecus erythrotis

Status	Endangered
Listed	October 19, 1976
Family	Cercopithecidae (Old World monkey)
Description	Medium to large size monkey, with long rusty-red tail, round head, short muzzle, pronounced cheek whiskers, and well-developed cheek pouches.
Habitat	Primary and secondary rain forest.
Food	Fruits, leaves, shoots, and insects.
Threats	Loss of habitat to logging, agriculture, and expanding human communities in a region where the human population has boomed. Hunting for meat.
Range	Cameroon, Equatorial Guinea (Bioko Island), and Nigeria.

Liza Gadsby

Description

The red-eared guenon, *Cercopithecus erythrotis*, measures 14.0 to 15.7 inches in length from the snout to the base of the tail. The tail is brown agouti at the base, gradually becoming all red toward the tip, and measures 18.1 to 30 inches long. The coat is dark brown with gray black limbs; the face is blue around the eyes, nose, and ears, and the cheek fur is yellow. This species weighs from 9 to 11 pounds.

Taxonomy is disputed. This species was elevated from *C. cephus*, which also formerly included *C. sclateri* as a subspecies.

Other common names are red-eared monkey, russet-eared guenon, and red-eared nose-spotted guenon.

Behavior

The red-eared guenon is very little studied, with almost nothing known about its habits. Forest guenons appear to form one-male troops. This single male's tenure may be quite short and, in a mating season when more than one female is receptive, other adult males join in mating. Newly arrived adult males have been seen to kill infants they find in the troop as part of their mating strategy, although generally infanticide does not seem to be common. This guenon associates with gray-cheeked mangabeys almost half of the time and have been observed to hybridize with mustached guenons in their natural habitat.

The red-eared guenon's diet principally comprises fruit, shoots, leaves, and insects. It will raid crops. Most food is caught or gathered with the hands.

Habitat

The red-eared guenon inhabits primary and secondary rain forests. It once inhabited a continuous coastal forest in Nigeria and Cameroon, with a focus on the delta of the Niger, as well as a forest on the island Bioko. This forestland has been broken into small patches by human activity. The forest inhabited by the monkey in Nigeria and Cameroon is disappearing so rapidly that it may be gone altogether in a year or two.

Distribution

This species is naturally rare and occurs in small isolated populations distributed through Bioko (also called Fernando Póo, an island belonging to Equatorial Guinea), northern Cameroon, and southern Nigeria.

Threats

The red-eared guenon is threatened by the replacement of its habitat with agricul-tural and expanding human settlements, and it is hunted for meat in Cameroon and possibly in Nigeria as well. It also has been exported to American zoos.

Conservation and Recovery

The governments of Cameroon and Nigeria have restricted killing monkeys, and in some territories monkeys are considered sacred and must not be harmed. Pressure to convert forests into agricultural lands presents the greatest threat to the red-eared nose-spotted monkey, and although most of the forests fall within government jurisdiction, enforcement of regulations varies greatly. Educational programs have been established to teach local people the importance of conserving the forests, as well as how to use the forests for sustainable development. On Bioko, the monkey is helped by the poor soil of some of its forest land, making the land unsuited to farming.

The red-eared guenon is in protected lands in Cameroon: the Douala-Edea Reserve and the Korup National Park. Cameroon has been decidedly hostile to foreign loggers since the early 1970s, when the logging companies where expelled from the country.

L'hoest's Guenon

Cercopithecus lhoesti

Noel Rowe

Status	Endangered
Listed	October 19, 1976
Family	Cercopithecidae (Old World monkey).
Description	Dark grey to brownish hair, with a chestnut saddle; eastern subspecies has a dazzling white chest.
Habitat	Dense forests
Food	Mostly fruits, leaves and insects.
Reproduction	Gestation of about 210 days.
Threats	Loss of habitat and hunting.
Range	Burundi, Rwanda, Uganda, Zaire.

Description

L'hoest's guenon, *Cercopithecus lhoesti*, is a guenon with an overall dark gray or brown coat. The western subspecies may be identified by its white moustache, whereas the eastern subspecies has the larger white bib on its chest. The L'hoest's guenon's tail is 18 to 30 inches long and has a hook at the end. Males are larger than females, reaching 22 inches in head and body length; females are as small as 18 inches. Males may weigh up to 13.1 pounds, with females weighing 6.5 to 8.9 pounds.

This monkey is also known as the mountain guenon.

Behavior

L'hoest's guenon dwells primarily on the ground (although it moves easily among tree branches and is often arboreal), not like some of its relatives such as the Diana monkey that are primarily arboreal. They live in bands of about 5 to 17 members with one adult male, and have ranges of about 10 square miles. Their diet requires fruit, but they also eat leaves and insects. Like other guenons, they have large cheek pouches, into which they stuff food, to be eaten after gathering when they have moved to sheltered areas. Although they live in forests, they will move into open areas to gather food, and thus they will sometimes raid farm crops.

A key to its survival has been the

L'hoest's monkey's high intelligence and adaptability. It is an opportunistic eater that will adjust to what fruits are available, including ones cultivated by humans. They often travel by day to an area that offers food and then retreat to dense forest for shelter.

Habitat

Both lowland and highland forests are home to L'hoest's monkey, and it may be found within its small range in montane, gallery forests, and lowland rain forests. Its primary requirement is that the forest be densely vegetated, although it has been reported on wooded mountain slopes that are less dense than the lowland rain forests.

Distribution

L'hoest's monkey lives around the borders shared by Burundi, Rwanda, Uganda, and Republic of Congo between the Ulindi River to the north and the Ituri River to the south. It probably did not historically range far from where it occurs now, although it may have extended farther west.

Threats

L'hoest's monkey is threatened by deforestation. It lives in a small area and is heavily dependent on thick forest growth; logging and human agriculture have been reducing the small amount of forest that is habitable to the monkey. Destruction of its habitat in Republic of Congo will likely make the monkey extinct in that country within a few years. During Uganda's long and bitter civil war, L'hoest's monkey was slaughtered for food by civilians and soldiers alike.

Conservation and Recovery

At present, Uganda is trying to regulate the hunting of L'hoest's monkey, which is primarily protected by the inaccessibility of its remaining habitat in the Ruwenzori Mountains. Poaching is a significant problem in Uganda, where the monkey has been a food source since colonial times. Further, logging is threatening the Ruwenzori National Park and the Semliki Forest Reserves because of poor enforcement of laws protecting them. In Burundi and Rwanda, expansion of human communities is the primary threat to the survival of the L'hoest's monkey's habitat.

Burundi has the strongest laws protecting the monkey from hunting, but it already may no longer survive there. L'hoest's monkey may still survive in Rwanda's Nyungwe Forest Reserve, but logging and mining are breaking up the reserve's habitat.

The monkey is protected by the African Convention in class B; by treaty it may not be hunted or captured without a permit from an appropriate government agency.

Aye-Aye
Family: Daubentoniidae

Nosy Mangabe, Madagascar (Aye-aye and lemur habitat)   George E. Schatz

General Characteristics of the *Daubentoniidae*

The *Daubentoniidae* has but one extant species, the aye-aye (*Daubentonia madagascariensis*). The aye-aye is a lemur and it probably descended from the same anient lemurs that perhaps 50 million years ago drifted to Madagascar on flotsam from continental Africa. Although lemurs were supplanted by more modern primates almost everywhere else, the lemurs on Madagascar flourished, filling many ecological niches. One of those niches is held by woodpeckers in America and other parts of the world, but on Madagascar, the woodpecker's niche is filled by the aye-aye, an animal that is the result of millions of years of evolution isolated from competitors. The aye-aye looks like a rodent to some people, and it was originally classified as one. Its teeth are designed for piercing wood, and its long middle fingers are used to probe into worm holes and into hard-shelled fruit such as coconuts. Its unusual little rounded ears, and other traits that make it so unlike any other existing lemur have combined to make the aye-aye not just a unique species, but a family all to itself. It is of special interest to biologists because its evolutionary history, which is at present little understood, may reveal much about evolution, as well as about how species evolve to fill ecological niches.

Aye-aye
Daubentonia madagascariensis

Noel Rowe

Status	Endangered
Listed	June 2, 1970
Family	Daubentoniidae (Aye-aye)
Description	Thick black fur with white-tipped guard hairs; thick, bushy tail and large batlike ears.
Habitat	Rain, deciduous, montane, and coastal forests; coconut groves.
Food	Coconuts, mangoes, larvae.
Reproduction	One young every 2 to 3 years.
Threats	Forest alteration and clearing.
Range	Eastern and Western Madagascar.

Description

The aye-aye, the sole member of the family *Daubentoniidae*, measures 15.7 inches long, with a tail length of 15.7 inches. About the size of a domestic cat, it weighs about 5 to 6 pounds. The aye-aye has thick, silky fur with long, coarse, guard-hairs. Color is variable, but generally, aye-ayes are patterned gray, brown, white, and black. The aye-aye has a pointed nose and long mobile ears. Probably the best documented characteristic of this species is its long middle finger which is slender and extremely useful. This finger is used in foraging techniques and for scrupulous grooming.

The skeleton of the aye-aye includes a clavicle, separate radius and ulna (front appendages), separate tibia and fibula (hind appendages), and partially fused tarsiers. The clavicle allows for arduous work to be applied to the shoulder muscles without great strain. This becomes advantageous for climbing and hanging. Pronation and supination of limbs is accomplished through the presence of a separate ulna and radius in the upper limbs and a separate tibia and fibula in the lower limbs.

This prosimian posed a taxonomic perplexity in that its dentition is similar to a rodent's and its physical characteristics are somewhat opossumlike, but naturalists have firmly placed it among the lemurs.

Behavior

The aye-aye breeds seasonally, giving

birth in October or November to a single young. Females reach sexual maturity at three years of age and then breed once every two or three years.

The aye-aye makes large nests out of twigs 30 to 50 feet high in the forest canopy, often setting the nest in a fork of a tree. The nest is comprised primarily of the traveler's tree, *Ravenala madagascariensis*. Each individual is known to have 5 or 6 nests. This species has been noted to be somewhat gregarious, forming small groups. Home range size for males has been noted to be 300 to 500 acres; for females 85 to 100 acres. The aye-aye generally sleeps in its nest during the day, but it is active at night and in the evening, feeding and grooming.

The aye-aye forage on three main categories of food: insect larvae, fungi, and fruit. This lemur probes into trees searching for insects. It climbs a trunk or branch while listening for beetle larvae in the wood. If it hears nothing, the aye-aye will tap along as it goes, possibly disturbing the larvae into moving, thus making a sound and giving away their location. Then this lemur will chip bark away at the tree with its teeth and probe holes with its middle finger, looking for larvae. The aye-aye also uses this chiseling technique to expose the yellow-clay-like tissue of *Afzelia bijuga* trees. An aye-aye in captivity ate two of its young, but whether this cannibalism is habitual or the unique product of the stress of captivity is unknown.

Habitat

The aye-aye inhabits both the eastern rain forests and the western deciduous forests of Madagascar, including Ankarana Special Reserve. The trees of these forests are draped with lianas. Madagascar is dominated by evergreen forest and grassland vegetation. It has a tropical climate with abundant rainfall and warm seasonal temperatures. The average annual temperature is 80 degrees Fahrenheit (26.6 degrees Celsius). The aye-aye's habitat is still relatively undisturbed by logging and can therefore support this species' reliance on aged trunks containing beetle larvae. The aye-aye may have value as an indicator of ecological health because of its dependence on trees.

Distribution

The aye-aye is endemic to Madagascar and inhabits both the eastern rain forests and the western deciduous forests, including Ankarana Special Reserve. Eleven aye-ayes were moved to Nosy-Mangabe Island Reserve and they apparently reestablished themselves.

In July 1994 the captive population of aye-ayes worldwide was 25 animals: 11 at the Duke University Primate Center (4 captive born); 7 at the Jersey Wildlife Preservation Trust; 2 at the Paris Zoo; and 5 in Madagascar.

Threats

Human encroachment into its habitat is the primary threat to the aye-aye. As this species relies on an arboreal habitat, forest alteration and clearing for human settlements and agriculture is particularly devastating. People also hunt the aye-aye for food. In some areas, it is regarded with superstitious dread as a bringer of bad times and is therefore killed on sight. Although very rare and hard to find, when sighted it is easy to kill because it does not fear humans and does not try to protect itself from them.

Prior to human settlement, Madagascar was covered with rich evergreen forests and vast grassland savannahs. Most of the original evergreen forests have been cleared for agricultural development and livestock ranching. The deforestation has resulted in erosion, mineral depletion, watershed loss, and a recent fuel emergency (a lack of wood for burning).

Conservation and Recovery

Given the suitable habitat of Nosy-Mangabe Island, in 1966 eleven aye-ayes were transplanted there in hopes of creating a propagation program, which at present seems to have been successful, although the aye-ayes have been poorly tracked. The aye-aye has received considerable attention from international conservation organizations since the mid-1960s and efforts continue to try to protect the animal in the wild. Meanwhile, Duke University is coordinating an international breeding program of captive aye-ayes.

The species is protected by law in the Malagasy Republic, prohibiting its capture or killing, but poaching continues.

Indris and Sifakas
Family: Indridae

Indri indri

Noel Rowe

General Characteristics of the *Indridae*

The *Indridae* family was once large, containing several genera and many species, but in historical times it has been reduced to three genera containing a total of only four species, each of which is endangered. The sifakas were and still are at times confused with their close lemurian relatives. In 1832 Bennett recognized this group as a distinct genera of the *Indridae* family and collectively described it as *Propithecus*. This group is of the superfamily *Lemuroidea* and the suborder *Stepsirhini*.

The woolly lemur (*Avahi laniger*) is the smallest of the species and lives in eastern Madagascar's rain forests. It has shown some adaptability to secondary forests, but its habitat has diminished so greatly that even secondary woodlands are rare. The diademed sifaka (*Propithecus diadema*) has subspecies spread through the island's eastern forests, and like the woolly lemur, it is nearing extinction because its forests are being destroyed. The Verreaux's sifaka (*Propithecus verreauxi*) is the most widely distributed of the surviving indrids, with its subspecies living in deciduous forests on north, west, and south Madagascar. These forests are fast disappearing, with the Verreaux's southern habitat almost entirely gone. The indri (*Indri indri*), for which its family is named, lives in the northeast rain forests of Madagascar. Each of these species is subject to hunting for meat or for their coats, and their forests have been virtually eliminated during the last forty years by logging for timber and for making charcoal, by clearing for plantations, and by slash-and-burn agriculture.

One reason why the once large and diverse family of indrids has been reduced to only four species that are themselves nearly extinct is their size: Indrids are among the largest of lemurs, and their size makes them desirable targets for hunters because they provide more meat than small animals would. Their legs are much longer than their arms — an adaptation for their principal mode of movement: leaping. They can leap over thirty feet from tree to tree, and even on the ground hop on their hind legs rather than walk. They can use their powerful hands and feet to climb out on branches and hang while they eat the leaves or fruits that attracted them. Indrids eat primarily leaves, and they have extended colons that are home to microorganisms that help them digest the leaves. The indri eats soil, perhaps for nutrients or as an aid in digestion, and the Verreaux's sifaka eats bark and wood.

Of the *Indridae* species, only the woolly lemur is nocturnal; the others may be found making spectacular leaps from tree to tree in the daytime. The indrids live in small groups that establish territories in which they feed and reproduce and which they defend from intruders of their own species, usually by loud cries.

The *indridae* are somewhat similar to the lemurs with the exception of the lack of one premolar tooth on each side of both jaws and also a lack of a pair of incisors on the lower jaw for a total of only 30 teeth rather than 36. Indrids in general, including this species, have long hind-limbs and short front limbs (typical features of vertical clingers and climbers. The enlarged hindlimbs allow for saltatorial locomotion (leaping). This group is recorded to be able to leap up to 33 feet. The big toe is long and stout, allowing this species to grip vertical trunks with great strength. This species runs bipedally when on the ground, although it is very rare.

Sifakas socialize in multi-male groups dominated by the females. The group usually consists of up to 10 individuals with an average of five. In a study by Jolly in the Berenty Reserve it was determined that an ideal group consisted of two to three adult males, two females and one or two youngsters. There is no sexual dimorphism exhibited in size or color; however, at estrus the females' genitalia turn a reddish pink color.

Marking behavior is an important part of this species' social organization. The marking process entails the use of urine or ano-genital secretions; the male also marks with glands on his throat. Branches are the most likely candidates for scenting. Marking is especially prevalent during mating and for territorial reasons.

Territorial fights result in leaping, staring and scent-marking along with low growls. As invaders stay close together the residents hop rapidly toward the invaders. When the residents reach the invaders, the invaders will retreat to their own home range. When approached by an aerial intruder, the group will elicit a series of barks followed by complete silence. Ground intruders elicit a two-syllable call ending with a loud click that actually sounds like "sifaka".

Sifakas display only one mating season per year. Most mating occurs in the months of January through March. During the mating season males may seek out females from other groups. Sexual maturity occurs at about two years of age. Estrus may occur at different times for females within the group or outside the group, therefore there is competition between males for estrus females. At time of estrus the females' genital area becomes a reddish pink and usually the female initiates mating. At this time the male approaches the female from behind in this species, as is the case for most quadrupedal mammals. Gestation lasts for 130 days after which time typically only one infant is born.

This group displays parental care by the female. The young will grasp her abdominal fur in the beginning. Later the youngster will ride on her back with its arms wrapped around her neck. After two months of age the youngster will begin to venture away from its mother. The mother gives a great deal of attention to her infant and spends many hours grooming.

Primates display a primarily omnivorous diet, displayed in the uniform development of the cusps and lack of specialization of dentition. Unlike most primates this browsing species eats a great deal of leaves. Atypical of this order, sifakas have a special resistance to the toxins many trees produce in retaliation to predation. This leaf eating habit accounts for its small territory size as this food source is rather plentiful. This species also feeds on fruit, pods, berries, acacia buds, bark and flowers. Bark may provide a water source or may be used as a fiber source. This species spends most of its time feeding in trees and sleeping. Activity is observed both night and day.

Sifakas are forest dwellers and spend most of their time clinging to trees and are particularly associated with the presence of kily.

Conservation and Recovery

Madagascar is the world's fourth largest island. It was separated from Africa about sixty million years ago. Madagascar has been coined a Noah's ark of ecological riches; as its species were not affected by competition from more advanced forms, they were allowed a unique evolution. This island is dominated by evergreen forest and grassland vegetation. It has a tropical climate with abundant rainfall and warm seasonal temperatures. The average annual temperature is 26.6 degrees Celsius.

Prior to human settlement Madagascar was covered with rich evergreen forests and vast grassland savannas. Man did not settle on Madagascar until the third or fourth century A.D. Most of the original evergreen forests have been cleared since anthropogenic inhabitance. The settlers of this land cleared areas for agricultural development and livestock ranching. The deforestation has resulted in erosion, mineral depletion, watershed loss and a recent fuel emergency.

Human encroachment is the primary threatening factor to this species. As this species relies on its arboreal habit, forest alteration and clearing is particularly devastating. Its solely herbivorous diet is also somewhat detrimental.

Presently Madagascar's population exceeds 9 million people with an annual growth rate of about 3.1 to 7.2%. Approximately 85% of the human inhabitants are agriculturalists, pastoralists or a combination. The agricultural economy consists primarily of rice. Rice is grown in any area of suitable habitat, and hill rice cultivation accounts for much of the slow and chronic deforestation. The forests are also being exploited for their natural fuel reserves and are being cleared for roads and towns. Poor felling practices in addition to poor management techniques do not alleviate the plight of forest dwelling primates.

In an effort to preserve its own natural diversity, the Malagasy Government has initiated forest protection practices and reexamination of its already extensive reserve network. A criterion will examine ecological needs of primates, their habitat and populations. Many sifaka species are present on reserves and receive protection, but the ecological needs of the fauna within the reserves extend beyond the physical boundaries of the reserves.

Laws Protecting Sifakas

All sifakas are listed in class A of the African Convention, which means that by international treaty, sifakas may not be hunted, trapped, killed, or traded without permission of the highest responsible government authority, and then only for significant scientific or national welfare reasons. Sifakas are also included in CITES, Appendix I: Trade Prohibited, which means that by international treaty, sifakas may not be traded internationally in whole or in part.

Avahi [=Woolly Lemur]

Avahi laniger

Noel Rowe

Status	Endangered
Listed	June 2, 1970
Family	Indridae (Indris and sifakas]
Description	Dense, dark gray or brown coat with a white underbody and sometimes pale highlights on the face.
Habitat	Rain forests and dry deciduous forests.
Food	Leaves, flowers, fruits, and bark.
Reproduction	Breeding seems to be seasonal, with births in August through September.
Threats	Loss of habitat
Range	Madagascar.

Description

The avahi, *Avahi laniger*, is one of the smallest lemurs, weighing 21 to 24.5 ounces when adult. An adult has a head-and-body length of 10.5 to 11.5 inches, with a tail of 11 to 14 inches. The avahi's head is round, with broad ears, large, round eyes, and a prominent, blunt nose. Most of its coat is gray-brown to reddish, with flecks of lighter shades; its underbody and sometimes its tail are white. The face is brownish, with variable amounts of white on the throat and cheeks, and around the eyes.

Behavior

The avahi is monogamous, with the mating pair of adults being the core of their social life. They move as family units consisting of the parents and their young. They do not move around much, perhaps because their low-quality diet does not give them much energy; even though they are nocturnal, they rest for most of the night, as well as all of the day. They feed on leaves, flowers, fruit, and bark just after sunset and just before sunrise.

Each family group has its own home

range into which it allows no interlopers. Conflicts between groups are common and result in loud cries and chasing through the trees. The avahi walks through trees branches and transfers from one tree to another by leaping from trunk to trunk while holding its body vertically through the air.

Births occur in August and September, resulting in one youngster per mother. The infant is carried on its mother's chest at first, but is eventually transferred to her back.

Habitat

The avahi occupies mostly rain forests, although it occurs in deciduous forests, too.

Distribution

The avahi subspecies, western woolly lemur (*Avahi laniger occidentalis*), lives in patches of forest on northwestern Madagascar. The other subspecies, eastern woolly lemur (*Avahi laniger laniger*), lives in forests along Madagascar's eastern coast. Both subspecies used to be more widely distributed but deforestation has limited them to scattered patches of forest.

Threats

The avahi's forests are being clear-cut by loggers and burned to make room for agriculture.

Conservation and Recovery

The avahi is protected under Malagasy law, by Class A of the African Convention, and Appendix I of CITES, but enforcement of these laws and restrictions has been very difficult. The avahi lives in several nature reserves, but it has been poorly protected in them, although conservation organizations have recently focused on protecting the animal in the Ankarafantsika Nature Reserve.

Indri

Indri indri

Noel Rowe

Status	Endangered
Listed	June 2, 1970
Family	Indridae (Indris and sifakas)
Description	Dense coat of long, soft hair, usually dark brown or black with white markings; hairless black face and short tail.
Habitat	Coastal and mountain forests of Madagascar.
Food	Leaves and fruits, as well as flowers and buds.
Reproduction	Gestation lasts 150 days, resulting in a single birth. Breeding seems to be seasonal, with births occurring from May to June.
Threats	Deforestation for timber, fuel, and agriculture.
Range	Madagascar

Description

The adult indri, *Indri indri*, weighs about 15.5 pounds and is about 2.5 feet in head-and-body length. Unusual for a lemur, it has a short tail, about 2 inches long. Although several larger species of lemur have become extinct within the last 200 years, the indri is now the largest surviving lemur; indeed, it seems to be the largest of all surviving prosimians. Like other members of its family, the indri has hind legs that are longer than its forelegs; this is an adaptation that allows it to leap from place to place. An adult indri can leap over 30 feet at a time, and indris often do not run but leap repeatedly to escape predators. They have been known to run on their hind legs on the ground, but they prefer to remain in trees. Their long hands help them to grip tree trunks and branches, and their large ears may serve to help them hear each other moving about. They are usually black or dark brown with white or pale gray areas; the amount of white and its pattern varies from one individual indri to another.

The indri is also known as babakoto

(meaning "little father").

Behavior

The indri has a throat sac that is a physical adaptation related to its behavior. The sac serves as a resonance chamber, enabling the indri to give out an enormous howl, as well as other loud cries. Naturalists report that indris have one to seven howling periods per day, related to the indris bestirring themselves after a period of rest, to one group meeting another at territorial edges, and to gathering members of a group together for rest. The howls and other cries serve to let all the indris in a given neighborhood know where they all are in relation to each other, and the noise is deafening. The cries also help to demarcate territorial boundaries and to warn of predators. Such howls can be heard for miles and receive responses from indris as much as two miles away.

A territory is 31.5 to 75 acres in size and may be occupied by one indri or groups of 2 to six members. By day they feed on vegetation, primarily leaves and fruit, as well as flowers and buds. At night they rest either singly or in small groups. It is possible that before people ventured into their territory, indris gathered in larger groups, but their now very small range does not allow for anything but small parties; these parties are families: two parents and their young. Human beings have driven indris into small areas not only through habitat destruction, but through their noise. Even though they give off howls that sound like humans in agony, indris are actually very sensitive to sound; some subtle noises seem to be related to mating, and noises from humans — even from airplanes passing overhead reports one

investigator — can disrupt the indri's breeding.

The indris are born black, with their coat lightening as they grow older. Although they start venturing about on their own ·at six weeks of age and start eating solid food at eight weeks, they continue to nurse until nine months old and sleep with their mothers until a year old. Females and the very young have priority over adult males in feeding.

Habitat

The indri lives in humid montane forests at elevations up to 4,265 feet. It requires the presence of evergreens unique to Madagascar.

Distribution

The indri inhabits patches of forest in northeastern Madagascar. It shies away from humans and retreats as far as it can into its little forested hideouts.

Threats

The indri is very dependent on its forest habitat, which has been almost entirely cut down by humans. Efforts to keep them in zoos, even in Madagascar have failed; even when provided with their natural foods, the indris die within days of incarceration. Stress is thought to be the culprit; perhaps the animal's sensitivity to sound plays a role in its inability to adapt to captivity.

Conservation and Recovery

The indri appears in wildlife reserves in the Malagasy Republic, most notably the Special Reserve at Analamazaotra, which was created in 1970 specifically for the protection of indris. This reserve has become isolated from the block of forest that once covered the region and its forest has shrunk greatly.

The indri is listed in CITES, Appendix I: Trade Prohibited, which by treaty prohibits international trade in the animal. It also is listed as class A in the African Convention, which prohibits the hunting, capture, or trade of the animal except under special circumstances and with the permission of the highest appropriate governmental authority.

Silky Diademed Sifaka

Propithecus diadema candidus

Stephen Nash illustration

Status	Endangered
Listed	December 2, 1970
Family	Indridae (Indris and sifakas)
Description	The fur is often entirely white, but it may be highlighted by silver or gray hair.
Habitat	Dry deciduous forests.
Food	Primarily leaves, supplemented by fruit, pods, berries, acacia buds, bark and flowers.
Reproduction	One offspring after gestation of 165 days.
Threats	Deforestation and hunting for food by humans, even within wildlife reserves, are the primary threats to the silky sifaka. Its foremost natural predators are hawks.
Range	Northeast Madagascar

Description

There are four subspecies of *Propithecus diadema: P. d. candidus, P. d. diadema, P. d. edwardsi,* and *P. d. perrieri.* These sifakas measure from 18.9 to 20.5 inches from the tip of the nose to the tail; their tail length averages 18.3 inches. They weigh 12.3 to 15.9 pounds.

The silky diademed sifaka has a white coat of dense soft fur. The coat is often highlighted on the crown, the limbs, and the back of the animal with pale-to-dark silver or gray hair. An adult is stunningly beautiful. The eyes are typically yellow. Verreaux's sifa, shown in the photo, resembles the silky diademed sifaka.

Other common names include silky sifaka, simpona, crowned sifaka, or diademed sifaka.

Behavior

The silky diademed sifaka subspecies has not been well studied, partly because of its rarity. From the sketchy observations of it, some general characteristics emerge. The silky sifaka tends to congregate in groups with a dominant male and female pair and their young of various ages. At what age the young leave their parents has yet to be established, but full adults — presumably their offspring — have been observed traveling with dominant male and female pairs. Recorded group sizes vary from three members to five members. Although most of the little evidence there is suggests that these groups are family units, a few naturalists suggest that the adult members besides the male and female pair are not offspring, but are instead merely silky sifaka that are well known to the dominant pair, and that they form loose group associations for the purposes of foraging and mutual protection.

Habitat

Rain forest is the preferred habitat of the silky diademed sifaka. Like other crowned sifakas, it probably eats the leaves and fruits it finds in its habitat.

Distribution

The silky diademed sifaka occurs within the Marojejy Nature Reserve, north of Maroansetra and in the rain forests between Maroansetra, the Morojejy Massif, and the Andapa Basin, in northeastern Madagascar. It also appears in the Anjanaharibe-Sud Special Reserve. Its density is very low, and it is very rare throughout its range.

Threats

Deforestation is driving this animal to extinction. The forests are logged for timber or the making of charcoal, an important fuel in the Malagasy Republic. Further, the silky sifaka is hunted for food, even in the Marojejy Nature Reserve.

Conservation and Recovery

The Malagasy department of Water and Forests has made the conservation of the Marojejy Nature Reserve a high priority, but keeping poachers out is difficult. The World Wildlife Fund has shown particular interest in the Marojejy Nature Reserve and may provide some of the funding for its protection. For the silky sifaka to survive, it may need more territory than the Marojejy Nature Reserve can provide, and therefore the Anjanaharibe-Sud Special Reserve probably should be included in plans to save the animal from extinction. Badly degraded forests still survive between the two reserves, and if they could be protected, a potentially good-sized area could be preserved for the silky sifaka, enabling it to maintain a good breeding population, but these forests are disappearing quickly.

Diademed Sifaka

Propithecus diadema diadema

David Haring

Status	Endangered
Listed	December 2, 1970
Family	Indridae (Indris and sifakas)
Description	Black head, neck, and face; silver or gray on the shoulders and lower back; golden hindquarters.
Habitat	Primary rain forest.
Food	Leaves, berries, flowers, bark.
Reproduction	Single young after gestation of 150 days.
Threats	Loss of habitat; hunting.
Range	Northeastern Madagascar

Description

The adult diademed sifaka, *Propithecus diadema diadema*, is about 21 inches from nose to tail, with a tail of about 20 inches. It weighs about 12 pounds. Like other subspecies of its species, the diademed sifaka has a coat of long, silky, brightly colored fur. Its face is black, with a white forehead, and the rest of its head is black, as well. Its neck is also black, but with a white throat. Varying with the individual diademed sifaka, the black hair on the head and neck turns to silver or gray along the shoulders or further down on the back. The underbody is white or a pale gold. The forelimbs are white; the hindlimbs are golden, as are the hindquarters, but the tale is white.

The diademed sifaka is also known as the simpona.

Behavior

The diademed sifaka lives in small groups of about five members, with a dominant female and more than one male. Observers disagree considerably about how big a group's territory is, from 49 acres to 124 acres. This animal seems to live in low densities throughout its range, so large group territories would seem plausible, although territory size could be governed by the density of available food.

As with other of its species, scent marking is important to this subspecies. It uses anal and genital glands to indicate territorial boundaries, sexual availability of females, and to just simply keep track of each other. Males also have scent glands on their throats. When different groups confront one another there is often a frenzy of scent marking of tree branches or whatever else is available. This marking seems to confirm and reenforce territorial boundaries. The confrontation may include rapid movements such as leaping from one branch to another, jumping in place, and cries. All this seems to satisfy the need for agreeable boundaries and honor and confrontations do not seem to involve physical violence.

Diademed sifakas have been known to lick the ground in particular spots. Why they do is unclear, although Preston-Mafham (in *Primates of the World*, p.150) suggests that the animal may be improving a mineral-poor diet or may be assimilating something that aids it in neutralizing the toxins commonly found in the leaves on which it dines. The diademed sifaka does indeed dine on leaves that would be toxic to other animals. It probably also eats berries, buds, and bark.

Females are the primary care givers for the young. Rearing is probably like that of other members of its species, with much grooming, some play, and slow weaning. Sexually mature males usually leave their groups to roam independently and eventually join another female-dominated group. This particular subspecies has been so little observed that present notions of its behavior could undergo great revision if close studies are eventually conducted.

Habitat

The diademed sifaka occurs in primary rain forest.

Distribution

The diademed sifaka ranges from near the town of Maroantsetra in the north, through the eastern primary rain forests of Madagascar to the Mangoro River in the south.

Threats

As is true for other creatures that inhabit the patches of rain forest in eastern Madagascar, loss of the forest poses the greatest threat to the diademed sifaka's survival. It has been found only in primary rain forests, which suggests that it may have a specialized need for the primary forest that a secondary forest does not satisfy. Its forest is being logged for timber and for making charcoal, and it is being cleared for agriculture.

The diademed sifaka is intensely hunted by humans mostly for food; this may account for the very low densities in the forest.

Conservation and Recovery

The diademed sifaka is protected under Malagasy law, although enforcement of the law is difficult. It seems as though no one has a clear idea of how many of the diademed sifakas survive; it is very rarely seen, even by seasoned observers. Small numbers exist in the Analalmazaotra Special Reserve and in the Zahamena Nature Reserve; some were seen in the Betampona Nature Reserve in 1972, but not since, and sanguine researchers hope that a few may still survive there, but it is likely extinct in that reserve. There is some hope that it will recolonize a reserve near PJrinet.

With the aid of international conservation organizations, the Malagasy Republic is trying to protect the reserves in which the diademed sifaka subspecies is still to be found; it faces poaching of the animal for food and possibly commercial sale, and it faces poaching of forest trees, which are illegally taken for timber and charcoal. Agricultural development also encroaches on the reserves, shrinking the actual remaining wildlands. The Malagasy government is also trying to find less accessible wildlands to which the diademed sifakas could be introduced. Efforts to breed this particular subspecies in captivity are so far inconclusive.

Milne-Edwards' Diademed Sifaka

Propithecus diadema edwardsi

Noel Rowe

Status	Endangered
Listed	December 2, 1970
Family	Indridae (Indris and sifakas).
Description	Large prosimian, mostly black or blackish brown with broad white patches across the base of the back and flanks, varying in size from one individual animal to another; ventral fur is thin and reveals its black skin; the large eyes are orange.
Habitat	Rain forest at both low and high altitudes.
Food	Primarily leaves, supplemented by fruit, buds, and flowers.
Reproduction	Gestation lasts 150 to 180 days, resulting in a single birth.
Threats	Loss of habitat for logging, fuel, and agriculture.
Range	Southeastern Madagascar

Description

The Milne-Edward's sifaka, *Propithecus diadema edwardsi* measures 15.4 to 18.3 inches from the tip of the nose to the base of the tail. Its tail length varies from 19.7 to 23.2 inches and it weighs from 7.9 to 9.5 pounds. The Milne-Edward's sifaka is mostly blackish brown with the exception of its broad saddle of creamy white across the base of the back and flanks.

Behavior

Sifakas socialize in multimale groups dominated by the females. The group usually consists of up to 9 individuals with an average of five.

The Milne-Edward's sifaka has one mating season per year, from November to January, with births occurring May to July. During the mating season males may seek out females from other groups. At time of estrus the females' genital area becomes a reddish pink and usually the female initiates mating.

Marking behavior is an important part of the sifaka's social organization. The marking process entails the use of urine or genital secretions; the male also marks with glands on his throat. Branches are the most likely candidates for scenting. The marking indicates territorial boundaries and whether females are sexually receptive.

Territorial fights result in leaping, staring, and scent-marking, along with low growls. As invaders stay close together the residents hop rapidly toward the invaders. When the residents reach the invaders the invaders will retreat to their own home range. When approached by an aerial intruder, the group will elicit a series of barks followed by complete silence. Ground intruders elicit a one-syllable call that sounds like a sneeze or "simpone."

The female is the primary parental care giver. Her youngster will grasp her abdominal fur in the beginning. Later the youngster will ride on her back with its arms wrapped around her neck. After four months of age the youngster will begin to venture away from its mother. The mother gives a great deal of attention to her infant and spends many hours grooming it. Socialization begins early, and at three weeks of age a Milne-Edward's sifaka will crawl on members of its group besides its mother. Males rarely carry or groom infants.

The Milne-Edward's sifaka is active during daylight and spends most of the day feeding. More than half the food consumed by Milne-Edwards' sifaka consists of leaves from trees, vines, and herbs; the remainder is split between seeds, fruits, and flowers.

Habitat

The Milne-Edwards' sifaka lives in low-land rain forest.

Distribution

This sifaka is distributed in rain forest south of the Mangoro River and north of Manakara. Its population density within its range is low, about 6 per square mile.

Threats

The Milne-Edwards' sifaka's forest has been almost entirely cut down for logging to provide wood for fuel, and to make way for agricultural development and expanding human communities. It requires a large range because of its low population density. Researchers have noted its rapid disappearance from most of its traditional range over the last fifteen years. Attempts to keep it in captivity have failed.

Conservation and Recovery

A new national park in the area of Ranomafana may offer protection to the animal, but adequate funding for sufficient staff to protect it is a continuing problem.

The Milne-Edwards' sifaka is protected in CITES, Appendix I: Trade Prohibited, meaning that international trade is forbidden by treaty, and is protected in class A of the African Convention, which severely restricts the hunting, capture, and trading of the animal.

Perrier's Diademed Sifaka

Propithecus diadema perrieri

WWF/Helmut Diller

Status	Endangered
Listed	December 2, 1970
Family	Indridae (Indris and sifakas).
Description	Large lemur, colored black over almost its entire body, with very dark brown hair on its underbody; the thin chest hair exposes black skin; the large eyes are yellow.
Habitat	Dry deciduous forests.
Food	Primarily leaves and fruits, as well as pods, berries, acacia buds, bark, and flowers.
Reproduction	One offspring after gestation of 165 days.
Threats	Human encroachment, forest alteration.
Range	Northwest Madagascar

Description

Perrier's sifaka, *Propithecus diadema perrieri*, measures 15.4 to 18.3 inches from the tip of the snout to the base of the tail. Its tail length varies from 19.7 to 23.2 inches and it weighs 7.9 to 9.5 pounds. Perrier's sifaka is colored black over its entire body except for dark brown hair on its underbody. Its hair is long, dense, and soft. The thin hair on the chest exposes its black skin. Its large eyes are yellow.

Other common names are radjako, and ankomba job.

Behavior

Sifakas socialize in multimale groups dominated by females. The group consists of up to 10 animals with an average of five.

Marking behavior is an important part of the sifaka's social organization. The marking process entails the use of urine or genital secretions; the male also marks with glands on his throat. Branches are the most likely candidates for scenting. Marking establishes territorial boundaries, tells sifakas of the presence of others, and indicates when a female is sexually receptive. The Perrier's sifakas live at low population densities, about 6 to 8 animals per square mile. (One study, conducted by D. M. Meyers and J. Ratsirarson for the World Wildlife Fund, found about 30 animals per square mile, but this is likely to be an anomaly, perhaps caused by humans pressuring animals into an unnaturally small area.) Group home ranges are about 69 acres in size.

Territorial disputes result in leaping, staring, and scent-marking, along with low growls. While the invaders stay close together, the territorial residents hop rapidly toward them. When the residents reach the invaders, the invaders will retreat to their own home range. When approached by an aerial intruder, the group will elicit a series of barks followed by complete silence. Ground intruders elicit a two-syllable call ending with a loud click that actually sounds like "sifaka."

Perrier's sifaka has only one mating season per year. Most mating occurs in the months of January through March. During the mating season males may seek out females from other groups. Sexual maturity occurs at about two years of age. Estrus may occur at different times for females within the group or outside the group, therefore there is competition between males for estrous females. At time of estrus the females' genital area becomes a reddish pink and usually the female initiates mating. Gestation lasts for 165 days, after which typically only one infant is born.

The mother is primarily responsible for taking care of her infant. The young will grasp her abdominal fur in the beginning.

Later the youngster will ride on her back with its arms wrapped around her neck. After two months of age the youngster will begin to venture away from its mother. The mother gives a great deal of attention to her infant and spends many hours grooming it.

Perrier's sifaka spends most of its time feeding in trees and sleeping. Activity is observed both night and day. A browsing species, the Perrier's sifaka eats a great deal of leaves and fruit (each comprises about one third of its diet); sifakas have a special resistance to the toxins many trees produce, allowing them to eat leaves that other browsers would have to avoid. This leaf eating habit accounts for the small size of its territory, because this food source is traditionally plentiful in its native habitat. The Perrier's sifaka also feeds on fruit, pods, berries, acacia buds, bark, and flowers. Bark may provide a water source or may be used as a fiber source.

Habitat

Perrier's sifaka is a forest dweller and spends most of its time clinging to trees and is particularly associated with the presence of kily trees (*Tamarindus indica*). It is restricted to a small area in northwestern Madagascar, almost exclusively in the dry forests of the Analamera Natural Reserve.

Distribution

In 1972, some 500 Perrier's sifakas were found in the Analamera Natural Reserve and to the north and east of the reserve. Since then, estimates of the animal's numbers have varied greatly, with 100 thought to be left at the end of the 1980s, but with at least one naturalist suggesting that while the numbers are probably very small, there was the possibility of as many as 2,000 still surviving.

Threats

Perrier's sifaka requires an abundance of trees for its survival, but its forest is endangered, primarily by agricultural development. The trees are also cut down to be used to produce charcoal. Local people also hunt the animal for food. All the crowned sifaka subspecies are severely endangered, but this subspecies is the most endangered of all. Its numbers are now so small and its distribution so patchy that it may no longer be able to breed often enough to sustain itself.

Conservation and Recovery

Nearly all of the remaining Perrier's sifaka live within the Analamera Special Reserve; some live outside the reserve, to the north and east, and some survive in Ankarana Special Reserve. Malagasy's Department of Water and Forest has established a management program for the Perrier's sifaka within these reserves and is trying to prevent human intrusion into the reserved forest (some locals graze their cattle within the forest). Increased tourism in the region may help to protect the Perrier's sifaka by providing much needed funds to pay for the protection of the reserves and to persuade local peoples that the animals are valuable enough to avoid killing.

Golden-crowned [= Tattersall's] Sifaka

Propithecus tattersalli

David Haring

Status	Endangered
Listed	December 2, 1970
Family	Indridae (Indris and sifakas).
Description	Coat is typically white with a golden crown and a golden chest; hands, feet, and face are hairless, with black skin.
Habitat	Dry forests with high canopies.
Food	Primarily leaves; possibly fruit, pods, berries, acacia buds, bark, and flowers.
Reproduction	Gestation lasts 160 days, resulting in a single birth.
Threats	Deforestation and hunting by humans.
Range	Northern Madagascar

Description

In 1988, specimens of the golden-crowned sifaka, *Propithecus tattersalli*, were taken in hopes of breeding it because it seemed threatened with imminent extinction (which it still is). It was then that scientists learned that it had a different chromosome count than the crowned sifaka (*Propithecus diadema*); it had been thought to be a subspecies of the crowned sifaka, but the chromosome count made it clear that the golden-crowned sifaka was a unique species. Based on the study of eight specimens of the animal, the adult golden-crowned sifaka weighs about 7.25 pounds. They measure from 17.9 to 19.7 inches in body length with a tail length of 17.7 inches for females and 15.7 for males.

Its coat is typically white with a golden crown and a golden chest. Its hands, feet, and face are hairless, with black skin. The ears are furred with hair tufts 0.4 to 0.8 inches long.

This sifaka is also known as ankomba malandy.

Behavior

Very little is known about the golden-crowned sifaka's behavior. It lives in trees, feeds day and night, and prefers young leaves over mature ones for its diet. It also eats fruit. Captive golden-crowned sifakas feed only during the day, which has led some naturalists to speculate that nighttime feeding in the wild is a response to the presence of humans, who prey on the golden-crowned sifakas during the day. These sifakas seem to live in groups of three to ten members, but these numbers are based on the observing of only eight groups.

Mating season occurs in late January with births in late June to July. Infants are weaned in December.

Habitat

This species lives in rain forest and deciduous dry forests, including gallery forests during the dry season. The habitat features 115 to 130-foot-tall trees, which form an open canopy above the forest. The next layer of trees reaches about 65 feet, and the third level are at 50 feet.

Distribution

There are no more than a few hundred golden-crowned sifakas, and they are confined to a small region of less than 150 square miles near Daraina, in the far northeast of Madagascar. The population is fragmented.

Threats

The golden-crowned sifaka's habitat is being logged for timber and for the production of charcoal. The land also has been cleared for gold mining, an important source of international revenue for the Malagasy Republic. Miners hunt the animal for food, even though the custom of local people forbids its hunting.

Conservation and Recovery

Although the golden-crowned sifaka is a beautiful animal and plainly in need of protection, it has the misfortune of living in an area where gold is mined. The gold provides the Malagasy Republic with much needed international income, and the Malagasy government has therefore not protected the animal's range.

Malagasy law forbids the hunting of the golden-crowned sifaka, but without giving the animal a protected range, the law is difficult to enforce.

In an effort to breed the animal, several golden-crowned sifakas were taken to the Duke University Primate Center, but they have not done well in captivity. In 1994 one pair bred for the first time but the infant died when six months old.

Coquerel's Sifaka

Propithecus verreauxi coquereli

David Haring

Status	Endangered
Listed	December 2, 1970
Family	Indridae (Indris and sifakas)
Description	White base coat with maroon areas on the insides of the limbs and the lower torso.
Habitat	Deciduous and evergreen forests.
Food	In the dry season, diet consists of mature leaves and buds; in the wet season diet includes young leaves, fruits, and flowers.
Reproduction	In captivity, gestation has lasted 162 days, resulting in a single birth. Breeding is seasonal, with births occurring in June.
Threats	Loss of habitat and poaching.
Range	Northwest Madagascar.

Description

The Coquerel's sifaka, *Propithecus verreauxi coquereli*, is one of the best studied of the sifakas, although much about its characteristics and habits remains to be discovered. There seems to be no gender-related variations in size; adults are 15.5 to 18.5 inches long, not counting the tail, with the tail adding another 20 to 23.6 inches. They weigh 8 to 9.5 pounds. These are tough creatures; they have been seen to fall over sixty feet to the bare ground and then get up and bound back among the tree branches. Their fur is soft and fluffy and is mostly white with maroon to reddish brown patches inside the limbs and on the lower part of its body.

Behavior

The Coquerel's sifaka's territorial behavior differs significantly from that of most other sifakas. Although groups of the Coquerel's sifaka have territories that they mark, they are casual about overlapping of boundaries and even outright intrusions by other Coquerel's sifakas. Intruders are not confronted; instead, the separate groups take care to avoid each other and in so doing establish flexible boundaries. A group consists of three to ten members, with four or five being the usual size. Females dominate the groups, with the males taking decidedly secondary positions in the group's affairs.

A group typically has only one infant in it. Infants are born in June (possibly in July and August, too, as is the case with other subspecies of Verreaux's sifaka, *Propithecus verreauxi,* but for the Coquerel's sifaka births have only been observed in June). Gestation lasts about 162 days, although there is some disagreement about this, with 130 days reported and 165 days reported; 130 days is certainly too short, and 162 days is the only reliably reported period. Mating will have occurred early in the year, with males leaving their normal groups and wandering into other territories; mating usually occurs between members of different groups. Apparently, the males will sometimes wander far from home, but they seem to return after mating season ends. The females provide most of the parental care and will carry their infants on their bellies for a few months; then, the youngsters ride on their mother's backs. Weaning occurs after six months, with the youngsters exhibiting much independence. They are mature at about two years of age; linked to this is a female's birthrate, which is usually once every two years, even though consecutive annual births have been reported in a few cases.

The Coquerel's sifakas feed in their separate groups. Communication among groups consists of scent markings, which tell which group has passed by and whether a female is sexually receptive. Loud cries may also serve to help the Coquerel's sifakas keep track of each other, although cries in general seem to be for alarms, with different cries indicating different kinds of danger. Their most important natural predators are hawks. However, their most deadly predators are humans, but no one seems to have as yet recorded a cry signifying that dangerous humans are near. Perhaps this indicates one reason why humans find the Coquerel's sifaka easy to kill: The Coquerel sifakas do not recognize humans as threats and are not sufficiently alarmed by the presence of humans.

Foods are taken seasonally. In the dry season nearly the whole of the Coquerel's sifaka's diet consists of mature leaves. These are supplemented by buds. This is not as limited a diet as it may appear; the Coquerel's sifaka eats leaves from dozens of different kinds of trees. As the season changes to wet, the Coquerel's sifaka's diet broadens, with immature leaves forming a significant portion of the food consumed. Fruits and flowers are also added to the diet.

Habitat

The Coquerel's sifaka is a forest dweller that spends most of its life in trees. Its forests are either deciduous or evergreen and provide a wide variety of plant life.

Distribution

The range of the Coquerel's sifaka is restricted by natural boundaries to an area north and east of the Betsiboka River in northwestern Madagascar.

Threats

The Coquerel's sifaka's range is being

denuded of trees. The forests are logged for charcoal production and are burned to make way for grass on which people graze livestock. Even in the Ankarafantsika Nature Reserve and the Bora Special Reserve, which harbor groups of the Coquerel's sifaka, the forest is being logged and burned away. Some of the local people have taboos against hunting the Coquerel's sifaka, but others hunt them for food. They are very easy to hunt and shoot. The Coquerel sifaka's limited and vulnerable range combined with habitat loss and hunting makes it the most endangered of the Verreaux's sifaka's subspecies.

Conservation and Recovery

The Malagasy Republic's Department of Water and Forests, with the aid of the World Bank, is trying to improve its protections in the Ankarafantsika Nature Reserve by creating education programs for the local people, motorized transportation for park rangers to help them patrol it more effectively, and fire breaks to try to inhibit the damage caused by deliberately set fires. In the case of the Coquerel's sifaka and the Ankarafantsika and Bora reserves, the number of rangers needs to be increased and the destruction of the forest stopped or soon there will be nothing to protect.

There has been some success in breeding the Coquerel's sifaka subspecies in captivity. Sifakas are notoriously hard to keep alive and to breed in captivity. Part of the secret seems to be not only to discover and give them the right mix of foods, but to give them open areas with trees in which they can move about freely. Tight enclosures without trees seem to doom the captive animals. At present, several captive-bred examples of the Coquer-

el's sifaka exist.

Crowned Sifaka

Propithecus verreauxi coronatus

Anne Zeller

Status	Endangered
Listed	December 2, 1970
Family	Indridae (Indris and sifakas)
Description	White coat throughout except for a dark brown or black head and throat and pale brown chest.
Habitat	Deciduous forests with high canopies.
Food	Leaves, fruits, and flowers, varying with the season.
Reproduction	Mates in January, February, or March. Gestation lasts 150 days, resulting in a single birth.
Threats	Loss of habitat to logging and agriculture; hunting for food and export.
Range	Northwest Madagascar

Description

A few naturalists say the crowned sifaka, *Propithecus verreauxi coronatus*, is not a true subspecies, that those animals called "crowned sifakas" are actually just variants of the subspecies Decken's sifaka (*Propithecus verreauxi deckeni*). The overall evidence would mitigate against this view: crowned sifakas and Decken's sifakas do not mix together but maintain separate populations; the Decken's sifaka is more elaborately colored than the crowned sifaka; and the crowned sifaka has a proportionately larger muzzle than the Decken's sifaka. The proper classification of the crowned sifaka has yet to be resolved by naturalists.

The adult crowned sifaka is about twenty inches in length, not including the tail; the tail adds another 22 inches. Weight varies from 4.5 to 11.25 pounds with no distinction in size between the genders. It has fluffy white fur over most of its body, with its head and throat being dark brown or black. Its chest is usually a light to medium dark brown.

Behavior

The crowned sifaka needs to live in a

forest with an abundance of leaves. Where leaves are about, group territories for the animal tend to be relatively small: about 1.5 to 6.5 acres (sifakas to the east may require over a hundred acres for a territory). Some of the leaves eaten by the crowned sifaka are poisonous, but the crowned sifaka seems to have evolved an adaption that allows it to digest the leaves without harm. Its lower digestive tract has elongated and provides a home for symbiotic bacteria that help to digest the leaves thoroughly. Although leaves are the primary part of the crowned sifaka's diet, it also eats fruits and flowers, and the proportions the leaves, fruits, and flowers take up in its diet vary with their seasonal availability.

Active both night and day, the crowned sifaka spends its time eating, sleeping, grooming, and marking. It has several scent glands, in the anal and genital areas and, for the males, on the neck. The glands mark branches or other available objects and serve as communication among the crowned sifakas. The markings indicate where an individual crowned sifaka is, helping others keep track of it; they indicate the sexual availability of females; and they mark off a given group's territory. A group consists of two to twelve members, with five being the most common: Two adult males, two adult females, and one youngster is a common mix. The females dominate the group and get first pickings of food. Territories overlap, and groups do not seem particularly worried by the overlapping so long as a central core area of the territory is not violated. When rival groups meet, they raise a ruckus, leap about, and leave scent markings. One group will sometimes charge another, with the other retreating a bit. The confrontations seem to serve to establish agreeable territorial boundaries without much violence.

Mating occurs early in the year and re-sults in a single birth after 150 days. The mother is the primary care giver for the newborn. After 6 months, a youngster is weaned, but it does not reach sexual maturity until it is two years old.

Habitat

The crowned sifaka spends most of its life in trees, although it does occasionally descend to the ground in search of water or to lick dirt in select spots, perhaps to supplement its mineral consumption or to consume something that helps it safely eat toxic leaves. It requires a deciduous forest with a high canopy. The forest is usually dry.

Distribution

The crowned sifaka inhabits forests to the northeast of the Mahavavy River in northwestern Madagascar.

Threats

Local people and outsiders hunt the crowned sifaka for commercial purposes. The crowned sifaka is very easy to kill and a single hunter can shoot down a dozen in an afternoon. They may be eaten or possibly sold for export.

Slash-and-burn agriculture is devastating the western forests in which the crowned sifaka lives. Humans set fire to the forest to encourage the growth of grass; the fires consume much acreage. Livestock then overgrazes the nearly burnt-out areas, making it difficult for even grass to return and nearly impossible for the forest to reclaim the land.

The crowned sifaka needs its forest in order to survive, and as its forest shrinks, so do its chances for survival.

Conservation and Recovery

The Malagasy Republic has trouble policing the crowned sifaka's forest. The area is somewhat remote from big towns and is hard for law enforcement people to get to. The local people need to learn a more efficient form of agriculture than that which they now employ. The Tsingy de Namoroka Nature Reserve harbors some crowned sifakas, but the reserve is poorly protected.

The crowned sifaka is protected under Malagasy law, which forbids its capture or killing.

Decken's Sifaka

Propithecus verreauxi deckeni

Anne Zeller

Status	Endangered
Listed	December 2, 1970
Family	Indridae (Indris and sifakas).
Description	Color variation within this subspecies is considerable. The classic example of the Decken's sifaka would be entirely white, but it shoulders, backs, or limbs may be golden, brown, silvery, or gray.
Habitat	Dry deciduous forests with high canopies.
Food	Fruit, pods, berries, acacia buds, bark and flowers.
Reproduction	Gestation lasts 150 days, resulting in a single birth taking place in June, July, or August.
Threats	Loss of habitat to grazing lands.
Range	Western Madagascar.

Description

The coloration of the Decken's sifaka, *Propithecus verreauxi deckeni*, has created confusion among naturalists who disagree about whether the coloration indicates different subspecies or not. The classic image of the Decken's sifaka is of one that is entirely white, with yellow eyes. Yet Decken's sifakas may have different colors on the shoulders, backs, and limbs, including gold, silver, gray, and brown. Some naturalists believe that Coquerel's sifaka (*Propithecus verreauxi coquereli*; please see separate entry) may not be a differ-

ent subspecies but actually part of the Decken's sifaka subspecies (most disagree with this, citing morphological differences such as in the size and shape of the muzzle). If this were true, then the Decken's sifaka may have black, dark brown, and pale brown fur on its chest, throat, and head.

There seems to be little difference in size between a male and a female Decken's sifaka. An adult Decken's sifaka is about 20 inches long, not counting its tail, which is itself about 22 inches long. The adult Decken's sifaka weighs about 12 pounds.

This species is also known as Tsibahaka.

Behavior

The Decken's sifaka is territorial, with groups having small territories of 2.5 to 7.5 acres. The density of its principal food source, leaves, in its natural habitat enables the Decken's sifakas to survive in relatively small territories (sifaka species to the east may need hundreds of acres of territory for the same size group to survive). Scent markings are important for communication among Decken's sifakas; a marking on a branch or twig can identify an individual group member, indicate whether an outsider has intruded into a group's territory, what other groups are in the area, what the territorial boundaries are, and whether a female is sexually receptive. When groups meet along a boundary, a frenzy of scent marking (in addition to jumping and loud cries) seems to serve as reenforcement of mutually recognized territorial demarcation. On the other hand, some territorial overlapping seems to be tolerated, so long as a central core area is not violated.

Females dominate the small groups, with a group usually consisting of five members, a mixture of adult males, adult females, and young. The group spends most of its time quietly pursuing food and sleep, allowing their scent markings to speak for them. When danger threatens, they make loud, barking cries. Their principal predators are hawks; when one is spotted a Decken's sifaka will bark and then others will take up its cry, including members of other groups within earshot of the first cry. The Decken's sifakas prefer to remain treebound and move about their trees both night and day.

Habitat

Decken's sifaka is a forest dweller and spends most of its time clinging to trees and is particularly associated with the presence of kily. The flora of Tsingy de Bemaraha, the natural reserve where Decken's sifaka occurs, consists of a dry western deciduous forest with plant species of *Aloe* and baobab *Adansonia*, as well as the red-flowered tree *Delonix regia*. This vast reserve, the largest in Madagascar, includes limestone pinnacles or tsingy. The climate is dry with only 4 or 5 months of rainfall and generally high temperatures which do not drop below 68 degrees Fahrenheit.

Distribution

Decken's sifaka is found on a large bulge of land that extends into the ocean from central western Madagascar. It may have as recently as the 1970s extended east into the central regions of Madagascar, but this is not certain.

Threats

The forests of Decken's sifaka are set afire each year to encourage the growth of grass for grazing livestock. This burning occurs even in nature reserves and is reducing the size of the Decken's sifaka's range.

Conservation and Recovery

The Decken's sifaka has been found in the vast Tsingy de Bemaraha Natural Reserve,

which covers 130,000 acres, the Namoroka
Nature Reserve, and the Ambohijanahary
Special Reserve. The clearing of land for
grazing has been especially bad in the
Ambohijanahary Special Reserve, which may
soon have little to reserve. At present, educating local people about the wildlife in the
reserve and about the need to protect the
wildlife has been the focus of conservation
efforts.

Verreaux's Sifaka

Propithecus verreauxi verreauxi

Rich Block

Status	Endangered
Listed	December 2, 1970
Family	Indridae (Indris and sifakas)
Description	Coat is white, usually with a black or reddish brown crown; with large yellow eyes.
Habitat	Forest dweller.
Food	Fruit, pods, berries, acacia buds, bark, and flowers.
Reproduction	After a gestation period of 165 days, one infant is born.
Threats	Deforestation. Its primary natural predators are hawks.
Range	Madagascar

Description

Verreaux's sifaka, *P. v. verreauxi*, measures 16.7 to 17.7 inches from the tip of the nose to the tail; its tail length varies from 22.0 to 23.6 inches. It weighs 7.6 to 8.0 pounds. It has dense, white fur, usually with black or reddish-brown hair on its crown; its skin is black; its large eyes are yellow.

Behavior

Although Verreaux's sifaka prefers to eat leaves and fruit, it is an opportunistic feeder

that will take advantage of what a region offers. This is reflected in what it will eat when in captivity: Grapes, apples, peaches, pears, melons, bananas, avocados, oranges, mangoes and pineapples are the staple fruits. The vegetables consumed in captivity consist of canned or fresh sweet corn, garbanzo beans, lettuce, broccoli, cauliflower, cabbage, carrots, sweet potatoes, cucumbers and celery. Cream of wheat cereal, wheatgerm, baby cereal, corn oil, honey and vitamin supplements in evaporated milk are also dietary supplements. In the winter white oak trees (*Quercus* species) are a popular food. In 1985 a wide variety of browse plants were introduced to improve the sifikas' diet. Of twelve introduced, five have been selected popular year round food items: the American hornbeam (*Carpinus caroliniana*), mimosa (*Albizia julibrissin*), eastern redbud (*Cercis canadensis*), winged sumac (*Rhus copallina*), and sweet gum.

Verreaux's sifaka spends most of its time feeding in trees and sleeping. Activity is observed both night and day. Females are dominant over males, but no submissive behavior has been reported. Males maintain proximity to females and will fight each other for dominance during mating season from January to March. Females ovulate only once and are receptive for only 12 to 36 hours, mating only with the dominant male. Birth occurs after gestation of 130 to 155 days.

Home range is from 1.5 to 6.5 acres, with a nucleus territory, which allows for some overlapping of groups, with territorial defense if the nucleus boundary is crossed.

Habitat

Verreaux's sifaka is a forest dweller and is found in gallery and evergreen forest to dry deciduous forest to spiny desert.

Distribution

Verreaux's sifaka is found in the south and southwest portions of Madagascar from west of Fort Dauphin, up as far as the Tsiribihina river in the northwest. They are commonly seen in the private reserve at Berenty and in the Special Reserve of Beza-Mahafaly. They live in population densities as high as 300 per square mile.

Threats

Deforestation by logging for timber and fuel has dramatically shrunk the forests on which the Verreaux's sifaka depends.

Conservation and Recovery

Verreaux's sifaka lives in several wildlife reserves and national parks in the south and west of Madagascar. It is the most common of the endangered sifakas and may survive if the reserves and parks are properly protected.

Lorises and Pottos
Family: Loridae

Pygmy Loris (*Nycticebus pygmaeus*)　　　　　　Noel Rowe

Potto (*Perodicticus potto*)　　　　　　Noel Rowe

General Characteristics of the *Loridae*

Lorises, which occur in southern Asia, and pottos, which occur in Africa, are primitive primates that resemble lemurs. They move on all four forelimbs and hindlimbs, which are of equal length. They have powerful grasps and can cling to branches for extended periods without fatigue. Exclusively nocturnal, they avoid predators by remaining very still during the day. Lorises and pottos are slow climbers, and move smoothly along limbs to avoid detection by either predators or their own prey. Almost completely arboreal, they have lost the ability to leap, and they descend to the ground only when confronted by tree predators. They are able to remain motionless for hours in order to discourage or confuse predators.

The Loridae detect their prey by smell, and they will eat foods that other predators reject, especially species whose foul odor is the main defense. They are also able to digest hairs that irritate and discourage other predators, and they will eat caterpillars, butterflies, ants, fleas, beetles, and poisonous millipedes that are generally safe from other predators.

Lorises and pottos breed slowly, usually giving birth to a single young once a year. The newborn clings to the belly of its mother for several days, at which time she deposits the infant on a limb while she forages and sleeps. When the infant is mobile enough, it will follow its mother, who teaches it what to eat and how to hide. Weaning occurs in 40-60 days.

As small, reclusive, nocturnal animals, the Loridae are seldom hunted by humans, so that the threat to their survival is loss of habitat. They are dependent on thick foliage for protection from their predators, and when they are forced into alternative habitat, they do not survive.

Lesser Slow [=Pygmy] Loris

Nycticebus pygmaeus

Ron Garrison

Status	Threatened
Listed	October 19, 1976
Family	Lorisidae (Loris)
Description	Light brown coat with grey marking around the eyes and a grey stripe along the spine.
Habitat	Tropical rain forests.
Food	Mostly insects, but also snails, lizards, birds' eggs, and birds.
Reproduction	1, occasionally 2, young after gestation of 186 to 193 days.
Threats	Loss of habitat to logging, and warfare.
Range	Viet Nam, Laos, Cambodia.

Description

The pygmy loris, *Nycticebus pygmaeus*, needs much more study to confirm its description. Females may weigh 13.1 ounces; males may weigh 16.3 ounces. The nose-to-base-of-tail length is 8.3 to 11.4 inches with a vestigial tail. Like the slow loris, its fur is short and light brown, with grey markings on the face and back. Unlike the higher primates, lorises have fur on their face and have moist noses. Notable in the slow lorises is the opposable thumb, which is fully opposable to all of the other digits, allowing for a variety of strong grips on tree trunks and branches.

Taxonomy is disputed. A proposed third *Nycticebus* species, *N. intermedius*, has not been accepted.

Behavior

The pygmy loris is a methodical hunter that slowly creeps up on its prey. Sometimes it displays surprising quickness when an insect tries to escape, sharply grabbing the insect in its hands. Its prey includes insects that have foul tastes and poisonous defenses that repel most potential predators. Such insects often advertise themselves with bright colors and foul odors, but the pygmy loris is primarily a nighttime predator and probably does not see the insects' colors. As for the foul smell, it seems to attract the pygmy loris; insects that rely on foul taste and poisons to repulse predators are often slow moving, which makes them particularly attractive to the phlegmatic pygmy loris. Such insects can be so toxic to predators that eating causes death, but the pygmy loris seems to have adapted its metabolism to either absorb or eject the poisons. This means that in its native habitat the pygmy loris has a wealth of insect protein available to it that is untouched by other predators.

Very little is known about the pygmy loris because it is what naturalists call a "cryptic" animal. By "cryptic," they mean that it is very good at hiding from scientific observers. In the case of the pygmy loris, it is the animal's ability to freeze in place that makes it cryptic, or very hard to observe. Whenever it senses the presence of a potentially dangerous animal, the pygmy loris instantly locks itself into whatever position it is in — it may be climbing a tree and have two legs in mid-air, taking a step, or it may be feeding on an insect, and be in midbite. Whatever its position, it freezes absolutely motionless, not even twitching for several hours at a time, or until the dangerous animal goes away. By not moving, the pygmy loris becomes part of the leafy background of its habitat, and predators, including humans, may gaze in the right direction and without movement to betray it, the pygmy loris may not be seen at all.

Habitat

The pygmy loris lives in the secondary forests of Indochina. It seems to be primarily arboreal, and it favors areas with large numbers of insects.

Distribution

The animal is distributed through most of southeast Asia, from Viet Nam, Laos, to Cambodia.

Threats

The pygmy loris may always have been rare, but it is hard to tell on scanty information about its natural history. Much of the world in which it lives has long been troubled by wars and the illicit drug trade, making it very difficult for naturalists to study it in detail over long periods. Deforestation is certainly the major threat to the animals — much of its territory is being denuded by clear-cut logging. Its habitat has been further reduced by expanding human communities in a region where the human population is exploding. Warfare has even further reduced the size of its habitat.

Conservation and Recovery

The pygmy loris needs to have its habitat protected. The small reserve in west-central Viet Nam seems inadequate to the purpose, although the reserves in Malaysia and Indonesia may have some of the species within them.

Tarsiers

Family: Tarsidae

Philippine Tarsier (*Tarsius syrichta*)   Noel Rowe

General Characteristics of the *Tarsidae*

Tarsiers have their origins in the Eocene epoch, over forty million years ago. They probably evolved out of an ancient primate family called *Omomyidae*, two species of which were very like present-day tarsiers: *Necrolemur* from Europe and *Tetonius* from North America. The lineage of the surviving tarsier species is ancient; they have probably lived where they live now for the forty million years since they evolved, since their related tarsiers flourished and spread through Europe, North America, Asia, and Africa, then competed with newer, more competitive primates, declined and disappeared. Four species (*T. bancanus, T. dianae, T. pumilus,* and *T. spectrum*) are recognized in Indonesia and another (*T. sangirensis*) is proposed, based on field data on vocalizations, measurements, and genetics recently gathered. One tarsier species is found in the Philippines, *T. syrichta*. Of these, the spectral tarsier is the most primitive, which means it has retained more of the traits of its ancient ancestors than have the other species. For example, the spectral tarsier still has scales of its tail, similar to rats and mice, but the other species have lost their scales, with their skin showing faint traces of where the scales would have been. The spectral tarsier is also the least adapted to an arboreal life. *Tarsier dianae* was first discovered in 1991 and was named for Dian Fossey and Diana, the goddess of hunting. *Tarsier pumilus,* the pygmy tarsier, was elevated from a subspecies in 1985 based on museum specimens.

The tarsiers have extraordinarily long hind limbs in proportion to the rest of their bodies — about twice as long. This trait provides the legs with great leverage; tarsiers can leap many feet. They are also excellent climbers and travel through trees by climbing and leaping. Their feet have claws on the second and third toes; these claws are used for grooming. The other toes, as well as all the fingers, have nails. Both fingers and toes have wide pads at their tips that aid in gripping tree branches. The fingers are long and dexterous and are useful for snatching insects. The eyes of tarsiers are circular and large. In fact, the western tarsier's eyes each outweigh its brain. The brains of the tarsiers are adapted to emphasize vision, and the eyes are large for gathering light during the night, when the tarsier's are hunting. The eyes provide stereoscopic vision but are virtually immobile, facing forward; the head must move in order for a tarsier to scan its surroundings. The ears of the spectral tarsier are large, but on the other tarsiers they are less so. The hearing of tarsiers is acute, and can alert the hunters to the movements of their prey before they see their quarry.

Tarsiers are carnivorous, eating a wide variety of arthropods, from ants to scorpions. Snakes and even birds are also common prey. Tarsiers leap on their prey, pin it or grasp it with their hands (they are adept at snatching flying insects), and then kill it by biting it several times with their large, pointy teeth. Then they carry their meal to a safe place, eating it head first. A curious trait of tarsiers is the individuality of their taste: Individual members of the same species will have greatly varying preferences for food with, for instance, one preferring a particular species of insect while another avoids that insect altogether.

In spite of their antiquity and primitiveness when compared to most other primates, the tarsiers until recently have been abundant in their ranges. At present, the Philippine tarsier is the most endangered species, but logging kills thousands of the other tarsiers every year and these still plentiful animals could become endangered in the near future. The forests of Borneo in particular are disappearing, making the western tarsier likely to be the next of its family to face extinction.

Philippine Tarsier

Tarsius syrichta

David Haring

Status	Threatened
Listed	October 19, 1976
Family	Tarsiidae (Tarsiers)
Description	Gray or gray-brown coat; around the eyes and along the nose are brown; the coat may have variegated patches of white.
Habitat	Secondary lowland and coastal forest.
Food	Primarily insects and lizards.
Reproduction	Gestation lasts about 180 days and results in a single birth.
Threats	Habitat loss.
Range	Philippine Islands

Description

Adult Philippine tarsiers, *Tarsius syrichta*, weigh 4.6 to 5.3 ounces, measure 4.3 to 5 inches from tip of nose to tail, and have a tail 8.3 to 9.1 inches long. The tail is nearly naked, and it lacks the scales found on the tails of spectral tarsiers. Its coat is very soft and is gray or gray-brown, although its face tends to be brown with little gray in it.

Like its relatives the spectral tarsier and the western tarsier, the Philippine tarsier has acute hearing, which it uses to help it locate its prey in the dark. However, in spite of the importance of hearing, the parts of the brain associated with sight dominate the Philippine tarsier's brain as a whole. Its eyes are large and dominate its face; they point forward with little mobility, something like an owl's eyes, and provide true stereoscopic vision. Their size is an adaptation to night hunting, enabling the Philippine tarsier to see in very dim light. (Like cats, it cannot see in absolute darkness; if there is absolutely no light, it would be as blind as we humans would be.)

Another significant feature are the hind legs, which are much longer than the fore-limbs. These legs give the Philippine tarsier great leaping ability, with a vertical jump of about 6 feet. This adaptation helps the tarsier evade predators and to spring upon prey from several feet away.

Behavior

The Philippine tarsier is exclusively carnivorous, a rarity among primates. It prey consists of insects and small animals such as lizards, snakes (including venomous ones), and birds. When it spots its prey, the Philippine tarsier leaps upon it, holds it down with its hand, and bites it until it submits or dies. The prey is then carried up onto a tree limb and then eaten head first. The Philippine tarsier's diet varies from one animal to another; for example, some seem to relish eating snakes, yet others seem to detest snakes.

Gestation lasts roughly 180 days, resulting in a single birth. For three weeks, the young is carried by its mother in her mouth. After about four weeks, the youngster begins hunting on its own.

The Philippine tarsiers are active in twilight and during the night, sleeping during the day. In addition to hunting, they drink water several times during the night. They sleep clinging to stalks, stems, and tree trunks.

Habitat

The Philippine tarsiers live primarily in secondary lowland and coastal forest.

Distribution

The Philippine tarsiers live on the southern islands of the Philippines, including Mindanao and Samar.

Threats

Their islands are being denuded by clear-cut logging. Human communities are expanding in their territory, further leveling forests. The Philippine tarsier is heavily dependent on trees and the abundance of small animals that the rain forest provides. Sometimes these animals are captured for pets, but without expert handling, they die quickly in captivity. They require live prey and cannot subsist on anything else.

Conservation and Recovery

The efforts of the Philippine government to protect what little is left of its rain forests, which were vast as recently as forty years ago, have met with much resistance from logging companies and others who profit from the destruction of forests. The resistance can be extreme, including the killing of endangered animals and even killing native people if they get in the way. Thus conserving the Philippine tarsier is very difficult and offers significant challenges to the government and to naturalists, whose lives are at risk.

New World Monkeys:
Squirrel, Spider and Woolly Monkeys, Capuchins, Howlers, and Sakis
Family: Cebidae

Telho State Park, Brazil   Luiz Claudio Marigo

General Characteristics of the *Cebidae*

The family *Cebidae* includes the squirrel and howler monkeys, the capuchins, sakis, bearded sakis, uakaris, spider, and woolly monkeys. Marmosets and tamarins, which are also called "New World monkeys" are of another family, the *Callitrichidae*. Some authorities prefer to call the *Cebidae* "Capuchinlike monkeys" rather than "New World monkeys."

Much about the evolution of the New World monkey family *Cebidae* is not known because fossil evidence has been hard to find; the cebids tend to live in climates that are not good for creating fossils. Their earliest known New World predecessor is *Branisella*, the remains of which have been found in Bolivia. This ancient monkey lived about 35 million years ago in the Oligocene epoch and already had many of the traits of modern New World monkeys, which means that monkeys must have been in the New World long before. While *Branisella* may not be the ancestor of the modern *Cebidae* (but it could be), it is likely that the cebids are descended from a common ancestor.

The modern family *Cebidae* is very diverse, with very small monkeys and very large ones, with colorful coated species and drab species, with species with prehensile tails and species without prehensile tails — and even species with stubs for tails. They live primarily in the rain forest of Latin America, but some live all the time in trees, while others live in the underbrush. Most live in lowland forests, but some live on mountainsides. They are linked together by a common anatomy and are most easily identified by their dentition, which includes three molars on each side of the jaw. Their noses also set them apart from other primates: The cebid monkeys have widely separated nostrils that point to the side, rather than downward. Monkeys with prehensile tails are found only among the cebids.

The species of *Cebidae* live in social groups that are usually small, focusing on a mating pair, and that have territories that are usually vigorously defended against other groups of the same species. One of the more interesting aspects of the cebids is that different species not only live in overlapping territories with one another, but they also share the same foods. For instance, a particular fruit tree could have several different species of monkey in it at the same time, all feeding on the same fruit and insects. In such a tree there is usually a hierarchy of the different species, with the larger species getting the choicer feeding areas; naturalists have observed different species occupying different levels in a food tree and such stratified feeding is common, especially in the upper Amazon region, where the number of different species is particularly dense. This vigorous competition for food has apparently been going on for a very long time, because different species have evolved ways for coping with the competition from other species. Some monkeys such as the red uakari (*Cacajao rubicundus*) have adapted by becoming large; they drive away smaller monkeys. One species, the night monkey (*Aotus trivirgatus*), has adapted by becoming active by night and resting by day. All the other monkeys are daytime feeders, so the night monkey is able to eat what it likes during the night and remain undisturbed. On the other hand, the relatively small squirrel monkey (*Saimiri sciureus*) has adapted by socializing in very large troops. The larger monkeys live in smaller groups and therefore do not have enough group members to drive off the hordes of squirrel monkeys that swarm around them. In yet another adaptation, the titi monkeys (genus *Callicebus*) have developed the somewhat insidious practice of eating green, unripe fruit that other cebids cannot digest. Thus a tree may be shorn of its fruit by titi monkeys before other species have a chance to share in the tree's bounty.

Cebids have in common color vision, stereoscopic vision. Often great leapers (like the spider monkeys, genus *Ateles*), and typically agile when moving through trees, cebids rely on their good depth perception to help them avoid making missteps. Even so, they sometimes fall; the smaller species seem to endure great falls to the ground without being harmed, but the larger ones can be injured. The color vision probably helps cebids to select palatable foods and to avoid unpalatable fruits and poisonous insects. They probably also use their color vision to distinguish members of their own species or even subspecies from nonmembers — very useful for breeding and for forming secure social groups.

The *Cebidae* species are vocal animals, and their range of calls include grunts, howls, and whistles. Their systems of calls can be complicated, with an appropriate combination of sounds and cadences serving to identify the caller's particular species. The calls also indicate sexual interest, territorial range, and the discovery of food. Members of social groups also use calls to keep track of one another while they are foraging.

Within groups, grooming is an important activity, and cebids will groom one another as often as they can. Grooming may help form bonds among group members; in addition, the grooming seems to have a relaxing effect on the one being groomed, so grooming may be a way for subdominant group members to foster relaxed relationships with more dominant members.

There is a clear difference in behavior between the immature and mature members of a species. The youngsters take every opportunity to be active. They are very curious about their surroundings and the activities of adults; they may learn much of how to behave and to survive from observing their elders. The larger the group, the more likely it is that juveniles will seek out the company of other juveniles and play, even while adult group members rest. Thus in very large groups, such as those of squirrel monkeys, juveniles may spend nearly all their nonfeeding time in the company of other juveniles and away from their parents.

Even though the species of *Cebidae* are fascinating in their ecology and habits, most of them have been poorly studied. This stems in part from a long period in which scientists were only interested in them as subjects for laboratory medical research, and it stems in part from the long-standing inaccessibility of much of their range. Naturalists face great problems today when trying to study cebids. One is that some are very nearly extinct. For example, the woolly spider monkey (*Brachyteles arachnoides*) presently numbers in the few hundreds, yet it once numbered in the tens of thousands, perhaps hundreds of thousands. It now lives in tiny patches of forest, the rest of its habitat having been eradicated by humans; there is little chance for discovering what the woolly spider monkey's wild behavior would be if it were able to live in its now lost natural habitat. All cebids are threatened to some degree by habitat loss to logging, agriculture, and expanding human populations. Another problem stems from the contradictory consequences of increased accessibility to the ranges of once remote populations of cebids. New roads, logging, and slash-and-burn agriculture are opening up new areas for exploration, yet by the time naturalists get to newly opened areas the populations of cebids tend to be gone, having been killed off for food by local humans, as well as by hunters employed by logging companies and construction companies to supply work crews with meat. Another significant problem is violence by humans on humans: In some areas naturalists — especially foreign nationals — are killed or kidnaped by guerrillas or bandits, and in others conservationists are murdered by landowners and industrialists because their efforts to preserve forest lands may interfere with ranch or industry profits.

Mantled Howler Monkey

Alouatta palliata

E. R. Luna

Status	Endangered
Listed	June 14, 1976
Family	Cebidae (New World monkey)
Description	Brown or black coat blended with golden brown hair on the back.
Habitat	Evergreen rain forests.
Food	Leaves, fruits and flowers.
Reproduction	Gestation lasts 186 days and results in one infant.
Threats	Habitat loss and human predation.
Range	Costa Rica, Ecuador, Mexico, and Guatemala.

Description

The mantled howler monkey, *Alouatta palliata*, is sexually dimorphic, with males being somewhat larger than females. An adult male measures between 20.0 and 26.6 inches from the tip of its nose to the base of its tail; an adult female measures between 18.9 and 24.9 inches. The adult male's tail is 21.5 to 23.8 inches long; the adult female's tail is 22.2 to 25.8 inches long. Adult males weigh 9.9 to 21.6 pounds, but adult females weigh 6.8 to 16.8 pounds. Males have a larger hyoid — a bone in the throat — than females; it is through a cavity in this bone that air is passed to create the animal's howl.

Mantled howler monkeys have jaws adapted for eating leaves. They have broad, flat teeth, and their lower jaw bones are deep, anchoring powerful muscles. Their intestines take up about one third of their body's volume, with the lower intestinal tract greatly enlarged. In the lower tract are bacteria that break down the leaf-matter into sugars that the monkey can metabolize. This is somewhat inefficient because most nutrient absorption occurs in the upper tract, the small intestine, and it may in part account for why the mantled howler monkey is a slow mover — it is conserving energy because it needs to conserve the sugars it metabolizes.

Mantled howler monkeys have long, dense fur coats. The base color is brown or black. On the back, golden brown hair mixes with the base coat (this is the "mantle"), and the flanks of the monkey are fringed with yellowish brown hair. Their tail is prehensile, and its underside has a hairless area, perhaps for secure gripping.

Behavior

The mantled howler monkey has an eerie

cry that can be heard for many miles. Once thought to be a cry made by males to impress and attract females, it now appears that the cry is intended to give information about a social group of mantled howler monkeys. The cries serve in part to tell other groups where a given group is, but additionally, it conveys information about the group's place in the local hierarchy. In a given region, different groups of mantled howler monkeys are ranked on a hierarchy of dominance; the cries let all the local groups know where a dominant group is; groups lower on the hierarchy can then avoid coming near the more dominant group.

Occasionally groups meet even when they do not intend to. Although each group has a well-defined territory in which it tries to contain all of its activity, territories can overlap. This overlapping seems to be ignored for the most part; dominant groups do not go rushing about chasing out invaders it hears howling within its territory. Even so, when groups meet, accidentally or otherwise, there is a great deal of thrashing about. This normally slow-moving creature jumps and runs hither and yon, howls vociferously, and fights. It is possible that such fighting proves fatal occasionally. The confrontations between groups use up a great deal of energy, but the mantled howler monkey's behavior is normally one designed to conserve energy, so even dominant groups are motivated to avoid direct confrontations.

Groups average about 18 members, but range from 4 to 21 members. Their territories tend to be small, beginning at about 12 acres. A territory of 150 acres has been reported, but this would be very unusual; the mantled howler monkey usually has a territory no larger than it can travel through in a day. Although the groups have well-defined territories, they rarely defend anything besides

especially bountiful fruit trees within their territories. Each group has a dominant male who is the focus of group activity; where he goes, the group goes.

The mantled howler monkey sleeps about 50% of each day. When moving, it is slow, carefully walking from tree limb to tree limb. Its diet consists of about 50% leaves, which it chooses slowly and carefully. It prefers young leaves, probably because they are less fibrous than mature leaves and therefore have a higher proportion of sugars to fiber. They also eat mature leaves from select plants that produce an unusually high amount of sugar and other nutrients in their leaves. Although mantled howler monkeys can live for several weeks on leaves alone, most of the time they need to eat other kinds of food, as well. Sugary fruits are favored and will comprise most of the mantled howler monkey's diet besides leaves. The mantled howler monkey has also been observed eating flowers.

Mating seems to occur year round because births have been recorded year round. Gestation lasts 186 days, resulting in a single birth. At first, the young cling very close to their mothers because they are helpless. As they grow, they become more independent and their coat changes colors until they are full grown, beginning at downy gray. Males cannot be distinguished from females until their second year of life, when their testes drop. When males reach adulthood, the scrotum turns white. The growing independence of the young monkey is revealed by its exploration and careful observation of the wildlife around it. Their fathers will share some of the responsibility for care of the young and will even play with them occasionally. A mantled howler monkey can be weaned between 1.5 and 2 years of age. Females become sexually mature at 4 to 5 years of age, but males do not become sexually mature until 6 to 8 years of age. The dynamics of male hierarchy are unclear at present, but newly mature males seem to leave their birth groups either voluntarily or are driven out. Such males may form small groups with other wandering males, and eventually they blend in with other mixed gender groups, sometimes rising to dominance. Even so, some males seem to remain with their birth groups, remaining subdominant. Others are rejected violently by new groups and are sometimes killed. Adult males often bear facial scars attesting to combat, although this combat has yet to be observed.

The mantled howler monkey is reported to be a friendly, easy-going animal, that does not mind the presence of humans. Its typical response to being disturbed is to move over a few feet to get out of the way.

Habitat

Although it prefers evergreen rain forests, the mantled howler monkey has shown some adaptability as humans have driven it out of its traditional range. It has moved into montane and coastal forests. Even so, it is limited by its need for dense forest cover and abundant leaves, with some fruit mixed in.

Distribution

The mantled howler monkey once ranged from southern Mexico through Central America to Ecuador. Loss of habitat is restricting it to northeastern Central America, especially Costa Rica and Guatemala. The remaining patches of forest in its range likely to be too small to maintain viable breeding populations.

Threats

Logging has denuded much of the mantled howler monkey's range in the last few decades. Expanding agricultural development has also significantly reduced the size of its native forests. In its southern range, slash-and-burn agriculture has nearly eliminated its forest.

The mantled howler monkey is also hunted for food and for capture to be sold as pets, to zoological collections, or to laboratories. The animal is friendly toward humans and seems to regard us as variations of its own kind. It thus shares its space with humans rather than fleeing or hiding. This makes it very easy to shoot or capture.

Its range includes the range of the Guatemalan howler (*Alouatta pigra*; see separate entry). In the past, they have coexisted without conflict, even sharing the same trees while feeding. Now they are competing for very limited and ever shrinking resources, to the detriment of each. The more adaptable of the two species, the mantled howler monkey has managed to take most of the resources for itself, excluding the Guatemalan howler.

Conservation and Recovery

Costa Rica has preserved some highland rain forests in which the mantled howler monkey may survive. With the ending of its long civil war, Guatemala may be able to devote time and resources toward saving its surviving rain forests, in which mantled howler monkeys are still found. The region in which it is found has been torn by human warfare for decades; it features poor people who often live by slash-and-burn agriculture; and the governments in the region are sometimes not motivated to curb the logging that is

clearing away their forests. Money and research are needed to help the nations involved
create wildlife preserves, manage the reserves,
and protect them. They also need alternative
sources of international currency to logging
and the selling of the monkeys. The mantled
howler monkey has been bred in the laboratory.

Guatemalan Howler Monkey

Alouatta pigra [=villosa]

Art Wolfe

Status	Threatened
Listed	October 19, 1976
Family	Cebidae (New World monkey)
Description	Soft, dense reddish black hair with red-to-brown roots; underside of the prehensile tail is bare.
Habitat	Rain forests and forests that flood.
Food	Leaves and fruit.
Reproduction	Gestation probably lasts about 185 days, resulting in a single birth.
Threats	Loss of habitat is close to exterminating the Guatemalan howler.
Range	Belize, Guatemala, and Mexico.

Description

Taxonomy is disputed. *Alouatta pigra* was elevated from a subspecies of *A. palliata*. Until 1988 this species' name was *A. villosa*.

Measurements of Guatemalan howlers are taken primarily from specimens in captivity. Adult males are notably larger than adult females. Not counting the tail, the adult male Guatemalan howler is 24 to 25 inches in length; his tail adds another 19 to 30 inches. He weighs about 25 pounds. Not counting the tail, the female Guatemalan howler is 18 to 20 inches in length; her tale adds another 25 to 26 inches. She weighs 19 to 20 pounds. The Guatemalan howlers' hair is soft and dense and is reddish black, with red-to-brown roots.

The underside of their tail is bare; the tail is prehensile and strong enough to bear the entire dangling weight of the monkey. The Guatemalan howler's larynx is very large, with a big vocal apparatus.

This species is also known as the Mexican black howler.

Behavior

Howler monkeys derive their name because of the enormous howl they often make. Their vocal apparatus is cavernous and enables them to let loose with deafening howls that can be heard miles away. Even though the Guatemalan howler is a vegetarian and little threat to humans, its howl is said to be frightening.

The Guatemalan howler has been little observed in the wild, so most of what is known of it comes from laboratory studies; such studies cannot reveal the full range of the animal's behavior. The Guatemalan howler moves about during the day in groups of about 7 members. A large male dominates the group and serves as the group's focus of attention. Like other howler monkeys, the Guatemalan howler probably has a territory of fixed size, but it does not defend its borders from interloping groups unless they accidentally meet. In general, the animal has a relaxed attitude toward outside groups and is usually nonviolent. The exception to this involves groupless males; young males usually leave their groups when they near maturity, and when they find a new group they may either be accepted or driven away. Apparently no naturalist has yet recorded what happens when a groupless male is rejected, but the corpses of the males suggest that they received severe head injuries from teeth or hands.

Guatemalan howlers are not leapers; they are climbers. They move by anchoring their prehensile tails on a branch and then climbing in the direction they wish to go, releasing and reanchoring their tails as they go. Their tails also play a role in socializing; group members will interlink their tails when at rest.

The diet of the Guatemalan howler is not well understood, but it seems limited primarily to leaves, with preferably ripe fruits occasionally eaten. This restricted diet makes it challenging to keep them in captivity, and it limits their ability to survive the loss of their native forests.

Habitat

The Guatemalan howler lives in lowland forests and seems to prefer wet forests, although it has occasionally been found in drier deciduous forests.

Distribution

The Guatemalan howler's range includes southern Mexico, all of Belize, and most of eastern Guatemala. It may have once ranged farther north into Mexico, but it seems unlikely that its range was ever much larger than at present.

Threats

Clear cut logging has destroyed most of the Guatemalan howler's habitat, with agricultural development taking most of the rest of it. It shares its range with the mantled howler (*Alouatta palliata*; please see separate entry), an animal that is somewhat more adaptable than the Guatemalan howler and which is pushing the Guatemalan howler out of its last refuges as the two species, which cohabited fairly well, compete for scarce habitat resources. It is possible that the Guatemalan howler still inhabits Guatemala's Tikal National Park; it is also possible that it has recently become extinct.

Conservation and Recovery

It is essential for the Guatemalan howler's survival that the little primary forest remaining be preserved from clearing. The animal seems unable to live in secondary forests or forests that have been disturbed by logging. Of great help would be careful studies of the Guatemalan howler in the wild; at present, naturalists do not know enough about its behavior to be able to suggest what specifically needs to be conserved to save the animal, and they do not know for certain what the animal's particular dietary and social needs are. A general suspicion that the Guatemalan howler has already been overwhelmed by the nearly as endangered mantled howler may be inhibiting efforts to find out more about the animal and may be discouraging efforts to preserve it.

Black-handed Spider Monkey

Ateles geoffroyi

Status	Endangered
Listed	June 2, 1970
Family	Cebidae (New World monkey)
Description	A lightly built, slender armed monkey with medium length, golden to reddish brown hair.
Habitat	Rain forests.
Food	Fruit, young leaves, buds, seeds, bark, and wood.
Reproduction	Gestation lasts 210 to 225 days, resulting in a single birth.
Threats	Loss of habitat, hunting.
Range	Mexico, Central America, Colombia and Peru.

Noel Rowe

Description

There are nine subspecies of the black-handed spider monkey, *Ateles geoffroyi*, all of which are threatened with extinction. Two of these subspecies are listed by the USFWS as endangered: the black-browed spider monkey (*Ateles geoffroyi frontatus*) and the red spider monkey (*Ateles geoffroyi panamensis*; see separate entries). The species vary in coloration, characteristics of fur, and possibly in behavior. The fur may be golden brown, dark brown, or red-brown, and it may be coarse, somewhat shaggy, or smooth, even sleek. The hair on the head and tail tends to be fluffy.

Black-handed spider monkeys have long, slim arms and legs, hence the name "spider monkey." Their feet and hands are black, hence the common name "black-handed spider monkey." Although favorite displays in zoos, they are little studied, and very little studied in the wild. They may or may not be sexually dimorphic. Measurement for females especially are widely varying. They have a head and body length of 15 to 21 inches, with tails of 24 to 33 inches, and they weigh between 16 and 19 pounds. Their thumbs are small, an adaptation for brachiation — swinging by the hands from tree limb to tree limb. Their tails are prehensile, with a bare patch on the underside for gripping branches and a bare, sensitive tip. The tail is strong enough for them to swing by it, although they rarely do, and it has a sensitive enough touch that it can pick up, hold, and carry small objects.

Behavior

In zoos, the black-handed spider monkeys are playful animals, bright and full of tricks, making them prime attractions for drawing visitors. Some subspecies dislike the company of humans and are stressed by their presence, and tricks such as begging for food with their tails are unnatural behavior, probably brought on by their dependence on humans for survival in an alien environment.

The black-handed spider monkeys move through their forest's canopy by brachiation and by walking, usually dangling with their back to the forest floor, with their hands, feet, and tails along tree limbs. They rarely come to the forest floor, but when they do, they walk upright on their feet. Most of the time they descend no farther than 40 feet above the ground, and they prefer to remain high in the canopy, where their agility makes them masters of movement in their environment.

They live in troops of as many as 80 members, although 20 seems to be the most common size. These troops form loose affiliation; in some subspecies membership is fluid, with monkeys joining and leaving troops frequently. Each large troop is divided into groups of 2 to 8 members; the animals in these groups remain in the same general vicinity with each other and often gather together. Individual monkeys will sometimes wander away from their groups, moving alone for days, but they and their other group members make high pitched cries that apparently let them keep track of each other even when they are apart. A few naturalists say that groups feature loud and violent contests for dominance among males and females, but most observations do not support this. In general, all the subspecies seem fairly relaxed in their attitudes toward individual rank. They form all-male groups, all-female groups, and mixed-gender groups, with conflict being primarily observed in all-female groups, from which in a few subspecies females may be evicted by interloping females or males.

Males are the primary defenders of groups from threats. Although some black-handed spider monkeys regard humans with curiosity, even friendliness, most perceive humans as dangerous and respond accordingly. Males will thrash branches about and will tear some loose and drop them on the threat. Falling from 60 or more feet, these branches, weighing about 10 pounds, can seriously injure a human and seem to be effective deterrents against ground-traveling predators (other than humans, these have yet to be identified). Both males and females will cry out and will urinate and defecate on the threats below.

Surprisingly little is on record about the mating habits of the black-handed spider monkey. Given that tens of thousands have been exported to zoos, observations of mating habits should be plentiful, but they are not. Gestation varies from 226 to 232 days. Births result in a single newborn. The infant is first carried on its mother's midriff, usually held by one of the mother's hands. Eventually, it shifts to its mother's back for traveling. Youngsters are playful, frolicking by themselves and with other youngsters. Females reach sexual maturity after 4 years of life, and males reach sexual maturity after 5 years.

Fruit makes up most of the black-handed spider monkey's diet. During the early part of the day, it seeks out fruits and feeds, resting about half the day after dining. They apparently rest throughout the night. About 10% to 13% of a black-handed spider monkey's diet consists of foods other than fruit: young leaves, buds, seeds, bark, and wood. The eating of wood is an interesting, unusual but observed phenomenon.

Habitat

The black-handed spider monkeys prefer to live in the canopies of rain forests.

Distribution

Black-handed spider monkeys have been widely distributed animals, found from Veracruz in Mexico south through Central America into northwestern Colombia, and according to one field study, into Peru. They are now at best very rare in Mexico and are probably extirpated from Mexico except its southernmost border area. They live in patches of rain forest through most of their old range.

Threats

Much of Central America has been clear-cut for timber by logging companies, and much of the little remaining rain forest has been disrupted by warfare. Slash-and-burn agriculture has virtually wiped out the black-handed spider monkey's habitat in areas such as northwestern Colombia; more modern agriculture has supplanted the rain forest in most of the rest of the animal's range. The black-handed spider monkey requires a dense, high forest canopy in order to survive, and with the destruction of its once vast forest has come a corresponding decline in its population.

Everywhere in its range, the black-handed spider monkey is hunted by humans for food, and their meat is an important source of protein for local people, especially the poor. Handsome, playful animals, the black-handed monkey has long been captured and sold for pets or zoo animals. During the 1970s, the U.S. alone imported tens of thousands of black-handed spider monkeys. The hunting by an exploding, chronically impoverished population, combined with the destruction of the rainforest, brought most of the subspecies to near extinction.

Conservation and Recovery

Efforts to conserve the black-handed spider monkey have been few and small. Costa Rica has established forest reserves that may protect its native subspecies, although the reserved areas may be too small to maintain healthy breeding populations of the animals. On the other hand, while nearly all of Costa Rica's lowlands have been urbanized or converted to farmland in the last few decades, its mountain forests are unattractive for agricultural development and the government has curbed logging in them. Black-handed spider monkeys may survive at low elevations in the mountainous patches of rain forest. In much of the rest of Central America, the black-handed spider monkey's survival depends in part on economics; as people prosper they need less and less to take sources of protein out of their wildlands. As they become more educated, they may increasingly appreciate their region's special natural heritage, and there are already signs that people have found ways to economically exploit their rain forests without destroying them. For instance, medicinal plants dependent on the rain forest are a significant source of revenue, and as the warfare ends in the region, the forests have become sources of money from international tourism.

Through its Endangered Species Act and the USFWS, the United States has taken steps to eliminate the importation of two of the black-handed monkey's subspecies, greatly enhancing their chances for survival in the wild because Americans have been among the most voracious consumers of the monkeys as pets and for zoological display. However, seven of the subspecies remain unprotected in the United States, a bad situation for those native to Mexico, in particular. The *IUCN Red List of Threatened Animals* lists the entire black-handed spider monkey species as vulnerable.

Black-browed Spider Monkey

Ateles geoffroyi frontatus

Irwin Bernstein

Status	Endangered
Listed	June 2, 1970
Family	Cebidae (New World monkey)
Description	Dark brown, to golden brown, to reddish brown coat; the hands, feet, and forehead are black.
Habitat	Prefers the canopies of rain forests, but has shown some willingness to live in the canopies of secondary forests.
Food	Fruit, young leaves, seeds, buds, bark, and wood.
Reproduction	Gestation of 210 to 225 days, resulting in a single birth every 2 to 3 years.
Threats	Loss of habitat and hunting for food and capture.
Range	Costa Rica and Nicaragua.

Description

The black-browed spider monkey, *Ateles geoffroyi frontatus*, is a graceful, long-armed, and long-legged animal. Its tail is prehensile, with a bare patch for gripping tree branches and a bare, sensitive tip. Its dimensions are not well recorded, being taken from a small number of specimens. Males tend to be 15.25 to 19.75 inches in length, not counting their tails, with their tails adding another 24 to 32.5 inches; they weigh between 16.5 and 17.75 pounds. Females tend to be 13.5 to 20.75 inches in length, not counting their tails, with their tails adding another 28 to 33 inches; they weigh between 16.75 and 18.5 pounds. The black-browed spider monkey's coat tends to be dark brown, almost black, with pale highlights, but can be light brown or dark reddish brown. Its hair is of moderate length and smooth; a well-groomed the black-browed spider monkey's fur is sleek and glistening on its torso, but fluffy on its tail and head (some other subspecies of the black-handed spider monkey have coarse hair, so the monkey's sleek fur helps to distinguish it). Like the other subspecies of the black-handed spider monkey, *Ateles geoffroyi* (see separate entry), the black-browed spider monkey's hands are black; its feet are also black, and it gets its common name from its black face, which features white or pink skin under the eyes and on the eyelids.

Other common names include Geoffrey's spider monkey, and spider monkey.

Behavior

The black-browed spider monkey tends to travel upside down, walking along using its hands, feet, and tail while dangling with its back to the ground. Sometimes it swings by its arms or tail from branch to branch, and sometimes it leaps from one tree to another. A physical adaptation to its brachiation (meaning traveling by swinging by its arms from branches) is the reduction of the size of its thumb to a near stub; the small thumb does not get in the way of a swinging hand's grasp of a branch. The fingers curl into a curved shape that hooks onto branches. Although the black-browed spider monkey sometimes runs on its legs on the ground, it spends most of its life high in trees, staying above 40 feet.

It lives in loose troops of usually about 20 members, although much larger groups have been reported. Within the large troop are groups of 2 to 8 members that tend to travel and rest together. Sources disagree greatly about the composition of the small groups, saying that they have a single adult male who must fight off groups of young male rivals to saying that they have multiple adult males who have a peaceful shift in dominance as a dominant male ages.

Individual black-browed spider monkeys are loosely affiliated with their group and may travel alone, away from the group for several days. They seem to keep track of each other with calls that sound like whinnies. Groups may consist entirely of males or entirely of females; curiously, the female groups seem to be sometimes violent while the male groups are not. Females in an all-female group may be driven off by other females or by males and supplanted. In mixed gender groups, the adult males do the defending against threats. They bark (as will the females), shake branches, drop branches on the threat, and urinate and defecate near the threat. This behavior is dangerous to humans, who are recognized as threats, because the branches can weigh several pounds and when dropped from a great height, such as the forest canopy, can do considerable damage to a head. Unfortunately for the black-browed spider monkey, such behavior makes it an easy target for a human using a firearm.

Nearly all of the black-browed spider monkey's diet consists of fruit. Only about 17% of its diet is taken up by young leaves, buds, bark, and wood. Their tail is so sensitive that it can pick up even a small bit of food and transport it to its mouth, as if the tail were another hand. This feat seems to have surprised zoo keepers on occasion when the tail would reach out of a cage and grab something. They are daytime animals, feeding mostly in the morning, resting about half the day and during nighttime.

Little is known of the black-browed spider monkey's breeding behavior. It seems to be able to breed in all seasons, and births tend to be single, with mothers reproducing once every 2 to 3 years. At first a youngster is carried on its mother's tummy; as it grows, it will move to being carried on its mother's back. Youngsters play a great deal, by themselves and with others. Play sometimes involves sticks, perhaps as practice for group defense when as adults they may hurl branches at threats. Females reach sexual maturity at 4 years of age; males reach it at 5 years of age.

Habitat

The black-browed spider monkey lives high in rain forest canopies, but it does not require a large contiguous rain forest. It will live in patches or rain forest within a larger forest of mixed types. It may be willing to live among new trees.

Distribution

Not much is known about the past distribution of the black-browed spider monkey, but it is now found in the remnant rain forests of Costa Rica and Nicaragua.

Threats

The black-browed spider monkey is hunted for food and for capture and sale as pets. They are an important source of meat for local people, although not for much longer as their number continues to decline; they have been determinated in easily accessible areas.

Although the importation of the black-browed spider monkey subspecies to the United States is forbidden by American law, it is still threatened elsewhere by an illicit market for exotic animals. Even so, the greatest threat to the black-browed spider monkey is its loss of habitat. It needs a rain forest and an abundance of fruits throughout the year. It forests have been largely cut down by clear-cut logging and for agricultural development, leaving its population patchy, small, and decreasing. Although black-handed spider monkeys are often found in zoos, the black-browed subspecies is rare even there and has little chance of sustaining a viable breeding population in captivity.

Conservation and Recovery

Costa Rica is making efforts to preserve some of its once vast rain forest. Much of this is at high altitude, but the black-browed spider monkey seems to be a low altitude animal not found at elevations over 2,200 feet. Nicaragua was in turmoil for a long time, exploited by a greedy dictatorship, embroiled in a prolonged civil war, then exploited by another dictatorship, and only in recent years freed from warfare. Under Sandinista rule, a large amount of rain forest was cleared in order to drive out a Native American population that was not cooperating with the government. It is now taking the nation time to mobilize its resources toward conserving what has so far escaped destruction from loggers, agriculture, and war.

Red Spider Monkey

Ateles geoffroyi panamensis

Roy Fontaine

Status	Endangered
Listed	June 2, 1970
Family	Cebidae (New World monkey)
Description	The red spider monkey has a reddish brown, somewhat coarse coat of hair.
Habitat	Wide variety of forest types from rain forests to dry forests to mangrove swamps.
Food	Mostly fruit, but also young leaves, buds, seeds, bark, and wood.
Reproduction	Gestation lasts 210 to 225 days, resulting in a single birth. Infants weigh about 12 ounces.
Threats	Loss of habitat, hunting by humans for food, hunting for capture and sale.
Range	Costa Rica and Panama.

Description

The red spider monkey, *Ateles geoffroyi panamensis*, gets its name from the reddish color of its fur; in sunlight the red highlights of the fur seem to glisten. It is an agile tree traveler with slim, long arms and legs. Males weigh 16.5 to 17.75 pounds; females weigh 16.5 to 18.5 pounds. From the tip of the nose to the base of the tail, males are 15.25 to 19.75 inches in length, with tails 24 to 32.5 inches long; females are 13.5 to 20.75 inches in length, with tails 28 to 33 inches long. The red spider monkey's tail is prehensile and has a bare patch for gripping tree branches and a bare, sensitive tip. Various sources of information on the black-handed spider monkey (see separate entry), of which the red spider monkey is a subspecies, note that little has been recorded of the monkey's dimensions, this even though tens of thousands of black-handed spider monkeys have been taken for zoological study.

The red spider monkey's coat can vary in shades of brown, becoming very dark, but its coat is usually reddish brown. Its somewhat coarse coat is typical of most black-handed monkey subspecies, although a few have smooth coats. The hair on the red spider monkey's head and tail is fluffy. Its hands, feet, and face are black.

Behavior

The red spider monkey may have some significant behavioral differences between it and other black-handed monkeys, but this is unclear. For instance, the subspecies that occurs in Peru varies its group sizes and composition according to altitude, with larger groups at low altitudes, and smaller ones at high (about 2,200 feet) altitudes; the groups at low altitudes have more than one adult male, but the ones at high altitudes have only one adult male. In the case of the red spider monkey, groups tend to be large with multiple males; it is possible that it does not live at high altitudes, remaining primarily in lowlands unless driven out by humans.

At one time, troops of the red spider monkey could have as many as 80 members, although about 20 members was the most common size. With the red spider monkey's habitat greatly reduced and shrinking daily, it is unlikely that any troop has a range large enough to sustain much over 20 members. These big troops are fluid in their membership, with individual animals joining, lingering, and departing regularly. The troops are divided into smaller groups consisting of 2 to eight members. These small group affiliations seem to be long lasting, although the associations seem loose, with individual animals wandering off on their own, sometimes for days. The group members seem to keep in touch with each other with high-pitched, whinnying calls. Groups may consist of male and female members, exclusively female members, and exclusively male members. The all-male groups may behave similarly to all-male groups in other species of monkeys, ganging up on a dominant male in a mixed gender group, possibly killing the dominant male, then killing the deposed male's young

and supplanting him with a new male from the all-male group, but this seems unlikely, although one or two naturalists favor it. The groups are too loose to allow for much conflict between males, and mixed gender groups with more than one adult male have been observed, suggesting that male rivalries, if any, can accommodate multiple males in a group without violence.

Males are the protectors of their group, although females should not be taken for granted. Males will take the forefront against perceived threats, shaking branches and breaking them off to drop on dangerous animals and humans. Both females and males will cry out, give hard glares at the threat, and urinate and defecate on the threat. These have apparently been unpleasant surprises for naturalists attempting to study the animals. Although the red spider monkey often regards human beings as threats, it sometimes regards them with almost friendly bemusement, observing the humans even as the humans observe them. This suggests that hostility toward humans is a learned behavior as opposed to an instinctive one, although the evidence is not conclusive.

Breeding practices for the red spider monkey are now well recorded. It probably is able to breed year round like other subspecies of the black-handed monkey. Gestation lasts between 210 to 225 days, probably closer to 225. One infant is born at a time, with mothers able to breed once every 3 years. Infants are carried on their mother's belly, with their mothers holding them in place with one hand while using the other for feeding or traveling. The infants eventually move to being carried on their mothers' backs, perhaps because their grip has become strong enough that they no longer need their mothers to hold them. As they grow, they play a great deal by themselves and with other youngsters. Females reach sexual maturity at 4 years of age, while males reach sexual maturity at 5 years of age.

Like other black-handed spider monkeys, the red spider monkey travels back-to-ground while hanging from tree branches, using its hands, feet, and tail to grip branches. It also brachiates, meaning it swings from tree limb to tree limb while traveling. Its hands have adapted to this mode of travel by having small thumbs that do not get in the way as the hands reach for a branch; the fingers curl to hook onto branches. Its tail is sensitive and able to pick up even tiny morsels of food. Traveling is done during daylight and seems to be motivated by a search for food. The red spider monkey eats mostly fruits, nearly 90% of its diet, with young leaves, buds, seeds, bark, and even wood composing a small part of the animal's diet.

Habitat

The red spider monkey lives in rain forests with high canopies, and it spends the better part of its life in trees seldom descending below 40 feet.

Distribution

Hardly anything is known of the red spider monkey's distribution. It is certainly found in Costa Rica and probably in Panama. It is restricted to a few patchy areas of forest as yet undisturbed by humans.

Threats

Logging has stripped away most of the red spider monkey's natural habitat. It is also ardently hunted for food.

Conservation and Recovery

Costa Rica is trying to preserve some of its rain forest, which is home to many unique animal and plant species. To some extent, the local people are trying to earn livings from the forest by harvesting medicinal plants and cooperating in the running of parks, rather than fell the forest in logging or in agricultural development.

Woolly Spider Monkey

Brachyteles arachnoides

Luiz Claudio Marigo

Status	Endangered
Listed	June 2, 1970
Family	Cebidae (New World monkeys)
Description	Fur is dense and thick and is light gray to medium brown, with males sometimes having some yellow hairs.
Habitat	Rain forest.
Food	Fruits, berries, flowers, seeds, and leaves.
Reproduction	Single infant is born June to August after gestation of 210 to 255 days.
Threats	Loss of habitat and human predation.
Range	Brazil

Description

The woolly spider monkey, *Brachyteles arachnoides,* is the largest New World primate. It has thick, dense fur that is overall light gray to medium brown; males sometimes have some yellow hair. They have a bare patch of skin on their prehensile tail, and a protruding belly. Adult males measure 22.8 to 24.0 inches from the tip of the nose to the base of the tail, with the tail adding another 29.1 to 33.1 inches. Adult females measure 21.5 to 23.6 inches from the tip of the nose to the base of the tail, with the tail adding another 29.1 to 33.1 inches. Adult males weigh 26.7 pounds; adult females weigh about 20.8 pounds. These dimensions make the woolly spider monkey the largest of South American monkeys. The southern species has a black face, while the northern species' face is individually mottled.

The woolly spider monkey is also known as muriqui and mono.

Behavior

The woolly spider monkey is diurnal and arboreal. They are reported to be one of the most nonaggressive primate species. They participate in very little social grooming, but individuals embrace each other with a greeting hug when meeting a friend of the same gender. They will alarm-call at large feline predators. Because they are quite large, they do not react to aerial predators. They will associate with brown howlers, *Aloutta fusca.*

During mating season, males compete via sperm competition rather than overt aggression. Estrous females mate promiscuously with several males lining up to mate with her. The male's ejaculate hardens to form a vaginal plug, later removed by the female and dropped. Adults scent mark by depositing urine on their hands.

Their subgroups will range up to a half mile away from the main group, a day's traveling. These small groups are usually composed of one gender, although males will drift in and out of female-dominated groups. Upon reaching sexual maturity, females leave their birth groups to join another group.

Habitat

The woolly monkey may well have lived throughout the lowland forests of southeastern Brazil, but now they live in mountainous forests up to 5,000 feet high. These are rain forests with high canopies, although the woolly spider monkey tends to stay below the canopy in the middle levels of trees. They have shown willingness to move into young forests with middle-sized tropical trees.

Distribution

The woolly spider monkey once lived in a forest stretching along the Atlantic coast of southeastern Brazil. This forest is now nearly gone, and the woolly spider monkey lives in small, scattered patches of forest.

Threats

The range of woolly spider monkeys is in the center of Brazil's thoroughly developed region, where cities, industry, and agriculture have taken over almost all of the land. The process of human development has eliminated nearly all of the woolly spider monkey's original forest, leaving it patches in hard to access areas of mountain forest and a few patches on ranches that are protected by private citizens. This has scattered the small population of woolly monkeys, making it difficult for them to maintain a viable breeding population, as well as to find enough food for foraging. Their small remaining patches of forest are subject to poaching, illegal logging, and expansion of farms, and could easily disappear overnight. Loss of habitat may be the foremost threat to the woolly spider monkey's survival, but poaching is also an important threat. The woolly spider monkey's meat is eaten by local people.

Conservation and Recovery

The woolly spider monkey is in imminent danger of extinction and requires extensive human help if it is to survive. It has become a symbol of Brazil's efforts to protect its natural heritage, and it has become a point of national pride. It is found most abundantly on national wildlife reserves, and its largest population is in the Serra da Bocaina National Park, where it seems to be breeding well. Poaching is so extensive that the woolly spider monkey is threatened even in the national parks, which means that its future survival remains doubtful. A few state reserves, a ranch, and a coffee plantation harbor small numbers of these animals.

White Uakari

Cacajao calvus calvus

Noel Rowe

Status	Endangered
Listed	June 2, 1970
Family	Cebidae (New World monkey)
Description	Entirely white coat; pink face is bare except for a sparse beard, and its crown is sparsely haired.
Habitat	Forest swamps.
Food	Fruits and leaves.
Reproduction	Probably gives birth at night to a single infant.
Threats	Loss of habitat; human predation.
Range	Brazil and possibly Peru.

Description

Adult male white uakaris, *Cacajao calvus calvus*, are 18 to 21 inches in length, not counting the tail; adult females are 14 to 21 inches in length, not counting the tail. The tail of the adult male is 6 to 7.5 inches long; that of the adult female is 5.5 to 6.5 inches long. The adult male weighs about 9 pounds, whereas the adult female weighs about 7.66 pounds. The hair of the white uakari is long and shaggy except on its tail, where it is bushy. The hair is white, giving the "white uakari" its common name. Its face is pink and bare, except for a few hairs on its chin; its crown is very sparsely haired, also with pink skin. The pink may fade to white if the white uakari is kept out of sunlight.

Behavior

The white uakari is a mysterious animal, with little known about its behavior in the wild and little observed of its behavior in captivity. It lives primarily in groups of 5 to 30 multimale-multifemale members, although much larger groups may be possible. Each group may be said to have a dominant monogamous male-female pair, but competition for rank seems virtually nonexistent (a few naturalists say that there is indeed competition for rank, involving much noise but no violence). Each group seems to have at its core a family unit consisting of the dominant couple and their offspring of various ages. Grown males and females of other groups may join a group, apparently without much fuss.

Births take place at night and result in one newborn. The infant is at first carried on its mother's hip, then after a few months on her back or the backs of its father or other adult group members. Between 6 and 7 months of age the youngster shows increasing independence, moving about on its own and playing with other youngsters and adolescents, and even sometimes adults if it can persuade them to join in the fun. The youngster is fully weaned between 13 and 22 months of age.

Males seem to have the job of guarding the group and will put on a show of jumping, thrashing branches, and urinating on their abdomens when they perceive a threat to the group.

Habitat

The white uakari lives in swampy, forested areas where the floor is usually covered by water. It seems to associate itself with rivers that frequently inundate the land around them.

Distribution

The exact distribution historically or at present of the white uakari is not yet recorded and is the object of much disagreement among naturalists, making it one of the animal's many mysteries. As a generalization, it lives in northwestern Brazil, and its range probably stretches into the middle of northern Peru. There is general agreement that the range is very limited and shrinking.

Threats

The rare white uakari was little threatened by humans before the twentieth century, but logging, mining, and other enterprises have brought roads into the white uakari's habitat, and those roads have given hunters access to the once remote animal. It has been extensively hunted for food and possibly to provide bait for fishing, and it is sometimes captured and sold as a pet. The hunting alone has been extensive enough to drive the species to near extinction. The loss of its habitat to logging and industry has further jeopardized its survival.

Conservation and Recovery

The white uakari lives in a region that is of great concern to humanity in general, because its trees and other plant life contribute significantly to the world's oxygen supply. International conservation organizations such as the World Wildlife Fund have been trying for decades to get the region's wildlife protected from further economic exploitation, but so far this effort has been largely unsuccessful, with short-term profits taking precedence over long-term human survival. With the help of some international organizations, Brazil has been creating parks and reserves for its wildlife, but Brazil needs more financial assistance to enable it to protect its wildlife areas and both Brazil and its neighbors need more persuasion to protect the lands in which the white uakaris and numerous other species, probably some of which are still unknown to science, live. The white uakaris of Peru, if any still live in Peru (there is much disagreement about this), have the misfortune of living in areas where government agents of any kind are sometimes killed by drug gangs and revolutionary guerrillas simply because they are government agents. This makes establishing and protecting parklands very hazardous and very difficult. The sometimes hostage-taking of scientists doing research in the area discourages the field research needed to establish the range and habits of the white uakari.

Red Uakari

Cacajao calvus rubicundus

Roy Fontaine

Status	Endangered
Listed	June 2, 1970
Family	Cebidae (New World monkey)
Description	Covered in long, brown fur; crown may be yellow brown; face is bare and pink-to-scarlet.
Habitat	Forest swamps.
Food	Seeds, fruits, flowers, and small animals, such as insects, lizards and birds.
Reproduction	Usually has single births.
Threats	Loss of habitat and hunting by humans.
Range	Brazil

Description

The red uakari, *Cacajao calvus rubicundus*, gets its common name from the color of its face, which in the wild is pink to red to scarlet; when a red uakari is kept out of sunlight for a long period, its facial color fades to white. An adult male red uakari weighs about 9 pounds, is 18 to 21 inches long from the tip of it nose to the base of its tail, with a tail 6 to 7.5 inches in length. An adult red uakari female weighs about 7.75 pounds, is 15 to 21 inches long, with a tail of 5.5 to 6.5 inches. The red uakari is often described as one of the ugliest of the primates because of its short,

wrinkled, red face, and its very sparsely haired crown. The rest of the red uakari is covered in long, shaggy, brown fur. Most of the fur is a rich, medium to dark brown, but the fur inside the limbs may be yellow-brown to golden brown, and the hair on the crown may be yellow brown.

Behavior

Of the known variants of uakaris (please see separate entries on the black uakari, *Cacajao melanocephalus*, and the white uakari, *Cacajao calvus calvus*), the red uakari is the most studied, although nearly all observations have been of captive animals, with few observations from the wild. The red uakari is active primarily during the day. It has been reported to live in groups with as many as 100 members, but it usually lives in groups with between 5 and 30 members.

Its social life is by and large peaceful. Although a few naturalists have reported finding linear hierarchies in red uakari groups, with one hierarchy headed by a dominant male and another headed by a dominant female, most observers report little hierarchical behavior. Instead, the adult males treat one another like equals in most situations, including the sharing of food, and the adult females do likewise. Each group has at its core an adult male and an adult female who are paired for life. Much of the rest of their group consists of their progeny at various stages of growth, from infants to full adults. A group sometimes will include animals that have joined it from other groups, perhaps because they seek mates of their own. Red uakaris seem remarkably relaxed about all of this, with confrontation between group members rarely recorded. Further, this peaceable attitude seems to extend to group territories; each group seems to have a territory of 25 to 40 acres (this is not well recorded and may be at variance with true sizes of territories in the wild), but it seems to care little about other groups wandering through. Red uakaris associate with common squirrel monkeys, *saimiri sciureus*.

The details of mating are yet to be sorted out. It seems likely the female of the male and female pair of a group gives birth to the group's youngsters, with other females not becoming pregnant and having their own young. Whether the mother's relationship with her mate is monogamous is uncertain. Births tend to result in a single newborn and usually occur at night. Mothers seem to pay little attention to their young even though the infants will crawl on them and nurse at will. At first, a mother carries her infant on her hip, moving it to her back when it is 3 or 4 months of age. Other group members, including the father, will also carry the youngster. At 6 to 7 months of age, the youngster will wander freely through the group and play with other young red uakaris, and it will sometimes persuade an adult to join in.

The red uakari feeds on seeds, fruits, and flowers, and may eat small animals such as insects, lizards, and birds.

Habitat

The red uakari lives in black-water swamp forest where the floor is covered with water most of the time.

Distribution

The red uakari occurs in Brazil, although its range may extend a little into Peru and Colombia. The western extremity of its natural range is Rio Huallaga in Peru; its northern extremity is Rio Japurá in Brazil; its southern extremity is Rio Juruá in Brazil. The Rio Japurá curves south to join the Amazon near the town of Telé, and farther west the Rio Juruá curves north to join the Amazon near the town of Fonte Boa; where these rivers meet the Amazon marks the eastern extremity of the red uakari's range.

Threats

Humans have hunted red uakaris for a

long time, but in the last few decades the hunting has greatly reduced the numbers of the animal. At one time, humans hunted the red uakari with bows and blowguns, never taking enough to significantly affect the animal's numbers nor its breeding and social life. With the arrival of rifles, killing the red uakari became easy. The males in particular do not hide, but instead confront threats with open demonstrations that make them easy targets. As logging has intruded on the red uakari's territory, the killing has increased because the loggers use the animal as a source of meat. This killing has reduced the numbers of the red uakari to the point of near extinction. Complicating the animal's plight is a small market for red uakaris as pets; it is captured and sold, either at home or abroad as an exotic novelty.

Conservation and Recovery

The red uakari's range was once deep within the tropic jungles of the Amazon. The area was (and is) wet, swampy, and inhospitable to humans. Because of this, the red uakari still exists in enough numbers in the wild to be saved if action is soon taken to protect it and its range. The relentless destruction of the great forest by slash-and-burn agriculture, logging, and expanding human populations has shrunk the forest so greatly that the red uakari's range is now exposed and the inhospitality of the Amazon rain forest no longer protects it from humans. The trade in the red uakaris as pets needs to be halted altogether (the red uakaris are protected from importation as pets in the United States). These are social animals that require the company of others of their own kind, and their capture as pets not only decreases their chances for survival by eliminating potential mates but it harms the individual animal which needs its natural social life. The entire range of the red uakari is a treasure trove of animal and plant life, much of it unique; the trees alone are of immense value to humanity if left alone, supplying as they do a great deal of the oxygen we breathe. Ideally, the entire region would be made into a protected area, with further exploitation forbidden, but at the least, the red uakari needs a protected range such as a national park, where it may live in enough numbers to maintain a genetically diverse breeding population.

Both Brazil and Peru have taken steps to protect the red uakari, but enforcement is very difficult.

Black [=Black-headed] Uakari

Cacajao melanocephalus

Luiz Claudio Marigo

Status	Endangered
Listed	June 2, 1970
Family	Cebidae (New World monkey)
Description	Overall coloration is black, with chestnut-brown mixed in on the legs and tail; the tail also has yellow hairs mixed in; the face is black.
Habitat	Forest swamps, usually near rivers.
Food	Fruits and leaves.
Reproduction	Single births.
Threats	Loss of habitat.
Range	Brazil, Colombia, and Venezuela.

Description

The black uakari, *Cacajao melanocephalus*, is probably sexually dimorphic, with males being larger than females, but it has not been observed enough for naturalists to be sure. In general, an adult black uakari is 18 inches long, not counting the tail, which is short, about 6.75 inches, and bushy. Its hair is long, and its scalp is fully covered by hair. The hair is almost entirely black, with some chestnut-brown marking on the legs and tail, and with some yellow mixed into the hair on the tail. Sometimes, instead of black hair on it back, the black uakari may have brown hair. Its face

is bare and black.

Behavior

The black uakari is active primarily during daytime. Because its forest floor is usually flooded, the black uakari spends most of its life in trees. It is a quick and nimble climber but has not been observed to leap. It lives in groups with 15 to 25 members. The groups typically include more than one adult male. These social groups are apparently without competition over rank or for food, with members sharing what they have without rancor.

Births probably occur at night and probably result in one infant. Youngsters are carried on their mothers' hips and are allowed to crawl over her and to nurse at will. Between 3 and 4 months of age, a youngster begins riding on its mother's back; between 6 and 7 months of age it starts climbing on its father and starts playing with other youngsters and older juveniles in its group. Adult males will sometimes play with the youngster and even carry it. Youngsters start eating solid food at six months of age but are not fully weaned until they are about 22 months old; they remain close to their mothers even after she gives birth to a new infant and concentrates her care on the newborn. Youngsters spend much of their time playing with each other, and adults will occasionally play with them, too.

There seems to be little or no rivalry among adult black uakaris, with the adults apparently holding roughly equal rank in their groups. The black uakari has been very little observed, so there may be subtle gradations in rank that have not yet been noticed. Adult males seem to have the job of protecting the group. When threatened, they wag their tail 2 to 3 beats per second. They have a high-pitched alarm call that sounds similar to the call of an Amazon parrot.

Habitat

The black uakari lives in swampy forests that are frequently inundated by the overflow from rivers. It generally lives near rivers and lakes, although it has been found near the largest rivers in its range, apparently preferring the proximity of small and medium sized rivers. It tends to live at elevations of over 1,500 feet above sea level.

Distribution

The black uakari's range is in northwestern Brazil, southeastern Colombia, and southern Venezuela — eastward from the Rio Japurá to Rio Negro and Rio Branco, north of the Amazon.

Threats

The black uakari is threatened by the loss of its habitat and by persecution from humans. Logging is responsible for the destruction of much of the animal's forest, an area that was virtually untouched three decades ago. At first glance, the black uakari appears ugly to many people, and this has resulted in its being killed by humans. Hunting by humans is extensive and is significantly contributing to the animal's decline more so than habitat loss.

Conservation and Recovery

Little has been done to conserve the black uakari species. It needs to have some of its natural habitat preserved and protected — a difficult task given the swampiness of its terrain. On the other hand, the species has some hope for short term survival because it lives in a range that most humans would find inhospitable.

White Nosed Saki

Chiropotes albinasus

Luiz Claudio Marigo

Status	Endangered
Listed	June 2, 1970
Family	Cebidae (New World Monkey)
Description	Predominantly black monkey with a long, thick tail and short body hair; nose and upper lip are red and covered in thick white hair.
Habitat	Prefers tall, virgin forest but will tolerate different types of forest from swampy to higher elevations.
Food	Fresh fruit and occasional nuts, berries, flowers and leaves.
Reproduction	Birth peaks are February to March and August to September after gestation of 152-162 days.
Threats	Hunted for food and for use as bait for cat traps; hunted for its tail which is sold as dusters.
Range	Brazil

Description

The White-nosed saki, *Chiropotes albinasus*, is a medium sized New World monkey ranging in length from 17 to 19 inches. Adults weigh between 4.9 to 7.3 pounds. Females are slightly smaller than the males.

The white-nosed saki is predominantly black with a long (15 to 17.7 inches), thick tail and short body hair. The body is covered by an oily substance making it completely water-proof. The nose and upper lip are red in color and covered in thick white hair. Adults have two tufts of straight hairs on the sides of the head, and a thick, bristly beard. Both sexes have bright pink genitalia which are quite noticeable against the black fur. Males have an extraordinary, bulbous swelling on the top of their head. Forward projecting incisors are used to break open hard shells.

White-nosed sakis live in social groups of 2 to 26, consisting of several family units of mated pairs and offspring. They engage in frequent mutual grooming and communicate with long whistles. When threatened they raise themselves on hind legs, gnash their teeth, and shake their beards, while swiftly attacking their enemy. Social groups move in search of food about 2 miles per day. White-nosed sakis walk on all fours, rarely jump, and are extremely cautious and careful when moving. When moving they raise their tails into a vertical position. Home range usually consists of 0.8-1.2 square miles.

Albinasus means "white nose," although the nose is really red. The species was named by taxonomists in 1848 from a preserved specimen. When the tissues of the nose are preserved they lose their color and turn white. Another common name for the species, which better describes its appearance, is the red-nosed bearded saki.

Behavior

The white-nosed saki's diet consists mostly of fresh fruit and occasional nuts, berries, flowers and leaves. Their forward projecting incisors allow them to eat numerous types of unripe seeds that other monkeys would avoid. This saki is active during the daytime. They wag their tails to express excitement and perhaps as a silent warning to other troop members.

During mating season, the female presents to the male by lying down and lifting her tail to show her red estrous coloration. After gestation period of 152 to 162 days, young are born. Although births occur year-round, the peak seasons are February to March and August to September.

Habitat

The white-nosed saki is found in the southern regions of the Amazon basin, between the Rio Xingu and the Rio Madeira, and southward as far as the Rio Jiparana and the Rio Theodore Roosevelt, in the states of Mato Grosso and Rondonia. This species prefers tall, virgin forest but will tolerate different types of forest from swampy to higher elevations. The white-nosed saki spends most of its time in the upper part of the canopy.

Distribution

The white-nosed saki was found originally south of the Amazon and north of the Maderia River in Brazil. They are no longer found in parts of the lower Tapajois. Part of the sakis' range has been destroyed by the Trans-Amazonian highway.

Threats

The white-nosed saki is endangered due to hunting pressures and deforestation for cattle ranching. It was heavily hunted for food in the Rio Tapajo's area in the 1930s and has disappeared from part of the lower Tapajois.

Conservation and Recovery

Efforts to raise or breed the white-nosed saki captivity have had some success.

Southern Bearded Saki

Chiropotes satanas satanas

Chiropotes satanas   Noel Rowe

Status	Endangered
Listed	May 15, 1986
Family	Cebidae (New World monkey)
Description	Black base coat is dense and short with brown shoulders; beard and swollen temples give the face a puffy look.
Habitat	Highland forests.
Food	Seeds, fruits, flowers, and rarely leaves.
Reproduction	Pregnancy lasts roughly 5 months and results in a single birth.
Threats	Loss of habitat and predation by humans.
Range	Brazil

Description

The southern bearded saki, *Chiropotes satanas satanas,* is one of three subspecies of the bearded saki. Size measurements of southern bearded sakis are difficult to ascertain. Of the specimens measured, males were 16 to 19.5 inches in length, not counting the tail, and females were 15 to 18.5 inches. The tail of the male is 14.75 to 16.75 inches long, and that of females is 14 to 16 inches long. Males weigh 4.8 to 8 pounds, and females weigh 4.2 to 7.3 pounds. The fur of the southern bearded saki is dense and short, the non-prehensil tail is thick and bushy; the coloration is black overall, with brown on the shoulders. Males have long beards — often longer than their faces. The temples are swollen, giving the face a puffy aspect. The southern bearded saki's incisors point slightly forward and are adapted for eating seeds. The hind limbs are longer than the forelimbs.

Other common names are southern black saki, or southern black-bearded saki.

Behavior

Southern bearded sakis are diurnal and arboreal. They seem to prefer upper canopy levels for feeding and lower levels for traveling; they rarely come to the ground. Seeds seem to be the primary part of its diet, although it also eats fruits, flowers, and rarely leaves. It forms social groups with 8 to 18 members; these groups are a mixture of adult males, adults females, and youngsters. Observations of captive animals at the Cologne Zoo indicate that the bearded sakis need intimate social contact and long-term associations with other members of their species. They seem to derive a sense of security from seeing the same faces every day. Group territories are 500 to 625 acres in size. When they travel, southern bearded sakis nearly always run through their treetop habitat, seldom leaping or climbing. They carry their tails forward, over their backs, when moving. When sitting, they wag their tails below the branch.

Gestation lasts approximately 5 months, resulting in a single birth. Infants receive a great deal of attention from both their mothers and their fathers, with a great deal of touching. Infants seem to require this physical intimacy. The infant is carried on its mother's back for about 8 weeks, at which time it begins to venture away from its mother for short periods; these absences increase in length for several months until the youngster becomes fully independent. Youngsters make faint chirps when they want attention, and both the mother and the father will respond to the youngster. The father, as well as the mother, provides companionship, care, and guidance. Southern bearded sakis reach maturity at about 4 years of age.

Habitat

Bearded sakis prefer highland areas, but the southern bearded saki seems to live at the lowest elevations of any of the bearded saki's subspecies. It prefers mature forests undisturbed by humans, and although its range is primarily rain forests, it will inhabit gallery forests and savannah woodlands, as well. The southern bearded saki lives in the highest areas of the forest canopy, seldom venturing below.

Distribution

The southern bearded saki lives in Brazil, in the eastern region of the Amazon.

Threats

The southern bearded saki lives in a region that has seen an explosion in its human population and rapid expansion of urban areas and farmlands over the last forty years. This expansion of human habitations and agriculture has been matched by clear-cut logging, nearly wiping out the southern bearded saki's habitat. The tiny remaining patches of southern bearded saki forest habitat could be cut down in a day.

Humans have long preyed on the southern bearded saki. Its tail has been sold in Brazil as a duster; people also eat the animal; it has been a resource for medical experimentation.

Conservation and Recovery

Efforts to protect the southern bearded saki have thus far been unsuccessful because its range exists directly in the way of a massive expansion of human settlements, and there is little hope for its short term survival. Brazilian law apparently does not offer the animal much protection; hunting it needs to be outlawed and it needs a protected reserve in which it can live undisturbed.

Bearded sakis have been successfully kept in captivity at the Cologne Zoo, but apparently nowhere else — the southern bearded saki is very difficult to keep alive. At the Cologne Zoo one bearded saki lived for about 18 years; members of the different subspecies have bred with one another there. Given that the Cologne Zoo's experience is rare, perhaps unique, captive breeding offers no hope for the southern bearded saki's survival.

Yellow-tailed Woolly Monkey

Lagothrix flavicauda

Roy Fontaine

Status	Endangered
Listed	October 19, 1976
Family	Cebidae (New World monkey)
Description	Short, dense, mostly mahogany brown fur, with yellow underparts and yellow under the tail to its hairless tip; it has off-white fur on its nose and around its mouth.
Habitat	Wet montane forests between 5,300 and 8,600 feet in elevation.
Food	Fruits and flowers.
Reproduction	Pregnancy lasts 225 days and results in a single birth.
Threats	Loss of habitat and human predation.
Range	Peru

Description

Most of the short, dense fur of the yellow-tailed woolly monkey, *Lagothrix flavicauda*, is mahogany brown, with yellow on the tail's underside and a yellow scrotal tuft of hair. The tail is prehensile and its tip is without hair, probably so it can get a firm grip on tree branches. Its nose has gray-white fur, and its mouth is surrounded by gray-white fur. This animal is very rare and has only occasionally been studied. It was rediscovered in 1974 and was thought to be extinct. Details on its size come from only a few museum specimens and may vary from the average sizes of the animals in the wild. Adult males are 16 to 21 inches in length from the tip of the nose to the base of the tail, and their tails are 22.5 to 24 inches long. Adult females are about 21 inches in length, not counting the tail, which adds another 25 inches. Their average weight is 22 pounds.

Behavior

Very little is known of this animal's behavior. It was rediscovered by naturalists in 1974, but its remoteness and location in a violent region have severely limited efforts to study it. It is active by day, and it lives in groups of 4 to 35 members, with an average of 13 members, and with a mixture of adult males, adult females, and young. The adult males are the group members who respond to threats; they shake branches, urinate, defecate, wag their hips, and display their genitals in their efforts to repel danger. This sort of display makes them easy targets for hunters with firearms. Males will sometimes bark when excited; group members make loud calls, perhaps for locating one another in the forest. Mating may be seasonal, but this is not certain. After a gestation of 225 days, a single young is born. Yellow-tailed woolly monkeys reach sexual maturity between 4 and 5 years of age.

Habitat

The yellow-tailed woolly monkey lives in high wet primary forests with an abundance of trees and vines; it seems unable to adapt to secondary forests. It lives at elevations between 1,641 and 9,843 feet.

Distribution

The yellow-tailed woolly monkey lives in the high Peruvian Andes near the headwaters of the Amazon.

Threats

Logging, slash-and-burn agriculture, mining, road building, and other industries are rapidly reducing the forest habitat of the yellow-tailed woolly monkey. Although it has been observed since 1976, its numbers, apparently always small, have dwindled greatly. Human hunting is also a significant problem; local people have traditionally used it as a source of meat. A handsome creature, it is hunted for its skins and is also killed and then stuffed for sale as a trophy or decoration. New roads have made it much easier for hunters to penetrate into the yellow-tailed woolly monkey's range. These factors and the animal's limited range make the yellow-tailed woolly monkey's situation dire.

Conservation and Recovery

Peru has declared the yellow-tailed woolly monkey an endangered species and has undertaken an aggressive program of education for the people who live in the animal's range, teaching the people about the animal's rarity and value as a living creature. Naturalists have also undertaken to educate school children about the animal and why it should be preserved. The World Wildlife Fund has contributed funds to help with the educational process. A captive breeding project is underway at the zoo in Lima.

Red-backed Squirrel Monkey

Saimiri oerstedii

Sue Boinski

Status	Endangered
Listed	June 2, 1970
Family	Cebidae (New World monkey)
Description	Pale yellow underside; white on its ears, face, and throat; black on its crown, cheeks and muzzle; red or orange on its back.
Habitat	Broad range of forest habitats, including forests that have been disrupted by logging, roads, and agriculture.
Food	Fruit and insects.
Reproduction	Gestation of 152 to 168 days, resulting in a single birth.
Threats	Loss of habitat, capture for sale, insecticides, and raptors.
Range	Costa Rica and Panama

Description

Because it somewhat resembles the Bolivian subspecies of the common squirrel monkey (*Saimiri sciureus*), the red-backed squirrel monkey, *Saimiri oerstedii*, is sometimes treated as a subspecies of the common squirrel monkey, but nearly all authorities consider the red-backed squirrel monkey and the common squirrel monkey to be two separate species, distinguished from each other by native ranges (one in Central America, the other in the Amazon region), coloration, and behavior, especially group behavior.

Adult males are larger than adult females. Information on body weight is sparse for both genders, but adult males seem to weigh 1 to 2 pounds and females seem to weigh 0.5 to 1.25 pounds; this would make them lighter than common squirrel monkeys. They also tend to be significantly smaller than common squirrel monkeys: Adult males are 11.75 to 13.25 inches in length, not counting the tail (common squirrel monkeys: 10 to 15 inches); the tail is relatively long, measuring 15.5 to 17.5 inches in length (common squirrel monkeys: 14.5 to 18.5 inches). Adult females measure 11 to 12 inches in length, not counting the tail (common squirrel monkeys: 9 to 15 inches); the tail adds 15 to 16 inches (common squirrel monkey: 15 to 18 inches). Although many New World monkeys have prehensile tales, the red-backed squirrel monkey is not one of them; its long tail is used for balance during leaps. Its thigh is relatively short when compared to its lower leg to allow for more power and leverage in leaping. It has short, narrow teeth for eating insects. Males have larger canine teeth than females.

Although its size is less than imposing, the red-backed squirrel monkey can look spectacular when in sunlight. Its fur is short and dense. On its crown and cheeks is a hood of black that sets off the white throat, face, and ears. Its muzzle is black. The pale coloration of its chest and abdomen, often yellowish or pure white, sets off its brightly colored back, which varies from red to orange in different red-backed squirrel monkeys. Its tail tends to have the back's coloration from its base to midway along its length, where it turns to black for the rest of the distance to its tip.

Behavior

The red-backed squirrel monkey is not as well studied as its South American relative, the common squirrel monkey. There are important gaps in what naturalists know of its behavior, especially its reproductive habits. When a female is in estrus, it will mate with several different males. The males will compete with one another to mate with the receptive female and will often fight each other for the privilege of mating, frequently resulting in severe injury to the combatants. If it is like the common squirrel monkey, then the red-backed squirrel monkey has a gestation period of 152 to 168 days. Typically, only one infant is born to a pregnancy. The mother is weakened by the birth and is sometimes left prostrate, but a close female "friend" is usually with her and tends to the infant, which is usually strong and vigorous. The youngster spends most of its first six weeks of life riding on it mother's back, although other adult females in a group will baby-sit the youngster while its mothers goes off to forage for food. After six weeks of life, a youngster will begin to venture from its mother and to play with other juveniles. Much of a juvenile red-backed squirrel monkey's time is spent in solitary explorations of its environment and energetic play with other youngsters. Apparently, much of the red-backed squirrel monkey's behavior is not instinctive but is learned; the exploration of its environment teaches a youngster what is good to eat and what is not, where good feeding places are, and how to hunt. Juveniles often practice stalking other small animals. Play with other youngsters teaches a juvenile how to respond to danger, how to properly socialize, and how to fight other red-backed squirrel monkeys. Females oversee the activities of youngsters, but males do not take part in child care. Indeed, they are often chased away by groups of females if they venture close to youngsters.

Common squirrel monkeys can live in huge troops sometimes consisting of hundreds of members, but red-backed squirrel monkeys live in troops of 30 to 40 members. The troops have a mixture of adult females and males, as well as youngsters of varying ages. The adult females tolerate one another's company fairly well, but they chase away males who get close to them except when they are receptive to mating, forcing the males to live on the periphery of the troop. The members of troops sleep together at night and forage during the day. The troops are subdivided into groups of 1 to 20 members, the size varying according to the density of food resources; the greater the density, the larger the subgroup size. The core of these groups are the adult female members. Movement from place to place is governed primarily by these females. The groups usually have adult male members, who remain at the edge of the group's activities, and juveniles. The care for youngsters is shared among the adult females.

The groups move about according to the availability of fruit, and memorizing where the best, often isolated, fruit trees are seems to be an important part of the red-backed squirrel monkey's behavior. A group will remain in a particular fruit tree (or if they are lucky, among several fruit trees) until nearly all of the fruit is exhausted (common squirrel monkeys seem to leave more fruit); then they will move on to another place where fruit may be had. Although the availability of fruit governs group movements, insects probably form most of the red-backed squirrel monkey's diet; their teeth are adapted for crushing insects. They eat a wide variety of insects and are agile and clever hunters. Their reflexes are lightning quick, and they can snatch flying insects out of the air. Unappreciated by humans, this activity is beneficial to human beings; disease bearing insects fall prey to red-backed squirrel monkeys. In a region where antibiotic resistant strains of yellow fever are making a comeback, the red-backed squirrel monkey could be an important natural limitation on the disease-bearing mosquitos who spread yellow fever.

Troops of red-backed squirrel monkeys have territories in which they range, but beyond confining their movements to their territories they exhibit little territorial behavior. Territories often overlap, but the different troops occupying them do not seem to mind; there seem to be no territorial conflicts. In fact, different troops will even share the same fruit tree for feeding, apparently maintaining their separate troop identities while not minding the presence of animals from other troops.

Individual troops of red-backed squirrel monkeys will often associate themselves with groups of capuchin monkeys (the genus *cebus*), probably because the capuchin monkeys are better at finding food trees. Juvenile red-backed squirrel monkeys are relentlessly curious about everything in their environment and are constantly studying it; in adults, this curiosity translates into an acute sensitivity to movement within their locality. Although they prefer to live in the lower levels of tall, canopy-forming trees, often descending to the ground to feed, their principal predators are raptors, birds that also prey on capuchin monkeys. Red-backed squirrel monkeys are quick to spread the alarm when they see a predator, and it is possible that the capuchin monkeys benefit from the squirrel monkeys' sensitivity to danger.

Red-backed squirrel monkeys move about mostly by leaping. Their hind limbs are adapted for creating springlike motions that propel them through the air from branch to branch. Even when on the ground, they will leap away from threats. A group of red-backed squirrel monkeys will leap in several directions, crying out all the while, creating a confusing image of moving bodies that may well bewilder predators. Human beings are treated as objects of curiosity by red-backed squirrel monkeys in areas that are remote from human activities. The animals will stare at a human and even follow the human's movements. In areas of forest that have been disturbed by humans, red-backed squirrel monkeys treat humans as predators, fleeing from the presence of humans. Even so, the red-backed squirrel monkey has managed to adapt to disturbed forests, although tall trees must be present. In such areas, the red-backed squirrel monkey may subsist entirely on insects — its sources of fruit having been foraged by humans.

Habitat

The red-backed squirrel monkey prefers

to live in virgin tropical forest with high canopies, although it lives primarily in the lower levels of the trees. Fruit-bearing trees and other fruit-bearing plants are scattered throughout the forest, usually sparsely, yet the presence of fruit is decidedly preferred by the red-backed squirrel monkey. It has shown an ability to adapt to other forest types, including forests that have been extensively disturbed by humans; roads do not seem to be barriers to their movements, perhaps because they are willing to travel on the ground. On the other hand, farms and urban areas are barriers to their traveling. It is primarily a lowlands dwelling animal, but can be found at elevations as high as 3,300 feet above sea level.

Distribution

It is probable that the red-backed squirrel monkey ranged throughout the forests of mid-to-southern Central America until the extensive clear-cut logging of recent times eliminated most of the forestlands. It is now found in Costa Rica and Panama and is disappearing from all but the highlands of Costa Rica.

Threats

Loss of habitat is the most significant of the threats to the survival of the red-backed squirrel monkey. Most of its traditional range has been cleared by logging or for agriculture. Its lowland habitat in Costa Rica has been almost entirely converted to agriculture in the last three decades.

Another great threat is local and international trade in red-backed squirrel monkeys. They are beautiful animals and are captured for sale as pets. Although their importation is banned by treaty in most nations of the world,

they are smuggled into many countries where people keep them as pets. The red-backed squirrel monkey may also possibly find its way into medical services, not so much for experimentation as for becoming the "hands" for paraplegics. A very intelligent creature, it can learn to fetch food, turn television channels, and other small tasks.

An important threat is the use of insecticides in its range. It lives in a region where deadly insect-born diseases are common, and insecticides have long been used to eliminate the insects that carry diseases. Red-backed squirrel monkeys may eat insects that have consumed insecticides, and this can result in still births and a disruption of the monkeys' reproductive cycle.

Conservation and Recovery

Protection of the red-backed squirrel monkey is urgently needed. At present, it is on the very edge of extinction. Costa Rica has made strong efforts to protect wildlife in its highland regions (nearly all of its lowlands have given over to human occupation), and its Corcovado National Biological Reserve harbors some red-backed squirrel monkeys. Costa Rica's wildlife reserves have become internationally famous thanks to nature television programs and wildlife photographers, attracting tourists and their money, as well as financial aid from wildlife preservation organizations. The tourists do not seem to be causing much harm to the red-backed squirrel monkeys, and the money is helping Costa Rica create some fine wildlife refuges.

The common squirrel monkey seems to breed well in captivity, which suggests hope for being able similarly to breed the red-backed squirrel monkey. The United States government severely restricts the importation of the red-backed squirrel monkey, banning it in most cases, but smugglers seem able to get around America's laws by pretending that the red-backed squirrel monkey is a common squirrel monkey. The red-backed squirrel monkey is listed in CITES, Appendix I: Trade Prohibited as the "Central American squirrel monkey."

Marmosets and Tamarins
Family: Callitrichidae

Black-faced Lion Tamarin   Luiz Claudio Marigo

General Characteristics of the *Callitrichidae*

The earliest known primate in the New World was *Branisella*, from the early Oligocene epoch about 35 million years ago. *Branisella* shows some of the traits of modern New World monkeys, which suggest that the earliest ancestors of the family *Callitrichidae* were much older, still. By the late Oligocene epoch, marmosets had arisen in South America, making their line an ancient one among primate families. At present, the family *Callitrichidae* consists of the marmosets and tamarins, all of which live in the rain forests of Latin America. The evolution of marmosets and tamarins is mysterious and is open to much speculation. It is likely that they are descended from a much larger monkey, and that their present-day small size is the result of adapting to a diet depending on insects. Marmosets and tamarins have claws on their digits except for the big toe, which has the usual primate nail. The claws are not throwbacks to an earlier era, nor are they remnants of a preprimate ancestor; instead, they are modified nails that have adapted to a life of prying open bark, wood, and insect shells.

The members of the family *Callitrichidae* are among the most beautiful of primates. They feature colorful, fluffy coats of fur, handsome head crests, puffed-out beards and manes, and long tails with thick fur. This has made them attractive to humans and hundreds of thousands of them have been collected for display in zoos and to be kept as pets. This has led to the dramatic decrease in populations of some species. Further, many marmosets and tamarins are used in medical research, further threatening several species. Humans also hunt some species for food, and in areas with new human populations the numbers of marmosets and tamarins have decreased greatly — disappearing altogether in many areas. These primates are also threatened by the destruction of their habitats — a problem so great that some species are in imminent danger of extinction.

Callitrichidids live in social groups that usually have only one breeding female. A mature female can breed as often as every five months, and usually gives birth to twins. She receives much help in rearing her young from other members of her group, especially the father. Some authorities believe that group assisted raising of the young teaches young group members how to mate, give birth, and then raise their young, so that when they become mothers and fathers in their own right they will know what they need to do to propagate their species. In addition to raising young, groups establish and maintain territories. They mark their territories with scent glands or urine and tend to travel through about one third of their territory each day. They communicate with gestures and body postures and keep track of one another, including other groups, by making high-pitched cries.

The exact diet of marmosets and tamarins varies among their different species, but in general the diet emphasizes insects and fruits. Most also eat spiders, snails, frogs, lizards, fruits, flowers, and sap. Techniques for foraging for food vary among the species, with some depending on eyesight to locate food and others depending on a more physical approach by tearing open old logs or reaching into promising holes; most forage in groups but some forage alone or in pairs.

Goeldi's Marmoset

Callimico goeldii

Noel Rowe

Status	Endangered
Listed	June 2, 1970
Family	Callitrichidae (Marmosets and tamarins)
Description	Covered with black or brownish, fluffy fur; the face is flattish, with a perpetual frown.
Habitat	Mature forest with patchy high canopies that allow sunlight to reach the floor, stimulating grass and shrub growth.
Food	Mostly fruits, but probably insects, spiders, frogs, snakes, and lizards.
Reproduction	Gestation lasts 150 to 160 days, resulting in a single birth. Fe-males can have two births per year.
Threats	Loss of habitat and capture for sale as pets or to zoos.
Range	Bolivia, Brazil, Colombia, Peru.

Description

Goeldi's Marmoset, *Callimico goeldii*, is a long-limbed monkey covered with black fur; sometimes the fur is brown-black, especially on the back of the neck and in rings at the base of the tail. One naturalist reports seeing white spots on the heads and backs of some. The fur is long and fluffy. The face is flattish, resembling a pug-nosed dog, with eyes set squarely in the front of the head. The ears are set well back on the sides of the head and are nearly covered from sight by hair. The cheeks have long whiskers that hang to below the jaw.

The adult Goeldi's marmoset's length is 10 to 12.25 inches, not counting the tail, which adds 10 to 12.5 inches. The tail is thus about as long as the rest of the body, and it has fur that fluffs out on all sides. The adult Goeldi's marmoset weighs 14 to 24 ounces.

The Goeldi's marmoset has features that puzzle naturalists, primarily the skull and arrangement of teeth, which resemble members of the family *Cebidae* (capuchin and capuchin-like monkeys), and claws and behavior that resemble members of the family *Callitrichidae* (marmosets and tamarins). Some taxonomists believe that this combination of traits found in two distinct families of monkeys means that the Goeldi's monkey is an evolutionary link between the *Cebidae* and *Callitrichidae*; others argue that the Goeldi's overall anatomy and behavior place it among the *Callitrichidae*, and they solve the nettlesome problem of the capuchinlike traits by giving the Goeldi's marmoset its own separate genus within the family of marmosets and tamarins. Yet other naturalists say that the Goeldi's marmoset is neither a link between the *Cebidae* and the *Callitrichidae*, nor a marmoset or tamarin; they say that the Goeldi's marmoset has its own separate evolutionary heritage and should be given its own unique family, *Callimiconidae*, and that the animal is in no way a marmoset or tamarin and therefore should be called "Goeldi's monkey." We here follow the United States Fish and Wildlife Service's terminology, calling the animal a marmoset.

Behavior

The Goeldi's marmoset is a cryptic animal, meaning that it hides very well and is very hard to detect. Researchers report sometimes stumbling across them while unaware of their presence. Part of how the Goeldi's marmoset avoids detection is how it moves in trees: It tends to climb up and down trunks, disturbing branches very little. When moving from tree-to-tree, instead of moving along branches, it climbs down close to the ground, under the branches, and then leaps while remaining vertical through the air and clasps onto a tree's trunk; it then climbs up the new trunk. Leaps as far as 13 feet have been reported.

Another way the Goeldi's marmoset escapes attention is by associating with red-bellied tamarins (*Saguinus labiatus*) and saddle-back tamarins (*S. fuscicollis*). These other species tend to be noisy as they move through the trees, calling attention to themselves and away from the Goeldi's marmosets.

Primarily fruit eaters, the Goeldi's marmosets join other marmoset species in trees with ripe fruit. The different species eat together without any interaction and share a tree's fruit without conflict.

The Goeldi's marmosets live in family groups of two to ten members. Each group has as its focus a mature male and one or two breeding females with whom the male mates. The other members of the group are their progeny. Females can become pregnant and give birth twice a year. A few weeks after birth, the infants are left to their fathers or to one of the older nonmating group members. These groups live in widely separate patches of forest, far from one another (perhaps a mile apart). How they exchange members for mating, and thus keeping the genetic stock diverse, needs clarification, but it is possible that females leave their birth groups and find new groups in which they can pair with a male. It is also possible that as they move from one fruiting tree to another, groups occasionally meet and then exchange members.

Habitat

The Goeldi's marmoset prefers old, mature forests that have high but broken canopies. Broken canopies allow sunlight to reach the ground, enabling grass and shrubs to grow. The Goeldi's marmoset often moves on the forest floor, even though it prefers leaping from trunk to trunk when it can, and it uses the grass and shrubs as cover. It may also find food in the shrubs, such as fallen fruit, or small prey, such as insects and frogs.

Distribution

The Goeldi's marmoset lives in patches in the northern Andes. It has been studied mostly in Bolivia, but it also occurs in Brazil, Peru, and Colombia.

Threats

For a long time after its discovery in 1904, the Goeldi's marmoset continued to live undisturbed through much of its range. It is so good at hiding that even local peoples often did not know that it lived nearby. Then, probably starting in the 1970s, people began catching it for sale in Europe, lowering the animal's already sparse density and probably making the finding of mates outside of one's own family impossible in some regions. In addition to this trade, loss of habitat has been diminishing the numbers of the Goeldi's marmoset. Forest has been lost to logging, mining, and road building. These activities have not only reduced the food supply for the Goeldi's marmoset but have reduced the cover it needs to evade predators such as raptors. New roads have also given people easy access to previously remote areas where the Goeldi's marmoset had been safe; some people have taken the opportunity to trap the animal.

Conservation and Recovery

Some good steps have been taken to help preserve Goeldi's marmoset, the most important of which have been studies of its natural history. As the needs of the Goeldi's marmoset become better understood, the easier it becomes to plan how to preserve them. At present, their numbers seem reduced to near zero in most of their host nations, with only Bolivia retaining numbers large enough to form a good breeding population. A natural reserve needs to be set aside where the Goeldi's marmoset and other wild species, including other marmosets, may still live undisturbed. Such a reserve needs to have old-growth forest and heavy ground cover. The Goeldi's marmoset is listed in CITES, Appendix I: Trade Prohibited.

Buffy Tufted-ear Marmoset

Callithrix aurita

Luiz Claudio Marigo

Status	Endangered
Listed	May 16, 1986
Family	Callitricidae (Marmosets and tamarins)
Description	Overall coloration is dark brown to black, sometimes with paler stripes crosswise in the back; around the eyes is white or pale brown (buff) hair; ears have large tufts that are buff.
Habitat	Primary and secondary tropical forests.
Food	Fruits, flowers, nectar, insects, spiders, frogs, lizards, eggs, small mammals, and tree sap.
Reproduction	Gestation lasts 140 to 145 days, usually resulting in the birth of twins.
Threats	Loss of habitat, disease, and capture for sale.
Range	Brazil

Description

The taxonomy of the buffy tufted-eared marmoset, *Callithrix aurita,* has been disputed, and it was elevated from a subspecies of *C. jacchus* to a full species only in 1988. It is 8.75 to 10 inches in length, from its nose to the base of its tail; its tail is 12 to 14 inches in length. It weighs approximately 14.1 to 15.9 ounces. The buffy tufted-ear marmoset or white-eared marmoset gets its common names from the large white-to-buff tufts of hair that spray out in large fluffs from its ears. These tufts stand out against the black back-ground of the sides of the animal's head. The buffy tufted-ear marmoset's head also features a white-to-buff patch of hair between and above its eyes. Its back is black or dark brown, with yellow hairs scattered through it. Its underbody is dark, but sometimes paler than its back. The tail is black to dark brown, with thin, pale rings around it. The fur is dense and fluffy over nearly all of the buffy tufted-ear marmoset's body, but somewhat shorter on the animal's face.

This species is also known as the white-eared marmoset.

Behavior

Little is known about the buffy tufted-ear marmoset's behavior in the wild, and laboratory observations are of limited value because the creature becomes highly stressed in captivity and may not behave normally, particularly when it is the subject of medical experimentation. The buffy tufted-ear marmosets move about mostly during daylight. Typically, they live in family centered groups of 2 to 8 members. These groups are territorial, each occupying a territory of about 25 acres.

Tree sap is likely to be a major component of the buffy tufted-ear marmoset's diet because it is a major part of the diets of some of its closest relatives and because it has teeth adapted for gouging through bark, but its eating of tree sap has not been observed. Although most marmosets primarily eat fruits and sap, it is possible the buffy tufted-ear marmoset has a large territory because it primarily eats insects, like the tamarins, and needs the larger territory because edible insects are harder to find than sap or fruit.

A group seems to have a dominant male and a dominant female, and they serve as the focus of their group. The rest of the group consists of the dominant pair's young and subdominant females. Observations are not clear on this point, but it seems that buffy tufted-ear marmosets resist mating with immediate family members; this would mean that males and females from different groups would have to mix in order for mating to occur. Births usually result in twins, with single births occurring about half as often as double births. Triplets have been observed in the wild, and quadruplets may occur in captivity, although four infants are beyond the ability of their parents to care for all of them. The young stay with their mother at first,

carried on her back, but after about two weeks the father will carry them on his back, too. Eventually, other older group members will aid in the care of the youngsters by carrying and feeding them. The young are weaned at 2 months of age and will reach sexual maturity in 12 to 14 months.

Habitat

The buffy tufted-ear marmoset seems a little more adaptable than most other marmosets and may be found in secondary forests as well as primary forests at elevations from 1,312 to 1,641 feet. For its population to be fully healthy, it needs a large forested area of several hundred acres because its groups each need large territories, and there need to be many groups in order for them to avoid inbreeding.

Distribution

The buffy tufted-ear marmoset lives in small patches of forest in southeastern Brazil, in the states of Minas Gerais, Rio de Janeiro, and Sao Paulo.

Threats

The buffy tufted-ear marmoset is threatened by habitat loss, disease, and human exploitation. Its forest is nearly gone and could disappear altogether on any given day; the last forest patches are now primarily threatened by clearing for agriculture, although logging for timber has contributed greatly to their destruction. Although it has been able to adapt to secondary forests, the loss of forest altogether would probably be beyond the buffy tufted-ear marmoset's ability to adapt. Already greatly reduced in numbers by the loss of its ancient habitat, the buffy tufted-ear marmoset's population has been further reduced in recent years by epidemics of disease. The buffy tufted-ear marmoset may be particularly susceptible to contagious diseases because of inbreeding created by its greatly reduced numbers. The animal has long been used in medical experimentation, partly because it is easy to control and maintain, even though the animal reportedly displays bizarre behavior because of the stress created by captivity. Little information about the animal has come from the medical experimentation because the experimenters were not interested in studying the animal itself. The buffy-tufted ear marmoset is also sold as a pet.

Conservation and Recovery

The buffy-tufted ear marmoset is not well protected. Disease has eliminated it from most protected reserves, and its capture and sale are not inhibited by legal authorities. The tiny remnants of its native forest need to be protected from further cutting if the buffy tufted-ear marmoset is to have any chance for survival in the short term or long term, and it needs to be protected from further human exploitation.

Buffy-headed Marmoset

Callithrix flaviceps

Luiz Claudio Marigo

Status	Endangered
Listed	January 23, 1984
Family	Callitrichidae (Marmosets and tamarins)
Description	Light brown back with side-to-side stripes, a yellow-to-orange under-body; crown, cheeks, and ear-tufts are a creamy brown (buff) mixed with white and gray hair; forehead is white; tail is covered by fluffy dark gray hair with light gray rings.
Habitat	Highland evergreen and semide-ciduous forests.
Food	Fruit, insects, buds, nectar, frogs, small lizards, birds' eggs, and nestlings.
Reproduction	Gestation lasts 140 to 150 days, usually resulting in twins.
Threats	Loss of habitat and capture for commercial sale.
Range	Southeastern Brazil

Description

Adult male and female buffy-headed marmosets, *Callithrix flaviceps*, are close in size. The buffy-headed marmoset measures 8.75 inches to 10 inches from the tip of the nose to the base of the tail. The tail adds another 12 to 14 inches. An adult buffy-headed marmoset weighs 10.75 to 12.75 ounces. It is an attractive animal with dense soft fur that fluffs outward around its face. Its cuddly appearance may account for its popularity as a pet. Its coat is a complex mixture of colors,

with an overall impression of gray. The back is primarily brown to gray-brown, with side-to-side stripes of dark gray or gray-brown. The underside is yellow to orange, often with gray hairs mixed in. Its face has a mixture of fluffy brown, gray, and white hairs, with white predominating on the forehead over the nose and eyes. Creamy brown dominates the animal's crown, ears, and cheeks, hence the common name "buffy-headed marmoset." The ears have tufts that are also creamy brown. The tail has hair of uniform length from its base to its tip; it is dense and fluffs out. The tail is primarily dark gray, with narrow light gray rings along its length.

C. *flaviceps* was elevated from a subspecies of C. *jaccus* in 1988.

Behavior

The buffy-headed marmoset is active primarily during the day. It lives in groups of 5 to 15 members. Each group has territory of 2.5 to 100 acres, with the size depending on the density of available food. The group has a hierarchy of dominant males and females. Only the dominant female mates; laboratory observations of a related species, the white-fronted marmoset (*Callithrix geoffroyi*), have shown that subdominant adult females do not ovulate, only the dominant one does. Without the presence of the dominant female, the subdominant ones will ovulate normally. The mechanism involved in this arrangement has yet to be identified. Neither males nor females will mate with their parents, their own young, nor with their own siblings. This means that a healthy population must have several separate groups that will mix enough that buffy-headed marmosets may join new groups and mate with unrelated animals.

The dominant female of a group seems to have a regular cycle of ovulation making it able to mate several times a year. Its gestation period is 140 to 150 days. Birth results in twins most of the time, although a single birth is common. Triplets are rare. Not much is known for certain about parental care and how individual buffy-headed marmosets develop. If it is like the common marmoset (*Callithrix jaccus*), then the infant buffy-headed marmoset is weaned at about 6 months of age and reaches sexual maturity between 14 and 18 months of age. The mother carries the young on her back, as many as three at a time. The father becomes particularly involved in the care of the young when they are weaning. The father will premasticate solid food for them until they are fully weaned. He will then find solid food for them and offer it to them, even calling to them with a trill. Perhaps this behavior serves to teach the young which foods are good to eat.

Feeding involves a considerable amount of time devoted to hunting small game, usually insects. The buffy-headed marmosets are careful searchers, particularly among decaying vegetation that may attract insects. They primarily eat small, very sweet fruits, and possibly flowers and buds.

By the time naturalists tried to seriously study the buffy-headed marmoset, its range had been reduced to about 5% of its former size (it is even smaller now) and the animal was nearly extinct. This created large gaps in what could be learned; we may never know how buffy-headed marmoset groups interacted when undisturbed, nor how large a group could become in a large forest. Information from laboratory research is tainted because the animals are severely stressed in a captive environment and they behave abnormally.

Habitat

The buffy-headed marmoset prefers to live in "marginal forests," meaning that it likes to live in woodlands along river banks and beside roads. It prefers to remain high off the ground, ranging from 10 feet high to the top of the forest canopy, about 100 feet high. They prefer mountainous areas above 1,300 feet in elevation.

Distribution

The buffy-headed marmoset once ranged through the southeastern coastal forests of Brazil. It now has a range limited to a few small patches of forest, primarily in two protected wildlife areas.

Threats

The buffy-headed marmoset is entirely dependent on trees and cannot survive without them. Its range has been almost entirely cleared of trees by clear-cut logging and agriculture, as well as a burgeoning human population. The last patches of native forest are in imminent danger of being cleared, at which time the buffy-headed marmoset will be extinct.

The buffy-headed marmoset has been extensively hunted for sale as pets. Many thousands disappeared into the pet trade, and many thousands of others were sold to laboratories for medical research.

Conservation and Recovery

The best way to preserve the buffy-headed marmoset is to put an end to the destruction of the trees on which it depends. In addition, all hunting and capturing of the animal needs to be ended.

The Fazenda Montes Claros preserve and Nova Lombardia Biological Reserve have small populations of the buffy-headed marmoset, but their numbers are probably too small to form viable breeding populations.

Black-faced Lion Tamarin

Leontopithecus caissara

Luiz Claudio Marigo

Status	Endangered
Listed	June 2, 1970
Family	Callitrichidae (Tamarins and marmosets)
Description	Covered by long, bright golden hair, with its head framed in a puffy, black mane.
Habitat	Cool, dry, dense forest.
Food	Probably mostly fruit, supplemented by insects, and small vertebrates.
Reproduction	Gestation may last 125-132 days, usually resulting in twins, although single births are common.
Threats	Habitat loss and hunting for food.
Range	Brazil

Description

The black-faced lion tamarin, *Leontopithecus caissara*, has long, silky, golden hair over most of its body. Its face is dark gray to black, and its head is surrounded by a large mane of black hair. It is said to have a larger frame than any other lion tamarin, which would make it over 14 inches long in head and body length and over 25 ounces in weight. Its heavily furred tail appears to be about as long as its body.

Behavior

Little is as yet known about this animal's behavior, and little is ever likely to be known about its wild behavior because only about two dozen had survived by the time naturalists discovered their existence in 1990. If they are like other lion tamarins, then they probably breed in monogamous pairs and their primary social units would be family groups with one or two breeding males, breeding females, and their young.

One reason they went undiscovered by

science until 1990 and why they are hard to study is their shyness. They know to fear humans and they flee humans on sight. They move with great agility through the trees among which they live, providing observers with only brief glimpses. They are primarily arboreal, rarely coming to the ground.

Habitat

Another reason why discovery of the black-faced lion tamarin did not occur until 1990 is that it lives where it is not supposed to occur. Scientific doctrine held that the animal's forest was too cool for monkeys. The forest was once dense, drier than Brazil's northern tropical forests, and temperate in climate, which is moderated by the Atlantic Ocean. The black-faced lion tamarin lives in primary lowland coastal forest with many epiphytic bromeliads and palms.

Distribution

The black-faced lion tamarin's traditional range is unknown. By the time it was discovered, the ancient Atlantic coastal forest of Brazil was less than 5 percent of its size when Europeans first settled there; the rest has been logged and cleared for agriculture and urban areas. At present, the black-faced tamarin lives on the 35,000-acre island of Superagui, in a tiny patch of forest.

Threats

Habitat loss is an immediate and ever-present threat to the black-faced lion tamarin's survival. When it was discovered by two naturalists who were investigating a one-hundred-year-old account of a monkey on the island of Superagui, its little patch of remaining forest was scheduled to be replaced by a beach resort and condominiums. All around its last bit of habitat are human habitations and resort areas. Another, lesser threat is killing the animal for food and capturing it for sale. The killing of the monkeys by local people may have stopped by now, partly because the few animals that survive are very elusive and partly because of efforts by naturalists to educate the public about the monkey's rarity and need for conservation. Lion tamarins are still kept as pets by some Brazilians, and the black-faced lion tamarin may be subject to capture and sale as a pet.

Conservation and Recovery

The only known population of black-faced lion tamarins lives in the Superagui National Park, where they are well protected but there may be too few individuals to form a good breeding population. For the species to survive, the destruction of their habitat needs to be halted completely. The Rio de Janeiro Primate Center hopes to breed the animal in captivity, but its scientists still know too little about its natural history to be able to succeed. They have had success breeding the golden-lion tamarin, and given time, may well succeed with the black-faced lion tamarin.

Golden-headed Lion Tamarin
Leontopithecus chrysomelas

Noel Rowe

Status	Endangered
Listed	June 2, 1970
Family	Callitrichidae (Tamarins and marmosets)
Description	Covered by long, silky black fur, except for a bright golden mane.
Habitat	Lowland tropical jungle, with seasonal heavy rains.
Food	Mostly fruit, as well as insects, spiders, and small vertebrates.
Reproduction	Gestation lasts 125-132 days, usually resulting in twins, although single births are common.
Threats	Loss of habitat and human predation.
Range	Brazil

Description

The fur of the golden-headed lion tamarin, *Leontopithecus chrysomelas*, may be somewhat coarser than that of its close relatives, the golden-lion tamarin and golden-rumped tamarin (*Leontopithecus rosalia* and *Leontopithecus chrysopygus*; please see separate entries). Its fur is long, even wispy on the torso; its body is black; a mane of golden fur surrounds its black face; the feet and outside of the tail are also golden color. The face is flattish, with a flattened nose that flares some-what to each side above the mouth. Their faces, hands, and feet are dark gray to black. Adult males and females do not seem to vary from one another in size; adults are 8 to 12 inches in head-and-body length, with 12.5 to 15 inch tails, and they weigh 15 to 25 ounces.

Behavior

Only about 200 golden-headed lion tamarins survive, which means that discussions of their behavior in large groups, or even whether they ever formed large groups, are mostly speculative. Like the other *Leontopithecus* species, the central unit of golden-headed lion tamarin society is a bonded, monogamous parental pair. The pair are the core of a family unit that includes infants and progeny up to two years of age; such a family unit may have as many as eight members, but rarely has more than five. The parental pair share equal dominance within their family unit and each member of the pair is intolerant of same-sex adult outsiders, fighting and even killing such outsiders. In spite of this intolerance, different family groups usually peacefully coexist with each other. Group territories greatly overlap each other, and family groups do not seem to mind the presence of other groups with their territorial boundaries. It is likely that, as is the case with the golden-lion tamarins, family groups will sometimes mix, with dominant members avoiding meeting each other.

The golden-headed lion tamarins breed seasonally, with birth occurring during the wet period from September to March. Pregnancies usually result in twins, although single births are possible. The father shares in the care of the young with their mother. A youngster is weaned between 2 and 3 months of age and will reach sexual maturity in about 18 months.

Golden-headed lion tamarins spend most of their lives in trees, living among tangles of branches 10 to 35 feet above the ground. During the day families move as a group, searching for food. They keep track of each other and warn of danger with whistles and cries; their cries are occasionally in pitches beyond human hearing. They seem to be methodical eaters, seeking out fruits but also using their long fingers to test for the presence of insects and other small animals in holes and flowers. Nectar is an important part of their diet. They seem to be crafty hunters who use lightning quick movements of their hands to snatch up prey. At night, they sleep in tree holes found only in the primary forest in their range.

Habitat

The golden-headed lion tamarin may be a little more adaptable than its *Leontopithecus* relatives. It prefers lowland forest, swamp, semideciduous and tall evergreen forest from sea level to 367 feet, but it also inhabits cocoa plantations; the plantations preserve some tall trees because the cocoa requires shade, and the golden-headed lion tamarins, perhaps with nowhere else to go, have taken up residence among the shade trees.

Distribution

The golden-headed lion tamarin's traditional range may have been a small one, although this is not certain, near the coast in the south of the state of Bahia. In that region are still some healthy stands of primary tropical forest suitable to the needs of the golden-headed lion tamarin, but these stands are disappearing quickly. For a time, the golden-headed lion tamarin had a 20-square-mile reserve in southern Bahia, but squatters took it over, reportedly destroying all of it, a catastrophe for the species because its numbers in the wild were greatly reduced and because its best chance for survival was taken from it.

Threats

The last of the golden-headed lion tamarin's natural habitat is disappearing because of logging, both legal and illegal, clearing for agriculture and industry, and expanding human communities. Although international trade in the golden-headed lion tamarin has abated because of enforcement of the CITES treaty, which forbids international trade in the animal or its parts, it is still subject to capture for sale as a pet or a restaurant delicacy within Brazil — even though Brazilian law protects the animal.

Conservation and Recovery

Private foundations have undertaken the task of educating local people about the golden-headed lion tamarin and its value to Brazilian culture in the hope that people will be convinced to stop preying on the animal and to stop destroying its habitat. Efforts by government and private interests to protect reserves for the golden-headed lion tamarins and other local wildlife in Bahia have so far failed, but a reserve of old-growth forest needs to be established and properly protected if the golden-headed lion tamarin is to have any realistic chance for survival. The Rio de Janeiro Primate Center is trying to raise golden-headed lion tamarins in captivity, in hopes of some day being able to introduce captive-bred ones into the wild. Few other golden-headed lion tamarins exist in captivity — too few for the species' genetic diversity to be preserved.

Golden-rumped [=Black] Lion Tamarin

Leontopithecus chrysopygus

Noel Rowe

Status	Endangered
Listed	June 2, 1970
Family	Callitrichidae (Tamarins and marmosets)
Description	Covered almost entirely by long, silky black fur, but with a golden rump and golden thighs.
Habitat	Dense tropical jungle, probably no higher than 1,000 feet above sea level.
Food	Fruit, insects, and small vertebrates.
Reproduction	Gestation lasts 125-132 days, usually resulting in twins, although single births are common.
Threats	Loss of habitat and human predation.
Range	Brazil

Description

The golden-rumped lion tamarin, *Leontopithecus chrysopygus*, has richly black fur, interrupted on its rump and thighs by brilliantly golden fur. The fur is long and soft on most of the body, but heavy and shaggy on the tail. Its hands, feet, and face tend to be dark gray, even black. The hands are long-fingered and dexterous; the feet have long toes for gripping tree branches. It is not as well studied as its close relative, the golden-lion tamarin (*Leontopithecus rosalia*; see separate entry), and is primarily known from a small group of captives at the Rio de Janeiro Primate Center. An adult golden-rumped lion tamarin is about 10 inches in head-and-body length, with a long tail of about 14 inches in length. It weighs approximately 18 ounces.

Another common name is the black lion tamarin.

Behavior

By the time serious study of the golden-rumped lion tamarins began (in the 1980s), there were far too few left in the wild, or anywhere else, for their social behavior to be fully recorded. In terms of group size, mixing of disparate groups, and the finding of mates, the golden-rumped lion tamarins were probably like the golden-lion tamarins: family groups no larger than 10 members; occasional mixing of groups, creating gatherings of about 40 members, during which pair bonding may occur.

Golden-rumped lion tamarins mate for life, with the mating pair forming the core of a family group. Within the group, the dominant male and dominant female are equally dominant. Both seem to resent the presence of outside mature members of their genders and will confront them, either fighting them or chasing them away. When family groups sometimes mix, the dominant members avoid each other. The family group may consist of only the bonded pair or of the pair and two or three years of progeny, up to 8 members, altogether. Breeding is probably seasonal, with births coinciding with the warm seasons in September through March. Typically, twins are born, although single births are common. The mother at first carries her young, but after 3 to 7 weeks, the father also carries them, and both parents care for their needs. Nearly mature siblings may also help care for infants. The young are weaned between 2 and 3 months of age; they will reach sexual maturity between 15 and 20 months of age, at which time they probably leave the family group, although it is possible that they may remain in the family group as subordinant adults.

The golden-rumped lion tamarins are arboreal, rarely coming to the ground, and they prefer to live between 10 and 40 feet above the ground in the dense branches of their habitat. They are active primarily during the day, sleeping in holes in tree trunks. Their diet is a mixture of fruits and small animals, especially insects, but including small vertebrates such as lizards and birds.

Habitat

The golden-rumped lion tamarin prefers lowland, semideciduous riparian forest from sea level to 328 feet. This inland habitat has a distinct dry season from April to September and is ecologically different from the habitat of other species of lion tamarins, which are found near the coast.

Distribution

The golden-rumped lion tamarin lived in what was once a vast forest in the central and western areas of the state of Sao Paulo. They now live only in the 145-square-mile Morro do Diabo State Forest Reserve in southwestern Sao Paulo and the 9-square-mile Caitetus Reserve in central Sao Paulo.

Threats

Nearly all of the golden-rumped lion tamarin's forest habitat was wiped out by the end of the nineteenth century, and its numbers became so few and they lived in areas so remote that they were not seen for decades at a time, and they have long been in peril of extinction. In the 1960s and 1970s, they were captured for sale as pets abroad; this trade was greatly curtailed by enforcement of the golden-rumped lion tamarin's listing in CITES, Appendix I: Trade Prohibited, which forbids nearly all international trade in the species. Even so, this animal numbered fewer than a hundred altogether by the 1980s. It has long been expected to become extinct at any time, and only strenuous efforts by naturalists have saved it from being exterminated in the Morro do Diabo State Forest Reserve; private interests have preserved it in the Caitetus Reserve. At present, it is still subjected to capture for sale as a pet within Brazil.

Conservation and Recovery

Protection of the golden-rumped lion tamarin's remaining habitat from the same forces that have erased nearly all of the animal's once vast forest is essential for the animal's long-term survival. The Morro do Diabo State Forest Reserve is reputed to be poorly protected from poachers; it is threatened by logging and clearing for agriculture. Only a few live in the Caitetus Reserve, which could be destroyed by new private ownership. The Rio de Janeiro Primate Center has the largest population of golden-rumped lion tamarins in captivity, and has had success in introducing captive-bred golden-lion tamarins into the wild.

Golden Lion Tamarin

Leontopithecus rosalia

Noel Rowe

Status	Endangered
Listed	June 2, 1970
Family	Callitrichidae (Tamarins and marmosets)
Description	Covered by long, bright, golden hair with red streaks on its cheeks and lower abdomen; its face is gray—dark on the nose, forehead, and brow, and light elsewhere.
Habitat	Lowland, dense tropical jungle.
Food	Mostly fruit, insects and spiders.
Reproduction	Gestation lasts 125-132 days, often resulting in twins,
Threats	Loss of habitat; captured for sale as a pet; hunted for food.
Range	Brazil

Description

The golden lion tamarin, *Leontopithecus rosalia*, is among the largest members of the family *Callitrichidae*. It weighs 13 to 25 ounces and has a head-and-body length of 8 to 13.5 inches, with its shaggy tail adding another 12.5 to 16 inches. It is easily distinguished from the other three lion tamarins (the golden-rumped lion tamarin, the black-faced lion tamarin, and the golden-headed lion tamarin; see separate entries) because its entire body is covered by a golden coat,

whereas the others have significant markings in other colors. Its body — save for face, hands, and feet — is covered by long, silky golden hair, with complementary streaks of red on its cheeks and lower abdomen. The sides of the face and under the chin are framed by a narrow white outline. The face is gray — dark along its nose, in the middle of the forehead, and along the brow, and lighter elsewhere, including under the chin. The nose is flat, blunt, and wide at the bottom, where the nostrils flare outward. Its hands are light to dark gray, with long, narrow fingers that it uses to probe into plants for insects. Its feet are also light or dark gray, sometimes with brushes of golden hair. When crouched on a branch, with its tail dangling and its puffed out hair around its face like a lion's mane, the golden lion tamarins look catlike, accounting both for its common name and the why early European explorers mistook it for a feline.

Behavior

Golden lion tamarins breed in monogamous pairs, and they live in family units of parents, infants, and still maturing young from previous years. These family units usually have 3 to 5 members, but may have as many as ten. Occasionally, these family units will mix with other such groups, forming bands of as many as 40 members. When this happens, the dominant males and females avoid meeting each other; if dominant golden lion tamarins of the same gender were to meet under other circumstances, they would almost certainly try to kill one another. This mixing of family groups probably facilitates the creation of new mating pairs. Although the family groups have territories to which they restrict themselves, the different territories overlap each other greatly, and the residents of a particular territory do not seem to care that other groups are in it.

Within their family unit, the parents are codominant, of equal rank. Mating in the wild is seasonal, with births timed for the warmest and wettest period of the year, from September to March. In captivity in the Northern Hemisphere the season for mating changes so that births occur from January to June. About 25% of pregnancies result in single births, with nearly all the rest resulting in twins; triplets do occur, but are rare. For the first few weeks, the mother carries the infants; after that, the father shares in caring for the young, and eventually older siblings in the family group may also help carry and feed the infants. Youngsters are weaned before 3 months of age, and they will reach sexual maturity before 20 months of age.

Golden lion tamarins are diurnal and live nearly all of their lives in trees. They move in a region of densely distributed branches, between 10 and 35 feet off the ground. The dense branches help them to hide when they want to, and they provide numerous places for sleeping: Golden lion tamarins prefer to sleep in holes in trunks or branches or among vines. When feeding, they manipulate food with their hands, holding onto it while they bite. The preferred foods are fruits of trees, but they have a varied diet that includes insects, spiders, and many small vertebrates. They are quick hunters with strong hands that can grip small prey firmly; they kill the prey by biting its head. They use their long fingers to probe flowers and other parts of plants for insects. As they move about they communicate with whistles and cries.

Habitat

Golden lion tamarins require primary or secondary lowland tropical forests with densely packed trees and high canopies. They occur from sea level to 984 feet in elevation.

Distribution

At one time the golden lion tamarin lived in the lowlands of southeastern Brazil. Although they now live only in the state of Sao Paulo, they once lived in the states of Bahia,

Espiritu Santo, Guanabera, and Rio de Janeiro. This region is the most urbanized and
industrialized of Brazil.

Threats

Nearly all of the golden lion tamarin's
habitat is gone, lost to agriculture, expanding
urban areas, industry, logging, and squatters.
The loss of suitable habitat could spell the
species' doom; it all could be logged in a few
days. During the 1960s and 1970s, the golden
lion tamarin was captured and shipped
abroad for zoos, pet owners, and scientific
laboratories. It is listed in CITES, Appendix I:
Trade Prohibited. Enforcement of the CITES
provisions has been by and large successful,
with export of the animal from Brazil having
been nearly halted. On the other hand, the
golden lion tamarins continue to be taken
captive for sale as pets within Brazil, and it is
still served in some urban restaurants — both
flagrant violations of Brazil's own laws.

Conservation and Recovery

Of the four lion tamarin species, the
golden lion tamarin has the best chance for
survival. Down to less than 100 in number in
the 1980s, it was rescued from almost certain
extinction by a cooperative effort of the Rio de
Janeiro Primate Center, the World Wildlife
Fund, and the Brazilian Forestry Development Institute, as well as captive breeding
efforts conducted by zoos. In 1974, the Brazilian government set aside 19 square miles of
land especially for the preservation of the
golden lion tamarin; called the Poço d'Anta
Biological Reserve, it is near the mouth of the
Rio Sao Joao and is administered by the

Brazilian Forestry Institute. Poaching threatened to exterminate the golden lion tamarins
during the 1980s, but with World Wildlife
Fund financial support and lobbying of the
Brazilian government for help protecting the
reserve, the poaching was curtailed enough to
delay what still may be the animal's extinction
in the wild. Satellite imaging was used to
locate pockets of forest where golden lion
tamarins might be found, and some were;
they were transplanted successfully to the
reserve. Even more heartening have been the
results of the captive breeding programs. The
National Zoo of Washington, D.C., compiled
a stud book and directed the transfer and
breeding of captive golden lion tamarins in
zoos, in an effort to maintain the animal's
genetic diversity. The result has been a steady
growth of the species' captive population.
(Captive breeding of the other lion tamarin
species has not met with the same success.)
During the 1990s, captive-bred golden lion
tamarins have been reintroduced to the wild
and have adapted to the wild environment
successfully; these golden lion tamarins have
begun breeding within a year of their introduction to their wild environment.

The golden lion tamarin's hold on existence is still very fragile; poachers or disease
could wipe them out in a month in the wild,
and zoo holdings may not form a viable
population for long-term breeding. The
poaching of the golden lion tamarin needs to
be altogether halted, and what little suitable
forest that remains for it needs to be protected
from further destruction. There are now
about 350 golden lion tamarins in existence.

Bare-faced [=Pied] Tamarin

Saguinus bicolor

Saguinus bicolor martinsi

Noel Rowe

Status	Threatened
Listed	October 19, 1976
Family	Callitrichidae (marmosets and tamarins)
Description	Overall coat is brown; tail is reddish on its underside and blackish on its upperside. The head is black and bare from crown to throat.
Habitat	Tropical and subtropical forests.
Food	Tree sap, insects, and fruit make up most of the pied tamarin's diet. It also eats flowers, nectar, frogs, lizards, birds' eggs, and nestlings.
Reproduction	Gestation lasts 140 to 145 days and usually results in twins, although single births are common.
Threats	Loss of habitat.
Range	Brazil

Description

An adult bare-faced tamarin, *Saguinus bicolor*, weighs 12.5 to 15.2 ounces. It is 8.2 to 11.1 inches long, not counting the tail, with the tail adding another 13.2 to 16.5 inches. The overall coat is brown. Its tail is reddish on its underside and blackish on its upperside, with white between the shoulders. The head is black and bare on the front, including the ears. There are 3 subspecies: *Saguinus bicolor bicolor* has a blackened tail; *S. b. martinsi* has a pale underbody and a dark brown back; and

S. b. ochraceous is a uniform light brown. The bare-faced tamarin has a pug face and large ears.

Behavior

Little has been recorded of the bare-faced tamarin's behavior. It is a case of naturalists studying the animal after it has become almost extinct, leaving too small a population for easy study. In addition, the bare-faced tamarin's range is a dangerous one for naturalists; local environmentalists reportedly have been assassinated by those making profits from the destruction of the forest.

Like most of its marmoset and tamarin relatives, the bare-faced tamarin is active by day, apparently resting by night. Groups consist of 2 to 8 members, dominated by a monogamous male and female pair. The monogamy seems to be rigidly adhered to. The groups have territories of 20 to 80 acres, with the size probably depending on the density of available food.

The father and mother of young share in child-care duties; it is likely that the group as a whole participates in the rearing of the young.

The bare-faced tamarins eat tree sap by clinging to a tree trunk and gouging out a chunk of bark with large teeth adapted for the purpose; the tamarins then drink the sap that runs out. They also are gatherers of food such as fruit, and they are stealthy hunters of small game.

Habitat

The bare-faced tamarin prefers primary tropical forest, but it can be found in secondary forests. It seems to be trying to adapt to whatever environment human beings create in its range, but it is unlikely the arboreal tamarin can long survive without trees.

Distribution

The bare-faced tamarin lives between the Rio Parú do Oeste and the Rio Negro in northern Brazil.

Threats

In ancient times, the bare-faced tamarin lived in a forest far from civilization, with a sparse human population. It now has the misfortune of living in an urbanized region with growing cities. Manaus in particular is expanding rapidly and urbanizing the bare-faced tamarin's natural habitat. Agriculture, too, is taking its toll as the area is cleared for ranching.

Conservation and Recovery

The best hope for the bare-faced tamarin is that its remaining range be preserved from further destruction. This probably would require a national park and the creation and enforcement of Brazilian laws protecting the animal. The bare-faced tamarin has been bred in small numbers in captivity.

Silvery-brown Bare-faced [=White-footed] Tamarin

Saguinus leucopus

Noel Rowe

Status	Threatened
Listed	October 19, 1976
Family	Callitrichidae (marmosets and tamarins)
Description	Face is bare and the head, except for the cheeks, is covered with short silvery hair; shoulders and thighs are white; back is dark brown.
Habitat	Primary and secondary tropical forest, usually on the forest's fringes.
Food	Tree sap, insects, and fruit, supplemented by nectar, flowers, frogs, lizards, and birds' eggs.
Reproduction	Gestation lasts 140 to 145 days, usually resulting in twins.
Threats	Loss of habitat.
Range	Colombia

Description

The adult silvery-brown bare-faced tamarin, *Saguinus leucopus*, measures 8.75 to 10.5 inches from head to the base of the tail, with the tail adding another 14 to 17 inches. It weighs 12 to 16 ounces. It is a colorful animal: Its legs are white, with the inner sides of the legs being red to brown. Its back is a caramel brown. The head features a dark, bare, flattish face, with the crown and neck covered by short, silvery hair. Its cheeks feature great tufts of white hair that soar upwards, forming a crest. The tail is dark brown to black.

Behavior

Some naturalists have already given up hope of ever learning much about the habits of the silvery-brown bare-faced tamarin. Its natural range has been destroyed, leaving it living in small, patchy populations in hard to access areas, and the naturalists deem the surviving population to be too small to show how the animal would behave in its natural environment, and they expect the animal to become extinct before anyone manages to study it in detail.

That said, there are some details of the silvery-brown bare-faced tamarin's life that are known. It is active during daylight. It lives in groups of 2 to 15 members, with groups having 20 acre territories (perhaps up to 80 acres where there is enough forest to allow a large size). Each group is dominated by a male and female pair that probably remain paired for life, although the female may mate with other males in her group (this is not certain but is inferred from the behavior of species closely related to the silvery-brown bare-faced tamarin). The dominant male participates in the care of the young; he will carry them and once they can eat solid food, he will help feed them. The young are weaned at 2 to 3 months of age, and they become sexually mature at 16 to 20 months of age. The diet of the silvery-brown bare-faced tamarin consists primarily of fruit.

These tamarins are extremely agile and active, and will come to the aid of wounded members of their troop.

Habitat

The silvery-brown bare-faced tamarin tends to live in lowland tropical forests. It prefers to live on the fringes of a primary forest, but it has shown some willingness to adapt to secondary forests, and it seems to prefer to be near streams.

Distribution

The silvery-brown bare-faced tamarin lives between Rio Cauca and Rio Magdalena in northern Colombia. It survives in patches of forest in areas that are hard for loggers and farmers to reach.

Threats

Although the native forest of the silvery-brown bare-faced tamarin has been slowly cleared off and on for decades, it was mostly cleared all of a sudden, with about one third of it being cleared in only six weeks; the animal went from having a small but secure range to having almost no range at all within several months. It has been hanging on in little, out-of-the-way patches of forest since the mid-1970s, and it has tried to repopulate secondary forests where its ancient primary forest once stood. Even so, its tiny remaining patches of forest are endangered, with people wanting to clear even the least accessible trees for timber or to make way for agriculture.

Conservation and Recovery

The silvery-brown bare-faced tamarin desperately needs protection from the Colombian government, probably the only entity that has any hope of saving the animal. The silvery-brown bare-faced tamarin's best remaining patches of forest need to be identified and then protected, perhaps as part of a national forest.

The animal is listed in CITES, Appendix I: Trade Prohibited.

Cotton-top Tamarin

Saguinus oedipus

Noel Rowe

Status	Endangered
Listed	October 19, 1976
Family	Callitrichidae (Marmosets and tamarins).
Description	Brown back, with a white-to-yellow underbody, arms and legs; tail is black with red and orange; head is black or dark gray, with long white hair sprouts.
Habitat	Margins of forests.
Food	Insects, spiders, fruits, and tree sap; also flowers, nectar, young leaves, frogs, lizards, birds' eggs.
Reproduction	Gestation lasts 140 to 145 days, usually resulting in twins.
Threats	Loss of habitat and capture for sale.
Range	Colombia and Panama.

Description

Adult cotton-top tamarins, *Saguinus oedipus*, weigh 14.5 to 15.2 ounces. They are 8.1 to 9.6 inches long, not counting the tail, with the tail adding another 13 to 15.8 inches. They get their common name "cotton-top" from a spectacular long mane of white hair that sprouts above the forehead, fluffs out in a great ball around the head, and extends down to the shoulders. Its underbody is usually white, but can be yellowish, and its back is dark brown. Its tail is dark red to black at its base, with the tail becoming all black to its tip beginning about halfway along its length.

The taxonomy is disputed. It formerly included the red-crested tamarin, *S. geoffroyi*, as a subspecies; in 1988 *S. geoffroyi* was elevated to a full species.

Behavior

The cotton-top tamarin is active primarily during the day. Its lives in groups of 3 to 13 members, with group territories of about 25 acres. The groups are not particularly picky about maintaining the integrity of their territorial borders and often cross into one another's territories, often even eating together, although the dominant members of each group take care to avoid each other. It is different when the cotton-top tamarins are in captivity. Then, they are intolerant of members of other groups.

Each group has at its center a male and female pair, and each gender has a hierarchy of dominance involving primarily the dominant pair's young. The dominant male tends to remain aloof from dominance rituals and is seldom (perhaps never) challenged. His sons work out among themselves who ranks where and even which males must leave the group to form or join another. In contrast to the dominant male, the dominant female participates in dominance rituals, as do the other females in the group. The ritual for determining relative rank is almost entirely vocal and rarely becomes physically violent. Rivals fluff out their fur and stare hard at each other while trilling long melodies. They slowly approach each other until they touch or nearly touch and then form round openings with their mouths, and each touch its mouth on the other, continuing to trill. Eventually, one yields to the other by dashing away. Very rarely, neither rival is willing to give way to the other and they will grapple with one another with enough force that one or both will be seriously injured, with one sometimes being killed.

In general, regardless of rank, all adult members of a group are important to rearing young and acquiring food. Typically, the dominant female breeds to the exclusion of the other females. Although she and the dominant male seem to be paired for life, she may mate with other unrelated males as well as her group's dominant one. This behavior may help to ensure genetic diversity within the species. Gestation lasts 140 to 145 days and usually results in twins, although single births are common; triplets rarely occur. Every older member of the group helps to carry the young and to find food for the young, sometimes bringing the food to the young, sometimes calling the young to come get the food. The young are taught how to move through the tree branches at about 3 weeks of age, with all group members keeping an eye on them as they learn. The young will be carried about for 70 to 80 days — a long time for tamarins; when the young are able to move through tree branches on their own, group members begin to refuse to carry them until none will carry them and the youngsters must move about on their own. Caring for the young can be very burdensome for a single mother, so the group helps to ensure both the young's and their mother's survival by participating in the basic chores of rearing youngsters.

The cotton-top tamarins eat primarily insects, spiders, fruits, and tree sap; they have dental adaptations for gouging through bark. They also eat flowers, nectar, young leaves, frogs, lizards, birds' eggs, and nestlings. The cotton-top tamarins are apparently good hunters, with sharp hearing that detects prey, and quick hands for snatching and sharp teeth for killing prey with a bite on the head.

Habitat

The cotton-top tamarins prefer marginal forests, along rivers and streams or along roads, although they have been sighted deeper in forests. Their forests vary from tropical to temperate. The cotton-top tamarin's principal requirements for a forest are an abundance of food and trees growing thickly enough together that their branches interlace; the cotton-top tamarin is arboreal and lives nearly all of its life in trees, which means it needs a densely branched forest in which to move around.

Distribution

Once reported to live from Costa Rica to Colombia, the cotton-top tamarin is now found in northwestern Colombia and possibly southern Panama.

Threats

Slash-and-burn agriculture and clear-cut logging have eliminated nearly all of the cotton-top tamarin's habitat.

For decades, the cotton-top tamarin has been sold as an exotic, expensive pet throughout the world, with the United States alone importing one to two thousand a year, and total exports probably reaching several thousand a year at one time. There are now few cotton-top tamarins left in the wild, so the numbers sold as pets has perforce dropped significantly in recent years. The trade has long been regulated in Colombia and the United States, but traders in the cotton-top tamarin have found ways to evade the regulations.

Conservation and Recovery

The cotton-top tamarin is one of the few members of the family *Callitrichidae* that

survives reasonably well in captivity. Given sufficient room to roam, trees to live in, and suitable food, the captive cotton-top tamarin breeds fairly well and often enough to sustain a small population.

Elephants

Family: Elephantidae

Asian Elephant (*Elephas maximus*)   Hanumantha Rao

General Characteristics of the *Elephantidae*

As the largest of land mammals, elephants have played a prominent part in the evolution of species. The skull, jaws and teeth have evolved into a specialized system for crushing plant material. The large head developed to support the trunk and tusks. The tusks are elongated incisor teeth that begin to develop at two years old and they continue growing throughout the elephant's lifetime, as does the elephant's body. The largest known individual was an African Savanna bull that weighed ten tons (22,000 pounds) and stood 13.1 feet at the shoulder. Tusks of old males have been recorded at 287 pounds and a length of 7.7 feet. The female's tusk is much smaller. The size and shape of the tusks also vary with habitat requirements; forest elephants, for example, have thinner, more downward-pointing, harder tusks that facilitate browsing in denser vegetation. The tusks are used for stripping bark from trees, digging for roots, as weapons, and for social interaction.

The trunk is an extension of the upper lip and nose. The trunk enables elephants to feed from the ground since their short necks prohibit them from reaching the ground with their mouths. The strength of the trunk also enables elephants in breaking branches off trees, or uprooting entire trees.

As massive and strong as it is, the trunk is a sensitive organ. The elephant's nostrils, located at the tip of the trunk, are acutely sensitive to smell and touch. The tip is comprised of fingerlike lips and fine sensory hairs that give the animal the capability of picking up tiny objects. Elephants use the trunks in a variety of ways, including drinking, bathing, vocalizing, and socializing. Because they smell and breathe through their trunks, elephants can raise the trunk high in the air to better detect odors or as snorklelike devices when submerged in water.

Although elephant skin is thick, it is sensitive to heat, parasites and disease. Elephants bathe frequently to reduce body heat and powder themselves with dust to remove or discourage parasites. During times of drought elephants can use their trunks to drill for water in dry river beds.

Locomotion and Territories

The massive body weight is supported by thick legs and a refined foot structure in which the heel partly rests on the ground, like humans. The fingers and toes are surrounded by a soft cushion of elastic fibers that provide a capability of walking silently. The foot spreads into a wide area and leaves almost no track.

Elephants cruise at a rate of 2.5 to 4 mph, can double this speed for hours at a time, and can charge at 25 mph. Their ability to travel gives elephants the option of walking long distances each day in search of food and water. They are able to detect rain showers from far away and will travel many miles to find newly fallen moisture.

Elephants require a large home range to ensure adequate food sources, water supplies and shade. In areas of sufficient resources, the territory may be as little as 300 square miles or as large as 600 square miles in arid areas.

Social Behavior

Elephants display complex social behavior. Females live in family units of adult relatives (sisters or daughters) and immature offspring. When young cows begin to breed, they remain with the family until it grows too large to accommodate all the family members, at which time individuals will break off to form subgroups. The oldest female is the matriarch, who may lead the family long after she is able to reproduce. Her wisdom of the home range and of potential danger is respected by the family members who follow her lead. She may decide, in the face of danger, to encircle the young and confront the intruder, or to retreat, in which case the family runs as a tight unit; if one member is hurt, wounded or sick, the family remains with the stricken individual. Male elephants are primarily solitary, forming temporary groups with little cooperative behavior.

Vocalization is an important function in communication. If a herd cannot see each other they will maintain contact with low growls. If they want to amplify sound, the trunk acts as a resonating chamber to produce bellows or screams, and the highly characteristic trumpeting. Vocalizations are used to convey a wide variety of emotions, and individuals who have been separated may greet each other with exuberant sounds. Elephants also communicate by touching each other with their sensitive trunk tips.

Reproduction

The reproductive cycle is correlated to food and water supplies. During the dry season or drought, females cease to ovulate when their body weight drops, and they must regain that weight before mating can occur. Females remain in heat only a few days and may come into heat at various times during the reproductive season. Males travel between families in search of receptive females, and often must compete with other males for copulation opportunities. For 2-3 months during mating season, males experience a hormone increase that results in more aggressive behavior and higher energy.

Females reach sexual maturity beginning at ten years of age (sometimes delayed for several years by dry conditions) and are most fecund between 25 and 45 years of age; gestation lasts from 18-22 months; following birth, which may be assisted by other family members, the infant requires a long period of dependency upon its mother. The infant nurses from two breasts for 3-4 years. Born with a body weight of about 265 pounds (African) or 220 pounds (Asian), the infant grows rapidly and may weigh 2,200 pounds by six years. The growth rate slows for the next ten years, but elephants continue to grow all their lives. Males experience a second rapid growth rate at 20-30 years of age, which increases their body size above females.

Threats

Elephants have been hunted to extinction since the 7th century BC and remain at the center of controversy regarding their protection and conservation. Although elephants are somewhat valuable as beasts of burden in some parts of the world, their primary economic value is their tusks. During the 1970s when the price of ivory rose, elephants were slaughtered by the tens of thousands. In Kenya alone, the population was reduced from 167,000 in 1973 to 60,000 in 1980. It is estimated that elephants are still being killed at the rate of 50,000-150,000 animals a year in spite of international trade bans imposed by CITES signatories. In addition to its value for ivory, elephants are further threatened because they are a nuisance to agricultural development in African countries. Elephants require large ranges which, more and more frequently, overlap farming areas in developing countries. Armed with semi-automatic weapons that have become available because of civil conflict, poachers and farmers kill elephants at an alarming rate.

Asian Elephant

Elephas maximus

Gale K. Belinky

Status	Endangered
Listed	June 14, 1976
Family	Elephantidae (Elephants)
Description	Flat forehead, small ears; wrinkled dark gray skin is sparsely covered with long, stiff hairs.
Habitat	Continuously forested areas.
Food	Grasses, bark, roots, leaves, bananas, paddy, and sugar cane.
Reproduction	1 calf after gestation of 644 days.
Threats	Hunted for valuable ivory; killed to protect crops from damage.
Range	Sri Lanka, Indochina, Malaysia, Indonesia, southern China.

Description

The Asian elephant, *Elephas maximus*, is smaller than the African elephant, *Loxodonta africana*, with the large males weighing up to 11,880 pounds and the females 5,984 pounds. Size varies throughout the range of *E. maximus*, with smaller individuals found in the east, and the smallest ones found in Borneo. The Asian elephant stands 98 to 117 inches high at the shoulder with the head and body measuring 215 to 250 inches. The top of the head is the highest point on the animal, and the forehead is flat. The ears are relatively small. The front feet usually have 5 nail-like structures and the rear feet have 4. The heart of both the Asian and African elephants is different from most mammals because its apex is cleft into two equal lobes.

Asian elephant trunks have one finger-like process on the tip, instead of two like the African species. This remarkably versatile organ can be used for a wide variety of functions, from feeding and watering to defense and offense. The tusks, usually found on the male, are also versatile and can be used to dig, to scrape bark off trees, to maneuver fallen trees, for protection, and possibly as a status symbol.

The skin of the Asian elephant is sparsely covered with long, stiff hairs. The wrinkled skin varies from dark gray to brown and is often mottled from around the front of the face to the base of the trunk and the ears. White colored animals have been recorded and were considered sacred. The thick skin provides protection from bites and bad weather. Because of the animals' large size, the mass to surface area is relatively small; so they can tolerate cold better than heat. To help dissipate excess heat, the skin is wrinkled to increase the surface area. Covering the skin with dirt and mud may also help Asian elephants regulate body temperature as well as protect against insect bites.

E. maximus is the only living species of the genus *Elephas*, which contains 10 extinct species. Different sources describe different numbers of subspecies for *E. maximus*. Chasen lists three subspecies, *E. m. indicus*, *E. m. maximus*, and *E. m. sumatranus*. Deraniyagala recognized 14 subspecies of *E. maximus*.

Behavior

Asian elephants generally congregate in herds of related females headed by the oldest, and usually largest, female. One or more males may join the herd, especially if at least one female is in estrus. Otherwise, the males usually remain solitary; although they sometimes form temporary all-male herds of up to 7 animals. The members of a herd communicate with each other through 8 basic vocalizations, including low-frequency calls that can be heard over long distances.

These non-territorial animals have varying home ranges depending on the season and type of herd. Adult males of Sri Lanka have home ranges of 6 to 11 square miles. The home range for a 23 member herd of females and young was 16 square miles during the wet season and 40 square miles in the dry season.

Usually, births occur at any time of the year; however, in a relatively low rainfall area in Sri Lanka births coincide with the rainy season. After a gestation period of approximately 644 days, females normally bear one calf, weighing 110 to 330 pounds. Newborns have a fuzzy coat of widely spaced brown hairs that decreases to a sparse covering of hair by adulthood. Standing shortly after birth, the infants follow their mothers around after only a few days. They begin to eat grass and foliage after several months, but may nurse for up to 18 months. The young stay with their mothers in the herd for several years. Males may be capable of some independent movement by four years of age, reaching sexual maturity by 10 to 12 years of age. Females reach sexual maturity at 15 to 16 years of age. Although some reports have Asian elephants living over 100 years, the oldest recorded captive animal was estimated to be either 69 or 77 years old.

Asian elephants eat a wide variety of plants including grasses, bark, roots, leaves, and small stems, as well as such cultivated foods as bananas, paddy, and sugar cane. Adults eat approximately 330 pounds of food per day. Using its trunk, the Asian elephant pulls up bunches of long grass and puts it directly in its mouth. If the grasses are too short, the animal uses its forefeet to scape together a loose pile, and then sweeps the pile into its mouth with its trunk. Asian elephants use either their tusks or molars to scrape bark off trees.

At least once a day, Asian elephants need to drink water. The animals also require salt and other trace elements. Asian elephants that live close to the coast get most of their salt requirements from the sea, and do not use salt licks as much as individuals located inland.

Asian elephants are most active during the morning, evening and night. They rest in the shade during the middle of the day.

Habitat

Asian elephants formerly ranged over a wide variety of habitats from thick jungles to grassy plains. Now, southern Indian and Sri Lankan populations are restricted to single-monsoon dry thorn-scrub forest. They prefer forest-grassland ecotone areas and do not live in large numbers in continuously forested areas with few clearings.

Distribution

In the past, Asian elephants had a very wide distribution from Syria and Iraq across Asia south of the Himalayas to Indochina and the Malay peninsula. Asian elephants could be found in China to at least the Yangtze River and in Sri Lanka, Sumatra, Borneo, and possibly Java. Asian elephants disappeared from southwestern Asia and most of China at least 2,000 years ago. The rest of the Chinese population disappeared slowly through the past centuries until only one small population in the southern part of Yunnan exists today.

Currently, scattered populations exist on the Indian subcontinent, and in Sri Lanka, Indochina, Malaysia, Indonesia, southern China. *E. maximus* is distributed more continuously throughout southeast Asia.

Threats

In addition to being hunted for its valuable ivory, the Asian elephant is increasingly being killed to protect crops from damage. Conflict between humans and the elephant will only increase as the number of humans increases.

Conservation and Recovery

Captive breeding programs have been set up to help increase the numbers of the Asian elephant. Several problems have to be overcome to effectively manage these animals. Mature bulls are very difficult to control and artificial insemination is used to help solve this problem. Inbreeding needs to be avoided as juvenile mortality is higher for offspring of closely related members of this species.

African Elephant

Loxodonta africana

Rick Weyerhaeuser

Status	Endangered
Listed	May 12, 1978
Family	Elephantidae (Elephant)
Description	Largest living land mammal; large ears, wrinkled skin, tusks.
Habitat	Forest and forest-grasslands and miombo woodlands.
Food	Strictly herbivorous.
Reproduction	Usually a single offspring after a gestation of 18 to 22 months.
Threats	Killing for illegal ivory trade; competition with humans for land.
Range	East, Central and West Africa.

Description

The African elephant, *Loxodonta africana*, is the largest land mammal living today. It ranges in weight from 8,820 to 15,430 pounds and stands from 10 to 13 feet in height at the shoulders, the highest point of the animal. From the tip of trunk to the tip of tail, the total length may be 23 to 29 feet. The skin is very wrinkled and light gray in color, but it can vary in appearance to reddish brown depending on the color of the soil and mud where the species may have bathed and dusted. The species has large ears that exceed the height of the neck. The back is concave and the belly slopes diagonally downwards from front to back. Its teeth have lozenge-shaped loops. Both sexes possess tusks; the males are slight-ly larger. The trunk is two fingered and not very rigid. The large ears, which is a distinguishing characteristic of the African elephant, function as heat diverters to release heat from the animal's massive body.

L. africana is a member of the *Elephantidae* family. This family is made up of two subspecies: the bush African elephant, (*Loxodonta africana africana*); and the forest African elephant, (*Loxodonta africana cyclotis*). These subspecies differ in mostly external characters: *L. a. cyclotis* is not as tall as *L. a. africana*; the ears of *L. a. cyclotis* are more rounded; and *L. a. cyclotis* has straighter and more slender tusks than those of *L. a. africana*. *L. a. cyclotis* also has darker skin, and more hair, especially on the trunk and around the mouth.

Behavior

Mating takes place in the usual quadruped position. The young are born after a gestation period of 18 to 22 months, the longest pregnancy of any known living mammal. The elephant usually gives birth to a single offspring, rarely twins. Newborns weigh about 165 to 255 pounds and measure approximately 39 inches in height at the shoulder. Individuals reach sexual maturity between the ages of 8 and 13 years. Adult males exhibit a period of heightened sexual activity known as must. During this period fluid is released from the temporal glands behind the eyes. This increased testosterone increases the animal's sexual and aggressive behavior. A female can give birth every 4 to 6 years, and has the potential of giving birth to about 7 offspring in her lifetime, which may be 60 to 70 years.

The African elephant is community oriented. It lives in families comprised of mostly females, usually mother, daughters, and juvenile males. The leader of the family is the oldest female, and she acts as the memory bank and teacher. Families may range in size from 2 to over a dozen individuals. If numbers reach over twenty, the family may splinter into two groups, but these groups stay in close contact. There are extremely strong bonds in these families, and all take part in rearing the young and helping with the sick and injured. Males tend to leave the family around the time of puberty. They may form bachelor groups for a short while.

Infants are is completely helpless at birth, and not only the mother, but others in its family take part in the care of the infant. Juveniles live on nothing but mothers' milk for the first two years of their lives.

Nearly three-quarters of the African elephant's life is devoted to feeding or moving toward a food or water source. The diet is strictly herbivorous. Most individuals consume 165 to 330 pounds of food and 20 to 40 gallons of water per day, but very large males may eat twice this amount. The species is adapted to be a browser rather than a grazer. Leaves of acacia trees are among the favorite delicacies, while other foliage and fruits are consumed, as well as grass species. The elephant is active during the day feeding, foraging, and bathing.

Habitat

The African elephant is found throughout much of the continent of Africa. It exists in a variety of habitats, including forest and forest-grasslands, bushland-thicketed mosaic and miombo woodlands, and Sudanian woodland and forests. It is usually not found in desert or sub-desert areas. The animal can be found in areas from sea level to mountainous regions above the snow line.

Distribution

The African elephant was believed to exist throughout the continent of Africa, including all areas except the 3,475,000 square miles of the Sahara Desert. It is believed that within the last three centuries the African elephant occupied virtually all of sub-saharan Africa except the very dry sub-desert steppe of the Sudanese Arid zone, the desert and sub-desert parts of the Somali Arid Zone, and the coastal desert of the South West Arid Zone. The elephant now has a range of approximately 2,002,500 square miles, or about 25 percent of its original range. In eastern Africa, the African elephant is found in Ethiopia, Kenya, Rwanda, Somalia, Sudan, Tanzania, and Uganda. Central Africa has African elephant populations in Cameroon, Central African Republic, Chad, Gabon, Republic of Congo (formerly Zaire), and Equatorial Guinea. Eight southern African countries provide 502,000 square miles of range. They include Angola, Botswana, Malawi, Mozambique, Namibia, Caprivi, Zambia, and Zimbabwe. Fragmented populations exist in west Africa in Sierra Leone, Togo, Liberia, Guinea, Ghana, the Ivory Coast, Burkina Faso, Mali, Niger, Benin, Guinea Bissau and Senegal.

Most individuals became extinct north of the Sahara by the sixth century AD, and most were eradicated from West Africa in the early twentieth century. The ivory trade may have caused the crash of the population in West Africa by 1914. The present elephant range is estimated to be about 2,002, 500 square miles. This is an area where individuals can be expected to occur, not the bounds of an area containing fragments of habitats suitable for the species. The African elephant's decline can be broken down into four areas of Africa: east, central, southern, and west Africa.

Threats

Overutilization is the major cause of this species' decline. Loss of habitat due to desertification and competition with humans is another major factor in its decline.

In eastern Africa, the African elephant was widely distributed until the turn of the century. Problems of land-use conflicts between people and elephants are complicated by rapidly increasing human populations, poverty, civil unrest, inadequate protection and management of elephants, and a lack of public awareness of the need for conservation. Land degradation has occurred because the dense human populations have put extensive pressures on natural resources and because of outdated agricultural practices.

In central Africa, this species is threatened by the expansion of roads, railways, and pipelines. Commercial plantations, logging, mining, and an expanding human population with its subsistence agriculture are also threats. All of these activities destroy potential elephant habitat, compete with the African elephant for land, fragment habitats, or provide access for poachers into otherwise inaccessible areas. The construction of the trans-Gabon railway has opened up virgin forests in some areas for logging, and planned or actual mineral and oil exploitation activities have introduced roads and human disturbances into areas that were formerly isolated and uninhabited.

Eight countries contain populations of the African elephant in southern Africa. In Botswana, a large portion of that population uses only a small area of land during the dry season. This riverine habitat is the rarest and most diverse habitat in the country. These high concentrations of individuals may cause sufficient foraging pressures resulting in significant habitat damage. In other countries, rapidly increasing human populations, a shortage of agricultural land, and one of the highest human populations densities in Africa adversely affect the elephant.

The African elephant was nearly eradicated from west Africa in the early twentieth century. It is now found in a series of highly fragmented habitats throughout that area. Increasing human population pressures and declining natural productivity in dry savanna habitats have confined remaining elephant populations to isolated pockets of habitat largely in parks and other reserves.

The decline of this species between 1650 and 1790 is believed to have been due to human settlement and population growth. Later declines from 1790 to 1870 were due to a massive elephant kill for the ivory trade. And, from 1870 to 1920, occasional individuals were killed because of crop depredation caused by the African elephant.

Conservation and Recovery

The combination of legislation, a fall in the price of ivory, and a drop in the demand for ivory associated with World War I, allowed elephant populations to recover. These populations had substantially recovered by mid-century in eastern, central, and southern Africa. The ivory trade increased substantially in the early 1970's as supply and demand pressures soared so that ivory exports from Africa reached pre-1914 levels. The wave of elephant killing for ivory in the 1970's and 1980's was the second of its kind in recorded history.

Much has been done in the past few years to protect remaining African elephants and to increase its population. Some were begun in the 1970's, when it became obvious that the illegal killing of the African elephant was widespread and that many populations, especially in east Africa, were in decline. The African elephant was put on Appendix II of CITES in 1977, and was classified as threatened by the USFWS in 1978. The African elephant was also listed as vulnerable by the International Union for Conservation of Nature and Natural Resources (IUCN) In 1978. These actions proved to be ineffective and the illegal killing of elephants for ivory commerce was considered out-of-control by the late 1980s.

In 1989, several conservation efforts to curtail the illegal killing of the African elephant were initiated. Individual countries increased their protected areas for the African elephant and developed strict anti-poaching campaigns. The United States established a moratorium on the importation of raw and worked ivory from all ivory producing and intermediary nations. A number of other major ivory consuming nations, most notably those in western Europe and Japan, enacted similar legislation. The African elephant was transferred from Appendix II to Appendix I of CITES in October of that year. These actions helped to cut off the major ivory trade, but black market trade still continues. In many areas, these increased protective measures have decreased poaching, but it still exists and in some areas, illegal killing is still heavy. Increasing the control of individual countries over their populations, and giving them guidelines to follow may help the battle with poachers. Studies have shown that local people are more successful in protecting the African elephant in their area. Money is often a limiting factor in the success of anti-poaching campaigns. Without proper funding, the equipment and personnel cannot be retained to do the job that is necessary. More funds, possibly from admission to state owned reserves and from other areas of government are needed to continue this battle. Public awareness of the plight of these animals is important to get the local support that is needed to protect the African elephant. Finally, improved systems for determining the numbers of African elephants are needed to better understand the current populations and threats facing this animal.

Rhinoceros
Family: Rhinocerotidae

Black Rhinoceros (*Diceros bicornis*)   Rick Weyerhaeuser

General Characteristics of the *Rhinocerotidae*

There are five surviving species of rhinoceros whose ancestors were abundant from 40 million years ago until the last Ice Age 15 million years ago. The Sumatran rhino has changed little from its ancient ancestors of 40 million years, as has the more primitive Javan rhino that has changed little from its 10 million-year-old ancestors. The two African rhinos, white and black, evolved from the same stock about 3 million years ago.

Rhinoceros means "nose horn." The horns are made of a hairlike substance that grows from the rhino's skin; unlike other horned animals, the rhino horn has no bony core but is made of keratin fibers. Like hair, the horn keeps growing, as much as 3 inches a year. If a horn is broken off, a new one will grow. Both African species and the Sumatran rhino have two horns in tandem, while the Javan and Indian rhinos have a single horn on the end of the nose.

Rhinos have poor vision and are unable to detect motionless objects a hundred feet away. Because the eyes are located on the side of the head, a rhino must turn its head side to side in order to see straight ahead. Its hearing, however, is quite good, as is its sense of smell.

Food and Water

All rhinos are herbivores that require a large intake of plant material to sustain their size. They are able to survive on high fiber foods but they prefer leafy materials. Although the African rhinos have lost their front teeth, they have broad lips that facilitate grazing on short grass. Black rhinos and Indian rhinos have a prehensile upper lip that further assists in food gathering. Javan and Sumatran rhinos are browsers rather than grazers, eating the leaves and shoots of saplings. Javan, Sumatran and African black rhinos also feed on some fruits. When water supplies are plentiful, rhinos drink every day, but they can endure periods of 4-5 days with no water during droughts.

In cool weather rhinos feed and rest alternately, for a few hours at a time, day and night. With the approach of the hot dry weather, the rest period near the middle of the day becomes more of a fixed point, until at the height of the dry season the animals are feeding in the cool of morning and evening, and dozing through the rest of the day. They feed more during the night at this time of year, to make up for lost time during the heat of the day.

Much of their resting time is spent wallowing to keep cool. Rhinoceros need water for drinking and wallowing at least every two to four days, and if their feeding areas are dry, they will walk up to six miles from their home range to find it. When there is no water for wallowing or grooming purposes, they will roll in dust, presumably to keep their skin clear of ticks and other parasites.

Mating

Male rhinos become sexually mature at 7 to 8 years; females at 4 to 5 years. Females may breed soon after becoming sexually mature but males do not breed until they establish territory or dominant status, which may take 2 to 3 years after maturity. Females produce one young, rarely two, but may bear additional young from 2 to 4 years after pregnancy. Rhinos breed and bear young year round, but African rhinos tend to mate during the rainy season. The young rhino usually remains with its mother until the birth of the next offspring, at which time the juveniles may form groups. Mature females who are not pregnant may form groups or may join a group of juveniles. Adult males are solitary except during breeding season when they may form a temporary relationship with a female in heat.

Male Asian rhinos and black rhinos are very aggressive, fighting each other as well as intruders. Males sometimes fight viciously. African rhinos fight with their front horns, while the Asian species attack with their lower incisor tusks or lower canine teeth. They will charge humans, vehicles or elephants in blind rushes designed to intimidate. The white rhino, however, has a mild temperament and will retreat rather than fight. When cornered by predators, a group of white rhinos will stand rump to rump, facing out in different directions in a posture of self defense.

Threats

Because of their size and toughness of their skin, rhinos have not been much threatened by natural predators; human predation has long reduced populations as a result of demand for rhino parts, especially the horns and tusks, and because of a decrease in their natural habitat. When Europeans introduced guns into Africa during the nineteenth century, rhinos were killed in great numbers, and by the end of the nineteenth century the white rhino was on the brink of extinction. The black rhino was extirpated in the Cape soon after the arrival of white settlers, remained steady throughout its range elsewhere in Africa, but declined rapidly in East, Central and West Africa during the 1970s because of the dramatic increase in the value of horns in India, China and countries in the far east. People in these countries believe that the horn is an aphrodisiac, a fever-reducing agent, and a cure for headaches, and for skin, heart and liver disease. The hooves, blood and urine are also used for medicinal purposes. Men in North Yemen consider daggers made from rhino horns a status symbol, and the production of oil in Yemen, which brought wealth to many people in that nation, resulted in the deaths of thousands of rhinos. During an eight year period, 8,000 rhino horns were imported in North Yemen.

The world population of rhinos is dangerously low for all species except the black rhino, which numbers about 15,000 individuals. The white rhino, which was on the verge of extinction, was repopulated through the Natal Parks Board conservation program and worldwide attention brought by international conservation organizations. The Sumatran rhino numbers only 150 animals and the Javan rhino has been reduced to 50 individuals. The population of the Indian rhino is about 1,500 animals.

Northern White Rhinoceros

Ceratotherium simum cottoni

Ron Singer, USFWS

Status	Endangered
Listed	June 2, 1970
Family	Rhinocerotidae (Rhinoceros)
Description	Gray with a massive head, a shoulder hump, and a long neck.
Habitat	Open, perennial grasslands.
Food	Short grasses and roots.
Reproduction	1 or 2 young every 2 to 3 years; gestation is about 16 months.
Threats	Habitat destruction, hunting.
Range	Republic of Congo and Sudan.

Description

After the elephant, the white rhinoceros, *Ceratotherium simum*, is the largest mammal in the world. Males stand 5 to 6.5 feet tall at the shoulder, weigh 3 tons or more, and have a head and body length of 12 to 14 feet. There are two races, or subspecies of this rhino, one in the northern grasslands of Africa, *C. s. cottoni*, and one in the south, *C. s. simum*. These animals are geographically quite distinct, but very similar physiologically. Both subspecies are tank-like creatures with a massive head that is hung near the ground almost all of the time, a shoulder hump, and a long neck. The long neck, distinguishing this species as a grazer, allows it to feed comfortably at ground level, and the square-ended, wide muzzle enables it to remove a full mouthful of grass with each bite.

Despite its name, this species is gray in color, "white" is probably a corruption of the Dutch wijd, or "wide," which would adequately describe the animal's broad muzzle. For this reason, the common name preferred today is square-lipped rhinoceros.

White rhinos have a pair of horns, with the front one being longer. Lengths average 37 to 79 inches for *C. s. simum*, and 37 to 40 inches for *C. s. cottoni*. Females' horns are longer and thinner than those of the males. Individuals with more than two horns have occasionally been recorded.

C. simum was discovered and described in South Africa in 1817, by Burchell. It was not discovered in Uganda until 1907. It is generally considered as being one species with two races. *C. s. cottoni* was not discovered until 1907.

Behavior

Rhinoceroses communicate with many sounds, and each of the five species of Rhinoceros have their own distinguishing noises. The northern white rhinoceros will make a husky panting sound when meeting another at a distance. Males and females court with wailing noises. Calves call to their mothers with whines and loud squeals when alarmed. The threat calls given by dominant males to intruders into their territories begin with a low growl, which is replaced by a fierce bellow as the threat becomes more intense. The most frequent signals used by this species are based on scent, conveyed by urine-spraying and dung-piles.

In spite of its huge size, the northern white rhinoceros, unless provoked, is normally an inoffensive animal that is easy to approach and to kill. It is generally found in herds of about a dozen. This species is territorial. Mothers are also very protective and defensive against any danger to their calf. Dominant males hold feeding territories from which they exclude all other adult males. These feeding territories will later become breeding territories, within which they will defend a mate. Breeding males occupy a solitary territory of 200-650 acres, which they mark with dungheaps and strong urine, which they spray frequently while patrolling the territory. Females entering the territory become the exclusive property of that male; if she leaves his territory he will not follow her into another. He attempts to confine her within his territory until she is receptive for mating. Subordinate males are permitted to enter and even reside in the territory but they are not permitted contact with females or the right to mark the territory. If the subordinate male breaks the rules and is confronted by the dominant male, he will stand defensively making loud shrieks, but he will not contest the territory holder's authority. Northern white rhinos rarely fight, but they often indulge in trials of strength, wrestling with their horns, or charging each other with their shoulders to settle disputes and to confirm their social position. If a territory-holding male is found in another male's territory, he will take the submissive role of a subordinate male unless he is close enough to his own territory to exert his dominance by backing steadily toward home. If a subordinate male challenges the territory holder and wins, the territory holder will leave and go to another territory where he becomes the subordinate male or challenges that territory holder for rights to the territory.

Females also have feeding territories, although theirs are much larger than those of the males. They may move through male territory without being challenged. Courtship in this species is a slow and cautious ritual, taking between five and twenty days to complete.

The northern white rhinoceros breeds year round, with peaks at times when there is a flush green grass. This occurs between February and June in northern Africa. The gestation period is about sixteen months. Calves are able to walk with the mother 2-3 days after birth, usually running in front of her (black rhino calves run behind). The calf stays with its mother for as long as two years. When a female gives birth to a new calf, she chases the previous calf away. By this time, it is two years old and fully weaned. Sexual maturity is reached at about six or seven years of age.

The northern white rhinoceros grazes on short grasses. It requires large quantities of food and it depends on permanent water. The horn is sometimes used for digging, when the grass is too short to graze and the animals have to turn their attention to roots as their main source of food.

Habitat

The northern white rhinoceros inhabits open, perennial grasslands on the plains of Africa.

Distribution

The southern race of this species, *C. s. simum*, was brought to the brink of extinction decades ago, but has recently recovered; the northern population, the northern white rhinoceros, has not fared so well and exists in only a fraction of its former territory. The living races are now restricted to two regions separated from each other by more than 2,000 miles.

The southern white rhinoceros was once widespread throughout Africa. Its range extended south of the Sahara wherever suitable savannah country could be found. Fossils indicate that it ranged to Morocco and Algeria, north of the present Sahara.

Until the latter part of the nineteenth century the northern white rhinoceros was widely distributed from the west bank of the Nile in the Sudan to Lake Chad. Since the beginning of the century, however, both

range and numbers have drastically declined. Today, this subspecies is extinct everywhere except in The Sudan and Republic of Congo (formerly Zaire), where a few hundred individuals survive.

Threats

The northern white rhinoceros numbers have declined rapidly over the years due to habitat destruction and hunting. This species has been hunted mainly for its valued horns. These threats still persist despite legal protection. Even those animals protected in reserves face the threat of illegal poaching.

It is possible that the decline is also partly due to changes in vegetation during drought when weaker animals were unable to recolonize in the face of competition from more efficient animals which could move more freely to exploit such food and water as was available. Its territorial behavior and rather slow rate of breeding make it a poor colonist, very slow to expand its range at the best of times.

Conservation and Recovery

The only way for the northern white rhinoceros to recover is in reserves where poaching can be kept to a minimum. In the Garamba National Park, in Republic of Congo (formerly Zaire), this animal is protected in every way possible, although poachers still manage to find ways to get their valued horns.

The southern white rhinoceros, once on the brink of extinction, has recovered through a conservation effort in the Umfolozi Game Reserve called "Operation Rhino." Over a twenty year period the numbers rose from 200 to 2,000 animals. The Umfolozi Game Reserve, however, is not large enough to sustain a larger population, and excess individuals are exported to zoos or sold to safari companies to be used as game animals.

Black Rhinoceros

Diceros bicornis

Rick Weyerhaeuser

Status	Endangered
Listed	July 14, 1980
Family	Rhinocerotidae (Rhinoceros)
Description	Short neck is gray in color; its muzzle has an upper pointed lip.
Habitat	Arid thorn-scrub country.
Food	Leaves and twigs, fruits, grass, green clover and other herbs.
Reproduction	Single young every 2 to 5 years.
Threats	Habitat destruction; hunting for valued horns.
Range	Tanzania, Zimbabwe, Zambia, South Africa, Namibia, Central African Republic, Mozambique, Cameroon, Sudan, Somalia, Angola, Malawi, Rwanda, Botswana, Ethiopia, Chad

Description

The black rhinoceros, *Diceros bicornis*, stands 4.9 to 5.6 feet tall at the shoulder, weighs about 1.5 to 1.75 tons, and has a head and body length of 10 to 12 feet. It has a short neck, and despite its name, it is gray in color. Its muzzle has an upper lip that is pointed and its tip is prehensile. The pointed lip and short neck distinguish this species as a browser. This animal has poor eyesight, but a sharp sense of smell and hearing.

Behavior

The black rhinoceros has a very aggressive temperament and has been known to charge vehicles and even campfires without provocation. It is the most aggressive rhinoceros species.

Adults are generally found alone, but they may be found in groups of up to five animals. Mothers can usually be found with their young. This species is very territorial, and is usually found in a definite locality, which the male will defend vigorously against rivals. Mothers are also very protective, and defensive, against any danger to their calf.

Rhinoceroses communicate with many sounds, and each of the 5 species make some distinguishing noises. The black rhinoceros snorts, snarls threateningly, and roars. Fighting rhinos grunt and scream. Males and females court with whistling noises. Calves and their mothers communicate with a variety of squeals. Adults approaching waterholes where others are already wallowing make a puffing or gasping sound which may serve to avoid conflicts by giving the group an early warning of their approach. The most frequent signals used by the black rhinoceros are based on scent.

The black rhinoceros does not appear to have a particular breeding season. Every two to five years, the female rhino, called a cow, bears a single young. The gestation period is about twelve to eighteen months. The newborn calf weighs between 55 to 88 pounds. On the calf's nose are two smooth, flat plates where its horns will grow. The calf stays with its mother for as long as two years, often departing shortly before its mother bears another calf, but sometimes remaining after its sibling is born. Sexual maturity is reached at about six or seven years of age.

The life expectancy of the black rhinoceros is not known, but in zoos they can live up to 40 years. In the wild, they may live up to 60 years.

The black rhinoceros uses its "hooked" lip for stripping leaves and twigs from bushes and shrubs. It will also pick up fallen fruits from the ground as well as take those which it can reach from trees, and it is able to feed on grass which is long enough to be twisted together into bundles. Green clover and other herbs are acceptable food if they are all that is available.

During the rainy season, the black rhinoceros ranges freely, feeding over a wide area. When the dry weather comes, it stays within three miles of permanent water. It needs to drink once a day or more, if possible.

The black rhinoceros has become largely nocturnal in most parts of its range, probably as the result of natural selection, which has eliminated the more diurnal individuals which were the most likely to be shot.

The black rhinoceros feeds at dawn, at dusk, and at night. When the noonday sun beats down, the animals lie in the shade or roll in the dust of dry riverbeds. When water holes are nearby, they cool off by wallowing in mud. The coating of mud or dust on their skin helps keep off insects and protects the large animals from the sun.

Habitat

The black rhinoceros is normally associated with arid thorn-scrub country in Africa. In Kenya, it can also be found in the high forests of Mount Kenya and the Aberdare Range, sometimes existing at an altitude of more than 10,000 feet above sea-level. This habitat provides plenty of browsing food, as well as cover in the thick brush. It avoids open grassland.

Distribution

The black rhinoceros was once widespread throughout Africa. Its range extended from Cape Province and southwestern Angola to eastern Africa, including Somalia, southwestern Ethiopia, and the southern Sudan. From there the range extended westward along a relatively narrow strip between the southern edge of the Sahara Desert and the northern limits of the dense rain forests of the Congo and Nigeria, as far as Lake Chad and Cameroon. Within this region there were areas where this species was absent.

Today, the black rhinoceros exists in a fraction of this territory. National Parks and other sanctuaries provide refuge and protection for this species. The largest number of black rhinoceros can be found in Tanzania. They also occur in varying numbers in Zimbabwe, Zambia, South Africa, Namibia, Central African Republic, Mozambique, Cameroon, Sudan, Somalia, Angola, Malawi, Rwanda, Botswana, Ethiopia, and Chad. The total population of black rhinos is estimated at 15,000 animals, by far the largest and most widespread of the extant rhino species.

Threats

The black rhinoceros numbers have declined rapidly over the years due to habitat destruction and hunting. In many areas these animals were exterminated by European settlers systematically to make room for human expansion, and because they were thought of as a nuisance, and sometimes dangerous. This species has also been threatened by hunting in the past, mainly for their valued horns. These threats still persist despite legal protection. Even those animals protected in reserves face the threat of illegal poaching.

Conservation and Recovery

The best, and most likely the only way for the black rhinoceros to recover, is in reserves where poaching can be kept to a minimum. In the reserves and parks of Africa these animals are protected in every way possible, although poachers still manage to find ways to get their valued horns.

Sumatran Rhinoceros

Didermocerus sumatrensis

Bruce W. Bunting

Status	Endangered
Listed	June 2, 1970
Family	Rhinocerotidae (Rhinoceros)
Description	Asian rhinoceros with two horns, measuring 3 to 5 feet tall at the shoulder, weighing about one ton, skin is relatively thin and smooth, with bristle-like hairs.
Habitat	Forested hill country, often at a considerable height, near water.
Food	Leaves, twigs, bamboo shoots, wild mangoes, and figs; lichens or fungus off rotting trees, and occasionally grazes on tall grass.
Reproduction	Single young; gestation period is guessed to be 7 to 18 months.
Threats	Habitat destruction; hunting.
Range	Burma, Indonesia (Sumatra and Borneo), and Malaysia

Description

The sumatran rhinoceros, *Didermocerus sumatrensis*, is the world's smallest and oldest rhinoceros, and it is the only Asian species with two horns. The front horn of the Sumatran rhinoceros is the larger of the two, being about 15 to 20 inches long on adult males. The hind horn is much smaller, usually little more than a large boss protruding only a few inches. On some specimens it is so small that it appears to be missing, which may account for earlier reports of one-horned specimens. Both sexes carry horns, but those on females are about one-third the size of the male's.

The Sumatran rhinoceros measures only 3 to 5 feet tall at the shoulder, weighs about one ton, and has a head and body length of 8 to 9 feet. The skin folds on this animal are rather inconspicuous when compared to the two other Asian rhinoceros species but the physical appearance is an armorlike barrier over the back. Also, the skin itself is relatively thin and smooth, with bristle-like hairs. Immature animals have a covering of hair, which appears to vary in density according to geographical locality, but which seems to diminish as the animals mature. Other rhinos are nearly hairless, except for tufts at the tips of their ears and at the ends of their tails. The Sumatran rhinoceros has a prehensile upper lip, distinguishing it as a browser. This species also has acute senses of smell and hearing.

Two subspecies of *D. sumatrensis* are recognized, the "typical" race, *D. s. sumatrensis*, being restricted to Sumatra and Borneo, and the race *D. s. lasiotis* (usually known as either Chittagong or hairy-eared) living on the mainland. The latter is reputed to be somewhat larger than the island race, and to have paler and somewhat longer hair, a shorter and more fully tufted tail, and a more strongly developed fringe on the edges of its ears.

The Sumatran rhino is the only surviving member of the family *Dicerorhinae,* which included the extinct Woolly rhino, and it has changed little from its ancestors that lived 40 million years ago.

The Sumatran rhinoceros is also known as a two-horned Asian rhinoceros, and a hair-eared rhinoceros.

Behavior

The Sumatran rhinoceros has been seen swimming from island to island. They are also strong climbers, able to go through the thickest bush and up slopes too steep for a man to climb except on all fours.

Rhinoceroses communicate with many sounds, and each of the 5 species make some distinguishing noises. The Sumatran rhinoceros has a more varied repertoire of voices than the other rhino species. A thorough study has not been made of the meaning of any sounds which it makes.

What little is known about the breeding of this species comes from captive births in zoos. The gestation period is guessed to be anywhere from seven to eighteen months, resulting in the birth of one offspring. Sumatran rhino calves are born with a long dense coat of hair that becomes sparse and bristly in older adults. Males are assumed to begin breeding by 10 years, with 80% of them participating in the breeding pool in a given year. Females may begin reproduction at 6 years, with pregnancy intervals of 4 to 5 years. When the sex ratio is 1:1, this rhino is a polygamous mammal. The Sumartra rhino may live to 32 years.

The Sumatran rhinoceros browses on leaves, twigs, bamboo shoots, and fruits, such as wild mangoes and figs. This species has been seen eating lichens or fungus off a rotting tree, and occasionally grazing on tall grass. As they grow older, and their teeth become more worn, individuals may choose to feed on thinner twigs, making up their diet with fruit.

Individuals spend the hot part of the day and the middle of the night wallowing or concealed in a sheltered place, emerging in the evening and again in the early morning, usually covered in mud, to feed.

Habitat

The Sumatran rhinoceros favors forested hill country, often at a considerable height, near water for bathing and wallowing.

Distribution

At one time, the Sumatran rhinoceros was distributed over a wide region, extending from parts of East Pakistan and Assam, throughout Burma, much of Thailand, Cambodia, Laos and Vietnam, Malaya, Sumatra, and Borneo, basically covering entire southeast Asia. On the two big islands, Sumatra and Borneo, its fossil remains have been found in prehistoric human sites far from its present limited haunts.

As of 1985, the Sumatran rhinoceros survives in limited numbers in Burma, Indonesia, and Malaysia. There is no recent estimate of the populations in Laos, Vietnam or Thailand, but there is no reason to suppose that even a single individual survived in any of those countries.

The 1996 population estimate is that 400 Sumatran rhinos survive on the Malay peninsula and on the islands of Sumatra and Borneo. It is the Borneo population of 70 individuals that most interests scientists. DNA studies indicate that this population is different from other Sumatran rhino populations, suggesting that they have been isolated for thousands of years.

Threats

The Sumatran rhinoceros numbers have declined rapidly over the years due mainly to hunting, but habitat destruction has also been a factor. This species was forced out of its hillside forest habitat and hunted mercilessly for its horns, and the rest of its body, since the typical Chinese apothecary shop uses the entire animal. As the human population increased and spread, this species' habitat diminished correspondingly, and pressure on the remaining population thus multiplied. During the last 100 years this multiplication has even further accelerated, the fate of the species being fully sealed in most areas by the introduction of more sophisticated weapons. Deforestation and agricultural clearing have forced the Sumatran rhinoceros out of its native areas.

Conservation and Recovery

The best, and most likely the only way for the Sumatran rhinoceros to recover is in carefully guarded reserves where poaching can be kept to a minimum. The social and political conditions over most of its range make poaching difficult to stop. In Indonesia, the government sponsors an active anti-poaching program, but it must be combined with education so that citizens will assist anti-poaching patrols. Poaching can also be reduced if logging companies in Sumatra will discourage poaching in their logging concessions.

All efforts to captive breed Sumatran rhinos have failed. Of the 39 animals that have been captured, 21 have died and not a single calf has been produced.

Sanctuaries for 50 Sumatran rhinos have been established in Malaysia and Sabah. The 40 square mile sanctuary in Way Kambas National Park in eastern Sumatra has a breeding complex with 10 natural enclosures. The rhinos now in zoos will be moved to this sanctuary during 1997.

Javan Rhinoceros

Rhinoceros sondaicus

Art Wolfe

Status	Endangered
Listed	June 2, 1970
Family	Rhinocerotidae (Rhinoceros)
Description	Body is covered with a dark gray, granular, scaly, thickly folded skin.
Habitat	Sparse forests.
Food	Trees and shrubs, bamboo leaves, and fruits.
Reproduction	Sexual maturity of females is believed to be 3 years.
Threats	Slow reproductive rate; hunting; overpopulation by humans.
Range	Island of Java

Description

The Javan rhinoceros, *rhinoceros sondaicus*, stands 6 feet tall at the shoulder, weighs about 3,500 pounds, and has a head and body length of 11.5 feet. It is covered with a dark gray, granular, scaly skin that is thickly folded to look like armor plating. Its muzzle has an upper lip that is pointed and its tip is prehensile. The pointed lip distinguishes this species as a browser. This animal has poor eyesight, but a sharp sense of smell and hearing.

The Javan rhinoceros is very similar in appearance to its close cousin the great Indian rhinoceros, *Rhinoceros unicornis*. There are a few differences, however. The Javan rhinoceros is a few inches smaller in size; females do not have horns; and the male's horn is normally less than half the length of its Indian relatives. The skin folds also differ; the Javan rhinoceros has an additional fold in front of the shoulder. Also, the skin structure lacks the "rivets" of the Indian rhino, instead it is marked overall with a pattern of scale-like disks. The tail on the Javan rhinoceros stands out more prominently from the hindquarters through lack of a deep fold across the rump.

The Javan rhinoceros was once considered to be the same species as the great Indian rhinoceros. It was not until the early 1800's that they were distinguished as separate species. This was formalized in 1822 with the necessary technical description by the French zoologist Desmarest. The Javan rhinoceros is also known as the lesser-horned rhinoceros.

Behavior

Very little is known about the Javan rhinoceros, except that they are good climbers. They are difficult to observe in the dense cover where they live.

These rhinoceroses may look awkward, but they are surprisingly nimble and quick. They can jump, twist, and turn quickly. Thick, spongy pads cushion the animals' feet as they move. This enables them to protect themselves in the thick scrub they live in.

The Javan rhinoceros does not use dung piles as territorial markers as other rhinoceros species do but relies entirely on urine scent. The urine is orange-red in color, and may be used as some sort of communication method.

The only account of the reproductive biology of the Javan rhinoceros, in *National Geographic* for June 1985, gives the age for sexual maturity of females as three years, and for males as "about twice that". The rut is said to occur sporadically and non-seasonally, accompanied by "frightful roaring and aggressive behavior by bulls". Gestation is given as 16 months, and the cow is said to remain with the calf for about two years.

The Javan rhinoceros is a browser that feeds on a variety of trees and shrubs, bending saplings over until it can reach the leaves at the crown, often grasping them with its prehensile upper lip. It will also feed from low-hanging branches and from bushes. The Javan rhinoceros is known to eat bamboo leaves and fruits of various kinds. Sometimes they push over trees up to 6 inches in diameter to get at the foliage and possibly the fruit.

Habitat

The Javan rhinoceros has been found in forested hill country at over 6,500 feet above sea level. Today, it exists solely in the sparse forests of the mountainous parts of the Udjong Kulon Reserve on the island of Java.

Distribution

The range of the Javan rhinoceros once extended throughout most of southeast Asia, from the Brahmaputra River valley in Assam, India and Bengal eastward to the southern border of China. They also existed on the islands of Java and Sumatra.

Today, only 50 or so animals exist on the western part of the island of Java, in the Udjong Kulon Reserve.

Threats

The Javan rhinoceros numbers have declined rapidly over the years due to hunting and people-pressure for space. During the last 100 years the human population of Java has increased more than tenfold, with the result that agricultural expansion has deprived the animal of much of its natural habitat, forcing it to retreat into more inaccessible areas, where the remnant has been persistently hunted for its horn. Also, in the mid-eighteenth century the Javan rhinoceros were so numerous that they caused serious damage to crops, inspiring the government of the time to offer a high bounty to hunters who would kill them: 526 were accounted for in two years.

The slow reproductive rate accounts for this species' slow recovery, if their recovery actually happens.

Conservation and Recovery

The only way for the Javan rhinoceros to recover is in the Udjong Kulon Reserve in western Java. In this reserve these animals are protected in every way possible. There is little hope that this small remnant population will maintain itself; few young have been observed.

Indian Rhinoceros

Rhinoceros unicornis

Bruce Bunting

Status	Endangered
Listed	December 2, 1970
Family	Rhinocerotidae (Rhinoceros)
Description	Large headed; with a small eye, thick hide with loose folds on its neck, behind its forequarters, and in front of its hindquarters.
Habitat	Plains of humid, subtropical climate.
Food	Grasses, shoots, reeds and water hyacinth.
Reproduction	Single calf every 3 or 4 years.
Threats	Alteration of natural habitat; hunting for valued horns.
Range	India, Assam, Bangladesh, Bhutan, Uttar Pradesh, Nepal, Pakistan

Description

The Indian rhinoceros, *Rhinoceros unicornis*, stands at least 6 feet tall at the shoulder and may measure as much as 14 feet in length. The species weighs 2 tons or more. It has a thick hide with several loose folds especially on its neck, behind its forequarters, and in front of its hindquarters. It seems to be encased in armor. It possesses convex tubercles on the sides and upper parts of its legs. It has a large head, a small eye, and a lower jaw containing a pair of sharp incisors that have developed into tushes.

This species is also known as the Great Indian one-horned rhinoceros.

Behavior

Despite its intimidating appearance, the species is normally shy and inoffensive, rarely aggressive unless wounded or with young. Females will use their horns to protect the young by butting and hooking attackers. The species is quick and nimble, charging at speeds of up to 30 miles per hour. In addition, it can twist, jump, and turn quickly. They possess a keen sense of hearing and smell, often finding trails by smell. Individuals communicate with each other by snorting, snarling, and roaring. Courting is accompanied by whistling noises.

Indian rhinos establish territories differently than other rhino species. Males are not dominant or subordinate, but are strong or weak with a continuum between them. Strong males urinates a backward jet and are the only males who copulate. They establish home ranges of up to 2.3 square miles, but the range may overlap with other strong males. Neighboring males do not compete, but strange males entering a territory will be viciously attacked. Receptive females entering a territory may be attacked by the male and noisily chased for more than a mile as part of the courtship ritual.

The reason that Indian rhinos establish territories differently from other species is because of habitat and food variances. Indian rhinos occur in flood plain habitats and the location of food sources changes in unpredictable ways, which discourages localized territories. Furthermore, the vegetation is so dense that individuals in close proximity may be isolated from each other, even within the same territory, making territorial disputes impractical.

Females give birth every 3 or 4 years. One calf is born. The youth will stay with its mother until she is ready to birth again. At this time, the offspring will wander off on its own.

The Indian rhinoceros feeds on grasses, shoots, and reeds in the early morning and evening. It is a grazer and roams around exploiting new vegetation. It will also feed on crops when within range.

In an adaptation to its diet, the upper lip is semi-prehensile which allows the species to feed on tall grasses; slender twigs can be folded out of the way to allow for grazing on short fresh grass. It will also eat bamboo shoots and water hyacinth.

The Indian rhinoceros is active during the day, normally feeding in the early morning and evening. The remainder of the day and night is spent resting and wallowing in mud, especially during hot weather. Wallowing may alleviate insect attacks which occur regularly in swamps.

Habitat

The Indian rhinoceros inhabits the flood plains of a humid subtropical climate. The dominant vegetation of this area are broadleaf deciduous shrubs. It is never far from water as it requires daily bathing. It wallows in water and mud.

Distribution

The genus *Rhinoceros* was one time widely represented by a number of living species. Many fossil records indicate that the genus existed in the Pleistocene Ice Ages. During this time, it seems to have ranged throughout Eurasia from Europe to Taiwan and Japan.

The Indian rhinoceros once inhabited the Ganges, from the Indus Valley west to Assam. Presently it ranges only over northern India, Pakistan, Assam, Bangladesh, Uttar Pradesh, Bhutan and Nepal. It occurs in Dudhwa National Park, Royal Chitwan National Park, Kaziranga National Park as well as Bardia.

The Indian rhino is restricted to 8 reserves in India and Nepal where populations are estimated at 1,500 individuals. Small isolated populations may still exist in remote areas of the natural range but this is suspected and not confirmed.

Threats

The Indian rhinoceros has been victim to increasing pressure on its native habitat by increasing human populations and alteration of this natural habitat. The species once ranged over the northern part of India and Nepal from Peshawar and Kashmir in the west, along the Himalayan foothills as far as the frontier with Burma. In the south, the range may have been limited to the plain of the Ganges River system although this is not known for certain.

Much of these lands have been converted to agricultural use. The Indian rhinoceros retreated to the hills and to the remotest and most inaccessible parts of their range. Recently, hunting has accelerated the decline of its already reduced numbers. A century ago, the Government of Bengal offered a bounty for each individual shot, which indicates the abundance of the species at that time. The Nepalese people built raised platforms of bamboo on the fields of the Terai. During harvesting time, they beat gongs and rang bells to scare the rhinos away.

Conservation and Recovery

Conservation efforts for the Indian rhino started as long ago as 1910 when the governments of Bengal and Assam prohibited its hunting because its numbers had been so much reduced. Sanctuaries in the upper Brahmaputra valley and Bengal were set aside for the rhino and its protection. Yet, this did not stop the many gangs of illegal hunters poaching the animal over the years. A lucrative trade has evolved around the horns of the rhino.

Tapirs
Family: Tapiridae

Asian Tapir (*Tapirus indicus*)   Rich Block

General Characteristics of the *Tapiridae*

Tapirs evolved in the Eocene epoch, about the time horses were also evolving. The ancient tapirs were very similar to modern ones, featuring the torpedolike design that enables them to move swiftly through dense underbrush, but such early tapirs as *Heptodon* had no proboscis — that is they lack the long, supple nose of the modern tapir. Tapirs evolved to their basic form in the northern hemisphere, then in the Pleistocene epoch they invaded South America. Today, there are four species of tapir still in existence: one lives in Southeast Asia (the Asian tapir, *Tapirus indicus*), and the other three live in Latin America (the Central American tapir, *Tapirus bairdi*; the mountain tapir, *Tapirus pinchaque*; and the Brazilian tapir, *Tapirus terrestris*). Although the tapirs have evolved adaptations to somewhat different environments, they are all remarkably alike in size, shape, and behavior.

Tapirs weigh 500 to 650 pounds, and are built low to the ground, standing between 29 to 47 inches at the shoulder. Their rumps and torsos are rounded; their necks are thick and strong; their heads are elongated. These general features enable the tapirs to propel themselves quickly through underbrush with their stout, powerful legs. This is one reason why people seldom see them. They can disappear in underbrush at the first hint of human presence. Their heads feature small, oval ears that can lay back on their necks, and their eyes are set deep back in their sockets, an adaptation for moving quickly through thorny brush that might poke eyes. Their noses are long and sensitive to touch; they are used to pull at plants during eating. The tapir's sense of smell is acute and perhaps its most highly developed sense. With its nose it can pick up the traces of other tapirs, of predators, and of food. Its hearing is also good, enabling it to keep track of movements in the dense underbrush of its habitat. On the other hand, its eyesight is not particularly good. A tapir's legs feature three toes pointing forward, and on the forelegs is a high fourth toe used on soft, mushy ground. Each toe has a hoof, and it is by the three-toes tracks left by the tapir that people are most likely to be aware of its presence. Sturdy legs and strong, hoofed toes make tapirs good at climbing and walking along slopes. All the young of the four species of tapir are notably similar in looks: They have brown coats dappled with white, making them hard to see when lying under bushes in a tropical forest. The similarity in the coats of their young is suggestive of how closely related the different species of tapir are, in spite of large geographical distances separating their ranges.

Tapirs prefer wooded environments with abundant underbrush that is so thick that most animals cannot penetrate it, although the mountain tapir lives in somewhat more open lands than the other three species. The mountain tapir also has a thicker coat than the other species because it lives on high mountainsides where the weather is cool. Tapirs are all territorial, and they mark their territories with urine. They all require that open water be near their territories, and they are good swimmers. They can stay immersed in water for several minutes at time. A creature of habit, each tapir walks the same path to its watering place whenever it journeys there or leaves to return to its territory; this makes it vulnerable to human hunters, who discover the path and then lie in wait or set a trap for the animal. Herbivores, tapirs will sometimes create paths to their favorite food bushes; they do not stay at one bush for long, but browse for a moment, then move on to the next bush, to browse, and then continue on.

The tapir species share mating rituals. The male and female will circle each other, sniffing each other's genitalia. They squeal loudly and they circle, becoming ever more frenzied, and circling ever faster. In addition, they poke each other with their noses, and nip at each other's ears, sides, and feet. Females are sexually receptive about every 60 days, and can breed year round. After a gestation of about 400 days, the female will give birth to a single young. Tapirs are typically solitary animals, and are usually seen traveling with one another only when a youngster is with its mother.

All the species of tapir are endangered by the loss of their forest habitat, usually to clear-cut logging, but also to agriculture and expanding human settlements. Humans hunt all four species for meat and for their skins, which make fine leather. The tapirs' principal natural predators are big wild cats such as jaguars.

Central American (= Baird's) Tapir

Tapirus bairdi

Alan Shoemaker

Status	Endangered
Listed	June 2, 1970
Family	Tapiridae (Tapirs)
Description	Dark brown, with a stiff, small mane; exceptionally large nose.
Habitat	Tropical rain forests and swamps.
Food	Grasses, leaves, buds, shoots, and fruits.
Reproduction	Single young after gestation of 14 months.
Threats	Loss of habitat, human predation.
Range	Central America, Colombia, Ecuador, and Mexico.

Description

A newborn Central American tapir, *Tapirus bairdi*, weighs between 14 and 22 pounds and looks much like the young of the other surviving species of tapirs. It has mottled horizontal white stripes with occasional spots over a brown background. This enables the young tapir to blend in so well with the forest floor of its natural habitat that one can gaze directly at it and not see it. The adult Central American tapir has a brown-to-tan coat, with light brown to near white fur on its neck and lower face, and the edges of its ears are white. It has a short, ruddy brown mane.

The Central American tapir is a big animal, among the extant tapirs second in size only to the Asian tapir (*Tapirus indicus* or *Acrocodia indica*; see separate entry). It can

weigh as much as 660 pounds and be as long as 6 feet 8 inches from nose to tail, with the tail adding another 5 inches; it can stand as high as 4 feet at the shoulders. This means it has considerably longer legs than do other species of tapir. These legs allow it to travel on a wide variety of difficult terrain from steep, rocky slopes to soft, swampy water lands, across which it moves with considerable skill. The hind legs each have three toes, with each toe having a broad hoof; behind the hooves is a calloused pad. The forefeet have four toes, one of which is small and rarely used — possibly for climbing. The other toes have broad hooves, and each forefoot has a calloused pad behind it.

Its fingerlike nose is one of the most interesting features of tapirs. The nose is actually a blend of upper lip and nose, with transverse nostrils at the front and the underside extending back several inches before blending into the upper palate. The nose is used to pull on branches, bushes, and shoots, and can pull loose leaves. The Central American tapir's nose is particularly large and has an evolutionary adaptation in its skull to support it, a bony nasal septum. The tapir's sense of smell is acute, and while foraging, it uses its nose to probe for the smells of food, predators, and other tapirs.

Behavior

The behavior of Central American tapirs has not been as well observed as that of the other species of tapir. They do not seem to be as solitary as other tapirs and have been observed gathering together to feed — although each tapir seems to have space around it that other tapirs may not enter without a fight. They also differ from the other tapir species by being active during the day as well as at night. They become primarily nocturnal only in areas frequented by humans.

Individual animals tend to create trails that they routinely follow, day in and day out, making them easy for hunters to track. They prefer to live in regions where there is abundant water, but have been found in areas far from water but with an abundance of food.

They are picky eaters, making them difficult to keep in captivity. There are many plants in their habitat that they do not use for food and will not eat if offered to them in zoos. Even so, these tapirs normally occur in areas rich in plant life and have perhaps 150 species of plants that they will eat. They insist on a wide variety of these plant foods for any feeding period. Their normal approach to feeding is to eat little — a few leaves, perhaps — from one kind of plant, then move to another and eat only a little of it, and so on. This has the beneficial effect of not depleting its sources of foods since its eating habits rarely destroy a plant. The diversity of foods makes it difficult to feed the Central American tapir in captivity since it must be provided with a little bit of almost everything it would find in the wild every time it is fed. In the wild, Central American tapirs show evidence that they know what they want and are not casual grazers or browsers. For instance, when a tree has desirable fruit in branches beyond the reach of the tapir's nose, providing the tree's trunk is medium sized or smaller, it will push the tree over by pressing its head against the trunk, spread its legs wide, and push until the tree topples. It then eats the fruit it wants. Other tapirs will sometimes come to join in the feast.

Like the other species of tapirs, Central American tapirs love water. They are very good swimmers and seem especially fond of deep water. On hot days, they will submerge themselves in water, leaving only the tops of their heads showing. They are able to be completely submerged for long periods — how long is yet to be determined — and they seem to walk on the bottoms of riverbeds much as hippopotamuses do. Submerging helps them to escape the heat of the day, but the water also offers relief from skin parasites.

The female Central American tapir probably is sexually receptive every 2 months. After a gestation period of 14 months, females will give birth to only one young — apparently no one has as yet seen a multiple birth. At first, the newborn is left in a sheltered area while its mother feeds. After a few weeks, the youngster travels with its mother. The youngster probably takes a year to be weaned. It is possible that at this time the youngster parts from its mother, but this is a detail that needs clarification through observation. The youngster probably will reach sexual maturity between 2 and 3 years of age, although this is an inference drawn from observations of the Brazilian tapir (*Tapirus terrestris*; see separate entry).

Habitat

The Central American tapir prefers forested areas and is comfortable at elevations from sea level to 10,500 feet. Its prefers rain forests with much water, but it will live in drier areas if the food sources are sufficient. The presence of a variety of fruits seems to be an important factor for the Central American tapir's choice of habitat.

Distribution

The Central American tapir once ranged from central Mexico south through all of Central America and into the Andes. It has disappeared from nearly all of its range and may be found only in forests in Central America, Colombia, Equador, and Mexico.

Threats

The primary threat to the survival of the Central American tapir is loss of its habitat, primarily to logging and the expansion of human communities. Hunting is also a significant problem. Another source of trouble is the Brazilian tapir, which in northern South America has competed for food with the Central American tapir and has supplanted the Central American tapir in much of its ancient range. (They are true species and do not intermate.) The Brazilian tapirs are being hard pressed by humans, probably prompting much of their migration into Central American tapir territories, although the two species probably always intermingled somewhat.

The Central American tapir is now very rare, very close to extinction in the wild. Wherever humans settle in the Central American tapir's habitat, they seem to quickly eradicate much of the local animal life, and local tapirs seem to be extirpated within a year of the opening of a new human settlement.

Conservation and Recovery

Zoos have had some success with breeding Central American tapirs, especially in the United States. However, the animal's natural genetic diversity may have been lost, making its long-term survival uncertain.

Asian [=Malayan] Tapir

Tapirus indicus [=Acrocodia indica]

Rich Block

Status	Endangered
Listed	June 2, 1970
Family	Tapiridae (Tapirs)
Description	Black on the head and back, covering their forelegs; they are black on their tail, along the bottom of the rump and covering the hind legs; and on the body in between, they are white.
Habitat	Rain forests.
Food	Grasses, leaves, buds, shoots, fruits, and water plants.
Reproduction	Gestation period is 14 months long, resulting in a single birth.
Threats	Loss of habitat and human predation.
Range	Burma, Cambodia, Indonesia (Sumatra), Laos, Malaya, Thailand, and Vietnam.

Description

A newborn Asian tapir, *Tapirus indicus,* looks much like the young of the other surviving species of tapirs. It has mottled white stripes with occasional spots over a brown background. This enables the young tapir to blend in so well with the forest floor of its natural habitat that one can gaze directly at it and not see it. This coat will be replaced by adult coloring in about 150 days, much earlier than with the other tapirs. At birth, the Asian tapir weighs approximately 19 pounds and will reach adult size in 9.5 months.

The adult's looks are distinctive and well adapted to its habitat. Its coloring is broken into three sections. The first, from the tip of its nose, over its shoulders, and down its forelegs is black. The second section, between forelegs and hind legs is white. The third, covering the hind legs, the rump, and the tail is black. This pattern is designed to fool its principal natural predators, tigers and leopards, which can fail to see the full outline of the tapir, especially at night when tapirs are most active; they instead see the start of a tapir, or a white barrel shape, or a rump — none which seems to register as food to the big cats' eyes.

The Asian tapir is a big animal, and can be as long as 8 feet from nose to tail, with the tail adding another 2 to 4 inches. Standing about 2 feet 10 inches at the shoulder and weighing as much as 660 pounds, it looks ungainly, and its short legs can give it an image of slowness. Yet, the Asian tapir is known to run away rapidly into dense undergrowth when humans approach. Its weight, low build, and long front-to-back proportions enable it to move like a torpedo through dense vegetation that most other animals cannot penetrate. Its eyes, set deep in the sockets, are surrounded by folds of flesh that protect them from thorns as the animals rush through the underbrush or when thrusting their heads toward food.

Its fingerlike nose is one of its most interesting features. As with other tapirs, the nose is actually a blend of upper lip and nose, with transverse nostrils at the front and the underside extending back several inches before blending into the upper palate. The nose is used to pull on branches, bushes, and shoots, and can pull loose leaves for eating. The Asian tapir's sense of smell is acute, and while foraging in the dark, it uses its nose to probe for the smells of food, predators, and the urine markings of other tapirs.

In Malaysia and Indonesia, the Asian tapir is sometimes called *bakar*, meaning "rhinoceros." This is because the animal is rarely seen and is known primarily by its tracks, which look like those of a rhinoceros. The hind legs each have three toes, with each toe having a hoof; behind the hooves is a calloused pad. The forefeet have four toes, one of which is small and rarely used — possibly for climbing. The other toes have hooves, and each forefoot has a calloused

pad. The legs and feet are effective not only for walking or running, but for climbing and descending steep inclines — something the Asian tapir does very well — and for swimming and walking on riverbeds while submerged.

There are two scientific names for the Asian tapir: *Tapirus indicus* and *Acrocodia indica*. The first one, *Tapirus indicus*, is the one preferred by most scientists, but some mammologists believe that the Asian tapir belongs in a genus separate from that of the New World tapirs. Hence they designate the New World tapirs as *Tapirus* and the Asian tapir as *Acrocodia*. They base their argument on morphological differences between the animals. The Asian tapir has a vestigial first metacarpal bone in its foot that the others lack; it has a higher occipital ridge in its skull; it has a higher nasal opening than the other tapirs. Further, the Asian tapir has a significantly heavier build, on average, than do the other species, and has thinner fur. There is scant fossil record to support this view, but it is possible that there was a splitting off from ancestral tapirs after the Pleistocene epoch, with the extinct *Tapirus hungaricus*, found in Europe, and *Mega tapirus augustus*, found in China, possibly being part of the same genus as the present-day Asian tapir, and *Tapirus helvetius* of the Micocene epoch possibly being part of the same genus as the New World species, possibly even an ancestor of the mountain tapir, *Tapirus pinchaque* (see separate entry). Other common names are Indian Tapir and Bakar.

Behavior

Asian tapirs are solitary creatures and need large areas in which to live. They are very hard to observe because they are nocturnal, very alert to the presence of humans, and able to run away, disappearing into the underbrush very quickly, but they leave traces of themselves with their dung, which they tend to deposit repeatedly in particular places and cover with leaves, and their tracks. Individual animals tend to create trails to their sources of water, walking the same track over and over again. Clues such as these indicate that in the wild the Asian tapirs live at a density of about 2 per square mile. This means that loss of habitat can seriously harm an Asian tapir population, and may account for some of the difficulties zoos have in breeding them, since keeping them in confined, close quarters is unnatural to them.

An odd aspect of the territories of Asian tapirs is that they overlap. This could indicate that territories were much more important to the ancestors of Asian tapirs than to the Asian tapirs themselves, perhaps even suggesting that Asian tapirs are evolving away from territoriality. On the other hand, the territories may overlap simply because some of the tapir's habitat is limited. For instance, the Asian tapir likes deep water and large swatches of mud; the territories may overlap because all the tapirs of a given region must use a localized deep-water source. The Asian tapirs mark their territories with trails that they follow repeatedly and frequently, and by urinating on plants. Like the rhinoceros, the males have backwards pointing flaccid penises and thus urinate backwards, as do the females. The deposits of urine serve not only to identify territory, but to provide a scent that identifies gender, which seems to be important for mating since tapirs of both genders remain solitary except for mating or when young are with their mothers before adulthood. This may also explain why territories overlap; if they did not, mating could be impeded.

On the other hand, Asian tapirs seem alert to one another even when far apart. Their very acute sense of smell seems to be able to catch whiffs of scents of other tapirs blown on breezes. Further, they can communicate with high-pitched squeals, and seem thus to communicate with each other over miles of terrain. Exactly what such communication expresses is unclear — for mating, perhaps, although the high-pitched noise seem to be used for much more.

Asian tapirs love water. They are very good swimmers and seem especially fond of wide, deep rivers. They are able to be submerged for several minutes at time — again making them hard for humans to observe — and they seem to walk on the bottoms of riverbeds much as hippopotamuses do. They eat underwater plants and gain relief from skin parasites while submerged. Muddy areas serve much the same purpose, relieving the itch from ticks and providing most swamp plants for browsing.

Asian tapirs are herbivores; their preferred foods include grasses, leaves, shoots, and fruit. They feed at night, while walking in unending zig-zag patterns through the forest. They do not strip plants clean; they eat a few leaves from any given plant and then move on, constantly walking and chewing. This prevents depleting their ranges of food; plants are rarely destroyed, and in the tropical jungle can often replenish overnight the leaves or buds they lost during the day.

The animal's mating rituals are still poorly understood: Exactly how Asian tapir's determine when to mate and with whom needs clarification. When they mate, they make a great deal of noise, squealing, whistling, and grunting. They bite one another on the neck and flanks and move about energetically while in coitus. The female is sexually receptive every 2 months. After a gestation period of 14 months, she probably gives birth to only one young — multiple births have not been recorded. The youngster probably takes a year to be weaned, although there is some evidence that this happens much earlier. It is possible that at this time the youngster parts from its mother, but, again, this is a detail that needs clarification through observation. The youngster will reach sexual maturity between 2 and 3 years of age, by which time it may have a territory of its own.

When threatened, Asian tapirs usually run away. However, they can fight, and can offer a nasty bite with their large incisors.

Habitat

The Asian tapir inhabits tropical jungles from Indonesia, through Indochina, and perhaps into southern India. They prefer very dense undergrowth and areas near large bodies of water. Their diet may require a wide variety of vegetation, which would mean that they would prefer regions with a wide diversity of plants. Warmth and humidity seem to be important to them, and zoos in temperate climates need to provide them with indoor accommodations during late fall and winter. How much the cold would adversely affect their health seems to be unknown, although they plainly dislike it.

Distribution

The Asian tapir may once have ranged throughout the tropical areas of Asia and through the islands to the southeast. Now they are restricted to Burma, Cambodia, Indonesia (Sumatra), Laos, Malaya, Thailand, and Vietnam. This range is shrinking rapidly. Logging in particular has shrunk its range in Indonesia, and war and social chaos has led to much destruction in Indochina. It is possible, in spite of good-will efforts to preserve it in most of those countries, that the Asian tapir will be restricted to Malaysia (provided that country is able to keep poachers out of its reserves) by the turn of the 21st century.

Threats

The primary threat to the survival of the Asian tapir is loss of its habitat, primarily to logging and the expansion of human communities, which are presently exploding in size throughout the Asian tapir's ancient range. It probably needs a large range in which to support a good breeding population, and its population is probably quickly affected by the destruction of forestlands. Hunting is also a significant problem. The Asian tapir's skin is thick, yet very supple; it is prized as leather for whips and harnesses. The meat is also edible, and tourists and others have reported seeing Asian tapirs being butchered and sold openly in villages (even at an airport). Hunters use battery-powered lamps and inexpensive small rifles to hunt tapirs at night. The Asian tapir relies somewhat on its protective coloring, which is supposed to fool predators, and thus they make large, immobile targets for hunters who illuminate them with lamps. The hunters can determine during the day where an Asian tapir may be found by discovering its trails that mark its territory and access to water and mud, then return at night to catch the animal. Further, the animal is hard to keep in captivity. Its diet is hard to supply, and it is selective about the foods it eats. The tapir may be one of the endangered species that zoos cannot preserve.

Conservation and Recovery

The Asian tapir has proven very hard to count. There is hope that in Malaysia it may still exist in the thousands. Malaysia has an extensive system of wildlife refuges, and the Asian tapir seems to be doing well in the ones on the island of Borneo. Indonesia's refuges on Sumatra seem to have many Asian tapirs left. Although poaching is a significant problem in both countries, the local people in general are cooperating with efforts to leave the tapirs in peace. In other nations, the plight of the Asian tapir is grim. Vietnam has a wildlife refuge near the old border between South and North Vietnam, but the number of tapirs there, if any, is unclear. Cambodia has terrible social problems of its own, not the least of which was the systematic extermination of the scientists who could have led efforts to preserve the native wildlife. The present government gives indications that it is aware of the value of its natural heritage, meaning there is hope that with social stability will come efforts to protect the tapir. Thailand has good wildlife reserves, although its most densely forested areas are dangerous because of the presence of illegal drug manufacturers and exiled Cambodian guerrillas. The state of affairs for that country's tapirs is hard to determine, but logging must be hurting them. The tapir may well be extinct in Burma.

Mountain Tapir

Tapirus pinchaque

Ron Garrison, San Diego Zoo

Status	Endangered
Listed	June 2, 1970
Family	Tapiridae (Tapirs)
Description	Dark brown fur, sometimes tinted by red, with white cheeks, lips, and ear edges; stands 2.5 feet and weighs 500 to 550 pounds.
Habitat	Mountain forests, 6,500 to 15,000 feet above sea level.
Food	Plants.
Reproduction	Gestation period is 13 months, resulting in a single birth.
Threats	Human and natural (jaguars and mountain lions) predation.
Range	Colombia and Ecuador.

Description

A newborn mountain tapir, *Tapirus pinchaque*, looks much like the young of the other surviving species of tapirs. It has mottled white stripes with occasional spots over a brown background. At birth, the mountain tapir weighs between 9 and 13 pounds. The adult's coat is thick, with dense underfur — adaptations for a cold climate. It coloring is dark brown, perhaps a bit reddish, with white lips, chin, cheeks, and ear edges. This coloring works well as camouflage in the high mountain forests of the Andes, matching the forests' floor cover.

The mountain tapir is a big animal, but is the smallest of the four surviving species of tapir. It reaches about 6 feet in length, from tip of nose to the tail, with the tail adding another 2 to 4 inches. Standing about 2.5 feet at the shoulder and weighing as much as 550 pounds, it looks barrellike, but its short legs can carry it quickly across steep terrain.

Its fingerlike nose is one of its most interesting features. As with other tapirs, the nose is actually a blend of upper lip and nose, with transverse nostrils at the front and the underside extending back several inches before blending into the upper palate. The mountain tapir's sense of smell is acute, and while foraging in the dark, it uses its nose to probe for the smells of food, predators, and the urine markings of other tapirs.

The mountain tapir is extremely rare and therefore is rarely seen and is known primarily by its four-toed and three-toed tracks. The hind legs each have three toes, with each toe having a hoof; behind the hooves is a calloused pad. The forefeet have four toes, one of which is small and rarely used — possibly for climbing. The other toes have hooves, and each forefoot has a calloused pad. The legs and feet are effective not only for walking or running, but for climbing and descending steep inclines.

This species is also known as the Andean tapir and the mountain woolly.

Behavior

Because of it rarity, the mountain tapir has been little observed by naturalists, so much of its behavior in the wild is unknown. They are very solitary creatures who seem to only get together for mating, or when the young are with their mothers. The males fight one another fiercely, sometimes doing great harm to one another, for the opportunity to mate with a receptive female. This makes keeping males penned together in captivity dangerous for the animals. Furthermore, the mountain tapir will eat only select foods, making it very hard for zoos to feed, since those foods may be unique to the Andean forests and unavailable in the temperate climates where many zoos are located.

The other species of tapir are territorial, and the mountain tapir probably is, too, although this is not a certainty. After all, the tapirs evolved in tropical, warm habitats, and the surviving tapirs other than the mountain tapir prefer those habitats, yet the mountain tapir has left the warm habitats for a cold one; it may have changed in its other behaviors, as well.

The tapirs are herbivores who eat primarily grasses. They probably do their eating at night. Along with a keen sense of smell, they have keen hearing. This would be important for hearing movement in the dark of predatory cats, as well as of other tapirs. They make high-pitched whistles, which may indicate to one another whether or not they are interested in mating. When threatened, mountain tapirs usually run away. However, they can fight, and can offer a nasty bite with their large incisors.

Habitat

The mountain tapir lives high up in the Andes of Colombia and Ecuador (although they may be extinct in Ecuador). They tend to stay within the mountain forests, although they sometimes venture above the tree line and will graze on grasses in open areas below the forests.

Distribution

The ancient range of the mountain tapir may once have been extensive, extending throughout the high elevations of the Andes. Now they are restricted to mountains in Colombia and Ecuador. Their range is not especially limited by human populations because they prefer habitats inhospitable to most people. Further, they have existed with Native American populations for eons. Therefore, their range is limited primarily by how accessible it is to hunters.

The numbers of mountain tapirs in the wild are not known, but it is probable that fewer than 100 remain.

Threats

The primary threat to the survival of the mountain tapir is hunting. The meat of the animal sells for high prices, and hunters track down and kill mountain tapirs for the money. Ecuador has tried to curb the hunting, but its mountain tapirs may have vanished by now. Colombia has serious social problems that make it difficult for naturalists to protect mountain tapirs. Those who venture into the tapir's range risk death not only from natural hazards, but from the hunters, drug manufacturers, and terrorists.

Conservation and Recovery

The best hope for the survival of the mountain tapir is in Ecuador's wildlands. Zoos have a small population, but they are proving hard to keep. Their diets are restricted, and their mating rituals are poorly understood. Thus it is hard to feed them and to breed them. On the other hand, much of what little that is known about the mountain tapir comes from the observation of zoo animals.

Brazilian [=South American] Tapir

Tapirus terrestris

Luiz Claudio Marigo

Status	Endangered
Listed	June 2, 1970
Family	Tapiridae (Tapirs)
Description	Weighs 400-550 pounds; coat is gray-brown to gray-black with a mane on their head and shoulders.
Habitat	Prefers woodlands and grasslands with ample water.
Food	Variety of plants but prefers fruits.
Reproduction	Sexual maturity at 2.5 years; gestation period is 14 months long, usually resulting in a single birth.
Threats	Loss of habitat, natural predation, and human predation.
Range	Argentina, Bolivia, Brazil, Colombia, Ecuador, Paraguay, Surinam, and Venezuela.

Description

The Brazilian tapir is the inspiration for the family name *Tapiridae*. In the Native American language Tupi, spoken by a number of tribes in Brazil, the animal is called *tapyra,* which was Latinized into *tapirus*. A newborn Brazilian tapir, *Tapirus terrestris*, looks much like the young of the other surviving species of tapirs. It has mottled white stripes with occasional spots over a brown background. This enables the young tapir to blend in with the forest floor of its natural

habitat. At birth, the Brazilian tapir weighs 9 to 16 pounds (usually near 12 pounds).

Adult Brazilian tapirs vary somewhat in color from gray-brown to black. Their coat is thick. They may be distinguished from the other species of tapirs by their short, narrow mane that runs from the top of their heads to between their shoulders, and by the prominent arch of their heads, created by a high ridge on their skulls.

The Brazilian tapir is not as large as its Old World relative, the Asian tapir (*Tapirus indicus* or *Acracodia indica*; see separate entry), which can reach 8 feet from nose to tail and top 700 pounds. The Brazilian tapir is 6 to 7 feet long and usually about 500 pounds at full maturity. Although its short legs may make it look ungainly, it has a sleek build and has quick reflexes. Its weight, low build, and long front-to-back proportions suggest that it evolved to cope with a densely vegetated rain forest environment in which those qualities enable it to move like a torpedo through dense vegetation the way the Asian tapir does. This lends credence to the view that it evolved north of its present territory in tropical rain forests and then migrated southward to live not only in tropical forests but grasslands and deciduous forests.

The Brazilian tapir's fingerlike nose is one of its most interesting features. As with other tapirs, the nose is actually a blend of upper lip and nose, with transverse nostrils at the front and the underside extending back several inches before blending into the upper palate. The nose is used to pull on branches, bushes, and shoots, and can dislodge loose fruits. The Brazilian tapir's sense of smell is acute, and while foraging in the dark, it uses its nose to probe for the smells of food, predators, the urine markings of other tapirs, and — if it is male — for the scent of females. Its hearing also seems very good, based on observations of the whistling calls of Brazilian tapirs in captivity. Its eyes are not as acute as its sense of smell and hearing; its senses seem to have evolved to be most effective at night, in the dark.

Accurate information about Brazilian tapirs in the wild is hard to come by and much of what is known about them comes from observing them in zoos. The problem stems from the animal's elusiveness and scarcity. Its primary response to danger is to run away, and it usually makes very good use of its environment to disappear before hu-mans can see it. Like other tapirs it is known in the wild primarily by its tracks, which look like those of a rhinoceros. The hind legs each have three toes, with each toe having a hoof; behind the hooves is a calloused pad. The forefeet have four toes, one of which is small and rarely used — possibly for climbing. The other toes have hooves, and each forefoot has a calloused pad. Its hooves are somewhat broader than those found on other species of tapir. The legs and feet are effective not only for walking or running, but for swimming and even walking on river beds while submerged.

Behavior

Brazilian tapirs are solitary creatures and need large areas in which to live in order to maintain a low and, for them, comfortable population density of about 2 tapirs per square mile. Individual animals are detectable through their dung and trails — they tend to create trails to their sources of water, walking the same track over and over again.

The males have backwards pointing flaccid penises and thus urinate backwards; they leave urine markers to attract females. When males and females sense one another's presence (the female perhaps by smelling a male marker), they whistle at each other. What the whistling signifies is not clear because it has been mostly observed in captive animals who are penned much closer to each other than they would be in the wild. The whistling seems to be an important part of determining the suitability of a prospective mate; the sound could carry far in the wilderness and could serve to communicate sexual interest to a faraway prospective mate.

When they mate, they make a great deal of noise by whistling. They bite one another on the neck and flanks and move about energetically while in coitus. The female is sexually receptive every 2 months. After a gestation period of 14 months, the tapirs tend to give birth to only one young, although two occur — but rarely. The youngster takes 10 months to be weaned. The youngster will reach sexual maturity at 2.5, by which time it may have a territory of its own.

Although Brazilian tapirs sometimes populate dry areas, they love water. They are very good swimmers and seem especially fond of wide, deep rivers. This trait probably accounts for how they would have migrated from the north through the Amazon rain forest. The many wide rivers and huge seasonal flooding would be attractive to them and something they could skillfully traverse. They are able to be submerged for several minutes at a time — again making them hard for humans to observe — and they seem to walk on the bottoms of river beds much as hippopotamuses do. They gain relief from skin parasites while in water. Muddy areas serve much the same purpose, relieving the itch caused by parasites.

They are herbivores who eat fruit and graze on grasses. They feed at night while walking in unending zig-zag patterns through their territories. The attraction of fruit and grasses makes them pests for some farmers.

Habitat

The Brazilian tapir has adapted to a variety of warm habitats. It lives in tropical jungles, dry forests, and grasslands, and may be found in dry areas as well as wet ones.

Their diet is somewhat flexible, enabling them to adjust to the variations of vegetation from one habitat to another. Warmth and humidity seem to appeal to them, and zoos in temperate climates need to provide them with warm indoor accommodations during late fall and winter.

Distribution

The Brazilian tapir has had a huge range, from the north coast of South America all the way into the grasslands of Argentina. This range has been shrinking for decades as human beings push wildlife out of their ancient regions. Logging in particular has shrunk its range. However, it is still possible, in spite of the competition from humans and their domesticated animals, to find Brazilian tapirs in the nations to which they are native, including Argentina, Bolivia, Brazil, Colombia, Ecuador, Paraguay, Surinam, and Venezuela.

Threats

The primary threat to the survival of the Brazilian tapir is loss of its habitat, primarily to logging and agriculture. Hunting is also a significant problem. It is a pest for some farmers and ranchers because it may eat their crops and compete with domesticated grazing animals for grass to eat. Thus farmers and ranchers will kill them. For the big cats — jaguars and mountain lions — of the Brazilian tapir's range, the tapir's are a food source.

Conservation and Recovery

Fortunately, the animal breeds well in captivity. Thus zoos and wildlife parks have been able to create a captive breeding population. As is often the case with animals bred in captivity, there must be concern about the possibility that the captive tapirs' genes are too limited and not diverse enough to sustain the population. The listing of the Brazilian tapir in CITES, Appendix II (trade restricted) may help the animal by restricting international trade in it body parts.

The tapir has proven very hard to count, but its population has been declining significantly. There is reason to hope that in the denser jungles of Brazil and Venezuela the tapir can evade the encroachment of human beings and survive in its natural state. The subspecies that live in grasslands or on the east coast of South America may already be doomed to extinction.

Bears

Family: Ursidae

Brown Bear (*Ursus arctos pruinosus*)   USFWS

General Characteristics of the *Ursidae*

The family of *Ursidae* is the family of bears. Bears evolved out of the same stock that gave rise to the family *Canidae*, the dogs, and the skeleton, especially the skull, of the bear resembles that of a dog. The earliest bears probably appeared during the Oligocene epoch about thirty-five million years ago. These early bears were about the size of a fox terrier. Bears proved to be a successful family of carnivores, spreading throughout the Northern Hemisphere, growing in size, and dividing into many species. Eventually, bears invaded the Southern Hemisphere where they did not do as well as they had in the Northern Hemisphere. Only one species of bear (the spectacled bear, *Tremarctos ornatus*) survives in South America. The continent of Africa supported one species of bear into the present era, but it occupied the northernmost region of the continent. Otherwise there are no bears and no fossil record of bears between the Sahara and South Africa; one of the great mysteries of bear evolution is how the now extinct species *Agriotherium*, an Asian bear, five million years ago found its way to South Africa, where remains of several of the bears have been discovered. Most ancient species of bear died out in prehistory, one of which, the cave bear *Ursus spelaus*, may have perished from overhunting by humans in Europe.

At present, bears do not live in high concentrations but are spread out over the Northern Hemisphere and into South America. Most of the surviving bear populations are endangered by habitat loss and overhunting. The largest modern bear is the polar bear, a beast that can weigh over a ton; the polar bear is also the only modern bear that survives entirely on a diet of meat. Most bears eat vegetation such as roots and berries; vegetation comprises about three quarters of their diet. They are carrion eaters and will take advantage of finding a dead animal. They are also quick, clever hunters that will kill small to medium-sized animals such as immature deer if they need to. Otherwise, they eat insects.

Early in their evolution, bears developed plantigrade walking, which is the same sort of walking people have: The entire foot from heel to toe is placed on the ground when walking. Their teeth also changed, differentiating them from other carnivores. Their sheering teeth, designed to slice through meat, have become broad and flat, an adaptation for chewing plants. Only the polar bear is re-evolving sheering teeth out of its molars, probably because it eats only meat. A bear's teeth grow throughout its life, probably an adaptation to the constant wear of the bear's often tough-to-chew food. The teeth create annual layers that can be seen through a microscope. Counting the layers in a tooth will show how old a bear is; especially thin layers indicate years of poor nourishment, whereas especially thick layers indicate years of bountiful food. The claws of bears are not retractable and curve downward. Their forepaws are supple and sensitive and are used to manipulate food, stones, and other parts of their environment, as well as to dig into the ground or into logs in search of food. The giant panda (*Ailuropoda melanoleuca*) has evolved its wrists into digits that function like opposable thumbs, helping it grasp the bamboo it eats. Bears are universally covered with fur, which varies in coloration and thickness from species to species. Although descended from brown bears (*Ursus arctos*), the polar bear has a white coat that is dense; it even has thick fur on the bottom of its feet. Most bears have coats that are fairly uniform in color, with occasional patches of other colors like those found on the Asian black bear (*Selenarctos thibetanus*), but the giant panda has a striking color pattern of large bands and circles of black and white.

The most highly developed sense in bears is smell. Because of their sense of smell, bears are very good trackers, and they can detect the presence of other bears, other animals, and food. When they approach a human, bears will sniff; this tells them the species (in this case *Homo sapiens*), gender, and age of what they are sniffing, as well as whether it has any food. Most bears do not regard humans as food, but they may regard humans as rivals. Humans that seem to behave like bears (for instance, crouching forward to take a photograph looks to a bear like another bear getting ready for combat) can seem like threats to bears, which will then either attack or flee; bears that have been foraging in garbage dumps can have their noses overloaded with foul smells, making it impossible for them to detect and identify a human's odor, increasing a human's danger of being attacked. A bear's hearing is not extraordinary, but a bear can identify a variety of sounds, including, perhaps, the movement of termites or ants in logs or the ground. The eyesight of bears has been much maligned, with many authorities saying that it is very poor, helping to account for why bears sometimes attack humans: A standing human might look like a standing bear to a nearsighted bear, and standing erect on the hind feet can be a threatening posture. Recent tests indicate that bears can see colors, which indicates visual acuity; notions of poor eyesight may stem from bears preferring to sniff and listen before they look.

Hibernation

Bears are often said to "hibernate," a word scientists prefer not to apply to bears. Authorities on bears take pains to point out that in science, hibernation involves a significant lowering of body temperature and slowing of metabolism: A hibernating animal is very hard to revive. Thus, scientists prefer to refer to a bear's "dormancy" rather than hibernation. When a bear is dormant, its body temperature drops a little, but its metabolism remains normal; even so, it not only does not eat but does not urinate or defecate during its dormancy. Not all bears have periods of dormancy; in fact, within a species some bears will become dormant while others will not, and even within subspecies individual animals vary from having a period of dormancy and not having one. In fact, some individual bears will have a period of dormancy one year but not in another. The controlling mechanisms for dormant periods seem to be environment and diet. Bears that live in warm regions may have dens or nests for sleeping and giving birth, but they do not become dormant in them. For the Asian black bear, living on the southern slopes of the Himalayas may mean remaining active all year long, but living to the north where snows fall and the winter temperature is frigid, Asian black bears may become dormant for months at a time. Among most bears, the period of dormancy is used for giving birth. When a female bear has fed poorly during summer and fall, its body will reject its fertilized egg, thus eliminating one of the principal reasons for retiring to a den and lying dormant for several months. Males especially may be up and about during winter if they have had little food during the warm months. Among polar bears, only females den. In other bears, the period of dormancy coincides with the disappearance of plant foods essential to a bear's diet, but polar bears restrict themselves to meat — a year round staple — and they have no annual periods of low availability of food. Thus they are up and active all year, with only pregnant bears needing to pause to give birth and suckle their young.

Reproduction

When bears mate, the female is not immediately impregnated. Instead, her fertilized egg is held in stasis, to be implanted near the end of a good feeding season. If the female bear does not eat well, her body will not implant the egg in her womb. To observers, the period of gestation may appear to be long, over 220 days, but in fact, because the implantation of the fertilized egg comes months after mating, gestation is short. This means that newborn bears are very undeveloped and small and will not have much hair. A pregnant female will den or go into dormancy in part because her cubs need to grow for weeks or months before they can move about on their own. During their mother's dormancy, cubs will suckle and grow in size and grow a fur coat that looks much like that of an adult. Females have the burden of raising cubs, which can take a few years. In most species, adult males may kill and even eat cubs; this seems to be a function of passing on the male's own genes. A female without cubs is eligible for mating, whereas a female with cubs will not be ready for mating until her cubs have grown up and left to live on their own. Thus, mother bears are very touchy animals. They are prepared to defend their cubs vigorously and are determined fighters. Humans, as potential predators, are unwelcome company for mothers with cubs. Once young bears reach sexual maturity, they leave their mothers and find territories of their own. Some naturalists have observed that bears remain close to their siblings and mother, avoiding conflict with them when they might otherwise seek to drive them away.

Territoriality

Bear territoriality is still not well understood, particular among polar bears. In general, bears, including giant pandas, create territories in which other adult members of their gender are unwelcome. Males tend to have large territories, and females tend to have smaller territories within a male's territory. The adult males try to exclude other adult males from their territories, and they will sometimes kill immature males that might someday become rivals. Adult females may exclude other adult females from their territories in order to preserve the foods they need for pregnancy and cub rearing for themselves. In vast ranges encompassing many large territories, bears seem to create hierarchies. These hierarchies are most evident when bears come together in large groups, for instance when brown bears gather for salmon runs. A subtle hierarchy may then be seen, with larger, stronger bears at or near the top, and smaller weaker ones at or near the bottom. Most conflicts are decided by size and strength, with the smaller, weaker animal usually yielding to the other. Young bears may often be seen wrestling with one another, giving each other harmless nips; this play helps to prepare them for the more serious conflicts of adulthood. For instance, a bear may choose not to yield a favored fishing spot to another, more dominant one. Or the bear may need to defend its territory against a rival that is trying to take it over, or it may be that rival, defending itself against a resident bear that is defending its territory. Usually, when serious conflict happens, the tussle is not particularly harmful; one bear shows itself to be larger, stronger, and more determined after a few minutes of wrestling, and the other flees. Sometimes the fighting becomes deadly, with neither bear yielding until one or both are badly wounded.

The Giant Panda

When first observed by a Western scientist, the giant panda was classified as a member of the genus *Ursus*, where it remained for decades. In the 1930s, some scientists questioned the giant panda's classification, noting that its coloration was unique among bears, resembling the coloration of raccoons. Its sixth digit, a wrist bone modified to act like an opposable thumb was also unique among bears. Further, the giant panda seemed to eat no meat, but instead ate the tough to digest bamboo. Studies of the fossil record (and recent genetic studies seem to confirm this) indicate that bears and raccoons share a common ancestor from which the two animal families branched away. Thus, the giant panda was reclassified as a kind of raccoon, and the popular name "panda bear" was discouraged. Then in the 1960s, a titanic study was published (*The Giant Panda: A Morphological Study of Evolutionary Mechanisms,* by D. Dwight Davis) that showed the giant panda's anatomy to be that of a bear, not a raccoon. Even so, many reference books continued to place the giant panda among the raccoons. During the 1980s, genetic studies were conducted that supported Davis's discoveries: the giant panda's genes were those of a bear, not a raccoon. Therefore, most present-day authorities classify the panda as a bear, but readers should note that older reference works may still place the giant panda among raccoons.

The giant panda's distinctive features seem to be products of its antiquity: It parted from other bears during the Pliocene epoch and evolved on its own in China, where it adapted to the large bamboo forests of the time.

North America Species

The Mexican population of the grizzly bear, *Ursus arctos,* has a powerfully built body with a distinctive, large shoulder hump. The animal's head is massive with small, rounded ears and small eyes. The face has a distinctly dished profile because the nose rises abruptly into the forehead. The front feet have long, slightly curved claws for protection and killing prey. Unlike the black bear, these foreclaws are not adapted for climbing trees. The claws on the back feet are only half as long as those on the front feet. The size of this species varies greatly, depending upon location. The male is usually larger than the female.

The brown fur of *U. arctos* has 2 distinct layers. The dense inner fur is shorter than the longer outer guard hair. For protection from the cold, the animal's fur is longer and coarser in the winter. In the summer, the guard hair and old inner fur are shed and the color fades.

These unpredictable animals usually walk slowly, but are capable of moving very quickly when aroused. Females with young are the most aggressive, although any *U. arctos* eating or guarding carrion should be avoided. These very strong animals can cause major injury with a bite or a swipe with their massive, long-clawed paws. *U. arctos* usually don't make much noise, except when wounded, threatened, or attacked. *U. arctos* primarily uses its excellent sense of smell to find food and detect danger, although its hearing is also excellent.

Although not much information is available on the behavior of the extremely rare Mexican population of *U. arctos,* in general, they are solitary animals. However, they are fairly sociable, living in overlapping home ranges without any territorial defenses displayed. Females forage and den with their young. Dominant males forage alone although they try to be near the home ranges of one or more females. The size of the home ranges are largely determined by the distribution of food, although age, sex, social status, and condition of the animal are also factors.

During the breeding season, females mate with one or more males. Several males may follow a female and fight with each other. After mating, the fertilized eggs lay dormant for several months until late fall when active gestation begins. Usually in mid-winter, 1 to 4 cubs are born, after an active gestation period of 6 to 8 weeks. The young are born blind and helpless, only weighing about 0.5 kilograms (1 pound). However, they grow rapidly and by three months weigh about 15 kilograms (33 pounds) with a full set of milk teeth. At birth, the cub's faces are short and rounded, eventually lengthening to the adult shape. Often during the first summer, the young have a whitish V-shaped neck patch that eventually fades by the second year. Cubs remain with their mother for at least the second spring, but often until their third or fourth year. Litter mates may stay together for 2 to 3 years after leaving their mother. Usually *U. arctos* reach sexual maturity at 4 to 6 years; although growth continues after puberty.

Although *U. arctos* do not technically hibernate, they generally spend the coldest part of the winter in a torpid, dormant state. During winters of little snow, some southern populations may sleep briefly or not at all. When they do sleep for the winter, *U. arctos* do not eat, drink, urinate, or defecate in the den. If disturbed, the animal can wake up relatively easily and make a quick escape.

U. arctos undergo certain changes to prepare for a winter sleep. The heart rate decreases from a rate of 40 to 50 beats per minute in the summer to 8 to 10 beats per minute during dormancy. Body temperature decreases 4 to 5 degrees Celsius during this time. While sleeping, *U. arctos* lose a large amount of body fat, with the females losing 40% of their Autumn mass and the males losing 22%. The energy needed for bearing and nursing young is the probable reason for the difference between males and females.

One of the least picky eaters of the animal kingdom, *U. arctos* eats almost anything, from vegetables to meat. Primarily a vegetarian, *U. arctos* usually eats a wide variety of plants, including grasses, herbs, flowers, leaves, roots, bulbs, shrubs, and many types of berries. The animal may not be able to digest fibrous or coarse forage very well. To supplement its diet, *U. arctos* will also eat insects, larvae, grubs, fungi, eggs, nuts, and cones. The animal eats small animals, such as birds and rodents. *U. arctos* will also eat bigger game, especially if the prey is already dead. It usually kills larger animals only when the prey is sick or injured. When living close to humans, the animal may kill domestic animals. *U. arctos* may cache their food to protect it from competitors or to slow decomposition.

U. arctos eating habits vary over the year. Before their winter sleep, the animals greatly increase the amount of food they eat in order to increase body weight and store fat. While in their dens, *U. arctos* do not eat or drink. After emerging from their dens in the spring, the animals normally do not eat for 10 to 14 days. Then, they need to eat and drink or they lose muscle tissue, suffer from dehydration, and become uremic.

U. arctos mainly feed in the cool of the evening and in the morning. During the day, the animals shelter in areas of dense cover or sometimes in a shallow excavation.

Giant Panda

Ailuropoda melanoleuca

David L. Chesemore

Status	Endangered
Listed	January 23, 1984
Family	Aeloropidae (Pandas)
Description	Dense black and white fur; about 4 feet in length with short legs.
Habitat	Native bamboo forests.
Food	Arrow bamboo and plants in the wild; cereal, milk, vegetables, and meat in captivity.
Reproduction	One cub weighing 3 to 4 ounces.
Threats	Hunting and collecting; loss of arrow bamboo.
Range	China: Western Regions.

Description

There are no known near-relatives to the giant panda. The giant panda, *Ailuropoda melanoleuca,* is conspicuously patterned black and white. This coloration functions as a protective measure in contrasting elements of snow and shadows. The giant panda is about 4 feet in length and weighs around 300 pounds. Its legs are strong and short. The forelegs are more powerful than the hind legs. The fur of this species is dense and thick and feels oily. The dense fur serves to keep the animal warm, and the oiliness prevents water from penetrating the skin. The feet are plantigrade, like those of a bear. Other physical characteristics are short ears, tail, and snout; a broad skull; and long claws. The head and forepaw are specialized for the handling of bamboo. The skull, which is comprised of the typical carnivorous dentition, has been modified for crushing and grinding food. The famous "Pandas thumb" is a modified wrist bone to serve in gripping. This species has been thought to be a true "bear" and disputes over its status are still ongoing. Many believe that the morphology of the teeth indicate this species to be more closely related to a raccoon than *Ursidae.*

Behavior

The giant panda probably mates in spring. The physiology of its reproductive characteristics has been studied more closely in captive specimens. Gestation of these captive pandas varies from 97 to 165 days. Implantation of the fertilized eggs is delayed; after implantation the young develops in utero for 45 to 60 days. The young are born fully developed, blind, nearly naked and almost helpless. Weight of the newborns varies from 3 to 4 ounces. Parturition in the wild occurs in January and results in one cub (twins are rare, triplets exceptional). By April the cub has milk teeth and weighs about 3 pounds and gains about 5 pounds a month until it is a year old. Maturation occurs between 4 and 10 years. Although most litters contain two cubs, the mother is able to care for only one, and she abandons the second cub which, in the wild, dies.

Food in the wild is believed to consist solely of arrow bamboo. However pandas have been known to eat over 25 wild plant species including: *Equisetum hiemale*, *Ligusticum sinense*, *Heracleum caudianus*, *Aster alpina*, *Allium*, *Saussurea*, *Notopterygium*, *Houtinyxia cordata*, and pandas certainly supplement or replace their diet of arrow bamboo when it is unavailable. In captivity, the giant panda has a varied diet that may be composed of cereal, milk, vegetables, orange juice and meat. The presence of claws may imply a carnivorous behavior (thought to be fish), but this has not been demonstrated.

The giant panda's food dictates nightly feedings for several hours to meet energy needs. Schaller observed that the giant panda was most likely to be active just before dawn from 4:00 a.m. to 6:00 a.m., and in the late afternoon between 4:00 p.m. to 7:00 p.m. The giant panda is most inclined to rest during the hours of 8:00 a.m. and 9:00 a.m. and around 7:00 p.m. just after dusk.

Habitat

The giant panda inhabits the native bamboo forests in the mountains of western China. It is found in forested areas where large trees are present that are suitable for scent-marking and shelter. Huge hollow trees are often used for maternity dens. The elevation is 6,000 to 12,000 feet. The annual precipitation exceeds 59 inches. The area of Yaoji is gentler and more arid than the mountainous Baoxing.

Distribution

The giant panda appeared during the Pleistocene era. The past range extended from parts of Burma, much of eastern China, and near Beijing. It is known from west central China in Wolong, Sichuan (most pandas occur in this province), and Gansu. Several natural reserves have been set aside which pandas occupy. They are Wolong, Wanglang, Jiuzhaigou, and Tangjiahe Natural Reserve.

A census in 1975 estimated the numbers of individuals in the wild to be 1050 to 1100. The 1997 estimate was about 1,000. The density of pandas in reserves is about one animal per 9.3 to 10.7 square kilometers. There are about 60 to70 species in zoos and forest department installations in China. Little is known about the reproductive rate, longevity, and mortality rate of the giant panda in the wild. Captive pandas have been known to live up to 30 years.

Threats

The giant panda is a highly specialized eater, preferring arrow bamboo. This plant flowers only every hundred years or so. In recent times this "mass-flowering" has caused the flower to die after seeding, and this phenomenon has caused widespread starvation of wild giant pandas. Pandas will supplement their diet with other foods, and they have been able to survive for many centuries even when the arrow bamboo supply has decreased.

The food supply problem, however, has been compounded by increased human population around giant panda habitat. While the isolated habitat itself has not been destroyed, the freedom of the panda to move from one habitat to another has been restricted by human settlements, thus restricting the panda's freedom to search for alternative food resources in more abundant areas.

Conservation and Recovery

As early as 1946 the Chinese people were aware of the declining status of giant panda. In 1957, the Third National People's Congress established forest reserves. In 1962, panda hunting was banned.

The Chinese Government is sometimes unwilling to work with foreign conservation organizations. The World Wildlife Fund International spent much time and effort in the direction of preservation of the panda; at times the Chinese government was uncooperative and efforts came to a standstill. In 1983 in a effort to prevent the starvation of pandas in Baoxing county during a mass-flowering of bamboo, refuge camps and rehabilitation stations were constructed. But World Wildlife Fund professionals were not allowed to oversee the project.

Captive breeding programs have been established in a number of zoos worldwide, but they have been largely unsuccessful. The species is so rare in captivity that zoos may have only one individual, or a pair of individuals that aren't well suited to mate. Females who are dependent on humans may not accept a male animal or may refuse a male who is too aggressive. Some males have not been able to adopt the correct mating posture. Breeders have attempted to overcome some of these mating problems with artificial insemination, but that has not proven very successful either.

American Black Bear

Ursus americanus

Louisiana Department of Wildlife and Fish

Status	Threatened
Listed	January 7, 1992
Family	Ursidae (Bears)
Description	Usually black but may be brown, gray, or white; hair is short.
Habitat	Very diverse habitat, from hot to cold, from arid to humid; prefers woodlands but also inhabits open plains and tundra.
Food	Grasses, grains, fruits, seeds, nuts, honey, insects, fish, birds, small mammals, and carrion. It seems to prefer berries, honey, and ants.
Reproduction	Usually two young.
Threats	Hunting by humans for trophies, commercial sale of body parts, loss of habitat.
Range	Canada, Mexico, U.S.

Description

The adult American black bear, *Ursus americanus*, is between four and six feet long, with a tail that is four to five inches long. It stands 2.5 to 3 feet at the shoulder. It weighs between 250 and 350 pounds, although larger ones have been occasionally reported. The American black bear's hair is usually short and black, but this varies among the bear's many subspecies. Common variations are brown and gray, although orange, and in the case of the Kermode bear (*Ursus kermodei*, also called the ghost-bear) that live in British Columbia, white or cream colored. The American black bear has sharp, somewhat curved claws on its forepaws that its uses for climbing trees and digging dens.

Behavior

Perhaps the most common image of the American black bear is one of it clinging high up on a tree trunk. The American black bear climbs trees to escape predators (which would be humans, brown bears [*Ursus arctos*], other American black bears, and possibly cougars) and to find food such as seeds, nuts, honeys, and bees. The American black bear is quick and agile for its size, and it can run fast if it chooses. The old adage that a person should flee an American black bear by running downhill because the bear has trouble running downhill appears to be untrue; the bear can outrun a human being over a short distance, even down, up, or along a hill.

It is an intelligent, sometimes thoughtful animal that avoids trouble as much as it can; it avoids humans and is very good at hiding from them. A mother bear with young to protect may mistake a human being for a dangerous male bear that may kill her young, and she will charge the human the way she would another bear. Even when American black bears confront each other, they rarely seriously injure one another; they are adept at swatting with their paws without using their claws. When a human annoys an American black bear, the bear may respond with a swat of the heal of a forepaw; the human would be well advised to leave at that moment. When American black bears and humans conflict in parks and reserves, it is usually because the human is ignorant of the bear's instincts for survival. For instance, a crouching human resembles the posture of a bear about to charge; the American black bear's inevitable response to this is to charge first. The American black bear is also motivated to take food wherever it finds it; its ability to eat almost anything has been crucial to its survival as a species. It will chase away humans, tear through tents, and even peel off car doors to get at the tasty treats humans have brought.

The American black bear favors berries and ants in its diet, but its legendary love of honey is true, and it will endure bee stings in order to have its fill of the amber liquid. It also eats a wide variety of vegetation, including seeds, nuts, roots, grains, and grasses. It seems to have trouble digesting grasses. It will kill and eat small game such as fish, birds, and rodents, and it will sometimes feed off carrion. Large animals usually do not suit it, and it only very rarely preys on hoofed animals or livestock.

The American black bear's climate is varied, but it usually features a cold season, winter. The bear spends summer and fall bulking up as best it can on the food available. Scarcity of food during summer and fall may doom an individual bear during winter. During the winter, the American black bear "hibernates." Most naturalists agree that what happens with the bear is not true hibernation because the bear's body does not undergo the severe changes of lowered body temperature and drastically slowed metabolism that true hibernation requires. Instead, the bear enters its den, usually among roots or under rocks, and enters a torpid state in which its metabolism slows a little but from which it can awaken quickly. American black bears that have been disturbed or did not feed enough before winter can be up and about even in deep winter snows.

Habitat

The American black bear requires large ranges; at its densest, the American black bear population reaches no more than 2 bears per square mile. Usually, the density is much lower; the higher densities, found in the United States, may reflect the bears being pressured into unnaturally small territories by the loss of habitat to logging, agriculture, and expanding human communities. The American black bear is highly adaptable, and may be found in lowland and highland forests, open brushlands, and even swamps.

Distribution

The American black bear has a wide distribution from central northern Mexico, through the central and western United States, through central Canada, and west into eastern and central Alaska. This immense range was once even larger, extending into the eastern United States and Canada.

Threats

In western United States and the western provinces of Canada, the American black bear is being slaughtered by commercial poachers. The bears are killed, then dressed and shipped overseas to serve the East Asian market for folk medicines; bear parts are thought to be aphrodisiacs and to alleviate some human ailments. All of this hunting is illegal throughout the bear's range, from Mexico to Canada, but the hunters are ruthless. In Canada and the United States, some of them have formed gangs and become organized crime; they put the lives of rangers and customs officials at risk.

Mostly in Canada, the American black bear is sometimes hunted for food, even though the bear's parasites pose a serious health risk to people who eat its meat. It is also hunted as a trophy animal. In the United States, permits are sometimes granted for the hunting of American black bears. Hunting without permits is illegal. Occasionally, unscrupulous people will trap and capture American black bears and keep them on ranches to be shot for a high price by visitors;

the bears are usually sick and wounded and incapable of running away or fighting. They may even be tied to a stake so that they cannot move.

In western North America hunting by humans is the greatest danger to the survival of American black bears, since even state and national parks, forests, and reserves offer no protection from humans willing to break the law. In the American Southwest, Midwest, and South, the American black bear also faces pressures from encroaching human developments. People need places to live and food to eat, so swamps are drained, trees cut down, and land cleared so that farms may be established and living communities built. Much of the American black bear's traditional range has been logged and is still being logged for timber for building and pulp for paper products. The loss of the land deprives bears of the environment they need to survive, so some of them starve. Increasingly, the clearing of lands inhabited by bears has created a modern relationship between bears and humans; the bears try to inhabit human communities. They are very good at hiding, and often only their track shows that they are living nearby, but they can frighten people by wandering into their yards looking for food). Usually people find the presence of American black bears too threatening and the bears are either captured and moved to protected forestlands far away or are killed. When food is scarce, as it is during a drought, or when there just is not enough room for all the bears that need it, American black bears move into human communities.

Conservation and Recovery

The American black bear population is so

diverse that it is hard to pin down just what it needs to survive. Most of the American black bear's subspecies are in imminent threat of extinction, and the threats are increasing at such a rate that it is possible only some American black bears in Alaska and northern Canada will survive for another generation, even though, at present, there are some healthy populations in protected American wilderness. In the United States, the American black bear is protected by a complex group of laws that govern how and when it may be hunted and that set aside lands for the bear to live undisturbed. The American black bear is further helped by changing attitudes of Americans toward it; still considered a pest by some, others see the American black bear as symbolic of America's frontier heritage, as well as a playful and unassuming animal that represents little threat to humans. This positive attitude can help save the animals because it motivates people to look for ways to help the bears, rather than kill them.

Canada protects its American black bears under law, although hunting may be permitted. The bears in Canada face the same problems that those in the United States do, but some of their range in Canada is remote enough that some bears escape human pressures. In Mexico, the American black bear is protected by law from hunting and capture. The American black bears in Mexico are particularly adept at evading humans.

The American black bear is listed in CITES, Appendix II: Trade Restricted.

Brown Bear (Italian population)

Ursus arctos arctos

Potawatomi Zoo

Status	Endangered
Listed	June 24, 1976
Family	Ursidae (Bear)
Description	Massive head and small, rounded ears and eyes, with a dished profile in its face; the front feet have long, slightly curved claws.
Habitat	Tundra, alpine meadows, forests and coastlines in the Italian Alps.
Food	Wide variety of plants, including grasses, herbs, flowers, leaves, roots, bulbs, shrubs, and berries.
Reproduction	Litter sizes range from 1 to 4.
Threats	Hunting; low populations and low reproduction rate.
Range	Italy

Description

The brown bear, *Ursus arctos arctos*, has a powerfully built body with a distinctive, large shoulder hump. The animal's head is massive with small, rounded ears and small eyes. The face has a distinctly dished profile because the nose rises abruptly into the forehead. The front feet have long, slightly curved claws for protection and killing prey. Unlike the black bear, these foreclaws are not adapted for climbing trees. The claws on the back feet are only half as long as on the front.

The size of this large bear varies greatly, depending upon the location. In southern Europe, the brown bear tends to be smaller, with some populations only averaging 154 pounds. In contrast, the brown bear on Kodiak island can weigh up to 1,716 pounds. The male is usually larger than the female.

The brown fur has two distinct layers. The dense inner fur is shorter than the longer outer guard hair. For protection from the cold, the animal's fur is longer and coarser in the winter. In the summer, the guard hair and old inner fur are shed and the color fades.

These unpredictable animals usually walk slowly, but are capable of moving very quickly when aroused. Females with young are the most aggressive, although any brown bears eating or guarding carrion should be avoided. These very strong animals can cause major injury with a bite or a swipe with their massive, long-clawed paws. The brown bear usually doesn't make much noise, except when wounded, threatened, or attacked. It primarily uses its excellent sense of smell to find food and detect danger, although its hearing is also excellent.

Brown bears are solitary animals, although they may live in overlapping home ranges without any territorial defenses displayed. Females forage and den with their young. Dominant males forage alone although they try to be near the home ranges of one or more females. The size of the home ranges are largely determined by the distribution of food, although age, sex, social status, and condition of the animal are also factors.

During the breeding season, females mate with one or more males. Several males may follow a female and fight with each other. Although the breeding season is mid-May to July, the fertilized eggs lay dormant until late November when active gestation begins. In January to March, 1 to 4 young are born after an active gestation period of 6 to 8 weeks. The young are born blind and helpless, only weighing about 1 pound. However, they grow rapidly and by three months weigh about 33 pounds with a full set of milk teeth. At birth, the cub's faces are short and rounded, eventually lengthening to the adult shape. Often during the first summer, the young have a whitish V-shaped neck patch that eventually fades by the second year. Cubs remain with their mothers at least through the second spring, but often until their third or fourth year. Litter mates may stay together for 2 to 3 years after leaving their mother. Usually brown bears reach

sexual maturity at 4 to 6 years; although growth continues after puberty.

Although the brown bear does not technically hibernate, it generally spends the coldest part of the winter in a torpid, dormant state. During winters of little snow, some southern populations may sleep briefly or not at all. When they do sleep for the winter, brown bears do not eat, drink, urinate, or defecate in the den. If disturbed, the animal can wake up relatively easily and make a quick escape.

The bears' bodies undergo certain changes to prepare for a winter sleep. While sleeping, brown bears lose a large amount of body fat, with the female losing 40% of her autumn mass and the males losing 22%. The energy needed for bearing and nursing young is the reason for the difference between males and females.

U. a. arctos is one of many subspecies of the holarctic brown bear, *Ursus arctos*. Hall and Ellerman and Morrison-Scott distinguish nine subspecies from the New World and seven from the Old World.

Behavior

One of the least selective eaters of the animal kingdom, the brown bear eats almost anything, from vegetables to meat. Primarily a vegetarian, it prefers to eat a wide variety of plants, including grasses, herbs, flowers, leaves, roots, bulbs, shrubs, and many types of berries. The animal may not be able to digest fibrous or coarse forage very well. To supplement its diet, the brown bear will also eat insects, larvae, grubs, fungi, eggs, nuts, and cones. It eats small animals, such as birds and rodents. It will also eat bigger game, especially if already dead. It usually kills larger animals only when the prey is sick or injured. When living close to humans, the bear may kill domestic animals. Brown bears may cache their food to protect it from competitors or to slow decomposition.

The brown bears's eating habits vary over the year. Before its winter sleep, the animal greatly increases the amount of food it eats in order to increase body weight and store fat. While in its den, it does not eat or drink. After emerging from its den in spring, the brown bear does not normally eat for 10 to 14 days. Then, it needs to eat and drink or it loses muscle tissue, suffers from dehydration, and becomes uremic.

The brown bear mainly feeds in the cool of the evening and in the morning. During the day, the animal shelters in areas of dense cover or sometimes in a shallow excavation.

Habitat

The Italian population of the brown bear is mainly restricted to scattered woodlands in the Italian Alps. Throughout its range, the brown bear lives in a wide variety of habitats including tundra, alpine meadows, forests and coastlines.

In the winter, the brown bear usually digs its own den and lines it with dry vegetation. In southern regions, the brown bear builds its den on north-facing slopes as protection against mid-winter thaws and flooding. In general, it prefers well-drained den sites on a sheltered slope, either under the roots of a large tree or under a big stone. The animal may use the den for several years.

Distribution

Historically, *U. a. arctos* lived in a wide variety of locations throughout the Old World. Now, however, the Italian population of the brown bear is restricted to one location in the Trentino Alps and another in Abruzzo National Park. Other populations of the brown bear still exist in Eurasia, although their ranges have diminished.

Threats

Since the brown bear has been known to kill humans, the animal has been ruthlessly hunted for centuries. Problems usually occur in areas where humans encroach on the animal's habitat. The animal normally avoids humans, but will attack when provoked, especially a mother protecting her cubs or an animal protecting its food cache. Hunting for its pelt and to protect livestock are other reasons for the decline in this subspecies.

Conservation and Recovery

The Italian population of the brown bear is protected in the Abruzzo National Park in Italy.

Kamchatka Bear

Ursus arctos beringianus

Alan Shoemaker

Status	CITES, Appendix II
Family	Ursidae (Bears)
Description	A huge bear with long legs, broad shoulders, and a broad, long head that is somewhat flatish on its forehead. Its fur is long and black.
Habitat	Extremely cold tundra.
Food	Seeds of coniferous trees; fish, birds, stranded whales, seals.
Reproduction	Usually 2 cubs after gestation lasts 6 to 7 months.
Threats	Hunting by humans.
Range	Russia: Kamchatka Peninsula

Description

Both male and female Kamchatka bear, *Ursus arctos beringianus*, are among the largest of bears. Adults are often longer than 9 feet from nose to tail, stand over 4 feet high at the shoulder, and weigh over 1,500 pounds, making them similar in size to Kodiak bears and just a little smaller than the largest polar bears (now known to grow larger than even Kodiak bears, once believed to be the largest). It is powerfully built, with long legs and broad shoulders. Its head is broad, long, and somewhat flatish on its forehead. Its fur is long and black (although a short-haired variant has been reported).

The Kamchatka bear is a legendary figure among the indigenous peoples of the Kamchatkan Peninsula, and scientists have yet to sort out all of the fact from the fiction. According to local people, the bears are known to grow to 2,500 pounds in size, but these incredibly huge animals live in the densest parts of the forest and are therefore hard for humans to find. One scientist has reported seeing a bear skin of enormous size, covered with short black hair. He also found very large footprints and a large skull that suggests the Kamchatka bears may well grow larger than has so far been observed; perhaps he found the remains of another subspecies of brown bear and not the Kamchatka bear.

Behavior

The Kamchatka bear is a somewhat mysterious animal because it lives in a remote region that is very inhospitable to humans. It is a solitary animal that seems at home in both coniferous forests and open tundra. Males and females establish large territories for themselves, with male and female territories overlapping, but with neither gender tolerant of members of the same sex in its range. Males will drive off adult males, apparently even ones it has sired, and will kill them if they do not leave. Females breed only a few times in a lifetime, and they often have their young with them when hunting. At about 4 years of age, the young leave their mother and move into new territories. Males will sometimes fight for the right to mate with a receptive female; these conflicts can result in serious injuries for both animals.

The seeds of coniferous trees form the bulk of the diet of the Kamchatka bear, making it somewhat dependent on the survival of the primeval forest on Kamchatka; it probably eats fruit when it can find some. It is known to fish, probably mostly for salmon, and to hunt birds and seals. It is likely that it will also kill and feed on stranded whales. While an important part of the bear's diet, all this meat may make up only about 20% of its total diet. Like other members of the brown bear (*Ursus arctos*) species, the Kamchatka bear builds up a reserve of fat that sustains it during hibernation.

Habitat

The habitat of the Kamchatka bear is very cold; in winter the temperature is about 75 degrees Fahrenheit below freezing, and the ground is free of frost no more than two months per year. The forest was once much larger than it is now; its timber was an important source of international currency for the

Soviet Union, and it remains such for the Russian Republic. The bear shares its environment with many exotic species of animal, including the Siberian tiger. There is at least one recorded conflict between a bear and a tiger, and in spite of its great size and strength, the bear is recorded to have been driven off by the tiger.

Distribution

The Kamchatkan Peninsula of Russia seems to be the entire range of the bear. At the present time there is a large enough population of the Kamchatkan bear to sustain its numbers and it is not endangered, but bears are pressured worldwide and the condition of this species should continue to be monitored.

Threats

The Kamchatka bear is still hunted for sport. During the era of the Soviet Union, high communist party officials would be taken on special hunts in the forest of Kamchatka, and they would kill bears. Although the Russian government is trying to put a stop to them, poachers hunt the bears and other wildlife on Kamchatka. The bear is valued as a trophy animal, and its fur for clothing and rugs. Bear parts are highly valued in folk medicine in Southeast Asia, and it is possible (but not certain) that the bear is hunted to be sold in Southeast Asia markets.

Conservation and Recovery

Russia has made much of protecting the

remaining forest on the Kamchatkan Peninsula, but the chaos that resulted from the
break up of the Soviet Union has made policing the forest very difficult. Poachers have
better equipment than the forest rangers,
although Russia has been increasing the
number of rangers by employing former
military personnel whose combat experience
may prove valuable in putting an end to the
poaching. The rangers need modern all-ter-
rain vehicles and better equipment overall.
Much of the ecology of the bear's range is still
poorly understood and stands in need of
more study so that the needs of its wildlife
can be properly understood.

The Kamchatka bear is listed in CITES,
Appendix II, meaning that by treaty international trade in the bear or its parts must be
regulated by the government and must be
overseen by international conservation
groups to be sure that the animal's survival is
not threatened.

Mexican Silver Grizzly

Ursus arctos nelsoni

Ursus arctos horribilis   Jan O. Murie

Status	Endangered (Probably extinct)
Listed	June 2, 1970
Family	Ursidae (Bears)
Description	Medium-size, silver-colored bear with a huge head, small ears, and a distinctive shoulder hump.
Habitat	All territories in Mexico including tropical rain forests, temperate grasslands, and mountains.
Food	Plants, fruit, and insects; occasionally carrion and small mammals.
Reproduction	From 1 to 3 (usually 2) cubs every three years.
Threats	Hunting and trapping.
Range	Mexico

Description

Once the largest animal native to Mexico, the Mexican silver grizzly, *Ursus arctos nelsoni*, weighed an average of 700 pounds. It measured 6 feet from nose to tail. The Mexican grizzly has a huge head, small ears, and a distinctive shoulder hump. Its brown coat varies in shades, and gives off a silvery cast.

Behavior

The home ranges of adult bears frequently overlap. The home ranges of adult male grizzlies are generally two to four times larger than that of females. Adult male black bear's home ranges are also significantly larger than the home ranges of females. The home ranges of both grizzly and black bear females appear to be smaller while they are with cubs, but ranges expand when the young are yearlings in order to meet increased foraging demands.

Bears usually disperse as subadults, however, the pattern of dispersal is not well documented. Dispersing young males apparently leave their mother's home range and their dispersal may be mediated by the avoidance of the home ranges of established adults. This increases their susceptibility to mortality and human/bear conflict by finding and utilizing unnatural food sources. Young females may establish a home range soon after family breakup, often within the vicinity of their mother's home range. Grizzly bear mothers may tolerate female offspring and may shift their home range to accommodate them.

Sexual maturity of the Mexican grizzly is reached at 4 to 5 years, although full growth is not completed until 8 to 10 years. Females give birth every 2 to 3 years, usually to 1 or 2 cubs, although multiple births have been recorded. Cubs remain under the care of their mothers for about 2 years.

The Mexican silver grizzly is omnivorous and feeds on a wide variety of nuts, acorns, roots, shrubs, insects, honey, and mammals.

Habitat

The species inhabited Mexico which is characterized by 3 distinct habitat regions: tropical rain forest, temperate grassland, and mountainous.

The foothill regions of this area are characterized by temperate grassland, but, heading up the mountains, this gives way to boreal forest and then tundra. On lower slopes, animals thrive on the rich vegetation. Higher up, however, larger predators are rare due to the cold, wind, and lack of prey. The Mexican silver grizzly probably inhabited the middle to lower elevations and rarely ventured as high as the tundra.

Distribution

This species once ranged over the entire western half of the North American continent.

Its range ran the entire length of the Rocky Mountains. It was considered abundant in 1855 when the boundary between the U.S. and Mexico was being surveyed, and it was particularly abundant in the San Luis Mountains. In 1892, when the second boundary survey was undertaken, the Mexican silver grizzly was still abundant in the San Luis Mountains but it was disappearing in Arizona and California. By 1932 the last specimens in the U.S. and Sierra Madre were killed. The last known population occurred about 50 miles north of the city of Chihuahua where 20 to 30 animals survived in 1965. That population has since disappeared.

Threats

This species has been the victim of steady and gradual extirpation by humanity since the first northward march of the conquistador Coronado in 1540, which traversed native habitats from Mexico City to the Seven Cities of Cibloa in New Mexico and into the plains of Texas and Kansas. The Mexican silver grizzly once roamed the entire western half of North America from the Arctic to northern Mexico, its territory running the length of the Rocky Mountains. The subspecies declined because of hunting, trapping, and poisoning by humans.

Conservation and Recovery

The subspecies was last reliably reported in 1964; however, in 1977 naturalists conducting a habitat survey reported seeing several bears in Chihuahua, Mexico that may be Mexican silver grizzlies. If they still survive, they are protected under Mexican law. If any wander into the United States, they are protected under American law.

Horse [=Brown] Bear

Ursus arctos pruinosus

USFWS

Status	Endangered
Listed	June 14, 1976
Family	Ursidae (Bears)
Description	Large, usually brown, and has a shoulder hump; in winter it is coarse and shaggy, but in warmer weather it is shed in patches until the fur is short and dense.
Habitat	Cool to cold forestlands, mostly in mountainous terrain, although it will inhabit forested flatlands.
Food	Roots, grains, flowers, buds, fruit, berries, carrion, birds, mammals.
Reproduction	One to four young, usually two.
Threats	Loss of habitat; hunting by humans.
Range	Tibet and the western provinces of China.

Description

The horse bear, *Ursus arctos pruinosus*, is an impressive animal both in its size and in its ferocity when threatened. Of the brown bear species (*Ursus arctos*), the horse bear is one of the smaller subspecies; adults grow longer than 7 feet from nose to tail, stand over 3 feet at the shoulder, and weigh over 500 pounds (as opposed to the Kodiak bear, *Ursus arctos middendorffi*, which reaches 10 feet in length, 5 feet at the shoulder, and reaches over 1,700 pounds), with males somewhat larger on average than females. Typical of the brown bear species, it has a long nose, a long face, and rounded ears. It claws are unsuited to tree climbing, but are long and curved and well suited to fighting and to digging (for roots or to create a den).

The horse bear's fur is brown; in winter it is coarse and shaggy, but in warmer weather it is shed in patches until the fur is short and dense. The winter coat tends to have a richer brown color than the summer one, which is paler.

Behavior

The social behavior of horse bears seems to be more relaxed than for most other brown bears. Although males and females have their own individual territories, these territories overlap considerably and the bears do not seem to mind the intrusion of others of their subspecies unless food is in short supply or one of them is a mother with cubs to protect. Human agriculture and settlements often severely reduce the food supply and often intrude into a mother bear's territory, which is why the bears often attack humans that intrude into their territories.

Typically, females are more aggressive than males, with males usually fighting only for access to sexually receptive females. When hungry, the bear can be very aggressive, and it is very protective of any food that it has found. If the food is carrion or a kill, it will discourage other bears from approaching the food, although larger, socially dominant males may force access to the food. If the kill is livestock, humans may appear to be threats to the bear's food. The horse bear is a quick moving predator, capable of sudden movement and sharp slaps with its forepaws, belying its usually slow, ambling gait when moving through the forest. It is very strong, and can kill most prey with one blow.

The horse bear's diet is highly varied and is adapted to what is available. The bear will eat almost anything, including fruits, grains, seeds, fungi, and roots, as well as carrion. When it hunts, the horse bear prefers small game, but it will kill large animals such as deer if other sources of food are in short supply. It usually feeds at dawn or dusk, resting in ground cover or its den much of the rest of the time.

The horse bear tends to mate in May, June, or July. A sexually receptive female may attract more than one male suitor. The males may then fight for the opportunity to mate with her, doing great harm to each other. It is possible that these conflicts help shape the bear's social order, helping to determine the relative dominance of the males. A fertilized egg does not become active until November, when a short period of gestation begins, resulting in a birth in January or perhaps February. The resulting young are small, about one pound, but grow rapidly. Births almost always result in two young, but one, three, or even four are possible. The life-cycle of the horse bear is not well known, but it seems that cubs take more than 2½ years to be fully weaned and reach sexual maturity at over 4 years of age, although they may part company from their mothers after 3 years. This means that female bears cannot breed often in their lifetimes (as much as 20 years barring illness or injury).

The horse bear will "hibernate" (many naturalists dispute whether the bear's dormant state is true hibernation) in cold winter months, but is known not to hibernate at all if the weather remains relatively warm. They are quick to waken from their dormant state and can be very aggressive when disturbed. To successfully "hibernate" the horse bear needs a large reserve of fat, so it must eat voraciously before winter and its snows arrive. Horse bears prefer to dig their dens under rocks or trees on mountain slopes.

Habitat

The horse bear prefers to live in cool forests, mostly in mountainous terrain, although it may be found in flatlands that otherwise meet its needs. The forests should have a great deal of vegetation, especially berries and roots. The bear prefers rocky terrain for its dens.

Distribution

The horse bear was once a widely distributed animal, with a range extending through the Tibetan mountains, the Tibetan Plateau, and into western China. As humans have pressed it out of its ancient range, it has been able to survive by being an opportunistic feeder and being able to adapt whatever its remaining territory offers. It now exists in small, dispersed populations, mostly in the mountains.

Threats

The greatest threat to the horse bear is encroaching agriculture. China is expanding farms up into the mountains flanking the Tibetan Plateau, taking over traditional horse bear territory, pushing the bears into ever more restricted and fragmented ranges. The bear is greatly feared by local people, and naturalists say that it kills as many as 1,500 people per year. In general, China does not allow its people to have firearms, so when farms expand into a bear's territory, the farmers have only farm implements with which to defend themselves against a large, ferocious, and angry bear that by instinct is compelled to defend its food supply.

The danger to humans posed by the horse bear is one reason it historically has been hunted. Another reason is that it poses a threat to livestock. At present, poaching is a significant threat to the bear's survival; its pelt is highly valued as a decorative rug, and its body parts are used in Southeast Asian folk medicines.

The bear once had a large and continuous range in a mountainous region that is inhospitable to humans, but the pressures of China's enormous human population have pressed the government to move large populations of people into previously sparsely inhabited areas and to farm areas previously avoided by humans. Millions of Chinese have been moved into Tibet and the adjacent Chinese provinces. The result of all this human activity and movement has been to break up the horse bear's range into small regions. Not only has this reduced the population of the bear, which — no matter how intimidating it may be — must inevitably lose in confrontations with humans, but it has fragmented the breeding population. It takes years for bears to breed and rear young, so they need a large, unbroken population to successfully sustain their breeding population. Most of the horse bear population, perhaps all of it, will die out in the next decade because males and females will not be able to mix enough to breed.

Conservation and Recovery

The horse bear needs a range that is protected from human intrusion. At present, it is treated as a pest and is in imminent danger of extinction, with individual bears too isolated from one another to breed.

The horse bear is listed in CITES: Appendix I: Trade Prohibited.

Asian Black Bear

Ursus [=Selenarctos] thibetanus

Rich Block

Status	Endangered
Listed	June 14, 1976
Family	Ursidae (Bears)
Description	Purplish-black, sometimes reddish brown fur is usually shaggy and extra-long hair on its neck and shoulders; head is short and rounded, featuring large round ears.
Habitat	Prefers forests but may be found in brushlands where there is heavy ground cover.
Food	Nuts, seeds, fruits, and bark of trees, but will eat berries, grain, insects, birds, mammals, and carrion.
Reproduction	Usually two cubs.
Threats	Loss of habitat and hunting.
Range	Japan, Russia, China, Laos, Tibet, India, and Nepal.

Description

Adult Asian black bears, *Ursus thibetanus,* measure from 4.5 feet to 5.5 feet in length. Males tend to be bigger than females, weighing between 110 and 265 pounds, whereas females weigh between 92 and 155 pounds. Their hair tends to be shaggy, but is thinner among southern subspecies than among northern ones. Most Asian black bears have manes of long hair in their shoulders and necks. Their heads have short snouts and big, round, hairy ears; their chins are white. They are often called moon bears because of the crescent of white hair that begins on one side of their ribs, dips below the ribs, and rises on the other side.

Behavior

Asian black bears are solitary animals with little social interaction except between a mother and her young. Individual bears have territories, but they do not seem to mind when territories overlap. They are opportunistic feeders who very much prefer what foods a forest has to offer. They are very good tree climbers and will make nests of twigs among tree branches in which they will sleep through much of daytime; these nests have been found from within a few inches of the ground to several yards above the ground. They can use the long, curved claws on their forepaws to dig dens, usually among roots or underneath rocks. These dens are used for what is known in other species as hibernation; however, scientists in general do not regard the Asian black bear's long torpid state and true hibernation because the bear's metabolism slows only a little while in that state. Where winters are cold, especially when snow covers the ground, Asian black bears will retreat to their dens and rest in their torpid state for as long as three months. The shorter the cold period, the shorter the rest. In southern areas of the Asian black bear's range such as northern India, Nepal, and southern Tibet, the bear may not hibernate at all during mild winters. However, pregnant females always retreat to their dens to hibernate, during which time they give birth. Even hibernating Asian black bears are easily awakened, and if recently awakened, they are very dangerous, being prone to attacking whatever they find, including humans.

They tend to avoid humans, but human encroachment into the Asian black bears' range has forced the bears into association with humans. The bears will roam into cultivated groves and denude the trees of fruit and bark, and they will dine on grain in cultivated fields. In Japan, they are regarded as major agricultural pests because immediately after waking from hibernation the Asian black bears strip and eat bark from trees, destroying orchards and forest. Thus hundreds of the bears in Japan are hunted and killed every year. A somewhat contradictory report comes from naturalists who have studied the Asian black bear in its southern range; according to them, the bear's stripping of trees has an effect like pruning — the trees return even more bountifully endowed with foliage and fruits the next growing season.

Although primarily vegetarians, Asian black bears will eat meat when it suits them. They will eat carrion if they stumble across it — a very dangerous activity in regions where tigers are still active; a tiger will make a kill, eat some of it and leave the rest for later; when it finds an Asian black bear dining on its kill, the tiger will nearly always kill the bear. Everywhere that agriculture has intruded into the Asian black bear's territory, the bear is said by locals to kill livestock. The bear is very strong and will fell an animal with a blow to the head. The bear is also said to kill human beings. It is a very easily irritated creature, and it does not like having human beings around to begin with. Humans that intrude on its dens or nests run a risk of attack, especially if the bear is caught by surprise. In spite of their dangerous tempers, the bears are easy to hunt; when resting in their nests in trees they are easy and helpless targets.

The Asian black bear is highly intelligent and has the ability to walk as much as a quarter mile entirely upright on its hind legs. These qualities have made it a favorite show animal. In circuses, carnivals, street shows, and even zoos, the bear will be seen riding bicycles, or even walking tightropes.

Habitat

The Asian black bear's habitat varies throughout its range; it is highly adaptable to a variety of climactic conditions. In general, it prefers deciduous forests with old, tall trees. It likes warm weather and its southern populations migrate southward during winter in order to take advantage of warmer weather.

Distribution

The Asian black bear's ancient range was huge, extending from northeastern Asia south into Indochina and southwest through central Asia, through the Himalayan Mountains, into India and Nepal, and onto Formosa. Much of this ancient range has been lost to the Asian black bear in only the last few decades; it now lives in patches of population in Japan, eastern Russia, China, Laos, Tibet, India, and Nepal. Most of the details about where these remnant populations are and how bears live in them is unknown; only the Japanese population has been thoroughly studied.

Threats

Both loss of habitat and hunting are threatening the Asian black bear's survival in all regions where it currently survives. Naturalists do not agree on exactly how many subspecies of the bear may have existed because the bear has been insufficiently studied, but they all seem to agree that some subspecies that were observed as recently as ten years ago are either now extinct or will be within a few years. Individual Asian black bears need large territories in which to forage for food; females are in especially great need of large ranges because they need to build up a great deal of fat in order to successfully carry their young to term. When the potential mother lacks sufficient fat, her fertilized eggs abort. Since a female Asian black bear can only breed and raise about eight young in a lifetime, loss of habitat severely restricts the

animal's chances of perpetuating itself.

The Asian black bear is regarded as a pest throughout its range, although both India and Nepal have made significant strides in changing local people's minds about the value of the animal. It has been extensively hunted for many years and has been virtually wiped out in regions near human habitations. In southeast Asia, it is valued in folk medicine. The bear's parts are used to create aphrodisiacs, to create medicines that are supposed to improve a person's vigor, and in other folk remedies. The bear is therefore relentlessly hunted for profit, and it has now become so scarce that poachers have moved much of their operations to North America, where they hunt the Asian black bear's close cousin, the American black bear, *Ursus americanus* (see separate entry).

Conservation and Recovery

Japan tries to regulate the hunting of its population of Asian black bears, aiming for a balance between the needs of agriculture for protection and the bears' needs for food and territory. The effort has not been successful so far, and the Asian black bear has disappeared from one of Japan's islands and may soon disappear from the nation altogether. In Southeast Asian territories, controlling the hunting of the Asian black bear has been nearly impossible because of the chaos created by interminable human warfare. Its exact status in Indochina in particular is unknown, but it may already be extinct there. In China, the Asian black bear is both a nuisance and a natural resource. Its best hope for survival in China would be in the west, where Chinese naturalists have studied the bear, but even there it is still regarded as a pest to be exterminated or a financial resource to be killed and exploited. As human agriculture expands westward into Tibet, the bear is squeezed into tiny, wildly separated mountainous territories where it cannot maintain enough contact among males and females to breed. Both India and Nepal have made important strides in protecting their wildlife, but preventing poaching of their bears is nearly impossible, and the poachers seem willing to kill park rangers or even local villagers who get in their way. In Nepal, local peoples seem more tolerant of the bear than elsewhere. Given the currently rapid destruction of the Asian black bear population, there is a good chance that within a decade (maybe only a few years) the only places any Asian black bears may be found will be in Nepal and in zoos.

Baluchistan Bear

Ursus [=Selenarctos] thibetanus gedrosianus

Ursus thibetanus   Rich Block

Status	Endangered
Listed	May 16, 1986
Family	Ursidae (Bears)
Description	Black to dark red-brown fur with a white crescent on its underside.
Habitat	Dry, cool, deciduous forested mountains.
Food	Mixed diet of plants and animals.
Reproduction	Usually 2 young after gestation of 7 to 8 months.
Threats	Habitat loss and hunting.
Range	Iran and Pakistan

Description

The adult Baluchistan bear, *Ursus thibeta-nus gedrosianus*, is 4.5 to 5.5 feet long from nose to tail, and it weighs 200 to 255 pounds. Males, which tend to be larger than females, have been recorded up to 6.5 feet long, weighing over 400 pounds. Its shoulders are large and prominent; its chest is large, but it hips are slim; its ears are large and thickly furred; its hair is especially long on its neck and shoulders. It has the typical color pattern of the Asian black bear species (*Ursus thibeta-nus*), of which it is a subspecies: black fur with a pale crescent under the chest; a brown muzzle; white fur under and beside the mouth. The Baluchistan bear's coloring may be lighter than that of the average Asian black bear, with its coat being a reddish-brown.

Other common names include the Asian or Asiatic Black Bear and Moon Bear.

Behavior

The Baluchistan bear prefers to live in forested lands, and it is an adept tree climber, although the largest males do have some trouble climbing trees. They often climb trees to hide from intruders such as humans, as well as to find food. This bear may be active during the day and at dusk, otherwise resting in a den in a cave or tree hollow. They eat fruits, nuts, grain, honey, insects, and carrion, and are frequent and deadly hunters. They will hunt large animals and can kill even water buffalo by breaking their necks. Agricultural lands are tempting for the Baluchistan bear, because in those lands it can find grains to eat and livestock to hunt.

The reproductive habits of the Baluchistan bear have not been well recorded. Its mating appears to be seasonal, favoring May. Females may be sexually receptive for only a couple of days. Gestation for various Asian black bear subspecies varies from seven to eight months. Births occur in the mother's den, resulting in two, occasionally three young. The young remain with their mother from one to several years, sometimes even remaining with her after she has given birth to another set of young.

The Baluchistan bear probably hibernates (some scientists argue that the bear's prolonged torpid state is not true hibernation) for only a short time. When winter comes, instead of sleeping the months away in its den, it moves southward to warmer areas. On the other hand, pregnant females always hibernate, making sure that their cubs are born in their dens.

Asian black bears in general are very aggressive animals that should be avoided by humans. They are known to attack people who intrude on them.

Habitat

The Baluchistan bear occurs in temperate mountainous deciduous forests.

Distribution

The Baluchistan bear once ranged throughout the Makran Range in Baluchistan, a region encompassing southeastern Iran and southwestern Pakistan. There is only a little hope that it survives in Iran, where it is persecuted as a pest. Its exact numbers are not known, but only one to three hundred survive in the more remote mountain areas of Pakistan.

Threats

People are most likely to be familiar with the Baluchistan bear's cousins in the Asian black bear species. These animals such as those found in India and Nepal often are the trained bears that people see in circuses and carnivals. In general, the Baluchistan bear's relationship with human beings has been an unhappy one. Most of the bear's natural habitat has been denuded of its forests, leaving it few places to live away from humans. It thus will inhabit agricultural areas in what was once its forest range. Local people kill it as a pest because it eats their crops and sometimes kills and eats their livestock. It is also hunted for its body parts, which can be sold for use in local folk medicine, and it is hunted for sport.

Conservation and Recovery

The Baluchistan bear stands most in need of a protected range where it can be free of human intrusions. Commercial hunting and sport hunting of the bear need to be stopped. All Asian black bears are listed in CITES, Appendix I: Trade Prohibited.

Camels

Family: Camelidae

Wild Bactrian Camel   USFWS

General Characteristics of the *Camelidae*

The camel family includes llama, alpacas, guanacos, vicunas, dromedaries and bactrians. There are more than 21 million camelids (South American species) and 14 million camels, of which ninety percent are dromedaries. Although the world camel population has declined as a result of a reduction of nomadic tribes, the overall population has remained stable except for bactrians and vicunas. The once vast range of the bactrian has been severely reduced, and there are fewer than 1,000 bactrians in the Altai Gobi desert. Some scattered populations may survive in Afghanistan, Iran, Turkey and Russia. The vicuna population, most of which is in Peru, declined from millions to 400,000 in the 1950s to less than 15,000 by 1970.

Camels have provided humans with the capability of colonizing desert environments and may have been domesticated as early as 13th to 12th centuries BC. The one-hump dromedary became the standard beast of burden in southwestern Asia and northern Africa while the two-humped Bactrian camel was domesticated much later for work in Turkestan, Iraq, India and China. Camels are also indigenous in the New World and probably originated in North America 40-45 million years ago and were not dispersed to South America and Asia until 2-3 million years ago. The South American camel was domesticated in the 3rd to 2nd centuries BC.

Camels have been a vital part of human's ability to survive in inhospitable climates and terrain. Camels are used not only as pack animals but also for their wool, milk and meat. Dromedary camels, for example, provide over a gallon of milk per day and is the main source of nourishment for their keepers. They can walk 20 miles a day at a leisurely pace, carrying a load of 220 pounds. They are such an important element in the economies of some cultures that they are bartered for land, exchanged for marriage rites, and are a part of dowries and reparations.

Camels are opportunistic herbivores, and will eat a wide variety of plants throughout their range or human-induced travels. Their food sources include thorns, dry vegetation, saltbush, even toxic plants that other mammals find unacceptable. Their ability to eat opportunistically, combined with their minimal water requirements and the energy-rich fats which they store in their hump(s), make camels one of the most enduring mammals. Inactive camels can survive ten months without water as a result of the manner in which their body processes waste and because of the structure of their sweat glands. Their body temperature can rise as much as 14 degrees centigrade without the necessity of cooling by sweating. The nostrils can be closed to prevent sand from entering the body, and the nostril cavities are designed for preventing moisture from escaping while exhaling. Its eyes are protected by long eyelashes and the translucent eyelids allow the camel to determine direction when its eyes are closed against sandstorms.

Camels are social animals who live in non-territorial groups. Bull groups occur throughout the year; cow groups consisting of females and their calves form only outside of breeding season; breeding camels comprise one male and several females with their calves. During droughts camels in the wild may form herds of several hundred individuals.

Camels mate year round but sexual activity increases with a favorable supply of plant growth. During mating season a dominant bull associates with as many as two dozen females and drives off any intervening males through a series of gestures, urination rituals or aggressive fights. Pregnant females separate from their group and give birth alone. Three weeks after birth they join another group of young mothers, which remain together until the young are weaned at 1.2 to 2 years of age. Gestation is 360-380 days after which time a single young is born. Females may reproduce every 18 to 24 months.

Wild Bactrian Camel

Camelus bactrianus

Rich Block

Status	Endangered
Listed	June 14, 1976
Family	Camelidae (Camel)
Description	Two humps, dark brown to sandy or gray colored with long hair, short legs, thick eyelashes; weighs 1,000 to 1,525 pounds.
Habitat	Mountainous regions to about 11,000 feet in the summer; in the winter it returns to the desert.
Food	Any available vegetation, including leaves, herbs, and grasses.
Reproduction	After a gestation period of 12-14 months, females give birth to a single calf every two years.
Threats	Competition for scarce water sources and grazing with herds of domestic animals.
Range	Mongolia and China: Gobi Desert; Lakes Lob Nor and Bagrach Kol.

Description

The bactrian camel, *Camelus bactrianus*, is dark brown to sandy or gray colored with long hair that sheds in large lumps when molting. It is less stoutly built than domestic camels, with short legs; the body length is 7 feet 5 inches to 11 feet 3 inches and the tail is about 22 inches long. It stands 5 feet 11 inches to 6 feet 11 inches tall and weighs 1,000 to 1,525 pounds. It has two humps. To sustain the harsh desert environment the bactrian camel has thick eyelashes, nostrils which can

be closed and broad padded feet.

The bactrian camel was described by Russian naturalist, Przewalski, in 1883 as *Camelus bactrianus ferus*. *C. bactrianus* has also been known as *C. ferus*, and is commonly known as the bactrian or two-humped camel.

Behavior

Sexual maturity occurs at about 3 to 4 years of age for females and 5 to 6 years for males. After a gestation period of 12 to 14 months, females will give birth to a single calf every two years. The calf will weigh about 77 pounds. The calf is usually weaned after 1 to 2 years.

In the wild this species may be found in herds of up to 30 individuals, but is usually observed in groups of 5 or 6 animals.

The bactrian camel can survive without water for months at a time. In order to replenish itself, it may drink up to 30 gallons of water at one time. The bactrian camel is even able to endure the brackish water of the Mongolian steppe, a water source intolerable to most species. It feeds on any available vegetation, including leaves, herbs, and grasses. The bactrian camel is probably most active during the day as is typical of the *artiodactyla* family.

Habitat

During the summer intense heat in the desert pushes the bactrian camel into the mountainous regions to about 11,000 feet. In the winter it returns to the desert. It can be observed in the grasslands and steppes of China and Mongolia.

Distribution

The bactrian camel was probably domesticated on the plateau of northern Iran and southwestern Turkistan around 2,500 BC. Once domesticated, humans evolved Bactrain populations in Iraq, India and China.

The bactrian camel is restricted to the Gobi Desert on the borders of Mongolia and China. In China this species' range lies between lakes Lob Nor and Bagrach Kol. There may be remnant populations in Afghanistan, Iran, Turkey and Russia.

Threats

Camels are such an essential element in nomadic existence that they are seldom threatened until their usefulness is diminished. However, camels are of little economic importance to developed countries or agricultural societies, and as the complexion of a country changes so does its demand for camels. The once vast range of the bactrian camel has been severely reduced and the nomadic populations have been displaced or resettled into communities. The need for and cultivation of bactrians has subsequently been reduced as well.

Conservation and Recovery

The fate of the bactrian camel depends upon the fate of the nomads and the arid lands they roam. These camels can be bred in captivity and are hardy survivors, but they are unlikely to be propagated except as exotic species in zoos and game reserves.

Vicuna

Vicugna vicugna

Luiz Claudio Marigo

Status	Endangered
Listed	June 2, 1970
Family	Camelidae (Camel)
Description	Smallest member of the camel family; two toes on each foot with thick, leathery pads instead of hooves; fur is tawny brown above and paler below, with long yellowish-red hair on the lower neck and chest.
Habitat	Semiarid rolling grasslands and plains of the altiplano zone.
Food	Grasses; succulent plants, roots, lichens, and mosses.
Reproduction	Single calf after a gestation period of 330 to 350 days.
Threats	Hunted for food and wool.
Range	South America: Andes Mountains, Peru, Bolivia.

Description

The vicuna, *Vicugna vicugna*, is the smallest member of the Camel family, weighing approximately 110 pounds and measuring 39 inches high at the shoulders and 60 inches long. Like all members of the camel family vicuna have two toes on each foot with thick, leathery pads instead of hooves, as well as long, slim legs. The stomach consists of three chambers. Unlike any other living *artiodactyl*, the vicuna's incisor teeth are more like a rodent's teeth, growing constantly and having enamel on only one side. The fur is tawny brown above and paler below, with long yellowish-red hair on the lower neck and chest.

Because the animals live in the rarified air of the high Andean mountains, the vicuna's blood possesses nearly three times as many red blood cells as humans. These blood cells efficiently extract enough oxygen for the vicuna to survive. Of all the senses, the animal's vision is the best developed, the hearing only moderately acute, and the sense of smell is poor.

The vicuna is the single species of the genus *Vicugna*. Although some authorities include *Vicugna* in *Lama*, Franklin believed the species warranted full generic rank because of its unusual incisors. Otherwise, the vicuna is similar to the guanaco, *Lama guanicoe*, except smaller and with a lighter colored coat.

Behavior

The vicuna is one of the few ungulates to defend a year round feeding territory and a separate sleeping territory. The two territories range from 7 to 30 hectares and are connected by an undefended corridor. The herd consists of 7 to 10 individuals dominated by a single male with several adult females and young. The dominant male fiercely defends the group by warning them with an alarm trill and interposing himself between the source of alarm and the retreating group. The dominant male forces juveniles out of the herd, driving young males away at 4 to 9 months and the females away at 10 to 12 months. Females usually join other groups. The males form bachelor groups of 15 to 25 males that usually don't have well-defined territories. Group members urinate and defecate in a common dung heap.

After mating in March and April, the female usually gives birth to a single calf after a gestation period of 330 to 350 days. The newborn weighs 4 to 6 kilograms (9 to 13 pounds) and can walk within 15 minutes after birth. In captivity, one vicuna has lived as long as 24 years and 9 months.

Vicuna graze mainly on low perennial grasses; although they can also eat broad-leaved succulent plants, roots, lichens, and mosses. The animals chew their cud while resting. The juveniles often lay on the ground to graze, with their legs tucked under their bodies. As vicuna live on very arid plains, water is scarce and they are compelled to return repeatedly to the few existing springs in their area.

Habitat

Vicuna live high in the semiarid rolling grasslands and plains of the altiplano zone in the Andes Mountains. They range from altitudes of 11,500 to 18,900 feet.

Distribution

According to fossil records, the vicuna once roamed the vast grasslands (pampas) of South America. Competition from other animal species forced the vicuna into the mountains where competition was lessened. In the Andes mountains, they could be found from the southern part of Ecuador south to Argentina and North Chile. Today, they can still be found in the Andes mountains, especially within protected parks and reserves. Seventy-two percent of the surviving 85,000 vicunas are in Peru.

Threats

The Incas considered the vicuna to be sacred and strictly banned the killing of these animals. Instead, the priests organized roundups of the animals and, under strict rules, had them sheared. After they were shorn, the vicuna were freed in order to ensure a continuous supply of wool.

Unfortunately, the Spanish were not so

foresighted and slaughtered the animals in large numbers for food and the exquisite wool. Local human populations continue to hunt the animals for food and to sell the wool to foreign tourists. The local humans also graze their domestic animals on the vicuna habitat, thereby decreasing the wild animal's food source.

Conservation and Recovery

Several reserves have been successfully established to protect these rare animals, including the Pampas Galeras National Vicuna Reserve in Peru and the national park of Sajama in Bolivia. Additionally, small numbers of vicuna are bred in zoos. However, the animals require greater care and attention in captivity than some other members of the camel family, such as llamas and guanacos.

Horses and Zebras
Family: Equidae

Grevy's Zebra   Ron Singer, USFWS

General Characteristics of the *Equidae*

All members of the horse family *Equidae,* which includes horses, asses and zebras, have many similar characteristics. They have long heads, slender necks and legs, moderately long, erect ears, a mane that covers the neck, and long tails. The mane and tail of asses and zebras have short hairs that stand erect. The eyes are set far back in the skull and provide binocular vision that is excellent during the day and good at night. The ears can be rotated to detect the direction of sound. Vocalization, including whinneys, nickers, squeals and brays, provides an important method of socialization. The most distinguishing feature between the species of horses is coat color and, with zebras, stripes.

All horses forage on fibrous foods, primarily grasses and sedges, but also bark, leaves, buds, fruits and roots. They only partly digest their intake of food and are required to consume more bulk in order to achieve their required nutritional value. However, they are able to eat a lower quality food and can be sustained in a habitat of marginal food quality, although they prefer high quality, low fiber foods. They forage both day and night.

Horses and zebras are highly social animals. Adult horses, and plains and mountain zebras form permanent groups comprised of a male and several females. The harem of females establish a home range, which may overlap with another harem's home range. During dry seasons or periods of poor food supplies, harems will combine and migrate up to sixty miles in search of a more hospitable habitat. The asses and Grevey's zebra form temporary groups with one or more sexes in a group that stays together only a few months. Males establish mating territories marked by piles of dung; if there is insufficient habitat for all males to establish a territory, bachelors will form groups until they can displace a territorial male or migrate to another habitat. Temporary social systems are more prevalent in drier habitats with widely distributed low-quality resources. If females must disperse to find food supplies, they cannot form permanent groups, and the males become solitary defenders of mating territories, waiting for females to pass through.

All female equids leave the harem when they become sexually mature at about two years of age; males disperse at about four years of age to join bachelor groups until they can steal females or displace a harem male. Competition for mating rites among males includes establishing superiority through defecating and sniffing or through combat. Mating occurs 7 to 10 days after a female gives birth, usually to one young, but she typically skips a year between birthing. The young are able to walk within an hour after birth and begin grazing in a few weeks, although they are not weaned for 8 to 13 months.

Zebras

Zebras are highly social animals. Hartmann's zebras live in groups of permanent membership, consisting of a male and a few females, some of which remain in the same harem throughout their adult lives. Each harem has a home range, which may overlap with neighbors. The size of the range is determined by the quality of the habitat. Typically, daughters remain with their mothers, creating groups of close kin. Females leave the group when they become sexually mature at age two, when neighboring harem males or bachelor males attempt to steal them. Males disperse by the fourth year to form bachelor associations, where they remain until they can defend territories, steal young females, or displace harem males. Reproductive competition among males for females is keen, and often results in fierce fighting. Females form amicable relationships that include mutual grooming. When food and water resources are scarce, however, a hierarchy prevails in which some females derive substantial benefit from their standing in the harem.

All zebras forage on fibrous foods. Although they feed primarily on grasses and sedges, they will eat bark, leaves, buds, fruits, and roots. They digest through a hindgut fermentation system, in which plant food is only partially digested; therefore, they need to ingest large quantities of food although the quality of food is not as important as the amount. Although they can survive on low quality diets, they prefer high quality, low fiber foods. Zebras forage most of the day and night, and spend about 60% of their time eating.

African Ass

Equus africanus [=asinus]

Roland Wirth

Status	Endangered
Listed	June 2, 1970
Family	Equidae (Horses and zebras)
Description	Coat is grey, with a white underside and a dark stripe across its upper back.
Habitat	Desert.
Food	Grass and shrubs.
Reproduction	Gestation of about 1 year, giving birth to one foal.
Threats	Human predation.
Range	Ethiopia, Somalia, and Sudan

Description

Because the U.S. Fish and Wildlife Service classified the African ass as *Equus asinus* rather than *Equus africanus* when listing it as an endangered species, it has been confused with the wild burros of Western America, which are classified as *Equus asinus* and are derived from the African ass. Since *Equus africanus* is the more common nomenclature for the African ass and helps to distinguish it from the burro, it is more commonly used.

As with other members of *Equidae*, the African ass's eyes are set well back in its skull. It is able to see from side-to-side, to the back except directly behind its head, and stereoscopically forward. It is apparently able to see colors and to see well at night — perhaps as well as cats. Its nose is narrower than that of other *Equidae*, and its legs and hooves are slimmer, too. The subspecies in Ethiopia and Sudan has a dark stripe across its shoulders, a distinctive marking that makes it easy to identify. The Somalian subspecies, *E. a. somalicus*, has a narrow, slightly angled horizontal stripes on its legs — this subspecies is likely to be extinct. The African ass's mane is short, dark, and stiff, pointing upwards. It is smaller and more compact than the other members of *Equidae*. It lives to 25 years in the wild and to 35 years in captivity.

Behavior

The African ass is shy of humans and avoids them. It is territorial, with males using dung to establish their borders. Males will fight one another for the rights to a sexually receptive female, and females too, will fight, kicking hard with their hind legs to dissuade male suitors.

Its territoriality resembles that of the Asiatic ass (*Equus hemionus*) and Grevy's zebra (*Equus grevyi*), although it is no more closely related to those species than it is to the other surviving members of the family *Equidae*: Przewalski's horse (*Equus przewalski*), the domestic horse (*Equus caballus*), the plains zebra (*Equus burchelli*), and the mountain zebra (*Equus zebra*). Territories are held by males, although other males may wander through them. Males with territories tend to be solitary, gathering with other African asses only at watering holes or with groups of females for mating. It determines a female's fertility by smelling her urine. Even if a female is found to be fertile, she will not necessarily be receptive to any given male that tries to mate with her and seems to exercise some choice as to which male she will mate with (perhaps after the male has fought off other suitors). Gestation lasts about one year, resulting in the birth of a single foal. The foal will be on its legs and ready to run in about an hour. In about 3 weeks, it will be able to graze. After several months, it will be on its own. If it is a female, it will associate with loose groups of other females, and slowly find its place in a social hierarchy, with dominant females being the first to drink at watering holes. Males will join loose groups of bachelor African asses and eventually take over an old territory or create a new one.

Because of their scarcity, it has been hard for naturalists to observe the behavior of African asses, and there are important details about their diet, interaction with their environment, and social interaction that are not known for certain. For instance, although they share similar habitat and geographic region with Grevy's zebra, their ranges seldom overlap. Each species seems to have a distinct region apart from the other, perhaps because of diet. Each animal eats grass and scrub plants. Each is adapted to arid regions with great flat plains and seasonal rainfall. The African ass grazes night and day, with about two-thirds of the total day spent in constant motion, moving from plant to plant (it seems to have good stamina at slow speeds).

Its primary natural predators are lions, hyenas, and wild dogs. The African ass responds to their attacks by running and dodging quickly (it has little stamina when running at full speed) or by delivering powerful kicks with its hind legs. Its most deadly predators are humans, and its only protection from them seems to be staying in isolated, remote, and inhospitable tracts.

Habitat

The African ass lives in an arid climate in northeastern Africa where the land is flat, water is hard to find, and grasses are scarce.

Distribution

The African ass once ranged over Ethiopia, Somalia, and Sudan, and may have ranged farther before human beings began encroaching on its habitat. It has probably been exterminated in Ethiopia and Somalia, although its semi-solitary nature may have helped a few survive in isolated ranges far from where researchers have been able to go in recent years. It survives in Sudan, and still has a big natural range there; the drought which presently afflicts the country may have dried up its waterholes, driving it toward human habitations. On the other hand, it is better equipped than most animals to survive in a dry climate. Its greatest threat comes not from lack of territory, but from hungry people desperate for food.

The African ass is the root-stock for the burros of the New World. These burros, perhaps a subspecies (naturalists disagree markedly with one another about how the burros' relationship to African asses should be signified), were brought by human beings. The ass had been first domesticated in North Africa and was brought into the Middle East and Europe and from there to the Americas, where it proved an able beast of burden, especially in dry climates.

Threats

Muslim tribesmen hunt the African ass because of their religious belief that the animal's flesh will cure disease. Tourists disrupt their habitat and will use automobiles to chase the animal down for photographs (or hunting); the ass has little stamina and will die of exhaustion after such pursuits. Its habitat has been the scene of warfare for much of the last three decades; this has prevented naturalists from being able to work to preserve it in the wild.

Further, warfare has brought with it starvation. The United States and other nations made a much-publicized effort in the late 1980s and early 1990s to feed the people of Somalia, who were starving to death by the millions. In the Sudan, starvation has been a weapon used in its decades-long civil war. Starving people are unlikely to reject a food source because it may be verging on extinction, and the African ass has long been a source of protein for the local peoples. Preserving the animal in its natural range is a daunting task, and the outlook for its survival is grim.

Conservation and Recovery

The African ass has been placed in Appendix I of CITES. The governments in its native range are unable to prevent its exploitation. At present, Somalia is without a national government, Ethiopia is trying to recover from a disastrous war with Somalia and a long civil war with the former province Eritrea. Its present government may soon take steps to protect its natural heritage, but its social problems are immense after years of dictatorial rule, with much of its population near starvation from day-to-day. One result of this very grim situation is that the people who displaced the African ass from its habitat are following the animals north in search of food.

Grevy's Zebra

Equus grevyi

Rich Block

Status	Threatened
Listed	August 1, 1979
Family	Equidae (Horses and zebras)
Description	Long, slender head with wide ears and a stiffly erect mane; it has narrow vertical black-on-white stripes along its body, curving at the haunches; its underside is white.
Habitat	Arid grasslands
Food	Primarily grasses, but will eat leaves, fruits, roots, and bark.
Reproduction	Mares will usually give birth to one foal after gestation of 12.5 months.
Threats	Loss of habitat, predation, hunting by humans.
Range	Northern Kenya

Description

Although Grevy's zebra, *Equus grevyi*, has the stripes commonly associated with zebras, it is no more closely related to other species of zebra than it is to horses or asses. It is of ancient lineage, the first of the modern members of *Equidae* to branch off from the ancestral equids, which means that studying its physiology and behavior can shed some special light on the ancestors of modern horses. It is the largest of the zebras and is notably heavier. Its stripes tend to be more even, from neck to hind leg. Each Grevy's zebra has its own unique pattern, but there is little by way of dramatic variation. The rare Grevy's zebra with a significantly unusual pattern — say nearly all black or white stripes on a black background rather than the usual black-on-white — tend to be ostracized by other Grevy's zebras, which means they are less likely to reproduce.

Exactly why the zebras have stripes is not known, and naturalists tend to debate what exactly the evolutionary advantage of stripes might be. Further compounding the mystery is the now generally held assumption that the equids from which all modern *Equidae* have sprung were probably striped, meaning that horses and asses lost their stripes, suggesting that they offered no particular evolutionary advantage to those species. The notion that the stripes are camouflage is easy to dispense with — Grevy's zebra live in open territory with green and tan for background, making their stripes easy to spot. Certainly, lions have no trouble seeing and tracking the zebras. Another somewhat more plausible explanation is that when gathered in groups, the zebras seem to blend into one another because of their stripes, making it hard for predators to single one out. The explanation might work for plains zebras, which tend to gather in herds, but Grevy's zebras tend to be solitary, gathering only occasionally into small groups. Another explanation is that the stripes seem to soothe the zebras; although to humans the stripes excite the eyes and can even be annoying to look at for long periods, Grevy's zebras seem to be calmed by the presence of other stripes. This could provide a reproductive advantage to properly striped Grevy's zebras when they gather to mate and to compete for mates.

Behavior

Adult males tend to live alone in territories of one to four square miles, although those without territories tend to gather into loose groups. The boundaries of these territories are marked by dung piles. Having a territory gives a male a mating advantage, since females will tend to mate with the male in whose territory they have wandered. Grevy's zebras will sometimes congregate into loose groups containing members of both genders, but the groups are not permanent and will shift and break apart, lasting only two or three months.

Mating is seasonal for Grevy's zebra, with females becoming receptive soon after giving birth, during the season when plant life is flourishing. Males will contest a territorial male's rights to a mare through ceremonious defecating; if this does not resolve the dispute, they could end up fighting, wounding necks and legs. Females create "pecking orders," with dominant mares getting first choice of food and water.

Gestation in Grevy's zebra is about a month longer than for other zebras, about 12.5 months. Males compete for the opportunity to mate with a fertile mare, sometimes fighting each other with their forelegs and teeth. The males determine whether a female is fertile by smelling her urine. Foals take a year to be weaned. If they are females, they will then form loose associations with other females and will gather into groups of females and males without territories, break from those groups, reform others, and so on, every two months or so. Males may gather into small bachelor groups, composed mostly of young stallions. As they increase in size, they may be able to challenge an established male for its territory or take over an abandoned territory (for instance, when the previous occupant has died). More observation is needed before the Grevy's zebra's system of forming territories is fully understood, but they tend to be patterns of intricately looping and weaving boundaries, which may, perhaps, change as some territory holders expand their boundaries at the expense of weaker territory holders.

Much of the Grevy zebra's behavior has yet to be understood. Its range in Ethiopia and Somalia was disrupted for decades by warfare, preventing their study. Political chaos in those countries damaged efforts to research any of those nation's wildlife, with some naturalists having their studies suspended for more than a decade. In Kenya, a relatively stable country that has long-established institutions for naturalist studies, Grevy's zebra has had to compete for attention with other endangered species. In those countries where poaching is not rigidly monitored by the government, poachers do not hesitate to interfere with, or kill researchers who may interfere with their illegal trade in wildlife.

Habitat

Grevy's zebra occurs in northeastern Africa, in deserts and near deserts. Their habitat typically includes grasses and low bushes, which provides their food supply but does not interfere with their view of the vast, usually flat range. Water is scarce, and who drinks first at the watering holes is determined by a loose social hierarchy. Seasonal rains can make Grevy's zebra's range temporarily lush, and birthing and mating are reserved for that brief period. Grevy's zebra shares its habitat with antelope, lions, hyenas, and wild dogs. Because they have different digestive systems, the antelopes and Grevy's zebra eat different plants, allowing them to coexist in the same territory.

Distribution

Grevy's zebra is probably the most ancient member of the seven surviving species of the family *Equidae*, which includes horses and asses, as well as zebras. Although they do not tend to gather into herds, their numbers were once vast before an international market for their coats developed. Even in the 1970s, they numbered in the tens of thousands. They ranged over the great plains of southern Ethiopia, through Somalia, and into northern Kenya. During the 1970s, Grevy's zebra disappeared from Ethiopia and Somalia. When the U. S Fish and Wildlife Service proposed putting Grevy's zebra on its endangered species list in 1977, the Kenyan Rangeland Ecological Monitoring Unit conducted a head count of Grevy's zebra in its territories in 1979 and found about 14,000 of them, about ten times as many as were then thought to exist. Even so, the Kenyan Minister for Tourism and Wildlife indicated some alarm; he said that in the Samburu District Grevy's zebra's numbers had shrunk from 7,000 in 1976 to 2,500 in 1977. This decline was probably due to hunting; a Grevy's zebra coat sold to collectors for about $2,000 U.S. dollars at that time.

Threats

Because Grevy's zebra is hunted for its beautiful coat, it may be hunted into extinction, much like the quagga, a zebra that disappeared in the 1880s. Predators other than humans include lions, hyenas, and wild dogs, with the lions tending to take adults and the hyenas and wild dogs tending to take foals. Adult zebras will sometimes try to distract lions from taking their young, thus exposing themselves; male Grevy's zebras will confront hyenas and dogs in defense of foals.

Conservation and Recovery

Kenya has prohibited the hunting of Grevy's zebra since May 1977. CITES lists Grevy's zebra in Appendix I: Trade Prohibited — meaning that the zebra and parts of the zebra are not to be bought and sold internationally. Yet, the trade continues. International buyers, who very likely know that they are purchasing the skins of a species nearing extinction, continue to pay thousands of dollars for coats obtained by poachers in Kenya. Kenya's fight against the poachers has been a violent one, but possibly a losing one.

Asian Wild Ass

Equus hemionus

Artiszoo, Amsterdam

Status	Endangered
Listed	June 2, 1970
Family	Equidae (Horses and zebras)
Description	Light buff to yellow colored on sides with black and white face, measuring 43 to 55 inches tall with narrow head, short mane and long ears.
Habitat	Lowland deserts of southwest and central Asia.
Food	Grasses, herbs, and bark.
Reproduction	One young per year.
Threats	Hunting for sport and food.
Range	India, China, Iran, and Pakistan

Description

The coat of the Asian wild ass, *Equus hemionus*, varies according to the season and its range. Generally it is reddish brown that fades to a light buff or yellowish-brown in winter. The underparts and muzzle are white and a distinctive stripe can be observed along the back. It has short legs and small feet. This species stands about 3 to 4.6 feet tall and weighs 440 to 575 pounds. The Asian wild ass has a comparatively narrow head, shorter mane and longer ears.

E. hemionus is divided into five geographically distinguished subspecies: the Dziggetai, *E. h. hemionus*; the Khur or Indian wild ass, *E. h. khur*; the Onager, *E. h. onager*; and the Kulan, *E. h. kulan*.

Behavior

The Asian wild ass will graze on grasses, herbs, succulent plants and bark. It can survive long periods without water. It is primarily nocturnal.

Although little is known about the social behavior of the Asian wild ass, after an observation of the kulan (a subspecies of *E. hemionus*) in the Badkhyz Reserve, it is believed the females will roam in a group. Males establish mating territories that are about 20 square kilometers in size. Group size and composition varies throughout the year and may grow to over a hundred animals in the autumn.

Mating occurs from April to October. After a gestation period of about twelve months, one 55 pound young is born. Six to eight months after birth the youngster will be weaned and after one year it will be sexually mature.

The Asian wild ass is the fastest member of the horse family, attaining speeds to 43 miles per hour.

Habitat

The Asian wild ass inhabits the lowland deserts and steppes of Southwest and Central Asia. The different subspecies of *E. hemionus* occupy a variety of habitats. The Indian wild ass can be found in dry salt plains at sea level while the onager, kulan, and dziggetai inhabit desert area.

Distribution

The Asian wild ass was found in Anatolia over 3,000 years ago. At the beginning of the twentieth century its range was from Gobi and Lake Baikal, west to Kazakhstan, Palestine, and south to the Thar Desert of India, and North Arabia. The four subspecies of *E. hemionus* are distributed as follows: *E. h. hemionus* from Mongolian Sinkiang, China; *E. h. khur* from Rann to Kutch in India; *E. h. onager* is from Iran; and *E. h. kulan* is known only from Turkmenistan. The Tukmenian kulans occur in the Badkhyz Reserve.

The only subspecies found in significant numbers is the Persian wild ass (*E.h. onager*); *E.h. kaing*, the largest of the subspecies, has been given some protection in China. The Indian wild ass, *E. h. khur*, occurs in extremely severe habitat in India and Pakistan, where its numbers have been reduced to 400-500 animals.

Threats

The Asian wild ass has been threatened by hunting for both sport and food but the greatest toll has been taken by the encroachment of humans who have converted their habitat to grazing lands for camels, horses and sheep.

Another problem is hybridization with domestic horses, with which asses easily breed.

Conservation and Recovery

The Badkhyz Reserve in Turkmenistan is the only protected area for any Asiatic wild asses. As the reserve is surrounded by land that is not being utilized, the herds are able to expand. Attempts have been made to reintroduce the Asian wild ass into its former habitat, and a number of animals were introduced into a protective reserve in Israel.

Asian wild asses can adapt to captivity, and zoos sometimes have one or two individuals, but these homely animals are not popular zoo citizens and captive breeding programs are not widespread.

Przewalski's Horse

Equus przewalskii

Status	Endangered
Listed	June 14, 1976
Family	Equidae (Horses and zebras)
Description	Stocky horse with short legs, and short mane that stands straight up; the upper body color varies from dark gray to brownish gray with a dorsal stripe from mane to tail; the belly and muzzle are lighter; its mane is erect, comprised of short, dark hairs.
Habitat	Plains, semideserts and deserts in the wild.
Food	Grasses
Reproduction	One foal per year.
Threats	Hunting
Range	Mongolia and China

Gale K. Belinky

Description

Przewalski's horse, *Equus przewalskii*, is about 8 feet measured from its snout to the base of its tail. It stands 4 to 4.75 feet tall and weighs about 440 to 750 pounds. This primitive horse is the ancestor of our domestic breeds. In comparison to the domestics, this species is rather stocky with short legs. Przewalski's horse's mane is short and stands straight up. The upper body color varies from dark gray to brownish gray with a dorsal stripe from mane to tail. The belly and muzzle are lighter. Its mane is erect, comprised of short, dark hairs (unlike domestic horses with flowing manes) that is framed by yellow hairs. The tail and legs have long hair. The legs are marked with dark stripes on the lower portion.

In 1881 I. S. Polyakov was presented with a skull of a horse discovered on the border between Mongolia and China by Kilolai Michailovitch Przewalski, a Russian naturalist. Polyakov subsequently described this species as the new taxon *E. przewalskii*. It is also known as *E. caballus* or *E. ferus*. Within the *Equidae* family there is only one genus and 7 species.

Behavior

After copulation and a gestation period of 340 days, the mare will give birth to a 66 pound foal. After no more than about 30 minutes the foal is able to stand and walk. The foal remains with its mother until it is about 6 to 8 months old when it is weaned. Przewalski's horse reaches sexual maturity at age two.

Przewalski's horse browses primarily on grasses. From 1897 observations, it is believed that the horses would spend the day in the desert and travel to grazing and watering areas at dusk, returning to the desert in the morning hours.

Habitat

Przewalski's horse inhabited plains, semideserts and deserts in the wild.

Distribution

Przewalski's horse was once widespread throughout Europe and Northern Asia. At the end of the 13th century this horse was extirpated from all of Western Europe. By the end of the 19th century it was restricted to the Altai Mountains in Mongolia. By the 1950s a few animals remained in the wild on the border between southwestern Mongolia and China in an area called Takhin-Shara-Nuru, but by 1970 Przewalski's horse appeared to be extinct in the wild. Some 200 individuals remain in zoos worldwide, descendants of animals captured at the turn of the century.

Threats

Przewalski's horse was hunted extensively by Paleolithic men. After its discovery in 1879 the Grum-Grzimajlo brothers were able to capture Przewalski's horse. Friedrich Falz-Fein of Askaniya Nova desired to keep the last of this primitive stock and arranged to breed them. Beginning in 1897 wild horses were captured for Falz-Fein. Of all that were imported only one stallion and four mares survived. These five individuals are the genetic link to any *E. przewalskii* species in existence today.

Conservation and Recovery

A successful captive breeding program has been in progress for Przewalski's horse since 1960. The Prague Zoo has maintained an international stud book listing all of the Przewalski's wild horses kept and born in captivity. This program has been so successful that reintroduction into the wild is planned. However, because of inbreeding for such a long time, the genetic diversity of the species has been greatly reduced and their ability to survive in the wild may have been diminished as a result.

Hartmann's Mountain Zebra

Equus zebra hartmannae

Gale K. Belinky

Status	Threatened
Listed	August 21, 1979; February 10, 1981
Family	Equidae (Horses and zebras)
Description	Yellowish-brown background; belly is white; the stripes on the muzzle are lighter around the eyes.
Habitat	Rocky areas and arid scrub bush.
Food	Grass, leaves, and shoots.
Reproduction	1 foal after gestation of 365 days.
Threats	Overhunting; competition with domestic species for resources.
Range	Namibia and Angola

Description

Hartmann's mountain zebra, *Equus zebra hartmannae*, is striped over the entire length of its body. These stripes are unique and distinguish mountain zebras from other zebra species. The pattern is known as a "gridiron" pattern and is observed just over the hips above the tail. This species' narrow, elongated hoof is also distinguishable in that it is resilient to skidding. The hoof of the Hartmann's mountain zebra and the Cape Mountain zebra grows 2.5 times faster than any other member of *Equidae*. Hartmann's mountain zebra weighs 660 to 816 pounds. This species stands 57 (females) to 59 (males) inches high. Tails grow to 23 inches long, with a tufted, black end.

Hartmann's mountain zebra's coat has a yellowish-brown background. The belly is white and the stripes on the muzzle are lighter around the eyes. The area around the nostrils is reddish. Hartmann's mountain zebra has wider stripes and the bristly mane tipped with black is longer than other zebra species.

Behavior

Hartmann's mountain zebra lives in family units of one stallion, several mares, and their foals. The remaining stallions live in stallion groups.

Sexual maturity occurs at about 3 years of age. Prior to mating a "mating territory" covering 0.7 to 3.6 square miles will be established. The gestation period is 365 days. After this time the female gives birth to one foal weighing 55 pounds. After 6 to 8 months the youngster will be weaned.

Habitat

Hartmann's mountain zebra habituates among rocky areas, semi-arid scrub bush zones, especially prairies and open mountain woods.

Distribution

Hartmann's mountain zebra is found in Namibia and Angola. Its range formerly extended north into Angola and south to Namaqualand, Cape Province, South Africa. In the 1950s its numbers were estimated to be 50,000, but it declined rapidly during the next 20 years. The current population is estimated at 7,000 animals in Nambia and 350 introduced animals at Cape Province. Very few Hartmann's mountain zebras remain in Angola.

Threats

Hartmann's mountain zebra is extremely threatened by hunting pressures. If hunting is allowed to continue, Hartmann's mountain zebra's status will most likely turn from threatened to endangered.

Hartmann's mountain zebra competes for water and food resources with domestic livestock, and the propagation of agricultural land has greatly reduced available habitat.

Conservation and Recovery

Because Hartmann's mountain zebra is listed under Appendix II of CITES, it is legal to import sport hunting trophies into the U.S. In listing the species as threatened, USFWS decided to exclude trophy hunting from the import prohibition. The reason for this alteration in policy is that USFWS believes that sport hunting is helping to preserve the species rather than deplete it.

Hartman's mountain zebra occurs over vast areas of privately owned ranches, where the zebras compete directly with the ranchers' cattle and sheep. Without the incentive of deriving income from hunting parties, the ranchers would not allow the zebras to remain on their land, but the revenue the ranchers receive from daily hunting fees and animals killed makes up an important income source. Because of this income incentive, the ranchers protect and breed the zebras.

Sport hunting of Hartmann's mountain zebra is controlled by the Namibian government, which issues hunting permits on the basis of surplus populations of animals.

Cape Mountain Zebra

Equus zebra zebra

Luiz Claudio Marigo

Status	Endangered
Listed	June 14, 1976; February 10, 1981
Family	Equidae (Horses and zebras)
Description	Donkey-like zebra with "gridiron" patterned stripes just over the hips above the tail which are narrow and broaden out at the rump.
Habitat	Rocky areas, semi-arid, and arid scrub bush.
Food	Herbivorous, feeding on grass, leaves, shoots.
Reproduction	Females give birth to 1 foal after a gestation period of 365 days.
Threats	Loss of habitat due to farming and sheep ranching.
Range	South Africa: Cape Province

Description

Like Hartmann's mountain zebra (see separate entry), the Cape mountain zebra, *Equus zebra zebra*, is striped over the entire length of its body except its hindquarters. These stripes are unique and distinguish mountain zebras from other zebra species. The pattern is known as a "gridiron" pattern and is observed just over the hips above the tail. Its stripes are narrow and broaden out at the rump. The Cape mountain zebra also possesses a dewlap under its chin. This spe-

cies' hoof is also distinguishable in that it is resilient to skidding. The Cape mountain zebra is the smallest of its race and stands about 48 inches high, measured from ground to shoulder. The Cape mountain zebra's physical characteristics give it a rather donkey-like appearance rather than a typical zebra.

Behavior

The Cape mountain zebra lives in family units of one stallion, several mares, and their foals. Juvenile males remain with the family for 2 to 3 years when they join other young stallions to form a group headed by an older male. The remaining stallions live in stallion groups for 5 to 6 years when individual males form a family group.

Sexual maturity occurs at about 3 years of age. Prior to mating, a "mating territory" covering 0.7 to 3.6 square miles will be established. The gestation period is 365 days. After this time the female gives birth to 1 foal which is 55 pounds. After 6 to 8 months the youngster will be weaned.

The Cape mountain zebra is herbivorous and feeds on grass, leaves, and shoots. It can tolerate the absence of water for two days, but normally drinks twice a day. During the dry season, it excavates river beds, digging as deep as two feet looking for water.

Habitat

The Cape mountain zebra has adapted to arid rocky slopes and mountain gorges with little vegetation.

Distribution

The Cape mountain zebra is found only in the Cape Province of South Africa in the Capetown Nature Park, which contains fewer than 200 individuals.

Threats

This zebra has been pressured by hunting and primarily from farming activities and sheep ranching. The latter two factors have resulted in habitat loss for the Cape mountain zebra.

Conservation and Recovery

As early as 1656 the Cape mountain zebra was afforded protection by Jan van Riebeeck and hunting laws were initiated. In 1806 the hunting laws were relaxed when the British took over the Cape.

With strict protection this subspecies bred to a stable population in the Mountain Zebra National Park at Cradock, which was created for the protection of the Cape mountain zebra. Individuals from this population are now being transplanted into two other reserves, and a species management plan has been established to increase the genetic diversity of the subspecies and to carefully monitor the populations.

Deer
Family: Cervidae

Pampas Deer (*Blastocerus dichotomus*)   Luiz Claudio Marigo

General Characteristics of the *Cervidae*

There are thirty-six species of deer in the family *Cervidae*, divided into four subfamilies, of which twelve species are threatened or endangered. Although all deer are similar in appearance with graceful, elongated bodies, slender legs and necks, short tails and angular heads, they vary greatly in size and antler structure, from 1,700 pound moose to 15 pound pudu. The antlers are bony structures that, unike horns, are shed and regrown every year. Some species have simple single-spike antlers with no branches to complex, colorful structures of red deer and reindeer, which have palmate antlers that give the appearance of a flat palm with fingers. Except for reindeer, females do not have antlers.

The coat color varies among species, including gray, brown, red and yellow, with the underparts usually lighter than the back and flanks. Often there is a rump patch which is fringed with dark hair. The young of many species have light colored spots on a darker ground, which improves their camouflage.

Deer use hearing, smell and sight to detect danger. While feeding, they raise their heads often to listen and sniff the air for predators. When alarmed, deer raise their heads, stare toward the source of alarm, rotate their ears forward, and flee rapidly. They raise their rump and tail when fleeing. They use smell to identify other deer. Most species have foot glands that leave scent trails and all species have facial glands that produce aromatic secretions. Deer also communicate with vocalizations, ranging from bleats by young deer, to alarm barks, to bellows by rutting males.

Deer feed by grazing on grass or browsing on shoots, twigs, leaves, flowers and fruit or herbs, shrubs and trees. The amount of food a species requires depends on its size, whether females are reproducing, and the availability of food sources. Most deer are capable of altering their diet and take advantage of the most plentiful sources.

Sexual maturity varies from one to four years of age and is partly determined by the nutritional value of the food sources. Males may gain sexual maturity at one year but are normally unable to compete for females until they are full grown at five or six years of age. Males spend much of the nonbreeding season building reserves for rutting and growing antlers. During rutting, they may fight, often viciously, for the opportunity to mate with five females. Genetic success is determined by how many females a male can impregnate, with a lifetime high of 24 and a lifetime average of about four young. Females can produce up to 13 young in a lifetime with an average of 4.5. Calf mortality can be high and a doe's genetic success is determined more by parental care than by frequency of reproduction. Mothers in the best physical condition during the rut are more likely to give birth to calves during the most favorable season (most mortality in calves occurs during the first winter), thus increasing the calf's chance of survival.

The social organization for deer is related to their type of food supply. Browsing deer tend to live singly or form small groups; in close proximity, large numbers of browsers interfere with feeding. Open habitats encourage herding, which provides more protection from predators. Males and females live apart except during mating season. Males may form temporary bachelor groups whose members change from day to day, while females may live in more permanent groups comprised of relatives.

Hog Deer

Axis porcinus annamiticus

NPIAW

Status	Endangered
Listed	June 14, 1976
Family	Cervidae (Deer)
Description	Short legged and thick set, with an overall coloration of yellow-brown, with an underbody that is darker than the rest of the body.
Habitat	Grasslands, brushlands, rice paddies, and tropical jungle.
Food	Grass, herbs, flowers, and fallen fruits.
Reproduction	Gestation lasts 180 days, resulting in the birth of a single fawn.
Threats	Loss of habitat and human predation.
Range	Vietnam and Thailand

Description

The Indochinese hog deer, *Axis porcinus annamiticus*, is stoutly and powerfully built, with a thick body and short legs. The shoulders are lower than the haunches. The head-and-body length of an adult is 40 to 50 inches, with the tail adding 6 to 10 inches; it stands 26 to 29 inches high at the shoulder. It weighs 80 to 100 pounds. A full set of antlers has 6 points with a length of 15 inches. These antlers are sharp and dangerous. The Indochinese hog deer's coat is coarse, and it is a bit shaggy along the flanks. Typical coloration is yellow-brown, darker on the underbody and lighter on the legs.

Behavior

The subspecies *Axis porcinus annamiticus* has been rarely observed and its wild behavior is only vaguely recorded. It seems to be a solitary animal that only casually joins herds of other Indochinese hog deer; individual deer join and leave herds constantly, spending most of their time alone. The population density is low, perhaps as a consequence of the solitary nature of the animals, perhaps because suitable food is sparse and spread evenly over large areas, or perhaps because humans have greatly depleted their numbers through hunting.

The hog deer gets its common name from the way it runs: It runs with its head lowered, like that of a hog, and with its shoulders lower than its hindquarters and its thick body, it can look like an antlered hog rushing through grass or brush. Unlike other deer, they do not leap over obstacles, but instead charge through them. Bucks are very aggressive and will often attack even humans when disturbed; some naturalists believe the bucks to be territorial and that they charge those who intrude into their territories, but other observers find no territorial behavior and regard bucks and does as solitary wanderers with fixed ranges.

The hog deer is adaptable and will adjust its behavior to the habitat and availability of food wherever it finds itself. Thus, in Indochina and Thailand, the subspecies *annamiticus* may be found where grass is twice as tall as human beings, in open lands covered by brush and bushes, amid rice paddies, and in jungles. Throughout its range, it seems to slowly travel to wherever food availability takes it. Its preferred food is grass, but it also eats herbs, flowers, and fruit fallen from trees.

Most breeding takes place in September through October, with some breeding occurring in August and November. During breeding season, as many as forty Indochinese hog deer may gather together in open feeding areas. The sexually mature males try to cull out sexually receptive females; when this happens, the pair leave the herd together. Bucks may contest the rights to a receptive female, but fighting seems rare. Mating results in the birth of a single young; if the fawn

dies early, it is possible (but not established) that its mother will mate and conceive again shortly thereafter.

Habitat

The habitat for the Indochinese hog deer varies, but it is nearly always warm and typically has water, either in lakes, rivers, or marshes. The Indochinese hog deer will inhabit grasslands, brushlands, and jungle, although it presently seems confined mostly to dense jungle because humans have hunted it out of its other habitats.

Distribution

The *annamiticus* (or Indochinese) subspecies of hog deer ranges throughout Indochina. It is now very rare and may have been exterminated in some of its host nations, although they have been reliably sighted in Thailand. Constant warfare in the range has made it almost impossible for naturalists to search for the Indochinese hog deer and other endangered animals in the region. Although it seems gone from Cambodia and Burma, it may possibly still live in west-central Vietnam.

Threats

The *annamiticus* subspecies of hog deer has lost most of its range to agriculture, expanding human settlements, and the destruction caused by warfare. If it is truly a solitary wanderer, the Indochinese hog deer needs a large range in which it can seek out food and others of its kind for breeding. It has been heavily hunted for its meat, and it has had the misfortune of living in a part of the world where people are frequently undernourished and who therefore treasure any palatable meat they can find. This hunting, more than anything else, is driving the Indochinese hog deer to extinction.

Conservation and Recovery

Vietnam has established a reserve on the western edge of the old border between North Vietnam and South Vietnam in which the hog deer may still survive. This reserve has not been well protected because of Vietnam's lack of financial resources to pay for park rangers. Thailand is making efforts to protect its endangered species, but the hog deer has the misfortune of favoring areas also favored by illegal drug manufacturers, making them very vulnerable to human predation.

Philippine Deer

Axis porcinus calamianensis

Jim Dolan, San Diego Zoo

Status	Endangered
Listed	June 14, 1976
Family	Cervidae (Deer)
Description	Fairly stocky body with a short head; coat is brownish with a dark stripe on the back.
Habitat	Forest edge with clear-cut areas.
Food	Young grasses and leaves.
Reproduction	One, rarely two, fawns after gestation period of 180 days.
Threats	Uncontrolled hunting.
Range	Philippine Islands: Busanga and Culion

Description

The Philippine deer, *Axis porcinus calamianensis*, is a small member of the true deer family, *Cervidae*, weighing 79 to 110 pounds. In general, the fairly stocky body with a short head measures 24 to 30 inches at the shoulders. Its body length measures 42 to 45 inches. The slender tail is of medium length, measuring 8 inches.

The coarse hair is longest on the flanks. Philippine deer do not have a mane on the throat or neck. The coat color is generally brownish with a dark stripe on the back, white underneath, and a whitish undersurface of the tail. Distinguishing features of this subspecies are the white spots on the throat and a white mark on the lips.

The Philippine deer's lyre-shaped antlers are carried on pedicels. In general, the antlers have three points per beam with the brow tine forming a right angle with the beam. The upper canines are usually missing and the lower teeth resemble incisors.

The Philippine deer greatly resembles the hog deer, *Axis porcinus*, in external appearance. The main difference in appearance is the distinctive white markings on the throat and lip of the Philippine deer. Geographically, the two species are distinct, with the Philippine deer found on a few islands in the Philippines and *A. porcinus* ranging from northern India to Indochina. However, some authorities disagree on the reason for this geographical gap between the two animals. Authorities such as Groves and Grubb suggest that Philippine deer are survivors of widespread Pleistocene populations of hog deer. Other authorities believe Philippine deer represent a more recent introduction of hog deer to the islands by ancient humans.

The exact taxonomy of the Philippine deer and other species of the genus *Axis* is controversial. Some authorities, such as Honacki, Kinman, and Koeppl, place all members of the genus *Axis* in the genus *Cervus*. Authorities such as Groves and Grubb consider Philippine deer to be a separate species, *Axis calamianensis*, not a subspecies.

Another common name for the Philippine deer is the Calamian hog deer.

Behavior

Adult males live alone or in small groups consisting of a female and her youngest offspring. After a period of 180 days, the female gives birth to one, rarely two, fawns. Little else is known about the behavior and reproductive habits of this rare species.

The Philippine deer's diet mainly consists of young grasses and leaves.

Habitat

Philippine deer live on Busanga, Culion, and a few other small islands of the Calamian group of the Philippines. They usually live on the forest edge; although they have been known to inhabit small, clear-cut areas.

Distribution

Currently, Philippine deer live exclusively on several islands on the Calamian group of the Philippines. These islands include Busanga with an area of 325 square miles, Culion with an area of 145 square miles, and a few even smaller islands.

Threats

Uncontrolled hunting has caused the population numbers of Philippine deer to dwindle. Because their range is restricted to small islands, they are extremely vulnerable to poaching and cultivation of habitat.

Conservation and Recovery

The Philippine deer's remoteness is both an aid and a hindrance to its preservation. It helps by making it hard for sports hunters to get to it; it hurts because it makes it hard for law enforcement personnel to watch over the deer and other wildlife on the islands, and consequently difficult to prevent the illegal hunting that does occur, as well as illegal logging. For about twenty years the Philippine government has tried to curb logging and to protect wildlife, with mixed success. On the large islands, logging companies have gone as far as hiring hunters to wipe out endangered species so that legal protection would be withdrawn from forested areas; in the late 1970s, the killing went as far as trying to exterminate indigenous peoples that the government sought to protect. Prosecutions have been rare, but have been increasing in number because the Philippines have been cooperating with law enforcement agencies of other countries to arrest and prosecute exporters illegally dealing in endangered species. This has included curbing the export of deer parts for trophies (to industrialized nations) and for folk medicine (to eastern Asia). If current efforts to halt logging on the Philippine deer's islands succeed, it has a fair chance for long-term survival.

Bawean (= Kuhl's) Deer

Axis porcinus kuhli

Ron Garrison, San Diego Zoo

Status	Endangered
Listed	June 2, 1970
Family	Cervidae (Deer)
Description	Small, brown heavy-set deer standing about 27 inches high at the shoulders.
Habitat	Tropical rain forest dominated by broadleaf-evergreen trees.
Food	Leaves and other vegetation.
Reproduction	One or two young every year in the spring.
Threats	Possible hunting and habitat loss, spraying of insecticides.
Range	Indonesia: Bawean Islands

Description

The Bawean deer, *Axis porcinus kuhli*, is a small, heavy-set deer that stands 24 to 40 inches high at the shoulders with a body length of 40 to 70 inches. It weighs 60 to 240 pounds. *A. porcinus kuhli* has a coarse brown coat with lighter underparts and a long, bushy tail.

Like other "hog" deer, Bawean deer run through the undergrowth with their head held down like a pig.

Behavior

In the mating season bucks use their antlers to detour rivals and attract does. At times of altercation, the bucks will wrestle with their antlers, crashing them together. Bucks are seldom hurt during fights. The buck who wins will remain with the doe for several days and will then leave in search of another.

Mating can occur year round but usually between July and November. The doe will give birth to one or two young every year in the spring (between February and June) after a gestation period of 180-210 days. When the fawn is strong enough the doe joins a group of other does with fawns.

The Bawean deer is diurnal and feeds in the early morning hours and again in the evening. Its diet includes grass, leaves and forbs.

Habitat

The Bawean deer inhabits a tropical rainforest biome dominated by broadleaf-evergreen trees with a warm, humid climate. The deer prefer a grassland habitat for grazing with a nearby dense forest for protection.

Distribution

The Bawean deer is known from the Bawean Islands, Indonesia where 200 to 500 animals are thought to survive.

Threats

Human pollution, destruction of natural habitat, possible hunting and poaching, and the spraying of insecticides have adversely affected this subspecies' population. The python is known to be a natural predator.

Conservation and Recovery

Local Indonesian and international conservation organizations have been working together to conserve the Bawean deer, as well as other endangered Indonesian wildlife. The pressing problem of habitat destruction probably needs to be addressed first. The Bawean deer requires a forest habitat, and logging and agriculture have eliminated most of the forest on Bawean Island. The Indonesian government is making a last-ditch effort to save what remains of its forests on most of its islands, and there are signs of success on Java that suggest it could be successful in saving some of the natural habitat on Bawean Island. Polluted waters are another significant problem that needs to be addressed. With a halt to logging would come diminished pollution from processing wood, but other human waste would still be a problem. A clean-up of the local environment would benefit local people as well as the wildlife and therefore could win the cooperation of the locals and local governments. To this end, an education program is needed that would show the benefits to people, as well as wildlife, if pollution were reduced. Although the Bawean deer is protected under Indonesian law, poachers threaten the deer. Although the deer is a food source, its primary appeal is in its commercial value: meat for sale, heads and tails for trophies, and body parts for use in folk medicine. Punishment for poaching can be severe in Indonesia, and conscientious law enforcement seems to be discouraging the hunting of the Bawean deer.

Marsh Deer

Blastocerus dichotomus

Luiz Claudio Marigo

Status	Endangered
Listed	June 2, 1970
Family	Cervidae (Deer)
Description	Coat changes from pale brown in winter to reddish in summer; the nose is surrounded by a dark black band; a lighter black stripe may be present, running from the nose to between the eyes or antlers; the legs are mostly black.
Habitat	Grassy savannas or marshes bordered by forest.
Food	Aquatic plants, especially grass and reeds.
Reproduction	One young after mating generally occurs in October and November.
Threats	Loss of wetlands.
Range	Argentina, Brazil, Bolivia, Paraguay, Peru

Description

The marsh deer, *Blastocerus dichotomus*, stands 3.5 to 4 feet tall at the shoulders and weighs up to 330 pounds. The color of its coat changes from pale brown in winter to reddish in summer. The nose is surrounded by a dark black band; a lighter black stripe may be present, running from the nose to between the eyes or antlers; the legs are mostly black. Each antler has 8 to 12 points, although many more points have been recorded in some individuals, and may grow as long as 2 feet. A distinguishing characteristic of the marsh deer is its light colored antlers.

Behavior

Although marsh deer are solitary foragers, they may form family groups comprised of a single male and several females and offspring. Mating generally occurs in October and November, producing one offspring, although newborns have been observed year round.

The diet of the marsh deer is aquatic plants, especially grass and reeds, which it forages at night.

Habitat

The marsh deer occurs in wetlands with dense vegetation, which provides camouflage as well as food sources. Its long legs and wide hooves give the marsh deer good mobility in its aquatic environment. Its preferred habitat is grassy savannas or marshes bordered by forest. During the rainy season when the marshes flood, the deer retreats to higher ground which, oftentimes, is grazing land for cattle.

Distribution

Marsh deer are distributed in scattered populations throughout wetlands in Argentina, Bolivia, Brazil, Paraguay and Peru. Its total population has been estimated at 20,000 to 40,000 individuals.

Threats

As with endangered deer throughout the world, the marsh deer has declined because of excessive hunting and habitat loss, but the marsh deer is especially vulnerable to agricultural development that drains wetlands to create pastures or farms. When the deer are forced onto higher ground during the rainy season, they come in contact with domestic cattle which pass diseases to the deer. Without natural immunities to these diseases, epidemics rage throughout flocks, rapidly reducing their numbers.

Conservation and Recovery

The habitats of the marsh deer are difficult to protect and are under constant pressure by agricultural development. Furthermore, these deer do not prosper in captivity because of their dependence on their marshy habitat. The only hope for the marsh deer's survival is the creation of reserves, but there is little sentiment for this remedy in the deer's host countries.

Visayan Deer

Cervus alfredi

Roland Wirth

Status	Endangered
Listed	September 1, 1988
Family	Cervidae (Deer)
Description	Small deer with short ears, tail, and antlers, fine, dense hair with yellowish white spots on shoulders, back and sides, and dark brown upper parts.
Habitat	Dense forest growth of the Philippines.
Food	Grasses, bark, twigs, and leaves.
Reproduction	Mating September to November.
Threats	Illegal hunting and deforestation, and military operations.
Range	Philippines (Leyte, Samar, Negros, Panay islands)

Description

The Visayan deer, *Cervus alfredi*, is a small deer standing about 25 inches at the shoulder. The ears, tail and antlers are relatively short. The hair is very fine and remarkably dense and soft. Coloration of the upper parts is generally very dark brown, and the underparts are buff. The shoulders, back and sides are marked throughout the year by yellowish white spots.

C. alfredi can be distinguished by its spotted adult coat from all other Sambar deer. It

also differs from the others in its fine and dense pelage, in having a relatively narrow skull, and in various other cranial characters.

C. alfredi was first described in 1870, and for many years after was considered a separate species. In recent decades, it was generally treated as a subspecies of the more widespread Philippine sambar (*C. mariannus*), or even of the common sambar (*C. unicolor*) found throughout Southeast Asia. In 1983, Grubb and Groves' detailed study of the taxonomy of the species again recognized *C. alfredi* as a full species. Moreover, they considered it the most, or perhaps second most, distinct kind of sambar deer.

Behavior

Deer feed early in the morning and also in the evening.

Visayan deer are known to migrate seasonally. In the winter months it is found at lower elevations, in the summer, higher elevations. Parturition probably begins in early summer and the copulation season runs through the end of September to early November.

Habitat

The Visayan deer is known only from the Visayan Islands in the central archipelago of the Philippines. The species appears to depend on dense forest growth.

The Visayan deer's range lies within the Oriental region. This region is between 68 degrees and 135 degrees East and between 10 degrees South and 32 degrees North. The vegetation comprises a tropical forest classification. Where forests are felled the soil erodes and ground temperatures rise. The top-soil is washed into the valleys by monsoon rains, causing flooding. This leaves behind a semi-desert area which is then over-run with coarse grass and vines.

Distribution

The Visayan deer originally inhabited eight islands in the central Philippine archipelago: Bohol, Cebu, Guimaras, Leyte, Negros, Panay, Samar, and Siquijor. It was fairly widespread in the early 20th century, but its decline began after World War II. The species has been extirpated from the islands of Bohol, Cebu, Guimaras, and Siquijor. It still survives on the other four islands of its original range, but only in relatively small and isolated patches of remnant habitat. Two extreme localized populations are known on Leyte, one in the north and one in the south of the island. There are also four small groups in south-central Samar and two in southern Negros. On Panay, this deer is still found in six parts of the western mountain chain. The largest population is in the Mount Madja-as/Mount Baloy area.

Threats

Loss of habitat and illegal hunting are two of the causes of the Visayan deer's decline. Upland logging began after World War II, eliminating much of the dense forest habitat on which the species depends. This clearing of the forest made the area much more accessible to settlers and hunters, greatly increasing the human population in this region. These new settlers practiced slash and burn agriculture, which involves clearing an area of forest, planting and harvesting crops, and then moving on to another area. This practice has accounted for nearly as much forest destruction as has commercial logging. By 1983 this practice was curtailed by the government, but the resulting unemployment forced many people to turn to slash and burn agriculture and to subsistence hunting.

Today, illegal hunting and deforestation continues. The species is sought as a source of food by both indigenous peoples of the region and increasing numbers of immigrants from crowded towns and coastal areas. It is not only shot, but is trapped, snared and run down with dogs.

Conservation and Recovery

Protection of the deer's remaining habitat and stricter enforcement of hunting limitations need to be implemented. To accomplish this, more money needs to be allotted for the Visayan deer's protection. Care must be taken to protect it from military operations in its range. A captive breeding program has been established, but so far has shown little success. More studies into the deer's reproductive characteristics and requirements could help this program to be more successful.

Another threat to the deer and its habitat is the activity by revolutionary forces, which further restricts the ability of the government to enforce protective laws and undertake conservation measures.

Swamp Deer [=Barasingha]

Cervus duvauceli

Philadelphia Zoo

Status	Endangered
Listed	June 2, 1970
Family	Cervidae (Deer)
Description	Brown, with yellow undersides; in the summer, males have reddish backs.
Habitat	Swamps, grasslands, deciduous forests,
Food	Grasses
Reproduction	Reaches reproductive maturity in its second year; may calve once or twice a year, with a gestation of about 250 days.
Threats	Loss of habitat to expansion of human settlements, predation, and humans hunting it for food and for its antlers.
Range	Central India to southern Nepal.

Description

Male swamp deer, *Cervus duvauceli*, grow to about 48 inches at the shoulder, with females standing slightly shorter at about 45 inches. Adults usually weigh between 375 and 400 pounds. Their antlers tend to have between 10 and 15 points. Fawns are spotted, probably to blend in with their usually shrubby, moist surroundings. Adults are golden brown on their sides and backs, blending into golden yellow on their throats and undersides. Adult males turn reddish brown on their backs in hot weather.

Behavior

Swamp deer seem to prefer to graze in the open, gathering in small groups to graze on grasses. They are alert, with males keeping watch for predators.

Habitat

The swamp deer's habitat tends to be wet, including central Indian grasslands, northern Indian swamp lands, and the deciduous forests of southern Nepal.

Distribution

At one time, the deer could be found in thousands of square miles of territory on the Indian subcontinent. The booming growth in India's human population has pushed them out of their southern territories. A subspecies, *Cervus duvauceli schomburaki*, once lived in Thailand, but it has been extinct for many years.

Human encroachment on the deer's traditional territory may have limited it to swamplands, although in the 1970s some could still be found in grassy plains. The deer seems adaptable to climates other than warm, moist ones, and has been found in the forests of Nepal.

Threats

Their preference for open areas makes swamp deer easy to see. This has made them easy prey for poachers, who sell the antlers to be carved into screws by boat builders and who eat the reportedly gamey, tough flesh. Although the animal is supposed to be protected in India and Nepal, the hunters are often driven by hunger, which may make persuading them to leave alone the swamp deer they find nearly impossible. Further, the deer's preference for inhabiting watery areas and its preference for eating grasses makes it a pest to rice farmers; the deer are attracted to the rice paddies and the rice plants. Because of this, as well as their having a reputation for raiding gardens, they are killed on sight as pests in some regions.

Conservation and Recovery

In the 1970s, there may have been no more than one hundred individuals left, but in wildlife parks in India and Nepal the deer population has grown to between 2500 and 4500, at present. Crucial to the animal's survival has been the maintenance of large parks that include not only the deer, but a variety of wildlife, especially the grasses on which the deer depends. An abundance of grasses within parks reduces the occurrence of deer wandering in search of grass on farmlands where it may be shot as a pest. Further helping the deer have been captive breeding programs in the United States; these programs have helped expand the deer's population and to help retain some of the genetic diversity it would otherwise have lost when its wild population nearly disappeared.

Bactrian Deer

Cervus elaphus bactrianus

Ron Garrison, San Diego Zoo

Status	Endangered
Listed	June 25, 1979
Family	Cervidae (Deer)
Description	Large deer measuring 98 inches in length and standing 43 to 51 inches at the shoulder, weighing up to 800 pounds, and bucks having antlers up to 5 feet long.
Habitat	River banks, open grasslands, and fringe areas in arid regions.
Food	Leaves and other vegetation.
Reproduction	One to two young each spring after gestation of 230 to 240 days.
Threats	Competition from livestock and poaching.
Range	Central Asia, northern Afghanistan, and Russian border

Description

The Bactrian deer, *Cervus elaphus bactrianus*, weighs 450 to 800 pounds, has a body length of 98 inches, and stands 43 to 51 inches at the shoulder. The tail is 7.5 inches long. The antlers may grow up to 5 feet long and weigh as much as 28 pounds.

Behavior

Rutting Bactrian deer fight for the possession of harems. Rutting takes place between August and September, and may extend to November. Fawns are born in the late spring.

A challenging stag approaches a harem holder and the two males roar at each other. Then they walk parallel to each other until one of the stags lowers his head and faces his opponent, at which time they lock antlers and twist each other around. If one succeeds in pushing the other rapidly backwards, the contest is ended and the loser runs off. The stags fight fiercely and serious injury results in as many as 25% of males during rutting season. As a result, smaller stags usually will not fight with animals of superior size or ability. Rutting males may fight as many as five times during the season.

The doe will give birth to one or two young every year in the spring after a gestation period of 33 to 34 weeks. The fawn is 11 to 17 pounds at birth. When the fawn is strong enough the doe joins a group of other does with fawns. After about 9 to 12 months the fawn will be weaned. Sexual maturity is reached at about 1.5 years.

The Bactrain deer grazes on whatever vegetation is available in its sparse habitat. It is most active at twilight and dusk but will feed during the day.

Bactrian deer are fairly social and form groups of 15 to 20 individuals.

Habitat

The Bactrain deer lives in a harsh environment of low rainfall and extreme temperatures along river banks and in open grasslands in arid terrain. It is the only deer that lives in a desert habitat.

Distribution

The Bactrain deer is known historically and presently from Central Asia, including Tibet, Kashmir, Turkestan and Afghanistan. Its present range is in the riparian forests and reed belts along the Amu-Darya and Syr-Darya rivers along the Afghanistan and Russian border. In the 1960s only a few hundred (400 to 500) deer were counted, but the captive population numbers 900 individuals, and there are certainly others in the wild. The total population is estimated at 2,000 animals.

Threats

Although the Bactrain deer is adapted to its harsh environment, competition from livestock and poaching has severely reduced population numbers. It is probable that many deer were killed during the Afghanistan/Russian conflict during the 1980s.

Conservation and Recovery

In 1970 Russia began creating protective areas and preserves for the Bactrian deer along the Amu-Darya river. Some of the wild deer were captured and relocated to seven preserves, where the population increased to some 900 animals by the early 1990s. The Tigrovaya Balka preserve holds the largest population of 450 to 500 deer.

Barbary Deer
Cervus elaphus barbarus

Status	Endangered
Listed	June 25, 1979
Family	Cervidae (Deer)
Description	Dark brown coat with spots along the back and a brownish-gray line; the horns are moderately branched with three points and may grow to a length of 39 inches.
Habitat	Thick oak and pine forests.
Food	Leaves and other vegetation.
Reproduction	One to two young every year in the spring.
Threats	Poaching and competition from sheep and goats.
Range	Tunisia/Algerian border

Cervus elaphus   Luther C. Goldman, USFWS

Description

The Barbary deer, *Cervus elaphus barbarus*, is about 39 inches tall at the shoulders and weighs up to 400 pounds. It dark brown coat usually has some spots along the back and a brownish-gray line. The horns are moderately branched with three points and may grow to a length of 39 inches. This species sheds its horns at the beginning of winter (November to December), which grow again over a three month period in the spring.

Behavior

The Barbary deer is primarily nocturnal and feeds in the early morning hours and again in the evening. During the spring, males require calcium to grow their antlers. Often there is a deficiency of calcium in the food sources, and the animal must use its calcium reserves, which weakens the animal and makes him less competitive during the rut.

Rutting lasts from mid-September through October. The doe will give birth to one or two young every year in the spring after a gestation period of 33 to 34 weeks. The fawn is 11 to 17 pounds at birth. The mother hides the newborn and attends to it only while feeding. The reason for her absence is that newborns do not have any scent, which gives them greater protection from predators, and the mother does not want to contaminate them with her own odor. When the fawn is strong enough the doe joins a group of other does with fawns. After about 9 to 12 months the fawn will be weaned. Sexual maturity is reached at about 1.5 years.

Habitat

The Barbary deer is restricted to thick vegetation in oak and pine forests in the mountains along the boundary of Tunisia and Algeria.

Distribution

The Barbary deer is the only deer which is an African native. During the Roman Empire era, the deer was plentiful in Morocco but was hunted to extinction during the classical era. Sightings were reported but not confirmed on the Barbary deer in Morocco during the 1920s. Until the 1850s the species was widespread and abundant throughout its range. This deer is currently restricted to the Atlas mountains, where the population is estimated at about 500 animals, and to a protected population in Tunisia, which numbers some 4,000 individuals.

Threats

The decline of the Barbary deer began with the Roman conquests of Morocco due to overhunting and deforestation of habitat. Continual habitat degradation combined with annual forest fires have steadily depleted the population. Nomads routinely fence water supplies to prevent wildlife from drinking it,

and this certainly has restricted the repopulation of deer and other wildlife.

Threats also include competition from livestock (sheep and goats), and poaching, which has severely reduced population numbers. Old regional laws granting landowners the rights to hunt any animals on their land are still honored so that national laws protecting species are disregarded.

Conservation and Recovery

Tunisia has protective measures that absolutely prohibit selling deer skins or body parts. Tunisia has also established nature reserves, where the Barbary deer is thriving.

Corsican Red Deer

Cervus elaphus corsicanus

Museum of Natural History

Status	Endangered
Listed	March 30, 1972
Family	Cervidae (Deer)
Description	Small deer weighing 165-176 pounds; the coarse fur is brown above, with paler underparts; the rump and buttocks have a prominent pale-colored patch; males have a long, dense mane.
Habitat	Scrub forest of southern Sardinia and, formerly, Corsica.
Food	Leaves and twigs in the forests; grasses in open areas.
Reproduction	1 sometimes 2 fawns after a gestation of 230 to 240 days.
Threats	Competition with domestic sheep for grazing; loss of habitat.
Range	Sardinia

Description

The Corsican red deer, *Cervus elaphus corsicanus*, is one of the smallest subspecies of the Red Deer, *Cervus elaphus*, weighing 165-176 pounds and measuring 33.5 to 39 inches at the shoulder. Other subspecies of *C. elaphus* can weigh as much as 748 pounds and measure up to 59 inches at the shoulder. The small size of the Corsican red deer is typical of many species and subspecies confined to islands.

Males have thick well-developed pronged antlers, with an extra tine above the brow tine.

Females do not have antlers. The coarse fur is brown above, with paler underparts. The rump and buttocks have a prominent pale-colored patch. Males have a long, dense mane.

The species *C. elaphus* contains many old world and new world subspecies, including *C. e. corsicanus*. Many authorities disagree on the exact number of subspecies. Groves and Grubb grouped the subspecies into 3 systematic units. The first group consists of the European red deer, including the rare subspecies *C. e. corsicanus* of Corsica and Sardinia, *C. e. barbarus* from North Africa, and *C. e. maral* from Asia Minor and the Caucasus. The second group contains 6 subspecies from south-eastern and central Asia, *C.e. yarkandensis* of Sinkiang, *C.e. bactrianas* of southeastern Asia, *C.e. hanglu* of Kashmir, *C.e. wallichi* of southern Tibet and Bhutan, *C.e. macneilli* of eastern Tibetan plateau and Sinkiang, and *C.e. kansuensis* of north-central China. The third group includes subspecies from eastern Kazakhstan, Sinkiang, Mongolia, Manchuria, Korea, Southern Siberia, and very disjunct populations in North America.

Behavior

Corsican red deer are gregarious animals, living together in herds. The females live separately from the males, except during the annual rutting season. During rutting season, males attract females with displays and vocalizations. The males spray urine onto their bellies and forequarters during the rut.

Corsican red deer give birth in the spring after a gestation period of 230 to 240 days. In general, females give birth to one, sometimes two, fawns weighing 11 to 17 pounds. The young are weaned at 9 to 12 months of age and reach sexual maturity at approximately 18 months of age. Corsican red deer can live 15 to 18 years.

Corsican red deer browse on leaves and twigs in the forests and graze on grasses in open areas. In general, subspecies of *C. elaphus* feed on various woody plants, grasses, and forbs depending upon the time of year. Most subspecies of *C. elaphus*, including *C. e. corsicanus*, are primarily active at night and at twilight. The animals make daily trips between covered resting areas and feeding places.

Habitat

Corsican red deer live in the scrub forest of southern Sardinia and, formerly, Corsica.

Distribution

The Corsican red deer was originally found on two islands in the Mediterranean Sea, Corsica and Sardinia. Ironically, the commonly named Corsican red deer has been extirpated from its namesake island, Corsica. On Sardinia, the species is only found in three separate areas.

Threats

Along with illegal hunting, habitat degradation has endangered the Corsican red deer. Because of the limited space on the islands of Corsica and Sardinia, increases in human population have greatly reduced the available habitat for this species. Unfortunately, the Corsican red deer has to compete with domestic sheep for the remaining grazing land.

Conservation and Recovery

Recently, efforts have been made to reintroduce the Corsican red deer to its former home on the island of Corsica using individuals from Sardinia. Unfortunately, no captive population of the Corsican red deer exists to start a breeding program.

Hanglu [=Kashmir Stag]

Cervus elaphus hanglu

Swamp Deer (*Cervus duvauceli*)   Philadelphia Zoo

Status	Endangered
Listed	June 2, 1970
Family	Cervidae (Deer)
Description	Brown in the winter to reddish-brown in summer with a grayish rump patch; antlers grow to 4 feet and generally have 10 points.
Habitat	Mixed broadleaf forests.
Food	Grasses, leaves, shoots from bushes and trees.
Reproduction	Rut occurs from October to November.
Threats	Degradation of habitat due to sheep herding; diseases.
Range	India: Kashmir

Description

Like its cousin, the shou (*C. e. wallichi*), the hanglu, *C. e. hanglu*, changes colors, from brown in the winter to reddish-brown in summer with a grayish rump patch. It strongly resembles the endangered swamp deer. It stands 4 feet at the shoulders and weighs up to 440 pounds. The antlers grow to 4 feet and generally have 10 points. The antlers are shed in March and April, just before the birth of the young.

Behavior

After shedding their antlers, mature males form groups and migrate to summer habitats at higher elevations, up to 12,000 feet. Immatures and juveniles remain with the females; older deer form their own group. The social hierarchy among males is determined by size, antlers, and strength. The social order seems to be quite complex with every member of the group occupying a specific place. The new horns are grown by September, at which time the males rejoin the females in preparation for the October rut. The males attempt to establish harems, which leads to battles over mating rights. At the end of the mating season in November, the males move to their winter feeding ground.

Habitat

During the winter the hanglu resides in mixed broadleaf forests at elevations below 9,000 feet and below the snow line; in summer it ascends to elevations of up to 12,000 feet.

Distribution

Historically, the hanglu occurred in wide ranges in the southern portions of the Himalayas, but today it is restricted to the Dachigam preserve in the north of Srinagar in Kashmir.

Threats

In the 1960s the Kashmiri government authorized sheep herding within the range of the Kashmir deer, which resulted in a serious reduction of food sources for the deer. Sheep farming also caused an increase in hunting, degradation of forest habitat, and the introduction of infectious diseases, causing the population to decrease in unprotected areas to as few as 25 individuals by 1970. Within the Dachigam preserve, poaching was a continuing problem.

Conservation and Recovery

Some protected zones were established for wildlife when sheep herding was approved by the government. Although the population in the unprotected areas was greatly reduced, once poaching was controlled in the preserve, the protective population rose, and there may be as many as 400 animals today.

McNeill's [=Szechwan] Deer

Cervus elaphus macneilli

Cervus elaphus

Luther C. Goldman, USFWS

Status	Endangered
Listed	June 2, 1970
Family	Cervidae (Deer)
Description	Changes colors, from brown in the winter to reddish-brown in summer; stands 4 feet at the shoulders and weighs up to 450 pounds; the antlers grow to 4 feet.
Habitat	Rhododendron forests.
Food	Shoots, buds, and leaves of rhododendron.
Reproduction	Mating season in November.
Threats	Hunting.
Range	China

Description

Like its cousin, the hanglu *(C. e. hanglu)*, McNeill's deer, *C. e. macneilli*, changes colors, from brown in the winter to reddish-brown in summer. It stands 4 feet at the shoulders and weighs up to 450 pounds. The antlers grow to 4 feet and generally have 5 points. The antlers are shed in March and April, just before the birth of the young.

Behavior

After shedding their antlers in March, mature males form groups and migrate to summer habitats. The new horns are grown by September, at which time the males rejoin the females in preparation for the October rut. The males attempt to establish harems, which leads to battles over mating rights. At the end of the mating season in November, the males move to their winter feeding ground.

McNeill's deer feeds on shoots, buds, and leaves of the rhododendron forest which it inhabits.

Habitat

The probable habitat for McNeill's deer are the rhododendron forests along the Yangtze and Yalung rivers, and in the Mekong forest.

Distribution

McNeill's deer may still survive in the rhododendron forests in the Sinkiang mountains in Chinese Turkestan and along the Tibetan border above 9,800 feet elevation. McNeill's deer is very rare if not extinct.

Threats

McNeill's deer was hunted for the velvet on its antlers which are believed to possess aphrodisiac qualities. Because only the younger deer have velvet on their antlers, the future generations of deer are killed before they can become established.

Conservation and Recovery

Other than international bans prohibiting exporting animal parts for commercial trade, there are no conservation efforts for McNeill's deer.

Shou [=Sikkim Deer]

Cervus elaphus wallichi

Cervus elaphus   Luther C. Goldman, USFWS

Status	Endangered
Listed	June 2, 1970
Family	Cervidae (Deer)
Description	Color in the spring is tan or brown, changing to a deep brownish red in summer. The antlers grow to 5 feet and generally have 5 points.
Habitat	Mixed forests with open areas.
Food	Leaves, shoots, and grasses.
Reproduction	One, sometimes two fawns after gestation of 230 to 240 days.
Threats	Low population numbers; hunting; war.
Range	Tibet, Bhutan

Description

The shou or Sikkim deer, *Cervus elaphus wallichi*, is one of the red deer. It stands about 4 feet at the shoulders and weighs up to 440 pounds. The color in the spring is tan or brown, changing to a deep brownish red in summer. The antlers grow to 5 feet and generally have 5 points; the upper parts of the antlers incline toward the front.

C. e. wallichi is also known as the Tibetan red deer and Wallich's deer.

Behavior

It is assumed that shous rut like other red deer, and that females produce one, sometimes two fawns after gestation of 230 to 240 days. The normal food for red deer includes leaves, shoots, and grasses.

Habitat

Shous inhabit mixed forests with open areas.

Distribution

The shou once occurred in the Chumbi valley and the Lingmothng area in Tibet, but is probably extinct in both ranges. It is thought to survive in the Tsari area in southeastern Tibet, and may occur along the border of Bhutan, where a small group was discovered in 1982. The only known captive animal is in the palace of the Dalai Lama in Lhasa.

Threats

Because of its low population numbers, the shou is highly susceptible to hunting. The shou's range falls within an area of long-standing military conflict between China and India, and the many troops stationed there hunt the wildlife with automatic weapons. The animals are also accidentally killed during skirmishes.

Conservation and Recovery

Because of the continuing military conflict in the shou's known range, no conservation measures are possible, and because there is only one captive animal, captive breeding is not possible. The future of this species is bleak.

Yarkand Deer

Cervus elaphus yarkandensis

Cervus elaphus   Luther C. Goldman, USFWS

Status	Endangered (possibly extinct)
Listed	March 30, 1972
Family	Cervidae (Deer)
Description	Coarse fur is brown above, with paler underparts; the rump and buttocks have a pale patch.
Habitat	Riparian forest with open scrub and grassy areas.
Food	Leaves and twigs in the forests and grasses in open areas.
Reproduction	1, sometimes 2, young after gestation of 230 to 240 days.
Threats	Hunted for its antlers, meat, and hide; loss of habitat to agriculture.
Range	China: Tarim River Basin

Description

The Yarkand deer, *Cervus elaphus yarkandensis*, is a relatively large subspecies of the Red Deer, *Cervus elaphus*, weighing 441 to 772 pounds and measuring 53 to 55 inches at the shoulder.

Mature males have thick well-developed pronged antlers, with an extra tine above the brow tine. Females do not have antlers. The coarse fur is brown above, with paler underparts. The rump and buttocks have a prominent pale-colored patch. Males have a long, dense mane.

Behavior

Yarkand deer are gregarious animals, living together in herds. The females live separately from the males, except during the annual rutting season in September and October. During rutting season, males of the *C. elaphus* subspecies attract females with displays and vocalizations. The males spray urine onto their bellies and forequarters during the rut.

Although little is know about the extremely rare Yarkand deer's reproduction, the gestation period is believed to be 230 to 240 days. In general, female *C. elaphus* give birth to one, sometimes two, young weighing 11 to 17 pounds. The young are weaned at 9 to 12 months of age and reach sexual maturity at approximately 18 months of age. Yarkand deer can live 18 to 20 years.

Yarkand deer browse on leaves and twigs in the forests and graze on grasses in open areas. In general, *C. elaphus* feed on various woody plants, grasses, and forbs depending upon the time of year.

Most subspecies of *C. elaphus*, including *C. e. yarkandensis*, are primarily active at night and at twilight. The animals make daily trips between covered resting areas and feeding places.

Habitat

In the past, Yarkand deer occurred in the riparian forest of the Tarim River Basin in China. They preferred open forest, scrub forest, scrub thickets, and some open grassy areas and glades.

Distribution

The Yarkand deer once inhabited the Tarim River Basin in Sinkiang, China but is presumed to have disappeared from its Tarim River Basin habitat in Sinkiang, although it has not yet been listed as extinct.

Threats

Although the Yarkand deer has been hunted for its antlers, meat, and hide, the main reason for the near extinction of this species is the loss of habitat to agriculture.

The Tarim River Basin home of the Yarkand deer has a very dense human population. Yarkand deer antlers are sought after for use in Chinese folk medicine.

Conservation and Recovery

The Yarkand deer is listed by IUCN as endangered and is protected by the government of China.

Eld's Brow-Antlered Deer

Cervus eldi

Montgomery Zoo

Status	Endangered
Listed	June 2, 1970
Family	Cervidae (Deer)
Description	Brown-antlered deer with dark brown or black pelage and foot structure adapted to marsh habitats.
Habitat	Marshes.
Food	Vegetation
Reproduction	A single fawn is produced after a gestation period of 8 months.
Threats	Overhunting, habitat loss, and competition with domestic livestock.
Range	Burma, India, Thailand

Description

The unique antlers of Eld's brow-antlered deer, *Cervus eldi*, have brow tines that form a continuous curve with the beam so that the antlers in profile appear bow-shaped. Only the males have these antlers. These long brow tines appear to be effective weapons when the stags are fighting during the rut. These antlers may grow up to 3 feet in length. The subspecies *C. e. siamensis* differs from the typical form *C. e. eldi* in having the beam palmated toward the crown, with several small snags appearing on the posterior edge. The subspecies *C. e. thamin* has less palmated antlers.

Eld's brow-antlered deer measures 59 to 67 inches long from its snout to the base of its tail and stands 47 to 51 inches tall. This deer's tail is 9 to 10 inches long.

In the winter, the brownish-red fur is course and long. The fur is shorter and lighter in color in the summer. Females are paler than the stags in all seasons. Adult stags have long thick hair forming a mane on the neck. Along the back, adults have faint spots. In fawns, these spots are more prominent and appear closer together. The ears, eyes, and chin usually have some white hairs around their edges. The subspecies *C. e. siamensis* appears to be more reddish than the typical form *C. e. eldi*. Another subspecies, *C. e. thamin*, is darker than *C. e. eldi*.

Eld's brow-antlered deer can be readily distinguished by foot modifications which enables it to walk easily in its marshy habitat. While the length of the foot is unchanged, the back part of the first phalanx is hardened resulting in a larger support surface. This modification helps pre-vent the legs from sinking into the mud.

There are three subspecies of *C. eldi*:

C. e. eldi (M'Clelland, 1842), Manipur Eld's deer

C. e. siamensis (Lydekker, 1915), Siamese Eld's deer

C. e. thamin (Thomas, 1918), Thamin Eld's deer

The local people call *C. e. eldi* "sangai" which means "the animal that looks at you".

Behavior

The mating season of the subspecies *C. e. eldi* lasts from the middle of March to the end of May, while the mating season for *C. e. siamensis* lasts from February to March. The males gather into groups during the mating season but live separately during the rest of the year. During this time, the males engage in fierce, sometimes dangerous, battles to determine the dominant males. Occasionally the participants have been killed, and dead males have been found hit in the eyes by the victorious male's brow tine.

After a gestation period of approximately 8 months, usually a single calf is born.

The diet of the swamp dwelling Eld's brow-antlered deer consists of wild rice and other plants typical of the watery environment. It prefers to rest in the shady edge of the forests during the hottest parts of the day.

Habitat

The different subspecies of *C. eldi* occur in distinctly different habitats.

The Manipur brow-antlered deer, *C. e. eldi*, is restricted to the wetlands at Keibul Lamjao National Park in Manipur, India. These wetlands consist of water-filled depressions with large areas of floating organic matter called phumdi. Grasses, sedges, and reeds grow on top of the phumdi. Eld's brow-antlered deer spend much of the year on the phumdi and move to higher hills during the monsoons.

On the other hand, the Thailand brow-antlered deer, *C. e. siamensis*, occurs in drier open plains and deciduous forests in Southeast Asia. Interestingly, stags are very fond of wallowing in mud, possibly indicating that the subspecies may have recently inhabited swampy areas. The subspecies could have been forced from these areas by habitat destruction. In the drier habitat, the Thailand brow-antlered deer avoids dense forests possibly because the males' hooked-shaped brow tine gets easily tangled in branches and hanging vines.

Distribution

C. eldi is known from three geographic locations. *C. e. thamin* occurs in Burma. *C. e. eldi* is restricted to Manipur in Keibul Lamjao

National Park. Lastly, *C. e. siamensis* is known from Hainan west to Thailand. This subspecies is extinct, or close to it, over most of its range.

Threats

The subspecies of *C. eldi* are declining in number due to overhunting, habitat loss, and competition with domestic livestock.

The marsh habitat of *C. e. eldi* has been reduced because of domestic stock grazing and illegal cultivation in the center of the Keibul Lamjao National Park. Other human activities such as grass and tree cutting, and burning during February to April, has also threatened this subspecies. Burning especially threatens this subspecies because this activity occurs during rutting season and interferes with the animals' breeding.

The forest in Thailand, home of *C. e. siamensis*, has increasingly been cleared because of technical advances in agriculture and human population increases. Many local tribes still practice shifting cultivation.

Conservation and Recovery

C. eldi has responded positively to recovery efforts. For example, in 1977 when Keibul Lamjao was declared a National Park, *C. e. siamensis* began to increase. Additionally, a captive breeding program for this subspecies has been set up in several zoos in India. Because of strict laws protecting *C. e. thamin* in Burma, its population has increased from a few hundred to a few thousand individuals.

Shansi Sika Deer

Cervus nippon grassianus

Cervus nippon   E. R. Degginger

Status	Endangered
Listed	June 25, 1979
Family	Cervidae (Deer)
Description	Large Chinese sika deer, standing 3 feet 6 inches at the shoulder, adult males weigh 220 pounds with almost invisible spots; body is dark grayish-brown, becoming a rich brown on its back and the lower parts of its legs; has a patch of long white hair edged with black below the heel of its outer hind leg.
Habitat	Forested regions of Shansi Province, China
Food	Grasses
Reproduction	Gestation period of 211 days.
Threats	Uncontrolled hunting.
Range	China: Shansi Province

Description

The Shansi sika deer, *Cervus nippon grassianus*, is one of the four larger races of Chinese sika deer, standing 3 feet 6 inches at the shoulder, the weight of an adult male being about 220 pounds. It is readily distinguishable because the spots, so distinctive a feature of the other races, are almost invisible on it both in summer and in winter. The general color of its body is dark grayish-brown, becoming a rich brown on its back and the lower parts of its legs. Below the heel of its outer hind leg is a patch of long white hair edged with black. All subspecies of *Cervus nippon* are to a greater or lesser extent spotted with white when in summer coat; and all possess a distinct throat and neck mane during the winter, together with a conspicuous erectile rump patch edged with black. The antlers have 6 to 8 points with the top points arranged palmate.

There has been taxonomic confusion in the past, but the consensus of opinion of most authorities recognizes seven subspecies, which vary in size and general appearance.

Behavior

The Shansi sika deer is a forest dweller in the wild state, but in captivity it readily adapts to open grasslands.

Habitat

The Shansi sika deer inhabits forested regions of Shansi Province, China.

Distribution

This subspecies at one time may have been distributed throughout the whole of the mountainous area of West Shansi, as well as in the mountains that extend in a north and south line between Shansi and Chihli.

Threats

Uncontrolled hunting has coincided with widespread degradation of forest habitat that were the sika's natural habitat, and without which the animal cannot survive in the wild state.

Conservation and Recovery

The status of the Shansi sika deer is a mystery: It is very rare and may even be extinct, at least in the wild. It is possible that it survives in a few Chinese zoos, but outside scientists have yet to confirm this. If the Shansi sika deer is to have any chance of survival in the wild, hunting of it needs to be halted altogether. Its habitat is nearly gone, so what little remains — if any — perhaps in the small mountains to the south, where a few other rare species are making their last stands, needs to be protected from human intrusion. If any of the deer survive in zoos, care must be taken that they do not crossbreed with other subspecies of the sika deer; crossbreeding is significant problem in Far Eastern deer populations.

Ryukyu Sika Deer

Cervus nippon keramae

Formosan Sika and Ryukyu Sika   D. W. Ovenden

Status	Endangered
Listed	March 30, 1972
Family	Cervidae (Deer)
Description	Mostly brown with white spots over the lateral portions of its fur.
Habitat	Diverse habitats consisting of deciduous woodland, thicket and polestage conifers, new plantations, rides and glades.
Food	Leaves and other vegetation.
Reproduction	Gestation period of 217 days.
Threats	Shortage of water; presence of goats; poor forage.
Range	Japan: Ryukyu Islands

Description

The Ryukyu sika deer, *Cervus nippon keramae*, has a head-body length of 98 inches. The tail is up to 7.5 inches. The Ryukyu sika deer weighs up to 1100 pounds. This species is mostly brown with white spots over the lateral portions of its pelage. This subspeices bears a close resemblance to the typical race that inhabits Japan.

C. n. keramae was first described by Kuroda in 1924, and is distinguishable from *C. n. nippon* by the small size of its body and skull, as by its antlers, which are smaller and have more warty appendages.

Behavior

This species browses on leaves and other vegetation. This species seems to utilize coniferous woodland during the day and migrates to deciduous woodland at night during the summer and winter months.

Habitat

Sika deer will utilize a variety of habitats including deciduous woodland, thicket and polestage conifers, new plantations, rides and glades. The Ryukyu sika deer has displayed adaptability and utilizes resources offered at any time.

all goats for the island.

Distribution

This deer was introduced into the Ryukyu Islands from Japan many years ago: the date of introduction is not known, but there is a record of deer on the islands in 1757. Its long isolation has resulted in the development of an insular form with distinctive characteristics. The sika exists on three small islands in the Ryukyu group: Yakabi-Jima, Aka-Jima, and Geruma-Jima.

Threats

The islands of Ryukyu are very small and support poor quality forage, much is comprised of *Miscanthus sinensis*; this is probably due to the presence of goats. There is also a shortage of water on the islands at times.

Some deer have fallen into a copper-ore separator tank that was built before World War II and is no longer utilized; others have fallen from the steep cliffs during the frequent sparring that takes place in the rutting season.

Conservation and Recovery

In January 1955, the Ryukyu sika was officially designated a natural monument, giving it full legal protection. Other measures that have been taken to safeguard the race include the demolition of the obsolete copper-mine construction and the building of an artificial catchment of the provision of water. Plans have also been made to improve the grazing on Yakabi-Shima by the introduction of leguminous plants and the elimination of

South China Sika Deer

Cervus nippon kopschi

C. nippon mandarinus　　　　　Craig W. Racicot, San Diego Zoo

Status	Endangered
Listed	June 25, 1979
Family	Cervidae (Deer)
Description	Yellowish umber brown to bright chestnut brown with a relatively distinct, dark dorsal stripe; white spots cover the animal; although they are less distinct on the upper part of the neck and shoulder and thighs.
Habitat	Deciduous woodland, thickets and polestage conifers.
Food	Grasses, broadleaf vegetation, and heather.
Threats	Habitat loss; overhunting.
Range	Southern China

Description

The South China sika deer, *Cervus nippon kopschi*, is generally yellowish umber brown to bright chestnut brown with a relatively distinct, dark dorsal stripe. White spots cover the animal; although they are less distinct on the upper part of the neck and do not extend very far down the shoulder and thighs. In winter, the spots are less noticeable. Both sexes have a dark mane in summer.

The narrow antlers stand erect over the head and bend slightly backward. The bay tine is absent. The hoofs are tapered in front and round in the rear.

This species is of the family *Cervidae* (the modern deer) and subfamily *Cervinae* (Eurasian deer). China was an important center of deer evolution and dispersal, and thus has a relatively large number of different deer taxa. It is believed that all sika deer species were derived from hybrids of the red deer group and the Japanese mainland group (*Cervus nippon nippon*).

C. n. kopschi was originally described in 1878 by Swinhoe as a separate species *Cervus kopschi*. Lydekker designated this deer as *Cervus hortulorum kopschi*.

Behavior

Little is known about the food habits of the South China sika deer. Other subspecies of *C. nippon* eat grasses and broadleaf vegetation. Data collected by Mann in 1983 indicate that activity levels do not fluctuate with either the time of day or year.

In general sika deer give birth to one, occasionally two fawns.

Habitat

In the past, the South China sika deer occurred in mountainous areas in southern China. As the subspecies may now be extinct in the wild, little is known about its exact habitat requirements. Many of the other subspecies of *C. nippon* are considered woodland deer and spend most of their lives associated with forests or appropriately wooded areas.

Distribution

Historically, *C. n. kopschi* occurred more or less continuously from the Yangtze River basin eastward to the coast and southward as far as the north of Kwangtun province. It was also recorded in 1842 on the island of Chusan off the mouth of the Yangtze. However, by the 1930's, this subspecies' range had contracted to a small area in the mountains of southern Anhui and closely adjacent northwestern Chekiang and southeastern Kiangsi. In 1965, some individuals were thought to possibly exist in the Yangtze valley.

Threats

This subspecies has been and still is threatened by habitat loss and overhunting. When hunted, sika deer of all ages and sexes are taken because they are killed with set-guns, snares and pit falls.

Conservation and Recovery

Rigid protection by the Chinese government may help the remaining, if any, populations in the wild.

North China Sika Deer

Cervus nippon mandarinus

Craig W. Racicot, San Diego Zoo

Status	Endangered
Listed	June 25, 1979
Family	Cervidae (Deer)
Description	Yellowish brown fur with dark underparts; white spots cover the deer in summer, with fewer spots appearing on the winter coat; tapered hoof prints in front and round in rear.
Habitat	Wooded areas and forests
Food	Grasses, broadleaf vegetation, and heather.
Reproduction	Gestation period of 217 days.
Threats	Habitat loss and overhunting.
Range	China: Shansi Province

Description

The North China sika deer, *Cervus nippon mandarinus*, has dark yellowish brown fur with dark underparts. White spots cover the deer in summer, with fewer spots appearing on the winter coat. The metatarsal tuft is the same color as the rest of the leg. The comparatively long tail is mainly reddish with little white. Subspecies of the sika deer, *C. nippon*, have hoofs that taper in the front and are round in the rear.

The species *C. nippon* is of the family *Cervidae* (the Modern deer) and subfamily *Cervinae* (Eurasian deer). Milne-Edwards originally described *C. n. mandarinus* in 1871 as a separate species, *Cervus mandarinus*. Lydekker considered this subspecies only a variation of the species *Cervus hortulorum*.

Behavior

Because this rare subspecies is little studied, it dietary habits in the wild are little known. Other *C. nippon* subspecies eat grasses and broadleaf vegetation.

Although the periodicity of the North

China sika deer is not reported, data collected by Mann on other *C. nippon* subspecies in 1983 indicate that activity levels do not fluctuate with either the time of day or year.

Habitat

The North China sika deer probably inhabited mountainous areas in northern China. Unfortunately little is known about its natural habitat because the subspecies is extremely rare in the wild and has only been found in a few small populations since 1918. Many of the other subspecies of *C. nippon* are considered woodland deer and spend most of their lives associated with forests or appropriately wooded areas.

Distribution

C. n. mandarinus originally may have occurred over a wide range in northeastern China. However, by 1918, it was only found in the wild on the Imperial Hunting Grounds north of Tung Ling (eastern Tombs) and in the Wei-ch'ang to the north of Jehol, both in the Chihli province, and to the north and northeast of Peking in the Shansi Province. Its range further constricted in the 1930s to northeastern Chihli in the Tung Ling and Jehol areas.

Presently this subspecies may occur in the Shansi Province, but not near Peking. Its status in the Chihli province is unknown.

Threats

Along with overhunting, destruction of its habitat seriously threatens this very rare subspecies.

Conservation and Recovery

Some North China sika deer are reportedly being bred on deer farms north of Peking. Otherwise, no known conservation measures are underway.

Formosan Sika Deer

Cervus nippon taiouanus

Status	Endangered
Listed	June 25, 1979
Family	Cervidae (Deer)
Description	Stands only 35 inches tall; light brown with white spots and a dorsal stripe; the coat is thicker and somewhat darker in the winter months.
Habitat	Deciduous woodland, thickets and polestage conifers.
Food	Grasses, broadleaf vegetation, and heather.
Threats	Habitat loss and overhunting.
Range	Taiwan

P. I. Wagner

Description

The Formosan Sika deer, *Cervus nippon taiouanus*, is relatively large for an island deer measuring up to 38.5 inches high at the shoulders. Most island mammals are much smaller than their mainland relatives.

In the summer, the coat is generally a bright chestnut color with prominent white spots and a reddish tint on the hind part of the neck. The winter fur becomes more drab and the spots less noticeable. However, the fact that the spots persist in the winter at all is a distinguishing feature for this subspecies. The black line bordering the white rump patch and running down the center of the tail is more distinct than in the similar Japanese Sika deer (*C. n. nippon*). The metatarsal glands are brownish.

The antlers measure up to 19.8 inches along the curve. Like all subspecies of *C. nippon*, the hoofs are tapered in front and round in the rear.

This subspecies is of the family *Cervidae* (the modern deer) and subfamily *Cervinae* (Eurasian deer). China was an important center for deer evolution and dispersal of many of the deer species. This subspecies was originally described by Blyth in 1860 as a full species, *Cervus taiouanus*. Other synonyms for this subspecies include *Pseudaxis taivanus*, *Elaphoceros taevanus*, and *Axis taivanus*.

Behavior

Because the Formosan sika deer has disappeared from its native habitat, its usual diet is unknown. However, in captivity subspecies of *C. nippon* feed on grasses and broadleaf vegetation.

In captivity, the activity levels of subspecies of *C. nippon* do not fluctuate with either the time of day or year.

Habitat

The Formosan sika deer typically inhabited grasslands in lowland areas at the coast, along rivers, and in the mountains and foothills below 300 meters in elevation on the Island of Taiwan (formerly Formosa). Because it has been changed into agricultural land and planted with cassava and *Aleurites* trees, this habitat has almost completely disappeared. And unfortunately, the Formosan sika deer seems to have disappeared along with the grasslands.

Unlike other subspecies of *C. nippon* which prefer woodlands, the Formosan sika deer did not associate with forests.

Distribution

This subspecies is endemic to the Island of Taiwan. In captivity, it occurs worldwide in parks and zoos. Small herds exist in Whipsnade and Woburn Park in England. In China, a number of deer are raised on Lu-tao island east of T'aitung for its antlers. Thirty years ago a herd was imported to the zoological gardens on the small Japanese island of Oshima. Subsequently these deer escaped from the gardens and established themselves on the island's slopes.

Threats

Along with overhunting, the Formosan sika deer has probably been driven to extinction in the wild because of habitat loss. Most of its grassland habitat on the Island of Formosa has been converted to agricultural lands.

Conservation and Recovery

The Formosan sika deer has been bred in captivity in both Europe and Asia for years. The population of this sika deer is becoming replenished as a direct result of captive breeding programs in zoos.

Persian Fallow Deer
Dama dama mesopotamica

Maurice Wilson

Status	Endangered
Listed	June 2, 1970
Family	Cervidae (Deer)
Description	Summer coat is fawn with white spots; winter coat is gray to brown without spots.
Habitat	Mixed forests, plains and low montane regions.
Food	Grasses, leaves, shoots, and bark.
Reproduction	Gestation of 229 to 240 days.
Threats	Timber harvesting; competition.
Range	Iran, Iraq

Description

The male Persian fallow deer, *Dama dama mesopotamica*, has branched and palmate antlers measuring to 27.5 inches. During the summer the coat of both sexes is typically fawn colored with white spots on the back and flanks. During the winter it is grayish brown without spots. In both seasons the rump patch is edged with black and there is a black line down the back and tail. The color of the belly varies greatly from white to intermediate colors. It measures about 4.3 to 5.3 feet from the snout to the base of the tail, which is 7.4 to 7.7 inches long. Bucks weigh 132 to 187 pounds, while the much smaller does vary from a petite 66 to 110 pounds.

The Persian fallow deer was relatively unknown until 1875, when Sir Victor Brooke discovered and subsequently described this species. It is classified as both *Dama dama mesopotamica* and *Capra dama mesopotamica*; as well as under the full species designation, *Dama mesopotamica*. The Persian fallow deer is also known as the Mesopotamian fallow deer.

Behavior

The Persian fallow deer feeds on grasses, herbs, leaves, shoots and bark. It is primarily nocturnal, being most active during the twilight hours. The deer may at times, however, be observed during the day.

Habitat

The Persian fallow deer is rather adaptable and can be found in mixed forests, plains and low montane regions. It prefers woodlands and woodland edges with scrub. Documented associations include poplar, tamarisk and acacia gallery forest.

Distribution

During the Pleistocene period, the Persian fallow deer was considered to be widely distributed through North Africa and the Near East from southwest Iran through Mesopotamia to Syria, Jordan, Lebanon and Israel. It is extinct from North Africa, became extinct in Greece in the nineteenth century, and is also extinct from Sardinia.

This deer has been introduced to many areas of Europe, Australia and New Zealand, where it has established wild populations. Currently, it survives in two small areas in Iran and Iraq along the Dez and Karkheh rivers.

The population in 1966 was estimated at no more than 40 individuals.

Threats

As is a primary threat to much of the world's fauna and flora, the Persian fallow deer fell victim to the timber harvesting of its natural habitat, and to war. Its range is considered valuable agricultural land and increasing human populations will further encroach on the Persian fallow deer's habitat. This deer is also threatened by competition for space and food with domestic animals.

Conservation and Recovery

In 1969, the Iran Game and Fish Department initiated a rehabilitation program for the Persian fallow deer. This program involved capturing wild fallow deer, placing them into a reserve, and breeding them. Reports from 1969 claim successful breeding of the five males and six females within the reserve.

The Iran Game and Fish Department also declared a total ban on hunting, and defined the remaining woodlands inhabited by the Persian fallow deer as protected areas. A 27,000 acre area along the Dez River has been designated a wildlife park. It is hoped that this will regulate encroachment by domestic animals.

The ten-tear war between Iran and Iraq during the 1970s and 1980s probably resulted in widespread destruction of wildlife and of the Persian fallow deer. There may be as many as 200 captive fallow deer in northern Iran, but it is not known if the stock is pure enough to repopulate the species.

North Andean Huemul

Hippocamelus antisensis

Alan Shoemaker

Status	Endangered
Listed	June 14, 1976
Family	Cervidae (Deer)
Description	Short, stocky limbs; wide, long, mule-shaped ears; its short tail ends in a roughly triangular point.
Habitat	Dry, rocky slopes and mountains.
Food	Moss, lichens, and grassy plants.
Threats	Agricultural development; competition and diseases from domestic animals.
Range	Chile, Peru, and Ecuador

Description

The genus *Hippocamelus* includes only two species, *H. antisensis* (the North Andean Huemul) and *H. bisulcus* (the South Andean Huemul; see separate entry) which are found only in South America.

The North Andean huemul is of a medium body size; it is only about 3 feet tall at the withers and about 5 feet long. Its limbs are rather short; however, they are stocky and allow it to climb the most difficult of Andean mountains easily.

The ears are shaped somewhat like those of a mule; they are large, wide and long. Another distinguishing trait is the short tail, which ends in a roughly triangular point.

The antlers have a relatively simple structure with only one branch. They are short,

usually reaching only 1 foot in length. Exceptional cases have been known where the antlers had a larger development and a greater number of points. The antlers of the North Andean huemul are bifurcated just above the nose.

The coat is rather rough to the touch, consisting of coarse and brittle guard hairs with a dense, soft undercoat. The shaft of each hair is hollow and has a zigzag edge; this provides good heat insulation and serves to repel water. The color of the coat is subject to slight differences tied to seasonal changes. During the summer, the coat is mainly brown. During cold periods, it takes on colors tending to gray. The body appears to be flecked by a yellowish-black color because of the light and dark streaks.

The muzzle is decidedly darker than the

rest of the body and is characterized by a band on the forehead that is even darker than the muzzle.

The upper part of the tail is dark brown, while the lower part and the end are white.

During the last century, the abbot Molinas classified these animals into the genus *Equus*, based on tales told by people who had seen them. Later, zoologists found a similarity to llamas and classified them in the family *Camilidae*. The systematic position of these deer is still uncertain; within the *Cervidae* family they were originally classified in the genus *Odocoileus*, but are now usually classified in the distinct genus *Hippocamelus*.

The North Andean huemul is also known as the guemal, the taruca, and the Chilean guemal.

Behavior

The North Andean huemul's diet consists mainly of moss, lichens, and grassy plants in high-altitude pastures. It pastures both during daylight hours, and at night. Huemuls in general are considered to be solitary animals; however, they may live in small groups of two or three animals.

Habitat

The North Andean huemul lives at high elevations and inhabits the dry, rocky slopes and mountains of northern Chile, Bolivia, Peru, and Ecuador. They are found most frequently at elevations from 4,600 to 5,400 feet on north and south slopes with an incline of 30 to 40 degrees as well as in rugged and diversified terrain. Scrub areas and areas with undergrowth are preferred to forest.

Distribution

Historically, the North Andean huemul was distributed from southern Ecuador or northern Peru southward on the plateau of the Altiplano and along the adjacent brushy slopes possibly to the 27th or even 29th parallel in Chile and Argentina. While the present day range of the animal extends over the same distance, only small, island-like populations have survived, mainly in Peru. It is assumed that the once numerous huemuls of Bolivia are completely extirpated.

Threats

The worrisome decline in the numbers of the North Andean huemul can be blamed for the most part on charcoal burners, who shot them and destroyed their cover; agricultural development in the river valleys; competition for food with domestic animals; and a vulnerability to the diseases that domestic animals carry.

Conservation and Recovery

It is hoped that the efforts being expended on the behalf of the vicuna (see separate entry) might in some way benefit the North Andean huemul.

South Andean Huemul

Hippocamelus bisculus

Mark MacNamara

Status	Endangered
Listed	June 14, 1976
Family	Cervidae (Deer)
Description	Coat is light brown in the warmer seasons, and mainly gray in colder seasons; body is flecked by a yellowish-black color because of the light and dark streaks.
Habitat	Dense, moist, and temperate rainforests.
Food	Mosses and lichens.
Threats	Loss of habitat due to cattle breeding.
Range	Argentina and southern Chile

Description

The South Andean huemul, *Hippocamelus bisculus*, is very similar in appearance to the North Andean huemul (*H. antisensis*; see separate entry). It is about 3 feet tall at the withers and about 5 feet long.

H. bisculus differs from *H. antisensis* in terms of certain morphological characteristics. The coat color of this southern species is slightly lighter; the main tint during the warmer season is always brown, while in the colder seasons it takes on mainly gray colors. The body appears to be flecked by a yellowish-black color because of the light and dark streaks. The coat is rather rough to the touch, consisting of coarse and brittle guard hairs with a dense, soft undercoat. The shaft of each hair is hollow and has a zigzag edge; this provides good heat insulation and serves to repel water.

The ears are shaped somewhat like those of a mule; they are large, wide and long. Another distinguishing trait is the short tail, which ends in a roughly triangular point.

The antlers have a relatively simple structure with only one branch. They are short, usually reaching only one foot in length.

Exceptional cases have been known where the antlers had a larger development and a greater number of points. In this southern species, the bifurcation is made at a farther distance from the basic nose, which presents a way to distinguish the southern species from the northern species.

H. bisculus was first described by the Jesuit priest Juan Ignacio Molina in 1782. According to him, the Araucania Indians may have named the animal huemul because the verb "huemin" (to follow one another) describes the custom of this deer to wander around in single file.

Later, zoologists found a similarity to llamas in these animals and classified them in the family *Camilidae*. The systematic position of these deer is still uncertain; within the *Cervidae* family they were originally classified in the genus *Odocoileus*, but are now usually classified in the distinct genus *Hippocamelus*.

The South Andean huemul is also known as the Chilean guemal.

Behavior

Only a few herbivores exist in southern Chile, and of these the South Andean huemul is the largest. Its diet consists mainly of mosses and lichens. Huemuls are generally are considered to be solitary animals; however, they may live in small groups of two or three animals.

Habitat

The South Andean huemul inhabits dense, moist, and temperate rainforests of southern Chile and Argentina. They are found most frequently at elevations from 4,600 to 5,400 feet on the north and south slopes with an incline of 30 to 40 degrees as well as in rugged and diversified terrain.

Distribution

The distribution area of the South Andean huemul extends into the southern part of the Andes chain in the central-southern regions of Chile and Argentina. It was possible, at one time, to find the South Andean huemul in the most southern extremities of the Andes chain, in the region between the Deseado and Santa Cruz rivers; however, none have been seen in this area for many years.

Threats

The South Andean huemul is threatened by the loss of its habitat as the territories in which this species lives have undergone large-scale transformations following the extension of agricultural activity and cattle breeding. Additionally, several members of *Cervus elaphus* were brought to this area by the first European colonists. These animals mated rapidly, and revealed themselves to be more competitive than the South Andean huemul; thus displacing the South Andean huemul to less favorable zones.

Conservation and Recovery

The passage of Chilean laws for the protection of the South Andean huemul has met with some success, which affords some hope for its conservation.

Musk Deer
Moschus spp.

Priscilla Barrett

Status	Endangered
Listed	June 2, 1970
Family	Cervidae (Genus *Moschus*)
Description	Hind legs are a third longer than the front legs; the dark brown to gray hair is long and bristly; it has a short neck and small head.
Habitat	Forests with dense vegetation bordered by brushland.
Food	Leaves, flowers, mosses, grasses, and lichens.
Reproduction	1 or 2 offspring are produced after gestation of 185 to 195 days.
Threats	Hunting for musk.
Range	Tibet, Nepal, Yunnan, Bhutan, Burma, Vietnam, Siberia, Mongolia, Korea

Description

The most important physical characteristic of *Moschus* spp. is the presence of a pouch of skin in front of the male genitals containing a musk gland, which produces a waxy substance that is in high demand for perfumes, soaps, and medicinals. The musk deer is also quite different from other *Cervidae:* it has no antlers; it has upper canines that grow to a length of 4 inches and resemble tusks; its hind legs are a third longer than the front legs; the backbone is sharply convex; it has a short neck and small head; its locomotion is by springing or hopping; the dark brown to gray hair is long and bristly, without value as a hide, and its meat is not edible. The smallest deer in the *Cervidae* family, the musk deer stands less than 3 feet high at the shoulders and weighs less than 40 pounds. It has upright ears, resembling a rabbit's ears, and a short muzzle that resembles the shape of a kangaroo's face.

Behavior

Musk deer are shy, solitary animals that form groups only during the mating season. In the northern ranges, mating occurs in November and December; 1 or 2 offspring are produced after gestation of 185 to 195 days.

Musk deer are territorial, marking their areas with the musk gland. Mature males may protect up to 3 females, who maintain separate territories within the male's territory. Young males will not enter into a marked territory. If there is a shortage of females, males will fight for mating privileges, and they can seriously hurt each other during mating and boundary bouts.

The musk deer is an adaptable eater and will feed on many varieties of leaves, flowers, mosses, grasses, and lichens, which they tear from the tree.

Musk deer are primarily nocturnal and spend the day hiding in undergrowth or windbreaks. These deer detect danger through their hearing, but they are not necessarily able to associate particular sounds with specific danger. The human voice, for example, may not alarm a deer while a fallen branch will.

Habitat

Musk deer prefer forests with dense vegetation for cover, bordered by brushland for foraging.

Distribution

Some taxonomists divide *Moschus* into five subspecies, all of which are endangered. *M. chrysogaster* occurs in the Tibetan Plateau and the Himalayas; *M. leucogaster* occurs in Nepal, Sikkim, Bhutan and Tibet; *M. fuscus* occurs in Yunnan and Burma; *M. berezovski* occurs in eastern and south China, and in northern Vietnam; and *M. moschiferus* occurs in Siberia, Mongolia, Manchuria, Korea, and Sakhalin. Because these populations are so widely scattered, population numbers are difficult to ascertain, but the total population may be as high as 100,000 individuals.

Threats

Because musk (and the musk pouch) is one of the most expensive animal products in the world, this deer is widely hunted. Females, which do not produce musk oil, are frequently snared in traps set for males. Encroachment on, or destruction of this deer's forest habitat has further applied pressure, as well as placing it in greater proximity to human predators.

Conservation and Recovery

An artificial scent has been developed which replaces the necessity of extracting musk from the animal, so that the demand for genuine musk has been reduced. Musk can be extracted from the deer without harming it, and in China, Nepal, and Russia, musk deer farms have been established to meet the demand for the scent. In Russia, hunters may shoot musk deer but are not permitted to trap or snare them. Other attempts to extract musk from wild populations without killing the animal have been attempted in these countries and in India.

Fea's Muntjac

Muntiacus feae

Reeve's Muntjac (*Muntiacus reevesi*)   Potawatomi Zoo

Status	Endangered
Listed	June 25, 1979
Family	Cervidae (Deer)
Description	Dark brown coat with yellow dots; lower parts are a lighter brown mixed with white; the muzzle is dark brown; the base of the ears and tufted head hairs are yellowish.
Habitat	Hilly or mountainous woodlands with dense, tropical vegetation.
Food	Foliage and bark to fruits and birds.
Reproduction	1 or 2 young after gestation of 6 months.
Threats	Hunted for its meat and hides; loss of habitat.
Range	Thailand, Myanmar

Description

Fea's muntjac, *Muntiacus feae*, has a dark brown coat with yellow dots; the lower parts are a lighter brown mixed with white. The muzzle is dark brown; the base of the ears and tufted head hairs are yellowish. The short, single-pointed antlers, which are shed every 1 to 2 years, incline backward.

Behavior

Muntjac deer are omnivorous feeders whose diet ranges from foliage and bark to fruits and birds. They are skilled at killing small mammals and birds by kicking them with their forelegs, and their large upper canines permit them to eat substantial prey. They will venture from their dense habitat to forage in cultivated fields and orchards. When threatened by their own predators, muntjacs sound an loud alarm which resembles a barking dog.

Both male and female muntjac deer are solitary and maintain territories which they mark with scents from their preorbital glands. Although food sources are available year-round, they are not plentiful, so that the deer occupy a small territory which they defend from all other adult muntjacs and cospecifics. Only during the rut do they allow other muntjacs to enter their territory. Fea's muntjac mates from December to March, producing 1 or 2 young after a gestation of 6 months. The young are forced to leave the mother's territory and establish a territory of their own when they are 6 months old. Because available territories are scarce, young deer that cannot find a territory become easy prey to natural predators, which include large cats, dholes, jackals, and crocodiles. Male muntjacs will accept immature males into their territory as long as they have not developed antlers, indicating their sexual maturity and capability of competing for males. When the young male matures, the two males may tolerate each other and share the territory as long as they rut during different periods.

Habitat

Fea's muntjac occurs in hilly or mountainous woodlands with dense, tropical vegetation, which it uses for protection and for food, and ready access to water.

Distribution

Of the 6 subspecies of *Muntiacus*, only *M. feae* is endangered. It occurs in peninsular Myanmar and Thailand. There are no population estimates but the only known populations are small and scattered.

Threats

Fea's muntjac is hunted for its meat and hides, and is vulnerable to hunting because it will venture from its territory to forage. Expanding farmlands have encroached on the deer's habitat and brought it in closer proximity to human predators. A small animal, it is also vulnerable to natural predators, including snakes. Because of the paucity of available territory, the deer's population cannot expand, and as the amount of territory diminishes due to agricultural expansion, so will the population.

Conservation and Recovery

Muntjac deer can be captively bred, and three programs have been established in Thai zoos to breed fea's muntjac.

Cedros Island Mule Deer

Odocoileus hemionus cedrosensis

Odocoileus hemionus   Milwaukee County Zoo/M. A. Nepper

Status	Endangered
Listed	September 25, 1975
Family	Cervidae (Deer)
Description	Medium-sized deer with a red summer coat changing to gray in winter, distinguished by large mule-like ears.
Habitat	Scrub grasslands to forests.
Food	Grasses, twigs, leaves.
Reproduction	Gestation period of 195-210 days.
Threats	Loss of habitat due to cattle ranching, hunting, poaching.
Range	Mexico: Cedros Island

Description

The Cedros Island mule deer, *Odocoileus hemionus cedrosensis*, is a medium sized deer with a red summer coat which changes to gray in the winter. The face and throat are whitish with a black bar around the chin and a black patch on the forehead. The belly, insides of the legs and rump patch are white. The Cedros Island mule deer weighs about 265 pounds and stands up to 39 inches at the shoulders. Mule deer are distinguished by their large mulelike ears. Its antlers are dichotomously branched with 8 to 10 points. It sheds its antlers between January and March, which are regrown by the end of August preceding the rutting season.

Behavior

The Cedros Island mule deer grazes during the wet season and browses on leaves and twigs during drier months.

Gestation is 195 to 210 days; longevity is 15 years.

Habitat

The Cedros Island mule deer occurs in grasslands and forests.

Distribution

The Cedros Island mule deer is restricted

to Cedros Island, off Baja California, Mexico where a few hundred individuals survive.

Threats

Cattle compete with the Cedros Island mule deer for grassland habitat and further restrict this subspecies' already limited range. Poaching remains a problem on this small island.

Conservation and Recovery

Until the authorities end hunting and poaching, the Cedros Island mule deer remains in continual threat of extinction.

Pampas Deer

Ozotoceros bezoarticus

Luiz Claudio Marigo

Status	Endangered
Listed	June 14, 1976
Family	Cervidae (Deer)
Description	Light brown fur with white underneath; the face is darker than the body with weak eye rings, white hazy spots on the lower lip, and a white throat spot.
Habitat	Low elevation grasslands or pampas.
Food	New green grass, shrubs and herbs.
Reproduction	1 fawn after gestation of over 7 months.
Threats	Uncontrolled hunting, loss of habitat, and transmission of disease from domestic livestock.
Range	Brazil, Uruguay, Mato Grosso, Bolivia, Paraguay, Argentina.

Description

The Pampas deer, *Ozotoceros bezoarticus*, is a small South American deer, standing 25 to 20 inches at the shoulder. The larger male weighs an average 88 pounds, and the smaller females average 13 pounds. The short, bushy tail measures 4-6 inches.

Pampas deer have light brown fur with white underneath. The face is darker than the body with weak eye rings, white hazy spots on the lower lip, and a white throat spot. The fur color doesn't change between summer and winter. The ears are relatively narrow.

Males have glands on the back hooves that emit a strong garlicky odor, detectable at a distance of 0.9 miles. Both sexes have small preorbital and tarsal glands, as well as large digital and inner nose glands. The male antlers usually have 3 tines with an undivided front prong and a divided upper prong. The antlers are cast off in August or September, and a new set becomes fully developed by December.

The genus *Ozotoceros* contains one species, *O. bezoarticus*. However, some authorities place this species in the genus *Odocoileus*, along with the white-tailed deer and the mule deer. The generic name *Blastoceros* is used by some authorities instead of *Ozotoceros*. However, *Blastoceros* is disliked by many because it is too similar to another generic name, *Blastocerus*.

The species *O. bezoarticus* is divided into 3 subspecies:

O. b. bezoarticus, Brazilian pampas deer
O. b. leucogaster, Chaco pampas deer
O. b. celer, Argentine pampas deer

Behavior

Pampas deer do not seem to be territorial. The animals usually live alone or in small groups, rarely exceeding 5 or 6 members. However, sometimes individuals will gather into groups of 50 or more on a common feeding ground. Both types of groups contain individuals of both sexes and are fluid in size and composition with males, especially, moving freely from group to group.

The rutting season occurs from December to February in Argentina and from February to April in Uruguay. During the rut, males aggressively compete for females. Sometimes several males will compete over a single doe. They use their antlers to thrash vegetation and rub the scent glands of their head and face on plants and other objects. Demonstrating aggression, they thrust with their antlers or flail with their forefeet. Fighting is frequent.

The females give birth to one fawn after a gestation period of over 7 months. Births usually occur from September to November; although they have been recorded throughout the year. Before birth, the female separates from her group, and afterwards keeps the newborn away from others. The young fawns are spotted at birth and weigh about 9.2 pounds. After about six weeks, the fawn begins to follow the mother and takes some solid food. By the age of 2 months, the fawn loses its spots. The fawn remains with its mother for about a year until sexual maturity is reached.

Although their diet has not been extensively studied, pampas deer have been seen to selectively graze on new green grass, instead of the drier more mature grass. The animals may also browse on shrubs and herbs. Pampas deer are active both at night and, especially if not disturbed, during daylight hours.

Habitat

Pampas deer live in low elevation grasslands or pampas drained by the Rio Plata and many of its tributaries. These animals can be found on a wide variety of habitats in the grasslands, including areas temporarily inundated by fresh or estuarine waters, rolling hills, as well as areas dry in the winter with no permanent surface water. In the past, many of these areas had grasses tall enough to hide a standing deer. However, tall grass no longer exists in many of these areas because of agriculture.

Distribution

In the past, pampas deer was widespread from the fifth to the fortieth latitudes in the South American countries of Argentina, Brazil, Uruguay, Bolivia, and Paraguay. The subspecies, *O. b. celer* was originally found throughout Argentina, but is now restricted to one small population along the coast and another population further inland. *O. b.*

leucogaster is still found throughout its original range of the Mato Grosso, Bolivia, Paraguay, and part of northern Argentina, although in smaller numbers. Originally, *O. b. bezoarticus* was found in Brazil and Uruguay. The subspecies is still found in Brazil, but its range has dwindled to nine isolated sites in Uruguay.

Threats

Indians had hunted pampas deer for centuries. However, the species remained common until Europeans settled the area and started farming and ranching. Pampas deer populations started to decline at this time due to continued uncontrolled hunting, loss of habitat, and transmission of disease from domestic livestock. Also the animal is very vulnerable to attack by domestic dogs because pampas deer evolved in an area that lacked large, fast predators. Before dogs were introduced, the biggest enemy of the species was the smaller, slower native fox.

Conservation and Recovery

Argentina protects several populations of the subspecies *O. b. celer*. Unfortunately, captive populations of *O. bezoarticus*, especially the subspecies, *O. b. celer*, are too small to set up an effective breeding program.

Pudu

Pudu pudu

Ken Kelly, San Diego Zoo

Status	Endangered
Listed	June 14, 1976
Family	Cervidae (Deer)
Description	Smallest of all deer, low-slung body with short thick legs, small round ears, small eyes, and short, spike-like antlers.
Habitat	Bamboo groves in rainforests.
Food	Trees, shrubs, vines; bark, twigs, buds, blossoms, fruits, berries.
Reproduction	1 fawn after gestation of 210 days.
Threats	Loss of habitat..
Range	Chile and Argentina

Description

The pudu, *Pudu pudu*, along with the closely related *Pudu mephistopheles*, is the smallest of all deer; weighing only 13 to 30 pounds. The low-slung body has short thick legs and measures 10 to 17 inches at the shoulder. The head has rather small round ears, small eyes, and short (4 inches) spike-like antlers. These antlers are shed in the middle of July and grow back by mid-November. The tail is very small, measuring only 3.2 inches.

P. puda has long, coarse, brittle hairs, generally brownish or dark gray in color. The middle of the back is dark brown, and the face is reddish-buff or brown. The ears, nose, chin, underparts, and limbs are reddish. *P. mephistophiles* has a reddish-brown coat and an almost black head and feet.

Behavior

When pursued, the pudu runs in a zigzag pattern. The animal uses tree trunks to get across streams or over cliffs and is said to move very nimbly over rocks.

This secretive animal is usually alone, except during breeding season. However, early reports suggest that the species may have lived in small herds in the past. Males maintain territories up to 60 acres.

Breeding season occurs in April through June. The female usually produces one fawn after an average gestation period of 210 days. The newborn weighs 2.2 to 3.3 pounds at birth and is covered with white spots. The fawns usually are weaned at 2 months. Females reach sexual maturity at six months, with males reaching sexual maturity later, at 8 to 12 months. The life span of the pudu is about 8 to 10 years. One individual was still alive after 12.5 years in captivity.

Pudus mainly browse on trees, shrubs, and vines. They also eat bark, twigs, buds, blossoms, fruits, berries, nuts, acorns, and cultivated vegetables.

When searching for preferred leaves and shoots, pudus may push over small plants and stand on top of them in order to eat the upper delicacies. The pudu rarely drinks water because it obtains most of its moisture from the lush vegetation.

The pudu is active mostly in the early morning, late afternoon and evening. However, the animal has been observed both during the day and at night.

Habitat

The pudu lives in the deep, humid forests of Chile and Argentina at elevations ranging from sea level to 5,400 feet. The habitat characteristically has a mild wet winter, with a short dry summer and an average yearly rainfall of 74 to 150 inches. The animal prefers the dark, dripping wet underbrush of the rainforest, especially bamboo groves. This luxuriant foliage provides protection from predators, like the puma, as well as food for the pudu. *P. memhistophiles* lives in the deep forests of the lower Andes in Ecuador and Peru.

In this lush vegetation, the pudu creates a network of tunnel-like trails. The animal has common resting places along these trails, usually with nearby dung piles that are used over and over again.

Distribution

Pudus were once widespread throughout the foothills, valleys, and lowlands of the southern Andes in Chile and Argentina. Although still found within this range, the population of the pudu has dwindled, especially in Argentina. *P. memhistophiles* occurs in the forests of the lower Andes in Ecuador and Peru.

Threats

Pudus are endangered because over 90% of the lowland area originally occupied by the species has been cleared and settled by humans. The lush vegetation needed by the pudu has been cut down for agriculture, livestock raising, and commercial timber plantations. Competition from roe deer and fallow deer introduced from Europe, as well as predation by domestic dogs has also contributed to the decline of this species. Domestic dogs and other animals also spread dangerous parasites such as bladder worm, lung worms, and round worms to the pudu.

Conservation and Recovery

Approximately 100 pudus are in captivity in North America and Europe. These animals could provide an invaluable gene pool for the continuance of the species.